The Dialectical Necessity of Morality

The Dialectical Necessity of Morality

An Analysis and Defense of Alan Gewirth's Argument to the Principle of Generic Consistency

Deryck Beyleveld

Michael Tonderum

March 1995

The University of Chicago Press / Chicago and London

Deryck Beyleveld is Reader in the Philosophy of Law, Centre for
Socio-Legal Studies, at the University of Sheffield.

The University of Chicago Press, Chicago 60637
The University of Chicago Press, Ltd., London
© 1991 by The University of Chicago
All rights reserved. Published 1991
Printed in the United States of America

00 99 98 97 96 95 94 93 92 91   5 4 3 2 1

Library of Congress Cataloging-in-Publication Data

Beyleveld, Deryck.
The dialectical necessity of morality : an analysis and defense of Alan
Gewirth's argument to the principle of generic
consistency / Deryck Beyleveld
p.   cm.
Includes bibliographical references and indexes.
ISBN: 0-226-04482-3. — ISBN: 0-226-04483-1 (pbk.)
1. Gewirth, Alan. Reason and morality. 2. Ethics. I. Title.
BJ1012.B48 1991   91-673
170—dc20   CIP

⊗ The paper used in this publication meets the minimum requirements of
the American National Standard for Information Sciences—Permanence of
Paper for Printed Library Materials, ANSI Z39.48-1984.

Contents

Foreword

Alan Gewirth

Deryck Beyleveld has done me the great honor of working out an exceptionally acute, systematic, and thorough analysis and defense of the argument for the supreme principle of morality that I presented in *Reason and Morality.* I am immensely grateful to him for his vast and insightful labors in producing this treatise. It is not only by far the most valuable contribution to the many critical discussions that my book has received since its publication in 1978; in its penetrating analyses and chains of argument Beyleveld's book is also an excellent example in its own right of how moral philosophy, at the level of principle that constitutes its most fundamental phase, should be done.

In analyzing my argument to the supreme principle of morality in Part 1 of this book, Beyleveld has rightly not aimed at giving a mere summary of the argument; instead, he has provided what may be called a rational reconstruction of it whereby its various parts are presented in their most compelling formulations, and their logical structure is spelled out in a helpfully formalized way. And in taking up and answering the many objections that have been brought against my argument, Beyleveld has done a remarkable job of sifting, organizing, and clarifying all the myriad components of the debates in which the argument has been involved. His book in its Part 2 is a model of its kind; at once extraordinarily patient, diligent, comprehensive, and cogent in its handling of objections. As he points out, I have published replies to very many of the objections that my argument has received. But these replies have been largely ad hoc in that they have taken up various objections as they have appeared. Beyleveld, on the other hand, while using to advantage my own replies, has confronted these objections as a whole; he has put each one in its proper place in relation to the overall sequence of my argument, and he has shown how each is to be answered by reference to appropriate parts of that sequence. He has also replied to many objections with which I did not deal. No author could wish for a more astute or perceptive defender.

From now on, anyone who wants to criticize any part of the central argument of *Reason and Morality* will have to take due account of Beyleveld's discussion of the issues.

In his introductory chapter, Beyleveld points out the very high philosophical stakes that are involved in the project I undertook in *Reason and Morality* and that justify the enormous labors he has put into writing this treatise. In accepting his invitation to contribute this foreword, I have thought it appropriate only to try to supplement his discussions by indicating something of my book's general intention in its broader philosophical context and my general reaction to some of the main kinds of objections that the book has received.

My chief aim in *Reason and Morality* was to show that a certain supreme moral principle can be given a stringently rational justification, in that self-contradiction is incurred by any actual or prospective agent who rejects the principle. The point of this aim was twofold. First, far from being arbitrary or subject to persons' contingent choices according to their own predilections or social conventions, moral requirements are categorically obligatory or normatively necessary, so that they cannot be rightly evaded by any actual or prospective agent regardless of her or his variable inclinations, ideals, or institutional affiliations. Such normative necessity can be upheld only through a stringently rational justification whereby it is shown that to reject moral obligations is to contradict oneself. No actual or prospective agent can reject these obligations and still fulfill the most elemental of rational requirements. Second, among the many different moral principles that have competed for persons' allegiance in all human ages, including ours, none is entitled to full rational acceptance if it involves a denial of the aforementioned supreme principle. Hence, the conflicting demands made by rival principles, far from being left in a relativistic welter of claims and counterclaims, can and should be assayed by reference to this principle. In this way a kind of determinacy is provided for morality, since valid moral obligations are organized under a single rationally justified principle so that they are not in any ultimate conflict with one another.

The appeal to contradiction as a way of validating some moral judgments and invalidating others has been a central feature of much moral philosophy at least from Plato's Socratic dialogues (including the first book of the *Republic*) through Kant to R. M. Hare in our own day. My line of argument differs from these others in one crucial respect. All the previous philosophers have used what I call a *dialectically contingent method*. Their method is *dialectical* (as against assertoric) in that it begins not from statements directly made by the speaker or writer but rather from statements or claims represented as being made by various interlocutors, and it then examines what these statements or claims logically imply, involving at some point a contradiction of the initial statement. But their method is dialectically *contingent* in that the initial statements or claims in question are left open to the optional choices of the protagonists; there is no necessity that these statements be made as against any others.

Because of this optionality, the dialectically contingent method cannot justify moral principles that are either categorical or determinate. While some of the specific grounds of this disability may vary from one philosopher to another (including the indeterminate contents of Kant's "maxims"), a general point is the following. If two statements are inconsistent with one another, it is indeed logically impossible to accept or act according to both of them simultaneously. But this still leaves open the question of which member of the inconsistent pair is to be accepted and which rejected. For inconsistency can be avoided and consistency maintained or restored by rejecting either of the two mutually inconsistent statements. Hence, for example, although one cannot consistently accept both (*a*) "All defaulting debtors ought to be jailed" and (*b*) "I, a defaulting debtor, ought not to be jailed," it is open to an interlocutor, depending on the relative strength of various of his or her contingent inclinations and ideals, to accept either (*a*) or (*b*).[1] The method thus provides no conclusive ground for accepting or rejecting either statement of the inconsistent pair. For this reason, the judgments and principles that can be justified by the dialectically contingent method are not determinate, nor are they categorical, because one can accept or reject one or another principle by consulting or shifting one's personal inclinations or ideals.[2]

In contrast to these historically influential but insufficiently efficacious appeals to contradiction, I have used a *dialectically necessary method.* This involves that logical necessity attaches to the content as well as to the form of moral argument, including the argument to the supreme principle of morality. The statements from which the argument begins are not left open to the optional choices of protagonists; on the contrary, they are statements that every person logically must accept simply by virtue of being an actual or prospective agent. The argument proceeds to show that, by accepting these agency-necessitated statements, every actual or prospective agent is logically committed to accept a certain supreme principle of morality. Any agent contradicts herself if she rejects the principle, but this stringent irrationality cannot be evaded, as can arguments using dialectically contingent methods, by shifting or otherwise consulting one's optional inclinations or ideals. On the contrary, because the very contents of the statements that enter into the argument logically must be accepted by any (every) agent, on pain of self-contradiction, the principle that emerges from the argument logically must also be accepted by every agent, so that the principle is categorical and determinate.

An important reason for confining the argument to such logically necessary contents is the following. As was mentioned above, both in their history and in their contemporary status moral principles are involved in fundamental conflicts about how persons ought to act, especially toward one another. Now if, amid these competing principles, there are statement contents that every agent logically must accept simply by virtue of being an agent, then this should bring a halt to the conflicts of principles in a rationally required way.

The necessary contents in question consist in the generic features that characterize all action and generally successful action. Because they are such generic features, they logically must be accepted by every actual or prospective agent. If any agent rejects these features, then he rejects the necessary conditions that are proximately involved in his agency, so that he is caught in a contradiction. These generic features are freedom and well-being, which are, respectively, the procedural and the substantive necessary conditions of action and generally successful action. It is on the basis of this necessary content that the argument to the supreme principle of morality establishes that every actual or prospective agent logically must accept the principle. The general line of the argument is that, by virtue of accepting these logically necessary conditions of agency for himself, every agent is logically committed to accept that he has rights to these conditions and that all other actual or prospective agents also have these rights. In this way morality is shown to have the categoricalness and determinacy referred to above.

The supreme principle of morality that I presented as justified by this line of argument is the principle of generic consistency (PGC). Addressed to every actual or prospective agent, it says: Act in accord with the generic rights of your recipients as well as of yourself. The generic rights are rights to have one's behavior characterized by the freedom and well-being that are the generic features of action and generally successful action. What the PGC requires, then, is that every actual or prospective agent act with favorable consideration for the freedom and well-being of other persons as well as himself or herself; and such action is a matter of the rights of the persons concerned. At certain important points the requirements in question are institutional rather than individual or personal, but they are all justified by the PGC. Thus the principle of generic consistency gets its name from the fact that the argument which establishes it com-

bines the formally necessary consideration of *consistency* or avoidance of self-contradiction with the materially necessary consideration of the *generic* features and rights of action. This combination
entails that the consistency required by the PGC, unlike other moral
appeals to consistency, operates at the logically necessary generic
level, in that the principle requires that each agent act in accord with
the generic rights of her recipients as well as of herself. All valid
moral rules are derivative, directly or indirectly, from the PGC, and
thus they also require consistency in the distribution of freedom and
well-being; any agent who violates the PGC incurs self-contradiction. The PGC provides criteria for resolving conflicts of rights; in
addition, it can account for the moral virtues and the meritorious-
ness of "imperfect" and "broad" duties, including acts of supererogation.

The argument for the PGC shows that the supreme principle of
morality is a principle of human rights and that the rational basis for
such rights is to be found in the fundamental needs of agency. The
chief originality of the whole argument for human rights consists in
the logically necessary dialectical derivation of the rights from the
necessary conditions of action and generally successful action. Since
the derivation establishes that the human rights are equal among all
humans, it follows that morally right actions and institutions must
maintain a certain mutuality of consideration whereby the agency
needs of all persons are given equal protection. At the same time,
through its applications to voluntary associations and political regimes, the argument for the PGC shows how various particularistic
concerns can also be morally justified, including those for one's family, friends, local community, and country, without violating the
equal rights of all persons.[3]

The dialectically necessary argument for the PGC thus refutes the
various kinds of moral skepticism and relativism, including the cur-
rently fashionable sociopolitical "postmodern" relativism which
holds that, while rational argument may proceed from *within* the
context of constitutional democracy, there is no way of rationally
justifying that context itself as against its various rivals.

The ambitious project of establishing the PGC, with the apodictic
claims I have made for it, has naturally attracted much critical attention. Contemporary philosophers, rightly suspicious of claims of
logical necessity with its purported conclusiveness and definitive-
ness, especially in moral philosophy, have pressed a wide array of
objections against the argument to the PGC. On the other hand,
some commentators have upheld the validity of the whole argument. For example, one commentator has written, "The major
strength of Gewirth's work is that he has successfully accomplished

two important tasks: one, the meta-ethical task of examining how moral principles and judgments can be justified; the other, the ethical task of actually showing which moral principles are justifiable. . . . In my view, Gewirth has provided all that is required in the way of a rational justification for the rights to freedom and well-being."[4]

The general pattern, however, has been that my argument, while receiving much favorable attention, has also been the object of considerable criticism, often on rather flimsy grounds.[5] The fact of the criticisms themselves I have not found particularly distressing. After all, the whole history of philosophy is a record of criticism and countercriticism; through such a dialectic philosophers come closer to whatever truth is to be found in their subject matter. Moreover, apodictic claims for ethics like mine do especially require the most searching scrutiny. And in any case, it is better to be criticized than to be ignored.

What I have found distressing are three other things. First, my argument, especially at certain crucial points, has been misinterpreted by critics, and this in ways that a more careful reading would readily have avoided.[6] Second, critics have presented objections without noting that I have already explicitly taken up and answered these very objections in *Reason and Morality;* hence they have incurred the fault of *ignoratio scripti:* ignoring what has been written in the book they are discussing.[7] Third, my various replies to my critics, far from being taken into account in subsequent discussions of my argument, have generally been ignored. This has had the unfortunate effect that the whole dialectic, instead of rising to stages of greater accuracy and discernment, has remained at a level where elementary errors of interpretation have been repeated, with no recognition of my corrections and replies.

Of course, the soundness of an argument is not established by the fact that critics have misinterpreted it or have ignored important parts of it. But such faults have greatly detracted from the cogency of the objections and of the whole debate.

I must acknowledge that some of the misinterpretations I have alleged may have arisen from unclarities of exposition on my part, including some unduly technical terminology. I must also regretfully note that in some sections of *Reason and Morality* I have given the reader too few signposts. Especially in Chapter 2, in the long section "Generic Rights and Right-Claims" I go on for forty pages (63–103) with no subordinate headings to guide the reader through the various steps of the argument and the various objections and replies. A similar lack of subordinate headings afflicts the next section, "The Criterion of Relevant Similarities" (104–128), as well as the section of Chapter 5 entitled "The Completeness of the Principle" (327–338), where the unlabeled subsection on "duties to one-self" (333–338) seems to have escaped the notice of many readers.

It must also be emphasized here that not all the criticisms my book has received have exhibited the faults mentioned above. In many cases, the objections have been directly philosophical, involving different analyses of basic concepts and opposed evaluations of arguments.

Beyleveld's treatise, with its penetrating and well-organized sifting of the various components of the objections my book has received, not only discloses in detail how critics of my work have incurred the faults I have cited above; it should also render much more difficult the repetition of these faults, through, among other virtues, its own fine clarities of exposition and its incisive and cogent replies to objections. On the more general philosophical issues raised by some objections, Beyleveld's intensive discussions also shed much needed light. He has gone into them using not only my theses but also his own impressive resources of critical analysis. As a consequence, his work in Part 2 of this treatise should lift the whole quality of the debate to much higher levels of accuracy and understanding. Toward this salubrious result his analysis of my argument in Part 1 of this book should also assist very strongly. Throughout his treatise, Beyleveld has found ingenious and perceptive ways to elucidate basic philosophical aspects of the argument. Thus, at the very outset, he points out that, according to the argument, "any PPA [prospective purposive agent] who does not assent to the PGC, or who violates its prescriptions in practice, logically contradicts that it is a PPA." This striking assertion at once puts into bold relief the central dialectical-philosophical contention of the whole theory: that one cannot consistently hold both that one is a prospective purposive agent and that it is permissible not to comply with the PGC. Beyleveld's treatise abounds in such clarificatory insights together with the rigorous philosophical argumentation required to support them.

In both parts of his treatise, Beyleveld has made definitive, and in many respects original, contributions to the understanding of the three stages into which he has divided my argument—where I show that every agent logically must accept, first, that her freedom and well-being are necessary goods for her; second, that she has rights to these necessary goods; and third, that all other prospective purposive agents also have these rights. By far the largest number of objections have been directed against Stage II of the argument, where I undertake to establish that every agent logically must hold or accept that she has rights to freedom and well-being as the necessary conditions of action and generally successful action. This is indeed an especially crucial phase of the dialectically necessary argument for the PGC, for it undertakes to establish that action has an ineluctable deontic component in that every agent is logically committed to accept on her own behalf certain rights-judgments and correlative 'ought' judgments. From this, it is then shown that every agent is also logically committed to accept the PGC. In dealing with Stage II, Beyleveld has worked out a massive analysis and rational reconstruction that runs through parts of Chapters 2 and 3 and all of Chapters 5, 6, and 7. No mere summary can do justice to the sharpness and wealth of detail whereby he explicates and defends Stage II in its various aspects. In view of the many objections this stage has received, and its crucial importance for my whole project of providing a rational justification of morality, Beyleveld's intensive attack on the entire range of issues involved in this stage is fully justified and, for the careful reader, immensely enlightening.

In addition to the various ways in which he has worked out a rational reconstruction of Stage II, Beyleveld has applied the same kind of massive and detailed analysis to Stages I and III of my argument. The overall result is an exceptionally fruitful and clarificatory explication of the whole chain of rational argument I have presented for the PGC as the supreme principle of morality. By showing how the argument, correctly understood, can answer the manifold objections that have been brought against it, Beyleveld has immensely strengthened the claim of the PGC to have the stringently rational status referred to above. Undoubtedly, my argument will continue to receive objections, but these will be more readily welcomed if they take more careful account both of what is written in my book and of the intensively clarificatory analyses that Beyleveld has presented here.

Beyleveld is very far from being an uncritical upholder of what I have written. Such a characterization is abundantly refuted by the critical acumen and original thinking he displays throughout this treatise. At several points he has given well-considered reformulations and emendations of my statements; and I think that he and I may still differ on certain points about human (as against universal agents') rights and about natural law (on which he has coauthored a noteworthy book which makes foundational use of the PGC).[8] It is all the more heartening that the powerful support my argument receives in this treatise comes from such a strong, independent-minded thinker. Beyleveld's book is an eminent contribution to the understanding of profoundly important issues of principle in moral philosophy.

Notes

1. This example is from R. M. Hare, *Freedom and Reason* (Oxford: Clarendon Press, 1963), Chapter 6. In his more recent book, *Moral Thinking: Its Levels, Method, and Point* (Oxford: Clarendon Press, 1981), Hare has not departed from the dialectically contingent method.

2. It is worth remarking that a similar disability is found in John Rawls's famous argument from the "original position" in *A Theory of Justice* (Cambridge, Massachusetts: Harvard University Press, 1971). This argument also uses a dialectically contingent method, since it begins from choices made by protagonists and it examines to what decisions these choices will lead, given certain background assumptions. Rawls does not try to show explicitly that if certain choices are not made, the protagonists will contradict themselves; but this is implicit in his argument. His method is dialectically contingent, among other reasons, because there is no necessity that his protagonists proceed from behind a "veil of ignorance" whereby they do not know any of their personal qualities. Because there is no rational necessity in such a procedure, the principles he derives from it are not categorical: persons can rationally reject the veil of ignorance, at least in their own cases, so that they can also reject, without self-contradiction or any less serious rational sanction, the principles that emerge from such a veil.

3. See my "Ethical Universalism and Particularism," *Journal of Philosophy* 85 (1988): 283–302.

4. Derek L. Phillips, *Toward a Just Social Order* (Princeton, New Jersey: Princeton University Press, 1986), 114. It is also relevant to note here that Phillips, after pointing out "serious weaknesses" in the theories of Rawls, Robert Nozick, and Jürgen Habermas (60, 71, 84 respectively), goes on to say that my justificatory argument is "superior to" these others and "avoids many of the weaknesses contained in their theories" (88–89).

5. A typical recent example is Brian Barry, *Theories of Justice* (Berkeley: University of California Press, 1989), 285–288. After saying that my argument "is a good deal deeper than most critics have conceded," and that the "considerations" I advance are "powerful ones," Barry goes on to criticize my move from the agent's claiming rights for himself to his having to accept that all other agents also have these rights (Stage III in Beyleveld's classification). In his criticism Barry confines himself to my earlier, compressed statement of the argument in a paper published in 1970, so that he completely ignores my "argument from the sufficiency of agency" and my full reply to what I call the "individualizability objection" (*Reason and Morality*, 109–112, 115–119). While it is perhaps too much to hope that Beyleveld's book will put a complete stop to such hasty treatments of my argument, it should be a great help toward this end.

6. Two examples out of many: (*a*) R. B. Brandt, after declaring that "[i]t would clearly be a tremendous *coup* if Gewirth could show it is irrational in this [stringent] sense not to accept important moral principles," says that he remains "unpersuaded," on the following ground: "The [agent's] right-claim is a demand made on others, based on a reason. Other persons, of course, can make similar demands on him, based on symmetrical reasoning, and in consistency he must concede that these demands are as valid against him as his

against others. What I do not see is why these reciprocal prudentially-based demands are demands which the persons addressed are in any way bound to honor. So I fail to see how Gewirth's theory gets off the ground" (R. B. Brandt, "The Future of Ethics," *Nous* 15 [1981]: 39–40). This objection misinterprets my argument because it construes me as saying that "other persons . . . can make similar demands"—which does indeed leave open the question of why the original agent should "honor" these demands. But my own argument proceeds not from what *other persons* may *demand* but rather from the *agent's* having to accept, through universalization, that all other prospective agents *have* the generic rights—and *this* is why he must "honor" or respect their freedom and well-being. Brandt's objection misinterprets me as using "judgmental universalization" ("other persons" may "demand"), whereas I in fact use "possessive universalization" ("all other persons *have* rights"). See, e.g., *Reason and Morality*, 112: "Since, then, to avoid contradicting himself the agent must claim he has the rights of freedom and well-being for the sufficient reason that he is a prospective agent who has purposes he wants to fulfill, he logically must accept the generalization that all prospective agents who have purposes they want to fulfill *have* the rights of freedom and well-being. This generalization is a direct application of the principle of universalizability" (emphasis added). See also page 133: "every agent must claim, at least implicitly, that he has rights to freedom and well-being for the sufficient reason that he is a prospective purposive agent. From the content of this claim it follows, by the principle of universalizability, that all prospective purposive agents *have* rights to freedom and well-being" (emphasis added). See also pages 48, 135, 146, 147, 171. So Brandt, in withholding his encomium that I have scored "a tremendous *coup*," has simply failed to follow my argument at a crucial point. The same mistaken interpretation is given by Kai Nielsen, "Against Ethical Rationalism," in *Gewirth's Ethical Rationalism*, ed. Edward Regis, Jr. (Chicago: University of Chicago Press, 1984), 65–66, and by Christopher McMahon, "Gewirth's Justification of Morality," *Philosophical Studies* 50 (1986): 264, 267, 271. I have previously exposed this misinterpretation in "Replies to My Critics," in *Gewirth's Ethical Rationalism*, 210–211, and especially in "The Justification of Morality," *Philosophical Studies* 53 (1988): 253–254. (*b*) R. M. Hare, referring to my argument from the agent's holding that he must have freedom and well-being to his holding that he has rights to these necessary goods of action, asks, "Can I not want something, without thinking that I ought to have it?" ("Do Agents Have to Be Moralists?" in *Gewirth's Ethical Rationalism*, 54. See also W. D. Hudson, "The 'Is-Ought' Problem Resolved?" in ibid., 127). This question misinterprets what the agent "wants" as contingent ("want something"), whereas I emphasized that the argument proceeds "only so long as the goods in question are *necessary* ones. . . . For it is only to *necessary* goods that the 'must' indicated above applies, and with it the requirement that they be kept inviolate. Other goods, by definition, are dispensable" (*Reason and Morality*, 81; emphasis added. See ibid., 77–78). I have also called attention to this misinterpretation in "Replies to My Critics," 207–208.

7. Three examples out of many: (*a*) In *Reason and Morality*, 68, I raised against myself the objection that since agents can act, it must be "pointless" for the agent to hold that she has rights to the generic features of her action,

"[f]or one cannot rationally hold that one has a right to do or have what one cannot help doing or having." I then gave two replies to this objection, each involving that actual or prospective agents may lack the full scope of the objects of the rights. Douglas Husak ("Why There Are No Human Rights," *Social Theory and Practice* 10 [1984]: 132) raises this same objection against me: "Presumably a great part of the world's population is without these rights; is it therefore logically impossible for them to act . . . ?" Husak fails to note that I have raised this very objection against myself and have given two answers. I replied to Husak in "Why There Are Human Rights," *Social Theory and Practice* 11 (1985): 237–239. (*b*) In *Reason and Morality*, 183, I raised against my argument the objection that "[t]o contradict oneself is to make an intellectual mistake, but this is different from making a moral mistake in the sense of doing what is morally wrong." I then gave a lengthy reply (184–187). E. J. Bond, in the course of a lengthy review ("Gewirth on Reason and Morality," *Metaphilosophy* 11 [1980]: 41), writes that in my argument "moral evil is reduced to logical error. . . . Gewirth and others like him would turn wickedness into a kind of intellectual incompetence." Bond gives no indication whatsoever that I have already raised this objection against myself and have given a detailed reply. (Bond's review is also full of other *ignorationes scripti*.) I replied to Bond in the same issue of *Metaphilosophy*, 56–58. (*c*) In *Reason and Morality*, 72, I raised against myself the objection that "rights-talk and rights-claims presuppose the existence of a community to which the talk or claims are addressed and which understands and recognizes such talk and the common rules that provide the justification or legitimacy of the rights." I replied to this objection on pages 74–75. The same objection is presented, without noting my own statement of the objection and my reply, by R. E. Ewin, *Liberty, Community, and Justice* (Totowa, New Jersey: Rowman and Littlefield, 1987), 52, 59–60, and by Neil MacCormick, "Gewirth's Fallacy," *Queen's Law Journal* 9 (1984): 345–351.

8. Deryck Beyleveld and Roger Brownsword, *Law as a Moral Judgment* (London: Sweet and Maxwell, 1986).

Acknowledgments

While writing this book I have received intellectual, material, and spiritual assistance from many quarters. In extending my thanks to various people, I apologize if I overlook any important contributions.

First, I would like to thank Alan Gewirth for writing the foreword, for drawing my attention to some items of criticism of *Reason and Morality* that I failed to locate in my own searches, for providing me with access to some of this material, for help in expediting publication arrangements, and for his encouragement and support during the period when I was putting the final touches to the manuscript.

Roger Brownsword, who read the whole of the first draft and made numerous helpful suggestions, and Stuart Toddington, who suffered my obsession with this project during sessions of supervision of his Ph.D. thesis, devoted countless hours of their time as sounding boards for my analyses and responses to criticisms. I am deeply grateful for their intellectual support.

Stuart Toddington and John Denham ("Harry") helped me to check the quotations against primary sources. For this supererogatory behavior they each deserve a medal. They are not, of course, to be held responsible for any residual transcription-errors.

Jesse Kalin made some very helpful comments about the manuscript as a whole, and I have taken advantage of some of these in my final revision.

It is difficult to quantify what I have learned from my undergraduate and MA students at the University of Sheffield; but attempting to explain Gewirth's argument to them has certainly sharpened my thinking.

The public lawyers at the University of Sheffield, and Norman Lewis in particular, while not concerning themselves directly with this project, were, as ever, unflagging in their moral support, for which I can hardly thank them enough.

I would also like to thank John Birds, who, as head of the Department of Law at the University of Sheffield, agreed to have some of the costs of this project paid by the department, and made essential word processing equipment available to me at a critical time.

Some expenses involved in completing this project were financed by a grant from the University of Sheffield Research Fund (GR/1241).

I am indebted to Lilian Bloodworth and Sue Turner for secretarial assistance and, in particular, for help with word processing.

My wife Janet (who also assisted me considerably with checking the final manuscript and other clerical tasks), and our daughter Thea, made many personal sacrifices to enable me to write this book. This book is dedicated to them.

Headings and Objections

[*]   This and other notes in the outline refer to this volume.

#30   To deny that I have a right to my freedom and well-being is not to imply that PPAO has a right to interfere with my freedom and well-being. The argument assumes that this is so.   166

#31   A PPA's need for freedom and well-being is motivation for a PPA to demand or secure noninterference with its freedom and well-being, but provides no justification for this demand or activity.   171

#32   The fact that a PPA need value its freedom and well-being only instrumentally means that a PPA need not claim a right to its freedom and well-being.   176

#33   Ethical egoism does not prescribe that PPAO has a duty not to interfere with my freedom and well-being. Because the ethical egoist maxim "Every PPA ought to act in its own self-interest" has only "regional force," Gewirth's argument that ethical egoism is internally inconsistent fails.   181

#34   The principle that "ought" implies "can" does not

Abbreviations

In various places, either for convenience or to facilitate formal presentations, I employ a number of abbreviations. These abbreviations are explained in at least the first instance of their use in the text. However, they vary in the extent and localization of their use. Readers might find it helpful to memorize the abbreviations ASA, LPU, PCC, PGC, PPA, PPAO, RM, and SPR, as these recur with great frequency and are not re-explained in every segment of discussion in which they are employed.

AC   "All categorically need": the statement that all prospective purposive agents have a categorical need for freedom and well-being in order to pursue/achieve purposes by their agency.

APGC   "Assertoric PGC": the principle of generic consistency stated directly.

ASA   "Argument from (/for) the sufficiency of agency": specifically, Gewirth's argument to demonstrate that if a prospective purposive agent must, because it is a prospective purposive agent, consider that it has a right to freedom and well-being (or contradict that it is a prospective purposive agent), then it must consider that the sufficient reason why (the property by virtue of which) it possesses this right is that it is a prospective purposive agent.

CP   "Contingent properties": contingent powers or properties of prospective purposive agents, which determine their pursuit and achievement of particular occurrent purposes.

DPGC   "Dialectical PGC": the statement that prospective purposive agents deny that they are prospective purposive agents if they do not accept/act according to the principle of generic consistency.

F&WB   "Freedom and well-being": respectively, the procedural and substantive generic (or categorical) conditions of a

	prospective purposive agent's pursuit/achievement of its purposes.
IC	"I categorically need": the statement that I categorically need freedom and well-being in order to pursue/achieve purposes by my agency.
IP	"I proactively value": the statement that I proactively value the purposes I act for.
LPU	"Logical principle of universalizability": this may be stated in a number of different ways, one statement being "From the inference that if some subject S possesses property P then S possesses property Q, it follows that if any other subject SO possesses P then SO possesses Q."
MyR	"My right": the statement that I have a (claim) right to my freedom and well-being.
NR	"No right": the statement that I do not have a (claim) right to my freedom and well-being.
OC	"Others categorically need": the statement that others (other prospective purposive agents) categorically need freedom and well-being in order to pursue/achieve purposes by their agency. (Also, on occasion, abbreviated as PPAOC.)
ORO	"Other-referring (-addressed or -directed) 'ought'": the statement that others (strictly) ought (at least) not to interfere with (prevent) my having freedom and well-being (against my will) (which, within the general context of use, is prescribed by me to others).
PCC	"Principle of categorial consistency": Gewirth's designation of the supreme principle of morality (equivalent to the principle of generic consistency) in his writings prior to Gewirth 1974a.
PGC	"Principle of generic consistency": the principle that may be stated as "All prospective purposive agents have a (claim) right to freedom and well-being," which Gewirth argues to be the supreme principle of morality and, indeed, the supreme principle of all practical reason.
PPA	"Prospective purposive agent": those who act voluntarily for purposes that they have freely chosen (purposive agents), as well as those who intend to do so, or those who have the capacity to do so, which they have some disposition to exercise.
PPAO	"Other prospective purposive agent."
PPAOC	"PPAO categorically needs": the statement that other

	prospective purposive agents categorically need freedom and well-being in order to pursue/achieve purposes by their agency. (Equivalent to OC.)
PPAOP	"PPAO proactively values": the statement that other prospective purposive agents proactively value the purposes they act for.
PPAOR	"PPAOs' right": the statement that other prospective purposive agents have a (claim) right to their freedom and well-being.
PPAORO	"PPAO-referring 'ought'": the statement that other prospective purposive agents (strictly) ought to pursue their freedom and well-being (which, within the context of use, is prescribed by me to other prospective purposive agents). (Not to be confused with ORO.)
PPAR	"PPAs' right": the statement that all prospective purposive agents have a (claim) right to their freedom and well-being, which is equivalent to the principle of generic consistency.
pvmp	"Property: valuing my purposes": the property of necessarily valuing my purposes.
pvPPAOp	"Property: valuing PPAOs' purposes": the property of necessarily valuing the purposes of other prospective purposive agents.
RI	"Right to interfere": the statement that other prospective purposive agents have a (claim) right to interfere with my freedom and well-being.
RM	*"Reason and Morality"*: Gewirth 1978a.
rpvp	"Relation: proactively valuing purposes": the proactive evaluative relation between a prospective purposive agent and its own purposes.
SPR	"Subjective viewpoint on practical reasonableness": a prospective purposive agent's personal view, theory, or criterion by which it assesses what purposes are permissible/impermissible/not impermissible for it (SPR for its purposes) or others (SPR for the purposes of others) to choose to pursue.
SRO	"Self-referring 'ought'": the statement that I (strictly) ought to pursue/defend my freedom and well-being (which, within the context of use, is prescribed by me to myself).
UR	"Undecided about rights": the statement that I am undecided/agnostic about the deontic status of others' interference with my freedom and well-being.
WB$_1$	"Well-being (sense 1)": the substantive necessary condi-

tions of my pursuit/achievement of all and any purposes (Gewirth's category of "generic-dispositional well-being"), these being universal and invariant for all prospective purposive agents—being specified independently of the content of a prospective purposive agent's particular occurrent purposes.

WB$_2$ "Well-being (sense 2)": the substantive necessary conditions of my pursuit/achievement of those particular occurrent purposes which I am, or would be, willing to pursue, these varying according to the content of a prospective purposive agent's particular occurrent purposes, subjective viewpoint on practical reasonableness, or "life plan."

1 Introduction

In *Reason and Morality* (Gewirth 1978a),[1] Alan Gewirth argues that purposive agents and prospective purposive agents (PPAs)[2] are rationally committed, by virtue of conceiving of themselves as PPAs, to assenting to a moral principle, "the principle of generic consistency" (PGC), which states that all PPAs have claim (or "strong") rights[3] to their freedom and well-being. Since Gewirth's criteria of rationality are confined to the canons of deductive and inductive logic, his contention is that any PPA who does not assent to the PGC, or who violates its prescriptions in practice, logically contradicts that it is a PPA.

The validity of this argument has profound implications for moral epistemology, substantive ethical theory, the philosophy of the human sciences, and all forms of social, political, and legal theory. The argument purports to establish the PGC as a rationally necessary proposition with an apodictic status *for any PPA* equivalent to that enjoyed by the logical principle of noncontradiction itself.[4] A PPA can no more coherently deny being bound in its practical reasoning and actions by the PGC than it can coherently deny being bound in its propositional thinking by the principle of noncontradiction. Acceptance of the PGC is claimed to be a necessary presupposition not only of rational (logically coherent) engagement in any form of moral discourse, but of rational engagement in any form of practical discourse. Unlike some other quasi-transcendental arguments for moral principles,[5] Gewirth's argument does not assume that a PPA is committed to some specific, optional form of practical discourse. Thus, if the argument is valid, a PPA cannot evade the PGC by pleading commitment to opposed principles of practical rationality or reasonableness. The PGC will be the substantive yardstick by which the rationality of all practical reasoning is to be judged. Thus, the argument purports to refute all moralities that prescribe in opposition to the PGC, and all forms of general moral relativism—including those based on amoralism (minimally, the view that there are no reasons that logically compel a PPA to engage in moral discourse) and adeonticism (which refuses to recognize any exclusionary reasons for acting of any kind). Furthermore, on the assumption that explaining human actions requires judgments to be made of the rational way to act,[6] the argument implies that such explanations require moral judgments to be made with the PGC as the ultimate criterion. In this sense, explanations of human action cannot be morally neutral. Inasmuch as human social phenomena must be characterized in terms of the significance that they have for human agents,[7] these phenomena (including legal phenomena) logically (and not merely morally) must be characterized from the specific moral viewpoint of the PGC. Thus, social science cannot be morally neutral, and the claims of an objectivistic form of legal idealism ("natural law theory")[8] are established over those of legal positivism and relativistic forms of legal idealism.[9]

Given the current state of philosophical opinion, it is not surprising that Gewirth's argument to the PGC[10] has been greeted with widespread skepticism. However, it is not Gewirth's moral objectivism per se that generates the greatest resistance. For, although there are strong relativistic currents in moral theory, moral objectivism (in one form or another) is enjoying something of a revival.[11] What modern philosophers find really difficult to accept is that morality can be given *apodictic* foundations—that something like the Cartesian or Kantian projects can be fulfilled in ethics, when philosophers have generally abandoned such views even for empirical science. To some it seems that Gewirth simply *must* be trying to square the circle. Indeed, as Kai Nielsen has said, most academic philosophers are likely to "sigh with ennui" when presented with this kind of argument: they will "want to ignore the whole thing and to turn their attention to more important matters" (Nielsen 1984, 59).

Now, there can be no doubt that there is, ideally, a need for the kind of demonstration that Gewirth attempts—and that to succeed in this enterprise represents the Holy Grail of moral philosophy. Indeed, there can be no doubt that the foundation of moral principles on any other grounds is, ideally, not good enough. Moral principles are held to be categorically binding on agents. They are used to justify the infliction of harms on agents who do not obey them, and they require the subordination of agents' self-interests to their requirements. If moral principles are grounded on claims that agents are not committed to as a matter of logical necessity, then these grounds possess a contingency that is antithetical to their supposed categorical character—with the result that the force of moral argument becomes strictly *ad hominem*, as it can rest on no more than variable inclinations, intuitions, ideals, or properties over which, in the final analysis, there can be no rational adjudication. The imposition of moral requirements on those who do not accept, or have, these grounding features remains ultimately arbitrary, and there can be no case for calling it anything other than dogmatic authoritarianism.

In short, that philosophers are inclined to seek contingent groundings for morality can only be justified on the conviction that the Gewirthian enterprise is unfulfillable.

Now, I do not propose to examine the philosophical developments that have led to the widespread presumption that the enterprise of ethical rationalism is necessarily doomed to failure. To do so would require a survey of developments not only in moral philosophy, but in the theory of knowledge generally, covering a period of at least two centuries. I shall simply note that this judgment can be refuted by producing a valid demonstration of Gewirth's thesis, and that one of Gewirth's greatest achievements, given the skeptical background, has been to produce an argument that philosophers have found difficult to ignore. As Kai Nielsen remarks, the very fact that Gewirth's argument has received considerable attention—albeit for the most part skeptical—attests to the "skill, the dialectical care, the thoroughness with which Gewirth has constructed his argument and the integrity of his project" (Nielsen 1984, 60).

However, while these scholarly qualities have compelled a hostile audience to take the argument seriously, they also create difficulties for anyone who wishes to defend it against criticism. To begin with, *Reason and Morality* is an enormously impressive philosophical achievement. It is immensely thorough and closely reasoned—its detail and complexity being occasioned by the fact that no one is more aware than Gewirth that he is swimming against the tide. Almost invariably, when one thinks that one has something new to add, a careful rereading reveals that the point has already been made. Furthermore, Gewirth undertook to answer almost every conceivable objection in *Reason and Morality,* and to most of the more important critical responses he has written specific rejoinders.[12] So, for anyone (like myself) who considers the argument to be essentially sound, there is a strong temptation to leave the matter in Gewirth's own capable hands. Why, then, did I decide to write this book?

Apart from the fact that this work represents the processes I have gone through in coming to the conclusion that Gewirth is right—and I naturally want these processes to be recorded and subjected to critical scrutiny—there are a number of reasons.

1. Although I do not claim to add enormously to the substance of Gewirth's argument, I do think that I can offer analyses, and addi-

tional arguments, which clarify its structure and inferences. Such restructuring of the argument, with emendations and supplementation, as necessary, in the light of all the critical commentary on Gewirth, seems to me to be opportune. It is now over a decade since the publication of *Reason and Morality*. During this period there has been extensive examination of the argument, and Gewirth has responded to many of his critics. In this debate it is possible to discern an emerging pattern, to see what the really critical moments in the argument are; and this facilitates a restatement of the argument with an eye to a defense of the enterprise as a whole. With this defense in mind, and my restructuring of Gewirth's argument in the background, I think that I can, on occasion, reply more forcefully to his critics than Gewirth has done. In addition, I can reply to critics to whom Gewirth has not responded.[13] However, these considerations alone might not be thought to justify a lengthy book—although they clearly justify a number of articles and footnotes to the debate surrounding *Reason and Morality*.

2. There are at least two considerations that justify a book-length project (and which also contribute to explaining the rather unusual structure of this book).

a. The critical debate is contained in diverse journals and books. Collecting all criticisms together, classifying them, and responding to them in a concerted fashion can serve a useful function for any persons wishing to know about the debate as a whole. Although Gewirth has responded to many criticisms, he has tended to do so in a piecemeal fashion. With all criticisms in view, suitably classified, it is possible to appreciate the significance of any objection within the overall context of the argument.

b. I deem it necessary to consider *all* criticisms that have been made and, in general, to treat different examples of the same general criticism individually. This is because Gewirth's enterprise requires his argument to be presented as a *proof*. It follows from this that all possible avenues of escape must be covered and closed. Although many critics have raised similar objections, it is unwise to assume that these are identical. To answer them conclusively, it is necessary to appreciate their different nuances and backgrounds. To conflate them is bound to result in some critics complaining that their particular versions have been distorted. Of course, replying separately to individual variants of the "same" objection leads to examining and appealing to specific considerations over and over again. However, this is not a process of needless repetition. Rather, it is a process of providing evidence that the argument can cope with the full complexity of the issues raised by particular objections and types of objections. Furthermore, this process has, I think, the positive aspect of producing a very rich and multifaceted picture, which enables the argument's power to be properly appreciated and the myriad issues that it raises to be displayed in all their complexity.

3. Believing, as I do, that Gewirth is right, I feel a personal responsibility to add what weight of support I can to his work. Anyone only casually familiar with the response to Gewirth is quite likely to gain the impression that it is a case of Gewirth versus the rest of the philosophical world. Is this because Gewirth has few supporters and many critics, or because Gewirth's supporters feel that they can safely leave the defense in Gewirth's hands? I don't know the answer to this question, but it seems to me that Gewirth's supporters need to stand up and be counted.[14]

4. I have a strong personal interest in attempting to elucidate and defend Gewirth in my own terms. In *Law as a Moral Judgment* (Beyleveld and Brownsword 1986), I and my coauthor attempted to spell out the consequences for legal philosophy of Gewirth's argument. Now, at one level our argument depends on the validity of Gewirth's argument. At another it doesn't. It can be read as an interpretation of the consequences of the hypothetically presumed validity of the argument. However, we have found it to be a fairly common response that, because we didn't undertake to defend Gewirth's argument step by step,[15] the whole book is fatally flawed (see, e.g., Ockleton 1988). In part, my response to this is that such criticism involves double-dealing. Many books are written in legal and moral philosophy in which certain fundamental premises are simply assumed and not argued for. Granted, the premises have to be at least entertainable rationally for the ensuing argument to have any live interest, but it is hardly the case that Gewirth's argument is not rationally entertainable, or that it is silly or disreputable. If every book spelling out consequences of a different moral thesis and moral epistemology had to defend its "axiomatic" theses against every extant criticism, then almost every such book would have to be considered fatally flawed, which at present escapes such criticism. Nevertheless, I am not content to rest with this response. I am perfectly willing to pick up the gauntlet. I do think that Gewirth's argument is valid. But if I cannot refer to Gewirth's work as the basis for my premises, and have to present proof positive myself for them, then I have no option but to produce something like the present work.

In the light of these comments, the general aim of the book can be stated as follows: I do not intend merely to summarize or paraphrase Gewirth's argument and replies to criticism. My aim is to present the argument as forcefully as possible by constructing (or

reconstructing), out of Gewirth's discussion, that sequence of inferences which I find most compelling, and to defend this sequence, in
particular, against all the criticisms that have been directed against
the argument. By doing so I hope to facilitate understanding (and
acceptance) not only of Gewirth's argument to the PGC, but also of
the legal theory that I (together with Roger Brownsword) have constructed on its foundation. At the very least, I hope to show that
extant criticism of Gewirth's argument is inadequate, that the argument is *very* much stronger than critics have tended to appreciate,
and that rejection of it is altogether premature. By clarifying it, I
hope to identify the issues upon which it really rests. Although I will
argue that these issues are to be settled in favor of the argument, I
will have achieved at least part of my aims if I can direct debate to
focus on a proper statement of them.

Gewirth's argument has three main stages. According to Gewirth,
a PPA logically must consider its freedom and well-being to be necessary goods (Stage I); hence, it must consider that it has a claim
right to its freedom and well-being (Stage II). In consequence, it
must consider that it has this right on the grounds that it is a PPA;
and, hence, it must accept "All PPAs have claim rights to freedom
and well-being"—which is the PGC (Stage III).

Part 1 presents Gewirth's argument to the PGC.

Chapter 2 begins with some preliminary remarks about Gewirth's
methodology. A thorough grasp of Gewirth's definitions, key distinctions, and procedures is essential if his argument is to be appreciated properly. I will later show that very many criticisms of the
argument rest upon inadequate understanding of, and inattention
to, these matters. I then present a sequence of steps for the three
stages of the argument. This sequence is constructed from the many
considerations that Gewirth advances in support of his argument.
During this presentation I refrain from commenting on objections
that have been raised against the argument, except where I deem
this to be necessary to elucidate the argument. Objections are dealt
with systematically in Part 2. I have decided against dealing with
the bulk of objections alongside the presentation of the argument for
two reasons. First, to do so would interrupt the flow of the argument
unnecessarily. Second, many criticisms that are directed at specific
inferences implicate interpretations of later inferences, and so cannot be considered adequately without an appreciation of the argument as a whole.

Chapter 3 summarizes the argument in two different ways. The
first summary displays the argument in the form of a reductio ad
absurdum of the proposition that a PPA may rationally hold any
criterion of practical reasonableness for its agency that conflicts

with the PGC, and is designed to clarify *the strategy* of the argument (the dialectically necessary method). The second is a partial formalization of the argument, which highlights *the logical operations* that it employs and structural features of their use.

Part 2 considers objections that have been raised against the argument.

I am concerned with objections to Gewirth's argument *to* the PGC (see note 10). I therefore ignore objections that have been raised against Gewirth's applications of the PGC,[16] unless these have a direct bearing on the argument to the PGC.[17] Gewirth (1981a) contends that the argument to the PGC justifies at least one absolute right. This is not so much part of the argument to the PGC as an interpretation of it. For this reason I do not pay any concerted attention to objections that have been raised against this interpretation.[18] Gewirth has also argued that the argument to the PGC is essentially an argument for a rights theory, and that the concept of rights cannot be replaced by that of duties (1986a). I also do not consider objections to this aspect of his theory.[19]

I have *attempted* to cover every published criticism of Gewirth's argument to the PGC that has appeared in English.[20] Although my concern is mainly with objections to the argument as presented in *Reason and Morality*, I have also included objections to later presentations of the argument, and to earlier presentations where the argument was not fully developed (and in which the supreme principle of morality is generally referred to as the PCC [principle of categorial consistency]).[21] In Gewirth's later presentations there are no substantial alterations of his position, so it is perfectly fair to treat criticisms of these articles as criticisms of the argument in *Reason and Morality*. There are, however, important differences between Gewirth's earlier writings and the argument in *Reason and Morality* and in later writings. In order to avoid becoming embroiled in explaining the differences, I have treated objections to these earlier writings as objections to my interpretation of the argument of *Reason and Morality*. In some cases this might not be fair to the critics of Gewirth's earlier work. My justification for this procedure is that I am not concerned with these objections *except insofar* as they can be construed as objections to my interpretation of the argument in *Reason and Morality*.

Ideally, one would like to group objections neatly as objections to various steps in the argument. This, however, is not always possible, as objections to one particular step very often implicate objections to other steps, and even to other stages. Thus the grouping of objections in various chapters is, to some extent, arbitrary. Some objections that are dealt with in one chapter might just as easily have been dealt with in another. Nevertheless, objections are by no means considered haphazardly. As far as possible, I try to follow the sequence of the argument, and later discussions often elaborate on and deepen earlier ones.

Where two or more critics press very similar objections, I have dealt with them separately, unless the objections really are identical. As I have already indicated, this is to meet the requirements of a proof, to avoid the dangers of conflation, and to be of use to students who wish to be able to use the book as a handbook of objections and replies.

On occasion, for these same reasons, when I have already discussed remarks made by a particular critic in conjunction with one objection, I reopen this discussion when it has relevance for a later, and different, objection.

Chapter 4 deals with objections to Stage I. These objections tend to focus on Gewirth's definition of "agency," on the claim that a PPA must value its purposes, and on the contention that freedom and well-being are generic conditions of agency.

Chapters 5–7 deal with objections to Stage II.

The focus of Chapter 5 is three interrelated sets of objections: those that charge the argument with deriving rights to freedom and well-being from the desire or need for these things; those that charge the argument with reducing morality to logic; and those that allege that the argument is an illegitimate "is-ought" derivation. Some of these objections can be construed as objections to the argument as a whole. I treat them as objections to Stage II, because moves that would justify these objections, if they are made at all, are basically made in Stage II.

Chapter 6 deals with objections that derive from the idea (in one form or another) that rights-claims presuppose a specific and contingent social context, and so cannot be logically necessary for a PPA to espouse.

Chapter 7 deals with objections that (by and large) can be related directly to my presentation of the steps for Stage II. These allege (variously) that the steps for Stage II exhibit logical gaps, involve equivocations, or can be evaded by PPAs who hold various practical viewpoints, or that the concept of prudential rights, or the concept of obligations on others relative to my interests (upon which the stage rests), are unintelligible. The most important of these objections implicates Stage III: it is that Stage II can be validly derived only if its conclusion is interpreted in such a way that it cannot support Stage III by purely logical universalization.

Chapter 8 deals with objections to Stage III. Correlative to what is the most important criticism of Stage II, the most important objections are those that allege that Stage III cannot be derived by logical universalization from a valid conclusion to Stage II without equivocating between moral and prudential rights, or without involving various assumptions that are either not dialectically necessary or even false.

Chapter 9 deals with miscellaneous objections.

Chapter 10 presents the argument as an argument for positive as well as negative rights—the presentation of Chapters 2 and 3 presenting the argument as one for at least negative rights—and considers objections to this thesis.

Chapter 11 summarizes the discussion of objections in Chapters 4–10, identifies the key issues upon which the validity of the argument rests, and summarizes the contentions adduced in the discussion of objections, which lead me to conclude that the questions that these raise are to be answered in favor of the argument.

In essence, the book consists of an analysis of the argument in Chapters 2 and 3, with a summary of my discussion and rejection of objections in Chapter 11, together with an "appendix in the middle," as it were (Chapters 4–10), which constitutes the evidence for the conclusions drawn in Chapter 11. Thus, there are, in principle, two ways in which this book might be read. Those who are interested in considering the argument from every angle should read the book in the normal sequential fashion. Others, with an interest limited to specific objections, are recommended to read initially Chapters 2 and 3; the sections of Chapter 5 entitled "The Argument from Attitudinal Consistency" (see #13) and "A General Analysis of Gewirth's 'Is-Ought' Derivation" (see #23); the section of Chapter 10 entitled "The Argument for Positive Rights"; and Chapter 11. They can then consult whatever chapters or objection commentaries they deem necessary. At the very least, Chapters 2 and 3 should be read before consulting my replies to critics. However, reading the book right through is highly preferable. Only in this way can an adequate picture of the argument as a whole be formed, and a sense of its richness will be lost if the alternative strategy is adopted. Although the structure of the book invites the second option, I suggest that it is only really appropriate for use after the book has been read sequentially.

Part 1

The Argument

2　The Argument Presented

In this chapter I present Gewirth's argument to the PGC in the way that I find most convincing. My terminology and explanations do not follow Gewirth invariably. The argument I present is not a mere summary of Gewirth's reasonings. At the same time, I do not think that any of the inferences are materially different from those that Gewirth draws: all the main steps are to be found in *Reason and Morality*.

For the most part, objections are not considered. To interrupt the line of reasoning to answer objections at every turn would interfere with the flow of the argument. Readers may thus find some of the explanations too terse. However, controversial matters are discussed fully in Part 2. An additional justification for postponing deeper analysis, when required, is that the significance of various issues is easier to appreciate when the complete sequence is in view.[1]

Preliminary Remarks

In order to understand Gewirth's argument, it is necessary to understand how he defines a number of key terms, and some general points about his methodology.

Action

Gewirth defines "action" as behavior done voluntarily in order to achieve a freely chosen purpose (goal or end), as voluntary intentional behavior (RM 22, 26–27).[2] He argues that any *rational* agent or prospective purposive agent (for which I shall indiscriminately use the abbreviation PPA) is committed to accepting a *moral* principle, the PGC.

The Main Steps of the Argument

The argument proceeds by a number of key steps, which may be divided into three stages. (See RM 48.)

STAGE I (RM 22–63)

A PPA claims (by definition)[3]

(1)   I do (or intend to do) X voluntarily for some purpose E.

By virtue of making this claim, the PPA rationally must consider that (claim) in logical sequence

(2)   E is good;

(3)   My freedom and well-being are generically necessary conditions of my agency;

(4)   My freedom and well-being are necessary goods.

STAGE II (RM 63–103)

By virtue of having to accept (4), the PPA must accept

(5)   I (even if no one else) have a claim right (but not necessarily a moral one) to my freedom and well-being.

STAGE III (RM 104–198, ESPECIALLY 104–128)

By virtue of having to accept (5) on the basis of (1), the PPA must accept

(9)   Other PPAs (PPAOs) have a (moral) claim right to their freedom and well-being.

If this is the case, then every PPA rationally must claim, by virtue of claiming to be a PPA,

(13)   Every PPA has a (moral) claim right to its freedom and well-being,

which is a statement of the PGC.

Reason

The criteria of rationality that Gewirth employs in drawing these inferences are confined to

the canons of deductive and inductive logic, including among the latter its bases in particular sense perceptions. (RM 22)

"A rational agent" means "an agent who thinks logically," i.e., one who avoids

self-contradiction in ascertaining or accepting what is logically involved in one's acting for purposes and in the associated concepts . . . [, and who exhibits] a certain minimal inductive rationality . . . . (RM 46)

Thus, what Gewirth purports to establish is that it follows *logically* from the concept of being a PPA that a PPA is rationally required to accept the PGC. No PPA can deny being bound by the PGC without contradicting that it is a PPA. Furthermore, for a PPA to violate the PGC in action is to contradict that it is a PPA, for such action implies the judgment by the PPA that it is not bound by the PGC.[4]

The Dialectically Necessary Method

The argument employs what Gewirth calls "the *dialectically necessary* method" within the *internal viewpoint* of a PPA. The method is dialectical, because it deduces its conclusions from claims made by certain persons about how they view things, rather than assertoric (in which case it would deduce conclusions from the assumed properties of things, rather than from anyone's subjective view of these properties). It is from the internal viewpoint of a PPA, because the claims it treats as premises are those made by a PPA about how *it* views *its own* agency. The method is necessary, rather than contingent, because (although the method is relative to PPAs in this way)

the dialectically necessary method propounds the contents of this relativity as necessary ones, since the statements it presents reflect judgments all agents necessarily make on the basis of what is necessarily involved in their actions. . . . The statements the method attributes to the agent are set forth as necessary ones in that they reflect what is conceptually necessary to being an agent who voluntarily or freely acts for purposes he wants to attain. (RM 44)

Since being a PPA is something that a PPA cannot logically deny, *acceptance of* the PGC *by a PPA* is presented as following with logical necessity from dialectically necessary premises (ones that a PPA cannot deny without self-contradiction), within the internal viewpoint of a PPA. Use of the dialectically necessary method implies that Gewirth is not attempting to establish the PGC itself as a truth. What he attempts to establish as a necessary truth is the proposition "A PPA contradicts that it is a PPA if it does not accept/act in accordance with the PGC." A prescription incompatible with the PGC is no more held to be a self-contradictory proposition than is an action violating the PGC. But it is held that a PPA contradicts its claim to be a PPA by violating the PGC or by accepting any PGC-incompatible prescriptions.[5]

In line with this method, the argument is presented in the first person. The reader is to imagine that he, she, or it ("it") is the "I" referred to in "I am a PPA," and in the judgments that are argued to follow from this. Central to the method is the claim that, in the argument only those propositions are accepted, either as definitively justified or as warranting favorable consideration, that emerge successively from the conceptual analysis of action and of the agent's necessary beliefs. . . . If, at any stage of this sequence, some particular agents or groups of agents have contingent beliefs or principles that are opposed to such propositions, this opposition will carry no justificatory weight. (RM 46–47)[6]

Only principles that emerge from such a sequence can be categorically obligatory, justified in a way that is not relative to arbitrary and contingent preferences.

Morality

Gewirth defines "a morality" as

a set of categorically obligatory requirements for action that are addressed at least in part to every actual or prospective agent, and that are concerned with furthering the interests, especially the most important interests, of persons or recipients other than or in addition to the agent or the speaker. The requirements are categorically obligatory in that compliance with them is mandatory for the conduct of every person to whom they are addressed regardless of whether he wants to accept them or their results, and regardless also of the requirements of any other institutions such as law or etiquette, whose obligatoriness may itself be doubtful or variable. Thus, although one moral requirement may be overridden by another, it may not be overridden by any nonmoral requirement, nor can its normative bindingness be escaped by shifting one's inclinations, opinions, or ideals. (RM 1)

This may be paraphrased as follows: If I think (according to a criterion of practical reasonableness, C, which I accept) that X ought to be done, then I regard this "ought" as a moral "ought" (and C as a criterion of moral reasonableness) *iff*

1. "X ought to be done" is addressed, at least in part, to every PPA (i.e., *this "ought"* is both self- and other-*referring, -addressing*, or -*directed*);
2. C takes favorable account of the interests of PPAs other than, or in addition to, myself (i.e., *the criterion* of this "ought" is other-*regarding*);
3. C prescribes that X ought to be done, whether or not the addressee of this prescription wants to do X (i.e., the requirement to do X is "conatively independent," independent of the particular occurrent wishes of the addressee). This condition may also be expressed by saying that C prescribes an exclusionary reason to do X, or that C prescribes that X *strictly* ought to be done; and
4. I regard C as overriding (i.e., I treat C as taking precedence

over other criteria I accept in cases where C and these other criteria conflict in their requirements).

Conditions 3 and 4 together embody the requirement that moral "oughts" are categorical. However, it is important to note that, according to this definition, an "ought" that I direct at an addressee can be categorical without being moral. It will be nonmoral, despite the fulfillment of 3 and 4, if C does not take favorable account of the interests of PPAs other than myself.[7]

Gewirth's task is to show that a PPA *rationally must*, within its internal viewpoint, adopt a moral point of view (rationalize its purposes by prescriptions that meet 1–4 above) without making the criterion of this "rationally must" a moral criterion; and that this must be a particular moral point of view: a PPA must rationalize its purposes by a criterion that takes favorable account *equally* of the interests of *all* PPAs (and not just the interests of some PPAs other than itself) *in their freedom and well-being* (rather than, or above, their other interests), thereby according all PPAs equal rights to their freedom and well-being—and, in effect, make its criterion of practical reasonableness the PGC.

Gewirth intends to answer three central questions of moral philosophy.

First, . . . the authoritative question: Why should one be moral . . . ? [Why should one adopt as one's criterion of practical reasonableness a criterion that meets Gewirth's definition of a morality or a moral (versus nonmoral) position? Answer: "Because not to do so is to contradict that one is a PPA."] If this question is not to be circular, the criterion of its 'should' must be other than the criterion of moral rightness whose obligatoriness is in question. [Gewirth proposes that the criterion be deductive and inductive reason.] Second, . . . the distributive question: Whose interests other than his own should the agent favorably consider in action? [Answer: "The interests of all PPAs."] . . . Third, . . . the substantive question: Of which interests should favorable account be taken? [Answer: "Their interests in freedom and well-being."] (RM 3)

Why choose to make the criterion for answering the authoritative question deductive and inductive reason? Because

the logical validity and necessity achieved by deduction and the empirical ineluctableness reflected in induction are directly constitutive of reason, and they give it a cogency and nonarbitrariness that provide a sufficient reason for relying on it. (RM 23)

In other words, because any attempt at justification *in any sense* "must make use of reason in the sense of deduction or induction or

both" (RM 22).[8] The use of any less stringent criterion will not satisfy Gewirth's "foundationalist" aspirations.[9]

Rights

The rights to freedom and well-being, which the argument maintains all PPAs must consider they have and which they must grant
to all other PPAs, are "strong" or "claim" rights. (See RM 65–67.)
These are correlative to obligations on the part of PPAs other than
the rights-holder, either not to interfere with the rights-holder having the objects (here, freedom and well-being) of the rights (*negative*
claim rights), or to provide the rights-holder with the objects of the
rights (*positive* claim rights). According to Gewirth, PPAs must generally consider that they have negative claim rights to freedom and
well-being, which they must also grant to others, and they must
claim and concede positive claim rights to freedom and well-being
under certain conditions. (See RM 67, 217–230.)[10]

Claim rights, whether negative or positive, are contrasted with
"weak" rights or "mere liberties." To say that X has a mere liberty to
do or have Y is to say that it is "all right" or "merely permissible"
("not impermissible") for X to do or have Y, but without any implication that it is "wrong," "not all right," or "impermissible" for others to interfere with X having or doing Y, or not to assist X in doing
or having Y. (See RM 67–68.)

It is also implicit in the argument that the claim rights with which
Gewirth is concerned are rights that a PPA can choose not to exercise
or "to waive." (See RM 334.) And it is also important to note, at the
outset, that Gewirth holds that claims to the having of rights can be
(formally) justified on grounds other than moral or legal ones. (See
RM 68–75.) This is parallel to Gewirth's claim that categorical
"ought" judgments need not be moral. Thus, Gewirth claims that
the rights-claim that concludes Stage II of the argument is not necessarily moral, but essentially prudential, being justified within the
PPA's internal viewpoint by the criterion of the PPA's own interests,
a criterion that does not necessarily take favorable account of the
interests of others. (See RM 145–146.)[11]

Freedom and Well-Being as Generic Features of Agency

According to Gewirth, the dialectical necessity of (2) "E is good"
entails the dialectical necessity of (4) "My freedom and well-being
are necessary goods," because it is true that (3) "Freedom and well-
being are generic features of my agency." It will facilitate my presentation of the argument if the terms "freedom," "well-being," and
"generic feature of agency" are explained beforehand.

By a PPA's "freedom," Gewirth means *the ability* of a PPA to control

each of his particular behaviors by his unforced choice ["occurrent freedom"] and . . . his longer-range ability to exercise such control ["dispositional freedom"]. . . . The loss of dispositional or long-range freedom, such as by imprisonment or enslavement, makes all or most purposive action impossible, while to lose some occurrent or particular freedom debars one from some particular action but not from all actions. Nevertheless, the loss of freedom in a particular case deprives one of the possibility of action in that case. (RM 52)

Dispositional freedom, at least in the extreme or ideal-typical case (for there is a continuum of degrees of necessity between dispositional and occurrent freedom), *is necessary in order to pursue or achieve any purpose at all.* My dispositional freedom cannot be interfered with without interfering with all my purposivity. In this sense, it is *a generic feature of my agency.* On the other hand, my occurrent freedom may be interfered with without affecting my ability to pursue or achieve all of my purposes. However, my occurrent freedom may also be given a generic-dispositional interpretation, in that *whatever purpose I wish to achieve,* I cannot pursue or achieve this purpose without it.

A PPA's well-being has three levels: "basic," "nonsubtractive," and "additive."

A PPA's *basic* well-being comprises

the proximate necessary preconditions of his performance of any and all of his actions . . . [viz.,] certain physical and psychological dispositions ranging from life and physical integrity (including such of their means as food, clothing, and shelter) to mental equilibrium and a feeling of confidence as to the general possibility of attaining one's goals. (RM 53–54)

Nonsubtractive well-being comprises whatever a PPA needs to retain what it already has that it regards as good, and whatever, before it acts (apart from its basic well-being), it has and regards as good. (See RM 54–55.)

Additive well-being comprises whatever a PPA needs to increase its existing level of purpose-fulfillment, and whatever it wishes to have (apart from its basic and nonsubtractive well-being).[12]

Freedom may be regarded as an aspect of basic well-being (in which dispositional freedom ranks higher than occurrent freedom [see RM 254], and life ranks higher than dispositional freedom [see RM 218, 343]), but Gewirth generally chooses to treat freedom as a distinct category from well-being.[13]

My basic well-being, like my freedom (both dispositional and occurrent [dispositionally interpreted]), is a generic feature of my agency in an all-inclusive sense, being necessary for my *pursuit* as well as my achievement of my purposes. Nonsubtractive and additive well-being may also be given generic-dispositional interpretations, not as particular purposes and the contingently necessary conditions for their specific achievement, but as *abilities and conditions* to retain and expand one's capacities for particular actions *in general*. As such, they are not generic features of my agency in the all-inclusive sense. They are not necessary conditions for my pursuit per se of my purposes, only necessary conditions for *generally succeeding* in achieving my purposes. (See RM 58–63.)[14]

Furthermore, although particular occurrent well-being (especially nonsubtractive and additive) will vary with individual circumstances and preferences, generic-dispositional well-being (whether basic, nonsubtractive, or additive) is invariable. (See RM 55–56, 59.) *Throughout the argument "freedom and well-being" is to be understood in the generic-dispositional sense.*[15]

The components of well-being

fall into a hierarchy determined by the degree of their indispensability for purposive action. The basic capabilities of action . . . are the most necessary of all, since without these [an agent] would be able to act either not at all or only in certain very restricted ways. Among these . . . there is also a hierarchy, headed by life and then including various other physical and mental goods, some more indispensable than others for action and purpose-fulfillment. Of the other two kinds of capabilities, the nonsubtractive rank higher than the additive because to be able to retain the goods one has is usually a necessary condition of being able to increase one's stock of goods. Thus the hierarchy of well-being corresponds somewhat to the 'hierarchy of needs' developed in psychological theories. (RM 62–63)

According to Gewirth, at various points in the argument

it will be important . . . to emphasize these degrees of necessity, but at many others it will be sufficient to refer without differentiation to freedom and well-being as necessary goods [and generic features of agency]. For, viewed generically-dispositionally, freedom and well-being are collectively the most general and proximate necessary conditions of all the agent's various purpose-fulfilling actions. Similarly, the [distinction] between . . . action and successful action, can be elided in some contexts . . . so long as the several ways in which the generic features are necessary for action are kept in view. (RM 63)

Finally, although this has greater bearing on arguments from the PGC than on the argument to the PGC, it is worth noting that when Gewirth argues for the rational necessity of the PGC, he argues (in effect) for the rational necessity for PPAs to accept a complex structure of rights corresponding to the hierarchy in which the components of freedom and well-being are arranged. In this hierarchy, importance is assessed by the criterion of degrees of necessity for acting. Correspondingly, in cases of conflict, the PGC specifies that rights to components that rank higher in the hierarchy override rights to components that rank lower in the hierarchy. (See RM 342–344.)[16]

The Argument

Stage I

STATEMENT (1) ENTAILS STATEMENT (2)

Given Gewirth's definition of "an action," any PPA may be characterized, dialectically, as claiming

(1)   I do (or intend to do) X voluntarily for (my freely chosen)[17] purpose E.

By virtue of this claim, I (who might be any PPA) am logically committed to claiming

(2)   E is good.

If I do X *voluntarily for* E, then I imply that I am for E, that I have a favorable attitude towards achieving E by my agency. That I claim "E is good" means that I attach a positive value to E. (See RM 40.) Because E is my freely chosen purpose, this attachment involves a value *judgment* (see RM 41),[18] at least dispositionally.[19] Furthermore, because I actually do X for E, or intend to do so, I do not merely judge that E has a positive value for me. I claim that I am actually motivated by this attitude to do X. I, therefore, claim that E is of sufficient value (for me) *to move me to do X.* (See RM 49.)

It does not follow from this that I must consider E to be morally good (for I may not think about my purposes in moral terms at all), and I may even consider E to be morally bad. (See RM 50–51.) Subjectively, *in choosing to pursue E,* I need only consider E to be morally good *if* I espouse a moral viewpoint according to which E is morally good, *and* my choosing to pursue E is the result of my choosing to be motivated by the value given to E by this viewpoint. It is perfectly possible, however, for me to consider E to be morally bad, to attach a positive value to E on nonmoral grounds, and to act in accordance with these grounds, despite the fact that to do so runs counter to my moral evaluation of E.

Indeed,

[t]he agent may or may not reflectively appraise or evaluate his purpose on

various criteria before, after, or perhaps even during the time he acts to attain it . . . . (RM 50)

However, a value judgment need not require reflective appraisal according to criteria independent of the desire that motivates the action. A PPA's "direct wanting to perform the action" involves a "judgment of at least immediate good on his part" (RM 50). Whether or not a PPA's wanting to perform an action reflects some *further* criterion for appraising its purposes, there is implicit in its acting for a purpose *some criterion* that the PPA follows according to which it regards its purpose as "good."

In other words, the judgment that I make in (2) reflects my motivations, which might be, but which are not necessarily, in line with any particular "rationalizing" viewpoint that I might happen to espouse as to what are, in a definitive sense, "good" or "acceptable" reasons for me to pursue purposes. Being a motivational judgment, it does not depend upon my espousing any particular moral, amoral, or even adeontic, rationalizing viewpoint (SPR, subjective viewpoint on practical reasonableness) for my purposes. (See RM 29.)[20] Only so interpreted is it a judgment that I am committed to by virtue of being a PPA *simpliciter,* rather than by virtue of being a PPA with a particular (contingent) SPR for my purposes that I invariably follow.[21]

In order to avoid any suspicion that the use of the term "good" will lead to equivocation, we may restate (2) as

(2a)   I attach a positive value to E on some ground, which motivates me to pursue E

(which I will generally express as "I attach a proactive value to E").

The meaning to be attached to (2) can be explained in a slightly different way. (1) also entails

(2b)   I wish (am motivated) to achieve E by my agency.

Now, just as (2) does not imply that a moral viewpoint guides my motivation to pursue E, (2b) does not imply that my motivation to pursue E is not morally guided; if I espouse a moral rationalizing viewpoint, it might be. "Wish" is to be understood in an "intentional" sense, and not necessarily exclusively in either an "inclinational" (or "hedonic") sense or in a "noninclinational" sense. (See RM 39–41, 49–51.) To say that I wish to achieve E in an inclinational sense is to say that my motivation to pursue E derives from my emotive inclination to pursue E: my choice to pursue E is a choice to follow my emotive inclination. To say that I wish to achieve E in a noninclinational sense is to say that my motivation to pursue E does not derive from an emotive inclination on my part to pursue E: my choice to pursue E is a choice to act on motivational grounds that might run counter to my emotive inclinations. (2b) is neutral with respect to the grounds upon which I attach a positive value to E. To say that I wish to achieve E in an intentional sense is simply to say that I attach a positive value to E, which may or may not derive from an emotive inclination on my part to pursue E, but which is the determining consideration in my choosing to pursue E. Understood in this sense, (2b) is equivalent to (2a).

STATEMENT (2) ENTAILS STATEMENT (4)

It is true, and I logically (where this includes inductive as well as deductive considerations) must recognize, that

(3)   My freedom and well-being are generically necessary conditions of my agency.

This may be restated as

(3a)   Whatever purposes I intend to pursue by my agency, I need my freedom and well-being in order to pursue (with any chance of success)/achieve these purposes by my agency.

In order to achieve particular purposes by my agency I need particular capacities and resources. Some of these needs are contingent upon the particular purposes that I choose to pursue: they are needed for my achievement of one or more of my purposes, but not for my achievement of every purpose that I might happen to have. On the other hand, I need my freedom and well-being (viewed as my general abilities to pursue, retain, and expand my purposes) to achieve any purposes whatsoever by my agency. My needs for freedom and well-being are generic features of my agency.[22]

It follows, from the conjunction of (2) and (3), that it is dialectically necessary for me to hold

(4)   My freedom and well-being are necessary goods.

If I contingently need M in order to achieve a particular purpose E by my agency, and regard E as good (in the sense explained above—because I intend to pursue E) then I logically must regard M as good (in the same sense) at least in its capacity as an instrumental requirement for my achievement of E by my agency, *conditional upon my persevering in my intention to pursue E by my agency*. However, I need my freedom and well-being in order to achieve E by my agency, *whatever E might happen to be*. Therefore, I logically must consider my freedom and well-being to be good at least as a means to my achievement of my purposes (instrumentally good), *conditional only upon my intention to pursue some (which may be any) purpose by my agency,* which means *subject only to my claim "I am a PPA."* What (4) specifically signifies is that I contradict "I am a PPA" if I do not regard my freedom and well-being as at least instrumentally good, *whatever purposes I am motivated to pursue.*[23]

Stage II

The task for Stage II is to show that if it is dialectically necessary, within my internal viewpoint as a PPA, for me to hold (4), then it follows, within this same viewpoint, that it is dialectically necessary for me to consider that I have a claim right to my freedom and well-being. According to Stage II, I contradict "I am a PPA" if I do not consider that I have a claim right to my freedom and well-being.

Gewirth points out that, if I consider that I have a right to anything, then I must consider that I have a right to my freedom and well-being. (See RM 63.) This follows quite simply from the fact that I need my freedom and well-being in order to achieve any purposes by my agency. Without my freedom and well-being I cannot exercise any rights that I consider that I have. So, by "'may' implies 'can,'" if I consider that I have a right to X, then I must consider that I have a right to my freedom and well-being, whatever X is. For, if it is a condition of a PPA's being entitled to do X that the PPA can do X, then it follows that, where a PPA is entitled to do X, it is entitled to the conditions under which it can do X. However, this observation does not constitute an adequate argument for holding what Stage III purports to establish, that I *must* consider that I have a moral right to my freedom and well-being. There are two reasons for this.

1.   I might consider that I have a right to X without considering that I have a moral right to X, because I might ground my claim to a right to X on nonmoral grounds, on criteria that do not take favorable account of the purposes of PPAs other than myself.

2.   I might not consider that I have any rights (moral or otherwise) at all.

Thus, in order to establish that it is dialectically necessary for me to accept the PGC within my internal viewpoint as a PPA, it must be shown that it is dialectically necessary for me to consider that I have a *moral* right to my freedom and well-being, *even if* I do not happen to consider that I have any moral rights, *or even if* I do not happen to

consider that I have rights of any kind at all. In fact, Stage II purports to establish that *I must consider* that I have a claim right (but
not necessarily a moral one) to my freedom and well-being, even if
I do not consider that I have any claim rights at all, *because* I must
consider that my freedom and well-being are necessary goods;
whereas Stage III purports to establish that *if* I must consider that I
have a claim right to my freedom and well-being *on such grounds,*
then I must consider that I, and all PPAs, have *moral* rights to our
freedom and well-being, even if I do not consider that I have a moral
right to my freedom and well-being.

Gewirth devotes forty pages to Stage II in *Reason and Morality.*
(See RM 63–103.) After a number of preliminary remarks he presents
what he calls his "direct argument." (See RM 78–79.) This may be
paraphrased as follows:

Because my freedom and well-being are necessary conditions of all my actions, in order to achieve my purposes, I (categorically) need my freedom
and well-being not to be interfered with by PPAOs (other PPAs). This may be
stated as "PPAO must not interfere with my freedom and well-being (if I am
to achieve any of my purposes by my agency)." However, because of my
conative attachment to my purposes, the significance of this "must" is not
merely factual (it does not merely express a means-ends relationship). I
must, for whatever my purposes, be opposed to whatever interferes with my
having freedom and well-being (because I categorically need my freedom
and well-being), and, thus, be opposed to PPAO's interfering with my freedom and well-being; and this opposition constitutes a practical requirement,
from my point of view, that PPAO strictly ought not to interfere with my freedom and well-being (because I categorically need my freedom and well-
being). Given the correlativity of strict other-referring "oughts" and claim
rights, this dialectically necessitates that I hold "I have a claim right to my
freedom and well-being."

In the pages that follow, Gewirth presents three alternative statements of this argument. (See RM 80–82.) In this argument, the key
move is from "My freedom and well-being are necessary goods" ($\equiv$
"I must (for whatever my purposes) be opposed to PPAO's interfering with my freedom and well-being") to "I must consider that
PPAO strictly ought not to interfere with my freedom and well-
being (as a means to my purposes)." The direct argument itself suggests that what licenses this move is that a reason for me to want
PPAO not to interfere with my freedom and well-being, or to oppose
PPAO's interfering with my freedom and well-being, is *for me* a reason why PPAO ought not to interfere with my freedom and well-
being. However, in one of his alternative statements, Gewirth can, or
so I interpret him, be read as claiming that it is contradictory for me
to hold "My freedom and well-being are necessary goods" together

with "It is not the case that PPAO strictly ought not to interfere with my freedom and well-being" (≡ "It is not the case that I have a claim right to my freedom and well-being"), because the dialectical necessity of the former claim makes it dialectically necessary (required) for me to be opposed to interference with my freedom and well-being, whereas if I make the latter claim I imply that it is dialectically permissible for me not to be opposed to interference with my freedom and well-being. (See RM 80–81.) I call this latter intimation "the argument from attitudinal consistency."

The rest of Gewirth's discussion is devoted to considering objections to Stage II from "an ethical egoist of the universalist sort," "an amoralist" (adeonticist), "the fanatic," "a radical social critic," and those who hold that the concept of a right is historically contingent. (See RM 82–103.)[24]

Now, I do not wish to suggest that Gewirth's "direct argument" with its alternative statements is inadequate.[25] In my opinion, however, the most convincing demonstration of Stage II that Gewirth provides is to be found in his reply to the objection from "the amoralist" (adeonticist).[26] (See RM 89–95.) Because Gewirth presents this demonstration as a reply to an adeonticist critic, and I wish to state the considerations he advances as a proof that holds independent of the contingent assumptions made by the adeonticist (or anyone else), I shall present this argument in a generalized form that is my own interpretation of Gewirth's reasoning.

THE KEY STEPS IN STATEMENT (4) ENTAILS STATEMENT (5)

The sequence that I find most convincing is outlined here.

We begin with (4) "My freedom and well-being are necessary goods," which may be restated as

(4a)   I consider my freedom and well-being to be (at least instrumentally) good, good for my purposes, whatever my purposes ≡ I (at least instrumentally) ought to value my freedom and well-being, for my purposes, whatever my purposes ≡ With the positive value that I, *as a PPA*, attach to my purposes as the criterion, I ought to attach a positive value to my freedom and well-being, at least *as instrumental to my purposes*, whatever my purposes.

Because the positive value I attach to my purposes (my criterion for this judgment) is proactive, this means that it is dialectically necessary, *within my internal viewpoint as a PPA*, for me to assent to

(4b)   I (at least instrumentally) ought to pursue my freedom and well-being, for whatever my purposes.

Since this "ought" is independent of my particular occurrent purposes, it is a strict "ought" on the criterion of my conative attachment to my purposes (my prudential criterion). It is restatable as

(4c)   I have (at least) instrumentally at least a prima facie duty (on my prudential criterion) to defend my freedom and well-being from interference ≡ I, at least prima facie, strictly ought (on my prudential criterion) to defend my freedom and well-being from interference, *as a means to my purposes.*

I am not, however, required to defend my freedom and well-being from interference as an end in itself. I may permit others to interfere with my freedom and well-being as a means to relinquishing my agency, and I may, myself, act to end my agency. Even in such cases, however, I am required to defend my freedom and well-being as the means to bringing about the relinquishment of my agency. *As a shorthand* for this complex requirement, we may say that (4c) is equivalent to

> I have (at least) a prima facie duty (on my prudential criterion) to defend my freedom and well-being *from such interference as is against my will.*[27]

Since "ought" implies "can," I must assent to

(4d)   PPAO (every other PPA) has at least a prima facie duty (on my prudential criterion) to (at least) refrain from such interference with my freedom and well-being *as is against my will* (i.e., a duty to refrain from such interference as is not willed by me as a means to relinquishing my agency).[28]

By the logical correlativity of other-referring strict "oughts" and claim rights, it follows that I must assent to

(5)   I (at least) have at least a prima facie claim right (on my prudential criterion) to my freedom and well-being.[29]

This sequence requires explanation.

COMMENTS ON STATEMENT (4a)
Two aspects of (4a) require comment.

1. From my internal viewpoint as a PPA, this "ought" is genuinely prescriptive: it is not merely a descriptive statement of a means-ends relationship. (See RM 79.) From "A needs M in order to achieve E,"

it might be said, it does not follow that A is required to consider M to be good (to attach a positive value to it) in any sense. This, however, depends upon whether the statement "A needs M in order to achieve E" is dialectical or assertoric, and if dialectical, upon who is claiming that A needs M in order to achieve E. Assertorically, it does not follow that A is required to consider that M is good, because there is no implication that E *is good, independent of the criterion that A follows in choosing to pursue E*. However, any PPA who *claims that E is good*, is, *conditional upon this claim (conditional upon retention of E as its purpose)*, required to consider that M is good; and where the speaker is A, who freely chooses to pursue E, A is logically required to consider E, and thus M (conditionally), to be good. From "I need M in order to achieve E (which I consider to be good)," it follows that I am required to do something, viz., to consider M (conditionally) to be good, and this requirement presents itself to me as an "ought." In general terms, to say that I ought to do X is to say that I have a reason to do X. Where I value E, and perceive that I need M for E, the value I attach to E is (for me) a reason that requires me to value M. Where M is my freedom and well-being, I, as a PPA who values my purposes (by definition), have a reason to value my freedom and well-being, whatever my purposes (conditional only upon my having some purposes, and as a PPA I necessarily have some purposes), because I need my freedom and well-being in order to achieve any purposes whatsoever by my agency.

2. The value that a PPA must attach to its freedom and well-being is at least instrumental. The instrumental value that a PPA must attach to its freedom and well-being is, however, a special sort of instrumental value. It is not an instrumental value that depends upon the PPA having specific purposes rather than others. Because a PPA needs its freedom and well-being to achieve any purpose at all by its agency, it must value its freedom and well-being *categorically as a means* to its purposes. Its freedom and well-being have, for it, categorical or intrinsic value *as the necessary means* to its achievement of its purposes by its agency; and its capacity to control its own behavior by its unforced choice, and its basic well-being, have, for it, categorical or intrinsic value as the necessary means to the very possibility of its agency. *If* "I value X categorically or intrinsically" means "I consider that I ought to value X, whether I do so or not," then a PPA must value its freedom and well-being intrinsically *in an instrumental manner*, for it is required to attach *instrumental* value to its freedom and well-being, whatever it wishes to do. I shall call this "intrinsic valuation in sense 1." This can be expressed somewhat differently. My freedom and well-being are of instrumental value to me, not just as being instrumental to this or that particular occurrent

purpose, but to my autonomous purposivity as such, to my *being a PPA*, in the achievemental mode; and my freedom (as my voluntariness as such) and my *basic* well-being are instrumental to my being a PPA at all. In other words, my freedom and well-being are of *intrinsic* value to me in the procedural context of my activity *as a PPA*.

There are, however, at least two further senses of "categorical" or "intrinsic" value, in which it is not the case that a PPA must value its freedom and well-being "categorically," "intrinsically," or "for their own sakes."

In the first of these senses, sense 2, to value X intrinsically is to value X, not because it is a means to something that one values, but as an end in itself. For a PPA to have to value its freedom and well-being intrinsically *in sense 2*, it is necessary for a PPA to have to value the fact that it is a PPA for its own sake, and not because having the capacities that make it a PPA is the necessary means to achieving whatever it might value by its agency. For intrinsic valuation in sense 2 to be necessary, a PPA would have to value its being the case that it has purposes that it chooses to pursue. However, a PPA might wish not to be a PPA. In relation to the fact that it, as a PPA, has purposes that it wishes to pursue voluntarily, such a wish is irrational. Outside of this procedural context, however, such a wish is not irrational. I contradict "I am a PPA" if I do not wish to pursue some purpose E voluntarily, but I do not contradict "I am a PPA" (≡ "I act voluntarily for some purpose E") if I wish that it were the case that I could not act voluntarily for any purpose E, or even if I act so as to bring it about that I am no longer able to choose to pursue any purposes by my agency. (This is discussed further under #4 [objection 4].)

In the second of these senses, sense 3, to value X intrinsically is to value X deontically or morally, either as an end in itself or as a means to something that is valued deontically or morally as an end in itself. However, a PPA need only value its freedom and well-being deontically or morally *in this sense*, on account of categorically needing its freedom and well-being in order to achieve its purposes, *if* there are some purposes that it values deontically or morally as ends in themselves. Of course, some PPAs do attach such deontic or moral value to some of their purposes, and such PPAs must attach deontic or moral value to their freedom and well-being. But it is not a premise of the argument that PPAs must be deonticists or adopt "a moral point of view," and it has not been shown at this stage that they must do so. Here, it must be noted, the difference between the deontic valuation involved in senses 1 and 3 is that, in sense 3, I ought to value X because X ought to be (rather than just is) valued for its own sake or as a means to what ought to be valued for its own sake, whereas in sense 1, I ought to value X as being a means to whatever I value, whether the things I value ought to be valued for their own sakes or not.

In *my* view, then, a PPA must regard its freedom and well-being as intrinsically good in sense 1, but need not regard its freedom and well-being as intrinsically good in sense 2 or 3, because its freedom and well-being are generic features of its agency. Furthermore, to say that a PPA must regard its freedom and well-being as at least instrumentally good is to say that it *might* regard its freedom and well-being as intrinsically good in sense 2 or 3, but need not do so, but must regard its freedom as categorically instrumentally good (intrinsically good in sense 1).[30]

STATEMENT (4a) ENTAILS STATEMENT (4b)

(4b) follows from (4a) simply by the proactive meaning of "good" in this argument. As a PPA, I do not value my purposes in a purely theoretical or abstract manner. I am, *by definition*, motivated by my positive valuation of my purposes to pursue these purposes. I regard the "goodness" that I attribute to my purposes as providing sufficient motivation to initiate action on my part. In Gewirth's terms, a PPA is a "conatively normal person," a being who

has the self-interested motivations common to most persons and is willing to expend the effort needed to fulfill them . . . . (RM 90)

This *proactive* positive valuation of my purposes must, logically, be carried over to the necessary instrumental conditions of my achievement of my purposes. In consistency with my proactive positive valuation of a purpose, I must make a positive proactive valuation of the necessary instrumental conditions for its fulfillment. Because my freedom and well-being are necessary instrumental conditions for my fulfillment of any purposes that I might be proactively motivated to pursue, and as a PPA I am proactively motivated to pursue at least some purposes, I instrumentally ought to pursue my freedom and well-being/defend my freedom and well-being from interference[31] for the sake of all and whatever proactive motivations I *might happen to have.*

It cannot, thus, be said that the instrumental "ought" prescriptions to which I am committed by virtue of my commitment to (4) are merely attitude/evaluation-directing and not *practical*-prescriptive (action-directing), even if it is held that, in general, adopting an attitude or making an evaluation is not really an action.[32]

STATEMENT (4b) ENTAILS STATEMENT (4c)

Not all "oughts" are duties (obligations or strict "oughts"). (4b), at least instrumentally, expresses at least a prima facie strict "ought," which makes it equivalent to (4c). It must also be emphasized that this "ought" is essentially prudential, and not necessarily moral. All of this requires clarification.

Strict "Oughts"

Gewirth does not provide an explicit definition of a strict "ought" as such. However, from his definition of "a moral position," and from his analysis of an *other-referring* strict "ought" (see RM 66–67),[33] the following definition can be constructed:

> I strictly ought to do X (according to criterion Z) ≡ (According to Z) I ought (in the sense of requirement)[34] to do X, whether or not I wish to do X.

> If there are no circumstances in which, according to criterion Z, I am not strictly required to do X, then "I strictly ought to do X" prescribes an *absolute duty* (according to criterion Z).
> If there are circumstances in which, according to criterion Z, I am not strictly required to do X, then "I strictly ought to do X" prescribes a *prima facie duty* (according to criterion Z).

However, although criterion Z might strictly require me to do X, I might not accept criterion Z as the criterion that determines what I have good reason to do. For me to consider that I strictly ought to do X, for me to consider "I strictly ought to do X" as subjectively binding, on the grounds that criterion Z strictly requires me to do X, I must accept criterion Z as the criterion of what I have good reason to do. Furthermore, if it is to be the case that I, as a PPA, rationally must consider that I strictly ought to do X, then it must be the case that a criterion that strictly requires me to do X is a criterion that I am rationally required to accept as the criterion of what I have good reason to do.

In this terminology, (4b) prescribes a strict "ought" or duty.[35] The criterion that validates this prescription is "I am a PPA," or more clearly, the proactive positive valuation of my purposes that I, as a PPA, (logically) make (my "prudential" criterion). I cannot, without contradicting "I am a PPA," eschew this criterion. So, it is rationally necessary for me to accept "I have a duty to defend my freedom and well-being from interference" as subjectively binding. Thus, (4b) and the other deontic judgments that flow from it are "doubly

strict." They are strict in being conatively independent *on* my "prudential" criterion, and this criterion is one that is *itself* strictly binding on me as a PPA. This "double strictness" implies that if the
argument is valid, then the PGC is a categorical norm on criteria that
are categorically binding for PPAs, which makes the obligations it
validates categorically binding for PPAs.

Instrumental Duties

This duty is instrumental. "I ought to defend my freedom and well-
being from interference" only prescribes a strict "ought," on my
prudential criterion, when this prescription is instrumental. It is
only *as a means to my purposes* that I am required to defend my freedom and well-being from interference, whatever my purposes.
Quite clearly, if my purpose is to commit suicide, or in some other
way to relinquish my agency, then I can only do so by interfering
with my freedom or well-being, or by allowing my freedom or well-
being to be interfered with. So, it cannot be true that I must consider
that I ought to defend my freedom and well-being from interference
as *ends in themselves*, whatever my purposes *on my prudential criterion*. Nevertheless, I need my freedom and well-being in order to do
whatever I wish to do to relinquish my agency. In order to relinquish
my freedom or well-being, I need to be free to do so, and I need my
well-being in order to be able to do so; and this means that it remains true that I must consider that I instrumentally ought to defend my freedom and well-being from interference, even when my
chosen purpose is to relinquish my agency.[36]

This strict instrumental prescription enjoins me to defend my
freedom and well-being from interference *except* when such interference is willed by me as a means to relinquish my agency. This means
that I must consider that I have an *intrinsic* duty to defend my freedom and well-being *from such interference as is against my will* (from
interference that is not willed by me as an end in itself).[37]

Now, it is clear from the definition of a strict "ought" or "duty,"
which I have given, that I cannot have a duty to do X, if I can release
myself from this duty simply by willing that I not be subject to it.[38]
It might, thus, be objected to this formulation that since I can release
myself from a prudential requirement to defend my freedom and
well-being from interference by willing such interference as an end
in itself, any such requirement cannot be conceived of by me as my
duty. However, this misses the point, which is that, although I can
release myself from a prudential requirement to defend my freedom
and well-being from interference *as an end in itself* by willing such
interference as an end in itself (and, indeed, cannot be subject to

such a requirement), I cannot release myself from a prudential requirement to defend my freedom and well-being from interference
as a means to my purposes. The class of "interference that is not willed
by me as an end in itself" coincides with the class of "interference
that thwarts the purposes I will," which coincides with the class of
"interference that removes the means to my purposes." Thus understood, I can have a prudential requirement to defend my freedom
and well-being from "such interference as is against my will," as I
cannot release myself from a requirement to defend myself from
such interference. This point may also be expressed by saying that
although I may, without contradiction, will/pursue interference
with my freedom and well-being as an end in itself, I cannot, without contradiction, will/pursue interference with my freedom and
well-being as a means to my purposes, even if I will interference
with my freedom and well-being as an end in itself.

The instrumental nature of this self-referring duty has important
implications for the specification of the PPA's prudential rights-
claim, and ultimately of the PGC. It follows from the instrumental
nature of this duty, that a PPA can release PPAO from its derived
duty (see [4c] → [4d]) not to interfere with PPA's freedom and well-
being, for, from PPA's viewpoint, PPAO has a duty not to interfere
with PPA's freedom and well-being against PPA's will. Quite clearly,
if my self-referring duty to defend my freedom and well-being from
interference were a duty to pursue my freedom and well-being as
ends in themselves, I could not release PPA from any duty of noninterference that logically follows from this duty. Thus, the rights-
claim in (5) is to a right for my freedom and well-being not to be
interfered with against my will; from which it will ultimately follow
that the PGC states that all PPAs have a duty not to interfere with
the freedom and well-being of all PPAs against their will; so that the
PGC grounds what is essentially a rights-ethics rather than an ethics
of duty.[39]

The Prima Facie Qualification and the Prudential Nature of This "Ought"

It is important to appreciate that it is not dialectically necessary for
me to hold that this duty is more than a prima facie one, but to
understand why this is so, it is necessary to understand what it
means to say that this "ought" prescription, as well as the other
deontic prescriptions of Stage II, is essentially prudential rather
than moral.

As a matter of contingent fact, I might espouse any one of a wide
variety of principles as to what purposes I have good reason to

choose (SPRs for my purposes). At the most abstract level, my espousal of a particular SPR for my purposes will classify me as an *adeonticist* (if I hold that it is not impermissible for me to choose to pursue any purposes that I am motivated to pursue, regardless of the motivating consideration), a *deontic amoralist* (if I hold that I have duties/rights, so that it is impermissible for me to choose to pursue certain purposes even if I am motivated to pursue them, but do not hold that I owe duties to other PPAs correlative to which they have claim rights against me), or a *moralist* (if I hold that I owe duties to at least some other PPAs, correlative to which they have claim rights against me).

I consider that I have a good reason to pursue a purpose if I wish to pursue this purpose and do not consider that such pursuit is impermissible (which makes my reason a nonexclusionary reason), or if I consider that I ought to pursue this purpose whether I wish to do so or not (which makes my reason an exclusionary reason, although, of course, if I am an adeonticist, I will not recognize any exclusionary reasons).

Now, it will not have escaped notice that the criterion that validates (4c) is motivational, rather than a criterion of good reasons. On the other hand, (4c) operates as a criterion of good (indeed, exclusionary) reason. How does Gewirth derive a conclusion that establishes a criterion for good reasons from a premise (my proactive valuation of purposes) that does not necessarily describe what I consider I have good reason to do? The answer to this question is important in its own right, and also because it has direct bearing on the "prima facie" qualification,[40] and the elucidation of "prudential."

The answer is quite straightforward. As a PPA I need my freedom and well-being for whatever purposes I am motivated to pursue. As such, I need my freedom and well-being for those purposes that I consider I have good reason to pursue (as well as those, if any, that I consider I do not have good reason to pursue, or even for those that I consider I have bad reason to pursue), regardless of what these purposes are, and thus regardless of my SPR. Thus, any value that my SPR attaches to purposes that it ratifies must (on pain of eschewal of this as my SPR) be attached to my freedom and well-being as the necessary conditions for my achievement of these purposes (and this will be the value of a good reason). *Provided that I have an SPR for my purposes that prescribes in accordance with (4c), I may view the "ought" of (4c) as qualified by that SPR. So qualified*, it would, thus, not be wrong to say that the proximate criterion on which (4c) is validated is my SPR, rather than my proactive evaluation of my purposes, *provided that* it is recognized that the reason why my SPR (whatever it is) validates (4c) (or, better, the reason why I rationally must hold an SPR that validates [4c]) is that I am required to value my freedom and well-being proactively in consistency with my proactive valuation of my purposes, whatever they might be (on instrumental grounds). It is for this latter reason that I deny "I am a PPA" if I eschew (4c), and my proactive valuation of my purposes, therefore, remains the ultimate (or direct) criterion on which (4c) is validated.[41]

Now, the argument does not proceed on the question-begging assumption that, as a PPA, I must be a moralist, rather than a deontic amoralist, or even an adeonticist. At least for the sake of argument, it must be granted that I logically, without contradicting "I am a PPA," may espouse any SPR for my purposes. (See RM 29, 49–50, 71.)[42] *On this assumption of dialectical consistency,* the validation that adeontic, deontic amoral, and moral SPRs for my purposes provide for (4c) is, however, different. If I am an adeonticist, and hold that it is not impermissible for me to act on any of my motivations, then I will recognize (following this maxim) no exclusionary considerations that require me to sacrifice my freedom and well-being. The duty I owe, on this maxim, to defend any aspect of my generic features from interference will in effect be conditional only upon the hierarchical importance of that feature as a need for my agency.[43] On the other hand, if I am a deonticist, then it is conceivable (but not necessary)[44] that I will hold, in certain circumstances, that there is a conflict between any duty to defend my freedom and well-being derived from *my* need for freedom and well-being and other duties I recognize, and that in some such cases a duty not to defend my freedom and well-being will be overriding. This is most clear in the case of an altruistic SPR for my purposes, where defense of my freedom and well-being threatens the freedom and well-being of PPAO. However, even in the case of an altruistic SPR for my purposes, I must still consider that I have a duty to defend my freedom and well-being from interference, even though this duty may be overridden in certain circumstances, because I will need my freedom and well-being in order to carry out my standard altruistic duties. Even on an altruistic SPR for my purposes, then, I must recognize at least a prima facie duty to defend my freedom and well-being from interference.

However, if I am required to espouse (4c) *because I am a PPA,* then the dialectical necessity of (4c) within my internal viewpoint as a PPA constitutes a reductio ad absurdum of the rationality of my espousing adeonticism. Adeonticism is shown to be incoherent for me to espouse as a PPA, because *as a PPA* I logically must recognize exclusionary reasons for action that my adeonticism eschews. (This is considered further under #28 and #29.) Nevertheless, this does not mean that it has been shown that (4c) prescribes a definitively prima facie duty, for there are deontic SPRs for my purposes that I might espouse, which prescribe that I have an absolute duty to defend my freedom and well-being from interference and which, at this point in the argument, have not been shown to be dialectically contradictory within my internal viewpoint as a PPA. Ultimately, with the PGC established as dialectically necessary, my duty to defend my freedom and well-being from interference will be seen to be definitively prima facie, but this cannot be stated at the present juncture.[45] By the same token (4c) cannot be held to prescribe a definitively absolute duty, because SPRs for my purposes that prescribe this have not been shown to be dialectically necessary. But, because they have not been shown to be dialectically contradictory, the duty in (4c) must be characterized as "at least prima facie."

Gewirth, as has been noted, refers to the duties and rights of Stage II as "prudential." This is because the criterion on the basis of which I am required to assent to (4c) and the prescriptions that are held to follow from it are both prudential. I strictly ought to defend my freedom and well-being from interference *for the sake of my achievement of* my *purposes*. I, as a PPA, advocate my achievement of my own purposes, so I logically must accept that I strictly ought to defend my freedom and well-being on the basis of this advocacy, because I need my freedom and well-being in order to achieve my purposes, whatever they might be. For me to deny that I strictly ought to defend my freedom and well-being from interference (that I have a strict reason of requirement to do so) is to deny "I am a PPA." This duty is a prudential one, rather than a moral one, because a moral duty is other-regarding in being owed to the achievement of PPAO's purposes, rather than, or in addition to, my own. For me to consider that I have a moral duty to do X is for me to consider that I strictly ought to do X on the grounds of my advocacy of the achievement of PPAO's purposes, rather than, or in addition to, my own.

It is, of course, possible that I will advocate the achievement of PPAO's purposes, in the sense of valuing the achievement of PPAO's purposes on grounds other than their possible instrumentality in enabling my own purposes to be achieved. If I do, then this will entail

1.   that I am required, by virtue of *this* (dialectically contingent) advocacy (rather than by virtue of "I am a PPA"), to recognize a *moral* duty for me to at least refrain from interference with

PPAO's freedom and well-being, on the grounds that PPAO requires its freedom and well-being for its achievement of any of its purposes;

2. that I am required, *by virtue of this advocacy*, to count the achievement of PPAO's purposes among my own, and to make my prudential criterion (indirectly) a moral one (pursue the purposes rationalized by a moral SPR for my purposes).

By virtue of this stance, I will be required to recognize counterconsiderations to my defense of my freedom and well-being—when such defense involves interfering with PPAO's freedom and well-being. In the extreme case, I will be required to consider my duty to defend my freedom and well-being from interference as overridden by any desire of PPAO that requires me to sacrifice my freedom and well-being.

However, even on such extreme terms, a conflict between my freedom and well-being and PPAO's does not negate the conclusion that I must consider that I have at least a prima facie duty to defend my freedom and well-being from interference. In particular, it does not permit me to conclude that I might very well have a duty on prudential considerations to defend my freedom and well-being from interference, but do not have a moral duty to do so, and therefore, on account of my acceptance of moral considerations, that I do not have any sort of duty to defend my freedom and well-being from interference.

There are three reasons for this. First, as has already been noted, I might actually have to do something in order to refrain from interfering with PPAO's freedom and well-being (or to actively promote it). In order to do so I need my freedom and well-being. In such a case I must, by virtue of 1, consider that I have a duty, indeed, a *moral* duty, to defend my freedom and well-being from interference.

Second, and most important, though it has been shown (at this stage) that I contradict "I am a PPA" by not considering that I have a strict reason to defend my freedom and well-being from interference, it has not been shown (yet) that I contradict "I am a PPA" if I do not accept 1 (or, indeed, if I do not accept any exclusionary reasons for my acting which could override my freedom and well-being). So, were the impact of my recognizing counterconsiderations to my freedom and well-being to be that I am not, on such terms, required to consider that I have at least a prima facie duty to defend my freedom and well-being from interference (which it is not), it must be pointed out that it has not been shown that I have any dialectically necessary reason to accept such counterconsiderations; and it would be irrational for me to regard reasons I know I must hold to be negated by considerations that I have, as yet, no reason to hold. It needs to be remembered that

[t]he use of the dialectically necessary method requires a certain sequence of argument. In this sequence, only those propositions are accepted, either as definitively justified or as warranting favorable consideration, that emerge successively from the conceptual analysis of action and of the agent's necessary beliefs. . . . If, at any stage of this sequence, some particular agents or groups of agents have contingent beliefs or principles that are opposed to such propositions, this opposition will carry no justificatory weight. (RM 46–47)

Third, even when I accept 1, I am still guided by my prudential criterion—it is just that my prudential criterion is here conceived by me to be a moral one.

Thus, it should be clear that the sense in which the duties and rights of Stage II are prudential does not necessarily preclude them being considered by me to be moral. They remain prudential even when I adopt a moral SPR for my purposes, for to say that they are "prudential" is to say that they are dialectically validated by my proactive valuation of my purposes, *regardless of the SPR I use to judge the permissibility (practical rationality) of my actions.* Another way of putting this is to say that the criterion for these duties is "directly prudential," being constituted by my proactive valuation of my purposes, regardless of how they are rationalized; but, "indirectly," it could be moral, *if* my proactive valuation is the result of my following a moral SPR for my purposes.

However, if we designate as "my prudential criterion" (call it IP) my necessary proactive evaluative relation to my purposes, and treat as a "prudential" claim any judgments that I am required to espouse in logical consistency with this criterion, then *all* the dialectically necessary value judgments in the argument are "prudential," *including the PGC itself!* Since Gewirth needs to distinguish "prudential" from "moral" claims, the criterion for the "prudential" claims of Stage II must be different from that for the "moral" claims of Stage III, while at the same time these criteria must, themselves, be dialectically necessary. The "prudential" claims of Stage II, in other words, must have a more specific "prudential" character than can be elicited simply by designating IP as my prudential criterion.

In addition to IP, the other characteristic that belongs to me *necessarily* as a PPA is that I categorically need my freedom and well-being for my purposes (call this characteristic IC). Now, IC and IP (together) require me to consider my freedom and well-being to be necessary goods, to act and prescribe for the sake of my having freedom and well-being. (4c) is "generally prudential" in being validated by IP, but it is "specifically prudential" in being required by IC. (4c) is upheld by me for the sake of *my* having *my* freedom and well-being. Any claims that I must make by virtue of having to claim (4)/(4c) will be specifically prudential, *insofar* as they are advocated for the sake of my having my categorical agency needs. We will later see that logical universalization will require me to accept that I have duties to PPAO because PPAO needs *its* freedom and well-being. These duties, though generally prudential, in being validated by IP within my viewpoint, will be moral rather than *specifically* prudential, in having as their criterion (or "ground") PPAO's categorical need for its freedom and well-being (OC).

Whereas Stage I demonstrates that I must take favorable account of my categorical agency needs in my SPR for my purposes, no attempt is made to demonstrate that my SPR for my purposes must take favorable account of PPAO's freedom and well-being until Stage III. Of course, the fact that I must prescribe for my own agency needs does not preclude me prescribing for PPAO's agency needs as well. Thus, my dialectically necessary commitment to specifically prudential prescriptions in Stage II does not preclude me from making moral prescriptions as well. But, unless Stage III is valid, such prescriptions will be dialectically contingent (depending on my general prudential criterion being indirectly—and contingently—moral).

Thus, to say that the claims of Stage II are prudential signifies not only that they are directly prudential, and could be nonmoral or moral indirectly, but also that they must be advocated on specifically prudential grounds at least. Insofar as these claims are dialectically necessary, they are to be designated as specifically prudential. And, this means that Stage III proceeds from Stage II on the premise of the dialectical necessity of the claims of Stage II having a specifically prudential character.[46]

STATEMENT (4c) ENTAILS STATEMENT (4d)

Statement (4c) prescribes a *self-referring* instrumental duty to defend my freedom and well-being from interference. If (4c) is dialectically necessary within my internal viewpoint as a PPA, then (4d) is dialectically necessary *within the same viewpoint.*

Gewirth's argument for this is quite brief. (See RM 91–95.) From "I ought to do X" it follows that "I ought (*in the same sense and on the same criterion*) to be free to do X, that I ought not to be prevented from doing X, that my capacity to do X ought not to be interfered with." If PPAO interferes with my freedom and well-being, then

PPAO interferes with my capacity to do X (whatever X is); so it follows from "I ought to do X" that "PPAO ought not to interfere with my freedom and well-being." From the dialectical necessity of (4c), within my internal viewpoint as a PPA, it follows that I contradict "I am a PPA" if I do not consider that I have at least a prima facie instrumental duty to defend my freedom and well-being from interference. The criterion for this "ought" is *my* interests. By this same criterion, it follows that PPAO has at least a prima facie duty not to interfere with my freedom and well-being (against my will). Thus it follows that I contradict "I am a PPA" if *I* do not consider that PPAO has at least a prima facie duty not to interfere with my freedom and well-being.

This may benefit from some expansion. From (3) it follows that

(4e)   In order to defend my freedom and well-being from interference (call any actions that constitute such a defense "X"), I categorically need to have my freedom and well-being ≡ No matter what actions constitute my attempt to defend my freedom and well-being, in order to succeed in these attempts I need my freedom and well-being generally (and I need my basic well-being to even make these attempts).[47]

From this it follows that

(4f)   I cannot discharge my at least prima facie duty (as presented by [4c]) to do X if I do not have my freedom and well-being.

By the principle that "ought" implies "can,"

(4g)   It cannot be the case that I ought to do X if I cannot do X.

However, according to the criterion of my interests, "I ought to do X." So, by this criterion,

(4h)   I ought to be able to do X.

Given (4e), it follows, by the same criterion of my interests, that

(4i)   My freedom and well-being ought not to be interfered with.

Who is this prescription directed at?

Y ought to do Z only if Y can do Z. "Y ought to do Z" is only directed at those who can do Z, in the sense of those who, if they do not do Z, are capable of doing Z instead, as a result of following the criterion according to which Z ought to be done. In this sense of "can," those who can do Z ought to do Z. Who are those who can do

Z (in this sense)? All PPAs.[48] Hence, by the criterion of my interests,

(4j)   PPAO ought not to interfere with my freedom and well-
        being.

It follows that it is dialectically necessary, within my internal viewpoint as a PPA, for me to hold (4d).

It must be emphasized that this "ought" is *other-referring* or *-directed*, but that it is not necessarily *other-directing*. Its criterion is *my* interests. It is *directing* only for those who accept my interests as their criterion. Only those who espouse my interests as their criterion must, from *their* point of view, consider that they ought not to interfere with my freedom and well-being. But, whether or not PPAO employs my interests as its criterion, this criterion prescribes that PPAO ought not to interfere with my freedom and well-being. PPAO's accepting this criterion is not necessary for this criterion to prescribe that PPAO ought not to interfere with my freedom and well-being. PPAO's accepting this criterion is only necessary for PPAO's *accepting* that it ought not to interfere with my freedom and well-being *from its own viewpoint*. What is necessary for it to be intelligible to say that this criterion prescribes that PPAO ought not to interfere with my freedom and well-being is not that PPAO accept this criterion, but that PPAO comprehend this criterion as one that it is capable of following. PPAO is capable of this. PPAO must assent to "If I (PPAO) employed PPA's interests as my criterion, then I would have to hold that I ought not to interfere with the freedom and well-being of PPA." *Acceptance* of this "ought" *by the addressee* as subjectively binding is thus conditional *upon acceptance* of this criterion *by the addressee, but the fact that this criterion prescribes this "ought" as binding on the addressee, is not.* Since my interests are necessarily my criterion, I must consider that PPAO is bound not to interfere with my freedom and well-being, meaning that *I* must hold that PPAO is bound not to interfere with my freedom and well-being with this criterion as my justification; which is not, however, the same thing as saying that I must consider that PPAO must consider itself bound not to interfere with my freedom and well-being on *its own view of its interests,* whatever this might be.[49]

STATEMENT (4d) ENTAILS STATEMENT (5)

Statement (4d) prescribes an *other-referring* strict "ought," or "duty." It follows, simply from the logical correlativity of other-referring duties and claim rights,[50] that it is dialectically necessary for me to hold, within my internal viewpoint as a PPA,

(5)   I at least (even if no one else) have at least a prima facie

claim right (which is not necessarily moral) to my freedom and well-being.

This right, although a claim right, and therefore other-*referring*, is
(like the duty prescription from which it is derived) still essentially
prudential rather than moral, because it has not been demonstrated
by the discussion of (4c) entails (4d) that my SPR for my purposes
logically must be an other-*regarding* criterion. (See RM 145.)[51] If I
happen to have an SPR that requires me to respect the needs of at
least some other PPAs, then, *on this criterion*, my claim will be a
moral claim, as my prudential criterion will (indirectly) be a moral
criterion, and I will have to grant it to those PPAs whose needs I
respect. Alternatively, I might happen to espouse an SPR that respects the needs of no one other than myself: in which case, I will be
required to claim this right for myself, but not, *on such a criterion*, to
accord it to anyone else (thus making it an amoral right). However,
thus far, it has not been demonstrated that it is dialectically necessary for me to espouse the former sort of SPR for my purposes, and
dialectically contradictory for me to espouse the latter kind. It has
only been demonstrated that, whatever SPR for my purposes I espouse, I logically must consider that I have a claim right to my
freedom and well-being, that I contradict "I am a PPA" by espousing
any SPR that does not prescribe that I have a claim right to my
freedom and well-being. But, so long as I espouse an SPR for my
purposes that prescribes that I have at least a prima facie claim right
to my freedom and well-being, as far as can be elicited from the
argument to this point, such an espousal is dialectically consistent,
whether or not, in terms of this SPR, this right is a moral right.

Stage III

If (1) entails (5), *within my internal viewpoint as a PPA*, then it follows
that I must guide my conduct by an SPR according to which I have
at least a prima facie claim right to my freedom and well-being,
because I am a PPA (or more fully, because I categorically need my
freedom and well-being,[52] and am conatively normal; in turn, because I am a PPA).

In other words, it follows from (1) → (5) that

(6)   I am a PPA → I must consider that I have at least a prima
       facie claim right to my freedom and well-being (≡ I must
       espouse an SPR according to which I have at least a
       prima facie claim right to my freedom and well-being).

The reason why *I* must espouse an SPR according to which *I* have
at least a prima facie claim right to my freedom and well-being is,

ultimately, that *I* contradict "I am a PPA" if *I* espouse any SPR that does not prescribe that I have this right. It therefore follows, from the fact that "I" stands for any PPA in this argument (*in the sense* that every PPA must correlatively, with regard to itself, go through the same reasoning as I must), that *every PPA* logically must espouse an SPR according to which *it* has at least a prima facie claim right to *its* freedom and well-being (see [11] below). *This, however, is not all that can be inferred from (6).*

According to any SPR I may consistently espouse, I have at least a prima facie claim right to my freedom and well-being. My SPR must have this content for the sufficient reason that I am a PPA. By having to espouse an SPR with a specified content, I am required to affirm this content: thus, I must hold that the fact that I am a PPA is the sufficient ground for "I have at least a prima facie claim right to my freedom and well-being"—that my being a PPA is the property I possess by virtue of which I have this right. It follows that (6) entails

(6a) From my internal viewpoint as a PPA, I am logically required to treat [I am a PPA → I have at least a prima facie claim right to my freedom and well-being] as a valid inference. (See RM 109–111.)

In other words, I must accept

(6b) My internal viewpoint as a PPA is a system of reasoning in which the inference [I am a PPA → I have at least a prima facie claim right to my freedom and well-being] is a valid inference.

The move from (6) to (6a) (from the premise that my being a PPA is a sufficient ground *for my being required to consider that I have a right to my freedom and well-being* to the conclusion that I am required to consider that my being a PPA is the sufficient ground *for my having a right to my freedom and well-being*) is absolutely critical for Stage III—and needs expansion. Gewirth infers (6a) from (6) by what he calls "the argument from the sufficiency of agency" (ASA) (RM 110).

Gewirth's statement of this argument is as follows:

The agent's description of himself as a prospective purposive agent is . . . a sufficient condition of the justifying reason he must adduce for his having the generic rights. If the agent were to maintain that his reason must add some qualifying restriction to this description, and must hence be less general than his simply being a prospective purposive agent, then he could be shown to contradict himself. Let us designate by the letter D such a more restrictive description. . . . Now let us ask the agent whether, while being an agent, he would still hold that he has the rights of freedom and well-being even if he were not D. If he answers yes, then he contradicts his assertion that

he has these rights only insofar as he is D. He would hence have to admit that
he is mistaken in restricting his justificatory description to D. But if he answers no, that is, if he says that while being an agent he would not hold that
he has these rights if he were not D, then he can be shown to contradict
himself with regard to the generic features of action. For, as we have seen, it
is necessarily true of every agent . . . that he . . . implicitly claims the right to
have freedom and well-being. For an agent not to claim these rights, at least
implicitly, would mean that he does not act for purposes he regards as good
at all . . . . But this in turn would mean that he is not an agent, which contradicts the initial assumption. Thus, to avoid contradicting himself, the agent
must admit that he would hold that he has the rights of freedom and well-
being even if he were not D, and hence that the description or sufficient
reason for which he claims these rights is not anything less general or more
restrictive than that he is a prospective agent who has purposes he wants to
fulfill. (RM 109–110)

The substance of this statement may be presented as follows: "I
am a PPA" logically requires me to consider that I have a right to my
freedom and well-being. Suppose that I claim a right to my freedom
and well-being, but that I contend that I have it only for the sufficient reason that I am D, which is more restrictive than being a PPA.
It follows that I would have to claim that I would not have a right to
my freedom and well-being if I were not D, even though I were a
PPA. But if I am a PPA, I must consider that I have a right to my
freedom and well-being, whatever contingent features I have as a
PPA. Hence, I may only adduce features that pertain necessarily to
me as a PPA as the sufficient reason for my having a right to my
freedom and well-being. Hence "I am a PPA" logically requires me
to consider that I have a right to my freedom and well-being for the
sufficient reason that I am a PPA.
     Thus (6) entails (6a)/(6b).[53]
     Now, according to the *logical* principle of universalizability,[54]

(7)   If S is a system of reasoning in which [A has property π
        $\rightarrow$ A has property ϵ] is a valid inference, then [B has
        property $\pi \rightarrow$ B has property ϵ] is also valid *in S*.[55]

Therefore, given that I must accept (6b), I must accept (by [7], and
substituting S = my internal viewpoint as a PPA, A = I, π = the
property of being a PPA, ϵ = the property of having a claim right to
freedom and well-being, B = PPAO)

(8)   My internal viewpoint as a PPA is a system of reasoning
        in which the inference [PPAO is a PPA $\rightarrow$ PPAO has at
        least a prima facie claim right to its freedom and well-
        being] is a valid inference.

Therefore, *from my internal viewpoint as a PPA,* it is dialectically necessary for *me* to accept

(9)   PPAO has at least a prima facie claim right to its freedom and well-being. (See, e.g., RM 146–147.)

Since every PPA is required to reason in this way (where PPA is "I"), it follows that

(10)   From *its* internal viewpoint as a PPA, it is dialectically necessary for *every PPA* to accept that PPAO has at least a prima facie claim right to its freedom and well-being.

Again, since every PPA must reason about itself in the same way, it follows from (6) that

(11)   From *its* internal viewpoint as a PPA, it is dialectically necessary for every PPA to accept that *it* has at least a prima facie claim right to its freedom and well-being.[56]

By the conjunction of (10) and (11), it follows that

(12)   From *its* internal viewpoint as a PPA, it is dialectically necessary for *every PPA* to accept that *every PPA* has a prima facie[57] claim right to its freedom and well-being.

This is equivalent to

(12a)   From *every PPA's* internal viewpoint as a PPA, it is dialectically necessary to accept that *every PPA* has a prima facie claim right to its freedom and well-being.

The principle

(13)   Every PPA has a prima facie claim right to its freedom and well-being[58]

is the principle of generic consistency (PGC).[59] Any PPA who denies that it is bound by the PGC denies that it is a PPA. Thus the PGC has assertoric force *for any PPA,* though this does not mean that the PGC can be stated as a true proposition "completely severed from its dialectical linkage to what agents must say or accept" (RM 158).[60] Once (9) (or [8]) is secured, it has been shown that my SPR for my purposes must be a moral one, and the rights referred to in (8) through (13) must be conceived of as moral rights. Because the ultimate and sufficient justifying ground of these rights is being a PPA, the PGC is an egalitarian principle that grants rights to their freedom and well-being to all PPAs equally. (See RM 127, 140.) Because it is only generic features of their agency that PPAs must value in a conatively independent manner (and thus about which they must reason deontically), it is only to possession of their freedom and well-being that the PGC grants rights directly.[61]

3 Two Summary Formulations

This chapter provides two summaries, each of which is designed to highlight and explain important features of the argument. The first focuses on its strategy; it portrays the argument as a reductio ad absurdum of the idea that a PPA rationally may espouse or follow any SPR for its purposes that is incompatible with the PGC. This is contrasted with two misinterpretations of the strategy of the argument. The second summary focuses on the logical structure of the inferences involved. It identifies the logical principles upon which the argument rests, and pinpoints some of the key features of their deployment.

The Argument as a Reductio ad Absurdum of Subjective Rationalizing Viewpoints

In arguing for the rational necessity of the PGC, Gewirth argues that, to be practically reasonable or rational,[1] a PPA must not act in any way that violates the PGC. PPAs must act in accordance with the PGC, which is the standard by which they must guide their conduct. He is, of course, well aware that different PPAs might (and do) have a variety of different views about practical reasonableness. Although it is a tautology to state that reason requires a PPA not to act impermissibly (against reason), PPAs might differ on the criteria by which they measure what is not impermissible. Some may be adeonticists (adeontic amoralists), who hold that it is not impermissible for them (or anyone else) to pursue any purposes that they choose to pursue, thereby denying that notions of claim rights and strict "oughts" have any nonideological application. Others will be deontic amoralists, who claim that they have claim rights (to various things) and that others owe them correlative duties, but refuse to grant such rights to anyone else. Still others will be moralists, who claim that others have claim rights and they themselves have correlative duties. These may be egalitarians, who grant that all PPAs have rights equally, but they may differ in the rights that they think PPAs have. Alternatively, they may be elitists, or racists, or sexists, or red-hairists (or whatever) who claim that only certain classes of PPAs have rights. Then again, moralists may claim that rights and duties depend upon the consequences of actions, or they may be deontologists, who claim that rights and duties depend on the intrinsic qualities of actions, etc., etc.

If Gewirth's argument is to succeed without begging the question against anyone who holds a non-PGC view of practical reasonableness, then he must be able to show that it is self-contradictory for a PPA to hold that it is not impermissible for it to do anything that violates the PGC, that a PPA contradicts "I am a PPA" by espousing any SPR for its purposes that prescribes in a way contrary to the PGC. As stated by a PPA of itself, the compound proposition "'I am a PPA' and 'I espouse a PGC-incompatible SPR for my purposes'" must be reducible to logical contradiction by conceptual analysis of its constituent propositions. Given Gewirth's employment of criteria of logic for the rationality of espousing an SPR for my purposes, I may espouse any SPR for my purposes that I can espouse without contradicting "I am a PPA." Given such a strict criterion, it might seem that very few SPRs for my purposes will be excluded; but, in direct opposition to such an expectation, Gewirth claims that, by employing this test, it can be demonstrated that I cannot rationally espouse any PGC-incompatible SPR for my purposes.[2] This claim, however, must not be misinterpreted. It is not claimed that it is logically *impossible* for a PPA to espouse a PGC-incompatible SPR for its purposes, or to violate the PGC in action. It is claimed that it is logically *impermissible* for a PPA to do these things (that a PPA is stating logically contradictory propositions by asserting that it is a PPA *and* by espousing a PGC-incompatible SPR for its purposes). By espousing a PGC-incompatible SPR for its purposes, or by violating the PGC, a PPA denies that it is a PPA; but it is not, of course, impossible for a PPA to say or to believe that it is not a PPA, or to say or believe things that imply that it is not a PPA. It is only impossible for a PPA who is rationally sound in its statements to say or believe such things.

There is one SPR for my purposes that can be excluded at the outset. I cannot hold that it is impermissible for me to choose to pursue any purposes whatsoever. If this SPR is applied to my agency, then it prescribes quite categorically that I ought not to choose to pursue any purpose *under any circumstances whatsoever.* But, how can I obey such an injunction? Am I commanded to commit suicide? If I am, since I can choose not to commit suicide, it commands me to choose to commit suicide. This is self-contradictory. If I have a duty to commit suicide, it cannot be impermissible for me to choose to do anything whatsoever. Does it command me to do nothing at all? But, again, I can choose to do something, so to choose to do nothing at all is to do something, at least by omission. Again, "this SPR for my purposes" is self-contradictory. It is not self-contradictory only if it simply says "Your being a PPA is impermissible" but in so doing requires nothing of me at all. As such, it gives me no guidance at all as a PPA, and is not an SPR for my purposes (agency). Thus, it is not a coherent SPR for a PPA to espouse for its agency. It may, perhaps, be entertained by a PPA as a purely theoretical speculation, but it has no place in rationalizing the phenomenology of a PPA's agency. Alternatively expressed, we might allow that this "SPR" is one that I can hold as a *thinking* being, but it is not one that I can hold as a *practical* subject or PPA.[3]

At the outset, then, any SPR for my purposes must prescribe that there are at least some purposes that it is not impermissible for me to choose to pursue. Given this, in attempting his reductio, Gewirth assumes, for the sake of argument, that it is dialectically consistent for a PPA to espouse any SPR for its purposes that renders at least some purposes nonimpermissible for it to choose to pursue.[4]

I suggest that the argument, by employing the dialectically necessary method, then applies the principle

(ω)   My view of practical reasonableness (my SPR for my purposes), which specifies purposes it is at least non-impermissible for me to value proactively, must strictly require me to value proactively (choose to pursue) any purposes (should there be any) that I am logically required to value proactively by virtue of my being a PPA.

(ω) is a purely *formal* principle of practical reasonableness from my internal viewpoint as a PPA. It says little more than that a PPA cannot rationally contradict that it is a PPA. Although there is nothing necessarily *practical* about propositions of this form, (ω) has practical form because "I am a PPA" logically commits me to some practical judgments (at least in the form of judgments of non-impermissibility). This fact, however, will have no substantive implications, *unless* "I am a PPA" logically commits me to practical judgments with determinate content. (ω) entertains the possibility that this might be so, but it remains purely formal because this conjecture is stated purely hypothetically.

However, in Stage I, Gewirth argues that "I am a PPA" logically requires me to assent to "My freedom and well-being are necessary goods." This involves the following sequence:

1.   I am a PPA → I value purposes proactively;

2.   In order to be/succeed as a PPA, I categorically need my free-
      dom and well-being; therefore
3.   I (logically) ought to value my freedom and well-being pro-
      actively for whatever purposes I value proactively, whatever
      they might be.

Since I deny that I am a PPA if I deny 3, my necessary recognition
of 3, on account of the importance of 2 for me, given 1, requires me
to value my freedom and well-being proactively for whatever purposes I might value proactively. Thus, given 3, my application of (ω)
yields a *substantive* principle of practical rationality, viz.,

(α)   I logically may entertain only such an SPR for my pur-
      poses as strictly requires me to value my freedom and
      well-being proactively for whatever purposes I might
      value proactively.

A strict reason to value my freedom and well-being proactively is
a strict reason to pursue my freedom and well-being. Since an
adeonticist SPR for my purposes renders nonimpermissible any
purposes I might wish to pursue proactively, this means that such
an SPR for my purposes, in order to qualify under (α), must specify
that I have a nonoverridable strict reason to pursue my freedom and
well-being for whatever purposes I might value proactively. So too
must any SPR for my purposes that grants me an absolute claim
right to my freedom and well-being. Other SPRs for my purposes,
however, might specify that some purposes are impermissible for
me to pursue. But, unless my SPR for my purposes holds that it is
impermissible for me to pursue any purposes whatsoever (and this
is already disqualified), it cannot validate considerations that override my strict (conatively independent) requirement to value my
freedom and well-being proactively in all circumstances. Thus, in
order for any SPRs for my purposes to qualify under (α), they must
specify that I have at least a prima facie strict reason to pursue my
freedom and well-being.
    (α) may, thus, be restated as

      My SPR for my purposes (to be dialectically consistent
      from my internal viewpoint as a PPA) must impose at
      least a prima facie *self-referring* duty (a duty *on me*) to
      defend my freedom and well-being from interference.

An adeonticist SPR for my purposes, however, specifies that I
have no duties. But, in order to qualify under (α), it must specify
that I have a duty to pursue my freedom and well-being instrumentally. This is incoherent, and constitutes a reductio ad absurdum of

an adeonticist SPR *within my internal viewpoint as a PPA*. An adeonticist SPR is dialectically inconsistent with "I am a PPA."

If a dialectically consistent SPR for my purposes, within my internal viewpoint as a PPA, prescribes that I have at least a prima facie duty to defend my freedom and well-being from interference, then since "I ought to do X" entails "I ought to be free to do X" (which is an application of the principle that "ought" implies "can"), it prescribes that PPAO has at least a prima facie duty to (at least) refrain from interference with my freedom and well-being (in order for me to achieve whatever purposes I might value proactively). Thus, (α) entails

(α₁)   My SPR for my purposes (or, more strictly, *my* SPR *for PPAO's purposes*, in consistency with my SPR for my purposes) must impose at least a prima facie *other-referring* duty (a duty *on PPAO*) to at least refrain from interference with my freedom and well-being.

The instrumentality here is for whatever purposes *I* am motivated to pursue proactively, and the imposition is on *my* thinking about what is nonimpermissible, etc., for *PPAO* to do, not an imposition on *PPAO's* thinking about what is nonimpermissible, etc., for *it* to do. More precisely, it is an imposition on what PPAO may or may not do, *and* on what PPAO may or may not *consider* that it may or may not do, *on my dialectically necessary criterion*, but not (as yet) such an imposition on PPAO's dialectically necessary criterion.

Since other-referring duties are logically correlative to claim rights, (α₁) entails

(α₂)   My SPR for my purposes must specify that *I*, at least, even if no one else, have at least a prima facie claim right to *my* freedom and well-being.

At this point, the end of Stage II, deontic amoralist SPRs for my purposes remain dialectically consistent within my internal viewpoint as a PPA. It has not been shown that I must consider that PPAO has a claim right to its freedom and well-being, because the duty prescription correlative to my rights-claim, though other-*referring*, need not be other-*regarding* on that account. However, it is in consistency with "I am a PPA" that I must regulate my practical thinking in terms of (α₂). On the grounds that I am a PPA (value my purposes proactively, and categorically need my freedom and well-being for my purposes) my SPR for my purposes must be one that requires me to consider that I have a claim right to my freedom and well-being. This means that, simply because I am a PPA, I am required to espouse an SPR for my purposes *in terms of which* "I, at least, have at least a prima facie claim right to my freedom and well-being" is justified; and this entails that *I* am required to *consider* that I have this right, and to consider that my being a PPA is a sufficient justification for my having this right (although it does not mean, without more being contained in this than meets the eye, that *PPAO* is required to consider that I have this right on the grounds that I am a PPA).

However, more *is* contained in this than might be apparent, for it follows from this, by the *logical* principle of universalizability, that my SPR for my purposes must be such that it requires *me* to consider that PPAO has at least a prima facie claim right to its freedom and well-being for the sufficient reason that PPAO is a PPA. For this reason (α_2) entails

(α_3) My SPR for my purposes must specify that *PPAO* has at least a prima facie claim right to *its* freedom and well-being.

This universalization is not moral, for, although *it entails* that I must take favorable account of the interests of PPAO in my SPR for my purposes, *it does not rest on assuming* that I espouse an SPR for my purposes that takes favorable account of the interests of PPAO. Furthermore, this universalization is not (specifically) prudential, as it does not rest on the (false) assumption that *I* categorically need *PPAO's* freedom and well-being in order to achieve my purposes. The universalization is purely logical.

There is an important point, concerning its being dialectically necessary for me, prior to this universalization, to claim at least a prima facie right to my freedom and well-being, that must be emphasized at this juncture. It is dialectically necessary for me to espouse an SPR for my purposes that grants me such a right. But this, at least at this stage, leaves it open for me to espouse a number of SPRs for my purposes that qualify this "at least prima facie" condition differently. A wide variety of overriding counterconsiderations to my right are still permitted, although not dialectically necessary. However, when the logical principle of universalizability is applied, it is *not* applied to judgments made by any contingent SPRs for my purposes that happen to specify that I have at least a prima facie right to my freedom and well-being, for I am not necessarily required to introduce their specific qualifications relating to the "at least prima facie" condition by virtue of being a PPA. The logical principle of universalizability is applied to the general statement that I am logically required to consider that I have at least a prima facie right to my freedom and well-being by virtue of my being a PPA (for only this general statement is dialectically necessary).

Thus, if at this point I have a dialectically consistent SPR for my purposes that states that my right to my freedom and well-being is overridden if counterconsideration X applies, the universalization does not yield that I must consider that PPAO has a right to its freedom and well-being which is overridden if X applies.

In other words, the universalization of Stage III is not a universalization of whatever judgments are validated by whatever is, as far as Stage II goes, some dialectically consistent SPR for my purposes that I might espouse, but a universalization of the proposition "I have at least a prima facie right to my freedom and well-being for the sufficient reason that I am a PPA," which it is dialectically necessary for me to hold. This is because the dialectically necessary method only operates, at every point, on premises that are themselves dialectically *necessary* for me to espouse. (See Chapter 2, note 23.)

Operating on this dialectically necessary basis, the logical principle of universalizability requires me to grant that PPAO has at least a prima facie right to its freedom and well-being, *because* PPAO is a PPA with the generic requirements of agency; and this means that the content of this prima facie qualification is not determined by the qualifications of any SPR for my (or PPAO's) purposes that specifies that I (or PPAO) have at least a prima facie right to my (or its) freedom and well-being that I (or PPAO) might happen to espouse in consistency with the argument of Stage II. Instead, this content is determined by the needs of consistency in holding that PPAO and I both have rights to our freedom and well-being.

In terms of this characterization of the move from Stage II to Stage III, it might be questioned that Stage II permits me to hold *any* SPR for my purposes *provided only* that such an SPR specifies that I have at least a prima facie right to my freedom and well-being. For, according to the argument for the sufficiency of agency (ASA), if Stage II establishes that I, *because I am a PPA, may only espouse an SPR for my purposes that specifies that I have at least a* prima facie *right to my freedom and well-being,* then it establishes that I may only espouse an *SPR for my purposes that specifies that I have at least a* prima facie *right to my freedom and well-being for the sufficient reason that I am a PPA.*[5] However, although this, in itself, prohibits me from espousing an SPR for my purposes in which *my having* an at least prima facie right to freedom and well-being is made conditional upon such factors as being Deryck Beyleveld, which do not pertain necessarily to all PPAs, it does not prohibit me from having any of a number of SPRs for my purposes that prescribe various counterconsiderations to my right to freedom and well-being (which I must consider that I have for the sufficient reason that I am a PPA).[6]

Once (α_3) is established, Gewirth has effected a reductio ad absurdum not only of my espousal of an amoralist SPR for my purposes,
but of my espousal of nondeontological moralist SPRs for my purposes. These are shown to be dialectically inconsistent options for
me. At the same time, because (α_3) must be conjoined with (α_2), my
moralist SPR for my purposes must be egalitarian— the conjunction
of (α_2) and (α_3) entailing

(α_4)   My SPR for my purposes must specify that *all PPAs* have
        prima facie claim rights to *their* freedom and well-being.

These rights are now definitively prima facie, in being conditional upon noninterference with PPAO's rights to freedom and
well-being by PPA and vice versa. It would be inconsistent to hold
that I have an absolute right to my freedom and well-being, but that
PPAO has a prima facie right to its freedom and well-being (or vice
versa), because a PPA's SPR for its purposes must be egalitarian
(given that being a PPA is the ground of the rights-claim); and it is
straightforwardly contradictory to hold that both I and PPAO have
absolute rights to our freedom and well-being (at least in the sense
that neither may defend its freedom and well-being from interference by the other, even when this requires interference with the
freedom and well-being of the other).[7] Once (α_4) is secured, the "at
least" qualification to the prima facie rights specified in (α_2) and
(α_3) must be removed.

Furthermore, since "I am a PPA" is the sufficient ground for (α_4),
and one of the essential features of "I am a PPA" (in this grounding)
is "I categorically need my freedom and well-being for my purposes,"[8] my SPR for my purposes has a specific and necessary egalitarian content. Rights are primarily and fundamentally owed to
PPAs' freedom and well-being, not to anything else. In other words,
my SPR for my purposes must be the PGC. No conflicting SPR for
my purposes is dialectically consistent within my internal viewpoint as a PPA. At one point, Gewirth asks,

If a rational agent is to claim any rights at all, could anything be a more
urgent object of his claim than the necessary conditions of his engaging both
in action in general and in successful action? (RM 63)

This question must be answered negatively, because, whatever
are claimed to be rights or duties, to exercise these rights and carry
out these duties the addressee of these claims needs its freedom and
well-being. If I have a right to X, or a duty to do X, then I must have
a right to the necessary conditions required to exercise this
right/carry out this duty.

Finally, because every PPA must reason in parallel fashion, (α_4) entails

(α_5)   The SPR for its purposes *of every PPA* must specify that *all PPAs* have prima facie claim rights to *their* freedom and well-being,

and this is equivalent to the statement that the PGC is dialectically necessary within the internal viewpoint of every PPA.

To conclude this presentation, I will very briefly contrast this interpretation of Gewirth's argument with two ways in which it might be (and has been) misconstrued.

1. The argument is not an attempt to argue that it is prudent for me to accept and act according to the PGC, that I will best serve my particular occurrent purposes, whatever they are, if I act according to the PGC. It rests, rather, on the contention that even a PPA who guides itself by prudence must accept canons of deductive and inductive reason, must value its purposes proactively, and must consider that it categorically needs its freedom and well-being. The argument of Stage II is also not just that my purposes, whatever they are, are best served if others do not interfere with my freedom and well-being. Gewirth argues that elements of the nature of agency and reason, which underlie even self-interested action, require a PPA to consider that it has a right to freedom and well-being if these elements are to be synthesized consistently. But, even if Stage II may be analyzed at least in part, if only in part, in terms of prudence, this does not apply to Stage III. If my purposes (whatever they might be) require *my* freedom and well-being (at least instrumentally), my purposes (whatever they might be) do not require PPAO to have *its* freedom and well-being. However, Stage III is effected by the employment of logical principles of reason, which are more fundamental than prudence and which require acceptance of the PGC when applied to the self-interested *judgment* that a PPA must correlate with the fact that it categorically needs its freedom and well-being. The argument, whether directed at an adeonticist, a deontic amoralist, or moralist, is that it is *illogical* for a PPA not to accept the PGC, not that it is imprudent or immoral for a PPA not to accept the PGC (although the validity of the argument implies that PPAs must consider it to be immoral for them not to follow the PGC).[9]

This misinterpretation is probably fed by the fact that Gewirth describes Stages I and II as "prudential." However, the prudential criterion is basically a property, my proactive evaluative relation to my purposes, which is necessarily connected with "I am a PPA," as particular occurrent purposes are not.

2. The argument does not allege that PGC-incompatible SPRs for my purposes are *in themselves* self-contradictory maxims, or, what amounts to the same thing, that all PGC-incompatible *SPRs* for my purposes logically presuppose the PGC. It maintains that it is inconsistent with "I am a PPA" for me to guide my conduct by PGC-incompatible SPRs for my purposes. It is *I* who presuppose the PGC *in treating maxims as action-guiding.* To portray the argument in the former manner is to ignore the role of (ω), and to miss the entire point of the dialectically necessary method. It is to portray Gewirth as attempting to argue that the PGC is an assertoric necessary truth rather than a dialectically necessary prescription.[10]

This misinterpretation has two probable sources. First, the description of the criterion of Stages I and II as prudential has led some commentators to construe the argument as an argument *from "egoism"* or some other nonmoral SPR for my purposes. Second, Gewirth's claims that even amoralists, egoists, and fanatics (or whatever) must accept the inferences of the argument have led some commentators to believe that Gewirth is claiming that the "principles" of amoralism, egoism, and fanaticism (or whatever) *themselves* entail the PGC. The argument to the PGC is not, however, an argument from *any* SPR for my purposes. It is an argument from features that necessarily pertain to any being that has any SPR for its purposes. Egoists (or whoever) are logically bound to the PGC by being PPAs, not by the principles that define their egoism (or whatever).

The Formal Structure of the Argument

Whereas the reductio formulation, just given, is designed to clarify the strategy of Gewirth's argument, the present summary is designed to exhibit the logical structure of his inferences.

The inferences that Gewirth draws in Stages I and II may be presented as follows:

(1)   I am a PPA = I do, or intend to do, X voluntarily for purpose E.

Where contents in curly brackets signify judgments, propositions, or inferences within *my* dialectically necessary viewpoint, (1) entails

(2)   {I value E proactively} ≡ {E is good}.

(I shall abbreviate the general claim that I must value my freely chosen purposes proactively as {IP}. IP does not stand for my proactive valuation of a specific particular occurrent purpose.)

(3)   In order to achieve any purpose whatsoever by my agency, I need my freedom and well-being ("my

F&WB") (abbreviated IC = I categorically need freedom and well-being).

[(2) & (3)] entails

(4)   {My F&WB are necessary goods} ≡

(4a)   {Whatever my purposes, I ought to value my F&WB pro-actively as necessary means to my purposes} ≡

(4b/c) {(Prudentially) I strictly instrumentally ought to pursue my F&WB} (abbreviated {SRO} = self-referring "ought").

By the application of "ought implies can," according to which "I ought to do X" entails "I ought to be free to do X," this entails

(4d)   {Others strictly ought not to interfere with my F&WB for the sake of my achievement of my purposes} ≡ {Others strictly ought not to interfere with my F&WB against my will} (abbreviated {ORO} = other-referring "ought").

By the logical correlativity of other-referring strict "oughts" and claim rights, this entails

(5)   {I have a claim right to my F&WB} (abbreviated {MyR} = my right).

Thus, in abbreviated form, we have

(A)   I am a PPA → {IP}.

(B)   {IP} & IC → {SRO}. But {SRO} → {ORO} (by "ought im-plies can," where the criterion of these judgments is the same); ∴

(C)   {IP} & IC → {ORO}. But {ORO} → {MyR} (by the correlativity of other-referring strict "oughts" and claim rights); ∴

(D)   {IP} & IC → {MyR}.

However, if {IP} & IC → {MyR}, then

(E)   {IP} → {IC → MyR}.

(E) is equivalent to [I am a PPA → {I am a PPA → MyR}]. So, the inference that (D) entails (E) is equivalent to Gewirth's argument for the sufficiency of agency,[11] for IP and IC merely represent different aspects of being a PPA.[12]

From this base ({IC → MyR}), Gewirth moves into *Stage III.*

IC may be written as "I am an X who has C (a categorical need for its F&WB [in order to achieve its purposes])," [13] and MyR as "I am an X who has R (a right to its F&WB)." ∴ {IC → MyR} may be written as

(F)   {(I am an X who has C) → (I am an X who has R)}.

(G)   {(I am an X who has C) → (I am an X who has R)} → {(∃X)[(X has C) → (X has R)]}.[14]

(H)   (∃X)[(X has C) → (X has R)] → (X)[(X has C) → (X has R)].[15]

(I)   All PPAs are Xs who have C (abbreviated AC). ∴

(J)   {IC → MyR} → {AC → PPAR} ("PPAR" standing for "All PPAs have claim rights to their F&WB" ["PPAs' right"]).

It may be noted that this is a more direct derivation of {AC → PPAR} than my presentation in Chapter 2 employs. The presentation in Chapter 2, following Gewirth, derives {AC → PPAR} in the following way:

(K)   PPAO is an X who has C (abbreviated OC). ∴

From {IC → MyR}, by (H),

(L)   {IC → MyR} → {OC → PPAOR} ("PPAOR" standing for "PPAO has a claim right to its F&WB" ["PPAO's right"]).

(M)   The union of {IC → MyR} and {OC → PPAOR} entails {AC → PPAR}.

However, either way, we now have

(N)   I am a PPA → {IP → (AC → PPAR)}. ∴

(O)   I am a PPA → {PPAR}.

From this we may infer (because all PPAs must accept parallel reasoning)

(P)   PPAR (= the PGC) is dialectically necessary within the internal viewpoint of every PPA.

It is important to note that

1.   from "I hold MyR" (on unspecified grounds), the logical principle of universalizability (LPU) does not require that I must hold PPAOR, or PPAR. This is because the reason why I hold MyR, those of my qualities that I hold to justify MyR, might not be qualities possessed by PPAO;

2.   from "I must hold (IC → MyR)," however, the LPU does require me to hold PPAOR, and PPAR. Since I am required to

hold that MyR is justified by my categorical need for my
F&WB, I must concede that PPAOR and PPAR, because PPAO
and all PPAs categorically need their F&WB; and

3.   from "I (as a PPA) must hold that [IP → (IC → MyR)]," the
LPU also requires (entails) that PPAO (as a PPA) must hold
that [IP → (IC → MyR)], where IP, IC, and MyR *in the consequent* refer to PPAO's proactive valuation of its purposes, categorical need for freedom and well-being, and right to freedom and well-being, rather than to mine. That is to say, PPAO
must value its purposes proactively, and on this basis hold
that the fact that it categorically needs its F&WB gives it a
claim right to its F&WB. (This inference might be presented as
$\{[IP → (IC → MyR)]\}_I → \{[PPAOP → (PPAOC → PPAOR)]\}_{PPAO}$,
where "PPAOP" stands for PPAO's proactive valuation of its
purposes, "PPAOC" stands for PPAO's categorical need for
F&WB, and the subscripts "I" and "PPAO" indicate whose
dialectically necessary inference this is.)

The difference between the universalizations achieved in 2 and 3
is that in 2 the LPU is applied to the inference that is dialectically
necessary *within* my internal viewpoint as a PPA, viz., (IC → MyR),
thus making (OC → PPAOR) dialectically necessary within *my internal viewpoint as a PPA.* (We may call this "internal application of the
LPU.") On the other hand, in 3, the LPU is applied to the inference
that, from IP, (IC → MyR) is a dialectically necessary inference
within my internal viewpoint; so that all PPAs (because they value
their purposes proactively) must consider (within *their* dialectically
necessary viewpoints) that the fact that *they* categorically need their
F&WB gives *them* a claim right to their F&WB. (We may call this
"external application of the LPU.")[16] External universalization is in
fact that achieved by noting that "I" stands for any PPA in the argument (in the sense that all PPAs are logically committed to parallel
reasoning). According to external universalization, whatever is dialectically necessary for *me* to hold relative to *my* position within a
transaction, within *my* internal viewpoint as a PPA, is dialectically
necessary for *any PPA* to hold within *its* internal viewpoint relative
to *its* position within a transaction. From the result of 3 the dialectical necessity of the PGC can still be derived by applying *internal*
universalization within the internal viewpoint of all PPAs. (All PPAs
must hold that the fact that they categorically need their F&WB
gives them a right to their F&WB; from which it follows that they
must grant that [AC → PPAR] *within their dialectically necessary internal viewpoints.*)

It is also important to note that the LPU does not specifically have to be applied internally to {IC → MyR}! It can be applied internally to {IC → SRO}, or, alternatively, to {IC → ORO}.

1. By internal application of the LPU, {IC → SRO} → {AC → All PPAs ought to pursue their F&WB in order to achieve their purposes}. This "ought" now has *moral* force. It represents my endorsement of all PPAs' pursuit of their F&WB. This is because, being validated by logical consistency with a judgment validated by IP, I have to consider it to be validated by IP.[17] Following on from this, by the application of "ought implies can," by which "I ought to do X" entails "I ought to be free to do X," and the logical correlativity of other-referring strict "oughts" and claim rights, it may be inferred that {AC → No PPA may interfere with the F&WB of any PPA against its will} ≡ {AC → the PGC}.

2. By internal application of the LPU, {IC → ORO} → {AC → All PPAs ought not to interfere with the F&WB of any PPA against its will}. By the logical correlativity of other-referring strict "oughts" and claim rights, it may be inferred that {AC → the PGC}.

This means that the argument for the sufficiency of agency (ASA), while appealed to by Gewirth in relation to [I am a PPA → {MyR}], could have been appealed to in relation to [I am a PPA → {SRO}], or in relation to [I am a PPA → {ORO}]. It does not matter, in presenting the argument, where we employ the LPU—*provided that we first establish the criterion of relevant similarities* as the property of being a PPA (or having a categorical need for one's freedom and well-being).[18]

What, then, are the major inferences/logical operations in the argument? The following seem to me to be the most important:

(i)   {IP} & IC → {SRO}.

This, according to my interpretation, is the most vital inference in the entire argument. If conceptual analysis of a PPA's internal viewpoint on its agency yields this result, then the rest of the argument may be viewed as a purely logical set of operations upon this premise.[19]

(ii)   [{IP} & IC → {SRO/ORO/MyR}] → [{IP} → {IC → SRO/ORO/MyR}].

This is the basis of Gewirth's contention that possession of prospective purposive agency is the property that I must consider to be sufficient justification for my having the rights to freedom and well-being which I must claim as a PPA, which is critical in his claim to have derived a *determinate* moral principle by use of the LPU.[20] It is

also critical in his claim to have closed the "is-ought gap" dialectically.[21]

(iii)   The internal application of the LPU as against the exter-
          nal application of the LPU.

This is used to effect the move from the (specifically) prudential
to the moral, and rests mainly on the validity of the ASA (in effect,
on the validity of [ii]), as the LPU itself can hardly be queried. Although the move from the prudential to the moral is frequently criticized, few objections actually portray the move as resting on this
operation.[22] My central claim in relation to this operation is that, if
it is valid, then, for the move from the "prudential" to the "moral"
to be dialectically necessary, it does not matter whether MyR is conceived by me to be *indirectly* moral or nonmoral. It only matters that
MyR be dialectically necessary for me as a PPA.

(iv)   The use of "ought implies can" to infer that [{SRO} →
          {ORO}].

The inference from {SRO} to {ORO} is the most frequently at-
tacked step, although it is rarely dealt with in terms of this principle.[23]

(v)   The use of the principle that other-referring strict
         "oughts" are correlative to claim rights to infer that
         [{ORO} → {MyR}].

This is basically uncontroversial, although there are those who
hold that ORO must be other-*directing*, or even moral/legal, for such
correlativity to hold.[24]

The argument can be invalid only if one or more of these opera-
tions/inferences are invalid. We must now see whether any of the
many critical discussions of the argument manage to demonstrate
that any of these operations is fallacious. In our examination we will
find that these operations are not always discussed, or are not discussed explicitly. Frequently, this is because the argument is interpreted as not resting on these operations. That it does rest on these
operations, and is misinterpreted if not seen to do so, and that these
operations are valid will be contentions that I will constantly make
and defend in the course of my defense of the argument.

Part Two

Objections to the Argument

4   Objections to Stage I

Most commentators are prepared to accept that Stage I is valid. The number of objections to Stage I is very much smaller than the number of objections to Stage II; and, although the number of objections to Stage III is rather limited, more commentators press them. Even those who have difficulty with the way in which Gewirth argues for Stage I are very often prepared to accept that a PPA must consider its freedom and well-being to be necessary goods. This said, it should be noted that what most commentators accept is that a PPA must want its freedom and well-being. However, Gewirth attaches specific meanings to the "must" and "want" here, which many of these commentators either do not appreciate or do not accept; so agreement with the conclusion to Stage I may be more apparent than real, such disagreement, where it exists, only tending to manifest itself in criticisms of Stages II or III. It, therefore, needs to be noted that I will not consider such "hidden" objections to Stage I in this chapter.

My discussion of each objection is very much "self-contained," and this applies to all the chapters. Furthermore, when two or more critics make an objection that can be placed under the same heading, I tend to treat them separately (unless the objections are identical) in order to place them in their context as much as possible. This means that I often repeat points made in relation to one critic when replying to another. This enables me to answer objections to Gewirth's argument in a way that can be consulted by anyone who seeks a reply to a criticism they have come across, without the assumption that the book is being read sequentially: it is justified by a desire not to conflate criticisms. At the end of each chapter, I draw attention to the main deficiencies in criticism. Chapter 11 summarizes the discussion of objections and draws some general conclusions.

#1   It is arbitrary, or a mistake, to make action the central subject matter of morality.

1 Trigg

Perhaps, . . . the most questionable element in Gewirth's argument is its starting point. Why should actions be regarded as the central subject[-]matter of morality rather than, say, the needs and interests of man? Why should the concepts of reason and action be preferred to, for example, conceptions of the nature of man as the foundation of morality? Gewirth merely asserts ([RM] p. 26) that action comprises the factual subject-matter of moral and other practical precepts. Moral judgements, however, may be action-guiding, but that might follow from their character rather than constitute it. (Trigg 1980, 151)

First, I do not see what the contrast between actions and human needs or interests is supposed to be. By making action the central subject matter of morality, the argument makes the purposes (interests) of PPAs central—because action is defined as voluntary purposive behavior. And what are needs for, as matters of concern to those who have them, if not for their agency? Furthermore, the argument makes generic needs the criterion, as well as the substance, of the moral rights that PPAs must accept.

Second, the search for foundations for morality is the search for a justification for morality. Justification requires reasons, so reason must be employed in any such enterprise, whatever the foundations are supposed to be. Why prefer the concept of "action" to conceptions of human nature as the starting point? Well, moral judgments prescribe actions,[1] and what Gewirth is primarily concerned to do is to ascertain which precepts for action are rationally justified, and which are not. By definition, PPAs (via their actions, *conceived of as voluntary purposive behavior*) are the subjects to which practical precepts are directed. So, what matters for the justification of morality is what PPAs can rationally do. Gewirth is concerned to base morality on a starting point that no rational PPA can deny, and no PPA can rationally deny that it is a PPA; so that anything that follows logically from its conceiving of itself as a PPA is something that it must accept. Gewirth suggests that there may be other possible starting points, but no starting point will do for his enterprise if it is not ineluctable for PPAs. (See 1984d, 221.)[2] Why not start from conceptions of human nature? Well, there are many conceptions of this. Which one do we start from? Furthermore, not all human beings are PPAs, and it is only to PPAs that practical precepts are directed.[3]

Finally, I must confess that I do not understand what Trigg means when he says that being action-guiding may be a consequence of morality's essence, rather than constituting it. But, whatever this is intended to mean, it is sufficient for Gewirth's enterprise (as should be clear from the preceding paragraph) that morality, for whatever reason, is action-guiding; and even if we can divorce what we are willing to call "a morality" from being action-guiding, this does not matter, because Gewirth is only concerned with what purposes we rationally may guide our actions by.

2 Den Uyl

Douglas J. Den Uyl, commenting on Gewirth 1967a, 1970a, 1970d, 1971a, and 1971b, agrees that a supreme principle of morality must be

derived from the most basic elements and requirements of action. Gewirth argues that the two most basic elements (and thereby necessary elements) of action are voluntariness and purposiveness. His arguments for this I believe are quite successful. [However, Gewirth fails to answer the question "Why are actions required?"] . . . It is not sufficient to answer . . . (as Gewirth might) by replying that men act to achieve their purposes since one can then ask why men want and need to achieve their purposes. The only fully fundamental answer . . . is that men act (and must do so) to sustain their existence. Gewirth's mistake comes from starting from the *fact* of human action and in regarding that fact as generic. With respect to human existence "action" is not the most generic category but rather "life" is. "Action" would thereby be the means of maintaining life or one's life and cannot be fully understood without reference to life. (Den Uyl 1975, 439)

Thus, the PCC[4] leaves room for more fundamental principles of morality.

However, one could equally well ask, "What do men need life for?" and answer, "In order to act." And what of the PPA who wishes to destroy life (especially its own life)? Den Uyl seems to think that "life" is a superior foundation for a supreme principle of morality, because it is "objective," whereas purposes are "relative." (See ibid., 440.) This, however, will not do. PPAs do not need life, and are not logically required to want it, except as categorically instrumental to their purposes.

In fact, properly viewed, the question "Why do men need to act (to achieve their purposes)?" does not arise. Those to whom practical precepts are directed *do* act (practical precepts are not directed at living beings as such but at PPAs), and we are interested in how they ought to/may act. Action is taken to be the most basic category in that how PPAs ought to/may act must be compatible with how they rationally (logically) ought to act as PPAs. As a *starting point* it is not taken to be basic in the sense of a basic moral value (the way in which Den Uyl seems to want to treat "life").

In any event, it is difficult to see how substituting "life" for "action" as the basic category (whatever this means) can generate principles more fundamental than the PGC. For life is the most necessary requirement for action (the most basic necessary good), in consequence of which the PGC attaches greater moral importance to life than to any other feature.[5]

3 Puolimatka

According to Tapio Puolimatka, Gewirth's starting point is arbitrary because it is not logically necessary to define "action" (and, hence, "being a PPA") as Gewirth does. This criticism, principally, involves the assertion that there are logically possible conceptualizations of action that are incompatible with Gewirth's definition. (See Puolimatka 1989, 32–35.)

Now, Gewirth derives his concept of "action," as "voluntary purposive behavior," from an interest in behavior as the address of practical precepts. According to Gewirth, although the word "action" is, and may be, used in many different senses, it is logically necessary for action to be conceived of as voluntary purposive behavior *if* the intention of practical precepts is

to guide, advise, or urge the persons to whom they are directed so that these latter persons will more or less reflectively fashion their behavior along the lines indicated in the precepts. (RM 26)

Puolimatka appears to agree that action must be defined as voluntary purposive behavior *if* the intention of practical precepts is characterized in this way, i.e., if practical precepts deal directly or indirectly with how persons may, or ought to, behave. He claims, however, that it is not self-contradictory (or, at any rate, that Gewirth has not shown it to be self-contradictory) to attribute a different intention.

However, to attribute a different intention is to allege that Gewirth's question "What purposes may I rationally (is it at least nonimpermissible for me to) choose to pursue/What precepts may I rationally choose to follow?" does not properly arise. For, given this question, it is obvious that "action" and "being a PPA" must be defined in the way in which Gewirth does. To ask this question, I *must* suppose that I am a Gewirthian PPA. Within the context of the question guiding his enterprise, Gewirth's definitions of agency and related concepts are not arbitrary, but logically necessary. Now, although there are various metaphysical theses, like determinism, which might disqualify this enterprise, unless these metaphysical theses can be proven, their "logical possibility" merely places limits on Gewirth's argument, which render its possible validity "transcendental" rather than "transcendent," in the way in which Kant intended this distinction. (What this amounts to is explained under #2 with respect to determinism.)

#2   The argument supposes that there is freedom of the will, but this presumption is false.

The argument does suppose that it is possible to choose to do things for reasons, and that this choice can itself be conceived of in a way that is not determined outside of the control of the agent. Whether or not beings can exist who are free in this sense is certainly debatable. However, the impact of such an assumption's being false is not on the inference from "I am a PPA" to "I rationally must accept the PGC." Its consequence is that there are, or can be, no PPAs. Indeed, if the assumption is false, practical precepts of any kind either can have no real objects,[6] or else the argument does not (as the objection presumes) suppose freedom of the will in any sense that is incompatible with determinism. Furthermore, if the argument is logically sound (on the hypothetical assumption that there are PPAs), any being who *claims* to be a PPA must accept that it is bound by the PGC *even if this claim is false.* In any event, the claim that the necessary freedom of will, which anyone who feels that he/she/it acts for reasons presupposes, is an illusion, is at least as contentious as the claim that Gewirth wishes to establish.

Gewirth (RM 36–37) gives four reasons why this objection does not invalidate his account of voluntary action.

1.   The thesis is far from being proved.
2.   Determinism, if it is to be plausible, must leave room for distinctions between forced choices (whether by direct or internal compulsion) and those resulting from deliberation.
3.   Why should the thesis be accepted as true or valid if the choice to believe it is based on determining causes rather than reasons?
4.   Determinism cannot account for the difference between the relation of physical or psychological causes and their effects, and the relation of logical or evidential ground and consequent.

Although I agree with Roger Trigg (1980, 151) that Gewirth's dismissal of hard determinism isn't conclusive (hence my rather different response, which appeals to the phenomenology of agency rather than to its metaphysical reality), my sentiments are with Hudson, who says of Trigg's comment,

I think this criticism less than fair. The four reasons he [Gewirth] ... gives for [rejecting determinism] ... comprehend the main grounds on which most philosophers would now be disinclined to accept a thoroughgoing harsh determinism. At the very least, Gewirth is entitled to raise the issue of what follows if the generic features of action are what we normally take them to be. (Hudson 1984, 112)

#3   PPAs do not have to regard their purposes as good. Indeed, they can pursue purposes that they consider that they ought not to pursue, thereby regarding their purposes as bad. Indeed, PPAs need not make any value judgments about their purposes.

1 Bond

In the first stage we are offered the equation: is sought = is desired = is thought good (valued). Of course if to will a thing is to want it, and if in wanting a thing one *thereby* values it ([RM] p. 50), then the claim that everyone regards his own purposes as good is a trivial consequence of this. But that we regard all our own ends as good is surely debatable, if not patently false. I would not dispute the claim that we necessarily desire our own ends, that there is no will without desire (though I would say that will follows, or may follow, desire rather than that they are the very same thing), but I would certainly dispute the claim that we necessarily think our own ends good. There is no reason at all why I cannot be in the grip of a powerful appetite ... yet regard its end as wholly base, ignoble, and unworthy. ... Gewirth would say at this point that if I did not regard my goal as worth aiming at I would not "unforcedly choose to move from quiescence or nonaction to action with a view to achieving the goal" ... ([RM] p. 49). But either this is question begging or these are mere dogmatic assertions. I certainly must have a *desire* for the object sufficient to motivate me, but this desire can exist without my valuing the object in the least. To desire, even to crave a thing, is not necessarily to see it as good. (Bond 1980a, 43–44)

There are at least two features of Gewirth's argument that this ignores.

1. Behavior that is not controlled by a person's unforced choice does not qualify as *action*, the object of practical precepts. Thus, counterexamples that adduce involuntary, compulsive behaviors do not tell against the first stage of the argument. Gewirth does not equate desire with a judgment of value; only the desires for their purposes that *PPAs* manifest in *choosing* these purposes are held to involve judgments.

2. Gewirth does not claim that a PPA must regard its purposes as definitively good. A PPA might choose to pursue a purpose, thereby judging it to have a positive value, and yet judge on various criteria

that it ought not to choose to pursue it. (See Gewirth 1980a, 62–64.)

To this, Bond replies,

Action *in order to satisfy an appetite* must be distinguished from action taken in order to achieve an end because we reflectively or judgmentally regard it as good. That is the distinction I was attempting to make. It is simply false . . . to suppose that all voluntary and purposive action is of the latter kind.

Professor Gewirth is wrong in supposing that I imagine him to understand by "value" only moral, or even only moral and hedonic value. . . . Nor did I imagine I could score a point by showing that an agent could do something he regarded as bad under some description. . . . I recognize this as being consistent with Professor Gewirth's account. My point is that an agent need not regard it as *good* under any description; he may just simply crave it. The reason why he would "unforcedly choose to pursue that particular goal" is that he has a *powerful inclination* to do so. Desire is one thing, evaluation another. (Bond 1980b, 72)

Gewirth, however, does not suppose that all voluntary and purposive action involves reflective appraisal in the light of further criteria. He holds that "direct" as well as "reflective wanting" involves judgment when *voluntary* behavior is involved. (See RM 50.) Either behavior under the control of an appetite is not voluntary, in which case it does not involve judgment, *but is then not action*, or

if, as Bond asserts, behavior stemming from a "powerful inclination" is voluntary, such inclination still leaves alternatives open for choice by the agent. This choice involves an at least implicit judgment of comparative worth or value, so that the separation Bond insists upon between desire and value judgment is untenable. (Gewirth 1980b, 140)

The crucial point is that, although I can act voluntarily by following my inclination (even a powerful one), I can only do so if I *choose* to follow this inclination (i.e., if I am not compelled by it); and, if I choose to follow it (rather than other considerations), then this implies that I value what it inclines me to do.

However, Bond claims that to appeal to PPAs' choosing their purposes is question-begging or dogmatic. I presume that he means that the very issue in question is how "action" is to be defined, or that Gewirth offers no argument for his definition of action. This, however, is not so. No other definition of "action" will do when the argument is concerned with what purposes PPAs may rationally *choose* to pursue.[7]

2 Heslep

Robert D. Heslep claims that PPAs do not necessarily value their purposes, because a PPA can have a "capricious desire," one that is desired for no reason or arbitrarily. "Esteem of a purpose" (valuing a goal) is one possible reason for desiring to achieve the goal; so if a PPA can have a purpose without reason, it can have this purpose without valuing it. The possibility of capricious desires constitutes a counterexample to Gewirth's thesis that PPAs logically must value their purposes. (See Heslep 1986, 382–383.)

Heslep claims that Gewirth offers three arguments, and suggests two more, for the proposition that a PPA necessarily values its purposes.

The three main arguments he attributes to Gewirth are that

1.   PPAs want to do what it is their purpose to do, either inclinationally or merely intentionally. In either case, a PPA's desire to attain its goal consists of a pro-attitude toward the goal. That PPAs have negative attitudes towards interference with their goals signifies that they have a positive interest in (approve) their goals. (See ibid., 380–381.)
2.   Any motivator other than a PPA's esteem of its purpose would be compulsive or coerced and render the action involuntary (which would contradict "I am a PPA"). (See ibid., 384.)
3.   A PPA esteems its purpose because it endeavors or at least intends to achieve it. (See ibid., 385–386.)

The two additional arguments he considers are that

4.   PPAs are rational in that they have reasons for acting. This entails that they value their purposes. "It follows that capricious purposes and desires, if there be such, are logically foreign to the agents of voluntary action." (See ibid., 387.)
5.   Capricious purposes might be nonexistent, and are certainly rare. So, even if they constitute a counterexample to Gewirth's claim, this fact is insignificant. (See ibid., 388.)

In response to 1, Heslep claims that, for two reasons, a PPA might desire X without having a pro-attitude towards X.

a.   A PPA might have a negative attitude towards interference with its goal not because it values the goal, but simply because interference involves "interruption of the agent's movement." (See ibid., 381–382.)
b.   In common speech, "[t]o describe A as wanting X is to say *inter alia* that A does not now have X; that A pays heed to X;

that *A* directs some effort toward obtaining *X;* and that *A*, given the opportunity and an absence of overriding conflicts, will obtain *X*. But it is not to say that *A* necessarily favors *X*." (See ibid., 382.)

To 2, he responds that capricious desires, which involve no esteem, need not be compulsive. They *can* be strong and irresistible, but they need not be so. (See ibid., 385.)

To 3, he responds that a PPA may endeavor, or intend, to achieve a purpose that it holds capriciously. (See ibid., 387.)

To 4, he responds that PPAs with capricious purposes are not rational in the sense of having reasons for acting. (See ibid., 387–388.)

Finally, to 5, he responds that the conceptual possibility of PPAs' acting for capricious purposes undermines Gewirth's radical justificatory intentions. (See ibid., 388.)

Each of these responses requires specific comment. Regarding 1: How does the fact that my movement is interrupted explain why I have a negative attitude toward interference with my acting? For it to do so it must be supposed that I have a pro-attitude to my freedom of "movement." But, as a PPA, my movement is for purposes, and so this pro-attitude must be carried over to my purposes. Regarding 2: This response is irrelevant. A capricious purpose may not be compulsive, in the sense that the urge to pursue it cannot be resisted, but this is beside the point. What matters is whether a capricious purpose (one that the PPA holds for no reason, and to which it thus attaches no value) can be one that the PPA has freely chosen to pursue. Regarding 3: Gewirth does not argue that PPAs value what they pursue or intend to pursue, but what they choose to pursue. Regarding 4: There is some inconsistency here. Heslep says that a PPA with capricious purposes has no reasons for *acting.* What he must mean is that it has no reasons *for having its purposes,* for its purposes, even capricious ones, are the purposes (reasons) for which it acts: and, in fact, Heslep himself refers to capricious agents as acting for "reasons of caprice" (see ibid., 387), and treats desires and purposes as reasons for acting. Regarding 5: If Gewirth employed such an argument, then Heslep's response would be sound. But, precisely because such an argument is incompatible with Gewirth's dialectically *necessary* method, he would never use it; so the suggestion should not be attributed.

In general, the basic problem with Heslep's criticism is that what he calls "a capricious purpose" is not one that is *chosen* by its pursuer. A "capricious purpose" is one held for no reason at all, and thus for no reason that leads its pursuer to *prefer* it over other alternatives; and it is for just this reason that a capricious purpose need, indeed, not be valued. Gewirth, however, defines a PPA as a being who pursues, or intends to pursue, purposes that it has chosen to pursue. It is from *this* voluntary aspect of agency that Gewirth infers that a PPA must value its purposes. This aspect is missing from Heslep's account of "Gewirth's arguments," which are not, in fact, separate—as they all amount to the same thing when this aspect is added to them.

The question, then, is not whether a being of some kind can pursue a capricious purpose, but whether such a being, in so doing, can exhibit itself as a PPA. According to Gewirth's conception of the voluntary character of agency, this question must be answered negatively. In relation to this conception, Heslep's criticisms must be regarded as question-begging. They simply rest on a different conception of what it is to be a PPA. Heslep treats voluntariness as purely a function of the relation between a purpose and an act, with voluntariness being constituted by the PPA's ability to resist acting for a purpose that it has. For Gewirth, what really matters is whether the PPA has chosen to have the purpose for which it acts or intends to act. If it has chosen the purpose, then Gewirth holds that this implies that it has a reason for doing so which consists of a positive evaluation of the purpose, either directly or indirectly (in the case of selection between purposes between which the agent is indifferent prior to making a selection).[8]

However, might it not be said that this just deploys a definitional stop against Heslep? If this is intended to suggest that Gewirth's claim rests on his definition of "a PPA" (via his definition of "action"), then the answer to this must be in the affirmative, though Gewirth's claim is no weaker for this than Heslep's counter-contentions. However, if this is intended to suggest that Gewirth's definition of "a PPA" is just an arbitrary stipulation, then the answer to this must be negative. For what matters is what conception of a PPA is best suited to the idea that a PPA is the addressee of practical prescriptions.[9] Gewirth's justificatory program is directed to the question of what purposes a PPA rationally may choose to pursue, and the whole idea of PPAs being the subjects of capricious purposes is inappropriate in this context.[10]

3 Lomasky

According to Loren Lomasky, the fact that A may be moved to do X and simultaneously value someone's preventing its doing X

is one reason why I think a derivation of rights from the bare fact of agency . . . must fail. . . . If agency is too spare a foundation for the derivation of rights, agency that has more determinate content may get one further along. (Lomasky 1984, 46 n. 16)[11]

Lomasky offers "project pursuit" as "the candidate for flesh that ought to cover and thus vivify the bare bones of agency" (ibid.).

Suppose that A is motivated to pursue E_1 yet fervently desires to be rid of the appalling desire for E_1. Then A has reason to bring about the state of affairs: A's not being motivated to pursue E_1. If that has directive force for his life such that it has implications for the value he assigns to a wide range of possible actions, if in other words it has the status of a project for A, then A values the ability to act so as to bring about the eradication of the desire for E_1. Even though the ability to pursue E_1 is disvalued, the *ability to be a project pursuer* has positive value for A.

. . . [P]rojects are taken to be those persistent desires which order a life and in terms of which other items are valued or disvalued. (Ibid., 46–47)

Later, Lomasky tells us that he is not saying

that all projects must be protected, but rather that human beings' capacity to commit themselves to projects is what undergirds the theory of human rights. The value of *being a project pursuer* must be acknowledged, not the value of any and every particular project. (Ibid., 54)

Lomasky appears to be claiming (*a*) that PPAs do not necessarily value all their purposes; (*b*) that PPAs necessarily value their projects; but (*c*) that PPAs are only rationally required to value what makes it possible for them to pursue projects in general; and it is this necessary valuation that is the basis of rights-claims.

If so, he has two criticisms of Gewirth.

1. PPAs do not necessarily value their purposes; they might find themselves motivated to pursue some purposes that they wish not to be motivated to pursue.
2. Rights-claims must be grounded in judgments of definitive value, which cannot be derived from the concept of being a PPA. They can only be derived from the concept of being a project pursuer.

1 is false, however, because PPAs (by definition) choose their purposes. A purpose that a PPA is motivated to pursue against its will is not a purpose that it chooses to pursue. Such compulsive purposivity lies outside Gewirth's conception of action or being a PPA.

Regarding 2: It is true that judgments of rights must be grounded in judgments of definitive value. But, although a PPA need not attach definitive value to all its purposes (any more than a PPA must attach definitive value to all its "projects"), it must attach definitive value to its freedom and well-being (which are the generic conditions of its "project pursuit," only because they are the generic conditions of its "bare" agency). Provided that 1 is false, the claim made under 2 (that judgments of definitive value can only be derived from the concept of a "project pursuer") must be false too (unless Lomasky's concept of a "project pursuer" is identical with Gewirth's concept of a PPA).

4 Puolimatka

Tapio Puolimatka contends that there are two reasons why a PPA is not logically required to value its purposes.

1.   A PPA could be agnostic about what is good. Thus, it could act for E and not claim that E is good. (See Puolimatka 1989, 56–57.)
2.   A PPA can have purposes it regards as bad and act because it is moved by these bad purposes. (See ibid., 57.)

Both of these suppose that the judgment "E is good" is meant to be a definitive assessment of E. The response is that the PPA must regard the purpose as good *according to* the criteria that move it to pursue the purpose, even if it regards the purpose as bad according to other criteria, or does not know what criteria to judge it by definitively. Puolimatka is, however, aware of this response, and objects that this supposes that PPAs can never act intentionally for evil. (See ibid., 58–59.)

This is not so. A PPA who thinks and acts for what it regards as bad purposes, regards the purpose as good *according to* the criterion that motivates it to act, and bad *according to* some criterion that it thinks *it ought to follow*, but which it does not choose to follow. Relative to the latter criterion, it chooses to act for evil; relative to the former, it does not.

However, Puolimatka says that a PPA could think an action bad on *every* possible criterion, yet still do it.

Again, this is not so. For Gewirth, to choose to pursue a purpose is to exercise a preference for it and (relative to this preference) to think it "good." This is the sense of "good" on which the argument proceeds. Unless the PPA is "acting" under compulsion, in which case it is not acting, simply by choosing to pursue the purpose the PPA regards it as good in the operative sense.

Puolimatka will, I suspect, not regard these responses as adequate. This is because he contends that the argument, if valid, must be valid on every possible sense of "good." He treats the sense of "good" that I have said is operative as "vague," and senses deriving from different SPRs for my purposes as "precise" interpretations of it. This means that he requires the argument to be a valid derivation of the PGC *from* every possible SPR for my purposes. (See ibid., 52–56.)

However, the argument does not derive the PGC from any, let alone all, particular occurrent SPRs. It derives it from the voluntary purposivity inherent in the adoption of, and action according to, any SPR for my purposes. This voluntary purposivity does not correlate with a vague sense of valuation. It is the precise *essence* of all proactive valuation, and receives its content as the ground for the material evaluations validated by the dialectically necessary method not from any particular occurrent SPR, but from the generic features of agency.

#4   **PPAs do not have to regard their freedom and well-being as necessary goods, because they can decide to commit suicide, engage voluntarily in life-risking endeavors, decide to sell themselves into slavery, or desire to live in a "desireless nirvana."**

Suppose an agent does, necessarily, value all his ends . . . . Must he, therefore, . . . value agency itself, and hence its generic properties? Perhaps, given that an agent has purposes, he must value his freedom (capacity for unforced choice) as a necessary means to attaining them (though even that could be challenged—he might prefer to have his desires catered to by others with no need for any effort on his own part), but need he value his purposiveness or his agency *per se*? Could he not say . . . "I do have these desires and, as a consequence, I necessarily value their ends. But I do not value in the least the having of these desires and purposes, which are a great burden to me. I would be much better off in a state of desireless *nirvana*. Far better not to be an agent at all; far better never to have to make another choice. Down with will! Better to move aimlessly and will-lessly in the great Tao!" If I am an agent, and therefore, as such, necessarily have ends which I desire, I need not desire, let alone value, this state of affairs itself, i.e. being an agent. And therefore I need not desire or value, *per se*, the generic properties (essential conditions) thereof. (Bond 1980a, 45)

1. However, as I have argued in Chapter 2, Gewirth does not hold that I must value my agency or the generic conditions thereof per se. I must value these things as necessary *means* to my purposes, which as a PPA I necessarily have, whatever my purposes (i.e., categorically instrumentally).[12]

2. Bond is mistaken when he suggests that it might even be the case that I need not value my freedom *instrumentally*. If I wish to sell

myself into slavery, or have others cater for my desires without my having to do anything, or whatever constitutes not having my freedom, I still need to be free to do the things necessary to bring this state of affairs about. Furthermore, such a state, having been brought about, needs to be maintained (unless my capacity to be a PPA has been destroyed), and a rational PPA will have to value its freedom in order to resist any interference with its "freedomless" state. As Gewirth says,

the rational agent would not completely surrender his freedom to other persons because he would be aware that there is no assurance that these others would continue to "cater" to his desires (see [RM] p. 125). (Gewirth 1980a, 64)

In fact Bond's suggestion is rather mysterious, for he later concedes that

in addition to his freedom, an agent must value those other qualities and conditions that enable him to achieve his ends, whatever those ends may be. These qualities and conditions may be said to constitute his well-being as an agent. This is true and unexceptionable. If there are certain qualities and states which are the enabling conditions of successful agency in general, no matter what an agent's ends may be, then, given that he has any end which he regards as good, an agent must value those qualities and states. Indeed they must *be*[13] good insofar as no genuinely good end can be accomplished without them. And they are good as *means* in any case, given that the agent *has* any end which, being an agent, he must have. (Bond 1980a, 47)[14]

#5   Gewirth equivocates between different meanings of "a generic feature of agency."

1 Bond

I have suspected throughout my reading . . . that Gewirth has confused two different senses of the word "generic" . . . . When he says ([RM] p. 52) that, in addition to his own particular purposes, the agent must value the *generic* features of all action, he appears to mean that he must value action (agency) itself and hence its *essential* or *defining* features (i.e. voluntariness and purposiveness). This is the first sense of the word "generic." But when the term is used as an element in the expression "generic-dispositional" ([RM] pp. 58–63), he appears to mean generic, not in the sense of "essential" or "definitional," but in the sense of "covering all acts of all persons" or "invariable with respect to different persons and actions" or "relating to action in general."

Now if there are certain capacities and conditions which are the *enabling conditions* of successful action in general, then they are generic in this second sense, but they need not be generic in the first sense, i.e. they need not be *defining* characteristics of action. Though they are necessary conditions of (successful) action in the sense that no successful action can *take place* without them, they are nevertheless not *logically* necessary conditions, as voluntariness and purposiveness are said to be. (Bond 1980a, 47–48 n. 3)

Bond is prepared to concede that freedom and well-being are generic features in the second sense, and that establishing this is sufficient for Gewirth to establish that PPAs must consider their freedom and well-being to be necessary goods. (See ibid., 47.)[15] So, what is the supposed import of this alleged equivocation? It would appear to be that Gewirth cannot establish that PPAs must consider their freedom and well-being to be necessary goods by analysis of the concept of action, a procedure which, according to Bond, requires Gewirth to establish what Bond considers to be

four equally implausible propositions: (1) An agent necessarily values all his ends. (2) In so doing he values agency itself and therefore its generic (essential) properties, voluntariness and purposiveness. (3) Purposiveness has three dimension[s], viz. basic, non-subtractive, and additive (apparent) goods. (4) For the sake of the theory, which requires invariability, the last two are to be viewed generically-dispositionally. (Ibid.)

It seems that Bond is not objecting to the validity of the conclusion to Stage I, but to the way in which Gewirth derives it, and to the validity of some of the propositions that he considers that Gewirth derives along the way.[16] In view of this, this objection is, perhaps, relatively unimportant. Nevertheless, I consider it to be mistaken.

I have discussed and rejected Bond's objection to (1) under #3 above; under #4 above, I have reiterated that I do not consider it to be a correct interpretation of Gewirth's position that I must value my agency itself (that I am a PPA for its own sake) and its generic features "intrinsically" in any sense other than categorical instrumental valuation. What about (3) and (4)?

Concerning (3), Bond says,

Gewirth tells us that *in* valuing his purposiveness as a generic property of his agency, an agent values the three kinds of goods. But are these dimensions or aspects of purposiveness? Basic goods are the necessities (other than freedom) for action of any kind. Non-subtractive and additive goods (or in strictness, *apparent* goods) constitute all the rest of the agent's aims and goals.[17] How, then, can they be aspects of purposiveness itself, and hence *generic* goods in that they are desired as part of the necessary desiring (because generic) of purposiveness itself? If this list is inclusive of all desired ends, and it seems that nothing could have been left out, then every desire can be seen as coming under one of the dimensions of desiring purposiveness itself. And that is absurd. Furthermore we are back at square one: an agent necessarily values all his ends. (Bond 1980a, 45)

In order to evaluate this, we need to be clear what Gewirth *is* arguing. According to Gewirth, a PPA is (by definition) a being who voluntarily pursues purposes of its choice. Thus, voluntariness and purposivity are generic conditions of agency in Bond's first sense. Because voluntariness and purposivity are defining conditions of action, a PPA *necessarily*, by definition, values its purposes, in the sense that it denies that it is a PPA if it does not value the purposes it has. Because this is so, a PPA denies that it is a PPA if it does not value its possession of those things that are necessary for it to pursue any purposes at all (basic *needs*) and those things that are necessary for it to pursue purposes with any general chance of success (nonsubtractive and additive *needs*). These three types of needs are different in being necessary (respectively) for purpose pursuit, purpose maintenance, and purpose improvement. In this sense, they are different aspects of purposivity. Since a PPA must value these needs, it must regard them as goods. Because they are generic conditions in another sense (categorically necessary conditions for agency/successful agency), *and* because a PPA must value its purposes, it must value these needs (have them as its purposes). This, however, clearly takes us beyond the assertion that a PPA necessarily values all its ends. And this indicates what is wrong with Bond's account. The three types of goods are not, insofar as they figure in this reasoning (and contrary to Bond's depiction), particular occurrent purposes, but capacities for agency. Furthermore, a PPA must value these capacities not just as goods, but as *necessary* goods (i.e., irrespective of its particular occurrent purposes). This means that a PPA denies that it is a PPA if it does not pursue its freedom and well-being as its purposes, which we can portray as "a PPA must value its freedom and well-being as aspects of its purposiveness." Bond says that this is absurd. The reason he does so, however, is that he treats the basic, nonsubtractive, and additive goods as particular occurrent purposes. So treated, to say that I must value these three types of goods as "aspects of my purposiveness" is to say that I contradict "I am a PPA" by not having *any* of my particular occurrent purposes as my purposes. This is, indeed, absurd. It is to say, not only that I must value any particular occurrent purpose I have, but that I cannot rationally pursue any purposes other than the particular occurrent purposes I do have/I must have every possible particular occurrent purpose as my purpose. No such absurdity is incurred, however, if the basic, nonsubtractive, and additive goods that I must value as aspects of my purposiveness are my needs for purpose pursuit, maintenance, and improvement generally.

Now, Bond in fact realizes that the three types of goods are to be regarded as general capacities (though this does not figure in his account of [3]), which brings us to (4). What Bond objects to in (4) is that he holds Gewirth's preference for a generic-dispositional view of the goods to be dictated solely by the needs of the theory for an invariant universally valued set of goods, and that this cannot be justified as an aspect of valuing purposiveness itself. (See Bond 1980a, 45–46.)

However, if "valuing purposiveness itself" means "necessarily valuing my purposes" (and this is all it does mean), then it is quite clear that *if* there are categorically necessary conditions for agency/successful agency, then I must value these as necessary goods, because I must value my purposes. So this really takes us back to Bond's objection to (1). Bond seems to think that it can be shown that a PPA must value its freedom and well-being as necessary goods without it being the case that it must value all of its purposes. It is enough, he says, for a PPA to have to value *some* of its purposes; and he seems to think that this means that, so derived, this conclusion is not derived from the concept of action. (See ibid., 48.)

There are some difficulties with this. If a PPA must value its freedom and well-being as necessary goods on the basis of valuing some purposes, then it must have to value some purposes. But then, to deny that its freedom and well-being are necessary goods is to deny that it values some purposes, and this is to deny that it is a PPA, which implies that "My freedom and well-being are necessary goods" *is* derived from the concept of action. This conclusion can only be avoided by holding that only a PPA who values some purposes must value its freedom and well-being, but that it is not necessary for a PPA to value any purposes.

This, perhaps, merits further analysis. But we need not go into it here. If, as I continue to maintain, a PPA must value all its purposes, then we have derived a PPA's commitment to the necessary goods from the concept of action, and there is no equivocation involved in doing so. Any suspicion of an equivocation only arises if we mistakenly reject (1) and/or misinterpret Gewirth's derivation of Stage I from it.

However, to return directly to the question of equivocation that Bond alleges: Gewirth does use "generic feature of agency" in more than one sense—in at least three ways, in fact, not only two. For example, Bond's second sense should include two senses, which refer, respectively to an enabling condition of the *possibility* of agency, and to an enabling condition of successful agency. However, none of these uses involves equivocation. Bond's contention that Gewirth derives Stage I by equivocation is the claim that this derivation involves treating what is generic in "the second sense" ("as relating to action in general") as generic in "the first sense" ("as relating to action's *essential* or *defining* characteristics"), and that these are not the same. (See ibid., 48 n. 3.) This is not the case. Gewirth states, in his reply to Bond, that his various uses are related, but not confused. He points out that "whatever is generic in the first sense must also be generic in the second" (Gewirth 1980a, 65); and that, in all his uses there is a linkage to the first sense, for

[i]n all these uses of "generic," the word signifies either the defining characteristics of action or whatever is directly derivative from or explicable by reference to those characteristics, so that there is no confusion of meanings. (Ibid.)

Instead, perhaps what is at issue is whether what is generic in the second sense (where this refers to what is a categorically necessary condition for pursuing/achieving purposes, rather than just to any generally occurring feature) is also generic in the first. So, what is more to the point are Gewirth's remarks about linkage. What is generic in the second sense may not be a defining condition of action, but it is enough for it to be a feature that a PPA who acts possesses by definition. And this is surely the case. I need my freedom and *basic* well-being in order to be able to act at all. No behavior with the defining conditions of action can occur without these features, and this is true by definition, as my freedom and basic well-being are the concrete specifications of the defining conditions of voluntariness and purposiveness. The other levels of well-being are not necessary for purposivity as such, but they are necessary for successful agency; so they are similarly *definitionally* linked to successful agency, and this is definitionally linked to purposivity as such, because PPAs act in order to *achieve* their purposes.

2 Puolimatka

1. Tapio Puolimatka claims that Gewirth

does not differentiate precisely and systematically between the meanings . . . [freedom and purposiveness] have as the necessary prerequisites of action and their other meanings. (Puolimatka 1989, 35)

This is shown by

a.   the fact that purposiveness does not imply well-being, as one might act to harm and destroy one's well-being;

b.   the fact that "the sense of 'purposiveness' signifying a neces-
        sary precondition of action is very different from Gewirth's
        broad concept of well-being" (ibid., 36). 'Well-being' "allows
        the incorporation of any elements . . . that agents regard as
        being good" (ibid.);

c.   the fact that PPAs can still act when deprived of some of the
        elements of their *basic* well-being, by torture, prison, or con-
        centration camps (see ibid., 37); and

d.   the fact that, although there is a sense of freedom which is a
        necessary precondition of action, it is compatible with forced
        choice situations and action under coercion; so when the PGC
        prohibits interference with generic freedom it does not pro-
        hibit coercing PPAs in various ways (see ibid., 39).

2. He also claims that, because behavior under forced choice is not
action, those acting under forced choice are not PPAs; from which it
follows that they could violate the PGC without contradicting themselves. (See ibid., 39.)

Regarding *a:* I *could* act to remove my freedom and well-being,
but this is different from saying that I *rationally* may do so. Furthermore, the argument only requires that I must value my freedom and
well-being in a categorically instrumental manner, not that I must
value these things for their own sakes. The presumed rationality of
suicide does not damage the argument.

Regarding *b: Generally* speaking, "well-being" *does* signify everything a PPA regards as good. But the argument operates only with
the generic-dispositional interpretation of "well-being."

Regarding *c:* This objection does not differentiate between basic
well-being and freedom. Ignoring this, torture, etc., does interfere
generically with my capacity to act, even if it removes it completely
only under extreme circumstances. It is because of these degrees of
interference that the basic goods are arranged hierarchically.

Regarding *d:* Inasmuch as the answer to this does not fall under
the answer to *c,* it must be pointed out that the PGC is derived from
the freedom I must value, regardless of my purposes. Whatever purposes I have, in relation to that purpose, I must value not being
subjected to coercion, etc., for in relation to that purpose this will
prevent my acting for it, or tend to do so. If I must regard the absence of coercion, etc., as a necessary good, and must claim a right
to my necessary goods, then I must grant this right to PPAO. The
supreme principle, so derived, will not permit me to subject PPAO
to forced choices or coercion.

Regarding 2: Presenting me with a forced choice restricts the actions I can perform, but it does not make me not a PPA. My being a
PPA is defined by my capacity to act for purposes I have freely
chosen. I can have this capacity in relation to one choice, while being
deprived of it in relation to another. Furthermore, even if we can
conceive of contingencies that present me with only forced choices,
I could still have the dispositional capacity to choose purposes
freely. My incapacity is a function of external interference, not of
internal inability. A forced choice that prevents me from carrying
out the requirements of the PGC *relating to that situation* will excuse
me from the PGC's requirements in *that situation*, but this will not
release me from its requirements in *my actions*, should actions be
possible for me.[18]

#6   There is nothing concretely specifiable that PPAs uni-
formly rationally must desire.

If we are going to start the way Gewirth does, namely from the *desires* of the
agent,[19] then . . . it is hopeless to try to come up with anything which all
agents as such *necessarily desire* if they are rational, other than simply the
satisfaction of whatever desire they have at the time. . . . [We cannot get] any
sort of uniform, concretely-specifiable "generically necessary good" of all
persons. (Narveson 1980, 659)

Narveson's overall view is that Stage I is problematic, that Stage
II is unsound (see #10–#12, #35.5 and #38), but that Stage III is sound
(see #47.4). We are here concerned only with his "queries" about
Stage I.

Why is Stage I problematic? To begin with, Narveson has no
qualms about accepting that if I act for a purpose then I necessarily
evaluate this purpose as "good," in the sense of considering that it
is worth aiming for. He accepts, without demur, that I necessarily
consider whatever purpose I have as a PPA as good. (See ibid., 657.)
This, of course, is proposition (2) in my presentation of the argument.

However, he expresses uncertainty about what Gewirth means by
(4) "My freedom and well-being are necessary goods." He recognizes that (4) is meant to go beyond (2) in some way, but he is not
quite sure in what way. Nevertheless, he is "on the whole" inclined
to think that (4) means, or at least entails, "I (if I have any purposes
at all) am committed to a positive evaluation of all my own (*future
and past*) purposes." To this he objects,

But how can we say that it *follows logically* from 'A wants x at t' that 'A at t values the satisfactions of his wants at t + n,' where n ranges over all intervals up to that between t and A's death? (Ibid., 657)

This is irrelevant, because (4) does not entail that I must value all purposes I don't have, on the basis of my valuing purposes I do have. "My freedom and well-being" (generically-dispositionally understood, and remember that Gewirth insists on such an interpretation) refers to general abilities or capacities that I require to pursue/achieve any of my purposes whatsoever. Narveson concedes that I necessarily value (at least instrumentally) the amount of freedom and well-being that I require for whatever purposes I have at any one time. (See ibid., 658.) So, he must concede that, if I value a purpose, I must value these general capacities (at least instrumentally), whatever my purpose might be. But to say that these are general (generic) capacities is to say that they *are the same capacities whatever my purposes might be.* So, whether or not I must now value purposes I will (or might) have, but do not as yet have, I must value these same general capacities, whatever purposes I value at t or at t + n. It follows that, in order to show that I must value my freedom and well-being, whatever my purposes, Gewirth does not have to suppose that I must value my future purposes (which I don't now have). He only has to suppose (which follows necessarily from "I am a PPA") that I value whatever purposes I actually happen to have.

However, the validity of (4) depends on the validity of (3) "My freedom and well-being are generically necessary conditions of my agency," on there being a set of concretely specifiable conditions, "my freedom and well-being," which are invariant conditions for my agency, whatever purposes guide it.

Narveson does not unequivocally deny that there are any invariant conditions for my agency, whatever purposes guide it. However, he interprets such conditions as "the necessary minimum which any agent, *qua* agent, can possibly want" (ibid., 658). On this basis he asserts that if we are to pinpoint an amount of freedom and well-being that I must value *whatever my purposes might be,* then this will be restricted to the amount of freedom and well-being required by a "suicidal masochist, . . . or by somebody who simply doesn't care about anything any more" (ibid.). This can amount to no more than freedom to kill myself, and whatever well-being (other conditions) I need to kill myself. If this is so, then, since the argument claims that rights are tied to generic needs, it can establish no more than that PPAs must be granted a right to kill themselves, etc., and Narveson says that this "would be as nearly as you like equivalent to conceding nobody any basic rights at all" (ibid.).

From this Narveson infers that Gewirth can only avoid his criticism (about past and future evaluation of my purposes) by adopting an interpretation of "my freedom and   well-being" that trivializes the argument. If the argument is not to be trivial then,

[i]nstead of conceiving of the "necessary" freedom and wellbeing which morality is fundamentally concerned with to be the same minimum for all, we should conceive it rather as variable among different agents and recipients. (Ibid.)

From such a conception, in which agents need not value anything other than their particular occurrent purposes and their particular occurrent conditions, we cannot generate a deontological ethics. At best, we are committed to a "contractarianism," or to a "utilitarianism." (See ibid., 659.)

However, Gewirth is not driven to Narveson's variable conception of the "necessary" goods, because Narveson misunderstands the relationship between a particular occurrent interpretation of my freedom and well-being and a generic-dispositional one. Narveson seems to interpret my generic-dispositional freedom and well-being as some kind of minimum particular occurrent freedom and well-being. My particular occurrent freedoms and well-being consist of conditions that are tied to my particular occurrent purposes. When my particular occurrent purpose is to commit suicide, my particular occurrent freedom is "my freedom to commit suicide." When my particular occurrent purpose is to buy a sports car, my particular occurrent freedom is "my freedom to buy a sports car," and so on. Narveson's discussion suggests that to pinpoint generic-dispositional freedom and well-being is to pinpoint some particular occurrent freedom and well-being that every PPA must want; and he says that this will be restricted to "a minimum," which is the freedom and well-being that a suicidal masochist, or someone who does not care about anything any more, must want. There is an immediate problem with this. I do not see that, at the particular occurrent level, there are *any* conditions that a PPA must want, whatever its purposes. Why should someone who does not wish to commit suicide specifically value freedom to commit suicide? So interpreted, there is no invariant minimum freedom and well-being that all PPAs must want. "Just so!" Narveson might respond. But this ignores another way of interpreting the idea of a generic-dispositional condition, which is, in fact, Gewirth's interpretation. For Gewirth, generic conditions of agency are "abstract" conditions in that their content does not depend on the content of my particular occurrent purposes, only on my having such purposes. What I must value, whatever my purposes, as my "generic-dispositional freedom," is noninterference with my capacity to choose my purposes. I need this capacity if I am to choose particular purposes, so my valuing this is independent of my valuing noninterference with any particular purpose. In other words, the freedom I must value irrespective of my purposes is my freedom to choose my purposes. Similarly, although I might only value my well-being (life, say) in order to pursue limited purposes, if I did not have my life, I could not pursue these purposes, whatever they might be. I must value my life for my purposes, *independently of my purposes*. So conceived, the generic conditions of agency are genuinely invariant, and far from trivial.[20]

Why does Narveson miss this interpretation? I think that it is because he considers that if "My freedom and well-being are necessary goods" is validly derived from "I necessarily value my purposes, whatever they are," then the antecedent does not commit me to valuing anything other than my particular occurrent purposes, because the freedom and well-being which I must value instrumentally are made conditional on the particular occurrent purposes that I do value.[21] By implication, he suggests that I am *necessarily* committed to valuing my freedom and well-being in no more, or less, than the sense in which I am *necessarily* committed to valuing my particular occurrent purposes.[22]

But, as Gewirth intends the consequent (expressible as "I necessarily value my freedom and well-being, whatever my purposes"), the "necessarily" in the antecedent and consequent do not have the same import. The consequent entails that I contradict "I am a PPA" if I do not have my freedom and well-being as my instrumental purposes. From the antecedent it does *not* follow that I contradict "I am a PPA" if I do not have my particular occurrent purposes as my purposes. In other words, that my judgment "I am a PPA" entails my judgment "The purposes I have are good," does not entail my judgment "I must have these purposes (or their particular occurrent conditions as my instrumental purposes)." But ["I am a PPA" entails my judgment "My freedom and well-being are necessary goods"] does entail my judgment "I must have my freedom and well-being as my instrumental purposes." Just because there is no necessity for me to value my freedom and well-being more than instrumentally does not mean that what I must value as my freedom and well-being is conditional upon the content of my particular occurrent purposes. Gewirth claims that there are instrumental conditions for my agency that are independent of my particular occurrent purposes, and which I, therefore, must value conditional only upon my being a PPA. Narveson has given us no good reason for thinking that this claim is mistaken.[23]

Finally, it is worth noting that Arthur C. Danto (commenting on Gewirth 1984b) echoes Narveson's claim that Gewirth's specification of the generic features is trivial when he claims that the sort of freedom to which I claim a right (according to Gewirth) is either what is necessary for action as such ("metaphysical freedom") or the kind of freedom that slaves lack ("political freedom"). However, the former is an empty category, for I can only be deprived of it by being killed; and the latter cannot be a necessary good, because I can act in various ways without having it. (See Danto 1984, 29.)

To this Gewirth replies (and I have nothing to add),

[T]he freedom I am primarily concerned with here is neither metaphysical freedom nor political freedom, but rather freedom of action. This freedom consists in controlling one's behaviour by one's own unforced choice, and hence without external interference, while having knowledge of relevant circumstances. Persons can, of course, be deprived of this freedom by violence, coercion, deception, and in other ways. Such freedom is a necessary, general condition of each particular action [and therefore of all actions]. If someone is deprived of it on one occasion, he may, of course still have it on other occasions; but still, for every particular action its presence is a necessary condition.

. . . [Although this is distinct from political freedom, there is a connection between it and political freedom.] This connection is especially involved in my thesis that freedom and well-being are necessary conditions not only of *action* but also of *successful* action in general, where such success consists in achieving the purposes for which one acts. For the absence of political freedom may sharply restrict persons' range of successful actions: not only slaves but also other subjects of repressive regimes. (Gewirth 1984c, 33)

#7   We don't know what the necessary preconditions of agency are.

Richard Brooks alleges that it is an empirical matter what the basic goods are, and that

[w]ithout the underpinnings of appropriate psychology or biology, Gewirth can hardly state these assumptions. The plain fact of the matter is that we don't know what are "the preconditions" of purposiveness and voluntariness . . . . (Brooks 1981, 293)

This goes too far. We do know that life is necessary for the possibility of agency, and know at least some of the capacities for the possibility of agency, some of the capacities for the maintenance of agency, and some of the capacities for the improvement of agency. That "preconditions of agency" are to be arranged into three categories, "basic," "nonsubtractive," and "additive," is in any case a conceptual matter, not an empirical one—even if discriminations according to the "degree of necessity" *within* these categories is in part an empirical matter. At the empirical level, it is untrue to say that Gewirth's specification lacks any underpinning in "appropriate psychology," as "the hierarchy of well-being corresponds somewhat to the 'hierarchy of needs' developed in psychological theories" (RM 63).[24] In any case, what matters in formal terms is that Gewirth provides a clear objective criterion for allocating importance within the hierarchy. We can run the argument to the PGC in terms of relatively unspecified generic-dispositional freedom and well-being, leaving *application* of the PGC as, partly, an empirical matter employing the criterion of degrees of necessity. If we do this, then the argument will be that PPAs must assent to the proposition that PPAs have rights to the generic features of agency (without it being specified *precisely* what this amounts to). Running the argument to the PGC in this "unspecified" manner will not affect its formal validity in any way, which is something W. D. Hudson appreciates when he comments (on the validity of the argument as an "is-ought" derivation—which can stand for the formal validity of the argument to the PGC) that Gewirth

may have overestimated the goods an agent needs in order to be purposive, but, if so, this is a small point so far as our present concern goes. (Hudson 1984, 109)

Because Gewirth provides the criterion of "degrees of necessity," it is not true, at least in principle, to say that he

fails to spell out and argue for specific prioritization of . . . factors necessary for well-being (e.g., intelligence, health, etc.); the substantive meaning of "well-being" thus remains ambiguous, perhaps inevitably. (Mahowald 1980, 447)

Finally, it should be noted that Douglas N. Husak objects to Gewirth's use of the criterion of "degrees of necessity" to set up his hierarchy for the resolution of conflicts between rights, on the grounds that necessity cannot admit of degrees. (See Husak 1984, 140 n. 15.)

However, when Gewirth talks of "degrees of necessity," the alleged variation is not in the relation of necessity itself, but in the range of effect of the necessary condition on the possibility of action and what can be achieved by it. Thus, for example, A is said to be "more necessary" than B if A is necessary for the very possibility of attempting to act, whereas B is only necessary for the possibility of generally succeeding in one's pursuits. A is also "more necessary" than B if A is necessary for the possibility of action, whereas B is only necessary for the possibility of increasing the range of purposes one can achieve by action. In addition, A is "more necessary" than B if A is necessary for a greater range of purposes than B.

General Comments

In this discussion there are six points, in particular, to which I have appealed in replying to criticisms, and which I consider critics have not appreciated fully.

1. PPAs are not merely beings who do, or try to do, what they want to do; the voluntary aspect of their agency extends to their choosing the purposes that they pursue.

2. Gewirth's definition of "action" does not derive from "ordinary usage," and it is not grounded as a description of the features that human behavior generally manifests (although much human behavior does, or is normally supposed to, manifest these features). Instead, its justification is that it is the sort of behavior that we must suppose to be characteristic of PPAs if we suppose that they are the addressees of practical precepts, and our interest is in what precepts they may rationally choose to follow.

3. A PPA's "freedom and well-being," as this is employed in the argument, refers to categorical needs for purpose pursuit/maintenance/improvement rather than to any particular occurrent purposes. (In the next chapter we will see that 3 assumes even greater importance in relation to Stage II.)

4. For PPAs to value their purposes it is not necessary for these purposes to be chosen as the result of conscious deliberation.

5. Although a PPA need not value all its purposes in a definitive manner, it does not follow that it need not value its freedom and well-being in a definitive manner.

6. The sense in which a PPA must value all its purposes is different from the sense in which a PPA must value its freedom and well-being. *If* a PPA has *purpose E,* then it must value *this purpose;* but *if* a PPA has *any purpose* (is a PPA), then it must value *its freedom and well-being.* A PPA is required to *have* its freedom and well-being as purposes, whatever its particular occurrent purposes. It is not required to have a particular occurrent purpose if it does not have it.

5 Objections to Stage II: Fact and Value

#8 **From the fact that I need/want/demand X, it does not follow that I have a claim right to X.**

There appears to be some temptation to interpret Stage II as resting on the validity of inferring "A has a claim right to its freedom and well-being" from "A needs/wants/demands freedom and well-being." For example, W. D. Hudson asks,

But how can the mere fact that anyone insists upon having something give him a right to it? (Hudson 1984, 127)

However, it must be emphasized that Gewirth insists that from the fact that I want or need X for my purpose E, it cannot be inferred that I *have* a claim right to X. (See RM 75, 160–161.) In the first place, Gewirth maintains that I am required to consider that I have claim rights only to the generically necessary requirements of my agency, to those things that I need for my purposes, *whatever they might be*, to my *categorical* (generic) needs. (See RM 77–78.) Second, he does not claim that it can be inferred from the fact that I categorically need X that I *have* a claim right to X. His argument is dialectical, not assertoric. As such, the alleged inference is from "I categorically need X" to "I (logically must) *consider* that I have a claim right to X." Additionally, the argument is from within my internal viewpoint as a PPA. So, the inference (in Stage II) is from "I categorically need X" to "*I* (not anyone else) *as a PPA* (logically must) consider that I have a claim right to X"; and the reason for this is that I am *logically required* to value ("want") my freedom and well-being proactively for whatever my purposes. Only to things that I am logically required to want, whatever my purposes, does Gewirth say that I must claim a right.

This chapter examines objections that revolve around the allegation that Gewirth cannot derive claim rights from wants/needs/demands.[1] These objections are dealt with in two sections. In the first

I examine contentions that I am not required to consider that I have a right to X on the basis of some statement of my desires or needs. Gewirth's contention, outlined above, is the basis of his claim to have derived "ought" from "is." In the second, "Morality, Logic, and 'Is-Ought,'" I examine objections to this claim. In addition, I examine objections revolving around the claim that the argument reduces morality to logic, because my discussion of these is necessary to deal with the relationship between "is" and "ought" in the argument. Although the objections considered in "Morality, Logic, and 'Is-Ought'" are generally not presented as objections to Stage II specifically, they are dealt with here because of their significance in relation to the connection between needs and deontic claims, which Gewirth presents in Stage II.

From Needs to Rights?

#9   The restriction of rights-claims to freedom and well-being is arbitrary.

Bernard Williams asks why, if I am going to prescribe that I have a claim right to my freedom and well-being,

I should not more ambitiously prescribe that no one interfere with whatever particular purposes I may happen to have. I *want* the success of my particular projects, of course, as much as anything else, and I want other people not to interfere with them. Indeed, my need for basic freedom was itself derived from that kind of want. (Williams 1985, 62)

Williams, hereby, implies that he regards the restriction of my rights-claims to generic features of my agency as somewhat arbitrary. However, the reason for this restriction is quite clear. Deontic prescriptions must be independent of my particular occurrent purposes (conatively independent). If I need my freedom and well-being for my purposes, whatever they are, then I need these things, and must value them instrumentally, *whatever I might want to achieve.* I am required to consider that I have a claim right to my freedom and well-being, in part, not because I just want to achieve my particular purposes, but because I rationally *must* want my freedom and well-being for my purposes, whatever my purposes, and *whether or not I in fact want my freedom and well-being.* This conative independency of evaluation can be logically required only of features that pertain to me in respect of my being a PPA as such, and not of contingent purposes that I might not have and yet not deny that I am a PPA.[2]

#10 I can value an end and not claim a right to it.

Jan Narveson asks,

Does my regarding the achievement of my purposes, no matter what they are, as good commit me to claiming a *right* to achieve them? . . . [No! Because] it is surely clear that we could both value, quite highly even, an end we have, and yet admit that we have no right whatever to pursue it. (Narveson 1980, 660)

But Gewirth does not hold that I must claim a right to every purpose I have. I must only claim rights to my necessary goods, and only my freedom and well-being (generically understood) are necessary goods. Gewirth does not derive a PPA's rights-claim to X from "I must, whatever X, value X if I have X as my purpose." He derives it from "I must (if I am to be rational) have X as my purpose (whether or not I have it as my purpose)."[3]

#11 Deontic judgments are not simply prescriptive judgments grounded on ends.

Narveson says that Gewirth, in arguing against the "amoralist,"

claims that if someone sees his basic goods threatened by something, Z, and believes that he can avoid Z if and only if he does X, then "given certain minimal qualifications, he must make or accept for himself such a prudential and prescriptive 'ought'-judgment as . . . 'I ought to do X,'" which, Gewirth says, "is a deontic judgment . . . [in setting] forth a prescriptive requirement for action, grounded on a justifying reason consisting in a certain end . . . " ([RM] 90). (Narveson 1980, 660)

Narveson objects that deontic judgments are not simply prescriptive judgments grounded on ends. And, whatever we "call the sort of 'ought' which one uses when one judges that one ought to use a #9 iron for this shot, . . . it is simply not true that those judgments *entail* rights-claims" (ibid., 661).

But, of course, Gewirth does not claim that *all* prudential "oughts" ("oughts" grounded on *my* ends) are deontic. And, in Narveson's example, he would not claim that I must consider that I have a right to use a #9 iron just because this is instrumental to some end I have: *though he would claim that I must consider that I have such a right if my use of this golf club were necessary to save my life!* He would say that what I need to do (X) to protect my basic goods yields a prudentially deontic requirement on me to do X because I need my basic goods for my purposes, regardless of what they might be, and hence must regard my basic goods as necessary goods

(meaning that I must value them proactively for my purposes, irrespective of my purposes); from which it follows that I must consider
that I strictly ought to pursue my basic goods; from which it follows
that I must consider that I strictly ought to do X. According to
Gewirth, from such a strict "ought" judgment rights-claims can be
derived.

**#12   From "I want X," no more follows than that I want
        others not to interfere with my having X.**

From "I ought to do X" (in the passage Narveson quotes from *Reason
and Morality* in #11 above), Gewirth argues that I must accept at least
an implicit requirement that there be no interference with my doing
X. Narveson agrees but says,

> [T]his is an inference from wanting to do X to wanting to *be* free to do it. It is
> not an inference to a "requirement" that one be free to do it, in the sense of a
> normatively-stated injunction to others not to interfere with one's doing X. It
> is quite true that, *qua* wanting to do X, I want others not to prevent me from
> doing it. But it is not true that, *qua* merely wanting to do it, I am *committed* to
> accepting some such statement as "Others ought to keep off," where 'ought'
> expresses a categorical norm. (Narveson 1980, 661)

Given that Narveson concedes that "I ought to do X" entails "I
ought to be free to do X," this objection rests entirely on the claim
that Stage I establishes only that I want to do X (what is necessary to
secure my freedom and well-being), and does not establish that I
ought to do X. This is not so. Stage I establishes that I rationally *must
want* to do X, whatever my purposes. Since my desires as a PPA are
proactive, the rational necessity of my desire for my freedom and
well-being is strictly action-directing for me at least. I, at least, must
consider that I (categorically) ought to do X. Thus, I must consider
that I ought to be free to do X, which yields (from my point of view)
a categorically binding requirement of noninterference on others.

**#13   It does not follow from the fact that I *must* want my
        freedom and well-being not to be interfered with that
        I must consider that I have a right to my freedom and
        well-being.**

According to Gewirth,

> [i]n saying that freedom and well-being are necessary goods for him, the
> agent . . . is opposed to whatever interferes with his having freedom and
> well-being . . . [. If] he accepts that it is permissible that other persons inter-
> fere with or remove his freedom and well-being [he] . . . shows that he re-

gards his freedom and well-being with indifference or at least as dispensable, so that he accepts . . . 'It is not the case that my freedom and well-being
are necessary goods' . . . . (RM 79, 80)[4]

Kai Nielsen retorts that

an agent, indeed a rational agent, could be "opposed to whatever interferes
with his having freedom and well-being" without believing for a moment
that he or anyone else is *entitled* to freedom or well-being. (Nielsen 1984, 72)

Similarly, Jeffrey Reiman (1990, 61) claims that to deny that I have
a right to freedom and well-being is not necessarily to regard my
freedom and well-being with indifference, or as dispensable.

Once again it has to be pointed out that "My freedom and well-
being are necessary goods" is a claim that *I am logically required* to
make. So, it is not just my wanting to have my freedom and well-
being, my *being* opposed to interference with my freedom and well-
being, that is the premise here. The premise is that I (if I am not to
deny that I am a PPA) *must want* to have my freedom and well-being,
that I (as a PPA) *must be opposed* to interference with my freedom and
well-being. However, Nielsen says that even if we

accept that as a purposive agent . . . "he [a human being] must want his
freedom and well-being" not to be "interfered with by other persons" ([RM]
80) . . . [h]e may view the situation simply as a clash of interests and not
conceptualize it in normative terms at all. (Nielsen 1984, 73)

Here, at last, we have an objection that is not directed at a straw
man; and, in fact, a number of commentators concede that a PPA
must want its freedom and well-being not to be interfered with by
PPAO, but go on to assert that it does not follow that a PPA must
claim a right to its freedom and well-being against PPAO.[5]

That this assertion is incorrect is shown by closer examination of
the argument from attitudinal consistency. If I logically must be opposed to interference with my freedom and well-being, then I logically must consider that I have a right to my freedom and well-
being.

The Argument from Attitudinal Consistency

We begin with the following premise:

(A)   I must consider my freedom and well-being to be neces-
        sary goods.

(A) entails

(β)   I *must have* a (proactive) negative attitude towards (be
        opposed to/resist) interference with my freedom and

well-being (where these are viewed as the preconditions of agency).

Now, our conclusion is to be that (A) entails that I must hold

(C)   I consider that I have a right to my freedom and well-being.

By the correlativity of rights and strict "oughts," (C) entails

(C_o)   I consider that my freedom and well-being strictly ought not to be interfered with by PPAO.

(C), therefore, entails

(B)   I have a negative attitude towards interference with my freedom and well-being.[6]

From (C) $\rightarrow$ (B) it may be inferred that (–B) $\rightarrow$ (–C). But it is clearly not the case that it can be inferred that (B) $\rightarrow$ (C).[7] What Gewirth requires, however, is not that (B) $\rightarrow$ (C), but that (β) $\rightarrow$ (C) $\equiv$ (–C) $\rightarrow$ (–β).
What does (–C) entail?

(–C)   = I do not consider that I have a right to my freedom and well-being.

(–C) is ambivalent. Compatible with (–C) are

(–C1)   I believe that others have a right to interfere with my freedom and well-being (that it is *permissible* for others to interfere);

(–C2)   I do not believe that I have a right to my freedom and well-being, but also do not believe that others have a right to interfere;

(–C3)   I do not have rights-talk in my vocabulary. (Both [–C2] and [–C3] entail "I believe that it is *neither permissible nor impermissible* for others to interfere with my freedom and well-being," which entails "I believe that it is *not impermissible* for others to interfere with my freedom and well-being"); and

(–C4)   I am agnostic on the question of my rights (I do not have an opinion on whether it is permissible, impermissible, or not impermissible for others to interfere with my freedom and well-being).

Now, if I hold (–C1), I believe that I strictly ought not to interfere with others' interference with my freedom and well-being. This entails "I have a *positive* attitude towards others' interference with my freedom and well-being," and this is a denial of (B). If I deny (B) then I deny (β). Clearly I cannot hold (–C1). However, (–C) only entails (–β) if (–C2), (–C3), and (–C4) also entail (–β).

But they do! Given (β), I *must* hold (B) (have a negative attitude towards interference with my freedom and well-being). If I hold any of (–C2), (–C3), or (–C4), I *could* hold (B), but *I am not required to do so.* But if I hold that I may hold (–B), then I deny that I must hold (B); and therefore I deny (β).

But this means that (–C) → (–β). This entails that (β) → (C). If I logically must have a negative attitude towards interference with my freedom and well-being, then I logically must consider that I have a right to my freedom and well-being.

A note of caution is necessary about this argument. The argument rests on inferring that if (–C) does not entail (β) then (–C) entails (–β). *Part* of the reason why this is valid, whereas (–p does not entail q) does not entail (–p → –q), is that (β) is necessary. However, it is not the whole reason. For "Napoleon was an emperor" does not entail (β),[8] but this does not entail (–β). So, from "X does not entail that I must hold Y," it does not follow *generally* that "X entails that it is not the case that I must hold Y." However, *if* "–X → I hold Y," then from "X does not entail that I must hold Y," it does follow that "X entails that it is not the case that I must hold Y." "'Napoleon was an emperor' does not entail (β)" does not entail that (–β), *because* "Napoleon was *not* an emperor" does not entail that (B). On the other hand, "(–C) does not entail (β)" does entail "(–C) → (–β)," *because* (C) → (B).

Gewirth says that if I do not consider that I have a right to my freedom and well-being, then I display indifference to my having my freedom and well-being. What he should, perhaps, have said, is that, if I do not consider that I have a right to my freedom and well-being, then I imply that I *may* display indifference. Nielsen replies that I *could* be opposed to interference without considering that I have a right to my freedom and well-being. This is true in the sense that I could have other grounds for being opposed to such interference. What he fails to say, however, is that, if I do not consider that I have a right to my freedom and well-being, then I *could* also not be opposed to such interference. But I am logically required to be opposed to such interference. So I may not adopt a stance that allows me not to be opposed to such interference, that allows me to be indifferent to such interference. Nielsen and Reiman are right to say that if I deny my right I do not necessarily display indifference, but all that Gewirth has to show is that if I deny my right then I deny that I *must be opposed* to interference. For me to deny my right does imply that I consider that it is not impermissible for me to be indifferent to interference or to be neutral on the question, and "My freedom and well-being are necessary goods" does not allow me to be indifferent to interference or to be neutral on the question. If "My freedom and well-being are necessary goods" entails "I logically may not be indifferent," and my denial of a right to my freedom and well-being entails "I logically may be indifferent," then my denial of my right entails denial of "My freedom and well-being are necessary goods."

We can summarize this as follows:

> As a PPA, I must believe either that I have a right to my freedom and well-being against interference by others (MyR), that I have no right against others' interference (NR),[9] that I am undecided about the deontic status of others' interference (UR), or that others have a right to interfere (RI).

> MyR → anti-interference.

> NR does not → anti-interference or pro-interference; it is compatible with both or with indifference.

> UR does not → anti-interference or pro-interference; it is compatible with a "neutral" attitude.

> RI → pro-interference.

> As a PPA I must be anti-interference. ∴

> As a PPA I must hold MyR.

It is possible that some will find this convincing at a purely formal level, yet still remain puzzled about why it is valid. In explanation we can start by asking, What, after all, is the difference between categorical and hypothetical imperatives? A hypothetical imperative has the form "*If* I want to achieve X then I ought to do Y." A categorical imperative has the form "I ought to do Y, whether I want to achieve X (for which the doing of Y is necessary, or which is constituted by doing Y) or not." Of course, it might be the case that I do want to achieve X. However, even if the hypothetical is *thus* written out, "I ought to do Y" (on the grounds that it is necessary to achieve X, and *I want to achieve X*), it is still not categorical. My reason for doing Y remains that I want to do X, and categorical reasons are not dependent upon what I happen to want to do. But the reason why this, in turn, is so is that it might be the case that I ought not to *want to achieve* X. So suppose that I *logically must* want to achieve X. I now logically must, if I am to do anything at all, have X as my purpose for which I must do Y. It would be categorically irrational for me not to do Y, for what is logically prohibited must be prohibited in terms of any form of reason. But this is equivalent to saying that I categorically ought to do Y, if I am to do anything at all. As a PPA it is not open for me not to do anything at all. So, from this vantage point, I categorically ought to do Y when this is necessary for me to achieve X, which I logically must want to achieve. Thus, it is readily seen that what I logically must desire is directly relevant to *deontic* claims.

Of course, this explains only how what I logically must desire, where this desire is proactive (as it must be for a PPA), yields *self-referring* deontic "oughts." The argument from attitudinal consistency alleges that there is no gap between my having to desire my freedom and well-being and my having to consider that I have a right to my freedom and well-being. So, this consideration does not explain completely how the argument from attitudinal consistency achieves its final result. Nevertheless, it should at least render it more plausible that the argument from attitudinal consistency should be able to achieve its result validly. For part of the problem is to explain how statements about desires can have deontic prescriptive implications of any kind. Furthermore, to move on from here to the final result requires only that it be the case that if I categorically ought to do X then I categorically ought to have the conditions for doing X.

However, it should now be apparent that an *explanation* of the argument from attitudinal consistency, *beyond its own terms*, requires the sequence that I have presented as Gewirth's central argument for Stage II. For this reason I have presented this sequence, rather than the argument from attitudinal consistency, as the central argument. Nevertheless, the argument from attitudinal consistency has independent force, for its *presentation* as a demonstration does not require explanation in terms of the central sequence. Thus, the two arguments may be regarded as mutually supportive, rather than as the same argument.

It might be objected that the argument from attitudinal consistency cannot be valid, because judgments about required pro-attitudes do not universalize as judgments about rights do. Thus, "I logically must (because I am a PPA) have a pro-attitude to my having X" cannot logically entail "I must consider (because I am a PPA) that I have a right to X." If this were so, it would have to be the case that "I logically must have a pro-attitude to my having X" universalizes to "I logically must have a pro-attitude to PPAO's having X," but this is not the case.

However, this objection is mistaken. I am required to have a pro-attitude towards my freedom and well-being because (formally) the criterion of my interests requires a pro-attitude to my freedom and well-being to be had not only by me, but by anyone (i.e., impersonally). (Subjectively) I am required to have a pro-attitude to my freedom and well-being not because the criterion of my interests directs only what *my* attitudes should be, but because I (must) accept this criterion, and, thus, regard the formal requirements of this criterion as binding. Although the criterion of my interests is *directing* only *for* those who accept this criterion (thus, prima facie necessarily only for me), what this criterion directs (requires for its satisfaction) is independent of my (or anyone else's) choosing (or having to choose) to follow this criterion; and it *directs* its requirements *to* all who are capable of satisfying it. My dialectically necessary viewpoint (being the viewpoint of my [generic] interests) is thus required to be that a pro-attitude towards my having freedom ought to be had (by anyone). By an argument analogous to the ASA, it follows that my dialectically necessary viewpoint must be that [I am a PPA → A pro-attitude towards my having freedom and well-being ought to be had (by anyone)]. But, then, internal application of the LPU requires me to hold [PPAO is a PPA → A pro-attitude towards PPAO's freedom and well-being ought to be held (by anyone, and, thus, by me)]. Since the pro-attitude in question is proactive, this means that I must accept that I ought to pursue PPAO's freedom and well-being (or, at least, not interfere with it). (See further #37.)

This can be approached in a slightly different way. Given that the pro-attitude in question is proactive, "I logically must (because I am a PPA) have a pro-attitude to X" is equivalent to "I logically must (because I am a PPA) consider that I strictly ought to pursue X." Thus, the objection rests on it being the case that "I logically must (because I am a PPA) consider that I strictly ought to pursue X" does not universalize to "I logically must consider that PPAO strictly ought to pursue X," where "PPAO strictly ought to pursue X" is a judgment made by me involving my endorsement, and not just a statement of what PPAO must endorse. For, if *I prescribe* that PPAO strictly ought to pursue X, then I must also prescribe that PPAO have the necessary conditions for pursuing/achieving X, and this means that I must grant PPAO a (moral) right to its freedom and well-being. However, "I logically must (because I am a PPA) consider that I strictly ought to pursue X" entails (by an argument analogous to the ASA) "I logically must hold 'I strictly ought to pursue

X because I am a PPA.'" By the internal application of the logical principle of universalizability, this *does* entail "I logically must hold 'PPAO strictly ought to pursue X because PPAO is a PPA,'" where this "ought" involves *my* prescriptive endorsement. Thus, the objection fails. (See also #37 and #47.3. For background considerations see #35.3.)

#14   Even if I cannot help valuing my freedom and well-being, it does not follow that I have a right to it.

For granted that every human being does in fact cherish both freedom and well-being— . . . necessarily and unavoidably, as being a part of the very notion of what it means to be an agent—still how does it follow from this that every human agent has a right to such freedom and well-being? Is there not somehow an illicit process here from fact to right, or from 'is' to 'ought'? Merely because I or anyone else happens to have or cherish something very dearly, surely that does not mean that I therefore somehow have a right to what I thus love and cherish, or even that it is right for me thus to love and cherish it. . . .
   . . . [Gewirth would grant that it does not follow from "I cherish X" that "I have a right to X." But he claims that the case is different when I necessarily cherish X.] But again, why should something's being necessarily the case make it any more a matter of right or obligation than its merely being actually the case? Is an inference from 'must be' to 'ought' any more valid than one from 'is' to 'ought'? Indeed, suppose that an old-time psychological hedonist were actually to bring off a demonstration to the effect that human beings not merely do not, but cannot, seek anything but pleasure. That still would not mean that pleasure was for that reason a good, in the sense of being something that human beings have a right to. (Veatch 1979, 410)

Veatch commits two errors in this passage. First, he attributes an assertoric inference to Gewirth, rather than a dialectical one. Gewirth does not claim that "I necessarily cherish X" entails "I have a right to X." At most, he claims that "I necessarily cherish X" entails "I logically must consider that I have a right to X." Second, although Veatch appreciates that Gewirth holds that I must claim rights only to what I must consider to be necessary goods, he misinterprets the sense of "necessity" that is involved. He interprets "I necessarily cherish X" to mean "I cannot help cherishing X." This is not what it means. It means "I logically ought (ought if I am not to contradict 'I am a PPA') to attach a proactive value to X." It cannot mean that it is impossible for me to claim to be a PPA and yet not to cherish X. As a PPA, I choose my purposes. If I cannot help valuing a purpose proactively, then I do not choose it, and this purpose does not belong to me as a PPA.[10]

   Furthermore, it should be noted that even if the inference from "I must consider my freedom and well-being to be necessary goods" to "I must consider that I have a right to my freedom and well-being" is not obvious, the inference to "I must consider that it is right for me to cherish/pursue my freedom and well-being" is straightforward. Indeed, it is straightforward that I must consider that I do wrong if I do not cherish/pursue my freedom and well-being. To say that I do wrong if I do not do Y, is to say that I ought to do Y. This is to say that I have some sort of reason to do Y. But, if I logically ought to do Y, then I must have a reason to do Y in any terms, and a reason not to fail to do Y in any terms, for no considerations can be binding on me if my acceptance of them requires me to deny that I am a PPA. There is, of course, still a gap between "I ought to cherish my freedom and well-being, for whatever my purposes" and "I must consider that I have a right to my freedom and well-being." But, at one level at least, the gap between "is" and "ought" is already closed, at least dialectically, when "My freedom and well-being are necessary goods" is given its proper interpretation in terms of the *rational* necessity of *proactive* valuing.[11]

Morality, Logic, and "Is-Ought"
Grounding Morality in Logic

This subsection examines some objections relating to Gewirth's use of criteria of deductive and inductive reason to ground the necessity for a PPA to accept the PGC.[12] The objections considered here and in the rest of the chapter are not necessarily directed at Stage II. For the most part they are directed at the argument as a whole. It is, however, necessary to deal with some of them in order to explain the relationship between categorical needs and the claiming of rights to freedom and well-being in the argument. Others are included here not for this reason but because they relate to objections that are included for this reason.

#15   The argument reduces morality to logic.

According to E. J. Bond,

Gewirth's argument follows what he calls a "dialectically necessary procedure," by which he means that we are to look at things internally (or intentionally), from the point of view of the agent, rather than attempt to deduce the principle in an objective manner. Thus we are not to say that a certain principle follows logically from certain analytic truths about action, but rather that certain judgments logically must be made *by* anyone who is a prospective agent. (Bond 1980a, 36–37)

This is entirely correct, but Bond goes on to say that, according to the argument,

[w]hat makes his [a PPA's] act immoral (what makes it true that his act is immoral) is that it contravenes the PGC, and since the necessity or binding-ness of the PGC is derived from logic, this is a *logical* error. Moral reasons (reasons determining that an act or omission of an act is wrong or obligatory) are *logical* reasons; indeed they reduce to *one* logical reason, avoidance of the implicit denial of the logically necessary but content-bearing PGC. . . .

The (moral) reason why I must not do some things is that, if I do, I will cause other persons hurt or harm. . . . Gewirth invites us to suppose that beyond this lies the *real* reason why these things are wrong, viz. that to suppose that hurting others is permissible is to "incur an inconsistency." Thus moral evil is reduced to logical error. The evil itself *lies in* the inconsis-tency. What Gewirth has done is to attempt to reduce the *practical* necessity of moral obligation to *logical* necessity, and sound practical reasoning . . . to sound *theoretical* reasoning . . . .[13]

. . . Avoiding inconsistency can only be a reason for not holding certain things to be true together. It cannot, *per se,* be a reason for *doing* anything . . . . Gewirth and others like him would turn wickedness into a kind of intellec-tual incompetence. . . .

But if logical necessity cannot require us to *do* anything (other than reject at least one of an inconsistent set of propositions), then no deontic statement with content . . . can be analytic or logically necessary . . . .

But if what I have said is true, then there must be something wrong with Gewirth's argument, since it has as its conclusion the claim that logical ne-cessity requires us to conform to the PGC . . . . Or, what is surely equivalent: The statement that everyone has rights to freedom and well-being is logi-cally necessary. (Bond 1980a, 40–43)[14]

However, as Bond himself states (in the first paragraph quoted), Gewirth's argument does not purport to establish that the PGC itself follows from analytic statements about action, but that it is logically necessary for a PPA to judge the permissibility of its actions accord-ing to the PGC. In other words, the argument does not purport to establish that the prescription "PPAs ought to act in accordance with the rights to freedom and well-being of all PPAs" is an analytic statement in itself, that what the PGC prescribes is itself an analytic statement. The statement that it *does* hold to be analytic is "All PPAs ought to espouse the statement that the PGC prescribes." This is a crucial feature of Gewirth's use of the dialectically necessary method, and Gewirth goes so far as to say that

the necessary truth of the dialectical statement 'Every agent logically must accept the *PGC*' does not entail that the *PGC* itself, in its assertoric form, is necessarily true or even plausible. (RM 154)

This means that the "ought" in "All PPAs ought to espouse the PGC" *is* a *logical* "ought"; but the "ought" prescribed by the PGC itself, the "ought" in "All PPAs ought not to interfere with the freedom and well-being of all PPAs," is *not* a logical one (but a moral one). Bond is quite right to say that no deontic statement with content can be logically necessary—*if* he means that no deontic proposition with content can be of the form "A = A." But Gewirth does not hold that the PGC itself is a logically necessary proposition:[15] the "ought" in "All PPAs ought to espouse the PGC" is not itself a practical-prescriptive "ought" beyond enjoining us not to hold two contradictory propositions to be true together (viz., "I am a PPA" and "It is not the case that I ought to respect the freedom and well-being of my recipients as well as of myself").

Bond is, therefore, wrong to say that the moral reason why I ought not to interfere with the freedom and well-being of all PPAs is a logical reason. The moral reason why I ought to respect the freedom and well-being of PPAs is that they categorically need their freedom and well-being in order to pursue/achieve their purposes. Avoidance of inconsistency (which is the logical reason involved in the argument) is the reason why I ought to espouse an SPR for my purposes in which "X categorically needs Y" is treated as a sufficient reason for "I ought not to interfere with X's having Y." Although PPAs who judge that it is permissible (or not impermissible) for them to violate the PGC are guilty of intellectual error, this intellectual error is not the evil they commit by violating the PGC. The evil they commit is to deprive PPAs of the generic features of their agency. The point is that there are a number of possible criteria of evil I might espouse, and the logical necessity of my espousing a particular criterion is a conclusive reason for me to espouse that criterion rather than others. But this does not convert the relation between the criterion and what it validates into a logically necessary relation. Irrationality (illogicality) is not what makes an action immoral. It is, however, the means by which we can know what actions are immoral. To think that the latter entails the former is to seriously confuse ontological and epistemological questions. Thus, Gewirth does not reduce morality to logic, the practical necessity of moral obligation to logical necessity, or sound practical reasoning to sound theoretical reasoning; he only purports to give us a logically necessary reason for adopting a particular criterion of moral obligation, and a sound theoretical reason for adopting a particular criterion of sound practical reasoning.

In effect, when Bond asserts that the statement "Logical necessity requires us to conform to the PGC" is equivalent to the statement "'Everyone has rights to freedom and well-being' is logically necessary," he either reads the latter in a way in which it is equivalent to the former—but which does not have the implication that morality is reduced to logic—or else he asserts to be equivalent two propositions that are not equivalent, which departs from his own declared understanding of the dialectically necessary method (indicated in the first paragraph quoted). Bond's objection thus rests on equivocating on his reading of "Logical necessity requires us to conform to the PGC." For Gewirth, this means "It is logically necessary for a PPA to espouse the PGC because not to do so is to contradict that it is a PPA." This is not equivalent to "It is logically necessary for a PPA to espouse the PGC because the PGC is a statement of the form 'A = A.'" For morality to be reduced to logic by Gewirth's position, his position must entail the latter proposition.[16]

If anyone is not convinced that the propositions that Bond alleges to be equivalent are not equivalent, then consider this: Suppose that A believes that all Europeans are six feet tall, and that Napoleon was a European. On the basis of these beliefs, it is logically necessary for A to believe that Napoleon was six feet tall. But it does not follow that "Napoleon was six feet tall" is a necessary truth (or even that it is true). To hold that it is, is to confuse the validity of a logical inference with the truth of its conclusion. Of course, if the antecedent in a logically valid inference is analytic, then the consequent must be analytic too. As a PPA, it is logically necessary for me to hold "I am a PPA," and Gewirth holds that it is logically necessary, on this basis, for me to espouse the PGC. Is this not equivalent to saying that "I am a PPA" is analytic and that, because the PGC follows from "I am a PPA," that the PGC is analytic too? No! For the analytic premise is not "I am a PPA," but "I (as a PPA) must hold that I am a PPA," and the analytic conclusion that follows from it is not the PGC, but "I must espouse the PGC." The PGC does not follow from "I am a PPA"; *my commitment to the PGC* follows from *my logically necessary commitments as a PPA*.[17]

#16   Immoral actions cannot be inconsistent; only judgments not actions can be consistent or inconsistent.

1 Bond

According to E. J. Bond, Gewirth holds

that immoral *action* is inconsistent, that immorality *itself* is a species of inconsistency. . . . But, of course, even if his arguments are sound, the most he is entitled to claim is that *judging* A to be permissible, where A contravenes the PGC, is inconsistent. Only judgments, not actions, can be consistent or self-contradictory. (Bond 1980a, 40)[18]

This objection is misdirected. What Gewirth claims is that *a PPA* who violates the PGC *is being inconsistent* in so acting. By so acting, a PPA implies that it judges such action to be not impermissible; and, according to the argument, a PPA cannot consistently make such a judgment (because such a judgment contradicts propositions/judgments to which a PPA is logically committed by virtue of being a PPA). (See RM 139.) Gewirth does not claim that *actions themselves* can be inconsistent. Inconsistency is not incurred *by actions*, but *by the propositional holdings of PPAs who act in certain ways.* (See Gewirth 1980a, 61–62.)

2 Geels

However, D. E. Geels (referring to Gewirth 1967a) presents an objection that threatens to render this reply inadequate.

Geels quotes William Wollaston (1964, 364) as saying,

[W]hoever acts as if things are so, or not so, doth by his acts declare, that they are so, or not so; as plainly as he could by words . . . And if the things are otherwise, his acts contradict those propositions, which assert them to be as they are. (Geels 1971, 663; ellipsis Geels')

Geels says that this is a fallacy, and that Gewirth is guilty of it. This is because

[t]here simply is no contradiction in saying that all acts of a given kind are obligatory, but that I will not so act. It is not contradictory to engage in deliberate and recognized wrongdoing. And to do what is morally wrong is not necessarily a matter of ignorance, of not knowing what is morally right. (Ibid., 667)

Geels could be saying one or more of three separate things.

1. It is logically possible for me to say "I ought not to do X," and yet to do X. The proposition "I say that I ought to do X, but do not do X," as a description of a state of affairs, is not a contradiction.
2. It is logically possible for me to consider/know that I ought not to do X, and yet to do X. The proposition "I consider/know that I ought not to do X, but I do X," as a description of a state of affairs, is not a contradiction. To violate a rule and to deny that one is bound by the rule are not the same thing.
3. By doing X I do not presuppose a rule *for its justification*, which contradicts my stated/considered/logically required judgment "I ought not to do X."

However, although 1 and 2 are both true, their truth does not entail that 3 is true, and for Gewirth to be guilty of a fallacy, 3 needs to be true. Geels seems to think that it is.

Suppose a certain judge explicitly and seriously asserts that all persons who violate a given statute and are convicted of so doing ought to be punished by a sentence of no less than five years at hard labor. Yet it happens that a friend of his is found guilty of the very violation and the judge refuses to apply the sentence of five years at hard labor to his guilty friend. Has the judge contradicted himself? Obviously not, for he may have changed his moral attitude or he may deliberately do what he believes to be wrong. . . . But this is not a logical inconsistency, for the judge has not asserted that one and the same proposition is both true and false, and he has not asserted a set of propositions to be true, all of which could not logically be true. [Geels 1971, 667] [Only] in a loose, "analogical" sense of contradiction as when someone says one thing and does quite another [has the judge contradicted himself.] (Ibid., 664)

The points about changing his mind and deliberate wrongdoing are irrelevant. Indeed, by suggesting that, in refusing to sentence his friend in what he has declared to be the required manner, the judge might be adopting a changed view on what he ought to do, Geels effectively concedes Gewirth's claim that actions display judgments. For what is at issue is whether the judge, by not sentencing his friend as declared, has implied his assent to a proposition that logically contradicts his declared rule. More pertinent is Geels' assertion that the judge is only involved in "analogical" contradiction.

What has the judge done? In declaring the rule he states that this is the rule to apply. He states, "I am guided by this rule." Yet, in not sentencing his friend according to this rule, he does not apply this rule. He acts in a way that is incompatible with his being guided by this rule. He acts as if he believed that this is not the rule to apply. True, the judge does not explicitly say, nor need he actually believe, that it is not the case that this is the rule to apply. But does the fact that he acts *as if* he believed something to be true, which he has declared to be false, merely yield "analogical" contradiction? Surely, we are only able to identify that he acts *as if* he believes that his declared rule does not apply because his failure to apply the rule evidences that his statement "I am guided by this rule" is false. This it can only do by implying a proposition that contradicts it. It is straightforwardly contradictory to say "I am guided by this rule" and not to apply it.

This can be shown in another way. The function of the declared rule is to justify the judge's behavior. To sentence his friend to five years hard labor would be justified according to this rule. Not to do so is unjustified according to this rule. Unless there are extenuating circumstances, the rules for which are justified by the same principle/s as justify the declared rule, not sentencing his friend to five years hard labor *presupposes* (is justified by) a rule/s that is/are *logically inconsistent with* his declared rule. That the judge might be engaged in deliberate "wrongdoing," and so not espouse these rules, does not mean that he is not logically presupposing these rules. It is between the rules (the nonimpermissibility of) his action presupposes and his declared rule that the contradiction lies, and there is nothing "analogical" about it.

#17   The argument makes intellectual error solely responsible for moral error.

Stephen Cohen (referring generally to some of Gewirth's earlier writing, and specifically to Gewirth 1972) grants that Gewirth does not conflate moral and nonmoral realms, and delineates moral behavior from intellectual calculations. However, he claims that

even if this is so, it is not clear that Gewirth has successfully answered his own objection that there is no difference in kind between intellectual and moral mistakes. . . . [Gewirth] does not meet the charge that given the PGC, with its derivation, intellectual error is solely responsible for immoral behavior. (Cohen 1979, 189)

Gewirth argues that the justification of the PGC is based not only on formal considerations of consistency, but also on its morally relevant content. Both the PGC and its justification concern only the sphere of moral behavior, interpersonal relations in situations of potential conflict. (See Gewirth 1972, 36.)

Cohen, however, maintains that

although Gewirth may have distinguished moral deductions from nonmoral ones in terms of the contents of their respective premises, it remains that immoral behavior is just as exclusively the result of a mistake in reasoning as is the claim that 2 added to 3 equals 6. (Cohen 1979, 189)

This is because the difference between the justification of $2 + 3 = 5$, and the justification of the PGC, is solely a matter of

what things, or types of things, are plugged into the premises and what conclusion is reached. There is no difference in terms of how the premises are dealt with in order to reach a conclusion. (Ibid.)

The common formal element entails that the argument shows that what constitutes a moral error is intellectually (logically) demonstrable (from within any PPA's viewpoint), and Gewirth certainly holds *this*. Cohen claims that it follows that intellectual error is *solely* responsible for acting immorally (and implies that the argument should be rejected because this calls for a radical reunderstanding of judgments of immorality). (See ibid., 190.)

In what sense does Cohen mean "solely responsible"? If he means that when an error is committed then it is intellectually demonstrable that this is so, then the entailment holds. However, this has no implications for "our" understanding of judgments of immorality. It only has implications for noncognitivists' understanding of morality, and unless noncognitivism is taken to be axiomatic, which is question-begging to say the least, no basis for rejecting the thesis is secured. Cohen must, therefore, intend a *causal* responsibility.

But does the fact of a common formal element, in the justification of the PGC and the inference that $2 + 3 = 5$, entail that intellectual error is solely *causally* responsible for immoral behavior?

To begin with, we must distinguish two cases:

1.   a PPA who does not see or accept that it is rationally committed to act according to the PGC and
2.   a PPA who acts in violation of the PGC.

In case 1 there are at least two possible explanations:

a.   the PPA has given no thought to what reason requires it to do; or
b.   the PPA has given this matter thought, but failed to conclude that it rationally ought to accept the PGC.

Only in case *b* can we say that an intellectual error (or inadequacy) is solely responsible for failure *to accept* the PGC. So it doesn't even follow that intellectual error is solely responsible for a failure *to accept* the PGC.

In any case, Cohen's allegation is stronger. He says that any PPA who violates the PGC (case 2) does so solely because of an intellectual error. This is false. A PPA might violate the PGC without having reasoned about the PGC: and, even if the PPA has thought about the PGC, it does not follow that if it violates the PGC it does so solely because it has made an intellectual error. No feature of the argument entails that those who accept that they rationally ought to accept the PGC cannot choose not to follow the PGC. As Gewirth says,

It is indeed possible to be an agent and to violate or fail to fulfill these obligations; but it is not possible to be an agent and fail to have these obligations, or to be a rational agent and fail to accept them as justified. (RM 171)

Thus, if a PPA accepts that it rationally ought to act according to the PGC, but chooses not to do so, the argument shows that it is intellectually demonstrable that this action is in error, but does not imply that the PPA chose to violate the PGC because of an intellectual error in determining what it ought to do.

Of course, a PPA who is a *rational* PPA, in the sense of acting as it rationally ought to do, cannot fail to act in accordance with the PGC, while remaining a rational PPA in this sense. So, if a PPA considers that it rationally ought to accept the PGC, but chooses not to act in accordance with the PGC, then such a PPA is not, in this sense, a rational PPA. It seems to me that it is reasoning along these lines, misapplied, which gives Cohen's charge whatever degree of plausibility it possesses. This reasoning is misapplied because the premise in such thinking is the tautology "PPAs who act as they ought to act, act as they ought to act." Gewirth's argument does not rest in any significant way on such an empty premise, and it is directed, not at PPAs who act as they ought to act, but at those who are rational in the sense of having *the capacity* to see how they rationally ought to act, and *the capacity* to be motivated to act accordingly, under the assumption that these capacities can exist without being effectively exercised.[19]

#18   Even if the PGC is dialectically necessary, it is not assertorically valid, as Gewirth claims or needs to claim.

1 Adams

E. M. Adams (who uses the abbreviation DPGC for the PGC in its dialectical statement, and APGC for the PGC in its assertoric statement) alleges that Gewirth attempts to derive the APGC from the DPGC by appealing to the premise "Agents ought to do what they logically must accept that they ought to do."[20] Adams contends that there is no defensible analytic interpretation of this principle that allows us to state the PGC itself as a necessary assertoric truth. In order to achieve this, the principle must be interpreted as a nonanalytic *ethical* truth about "the constitution of agents as reflected in their normative self-image" (Adams 1980, 590). However, although

an analysis of the semantic and knowledge-yielding powers of agents to explain their ability to fund their value and deontic language with meaning . . . might make such a natural law theory of ethics epistemologically defensible (ibid., 591),

Gewirth does not provide such an analysis. (See ibid., 589–591. See #59 for further discussion of this claim.)

Adams' discussion of the presumed analyticity of "Agents ought to do what they logically must accept that they ought to do" is rather complex. However, we need not consider it here, for this objection is misdirected. The fact of the matter is that Gewirth does not, as Adams contends, attempt to reduce "ethics to logic." (See ibid., 590. See discussion of #15.) It is true that Gewirth contends that the PGC can be stated assertorically, but this is for practical purposes only, and his argument for this does not involve the use of the principle that Adams attributes in the way he claims.

First, then, what does Gewirth mean when he says that the PGC can be stated assertorically? If the argument is valid, then every PPA must accept that it ought to act according to the PGC. Every PPA must consider it to be true that every PPA ought to act according to the PGC. This is the DPGC. But this means that, for *practical* purposes, the justification of the DPGC has, *for PPAs,* the same effect as a justification of the APGC would have. Since only PPAs have practical purposes, *for all practical purposes* the APGC can be treated as a necessary truth. This does not, however, mean that the PGC has been justified assertorically, that its linkage to what agents logically must accept can be severed completely. Gewirth sums this up in a sentence.

Since no agent can deny the *PGC,* on pain of contradiction, the *PGC* is necessarily true *within the whole sphere of practice.* (RM 157; my emphasis)

Second, what role does Gewirth attribute to "Agents ought to do what they logically must accept that they ought to do"? Gewirth considers an argument that the APGC can be inferred from the DPGC by this principle. He puts it thus:

This premise is . . . obvious; for what stronger ground can be given for someone's having a duty than that he logically must accept that he has the duty? For since he logically must accept that he has the duty, he contradicts himself if he denies that he has the duty. And from this it follows that he necessarily has the duty, so that the following assertoric statement is necessarily true and must be accepted for himself by every agent: 'I ought to act in accord with the generic rights of my recipients as well as of myself.' (RM 153)

This argument is the basis of Adams' attribution. However, as Gewirth's ensuing discussion reveals (RM 153–161), this assertoric necessity is not to be taken theoretically, only practically. What Gewirth means, when he says that it follows from this premise that a PPA *has* a duty to obey the PGC, is that the PGC "is necessary and universal in the context of action" (RM 158). Taken out of context, the passage on page 153 can be misleading; but it is quite clear that Gewirth has no intention of divorcing the PGC from its dialectical linkage by this argument. Although Gewirth, in stating the matter,

often uses an assertoric formulation, of such formulations he states
(after his discussion of page 153),

In my subsequent discussions I shall usually state and refer to the *PGC* in its
independent assertoric statement. This will involve no distortion or fallacy;
for since the whole of moral discussion is assumed to be addressed to actual
or prospective rational agents, it will not be necessary at each point to reit-
erate that the moral principle in question is such that it logically must be
admitted by every agent. (RM 159)

Nevertheless, how are we to interpret the argument of page 153?

Apart from the possibility that Gewirth contradicts himself here
(though there can be no doubt about his overall intentions), there is
at least one possible interpretation that removes any inconsistency.
This involves viewing this premise in a far broader context. We can
interpret it as saying that a PPA ought to hold itself practically
bound by principles that it logically must accept, so that the practical duties that it must consider that it has must conform to the practical duties that are prescribed by the practical principles that it
logically must accept. As such it is equivalent to (ω) in my presentation of the argument as a reductio, and this interpretation is supported by Gewirth when he says,

My argument . . . does not rest on the premise, 'What logically must be
accepted by every agent is right,' unless the criterion of 'right' is taken to be
rational or logical . . . . But so interpreted the 'premise' is not a normative
moral one but is rather the premise assumed by all uses of reasoning. (RM
156)

Looked at in this way, the "assertoric" formulation in the argument of page 153 is not to assert the PGC *in itself* as a necessary
truth, but to emphasize the fact that a PPA *has to accept that it has* a
practical duty on the basis of *logically* having to accept a practical
principle; for the fact that the DPGC is logically necessary might be
thought to have only theoretical significance as something that a
PPA must think. What Gewirth is really saying is that, if I must
consider that the PGC is binding on my agency, then *as far as I can
ascertain* it *is* binding on my agency.

This interpretation is also suggested by consideration of a parallel
"inconsistency." Gewirth frequently says that the PGC is analytically true. As I interpret this, in line with his generally stated position that the PGC cannot be completely severed from its dialectical
linkage, this is elliptical for saying that "All PPAs must accept the
PGC" is analytically true. That this is his considered position is clear
from his statement that it is not the PGC itself which he holds to be
(analytically) true, but the "complex judgment" that the PGC logi-

cally must be espoused by every agent. (See Gewirth 1984d, 219.) This, however, might be thought to contradict (or at least to retract from) the following statement:

The predicate of the *PGC* logically follows, although through several intermediate steps, from the concept of being a rational agent, where 'rational' means adhering to the criteria of deductive and inductive logic. This logical following holds for both the dialectical and the assertoric statements of the principle. (RM 171)

Here, it would seem, Gewirth holds both the dialectical statement

(1)   PPAs (logically) ought to consider that PPAs (morally) ought to respect the freedom and well-being of all PPAs (the DPGC),

and the assertoric statement

(2)   PPAs (morally) ought to respect the freedom and well-being of all PPAs (the APGC),

to be analytically true.

As Gewirth explains this passage, (1) signifies that it is not possible to be a rational PPA and fail to accept the PGC as justified, whereas (2) signifies that it is not possible to be a PPA and not have the obligations prescribed by the PGC. (See RM 171.)

This *can* be interpreted as contradicting Gewirth's considered position. It can also be read differently. To say that (2) is analytically true can be interpreted as saying that PPAs contradict that they are PPAs not only by not *considering* that they logically ought to accept the PGC (implied by [1]), but also by not *accepting* the PGC and by not *acting* in accordance with it. On this interpretation, (2) is true because a PPA, by violating the PGC, implicitly denies that it must consider that it is bound by the PGC, and hence denies (1). But, precisely because the justification of (2) is then (1) (and ultimately "I am a PPA"), (2) cannot be interpreted as true *tout court*. And, on this interpretation, (2) is not the statement that the PGC is analytically true *tout court*, but the statement that it is analytically true that a PPA contradicts that it is a PPA by violating the PGC as well as by not considering that it ought not to violate the PGC.

2 Stohs

Mark D. Stohs also holds that Gewirth attempts to derive the assertoric PGC *tout court* from its dialectically necessary statement by use of the principle "What logically must be accepted by every agent is right (true)." (See Stohs 1988, 62.) Later, claims Stohs, Gewirth retracts this. I have already commented on such suggestions in my discussion of Adams' objection, and it is unnecessary to repeat my analysis, although it is worth adding that this statement of the "transforming premise" would not be accepted by Gewirth, who would only accept "What logically must be accepted by the agent must be regarded as true by the agent." My specific interest in Stohs' objection is in his claim that Gewirth cannot set up an objective moral theory, *unless* he can establish the PGC *in itself* as a necessary truth (which, I admit, cannot be done).

According to Stohs, if the PGC is not established assertorically, then it is not rationally justified (objective) in Gewirth's own terms, and the argument does not show that moral relativism is false. His argument is that Gewirth holds that to justify something is to show or "establish its rightness or correctness" (RM 13). "Hence, to show that the PGC is justified, it must be shown that it is correct, i.e., true" (Stohs 1988, 55). However, the dialectically necessary method only shows that the PGC must be held by all PPAs (that the PGC is true from the viewpoint of PPAs), not that it *is* true. (See ibid., 62–64.)

Up to a point, this is a fair comment. However, although Gewirth does not establish that moral relativism is false *tout court*, his argument establishes that no PPA may accept moral relativism (which is to say that *it is true* that no PPA *may accept* moral relativism); and for all practical purposes this is sufficient to render moral relativism unjustified. Stohs seems to suggest that if the PGC in itself cannot be established assertorically, then Gewirth's justification of the PGC employs a different, and weaker, sense of "justification" from that of establishing "rightness or correctness." This is incorrect. The statement "The PGC must be accepted by every PPA" is a necessary truth and therefore justified in "the strong sense." The truth of the matter is that the PGC is *dialectically* justified, and that moral relativism is *dialectically* unjustified. Gewirth does not set out to justify the PGC *in itself* assertorically, so he does not have a "weak" justification for it. He sets out to establish the PGC dialectically, for which he provides a "strong" justification. Justification of the PGC as assertorically true for practical purposes is not "weak" justification of the PGC itself. It is *no* justification of the PGC as being true in itself. But such a justification is simply not required for Gewirth's purposes, because action is the context of all practical precepts.[21]

#19   The derivation of the PGC rests on a problematic "conative theory of truth."

According to Edward Regis, Gewirth's theory depends upon a "conative" theory of knowledge or truth. The truth of the PGC is not derived assertorically, but dialectically; and this involves a "distinctively new criterion of truth." Within the standpoint of agency adopted by the dialectically necessary method,

the agent propounds his claims not, as is usual, on grounds of assertoric or probative evidence that they are true, but on the grounds that he *needs* them to be true in order to secure his freedom and well-being. Within the dialectically necessary method, a claim is backed not by evidence but by need, and what warrants claims is not reason but conation. . . .
. . . This epistemology is problematic because, in general, the truth of an assertion is not a function of the wishes or needs, even the agency needs, of its utterer. (Regis 1981, 794)

This objection rests on the idea that the argument to the PGC attempts to establish the PGC (and intermediate prescriptions) as assertorically true by nonassertoric means. In fact, the only assertoric truths established are of the form that I (and other PPAs) rationally must accept the PGC; and this demonstration attends to the assertoric truth of premises ("I categorically need my freedom and well-being"), and observes standard deductive and inductive rules of evidence and inference. If we think of the PGC as *valid on necessary premises for PPAs,* rather than as "relatively true" (as Gewirth frequently portrays it), then there can be no possible confusion on this point.[22] However, even if we use Gewirth's locutions, we get the same result by distinguishing "relational" and "nonrelational truths."

The truths attained by the dialectically necessary method are relative to the conative standpoint of the agent. . . . [C]ertain value judgments and right claims made by agents are true when they are viewed from within the conative standpoint that agents must adopt . . . [which] are not necessarily true outside this standpoint. But the truths in question are relational; they are propounded as relative to the agent's standpoint, not as true *tout court* (see [RM] 158). (Gewirth 1982e, 407)

Because Regis does not appreciate this relational validity, his charge that Gewirth has a conative theory of truth is misleading. As Gewirth says,

The agent's right-claim . . . *is* based on the "assertoric or probative evidence" that freedom and well-being are the proximate necessary conditions of his acting for any purposes he may regard as good. But there is a difference between holding that this evidence is sufficient to ground the *assertoric* ascription of the rights *tout court* and holding that this evidence, combined with the agent's conative standpoint, is sufficient to ground the *dialectical* ascription to any agent of *claims* to have the rights. (Ibid., 409)[23]

#20   If PPAs are logically required to conform to the PGC, then the PGC is analytic, and hence purely linguistic.

Gregory Lycan (writing about Gewirth 1967a) says that Gewirth asserts that PPAs necessarily follow the PCC. But, if this is so, then the PCC is analytic—hence "stipulative, or definitional, or otherwise purely linguistic" (Lycan 1969, 140).

However, what is analytic is not the PCC itself, but the statement that a PPA (in order to be rational) must abide by the PCC. Of more interest here is the claim that if a statement is analytic then it is purely linguistic (true by convention). Gewirth replies to Lycan in Gewirth 1970b, 383, and this matter is dealt with more fully in *Reason and Morality*, 171–177, Gewirth's treatment drawing generally on Gewirth 1953.

According to Gewirth, a statement like "PPAs (in order to be rational) must conform to the PGC" is analytic in being true by virtue of meanings. (See RM 173.) However, he distinguishes two types of analytic statements: those that are "purely linguistic," true because we choose to assign the same meanings to the words that sign the subject and predicate, and thus "true by convention" (like "All bachelors are unmarried"); and those that

arise because persons can conceptually understand extralinguistic properties and make linguistic classifications based on that understanding (RM 174–175)

(like "Every [Euclidean] triangle has angles that are equal to two right angles"). Gewirth assimilates statements like "PPAs (in order to be rational) must conform to the PGC" and "Behavior to which practical precepts are directed is voluntary purposive behavior" to the latter type. These, though knowable a priori, nevertheless *describe* their subject matter.

Although I agree with this, it is worth noting that this account of two types of analytic statements looks very much like the distinction drawn by Arthur Pap (1958, 127–129) between "strictly analytic" and "broadly analytic" statements. According to Pap, all statements that are true (or false) by virtue of the meanings assigned to their terms are broadly analytic. These are reducible to the principle of identity ("A = A") (if true), and to contradiction (if false), by analysis of the meanings of their constituent terms. Strictly analytic (true) statements are a subclass of these—representing those statements that are reducible to the principle of identity by recognizing that their constituent terms have the same meaning as a matter of purely conventional designation. Non–strictly analytic (true) statements are also reducible to the principle of identity, but only via an understanding of the factual (extralinguistic) properties that the subject term designates. The distinction between strictly and non–strictly analytic statements can be expressed in a number of different ways. In the latter, nonlogical constants occur essentially; in the former they do not. Strictly analytic statements are logical necessities, whereas non–strictly analytic statements are conceptual necessities. Or we might even say that non–strictly analytic statements are synthetic (factual/extralinguistic) a priori, whereas strictly analytic statements are not synthetic. A statement like "PPAs (in order to be rational) must conform to the PGC" is a priori because PPAs can know that they (logically) ought to follow the PGC by an analysis of the concept of agency. The statement is synthetic because this analysis depends on an understanding of extralinguistic properties.

Gewirth, however, tells us that this statement is not synthetic *because* it is analytic. (See RM 175.)[24] I have two comments to make about this, one relatively uncontentious, the other highly contentious.

The uncontentious point is that the difference between Gewirth's analysis and that which I have attributed to Pap is purely terminological. Gewirth chooses to define "synthetic" as (in my terms) "non–broadly analytic" (thus, treating "synthetic," implicitly, as equivalent to "empirical"). On the other hand, my characterization of synthetic a priori statements rests on defining "synthetic" as "non–strictly analytic" or "nonlogical" (any statement being synthetic in which not only logical constants occur essentially). Gewirth, by implication, says (RM 173) that if "analytic" is defined as I define "strictly analytic," then there can be truths that are neither analytic nor synthetic. In my alternative terminology, it follows that there can be truths that are neither analytic nor empirical, but, in this terminology, a statement can be synthetic without expressing an empirical knowledge claim. Nevertheless, behind such terminological preferences, there is agreement. An analytic statement that is not empirical/contingent can be based on conceptual understanding that is not open to arbitrary preference/purely formal/devoid of material implications. Provided that we agree about this, it does not matter in the least whether we choose to call the statement that PPAs must recognize/conform to the PGC "synthetic a priori," "some special sort of analytic (but not synthetic) statement," or "neither analytic nor synthetic."

The more contentious point is that I consider Gewirth's dialectically necessary statements to have a character that is, in some ways, analogous to Kant's synthetic a priori judgments. No more than Gewirth's dialectically necessary conclusions are Kant's transcendental deductions intended to be assertoric conclusions. They are also not intended to be innate, or true by intuition, though they are sometimes characterized in all these ways. Kant argues that *if* we suppose (*claim*) that we can have empirical knowledge of a world that exists independently of ourselves, then *we must hold* certain propositions to be true of the nature of that world a priori. This framework is inherently dialectical, not assertoric. It is strictly analogous to Gewirth's claim that *if* we suppose that we are PPAs then there are certain propositions that we must consider to be true of ourselves. According to Kant, we can't *categorically* know that there is a world independent of ourselves. Similarly, we can't categorically know that we are PPAs.[25] However, the phenomenology of our experience and agency makes it, in practice, impossible to assume that we are not experiencing a "real" world, or that we are not PPAs. This fact gives our starting point phenomenological necessity, but the fact that it must still be counted hypothetical means that the framework of our empirical and practical knowledge can only be grounded dialectically, on a phenomenologically necessary assumption, not assertorically.[26]

#21   The argument makes the PGC a logically inviolable rule, and thus no rule at all.

Lycan also claims that if a PPA necessarily conforms to the PCC, then this makes the PCC a logically inviolable rule. He maintains that there must be something wrong with this, because the issuing of rules as a practice presupposes that rules can be broken. A logically inviolable "rule" is, effectively, no rule at all. (See Lycan 1969, 140–142.)

Replying to Lycan, Gewirth says that there is an interpretation of "A PPA cannot violate the PCC" under which this is true, and an interpretation under which this is false. If the argument is valid, then a PPA is to be defined as a being whose conduct is regulated by the PCC/PGC. A PPA has, as it were, a defining role—to conform to the PGC. If a PPA violates the PGC, then it departs from its role, and to do so is not to behave as a PPA. A PPA can only act as a PPA according to its role if it conforms to the PGC. In this sense it is true that a PPA necessarily conforms to the PGC and cannot violate it.

However, this does not mean that PPAs (now considered as those who have the capacity to occupy the role of PPAs, in the sense that has just been elucidated, rather than those who act in accordance with this role) cannot fail to act as PPAs according to their defining role.

This, I think, is a fair interpretation of the following passage:

It is a widely accepted view that if some person's act is to count as a case of applying or acting in accordance with a rule, then it must be at least logically possible that he violate or not conform to the rule. I shall refer to this as the *violability requirement* for rules. It is important, however, to specify precisely which persons are referred to in this requirement. In one respect, it is logically impossible that constitutive rules be violated by persons *qua* participants in the modes of activity or practice constituted by the rules. For example, no tennis player, *qua* person who plays the game according to its constitutive rules, can violate the rule which says that a player may not throw the ball with his hand (as against hitting it with his racket) during a rally. To be sure, someone who is on a tennis court with a racket can throw the ball while his opponent is momentarily distracted . . . , but then he is operating in some other capacity, not specifically *qua* tennis player in the sense just defined. (Gewirth 1970b, 384)

> The general point of this distinction is that

[i]n so far . . . as the violability requirement purports to deal with all rules, including constitutive ones, it is false unless its reference is extended beyond the range of persons defined as participants according to constitutive rules in modes of activity or practice constituted by the rules. And if it is so extended, then the categorial rules of action [the rules of the PCC] fulfil the requirement. (Ibid.)

This requires some expansion. The reference point of Gewirth's argument is PPAs, defined as those who are capable of directing their behavior according to practical precepts that they choose to follow. These are also assumed to be rational for the purposes of providing them with a justification for acting in certain ways rather than others. They are assumed to be rational in the sense that they have the capacity to understand and draw logical inferences. I shall call this focus "PPAs *in referentia*." Gewirth argues that if PPAs *in referentia* exercise their reasoning capacities so as to draw only valid inferences (correctly), then they will appreciate that they are rationally bound to act in accordance with the PGC. Not to appreciate this is to deny that they are PPAs *in referentia*. However, because the criterion of rationality is logic, this means that we have formed a conception of PPAs *in referentia* as beings who, if they act as reason requires, will not violate the PGC. Those PPAs *in referentia* who act as reason requires, act as what I shall call "PPAs *in essentia*." PPAs *in referentia* occupy a role, which *requires them to act* according to the PGC. PPAs *in essentia* (by definition) *act* according to this role. Now, if a PPA violates the PGC, then it *is not* a PPA *in essentia*. But, although it, thereby, also *denies* that it is a PPA *in referentia*, this does not mean that it cannot *be* a PPA in *referentia*.

Now, when Gewirth says that PPAs necessarily espouse and follow the PGC, this is to be taken as elliptical for "PPAs *in referentia* logically ought to espouse/follow the PGC" or as "PPAs *in essentia* do (by definition) espouse/follow the PGC." In other words, in "A PPA necessarily conforms to the PGC," where the subject is a PPA *in essentia*, the must is definitionally descriptive; but where the subject is a PPA *in referentia*, the must is logically prescriptive. Of PPAs *in essentia* it is true that they cannot violate the PGC, that the PGC is thus not a practical directive directed to them. But this doesn't matter, because the argument is directed at PPAs *in referentia*, exhorting them to act as PPAs *in essentia*. When Gewirth says that the violability requirement holds when "extended," I take him to be saying that its practical prescriptions are directed at PPAs *in referentia*, the specification of these prescriptions being based on what PPAs *in essentia* do (by definition). With this understood, the argument does not have the consequence that those who can act according to the PGC cannot fail to do so, and Lycan's objection only gets off the ground if the argument has this consequence.[27]

In any event, in *Reason and Morality*, Gewirth provides a different (though not incompatible account) of how an analytic moral principle (one that a PPA is logically required to accept) can be violated. Here Gewirth simply points out that, although a PPA who violates the PGC denies in effect that PPAO has the generic rights, and thereby contradicts itself, this self-contradiction

pertains to his negative judgment, not to his action taken by itself. Hence, one can violate an analytic moral principle even though to deny the principle, or to affirm its opposite, is to contradict oneself. (RM 180)[28]

#22   Establishing Stage II involves showing that it is necessarily true that PPAO has a duty not to interfere with my freedom and well-being; but this is contingently false.

Kai Nielsen raises such an objection, which may be put as follows: In order to establish that I rationally must consider that I have a claim right to my freedom and well-being, Gewirth has to show that it is necessarily true that PPAO has a duty not to interfere with my freedom and well-being. However, suppose that I am Hitler. In such a case, what Gewirth has to show is contingently false, and so cannot be necessarily true. (See Nielsen 1984, 71.)[29]

It should be clear from my reply to criticisms considered in this section that it is simply not true that Gewirth has to show that it is necessarily true that PPAO has a duty not to interfere with my freedom and well-being.

As Gewirth replies to Nielsen,

[W]hat I said to be necessarily true is that each agent must *hold* or *accept* that other persons ought at least to refrain from interfering with *his own* freedom and well-being. (Gewirth 1984d, 206)[30]

However, it is possible that Nielsen recognizes this, and that his objection is that it is contradictory for me to say, if I am Hitler, that I must consider that PPAO has a duty not to interfere with my freedom and well-being, and that I must consider that PPAO has a right to its freedom and well-being. If I am Hitler, who interferes with the freedom and well-being of PPAO, then, according to the PGC, PPAO has a right to defend itself, even if this involves interfering with my (Hitler's) freedom and well-being. According to the argument it is contingently false that I must consider that PPAO has a duty not to interfere with my freedom and well-being (when I interfere with PPAO's freedom and well-being). So, it cannot be necessarily true that I must consider that PPAO has a duty not to interfere with my freedom and well-being.

If this is Nielsen's objection, then it is a claim that, if Stage II is valid, then Stage III cannot be valid.

However, all that can be inferred from the juxtaposition of the conclusions of Stages II and III is that a PPA (at the end of Stage II) must consider that it has at least a prima facie right to its freedom and well-being. A contradiction of the type suggested only arises if, as the conclusion of Stage II, it is claimed that a PPA must consider that it has an *absolute* right to its freedom and well-being. In other words, such an objection rests on wrongly taking a "contingency," which properly bears on the question of whether a right/duty is absolute or prima facie, to bear on the question of the necessity/contingency of a PPA's having to consider that it has a right/duty of any kind at all.

Deriving "Ought" from "Is"

#23 The argument is an illicit "is-ought" derivation.

Before replying to specific critics who press some variant of this objection, I shall provide a brief general analysis of the argument as an "is-ought" derivation.

A GENERAL ANALYSIS OF GEWIRTH'S "IS-OUGHT" DERIVATION

According to Gewirth, an important consequence of his argument is that in the logical structure of action both the gap between fact and value and the gap between 'is' and 'ought' are bridged. (RM 102)

Since the agent's assertion that he acts for purposes is an empirical, descriptive statement, I have . . . derived 'ought' from 'is' . . . ; but the 'is,' action with its generic features, has been seen to be a context that implicitly contains an 'ought,' and the argument has shown how this 'ought' is made explicit. (RM 149)

Now, the doctrine of "the is-ought Gap"[31] has a very strong hold on much modern thinking, and there are many who will refuse to accept that Gewirth's argument is valid if it is construed as crossing this gap.

However, at a later time, Gewirth asserts,

My main concern is not with the 'is-ought' problem; it is, rather, to show that every agent logically must accept certain moral 'ought'-judgments. Hence if being an agent, or engaging in action, is not something that can be stated as a "pure, unadulterated statement of fact," this does not affect my general thesis. What it would show instead is that the *factual world* of human action is "loaded with values" for every agent; and this is something I would gladly accept so long as the facts and values in question are acknowledged to be ineluctable for every agent. It is the *necessity* of the argument that is crucial, not its crossing some logical gap. (Gewirth 1984d, 223–224, in reply to Hudson 1984)[32]

This latter statement is correct. Gewirth wishes to establish that it is rationally necessary for a PPA to accept the PGC, or that it follows logically from "I am a PPA" that "I must accept the PGC." If he can do this without attributing to a PPA evaluative assumptions *which require independent justification*, then it does not matter if such assumptions are implicit in the demonstration.[33] Indeed, if the argument is valid, then "I am a PPA" can hardly be morally neutral dialectically, for the argument then establishes that, dialectically, "I am a PPA" is equivalent to "I am rationally bound by the PGC in my actions." However, this latter statement does not actually disclaim that he has crossed the "is-ought gap." It only states that Gewirth does not really care whether he has done so or not.

Although Gewirth can sidestep the question in this way, the question still remains, "Has Gewirth crossed the 'is-ought divide'?" If this means "Has Gewirth derived a moral 'ought' (the PGC) from an 'is' ('I am a PPA')?" then I think it is clear that *he has not*. Strictly speaking, to derive the PGC from "I am a PPA," "I am a PPA" must entail the PGC. However, as I have emphasized in my discussion of objections in the previous section, the dialectically necessary method does not seek to demonstrate the PGC as a necessary truth *tout court*, but as a necessary presupposition which every PPA must accept. What is derived from "I am a PPA" is "I logically ought to espouse the PGC," and this latter proposition is not a moral "ought."

Nevertheless, we *can* say that Gewirth has derived (rationally necessary) espousal of the PGC from "I am a PPA" within any PPA's internal viewpoint; and we can say that he has derived a *dialectical* moral "ought" from a dialectical "is," or that he has *dialectically* derived a moral "ought" from an "is." But, if we use such expressions, we must be careful to understand what we mean, and we must not be misled by misinterpreting Gewirth's claim, made at the end of his argument, that the PGC can be stated assertorically.

Gewirth tells us that

the *PGC* has a certain relative status: its truth or correctness cannot be completely separated from what agents must accept. But this relativism is not in any important way a limitation on the status of the *PGC* as a moral principle. Since the *PGC* logically must be admitted by every agent, it is necessary and universal in the context of action, and it is this context that is relevant to morality. Thus the *PGC* has as much necessity and universality as can be attained by any substantial normative moral or practical principle. (RM 158)

As I stated under #18, what I take this to mean is that, because there is no rational alternative to accepting the PGC within any PPA's internal viewpoint, the PGC can be stated with assertoric effect to all PPAs. It follows that, *dialectically (within any PPA's internal viewpoint)*, [I am a PPA → the PGC] is a valid inference, and this means that the PGC is a valid prescription for any PPA on the grounds that it is a PPA. By the same token, *for any PPA*, an "is" ("I am a PPA") is a sufficient ground for a moral "ought" (the PGC). Dialectically, "ought" has been derived from "is." *However*, this is not the same as saying that, after all, the PGC can be established assertorically, that a moral "ought" can be derived from an "is" assertorically. The transposition of the conclusion of the argument to an assertoric formulation is not logical, but is based on the universality of its dialectical grounds. What Gewirth claims is that rational PPAs must act according to the PGC, because they are PPAs. *For all practical purposes* this has the same effect, *for PPAs, as if* the PGC could be derived from "I am a PPA" assertorically, because, as far as PPAs are concerned, [I am a PPA → I logically must espouse the PGC] has the same practical effect as [I am a PPA → the PGC], as ["is" → "ought"].

The important point about this, however, is that its validity is only practical, and independent of whether, assertorically, "ought" can be derived from "is." Those who wish to question the validity of Gewirth's argument cannot do so on the basis that it constitutes denial of the claim (which I think Gewirth accepts, as I do) that moral "ought" cannot be derived from "is" *assertorically.*

However, might it not be the case that the validity of the dialectical derivation rests on illicitly assuming that "ought" can be derived from "is" assertorically at some point in the argument? Such a charge might take the form of claiming that the argument rests on the claim that it follows from the fact that I want or need X that I have a right to X, which is objection #8, around which this chapter is organized. By now it should be clear that there is no straightforward way in which Gewirth assumes anything of the kind. However (see Chapter 3, "The Formal Structure of the Argument"), the argument concludes that PPAs rationally must hold [A *categorically* needs X → A has a right to X] to be a valid inference within their internal viewpoints; and along the way to "demonstrating" this we encounter claims like "I, as a PPA, rationally must hold [I categorically need X → I have a right to X], and [I categorically need X → I strictly instrumentally ought to pursue X], to be valid inferences within my internal viewpoint." It is these claims that I take to be the basis of the present charge. If the objection is not directed at these claims, *as formulated*, then it is misdirected. The charge must be that these claims cannot be true unless the inferences in brackets are assertorically valid (which they are not).

To simplify matters, let us suppose that it is true that I, as a PPA, rationally must espouse an SPR for my purposes according to which [I categorically need X → I strictly instrumentally ought to pursue X] is a valid inference. Let us call [I categorically need X → I strictly instrumentally ought to pursue X] β. According to Chapter 3, "The Formal Structure of the Argument," within an SPR for my purposes that recognizes β, the application of "ought implies can" to β yields [I categorically need X → PPAO strictly ought not to interfere with my having X]. Within this SPR, the logical correlativity of other-referring strict "oughts" and claim rights yields [I categorically need X → I have a (claim) right to X]; from which the internal application of the logical principle of universalizability (LPU) yields [A categorically needs X → A has a (claim) right to X]. By external application of the LPU, it can now be inferred that every PPA rationally must espouse an SPR for its purposes in which [A categorically needs X → A has a (claim) right to X], and this is the conclusion of Gewirth's argument. If this is valid, then the "ought" of the PGC is derived by a series of logical operations from the "ought" in "I strictly instrumentally ought to pursue my freedom and well-being"; and the question of the *dialectical* derivation of "ought" from "is" is the question of how it can be the case that I am rationally required to consider β to be valid because I am a PPA.

In order to escape the charge that the dialectical derivation of β from "I am a PPA" rests on an illicit assertoric assumption of β,

Gewirth has to explain how it is the case that I, as a PPA, rationally must assent to β, without it being the case that β is assertorically valid *tout court*.

The first thing that must be said is that the fact that β is not assertorically valid *tout court* does not entail that a PPA *may not* espouse an SPR for its purposes in which β is treated as valid. To espouse β as my SPR for my purposes is not to contradict "I am a PPA," and β is not, in itself, a contradiction. Furthermore, all sorts of systemic rules of the form [A → B] are espoused where A does not logically entail B. That is to say, different SPRs and normative systems exist that hold many different factual characteristics to be sufficient reasons for the ascription of normative claims. In any normative thought, "oughts" are, in a sense, derived from "is," and this cannot be illicit unless all normative thought is illicit.

What makes Gewirth's derivation contentious is that he does not merely claim that I rationally *may* espouse β ("play the β game," if you like). He claims that I rationally *must* play the β game. Now, while it is true that if A logically entails B, then I rationally must espouse [A → B] (i.e., "A is a sufficient reason for B"), it does not follow that if A does not logically entail B that I cannot be rationally required to espouse [A → B]. I can be rationally required to espouse [A → B] if I necessarily possess a property C, which I would deny possessing if I did not espouse [A → B].

According to Gewirth, the property I deny if I do not play the β game is that of being a PPA. The argument is addressed to PPAs, and no PPA may deny that it is a PPA. As a PPA I necessarily have one property, that of being conatively normal (proactively valuing my purposes), and there is another that I must accept, that of categorically needing my freedom and well-being. If I want to pursue a purpose E, and M is the necessary means to E, then my proactive commitment to E requires me (gives me a reason of requirement) to pursue M. Given my commitment to E, I ought to pursue M. This "ought" is not, however, necessarily strict, because, in general terms, I can evade it by giving up E in favor of purposes for which M is not a necessary condition. However, if M is a categorically or generically necessary condition for my purposes, I can only evade this "ought" by eschewing all purposes. Where M is my freedom and well-being, M is a generically necessary condition of my agency, and I strictly ought (instrumentally) to pursue M. Not to accept that I strictly ought (instrumentally) to pursue my freedom and well-being is to deny that I am conatively normal/that I categorically need my freedom and well-being, which, in turn, is to deny that I am a PPA. I am, therefore, logically required to play the β game.

Quite simply, what happens here is that my conative normality, my proactive motivation to pursue my purposes, imbues the fact that my freedom and well-being are generically necessary conditions of my agency with more than factual significance *in my eyes*. It renders this fact a strict reason of requirement *for me* to pursue my freedom and well-being, which means that it validates β. *However*, this only works *dialectically within my internal viewpoint as a PPA*, because, outside of this context, a proactive commitment to my purposes cannot be assumed.[34]

In consequence, the "gap" between "is" and "ought" is, within my internal viewpoint as a PPA, bridged dialectically, though not assertorically, at the point where it is established that I must consider my freedom and well-being to be necessary goods.[35] From this point on, I contend, the rest of the argument is to be viewed as a set of logical transformations of β, which now defines my dialectically necessary SPR for my purposes, to an SPR for my purposes (and thus to any PPA's SPR for its purposes) that makes "A categorically needs X (its freedom and well-being)" a sufficient justification for "A has a right to X."

SOME SPECIFIC CRITICISMS

#23.1 Gewirth has merely deduced a factual conclusion that he has illicitly translated into prescriptive language.

1 Paul

According to Jeffrey Paul, the conclusion that all PPAs must accept the PGC

> describes a universal belief or a judgment about a normative rule, rather than a normative rule itself. . . . [It] is a factual proposition which describes the affirmations necessarily made by all rational agents, rather than an axiological one which sets forth a categorical moral principle. (Paul 1979, 444)[36]

Gewirth cannot infer the truth of the PGC from "All PPAs must accept the PGC." Consequently, he has not solved the "is-ought" problem.

According to Paul, Gewirth infers the PGC ("All PPAs have a right to their freedom and well-being") from "All PPAs must claim a right to their freedom and well-being" together with "All agents have the same basis for claiming a right to their freedom and well-being." This, however, cannot be valid, because the PGC is a prescription that states that all PPAs *have* the generic rights, whereas the premises only state that all PPAs must

claim them and acknowledge a similarly based *claim* on the part of all other

agents. . . . Even if claims to rights are universally and necessarily made by
agents, it does not follow that rights are universally possessed by them.

. . . The mere universalization of a claim cannot materially transform it into
something other than a claim. (Ibid., 444)

At this point in his paper, however, Paul's argument seems to
switch tack. Thus far, it seems that Paul is arguing that "All PPAs
logically must consider (claim) that they have rights to their freedom
and well-being" cannot support "All PPAs *have* rights to their freedom and well-being." This, I concede, is true. However, Gewirth
holds only that the premise "All PPAs logically must consider that
they have rights to their freedom and well-being" (derived from "I
logically must consider that I have rights to my freedom and well-
being" by *external* application of the LPU) supports, by *internal* application of the LPU, "All PPAs *logically must consider* that all PPAs
have rights to their freedom and well-being," and that this has assertoric effect for all PPAs (i.e., for all *practical* purposes *the PGC* can
be stated as an assertoric truth), and I have suggested that this is
what Gewirth means when he talks about the PGC being analytically true. (See #18.1.)

Now, if Paul accepts "All PPAs logically must consider that all
PPAs have rights to their freedom and well-being," then my response to him is that Gewirth does not use the LPU to try to infer the
PGC as an assertoric truth *tout court*. At the same time, if Gewirth
can infer that acceptance of the PGC is dialectically necessary for all
PPAs, then he has effected a dialectically necessary inference from
"is" to "ought," even though this does not establish the PGC as an
independent assertoric truth. Because this still means that PPAs who
violate the PGC contradict themselves, Gewirth has done all that is
necessary to establish that requiring PPAs to follow the PGC is a
justified demand. (See #18.2.)

However, in trying to explain where Gewirth has "slipped up" in
trying to derive an assertoric "categorical ought" from an "is"
(which, to repeat, Gewirth does not attempt to do), Paul says that

the particular step in Gewirth's argument that he contends transforms descriptive statements into categorical normative ones . . . is the agent's universalization of his own favorable attitudes towards and claims about his purposes to others. (Paul 1979, 444–445)

Paul goes on to question that PPAs must take favorable account
of the generic interests of PPAO, and this suggests that he either

1.   does not accept "I logically must consider that I have rights to
     my freedom and well-being";[37] or
2.   accepts the proposition rejected in 1, but does not accept that

it can be universalized to "All PPAs logically must consider
that all PPAs have rights to their freedom and well-being"; or

3.   accepts "All PPAs logically must consider that all PPAs have
rights to their freedom and well-being," but does not accept
that this entails that PPAs must take favorable account of the
interests of PPAO.

There is some evidence for 1.

[I]f the purposes of the rational agent only *seem* good to him and those
seeming goods are merely non-moral values of any kind, then the agent is
dialectically committed only to *view* or *regard* positively what is instrumental
to his purposes and to *claim* or *advocate* his having freedom and basic well-
being. . . . As the agent has never established that his purposes are good in
themselves, he cannot validly infer that he actually has rights to the necessary conditions of those purposes. (Paul 1979, 445)

But why (as this seems to suggest) are all things that are good
morally good? Can't something be prudentially good? Can't something merely seem morally good? Does this claim that there cannot
be any rights that are not moral rights? Does it claim that a PPA
cannot consider that it has a right unless it considers that it has (or,
independent of what it considers, that it actually has) a moral right?
These features create problems for interpreting what Paul is actually
claiming. I shall consider such matters generally elsewhere.[38] Here I
shall interpret him as saying that unless my purposes *are* good, I
may not infer that I have a right to freedom and well-being. However, there is still an ambiguity here. I may, indeed, not infer that it
is assertorically the case that I have a right to my freedom and well-
being. I cannot consider that I *have* a right *tout court*. But this does
not mean that *my* position is not required to be that I have a right,
that I am not required to *consider that I have* a right. The point here is
that I am not required to consider that I have a right *independent* of
my dialectically necessary premises, but this does not mean that I am
not required to consider that I have a right *on* my dialectically necessary premises. Or, to put it differently: though I am not required to
consider that I have a right *because* I have a right, this does not mean
that I am not required to consider that I have a right *because* it is
dialectically necessary for me to espouse premises that would entail
that I have a right *if they were assertorically true*. All that Gewirth
needs to establish, in order to establish "I logically must *consider that
I have* a right," is the latter, not the former. (See discussion of the β
game, above.) So, consideration of 1 leads us on to 2.

There is also evidence for 2.

[E]very agent must *claim* (emphasis added), at least implicitly, that he has rights to freedom and well-being for the sufficient reason that he is a pro-spective purposive agent. From the content of this *claim* (emphasis added) it follows, by the principle of universalizability, that all prospective purposive agents *have* (emphasis added) rights to freedom and well-being. If the agent denies this generalization, he contradicts himself. For he would then be in the position of both affirming and denying that being a prospective [purpos-ive] agent is a sufficient condition of *having* (emphasis added) rights to free-dom and well-being. (Paul 1979, 445, quoting RM 133; Paul's emphases)

Again, a lot depends on how we read this passage. One way of reading it is as claiming that "All PPAs must consider that they have rights to their freedom and well-being" entails that the PGC is true *tout court.* As Paul says, this is invalid. But if this is what Paul is arguing, then it is irrelevant to establishing that on the basis of the premise it cannot be inferred that all PPAs must *claim* that all PPAs have rights to their freedom and well-being, and on this basis have a favorable attitude towards PPAO's generic interests.

Another way of reading Gewirth's passage is to take it as claim-ing that from "I/all PPAs must consider that I/they have rights to freedom and well-being" it follows that "I/all PPAs must consider that all PPAs have rights to their freedom and well-being." "How," it might be asked, "can it be read in this way?" Quite simply. Take away the emphases that Paul introduces, and put one on the word *content* in the second sentence. The *content* of the claim is that I have a right to my freedom and well-being. Now, apply the LPU to this content instead of, or as well as, to the act of claiming this content. The claim is now transformed to "All PPAs have rights to their free-dom and well-being." This way, Gewirth is claiming, as I agree he must, that all PPAs must claim that all PPAs have rights to their freedom and well-being, not that all PPAs have rights to their free-dom and well-being. When he says that PPAs have rights to their freedom and well-being, the dialectical context is taken for granted. However, if Paul is objecting to this, as he must to deny that PPAs must take favorable account of the interests of others (with one pro-viso), then he provides no argument for it. His arguments have va-lidity only as an objection to detaching the PGC entirely from its dialectical context.[39]

The one proviso is the possibility that Paul holds 3. This, how-ever, is too implausible to be attributed seriously.

In sum, I agree that Gewirth cannot detach the validity of the PGC from its dialectical context, but he really should not be read as trying to do so. In trying to show why Gewirth errs in arguing what he does not argue, Paul is led to question the validity of Stage III.[40] This he does unsuccessfully because he does not interpret Stage III merely as a universalization from dialectical premises to a dialectical conclusion, but as an attempt to achieve an assertoric transformation of dialectical premises; and this is a misreading of the role that Gewirth attributes to the LPU.[41]

2 Allen

According to Paul Allen III,

Gewirth is right in his contention that the agent inevitably regards his freedom and well-being as good and that the agent is then logically required to conclude that he ought to allow others their freedom and well-being. However, I cannot agree with Gewirth's claim to have derived an "ought" from an "is." (Allen 1982a, 213)

According to Allen, Gewirth's derivation running [I do X for purpose E → I regard E as good → I regard my freedom (and well-being)[42] as necessary goods → I consider that I have a right to freedom → I consider that PPAO has a right to its freedom] is valid. He claims, however, that the statements in this chain are *descriptive*, not prescriptive, and contain no "oughts."

He claims that the following inferences are also valid: [My purposes are good → My freedom is a necessary good → I have a right to freedom → PPAO has a right to freedom]. These claims are *prescriptive* and contain "oughts."

However, in order to derive an "ought" from an "is," Gewirth has at some point to switch from the descriptive track to the prescriptive one, but, says Allen,

I do not think it is possible to start out on the descriptive track and end up on the prescriptive one. But . . . this is just what Gewirth claims to do. (Ibid., 215)

According to Allen, Gewirth is led into the error of thinking that he has derived "ought" from "is" right at the beginning of the argument when he

omits the "I regard" and says: "From the standpoint of the agent, 'I do X for purpose E' entails 'My purpose is good' . . . ." [The problem is that] Gewirth states without any further justification that from the agent's standpoint, "I do X for purpose E" entails not "*I regard* my purpose as good," which has been justified, but the value-judgment "My purpose is good," which has not been justified. (Ibid., 215–216, 217)

Gewirth assumes that the following two sentences are equivalent . . . :
"I do X for purpose E" entails "I regard my purpose as good."
"I do X for purpose E" entails "My purpose is good." (Ibid., 219)

As a result, Gewirth regards the PGC itself as true, whereas all he has shown is that "Every PPA must accept the PGC" is true, and this is descriptive not prescriptive. (See ibid., 220.)

I must agree that Gewirth has very thoroughly demonstrated that . . . absolute inescapable logical necessity binds every agent to conclude that he ought to respect others' freedom, on pain of contradiction. What Gewirth does not establish, however, is that it follows from this that the agent really has the duty. (Ibid., 222)

It does not follow, as Gewirth claims, that I have a duty if I logically must accept that I have a duty.[43]

In brief,

our thesis for this paper as a whole is . . . that Gewirth has not shown how to derive "ought" from "is." Even though the agent necessarily concludes "I ought to respect others' freedom," he infers this "ought" from a prescriptive premise only—"My purpose is good." And although every agent inevitably holds this prescription, he does not logically infer it in turn from a higher descriptive premise such as "I do X for purpose E," as Gewirth claimed. Therefore, the agent has not derived his "ought" from an "is." (Ibid., 223)

Allen concludes,

[W]e can account for "My purpose is good" (as Gewirth has successfully done) by explaining that whenever one acts purposively, he necessarily regards his purpose as good and thus inevitably does the prescribing expressed by "My purpose is good." In giving this account of the premise "My purpose is good," we might say we have explained a phenomenological truth or articulated an existential insight, or something of that sort. But as I have argued, we should not claim that the agent has logically inferred that prescription ("My purpose is good") from the descriptive statement "I do X for E." (Ibid., 225)

I have the following comments to make.

1. I agree, in substance, with Allen's concluding comments. However, I disagree that Gewirth has claimed to establish anything more than Allen says he can establish.

2. Allen makes two claims as his basis for saying that Gewirth attempts to establish the PGC as an assertoric truth *tout court.*

a. Gewirth treats [I do X for purpose E → I regard E as good] as equivalent to [I do X for purpose E → My purpose is good].

b. Gewirth claims that "I logically must accept the PGC" entails "I must act in accordance with the PGC." (See RM 153.)

Now, *a* is quite simply false. Gewirth regards [I do X for purpose E → I regard E as good] as equivalent to [*From my standpoint as an agent*, "I do X for purpose E" → "My purpose is good"]. The latter proposition says nothing more, and nothing less, than [I do X for purpose E → I regard E as good], and this proposition Allen considers to be valid. To be fair to Allen, he does interpret Gewirth as inferring from "From my standpoint, E is good" the assertoric truth of the value judgment "E is good." But Gewirth does no such thing. He does not think that [From my standpoint, "I do X for purpose E" → "E is good"] means "E is good" is true, but that I must make the value judgment that E is good. Of course, it also means that I must *regard* "E is good" *as true* (as a premise for my thinking). But how can I regard E as good, without regarding "E is good" as a premise for my thinking? It seems that Allen would have Gewirth infer from "I do X for purpose E" only that it seems to me that I regard E as good. Apart from the fact that there are no grounds for such a double displacement, if it is required then the rest of the argument won't work.[44]

In relation to *b*, I have already argued[45] that Gewirth does not infer that "I have a duty to act as the PGC prescribes" is an assertoric truth *tout court* (valid independent of any PPA's standpoint), but only that it is *from a practical point of view* expressible with the effect of an assertoric truth (because it is valid from every PPA's standpoint), and that "'I have a duty to act as the PGC prescribes' is true" is to be read as so dialectically circumscribed, or as the claim that I contradict "I am a PPA" by implicitly denying (considering that it is not the case that) "I have a duty to act as the PGC prescribes" if I do not act as the PGC prescribes.

3. With all Gewirth's qualifications about the validity of the PGC not being wholly detachable from its dialectical context in agency, I see no harm in saying that his derivation is a dialectical derivation of "ought" from "is." For, even if the PGC is not knowable to be true *tout court*, every PPA must *consider* that it is true on the basis of premises that the phenomenology of its agency does not permit it to eschew. As long as we recognize that this is a statement that holds only within the standpoint of PPAs, "ought" has been derived from "is."

4. Although I agree that from "My purpose *is* good" we can infer that I *have* a right to my freedom and well-being (on the prescriptive track), this is in fact denied by some commentators, and requires more attention than Allen provides.[46]

5. I am not wholly convinced that the "descriptive" track is nonnormative. It seems to me that it is directly *logically* prescriptive, even if not prudentially or morally so; that it is also indirectly (dialectically) prudentially/morally prescriptive; and that it is just this

that Gewirth is trying to bring out when he says that it can be inferred that I have a duty to act according to the PGC. If it is not so taken, then the argument does not have a conclusion that Allen asserts to be of "great significance for moral theory" (ibid., 225).[47]

3 Seay

I am inclined to agree with his [Gewirth's] conclusion that the Principle of Generic Consistency does provide an ethical first principle that is categorically binding on all persons insofar as they are agents; yet I am not convinced that he has succeeded in providing a logical derivation of value judgments from factual statements. (Seay 1983, 134)

According to Gary Seay, Gewirth is not a "cognitivist" or a "naturalist" because his use of the dialectically necessary method has the consequence that the PGC is not established as an analytic truth—because its logical negation is not a contradictory proposition.

To say that the PGC is a dialectically necessary practical principle . . . is to say that its obligatory force is grounded in a kind of reflexive necessity. I must assent to it just to the extent that I have purposes I want to fulfill and undertake to act for the sake of those purposes. But if I had no purposes at all, then I would not be logically bound by the PGC—since in that case I would indeed not be an agent . . . . (Ibid., 137)

The argument shows that from my *acting* for purpose E, I am logically required to judge that E is good; and ultimately, this judgment requires me to make the judgment prescribed by the PGC. But this is not a derivation of a judgment from a fact, because,

[r]easoning from the point of view of the agent, it is not my *statement* 'I do X for purpose E' that commits me to the value judgment 'E is good,' but *my acting for purpose E*. The value of E (from my point of view) is something I give it in making it the object of my action. It is in no sense entailed either by the fact of my action or by the statement which describes that fact. (Ibid., 139)

I think that Gewirth is correct to find the source of value in the specific purposes of individual agents; but at the same time, it seems to me that he has seriously misconstrued the nature of the relation between purposive action and evaluative judgments. The relation is not a logical one, and the use of the dialectical method should only make this more clear. For, from the point of view of the agent, it is his specific intention that brings the action into being; yet the commitment to a purpose is already present in the intention; hence the element of value must be perceived by the agent as added to his object by him at the very beginning, in deciding to undertake the action. What Gewirth's dialectical argument discloses is not a derivation of value from fact, but a derivation of value from an antecedent value. (Ibid., 140)

In many respects this is an admirable statement of the position.

However, Gewirth has not misconstrued the relation between purposive action and evaluative judgments. The dialectically necessary method does not begin with actions, but with *statements* to which a PPA is committed *by virtue of voluntary purposive agency*. Within the point of view of the PPA, [I do X for purpose E → E is good] is a *logically* required inference; and "I do X for purpose E" refers to the fact of my agency, even though, within my point of view as a PPA, this fact is imbued with evaluative significance.[48] *Within the PPA's standpoint*, value is deduced from fact and ultimately "ought" from "is." It is just that, within my viewpoint as a PPA, the facts of my agency are not value-neutral. When Seay says that my statement "I do X for purpose E" is not what commits me to the value judgment "E is good," he is right if he means that the fact that I do X for purpose E does not justify that E *is* good *assertorically*. But he is wrong if he thinks that the fact that I make this statement does not commit *me* to *holding that it is the case that E is good* (though this judgment need not be a judgment of definitive goodness). Dialectically, the relation between purposive action and evaluative judgments is a logical one, but only within my viewpoint as a PPA. Gewirth would be misconstruing the matter only if he held that such a relation holds quite independently of my viewpoint as a PPA. And he doesn't.[49]

#23.2 Gewirth's premises are not rich enough to generate the PGC, even in its dialectical formulation.

1 Adams

E. M. Adams agrees that the PGC is dialectically necessary, *but not on Gewirth's premises*. He maintains that the normative structure of agency, as portrayed by Gewirth, is not rich enough to make it dialectically necessary for PPAs to accept the PGC (to prove the DPGC). For Stage II to be valid, in a way that is capable of yielding the DPGC by universalization, something more must be added to "My freedom and well-being are necessary goods," where this is interpreted in the way in which Gewirth does. Gewirth grounds his notion of "good" in the notion of "desire." In consequence, "My freedom and well-being are necessary goods" has a meaning that does not permit "I have a right to my freedom and well-being" to be derived, within my internal viewpoint, by logic alone. Stage I is valid, and it is true that a PPA must regard its freedom and well-being as necessary ("unconditional," "indispensable") goods. But this does not

warrant the conclusion that . . . he must, on pain of inconsistency, regard them as rights, which entail obligations on the part of others. All the connection between "good" and desire would seem to warrant at this point would be that the agent, with his judgment that his freedom and well-being are indispensable goods, would, on pain of inconsistency, desire, and even regard as an indispensable good, that others not interfere with his freedom and well-being and that they assist him under certain circumstances in the maintenance and enhancement of them. But this conclusion falls short of the claim that one's freedom and well-being are rights that impose obligations on others. The concepts "good" and "necessary goods" would have to be far richer or the concept "obligations" far weaker in meaning than Gewirth has indicated in order for the agent's movement to the rights-claim to be justified on purely logical grounds. (Adams 1980, 585)

However, Adams believes that there are features dialectically connected with being a PPA, which Gewirth does not appreciate (or make explicit), from which, together with "I categorically need my freedom and well-being," "I must consider that I have a right to my freedom and well-being" may be inferred.

The proof of the DPGC requires . . . a deeper and richer normative structure than Gewirth acknowledges; but the deeper and richer normative structure is there, I think, in the constitution of rational agents to be elicited dialectically, and so the principle is defensible. (Ibid., 591)

What is this deeper and richer normative structure? According to Adams, what is deficient in Gewirth's account stems from an analysis of "good" in terms of "desire." As I understand his thinking, what is missing from "My freedom and well-being are necessary goods," if analyzed on this basis, is the idea of "due," "entitlement," or "justification." For "My freedom and well-being are generic features of my agency" to generate any "oughts" from which statements of rights can be derived, it must be conjoined with an "ought," not merely with a statement of a desire. For the argument not to be question-begging, this "ought" premise must be dialectically connected with the idea of being a rational agent. According to Adams, the necessary "ought" judgment is implicit in the idea of being a rational agent who chooses purposes to pursue. We do not choose purposes just because we desire them. We choose our purposes because we consider that it would be good for them to be fulfilled. Furthermore, Adams holds that "ought" judgments are more basic than predicative value judgments (both being more basic than purposes). What he means by this is that a rational agent chooses to pursue a purpose because it judges that it would be good to achieve a situation X (that purpose) *because* it considers that X fulfills some need, or requirement, or makes some aspect of the situation more the way it *ought* to be. Of course, PPAs' views of what ought/ought not to be, etc., will differ. However, Adams does not

propose to identify the missing normative element with the contingent normative viewpoints of PPAs. If his analysis of "good" in
terms of "ought" is correct, then rational PPAs, whatever their contingent normative viewpoints,

as reflective beings, have a normative image of themselves as beings who, by
their own constitution, are under an imperative to develop and to use their
powers and to be self-directing in such a way that they will stand justified
under rational criticism. (Ibid., 587)

According to Adams, it is this general imperative without which
the argument is illicit even as a dialectical "is-ought" derivation.

A rational agent . . . is not merely a being who reasons from his multiple
wants and the value judgments implicit in them. More importantly, he has a
normative image of himself as a being who ought to define and to live a life
that would stand justified under rational criticism. He faults himself and
finds himself faulted by others when he fails to fulfill this imperative embodied in his self-image. He regards this imperative of his being as a responsibility. It is, I suggest, because the agent recognizes that his basic freedom and
'well-being' are necessary conditions of his fulfilling this responsibility, not
simply because they are necessary conditions of his achieving any of the
several things he wants, that he claims them as his rights and insists that
others are obligated to respect them. And, of course, consistency requires
that he acknowledge his obligation to respect the similar rights of other
rational agents. (Adams 1984, 21–22)

Adams, then, appears to be saying that sequence 1 isn't valid, but
that sequence 2 is:

1.   "I am a PPA" → "I consider my purposes to be good (because
      I desire them)"; "I categorically need my freedom and well-
      being in order to pursue/achieve any purpose that I might
      desire." ∴ I must consider that I have a right to my freedom
      and well-being (that others ought not to interfere with my
      freedom and well-being). ∴ I must consider that PPAO has a
      right to its freedom and well-being.
2.   "I am a PPA" → "I must consider that I ought to act rationally
      (in a way that will stand justified under rational criticism)";
      "I categorically need my freedom and well-being in order to
      act rationally." ∴ I must consider that I ought to have my
      freedom and well-being." ∴ I must consider that PPAO has a
      right to its freedom and well-being."

As far as Adams' criticism of Gewirth is concerned, I have three
comments.

1. Gewirth does not say that PPAs value their purposes because

they desire them. They value their purposes because they choose to pursue them, have a reason for pursuing them. It is desire for a reason that entails a value judgment, not just any desire; but, of course, it is only such purposivity that characterizes PPAs. (See #3.)

2. In relation to Adams' specific contention, that there is a gap between what I rationally (on pain of contradicting that I am a PPA) must desire, and what I must consider that I have a right to, I simply appeal to my discussion of the argument from attitudinal consistency. (See #13.)

3. Interpreted in one way, there is really no difference between Adams' sequence and Gewirth's. Gewirth recognizes that there are criteria according to which PPAs choose their purposes. These criteria, it is true, are treated by Gewirth as motivational, rather than as justificatory. But he does recognize that PPAs have justificatory frameworks, what I have called "SPRs for my purposes," and it is when these are violated that a PPA will act for purposes that it does not consider to be definitively good. Simply by posing the question of what SPRs for its purposes are rational (logically consistent) for a PPA to espouse, Gewirth recognizes that PPAs, viewed as rational (in the sense of logical), will recognize that they "ought" to act in a way that will survive rational criticism. This means that they accept that they "ought" not to act in ways that they consider to be impermissible according to their SPRs for their purposes, and in ways that are in accordance with SPRs for their purposes that they cannot, as PPAs, logically espouse. This "ought" is formal, however, and that is why it is dialectically necessary for a PPA to adhere to it. This "ought" does not function as the major premise in the derivation. Its function is to synthesize rationally the elements that generate the moral "ought," not to be this "ought" itself.[50] According to the argument, a material "ought" only appears with the recognition that I ought to pursue my freedom and well-being if I am to order my proactive commitment to my purposes and my recognition of the generic features of agency consistently. This "ought" is not logical but prudential, though I deny the logical "ought" if I do not espouse it.

If this is what Adams has in mind, then his own view does not differ materially from Gewirth's (although Adams' analysis of "good" in terms of "ought" is either vacuous or else begs the question against the adeonticist).[51] But then it is false to say that Gewirth does not have a rich enough structure, for Gewirth has the structure that Adams suggests.[52]

We should note that if I logically must be proactively motivated to pursue my freedom and well-being, for whatever purposes I might be proactively motivated to pursue, then it will be true that I ought to pursue my freedom and well-being for whatever purposes survive my criteria of "rational criticism," whatever these criteria might be. It is this fact that gives Gewirth's motivational starting point its justificatory implications.[53] If what Adams is pointing out is that the argument requires this justificatory feature, then he is correct. However, Gewirth's analysis provides for it.

On the other hand, if what Adams contends is that the argument requires it to be true that I have either a *moral* duty to be rational, or else that my criteria of "rational criticism" must impose *moral* duties, and that the dialectically necessary claims about rights and duties are to be derived from such allegedly dialectically necessary moral duties, then I do not see how these are to be justified as dialectically necessary (and hence not question-begging) unless—in the latter case—Gewirth's analysis is correct.[54]

2 Gamwell

According to Franklin I. Gamwell, picking up on Gewirth's statement that a PPA may rationally avoid the PGC only by "disavowing and refraining from . . . the whole sphere of practice" (RM 29), a "person" can avoid being bound by the PGC if it chooses not to be a PPA. He argues that this is a fatal concession. According to Gamwell, it follows that PPAs are not logically required to accept the PGC, *unless* it is presupposed that persons are morally required to be PPAs. However, such a suppressed premise would make the argument question-begging as an "is-ought" derivation, for it would then "presuppose rather than derive a moral principle" (Gamwell 1984, 65; though Gamwell believes that such a premise can be justified independently as a moral premise for the argument).

In essence, Gamwell's argument is as follows:

1. (*a*) The PGC need only be accepted by those who have made the "constitutive choice to be a prospective agent." (This choice is contrasted with choices made by a PPA between possible purposes to pursue as a PPA). ∴ (*b*) Gewirth's argument presupposes that the constitutive choice need not be made (i.e., that it is not morally required); whether or not to make it is a matter of preference. (See ibid., 61.)

2. Gewirth's argument presupposes that the constitutive choice must be made "without qualification" (meaning that there are no circumstances under which the PPA would choose to permit PPAO to interfere with its agency, or choose to relinquish being a PPA). If the constitutive choice can be made *with* qualification, then the argu-

ment will not work. If the constitutive choice is made with qualification, then a PPA will be required to value only those of its purposes that are consonant with its ideals. A fanatic might choose to relinquish its agency if it failed to live up to its ideals, and thus would not be required to claim a right to its freedom and well-being (see ibid., 61–62); an egoist might only wish to live in a "Hobbesian state of nature" with other PPAs. It would choose to live only if PPAO were permitted to interfere with it (?), and would not, by universalization, be required not to interfere with PPAO's freedom and well-being. (See ibid., 64–65.)

3. But "prospective agents *must* choose to be such without qualification only if human agency as such is morally required" (ibid., 65).

Regarding 1: Gamwell's idea of the "constitutive choice" is radically ambiguous. A person is, or is not, a PPA. A person cannot choose, in any sense relevant to practical precepts, to be or not to be a PPA, without already being a PPA. As Gamwell defines the constitutive choice, it is not a practical one, because it is not made by a PPA. So defined, Gewirth makes *no* presuppositions about the "constitutive choice." So, 1(*b*) is false. Furthermore, under this definition, 3 is incoherent. Moral precepts can only be directed at PPAs.

Regarding 2: This seems to change the nature of the "constitutive choice." Here, this is not the choice to *be* a PPA, but the choice whether or not to *continue to be* a PPA—which makes it a choice between particular occurrent purposes given to me *as a PPA*. "Unqualified" or "qualified" choices to "be a PPA" reflect different SPRs for my agency. Now, reasoning from *particular SPRs*, rather than from the necessary features of their agency, PPAs might well not be required to claim rights to their freedom and well-being, or not be required to grant to PPAO rights to PPAO's freedom and well-being. But Gewirth's argument is not *ad hominem*, or dialectically contingent, but dialectically necessary. It is as a PPA per se, not by virtue of any SPR for my purposes, that I must accept the PGC. When I choose to permit PPAO to interfere with my freedom and well-being (to end my agency, or as the price for permitting myself to interfere with PPAO's agency), I exercise a particular occurrent preference. If I must claim a right to my freedom and well-being *as a PPA*, by virtue of features necessarily connected to me as a PPA, then I cannot, by virtue of this preference, be said to deny that I have a right to my freedom and well-being. The claim I must make is that PPAO ought not to interfere with my freedom and well-being *against my will*. I do not deny my right to freedom and well-being when I decide to die, allow myself to be killed, or allow attempts to be made that threaten my life. I *waive* (some of) my rights (which characterization presupposes that I think I have them to waive). *As a PPA,* I must consider that I have the generic rights; but *in terms of some SPR for my purposes* that I contingently uphold, I *might* be prepared to waive these rights under certain circumstances. When universalizing to Stage III, I must universalize from the rights I *must* claim, not from specifications I merely *might* adhere to that are introduced by my (contingent) SPR for my purposes. So, I must grant PPAO a right for its freedom and well-being not to be interfered with against its will, even if I am prepared to will interference with my own freedom and well-being.

Regarding 3: First, I see no reason why an *assertoric* principle is necessary. *If* an assumption is needed, it is surely enough for it to be that PPAs *suppose* that they have a duty to be PPAs. Second, I do not see why this duty need be a *moral* duty (as Gewirth defines this). Third, the assumption that I have a *right* to be a PPA will do just as well as the assumption that I have a *duty* to be a PPA. These points alone indicate that there is something drastically wrong with Gamwell's criticism.

It seems to me that Gamwell sets off on the wrong foot by misinterpreting Gewirth's "get out" clause. Gewirth does not suggest, as Gamwell avers, that PPAs who would like not to be PPAs, or who intend to terminate/relinquish their agency, can evade the PGC. He claims that only beings who *are not* PPAs can rationally evade the PGC. The argument is that PPAs who violate the PGC deny that they are PPAs. PPAs are required to espouse the PGC regardless of the specific purposes they wish to pursue, simply by virtue of having purposes that they wish to pursue. If this is not correct, then Gamwell's argument does nothing to show that it is mistaken.

#23.3 The argument presupposes that PPAs must consider it to be good that they are what they are, which is implausible, or else trivializes morality.

W. D. Hudson grants that dialectically, from within my viewpoint as a PPA, "I do X for purpose E" does entail "E is good." But he says that this does not entail that I consider that it is good that I consider E good, or good that I pursue E. Even within my viewpoint as a PPA, my judgments of good are not definitive. (See Hudson 1984, 122–124.)

Hudson now asks whether this doesn't make the move from "I do X for purpose E" to "E is good" a Pyrrhic victory. "When 'ought' is said to follow from 'is,' that is normally taken to settle the value question" (ibid., 124). But the dialectically necessary method leaves it open.

The reply to this, of course, is that "ought" is only derived dialectically in relation to my freedom and well-being. Although, within my viewpoint as a PPA, the value I attach to my purposes is not definitive, it is also not the case that strict "ought" judgments attach to them. The case of my freedom and well-being, the generic features of my agency, to which "ought" judgments are attached, is different, because these are things I must value, whatever I value (and thus whatever I value definitively). In relation to my freedom and well-being, it does not make sense for me to say "I consider my freedom and well-being to be good, but I do not consider it to be good that I consider my freedom and well-being to be good." I *must* consider my freedom and well-being to be good, *whatever I value.*

Hudson grants this![55] Indeed, he says that this amounts to a "very firm grounding" at the end of Stage I of "good" (by which he means "definitive good" or "ought") in "is." But, says Hudson, this means that Gewirth

seems to see the agent as under a logical necessity to value what he is.

But why should it be thought self-evidently true that an agent must think it is good for him to be what he is, as Gewirth seems to assume? . . . Or does it simply take the point out of morality? What, after all, could be the point of discovering that what you ought to do is make sure of being what you are? Is not this to trivialize morality in the attempt to give it a firm foundation? (Ibid., 125)

Related to this, Hudson considers the following objection to Gewirth's argument:

There is no point in claiming a right to certain capabilities, if the claimant has to possess these capabilities in order to make the claim. To claim a right is to perform an act. In order to make this claim, therefore, an agent must already have the capability to act. So what is the point of claiming a right to that capability? (Ibid., 126)

To begin with, does Gewirth think that a PPA must consider it to be good that it is what it is? Well, a PPA must consider the purposes it has as good, but not that it strictly "ought" to have every purpose it has. However, "one's being a PPA" is not defined by the particular occurrent purposes one has, but by one's voluntary pursuit of particular occurrent purposes. Must a PPA consider that it is good that it is a being who voluntarily pursues purposes, or that it is good that it has the capacities of freedom and well-being which enable it to be a PPA? Well, not as such—PPAs are not prohibited from pursuing their own destruction. But they must consider their freedom and well-being to be good *for* what they are (beings who voluntarily pursue purposes), because their freedom and well-being are categorically necessary for whatever purposes they value as PPAs. PPAs must consider that they ought to have their freedom and well-being in order to be able to achieve any purposes by their agency.[56] This, I think, answers the implausibility side of the objection.

However, does this not amount to saying that PPAs must consider that they ought to be PPAs in order to be PPAs? If so, is this not trivial? Does it not take the point out of morality? Hudson, himself, comprehends Gewirth's reply.

> Gewirth's reply to this criticism would be that the agent is not simply a present but also a prospective agent ([RM] 68). As such, he claims the right to freedom and well-being in order to secure them for the future. True, if an agent is to make this claim he must already possess the necessary conditions of action; but his possession of them now does not in itself guarantee that he will possess them in the future. The point of his claim is to make sure of them for his prospective rather than his present agency. (Hudson 1984, 126)

Hudson concedes that this takes much of the force out of the triviality objection. The point, of course, is that a PPA need not consider that it ought to be a PPA to achieve whatever present purposes it might have, but in order to achieve whatever purposes *simpliciter* it might have.[57]

In his reply to this triviality objection, Gewirth (1984d, 224–225) is rather more expansive. In addition to pointing out that a PPA's normative claims bear not only on what it is, but also on its future agency (which Hudson already appreciates), and that a PPA is not only concerned with its agency itself, but also with the goods it can derive by being a successful agent, he emphasizes that being a purposive autonomous being is something that is essential to morality, and something that can be threatened. So, to strive to maintain such capacities must constitute a basic part of the point of morality. These points were already made in relation to a triviality objection in *Reason and Morality* (68) (which is the basis of Hudson's attribution of a reply). But Gewirth now offers a further consideration. Morality, as such, enters into a PPA's thinking only when it appreciates that it has to seek to maintain the purposivity and autonomy of PPAO. Such activity enhances rather than trivializes morality. In relation to the "triviality" of an imperative to seek its own freedom and well-being, it is essential to the demonstration that a PPA must engage in such other-regarding activity that it be required to act to maintain its own purposivity and autonomy. So, such an imperative cannot trivialize morality.[58]

#24   The argument is incompatible with the autonomy of morality.[59]

Closely related to the question of "is-ought," and also to the question of whether Gewirth reduces morality to logic, is that of the autonomy of morality. If assertoric "is-ought" derivations are possible, then this implies that morality is not an autonomous field of reasoning, and the same would be the case if the moral "ought" is a logical "ought." If what I have said so far is correct, then one of the consequences of Gewirth's use of the dialectically necessary method is that he is able to construe moral questions as objective ones, without appealing to the idea that moral truths are known by intuition, and at the same time preserve the autonomy of morality.

To recapitulate: according to the argument, the reason why I ought not to interfere with the freedom and well-being of any PPA is, in the first instance, that it is in the interests of PPAs for me not to do so, whatever their interests (categorically in their interests,[60] because PPAs categorically need their freedom and well-being). This "ought" is a moral "ought," in the sense that it is validated by an other-regarding criterion. This, however, does not constitute a naturalistic reduction, because, strictly speaking [PPAs categorically need their freedom and well-being $\rightarrow$ PPAs have a right to their freedom and well-being] is not held to be a truth; it is justified not because it is true *tout court,* but because it is logically necessary for PPAs to regard this inference as valid; and even if we choose to say that this means that it is "true for PPAs," this does not mean that it is being asserted that "PPAs categorically need their freedom and well-being" makes "PPAs have a right to their freedom and well-being" true *tout court.* All that is true is that PPAs rationally must consider that PPAs have rights to their freedom and well-being. Thus, the argument does not prove the PGC itself at all; it only proves that PPAs rationally must espouse the PGC.

The criterion of rationality for espousing this criterion cannot be moral, for this would make the argument question-begging. Two obvious alternatives are criteria of prudence (criteria of my particular occurrent self-interest) and logical criteria. To argue for the espousal of the PGC on grounds of prudence is to argue that, to achieve my purposes, I categorically need to refrain from interfering with the freedom and well-being of all PPAs. This is not necessarily true, and, in any case, it begs the question as to why my purposes (or interests) should be given precedence over the purposes of others. This latter point is important, because Gewirth desires a justification for the espousal of the PGC that no PPA can rationally evade. It is also reductive. If the reason why I must espouse the PGC is that it is categorically in my interests to do so, then morality would not be autonomous, but a species of prudence. This is because, according to the doctrine of the autonomy of morality, there is, in principle, a standing conflict not only between what I am morally required to do (to do on a criterion that takes account of the interests of others), and what I am required to do prudentially (on a criterion that takes no favorable account of any interests other than my own), but also between what I am required *to consider* that I am morally required to do, and what I am required to consider that I ought to do for self-interested reasons.[61] If prudence is the reason for espousing morality, then this conflict must be spurious.

However, Gewirth's argument is logical, not prudential in this way. (See RM 146.)[62] Logical criteria have a universality within the sphere of reasoning, which means that logical requirements cannot be evaded by anyone who engages in reasoning, whatever its form. This has two consequences: (*a*) the use of logical criteria is not question-begging; and (*b*) there can be no conflict between what I am required to do logically (if anything) and what I am required to do on more restrictive criteria of rationality. This latter consequence means that if Gewirth's argument does not make the material criteria of morality itself purely formal logical criteria (and I have insisted that it does not), then the fact that there are logically necessary grounds for espousing morality is not reductive in removing the distinctive character and sphere of moral criteria.

As Gewirth says,

The justification of the *PGC* through deductive and inductive rationality does not violate the autonomy of morality properly understood. . . .
. . . For rationality is internal to morality, not external to it. Moral judgments appeal to reasons and lay claim to justification or correctness. Hence, to evaluate them by consideration of the ultimate criteria of rational justification is to use and respect their own internal structure. That the same criteria are also applicable to other fields does not remove the autonomy of morality. It shows rather that morality is part of the whole vast area of rationality. On the other hand, the distinctiveness and practical supremacy of morality are preserved because the general, ultimate criteria of rationality are here applied to the generic features that distinctively characterize purposive action with its conativeness and its consequent evaluations and right-claims. (RM 360, 361–362)

General Comments

It seems to me that the critics considered in this chapter have not attended sufficiently to the following features of Gewirth's argument:

    1. Rights-claims are not attached to all my purposes, but only to

the generic features of my agency, because only these do I have to value as necessary goods, i.e., in a conatively independent manner.

2. The inference from categorical needs to rights is held to be valid only dialectically within my internal viewpoint as a PPA; it is not held to be a valid assertoric inference.

3. Directly related to this, Gewirth does not argue for the assertoric truth of the PGC divorced from its dialectical context. He does not argue that the truth of the PGC itself can be derived from the dialectical necessity for PPAs to accept the PGC. The PGC can be stated as a necessary truth only within the standpoint of agency. It can be stated assertorically only for practical purposes. If misportrayal of Gewirth on these matters is not to be attributed simply to failure to attend to Gewirth's clearly stated qualification that any assertoric formulation that he employs is to be taken to be elliptical, then it may be attributable to confusing the attribution of logical necessity to propositions and the attribution of logical necessity to the making of statements; or to failure to attend to Gewirth's distinction between relational and nonrelational truths.

4. Gewirth does not allege that actions are contradictory, but that actions presuppose judgments for their justification, which are capable of contradicting judgments that a PPA is logically required to make.

5. Gewirth argues that it is logically demonstrable what constitutes moral error, not that all immorality is necessarily the consequence of its perpetrator's making a logical error.

6. Gewirth does not argue that it is logically impossible for PPAs to violate the PGC. He argues that it is logically impermissible for PPAs to violate the PGC. Although a PPA denies that it is a PPA by violating the PGC, this does not mean that a PPA cannot be a PPA if it denies that it is a PPA. I have attempted to clarify this by drawing a distinction between PPAs *in essentia* and PPAs *in referentia*. PPAs *in referentia* are the subjects to which the argument, and practical prescriptions, are directed.

Of lesser significance, (*a*) I have noted a possible confusion about the sense in which Gewirth intends the term "claim" in "A PPA must claim . . . ." This states that a PPA must consider that . . . , rather than that a PPA must make a demand. (*b*) Discussion has also revealed further examples of failure to appreciate that Gewirth does not derive evaluation from desire but from the free choice of purposes, which was a central theme of the last chapter. (*c*) The argument does not suppose that PPAs have a reason to be PPAs (let alone a moral one). (*d*) That a PPA might choose to endanger or give up its freedom and well-being does not show that a PPA need not claim a right to its generic features; it only shows that the rights it must claim are waivable.

Finally, I have expanded Gewirth's argument from attitudinal consistency, and have claimed that it is adequate to demonstrate the validity of Stage II. This argument may be taken as complementary to the sequence that constitutes the argument for Stage II as presented in Chapter 2.

6 Objections to Stage II: The Social Context of Rights-Claims

In this chapter, I examine a number of objections that derive from, or revolve around, the idea that rights are, in some sense, social phenomena, and that rights-claims have, in some sense, an irreducible social context.[1]

#25 I cannot be rationally required to consider that PPAs have a claim right to their freedom and well-being, because, throughout history, persons have acted in violation of such a rights-claim.

This is an "objection" that is quite frequently put to me by some of my undergraduate students. It can be interpreted in a number of ways, which depend on what thinking lies behind it.

1

It is possible that the objection derives from thinking that "I have a right to X" means something along the lines of "Others permit me to do X" / "Others agree that they ought not to interfere with my doing X." If so, then in order to dismiss the objection, we only need to distinguish "having rights" in prescriptive (or "normative") and recognitional (or "effective") senses. In the prescriptive sense, Y can have a right to have/do X, even if Y is not permitted by others to have/do X, or others do not consider that they ought to permit Y to have/do X. In the prescriptive sense, Y has a right to have/do X *iff* others strictly ought to permit Y to have/do X (if there is an exclusionary reason why others ought to permit Y to have/do X). If I consider that there is an exclusionary reason why others ought to permit Y to have/do X, then I consider that Y has a right to have/do X. If I rationally must espouse a criterion according to which there is an exclusionary reason why others ought to permit Y to have/do X, then I rationally must consider that Y has a right to have/do X. If I am rationally required to espouse a criterion according to which all PPAs have a right to have/do X, then I am rationally required to consider that all PPAs have a right to have/do X, etc.

But, in the recognitional sense, I have a right to have/do X only if others permit me to have/do X or, at least, agree that they ought to do so.

Now, Gewirth does not claim that I must consider that all PPAs have a right to their freedom and well-being, *in the recognitional sense of "a right."* He wants to establish that all PPAs have rights to freedom and well-being in the prescriptive sense (or, more precisely, that all PPAs *logically ought to consider* that all PPAs have such rights, whether or not they in fact do so). Indeed, if PPAs' freedom and well-being were not interfered with, or if all agreed that they ought not to be interfered with, it would not be a pressing matter to argue that their freedom and well-being rationally ought not to be interfered with; and if Gewirth were unaware that PPAs' freedom and well-being are constantly under threat, he would hardly have an interest in establishing that their freedom and well-being rationally ought not to be interfered with.[2]

2 Trigg

Another possibility is that the objector reasons as follows: Gewirth claims that a PPA contradicts that it is a PPA if it violates the PGC (which he, indeed, does do). This means that Gewirth claims that it is logically *impossible* for a PPA to violate the PGC. However, it is logically possible for PPAs to violate the PGC, for they sometimes do. It must, therefore, be wrong to claim that PPAs contradict that they are PPAs if they violate the PGC.

Such reasoning, however, misportrays the argument. Gewirth does not claim that it is logically *impossible* for a PPA to violate the PGC. "I contradict 'I am a PPA' if I violate the PGC" does *not* mean "It is logically *impossible* for me to violate the PGC": it means "It is logically *impermissible* for me to violate the PGC." This, in turn, is equivalent to "It is logically *impossible* for me to violate the PGC, *if I am rational* (i.e., if I act as premises contained in 'I am a PPA' logically entail that I may act)." It is logically impossible for a *rational* PPA (in the sense of a PPA who acts as reason requires) to violate the PGC, for, if the argument is valid, then a PPA who violates the PGC is not a *rational PPA* (in this sense). But this is not the same as "A PPA who violates the PGC is not a PPA." For it to be the same, it must be logically impossible for PPAs to be irrational. Gewirth makes no such assumption, and his argument entails no such conclusion.

If the objection has this basis, then it is perhaps prompted by thinking, like Roger Trigg, that according to Gewirth

anyone rejecting the PGC is not so much an irrational agent as not an agent at all . . . . (Trigg 1980, 150)

However, the only possible basis for holding this is to hold that "A PPA who violates the PGC *denies that it is a PPA*" entails "A PPA who violates the PGC *is not a PPA*." But this does not follow, because "I deny that X is the case" does not entail "X is not the case."[3]

3 Narveson

Yet another possibility is that our critic has in mind something akin to an objection made by Jan Narveson.

Let us suppose that Gewirth is correct, and that reflection on the logically generic features of agency will show anyone who takes the trouble that there are these "categorically obligatory" duties[4] . . . . And then let us look out at the wide world and note the behavior of our fellows. It is not obvious that every apparently rational person has noticed what Gewirth is trying to prove. How is this? Is he going to say that they aren't, then, terribly rational after all? Or is it just a matter of not having done their homework? . . . Even apparently quite rational people have root disagreements with Gewirth's views. Well, given the Gewirthian arguments, shouldn't this be *puzzling*? (Narveson 1980, 652–653)

Is a "rational person" one with the commitment/ability to reason logically, or one who actually reasons in a logically valid way? Certainly, if Gewirth is right and "apparently rational" people don't see that he is right, then we would want to explain why they don't see that he is right. If a rational person is one who reasons validly, then I see nothing wrong in saying that those who do not accept the argument are not rational. Indeed, in this sense of "rational," they cannot be rational if Gewirth's argument is valid. On the other hand, if a rational person is one who has the commitment/ability to reason logically, then persons can be rational while making logical errors. I see nothing wrong in saying that they have not done their homework, or at any rate, that they haven't done it carefully enough. In this latter sense, even if "apparently rational" persons are rational, and even if they have "done their homework," the fact that some of them do not agree with Gewirth shouldn't be all that puzzling. And it certainly doesn't generate, as Narveson seems to suggest it does, much of a case for saying that Gewirth is wrong. Apparently rational persons are unable to prove theorems in formal logic, or in higher mathematics. There are complex considerations here, and in Gewirth's argument, which make the inferences difficult. An argument can be logically sound, without being easy to follow. More importantly, perhaps, a conclusion can be necessarily true, even if not everyone, and indeed no one, knows it to be true, believes it to be true, or has even thought of it. No one knows whether Fermat's last theorem is true; and there must have been a time when no one believed it was true, simply because there must have been a time when no one had thought of it. But, if it is true (or at any rate valid on the axioms of arithmetic), then it is necessarily so. If so, then rational persons are logically committed to accept it on the axioms of arithmetic. I do not see that the case here is all that different from the case presented by Gewirth's argument.

Furthermore, when we are dealing with an argument for a morality involving the sacrifice of self-interest, there are strong motivations not to accept that immorality is irrational, or even to set up self-interest above rationality. It is not stretching things to imagine that some with apparently rational commitments do not in fact have them.

All in all, one could equally well argue that because "apparently rational" persons agree with Gewirth, this is a case for saying that he is right; but I don't consider this to be much of an argument either.

4 Husak, Grunebaum, Regis

Finally, our critic might be prompted by the following kinds of claims:

1.

One might well wonder how the alleged human rights of freedom and well-being could be necessary conditions for purposive agency. Presumably a great part of the world's population is without these rights; is it therefore logically impossible for them to act—or to attain any of their purposes? (Husak 1984, 132)

2. According to James O. Grunebaum, "I wish to pursue E" entails "I do not want others to interfere with my pursuing E," but neither statement is equivalent to "I believe that others ought not to interfere with my pursuing E." Gewirth says that the case is different with necessary goods. This is not so. A PPA need not claim a right to its freedom and well-being on the grounds that it cannot pursue any of its purposes without its freedom and well-being because a

reluctant protagonist need not believe that his capacity for such action [pursuit of his purposes (what he regards as good)] depends either on his having a right to act or on his claiming a right to act. (Grunebaum 1976, 277)

Gewirth's argument shows that a reluctant protagonist must want freedom and well-being, but not that there is a logical requirement on him to claim a right to them.

3. According to Edward Regis, the argument of Stage II must fail because, although *to be* a PPA, a PPA must have its freedom and well-being, and have its freedom and well-being not interfered with,

it is neither a necessary nor a sufficient condition of enjoying freedom and well-being that one claim (or have) a *right* to freedom and well-being. (Regis 1981, 793)

To 1, Gewirth replies,

The objects of human rights are not only the necessary conditions of *action* but also the abilities and conditions needed for *successful action* in general. (Gewirth 1985c, 237)

These comprise freedom and the three levels of well-being. When Husak talks of a great part of the world's population being without rights,

this is not because they cannot act *at all* or achieve *any* of their purposes, but rather because they do not have the abilities and conditions required for *successful* action in general: such abilities and conditions as adequate health, education, income, and freedom from torture and other oppression. (Ibid., 238)

The objection also overlooks that "human rights are rights to the necessary conditions of *prospective* as well as *present* agency (see also *RM* 111–112)" (ibid., 239).

To 2, he replies that Grunebaum does not differentiate between particular occurrent purposes and necessary goods in relation to rights-claims. (See Gewirth 1976, 289–290.) And he makes a similar reply to Regis. (See Gewirth 1982e, 407.)

However, while each of these objections has at least some aspect that renders Gewirth's responses fair comment, I believe that there is a central aspect of each that is akin to Regis' remarks, and that Gewirth has missed what lies behind Regis' criticism. Gewirth reads Regis (and Husak and Grunebaum) as claiming that a PPA does not deny that it is a PPA if it does not consider that it has a right to its freedom and well-being. What these critics are claiming, however, is (a) that a PPA can *be* a PPA and not claim that it has a right to freedom and well-being, and (b) that a PPA can be a PPA without *being accorded* a right to freedom and well-being.

I can, indeed, *be* a PPA and not claim that I have a right to my freedom and well-being (where "claim" bears the sense of "address a prescription," or [alternatively] "consider that it is the case that . . . "). And, it follows that I can have my freedom and (basic) well-being (which I need to be a PPA), even if I don't claim a right to my freedom and well-being, or if others fail to recognize my right to freedom and well-being, or try to remove my freedom and (basic) well-being (but fail to do so). The proper response to *this* as a criticism is simply that it is misdirected. It is irrelevant to what Gewirth is arguing. What the critics have to show is that a PPA is not behaving as it ought to, if it is to be rational, if it does not consider that it has a right to its freedom and well-being (because it then denies that it is a PPA). But, because it can deny that it is a PPA, and still be a PPA, the fact that it can be a PPA and not consider that it has a right to its freedom and well-being is beside the point.

Furthermore, Gewirth argues that I must consider that I have a right to freedom and well-being because I categorically need freedom and well-being, because I must have freedom and well-being in order to act. He can be construed as arguing that I need a right to freedom and well-being in order to act only if he treats "I have a right to X" as equivalent to "I have X." But, in this sense, which he does not employ, it could not be the case, if I need freedom and well-being in order to act, that I do not have a right to freedom and well-being. The only senses in which it can be the case that I can act while not having a right to freedom and well-being are if "having a right to X" means either "others agreeing that they ought not to interfere with my having X," or "it being the case that others ought not to interfere with my having X." But Gewirth does not argue that I must have a right to freedom and well-being, in order to act, in either of these senses. For Gewirth, for me to consider that I have a right to X is for me to consider that others ought not to interfere with my freedom and well-being. That I must consider that others ought not to interfere with my freedom and well-being, on pain of contradicting "I am a PPA," does not mean that I cannot be a PPA if I do not consider that others ought not to interfere with my freedom and well-being. In addition, Gewirth holds that for me to consider that I have a right to freedom and well-being is not for me to consider that others agree that they ought not to interfere with my freedom and well-being. I might well be able to act if others do not agree that they ought not to interfere with my freedom and well-being, and attempt to so interfere (for their attempts might be unsuccessful). But this is irrelevant to the argument.

**#26   Claims about the possession of rights, unlike claims
        about necessary goods, presuppose the existence of a
        socially established set of rules that is historically con-
        tingent.**

1 MacIntyre

Claims to the possession of rights, as against claims about goods
necessary for rational agency,

> presuppose . . . the existence of a socially established set of rules. Such sets
> of rules only come into existence at particular historical periods under par-
> ticular social circumstances. They are in no way universal features of the
> human condition. . . . [T]he objection that Gewirth has to meet is precisely
> that those forms of human behaviour which presuppose notions of some
> ground to entitlement, such as the notion of a right, always have a highly
> specific and socially local character, and that the existence of particular types
> of social institution or practice is a necessary condition for the notion of a
> claim to the possession of a right being an intelligible type of human perfor-
> mance. (As a matter of historical fact such types of social institution or prac-
> tice have not existed universally in human societies.) Lacking any such social
> form, the making of a claim to a right would be like presenting a check for
> payment in a social order that lacked the institution of money. Thus Gewirth
> has illicitly smuggled into his argument a conception which does not in any
> way belong, as it must do if his case is to succeed, to the minimal character-
> isation of a rational agent. (MacIntyre 1981, 65)

MacIntyre's key assertion is that the claiming of a right to X is not
an *intelligible* type of human performance unless there is in existence
"a socially established set of rules." He also says that claiming a
right to X presupposes the existence of "particular types of social
institution or practice" which have "a highly specific and socially
local character." In composite, I take it that he is asserting that the
claiming of a right to X presupposes that persons justify their claims
to X by appealing to a socially established set of rules. If this is not
true, then it hardly matters whether or not there are/have been
human societies in which there are/have been no socially established rules.

According to Gewirth, when a PPA says "I have a (claim) right to
X," the PPA addresses a practical strict "ought" to PPAO ("PPAO
strictly ought not to interfere with my having/doing X") which has
four features:

1.   PPA sets forth a practical requirement that PPA endorses for
      the conduct of PPAO;
2.   PPA has a reason on which it grounds this requirement;
3.   PPA holds that this requirement and reason justify in some

way preventing or dissuading PPAO from violating the requirement; and
4.   PPA holds that fulfillment of the requirement is due to itself.
(See RM 79.)

I take it that MacIntyre is claiming that it is unintelligible to suppose that a PPA might engage in a performance that is characterized
by 1–4, unless the reason referred to in 2 is that this requirement is
grounded in a "socially established set of rules"; so that if there is no
such set of rules, to suppose this performance will be unintelligible;
but that there are (or have been) societies (comprised of PPAs) without such a set of rules. In such societies, PPAs cannot be required to
think that they have rights *on the basis that they are PPAs alone;* therefore, PPAs cannot necessarily be required (by virtue of being PPAs)
to think that they have rights.
    I am not sure what MacIntyre means by a set of rules being "so-
cially established," but I imagine that for a rule to be "socially established" has something to do with its being generally assented to or
effectively enforced. However, whereas I can see that an appeal to a
reason grounding a rights-claim to X is unlikely to secure noninterference with X unless PPAO agrees that this is a good reason, or
unless other PPAOs will enforce the claim on PPAO when this reason is appealed to, I simply do not see why acceptance of PPA's
claim (or reason for its claim) by *any* PPAO is a necessary condition
for the *intelligibility* of PPA's performance in claiming a right, as
against its being effective.
    Were Gewirth operating with a recognitional (or "effective")
sense of having a right, as against a prescriptive (or "normative")
one, this objection would have to be conceded. But he isn't. (See RM
100.) MacIntyre might be trying to deny the intelligibility of the
prescriptive notion of a right. But a moment's reflection is all we
need to dispel the possibility of his succeeding in such an enterprise.
Quite simply, if we are to socially establish rules, we need to understand what it is for something to be prescribed. Rules do not become
rules (achieve their abstract sense as rules) when they become socially established; they only become socially established rules.[5]
    According to MacIntyre, speaking generally of the Enlightenment
project in ethics, rather than specifically about Gewirth (whom Mac-
Intyre takes to be the best advocate of this project [see MacIntyre
1981, 20]),

[i]t would of course be a little odd that there should be such rights [those
which are "alleged to belong to human beings as such and which are cited as
a reason for holding that people ought not to be interfered with in their

pursuit of life, liberty and happiness"—rather than rights conferred by positive law and custom] attaching to human beings simply *qua* human beings in light of the fact . . . that there is no expression in any ancient or medieval language correctly translated by our expression 'a right' until near the close of the middle ages: the concept lacks any means of expression in Hebrew, Greek, Latin or Arabic, classical or medieval, before about 1400, let alone in Old English, or in Japanese even as late as the mid–nineteenth century. From this it does not of course follow that there are no natural or human rights; it only follows that no one could have known that there were. (Ibid., 66–67)

Well, *if* X has no concept of a right, then X indeed cannot know that there are human rights, or any others for that matter. But, first, what evidence does MacIntyre provide for *the concept* of "a right" being missing in various historical periods? And, second, what is the relevance of it being the case that some PPA might not have the concept of a right?

The only evidence MacIntyre provides for his assertion that the concept of "a right" is of relatively recent origin is that the use of *the term* "rights" is of fairly recent origin. Now, this will not do, even on MacIntyre's own admission, for, *on Gewirth*, MacIntyre says,

Gewirth readily acknowledges that expressions such as 'a right' in English and cognate terms in English and other languages only appeared at a relatively late point in the history of the language toward the close of the middle ages. But he argues that the existence of such expressions is not a necessary condition for the embodiment of the concept of a right in forms of human behaviour; *and in this at least he is clearly right.* (Ibid., 65; my emphasis)

However, even without this damaging admission, MacIntyre would not be on strong ground. As Gewirth points out in his reply to MacIntyre (see Gewirth 1985a, 747), MacIntyre ignores crucial aspects of Gewirth's discussion of this matter in *Reason and Morality* (98–102), where Gewirth argues for rather more than what MacIntyre attributes to him (and where he *does not*, contrary to what MacIntyre states, acknowledge the absence of cognate terms for "a right"). Gewirth argues generally that the concept of "rights" (in general) is historically universal (even if that of "human rights" is not), and specifically that the concept of rights is found in primitive societies, Roman law, Greek philosophy, and feudalism, and that it is not restricted to modern Western societies.[6] In part, his argument relies on interpretations of (cited) historians and anthropologists. These can be questioned (but MacIntyre does not do so, as he does not consider them). Furthermore, MacIntyre needs to claim (as, indeed, he does) that cognate notions are also absent in various societies. But, what are these cognate notions? They are, surely, notions of "duties," "authority," of "justified redress of wrong," and so on. If languages or societies lack all such concepts, then they can be said to lack the concept of "a right." If they have any of these concepts, then they (at least implicitly) have the concept of "a right." Is MacIntyre really alleging that there are (or have been) languages and societies that lack these cognate notions? The evidence that Gewirth cites is quite sufficient to make out a case, which MacIntyre has not even attempted to answer, for holding that these cognate notions are to be found in places where MacIntyre denies that they exist.

Of course, to argue that the concept of rights has a universal social footing is not to argue that every PPA has the concept of rights. But Gewirth does not have to argue that every PPA has the concept of rights, only that every PPA *rationally ought* to have the concept of rights (and, indeed, rationally ought to consider that it has a right to its freedom and well-being). As Gewirth says,

It is important to be clear about the sense in which I say that every agent must "claim" or "accept" that he and all other agents have the generic rights. This sense is not necessarily an empirically or phenomenologically descriptive one: it does not necessarily refer to the conscious thought-processes or explicit utterances of agents. It signifies rather what agents are logically committed to hold or accept insofar as they are rational in the sense of being able to follow out the implications of the concepts of action and agent, and hence of their own activity as such. Denials of any of these implications are thus failures of rationality, which are themselves often the effects of unjust social institutions. . . .

. . . The fact that some agents have not exercised their rational powers in . . . [some historical] context does not establish either that the propositions in question are not rationally justified or that the agents did not possess the requisite rational powers. (Gewirth 1985a, 748)[7]

2 Pollis

Adamantia Pollis, reviewing Gewirth 1982b, though her remarks are directed equally at *Reason and Morality*, claims that

[t]he book is a highly ethnocentric, ahistorical work. It ignores philosophic traditions, particularly from the East—for which objectivity and individuality are irrelevant, if not meaningless. Claims for the universality of his philosophic foundations and his moral premises, moreover, are highly tenuous since they are contingent on individualism, objectivity, and rationality. In the West, the notion of an autonomous individual emerged only with the modern political philosophers within a particular historical epoch, while the autonomous individual is conceptually and empirically non-existent either in the philosophic traditions or in the cultures of the vast majority of humankind. Gewirth's philosophizing is undergirded by no ontology, which might have, at least in part, compensated for his ethnocentrism. Furthermore his philosophy stems from the positivist tradition which allows him to assume that there are "objectively important needs" and that rationality governs

action. The presumption that action is governed by rationality excludes from the egalitarian and universality of rights [sic] those individuals he deems as possessing minimal rationality. Irrationality, feeling, and emotions are denied legitimacy. If his moral grounding of human rights stemmed from an ontology which incorporated universalistic elements derived from the extant diversity of human rights conceptualizations, his argument would have greater merit. As it is, his justification for human rights is an ideological exposition of little value to those concerned both with their substance and universality. (Pollis 1984, 185)

There are a lot of assertions here, containing no analysis or explication, so it is difficult to comment on this. I shall merely make a number of observations.

1. Gewirth's theory is "ahistorical" *in the sense* that he does not derive the PGC *from* an assumption of *any* cultural norms. He derives the PGC dialectically from features that belong to PPAs *necessarily*, hence universally. These features are "transhistorical" rather than ahistorical (here meaning not attending to the diversity of features of historically existing PPAs), belonging to PPAs regardless of the historical diversity that they manifest. (See #54). They exist *within* historical diversity, not outside of it. Furthermore, a theory cannot be both ethnocentric and ahistorical (in either of the senses of the latter term indicated), for to be ethnocentric it must rest on contingent, historically specific characteristics.

2. When Gewirth says that there are universal human (or PPA) rights, he does not claim that these are universally recognized. He says that they *rationally ought* to be recognized as belonging to all PPAs by all PPAs. So, to point to the absence of their universal recognition is irrelevant. Is the test for the justification of a moral principle supposed to be the recognition of that principle in human societies? In general, Pollis writes as though Gewirth were engaged in a social anthropology of the recognition of rights-claims, rather than in moral epistemology. Perhaps she holds that the latter can, or must, be reduced to the former. This is a large subject, but since Pollis presents no argument for this, I shall say only that I consider that such a view dispenses with any distinction between valid and invalid belief. Apart from anything else, this relativizes the criteria of "can" and "must" in the thesis itself, in such a way that there can be no point in *arguing* with those who have different beliefs.

3. When Pollis says that "autonomous" individuals do not exist in certain societies, she presumably means that PPAs exist who do not have their right to freedom recognized. She cannot mean that PPAs exist without the generic freedom necessary for them to be PPAs. Her claim is irrelevant, because Gewirth operates with a normative,

rather than a recognitional, concept of "having a right." The PGC is not derived from recognition of rights, but dialectically from the generic features of agency. On the other hand, her claim (like MacIntyre's) that individuals in certain societies had no concept of "autonomous individuals" is irrelevant—unless (and contrary to appearances) she is claiming that to claim a right to freedom in certain societies is literally unintelligible. To sustain this, the normative conception of rights must be held to be unintelligible. For this to be the case, prescriptions must be unintelligible if their addressees do not accept them. However, I consider that this contention is untenable. (See, e.g., #35.2.)

4. It is untrue that Gewirth's theory is "undergirded by no ontology" which incorporates "universalistic elements derived from the extant diversity of human rights conceptualizations." The subject of Gewirth's argument is a PPA. PPAs are the addressees of all practical precepts, regardless of their diversity. As such, what a PPA is logically required to believe is a justification for practical precepts that cannot be overridden by contingent commitments. PPAs, whatever their contingent commitments, are still PPAs, with *as such* universal features. (See #54.) The generic features of agency constitute the ontological basis for the theory.

5. Gewirth does not *assume* that there are "objectively" important human needs. He *argues* that there are needs that all PPAs must value for themselves (the necessary goods), and *tries to demonstrate* that all PPAs rationally must value these needs in others.

6. The only sense in which Gewirth assumes that action is governed by rationality is that action is purposive behavior, behavior done for purposes (reasons). He does not assume that PPAs *do* act rationally (in the sense of what reason [logic] normatively requires). (See #45.1. On 5 and 6: Pollis' statement that it is Gewirth's "positivism" that leads him to an "objectivistic" stance on norms, and a "rationalistic" one on actions, is peculiar. "Positivism" [as used in law, sociology, and philosophy] more frequently betokens "subjectivism" and "behaviorism." If there is anything common to schools of thought usually called "positivistic," then it is adherence to doctrines of value-freedom of science, empiricism, and determinism [and there is frequently, almost characteristically, an association with moral relativism]. None of this fits Gewirth's philosophical stance. Pollis, of course, is at liberty to define the term any way she likes; but without providing a definition her attribution is uniilluminating at best, and at worst an attempt to condemn by misassociation.)

7. Gewirth does not deny rights to those with minimal rationality. This is a complete distortion of his position on the rights of marginal

agents, and the way in which rationality enters into his argument. (See #45.)

8. Gewirth does not deny feelings or emotions legitimacy. On the contrary, it could be said that the theory provides a specification of what constitutes *rational emotions and feelings*. Indeed, Gewirth has written of his theory as an attempt to demonstrate the unity of reason and love. (See RM xii.)[8]

9. Gewirth *does* deny that the irrational (as against the merely nonrational) has legitimacy. But what is legitimate is what is justified, and what is justified is what is held for "good reasons." Gewirth's operative criteria of rationality are those of deductive and inductive logic, which undergird reason giving in all its senses. Pollis, herself, writes of what is wrong with Gewirth's argument, and purports to give reasons to support this judgment. But this, itself, presumes the criteria that she, apparently, wishes to question. (See #61.)

10. In arguments *from* the PGC on issues of human rights, the PGC is a moral premise that grants individual PPAs rights. But the foundational argument *to* the PGC operates on no moral premises, and does not *assume* that individuals have rights. It makes no assumptions about individuals that do not apply within every culture. (See #54.)

#27   **PPAs do not necessarily have to claim rights, because rights and rights-related duties can only arise in a social context; and Robinson Crusoe before the arrival of Friday did not live in such a context.**

Martin P. Golding[9] objects to Stage II, on the grounds that rights and rights-related duties can only arise in a social context, in a rather different way from MacIntyre or Pollis.

Consider the situation of Robinson Crusoe before the arrival of Friday. Robinson of course acts, and I am willing to grant that freedom and well-being are necessary conditions of his action: they are necessary goods for Crusoe, to use Gewirth's terminology. Still, it cannot be maintained that Robinson either has or does not have rights to freedom and well-being, for the question does not arise. The "dialectically necessary method" whereby Gewirth argues that a prudent, self-interested agent[10] *must* claim rights has no foothold in the situation of Robinson Crusoe. It may be true that the "necessary content of morality is to be found in action and its generic features," but rights cannot be derived from the generic features of action alone. Once Friday arrives the situation changes and Robinson now *can* claim rights, and perhaps[11] he also must claim them. (Golding 1984, 131)

Gewirth, of course, does not claim that the having of rights can be derived by his argument, only that a PPA must consider (claim) that it has rights to its freedom and well-being. However, we can let this point pass here, because Golding claims that rights-claims are not even *dialectically* necessary—because a PPA (e.g., Robinson) can act in a context in which it makes no sense for him to "claim" that he has rights to the generic features of agency, or at least in which Robinson could not be justified in claiming that he has a right.

Golding is mistaken about this. It is true that rights-claims are directed at others, in the sense that they specify that others ought not to interfere with what the claimant claims a right to. Before Friday arrives, there is no one on the island to whom Robinson can *address* the claim that he has a right to his freedom and well-being. It does not follow from this, however, either that Robinson cannot consider that he has a right to his freedom and well-being, or even that he cannot *have* a right to his freedom and well-being, *before Friday arrives.*

Why?

1. When Gewirth talks about a PPA "claiming" a right to its freedom and well-being, he means that the PPA considers that it has a right to freedom and well-being. He does not refer primarily to the act of a PPA laying claim to a right to freedom and well-being. After all, a PPA may waive its right and, if so, may certainly omit to lay claim to it. But, of course, it can only waive a claim to a right, or omit to lay claim to it, if it considers that it has a right to waive or not to lay claim to. So the fact that there may be no one around to whom Robinson can address his rights-claim does not mean that he cannot consider that he has this right. The conditions that justify my considering that I have a right to X are conditions that justify my laying claim to a right to X. But conditions that enable me to address a rights-claim are not conditions that justify my considering that I have a rights-claim to address.

2. There is a sense in which having a right or a duty is inherently hypothetical. To say that I have a right to do X is to say that, *if* there are any PPAs with whom I interact, then I am justified in laying claim to their having a duty not to interfere with my doing X, in requiring them not to interfere with my doing X. However, this social condition, this other-reference, which *is* part of the meaning of rights-claims, must not be misinterpreted. In considering that I have a right to X, I consider that I have justification for requiring noninterference with my doing X by any PPA with whom I *might* happen to come into social contact. After Friday comes along, Robinson can say, "I interact with Friday, and Friday has a duty not to interfere

with my freedom and well-being." But *before* Friday comes along, Robinson can say, "If Friday (or any other PPA) were to come along, then Friday (or any other PPA who came along) would have a duty not to interfere with my freedom and well-being." The social condition for the intelligibility of considering that I have a right to X is not constituted by the *actual* presence of others with whom I interact, but by the (logically) *possible* presence of an interactive situation. For Robinson to consider that he has a right to his freedom and well-being is for him to consider that others, if they were to come along, would have a duty not to interfere with his freedom and well-being. There is nothing unintelligible about Robinson's considering that he has a right to freedom and well-being just because he happens not to be in interaction with any other PPA at the time (or even if he is unlikely to be in the future). Thus, the possibility of PPAs existing in nonsocial contexts does not constitute a refutation of the claim that PPAs logically must consider that they have a right to their freedom and well-being. Indeed, I suggest that it is possible for Robinson to consider that he has a right to freedom and well-being against PPAs when they come along, only *because* for him to consider that he has a right to his freedom and well-being is for him to consider that he has justification for requiring their noninterference with his freedom and well-being independent of their actual presence.[12]

General Comments

Three main new points emerge from this chapter.

1. It is important to attend to a distinction between prescriptive and recognitional senses of a right, and the argument is essentially concerned with the former.

2. Although rights-claims presuppose a social context in directing that others ought not to interfere with what the claimant has a right to do, this social context constitutes only a subjunctive condition for the having of rights. I have a right to (or consider that I have a right to) X if it is the case (or I consider that it is the case) that *if* I were in social contact with PPAO then PPAO *would* have a duty not to interfere with my doing/having X. My having a right to X (or my considering that I have a right to X) does not depend on my *being* in social contact with a PPAO.

3. Gewirth holds that a PPA must consider that it has a right to its freedom and well-being, rather than merely, or instead of, that it must press a claim to such a right, when he says that PPAs must "claim" a right to their freedom and well-being. This has been noted before, but assumes greater importance than previously.

The point that Gewirth does not argue that PPAs cannot deny that they have rights, but only that they deny that they are PPAs if they do not consider that they have rights to freedom and well-being (with its various ramifications), which was seen to be of great importance in Chapter 5, has been seen to be equally important in replying to the objections of Chapter 6.

7   Objections to Stage II: Must Agents Prescribe to Others?

This chapter deals mainly with objections that are directed at the logical validity of specific inferences that constitute Stage II, in particular, at (4) "My freedom and well-being are necessary goods" entailing (4c) "I ought to pursue my freedom and well-being," and at (4c) entailing (4d) "PPAO ought not to interfere with my freedom and well-being"—although some wider ranging objections are also considered. It is not possible to separate some of these objections from objections to Stages I and III entirely. Some of the more important objections are inseparable from considerations relating to Stage III, in particular. Although it is, therefore, necessary to comment on Stage III objections at times, I have generally attempted to isolate those aspects of composite objections that relate specifically to Stage II, leaving discussion of their Stage III aspects for the next chapter.

#28   PPAs need not accept even prudential self-referring "ought" judgments, because they may regard all "ought" talk as mystificatory.

According to Gewirth,

a rational and conatively normal person must make or accept for himself at least instrumental prudential [strict] 'ought'-judgments. For suppose something Z threatens his basic goods and hence his basic well-being, and he believes that the necessary and sufficient condition of his avoiding Z is his doing X. Then, given certain minimal qualifications, he must make or accept for himself such a prudential and prescriptive 'ought'-judgment as . . . 'I ought to do X.' The qualifications in question are that he believes doing X is in his power and that he does not believe there is any superior counterconsideration to his doing X. (RM 90)

Kai Nielsen retorts that

he is not logically required to do anything of the sort. He could perfectly well stick with the considered expression of his intentions and assert instead 'I

will do X' or 'I certainly will do X' and eschew any 'ought'-judgments, prudential or otherwise. (Nielsen 1984, 79)

Nielsen hereby denies that (4) "My freedom and well-being are
necessary goods" entails (4c) "I have a prudential duty to pursue my
freedom and well-being/resist interference with my freedom and
well-being." If (4c) is not dialectically necessary, then my favored
sequence for Stage II is short-circuited at the very beginning. So,
why does Nielsen think this? Nielsen, quite correctly, holds that an
adeonticist ("amoralist" in his terminology) eschews all talk of
claim rights or duties, moral *or otherwise*, in relation to its purposes.
It does not consider that it is *either* permissible *or* impermissible, in
any exclusionary reason sense, for it to do anything that it is motivated to do. (See ibid., 68–69, 73, 74, 79–80.) The adeonticist operates
according to

the maxim 'I will do what I can to get what I want,' while regarding talk of
'ought' as mystificatory. (Ibid., 79)

Gewirth, of course, does not question this. For Gewirth, an a-
deonticist is a PPA who rationalizes its purposes according to the
maxim "It is not impermissible (meaning 'neither permissible nor
impermissible' [in *any* exclusionary reason senses]) for me to pursue
any purpose I am motivated to pursue"; and an amoralist (generally), who need not be an adeonticist, is a PPA who rationalizes its
purposes according to the maxim "It is not morally impermissible
for me to pursue any purposes I am motivated to pursue" (on the
grounds that it does not recognize any *moral* rights or duties). What
Gewirth questions is whether the adeonticist can consistently adhere to its maxim, given that, as a PPA, it must regard its freedom
and well-being as necessary goods.

So, what are we to make of the following statement? The a-
deonticist

recognizes that he must value his freedom and well-being as conditions
necessary for achieving any of his purposes. He will see that it is a very vital
interest of his to secure a situation where his freedom and well-being will not
be interfered with. He will, *if he is rational,* take the steps necessary to protect
his vital interests . . . . (Ibid., 73; my emphasis)

How is this consistent with eschewing all "ought" talk? Surely,
what Nielsen attributes to the adeonticist is equivalent to saying
that the adeonticist must accept "I am strictly prudentially irrational
(I act against my purposes, whatever they might be) if I do not
defend my freedom and well-being from interference"; and this is
equivalent to "I prudentially strictly *ought* to defend my freedom

and well-being from interference." Thus, on the interpretation of a "strict" or "deontic" "ought" as one that is binding irrespective of the addressee's particular occurrent wishes, the adeonticist must, even according to Nielsen, accept "I strictly ought to defend my freedom and well-being from interference." For this is what the a-deonticist is required to do according to the criterion of its purposes, whatever these might be; and, because of the proactive value that a PPA attaches to its purposes, this is a prescriptive constraint or requirement on the adeonticist's actions, not merely a means-ends statement. Thus, if the adeonticist, *as adeonticist*, does not hold that it strictly ought to do anything, then this merely serves to show that adeonticism is an inconsistent maxim for a PPA to espouse. For, *as a PPA*, it must consider that it strictly ought to pursue its freedom and well-being.

In order to make more sense of Nielsen's criticism, we need to note that he has a persistent tendency to interpret all "oughts" as moral "oughts." Now, it is certainly the case that Gewirth cannot, without appealing to the later steps in his argument, hold that (4) entails "I morally ought to pursue my freedom and well-being"; however, the "ought" of (4c) is not alleged to be moral, but prudential (self-regarding). Gewirth's target at this stage is not the amoralist, as I define this, but the adeonticist. So the fact that Gewirth does not, in the passage Nielsen criticizes, establish that PPAs must be moralists, is neither here nor there. If we take (4c) as Gewirth intends it to be taken, then Nielsen would appear to concede that (4c) is dialectically necessary.

#29   **In order to show that a PPA must accept even pruden-
       tial "ought" judgments, it must be assumed that PPAs
       are conatively normal. This, however, is a contingent
       attribution, which violates the dialectically necessary
       method.**

The conative normality of a PPA is a crucial factor in the argument that a PPA rationally must accept (4c). Kai Nielsen, however, claims that even if an amoralist, *provided that it is a rational conatively normal person*, is required to defend its freedom and well-being from interference, whatever its purposes, the assumption of conative normality involves Gewirth abandoning his strict ethical rationalism (adherence to his dialectically *necessary* method).

[T]he point I want to make here is that in making the assumption that the amoralist is a "conatively normal person"—a person, as Gewirth explains it, who "has the self-interested motivations common to most persons and is willing to expend the effort needed to fulfill them"—Gewirth deploys a proposition about the assumed motivation of the agent that is plainly a contingent one. But this is incompatible with both his avowed aim of sticking to the dialectically necessary method and with his commitment to *full apodictic procedural rationalism.* On the one hand, he cannot excise that assumption about conative normalcy for he needs it to make his argument work. On the other hand, to fulfill his own severely rationalistic requirements for a proof of what he takes to be the supreme principle of morality, he must proceed by a chain of entailments to a necessary proposition from a series of necessary propositions . . . . (Nielsen 1984, 78–79, quoting RM 90)

However, in stating this objection, Nielsen overlooks that a "person" who is not proactively motivated to pursue his or her purposes is not a PPA (something that Gewirth states in the words immediately following the definition of "conative normality" cited by Nielsen). It is contingent whether or not a person (if we define "a person" as "a member of *Homo sapiens*") is conatively normal (proactively motivated to pursue his or her purposes); but a person is not necessarily a PPA, and PPAs are conatively normal by definition. So, "PPAs are conatively normal" is not a contingent assumption. Because Gewirth's argument proceeds from "I do, or intend to do, X for purpose E" (which proclaims "I am a PPA"), not from "I am a person," there is no departure from the dialectically necessary method in assuming, as Gewirth does, that an amoralist *PPA* is a conatively normal person. (See Gewirth 1984d, 213.)[1]

Of course, if Gewirth introduces "conative normality" to mean "having the SPR for its purposes that most PPAs (perhaps) have (i.e., a moral one)," then the assumption of conative normality would be contingent (and question-begging). But this is not what Gewirth means by this phrase, and it is not a meaning that needs to be attributed to show that the adeonticist (amoralist) PPA must embrace deontic talk.[2]

#30   To deny that I have a right to my freedom and well-being is not to imply that PPAO has a right to interfere with my freedom and well-being. The argument assumes that this is so.

According to Bernard Williams,

[t]he argument [for Stage II] suggests that if I do not prescribe that others ought not to interfere with my freedom, I shall be logically required to admit that they *may* interfere with it . . . . (Williams 1985, 61)

According to Williams, this is a false dichotomy: to hold that it is permissible for PPAO to interfere (that PPAO has a claim right to interfere) with my freedom is not the sole alternative to holding that it is impermissible for PPAO to interfere with my freedom. I can also deny that PPAO ought to interfere with my freedom by not being in the "business of making rules," by holding that it is *neither permissible nor impermissible* for PPAO to interfere.

Williams' objection may be put as follows. If a PPA must accept "My freedom and well-being are necessary goods," then a PPA must (ought to) want its freedom and well-being not to be interfered with, and must resolve to do what it can to secure its freedom and well-being. If a PPA holds that PPAO has a claim right to interfere with its freedom and well-being, then it must accept that it ought not to interfere with PPAO's interference with its freedom and well-being. This entails that it ought not to do what it can to secure its freedom and well-being, and that it ought not to want its freedom and well-being not to be interfered with. There is, thus, a clear contradiction between "My freedom and well-being are necessary goods" and "PPAO has a claim right to interfere with my freedom and well-being."

However, an "egoist" simply does not think in terms of PPAs' actions being permissible (PPAs' having claim rights) or impermissible (PPAs' having duties to others). The rational egoist regards its freedom and well-being as necessary goods, on the basis of which it must want its freedom and well-being not to be interfered with, and must resolve to do what it can to secure its freedom and well-being, but denies both that it has a claim right to its freedom and well-being, and that PPAO has a claim right to interfere with its freedom and well-being.

Another way of putting this would be to say that the egoist considers that it does no wrong to pursue its freedom and well-being, but also that PPAO does no wrong to pursue its freedom and well-being, even if this involves interfering with the egoist's freedom and well-being. And Williams, in effect, puts it this way when he quotes Max Stirner's (1982) view of the egoist's position.

The tiger that assails me is in the right, and I who strike him down am also in the right. I defend against him not my *right*, but *myself*. (Williams 1985, 62)[3]

If we say that "X has a right to do Y" means "X does no wrong by doing Y," then we might say that "X has a *weak right* (or mere liberty) to do Y" means "X does no wrong by doing Y; while *at the same time*, Z does no wrong by interfering with X doing Y." On the other hand "X has a *claim right* (or 'strong' right) to do Y" means "X does no wrong by doing Y; *and* Z does wrong by interfering with X doing Y." In these terms, Williams is saying that the egoist must prescribe only that it has a mere liberty to its freedom and well-being. This means that Williams' basic charge against Gewirth is that Gewirth equivocates between mere liberties and claim rights in purporting to secure Stage II.

This objection raises two main questions. (*a*) Does Gewirth's argument for Stage II suggest that to deny that I have a claim right to my freedom and well-being is to grant PPAO a claim right to interfere with my freedom and well-being? (*b*) Is it dialectically consistent for an egoist, *as a PPA*, to claim that it has only a mere liberty to pursue its freedom and well-being?

Regarding (*a*): On pages 78–82 of *Reason and Morality*, Gewirth presents a number of interrelated arguments for

the step from (3) "My freedom and well-being are necessary goods," to a right-claim that logically must be made or accepted by every agent. (Gewirth 1984d, 205; Gewirth's numbering, here and in the quote that follows)

Gewirth says that these arguments may be summarized, collectively, as follows:

First, I argue that by virtue of accepting (3), every agent has to accept (4) "I must have freedom and well-being." This 'must' is practical-prescriptive in that it signifies the agent's advocacy of his having what he needs in order to act either at all or with general chances of success in achieving the purposes for which he acts. Now by virtue of accepting (4), every agent has to accept (5) "I have rights to freedom and well-being." For, if he denies (5), then, because of the logical correlativity of claim-rights and strict 'oughts,' he also has to deny (6) "All other persons ought at least to refrain from removing or interfering with my freedom and well-being." By denying (6), he has to accept (7) "Other persons may (i.e. It is permissible that other persons) remove or interfere with my freedom and well-being." And by accepting (7) he has to accept (8) "I may not (i.e. It is permissible that I not) have freedom and well-being." But (8) contradicts (4). Since every agent must accept (4), he must reject (8). And since (8) follows from the denial of (5), every agent must reject that denial, so that he must accept (5) "I have rights to freedom and well-being." (Ibid., 205–206)

Williams, I suspect, reads (7) as stating that PPAO has a claim right to interfere with my freedom and well-being. If it is necessary to do this, then the argument suggests that to deny that I have a claim right to my freedom and well-being is to grant PPAO a claim right to interfere with my freedom and well-being. But why should (7) be read in this way? Williams, I think, reads it in this way because he contends that (4) can only be validly read as stating "I ought to want my freedom and well-being not to be interfered with" / "I ought to pursue my freedom and well-being" (not as "I ought to have my freedom and well-being"), and that, if so, the argument is only valid if the denial of (6) is (7) in which "permissible" is given a claim rights sense.

However, *if* (4) can legitimately be read as "I ought to have my freedom and well-being," then (7) will contradict (4), whether "permissible" is given a claim rights sense or the sense of "not impermissible." Furthermore, no equivocation will be involved if "It is not impermissible for PPAO to interfere with my freedom and well-being" contradicts (contrary to Williams' assertion) "I ought to want my freedom and well-being"/"I ought to pursue my freedom and well-being."

Pointing this out, however, leads directly on to (*b*). The answer to (*a*) really depends on the answer to (*b*).

Why does Williams think that the egoist's position is dialectically consistent? Williams' reasoning might be that from

(A)   It is not impermissible (and no more) for me to pursue any purpose I want to achieve,

and

(B)   I categorically need my freedom and well-being in order to achieve any purpose I want to achieve,

no more can be inferred than

(C)   I have no more than a mere liberty to defend my freedom and well-being from interference, whatever my purposes.

However, while it is the case that this is all that can be inferred *assertorically, dialectically, from my internal viewpoint*, given that, *as a PPA*, I am proactively motivated to pursue my purposes (i.e., I am "conatively normal"), it can be inferred from (B) that

(D)   I ought to defend my freedom and well-being from interference, for whatever my purposes.

Now (D), which Williams effectively concedes (by conceding that I ought to act to secure my freedom and well-being), is stronger than "It is not impermissible for me to pursue my freedom and well-being." This "ought" does not just state that I have a prudential reason to defend my freedom and well-being from interference, for whatever my purposes (that it would be [instrumentally prudentially] *reasonable* ["all right," "not wrong"] for me to defend my freedom and well-being from interference, whatever my purposes).[4] It states, "I am categorically instrumentally prudentially irrational if I do not defend my freedom and well-being from interference," which is equivalent to "I have a prudential instrumental duty to defend my freedom and well-being from interference." The presence of (A) in the egoist's thinking does not cancel this requirement. The egoist is required to hold "I do wrong not to pursue my freedom and well-being" together with "PPAO does no wrong by interfering with my freedom and well-being." If *this* is consistent, then Gewirth's argument for Stage II fails. But is it consistent? Certainly, it is consistent for me to say "It is impermissible *from my point of view* (on the criterion of my purposes) for me not to pursue my freedom and well-being; and it is not impermissible *from PPAO's point of view* (on the criterion of PPAO's purposes) for PPAO to interfere with my freedom and well-being." But the argument is conducted strictly within my internal viewpoint as a PPA. What might be the case on the criterion of PPAO's purposes, or how things might be from PPAO's point of view, is either question-begging or irrelevant.[5] What matters is what follows on the criterion of my purposes from my point of view.

Now, Gewirth argues (in inferring [4d] from [4c]—my numbers) that from "It is impermissible for me not to pursue my freedom and well-being," it follows within the same viewpoint, and on the same criterion, that it is impermissible for PPAO to interfere with my freedom and well-being. This is because I *categorically* need my freedom and well-being; as such I need it to pursue/secure my freedom and well-being; and if I believe that I ought to do X, I must believe that I ought to have the means to do X. If this is so, and Gewirth complains that Williams does not consider this aspect of his argument (see Gewirth 1988a, 146), then the egoist's position, which holds that it is not impermissible for PPAO to interfere with my freedom and well-being, is dialectically inconsistent.

In other words, by saying that a PPA might not be "in the business of making rules," Williams suggests that whether or not a PPA considers itself/others bound by rules is a matter entirely at a PPA's discretion. But, as Williams himself effectively concedes, a PPA has no discretion to reject the rule that it (instrumentally) ought to pursue its own freedom and well-being; and the question of whether or not a PPA must consider (within its own viewpoint) that PPAO is bound by the rule "PPAO ought not to interfere with my freedom and well-being (against my will)" is solely a question of whether a rule addressing a requirement of noninterference to PPAO follows logically from the self-referring rule that the PPA must accept.

It is no argument against this (which argument might also be suggested by the phrase "not being in the business of making rules") that a PPA might will that PPAO interfere with its freedom and well-being, or (at least) not will that PPAO not (try to) interfere with its freedom and well-being (where the PPA wills the end of its agency as an end in itself, or wills the opportunity to [try to] overcome attempted interference as an end in itself). These stances only contradict "PPAO ought not to interfere with my freedom and well-being" where this rule is categorically intrinsic. They do not contradict it as categorically instrumental (correlative to a formulation as "PPAO ought not to interfere with my freedom and well-being *against my will*"—for interference, or attempted interference, is not, in these cases, against my will. See Chapter 2).

Furthermore, I have elaborated Gewirth's argument from attitudinal consistency to demonstrate that "I must want my freedom and well-being not to be interfered with" contradicts "It is not impermissible (from my viewpoint) for PPAO to interfere with my freedom and well-being." (See #13.)

Thus, Gewirth does not have to assume (falsely), in order to secure Stage II, that to deny "I have a claim right to my freedom and well-being" is for me to grant PPAO a claim right to interfere with my freedom and well-being.[6]

#31   **A PPA's need for freedom and well-being is motivation for a PPA to demand or secure noninterference with its freedom and well-being, but provides no justification for this demand or activity.**

1 Regis
According to Gewirth, the "ought" correlative to a rights-claim to its freedom and well-being, which a PPA addresses to others (my [4d]), has four features in the eyes of a PPA:

1.   it is a requirement that the PPA endorses for the conduct of PPAO;
2.   it is a requirement grounded in a reason (the PPA's categorical need for its freedom and well-being);
3.   this reason justifies the PPA in preventing interference with its freedom and well-being by PPAO; and
4.   noninterference with its freedom and well-being is due to the PPA. (See RM 79.)

Edward Regis objects that a PPA is not required to view the matter in line with any of these features.

Regarding 1: He says that, although a rational PPA will probably want noninterference with its freedom and well-being, it does not follow that it will on that account demand noninterference. It may do so, but this is not sufficient. Gewirth denies that a PPA can rest content with the realization that its freedom and well-being are factually necessary for achievement of its ends. Its ascriptions of necessity must carry its endorsement. But what does it mean to endorse necessity? (See Regis 1981, 787–788.)

In reply, it is to be pointed out that, as means to its actions for purposes, it is not a case of a rational PPA probably wanting its freedom and well-being. It, quite categorically, must want its freedom and well-being and, hence, *must* demand noninterference, and take whatever steps it can to secure noninterference. (See Gewirth 1982e, 405.) The significance of the fact that a PPA categorically needs its freedom and well-being is not merely factual. It requires a PPA to act in specific ways, correlative to which it must judge that it ought to do so. Because it must have its freedom and well-being in order to comply with this "ought," must have PPAO not interfere with its freedom and well-being, it must judge that PPAO ought not to interfere with its freedom and well-being. This "ought" is prudentially grounded, grounded in the PPA's interests. When Gewirth says that a PPA endorses "its ascriptions of necessity," he means that it endorses this "ought"—he does not mean that the PPA endorses "necessity" (which, I suppose, would mean that it prescribes that it ought to need its freedom and well-being); and this means that the PPA employs the criterion of its purposes as the criterion for what it and others ought to do.

Regarding 2: Regis says,

Gewirth shows at most that the agent's reason can motivate his issuing the requirement, and offers nothing to show that his reason justifies it. (Regis 1981, 788–789)

Here, again, it must be pointed out that we are not dealing with a case of something that *can* motivate a PPA. A PPA *must* be motivated to defend its freedom and well-being, or give up all purposes and cease to be a PPA. Now, as Gewirth says,

[t]o justify something is to show or establish that it is right or correct according to [required/allowed by] some relevant criterion, and the criterion is here prudential, consisting in the agent's need for the necessary conditions of action. (Gewirth 1982e, 405)

It is true, of course, that a PPA can want to do X, for which it needs Y, and so can say that its desire for X justifies its having Y. So it could be said that this is not justification in the relevant sense ("strict justification"), because the PPA can regard X itself as more definitively unjustified. However, this misses the point that a PPA cannot have this attitude towards its freedom and well-being as generic features of its agency. For, whatever its purposes, it has at least prima facie justification for having its freedom and well-being, and can only fail to accept this justification by denying that it is a PPA. A PPA can, in fact, only deny that it has at least prima facie strict justification for having its freedom and well-being by holding that it is impermissible for it to do anything at all, and this is not a coherent view for a PPA to espouse. (See Chapter 3, the first summary.)

Of course, this justification will not be assertoric, or *necessarily* justification, from every PPA's point of view. It is necessarily justification only from the PPA's own point of view. But, since the argument is conducted strictly within a PPA's internal point of view, no other justification is required or relevant.

Regarding 3: Regis maintains that a requirement with the reason for *issuing* it cannot justify *enforcing* the requirement. (See Regis 1981, 789.)

Here, Regis fails to perceive that the reason for enforcing the having of my freedom and well-being is in fact logically prior to my reason for issuing the claim that I ought to have my freedom and well-being, or any reason I might have for demanding my freedom and well-being.

What does it mean to enforce a demand? It means, surely, to take steps that will prevent or punish (with a view to prevention) action contrary to the demand. Now, by being required to defend my freedom and well-being from interference, I have justification for "enforcing" noninterference with my freedom and well-being, and it is from this justification that my justification for considering that I have a right to my freedom and well-being is derived. We are simply not dealing with a situation, which might exist in some other contexts, where I have a reason to hold that X ought to do Y, but require additional reason to enforce X's doing Y.

Finally, regarding 4: Regis claims that this must be unsatisfied because 2 is unsatisfied. (See ibid.)

My response to this can be brief. Since 2 does not fail, 4 does not fail either.

2 Veatch

According to Henry B. Veatch (commenting on Gewirth 1972 and 1974a), Stages I and III are unassailable, but an "amoralist" can evade Stage II because it does not regard its purposes as good in the sense of being justified (in the sense of having a right to them). It merely wants its purposes to be fulfilled. This means that Gewirth equivocates between "moral" and "nonmoral" senses of good (which Veatch treats as synonymous with "justified" and "neutral with respect to justification"). (See Veatch 1976, 284 n. 11.)

To this, Gewirth replies that Veatch does not attend to the fact that the rights-claims in the argument only attach to necessary goods, so that it is irrelevant that a PPA might not consider that it has rights to its particular occurrent purposes. Furthermore, he objects to Veatch's definition of "moral" versus "nonmoral," for this restricts rights to moral rights. Gewirth emphasizes that the rights-claims of Stage II are prudential (justification on self-regarding grounds being claimed) rather than moral, and that they become moral claims only in Stage III. (See Gewirth 1976, 290–293.)

This is a fair comment. However, it is possible that Veatch is claiming that a PPA might try to evade the argument by eschewing altogether the category of "justification" (whether moral, prudential, or otherwise as Gewirth defines these). If so, Veatch's objection is that Gewirth equivocates between a PPA having a motivating reason to pursue/demand its freedom and well-being, and a PPA having a justifying reason to pursue/demand/have its freedom and well-being.[7]

If so, my response is the same as that given to Regis under #31.1.2.

3 Nielsen

Kai Nielsen makes two claims that can be considered under this heading. The first is that,

while all right-claims may be demands, not all demands are right-claims. Rational agents, where this is necessary, will make demands that the essential prerequisites of their action not be interfered with, but they need not make these demands by way of a right-claim either moral or prudential. (Nielsen 1984, 71)

The second is that to attempt to derive "I ought to pursue my freedom and well-being" from "My freedom and well-being are necessary goods" is to

say that ought-talk here just comes to expressions of intentions [which] is to commit oneself to a very problematic reductionist meta-ethical thesis indeed. (Ibid., 80)

Both of these claims, in effect, contend that Gewirth tries, without any possibility of success, to derive reasons of justification from reasons of motivation.

In response to the first claim, it must be conceded that not all demands are rights-claims. I can demand something without claiming/considering that I have a right to it. However, a demand that is based on a justifying reason (and a demand that a PPA must make on pain of contradicting itself has the strongest possible justifying reason [for that PPA]), is hardly a mere demand. If I am simply motivated to do something, then this motivation does not provide me with a justifying reason of any kind. On the other hand, if I rationally must be motivated to do something, then the case is very different. Nielsen seems to think that a PPA can fulfill the need to be consistent with "My freedom and well-being are necessary goods" if it demands that PPAO not interfere with its freedom and well-being, and acts to secure noninterference with its freedom and well-being, without considering that it has a right to its freedom and well-being or that it ought to defend its freedom and well-being (this "ought" being the claim from which the rights-claim is derived). (See #28.) The problem with this is that we are not dealing with a case of a PPA's just happening to think that its freedom and well-being are good for whatever its purposes. We are dealing with a case of a PPA's rationally having to think so. Action to secure its freedom and well-being, coupled with belief that its freedom and well-being are good for whatever its purposes, might be consistent without an accompanying judgment that it ought to defend its freedom and well-being from interference. But this will not stand up when it is appreciated that a PPA rationally must regard its freedom and well-being as necessary goods. This puts a strict "ought" constraint upon its acting to secure its freedom and well-being, recognition of which can only be expressed as an "ought" judgment.

One possibility that might explain why Nielsen is willing to accept that a PPA, if rational, must pursue its freedom and well-being but need not accept that it prudentially "ought" to do so (leading to its claiming a prudential right to its freedom and well-being), is that he holds that the notion of an "ought" involves more than the notion of a "reason." It involves the idea of justification or warrant. Nielsen cannot say that I just have a motivating reason to pursue my freedom and well-being, for I also have a reason to be motivated to pursue my freedom and well-being—as explained above. What Nielsen may be claiming, however, is that justification relative to my purposivity is only justification for me, and that the relevant justification for rights and duties is justification for everyone. On the latter notion, Stage II cannot establish that I must consider that I have a right to my freedom and well-being, unless it establishes that I must consider that PPAO must consider (on grounds accepted by PPAO) that it ought not to interfere with my freedom and well-being. This it cannot do (see #35). However, unless the notion of justification in the eyes of one person only is an incoherent one, it hardly matters whether it is proper to talk of (4c) and (4d) as prescribing duties and (5) as prescribing rights. All that matters is whether (4c), (4d), and (5), involving the notion of justification for me, requires *me*, by *internal* application of the logical principle of universalizability, to accept that PPAO's categorical need for its freedom and well-being is *justification for me* why I should not interfere with the freedom and well-being of PPAO. If this is valid, then subsequent *external* application of the logical principle of universalizability will require PPAO to accept that my categorical need for freedom and well-being is justification for it why I ought to have my freedom and well-being, and the PGC will be secured. The issue, here, is whether justification claims need to be acceptable to others before they can be universalized. Nielsen, in fact, claims that this is so. I discuss, and reject, this under #47 and (specifically in relation to Nielsen) under #48.

Here, we need to consider, briefly, whether the notion of justification for one person only is coherent. It does not seem to me that it can be incoherent—for the simple reason that the idea of justification for everyone presupposes the idea of justification for each. What is involved in PPAO's considering that it ought not to interfere with my freedom and well-being is that on its criteria, it ought not to do so. If this makes sense, then the idea that PPAO ought not to interfere with my freedom and well-being on my criteria must make equal sense.

The second claim is false. Gewirth does not reduce "ought" talk to expressions of intentions. He analyzes the PPA's self-referring "ought" of (4c) in terms of *rationally required* intentions. There is nothing in the least problematic about saying that "ought" talk expresses what PPAs are *required* to do (intend to do) on some criterion of rationality (indeed, what else does it express?); and if they are rationally required (in Gewirth's logical sense) to do something, then they are required to do this on whatever more restricted criteria of rationality they might happen to espouse.

#32   **The fact that a PPA need value its freedom and well-being only instrumentally means that a PPA need not claim a right to its freedom and well-being.**

According to James O. Grunebaum (considering Gewirth 1974a), a "reluctant protagonist," who assents to the logical implications of his prior statements, and offers no unnecessary responses, need not accept Stage II. This is because a PPA is required to value its freedom and well-being *only* instrumentally. Its freedom and well-being must be valued instrumentally as means to its actions, which must be valued as means to its purposes. However, a PPA is

not required to place any categorical or intrinsic value on his freedom or
basic well-being or on his actions (Grunebaum 1976, 276),

because it is not required to place any intrinsic or categorical value
on its purposes. This means that its claiming a right to its freedom
and well-being will depend upon its claiming a right to at least some
of its particular occurrent purposes. Without begging the question
from the start, PPAs cannot be assumed to claim that they have any
rights.[8]

Gewirth responds that this is not so, because from the fact that a
PPA's freedom and well-being are at least instrumentally necessary
for all its actions for purposes,

> it by no means follows that the agent values his freedom and his basic well-
> being only instrumentally. For he performs some of his actions for their own
> sakes, and since freedom and basic well-being are generic features of all
> action, he therefore at least implicitly values these features for their own
> sakes. Hence, he will not limit the value they have for him to what pertains
> only to some, not to all actions . . . . (Gewirth 1976, 289)

This reply creates two problems. First, it might appear to contradict my claim that a PPA need not value its freedom and well-being
any more than instrumentally, meaning that it need not value it
intrinsically. (See Chapter 2.) Second, any sense in which it might be
true that a PPA must value its freedom and basic well-being "for
their own sakes" does not seem to tackle Grunebaum's objection
directly, for Grunebaum appears to be saying that, in order for a PPA
to have to claim a right to its freedom and well-being, it must have
to claim a right (perhaps even a moral right)[9] to at least some of its
particular occurrent purposes. For Grunebaum, to attach a "categorical" or "intrinsic" value to a purpose is to value it either *deontically*
or morally, either as an end in itself or as a means to something that
is valued either deontically or morally as an end in itself. Gewirth
cannot mean that PPAs (necessarily) perform some of their actions
for their own sakes *in this sense* without begging the question against
adeonticists and amoralists. Gewirth's reply bears clearly only on a
claim that a PPA must value its freedom and well-being *only* instrumentally. But even this seems to miss the mark, as Grunebaum does
not say that a PPA must value its freedom and well-being only instrumentally, but that a PPA need not value its freedom and well-
being more than instrumentally. To counter Grunebaum's objection
it is necessary to show that a PPA need not value any of its particular
occurrent purposes in Grunebaum's sense of "intrinsic" for it to be
committed to claiming a right to its freedom and well-being. It is not
enough to show that a PPA must value its freedom and well-being *at*

least instrumentally—which, whatever else, is Gewirth's clearly stated position.

First, then, what is Gewirth's position? In "The 'Is-Ought' Problem Resolved," he states that

because freedom and basic well-being are at least instrumentally necessary to all the agent's actions for purposes, . . . [the agent must claim] "My freedom and basic well-being are good as the necessary conditions of all my actions." (Gewirth 1974a in Gewirth 1982b, 118)

This is equivalent to my view that a PPA must consider that its freedom and basic well-being are categorically instrumentally good. In a sense, a PPA must attach categorical or intrinsic value to its freedom and basic well-being, but only *as* the necessary means to the very possibility of its agency. In this sense (sense 1), a PPA must attach intrinsic value to its freedom and basic well-being, whether or not it attaches intrinsic value in Grunebaum's sense to any of its particular occurrent purposes.

However, in *Reason and Morality,* Gewirth claims that a PPA must consider its *freedom* to be "intrinsically" good as well. Of freedom as an *instrumental* good, he says that

the agent's control of his own behavior serves . . . as a means to attaining his ends. He not only controls his behavior, but he wants to control it with a view to such attainment, so that any threat to this control is perceived as a threat to his getting what he regards as good. (RM 52)

Of freedom as an *intrinsic* good, he says that

the agent also regards his freedom as intrinsically good, simply because it is an essential component of purposive action and indeed of the very possibility of action. This is shown by the fact that when he is subjected to violence, coercion, or physical constraint, he may react negatively, with dislike, annoyance, dissatisfaction, anger, hostility, outrage, or similar negative emotions, even when he has no further specific end in view. (Ibid.)

One difficulty created by this is that I do not see how this sort of "intrinsic" valuation goes beyond what I have called "categorical instrumental valuation." Perhaps it is not intended to do so. If so, then the problem can be partly resolved by reading Gewirth's use of "instrumental valuation" as "valuation dependent upon the valuation of my particular occurrent purposes" (in such a way that I am required to attach only the kind of value to my freedom that I attach to the purposes for which it is a necessary condition), and his use of "intrinsic valuation" as "valuation that is required by my having purposes (which depends upon my purposivity as such), but that is independent of what my specific purposes might be." However, although this makes Gewirth's "intrinsic valuation" equivalent to my "categorical instrumental valuation," unless there is here a retraction of the view that a PPA must consider its freedom and well-being to be *at least* instrumentally good, there is at least terminological confusion, even if no contradiction, between this view and that of the 1974 article. For why say that I must consider my freedom to be *at least* instrumentally good, if I *must* consider it to be intrinsically good as well?

Indeed, there is a further problem interpreting Gewirth here. Gewirth never appears to state, at least so far as I have noticed, that a PPA must consider its *basic well-being* to be intrinsically good as well. But, if my freedom must be regarded as intrinsically good because it is a precondition of the very possibility of my agency, then I must also be required to regard my basic well-being as intrinsically good.

I confess that it is possible that I have misunderstood Gewirth in reading his "intrinsic valuation" as my "intrinsic valuation in sense 1," and that Gewirth does not, in his intended sense, hold that I must value my basic well-being intrinsically. If so, I have missed what he means by "valuing my freedom intrinsically." It is possible that Gewirth is here drawing attention to his contention that voluntariness represents the procedural aspect of agency, whereas purposiveness represents the substantive aspect of agency. In part, this means that

purposiveness . . . , unlike voluntariness, involves intrinsic reference to the end or goal the agent envisages for his action . . . [(RM 39), and that] voluntariness or freedom, unlike purposiveness, is not conceptually tied to ends or purposes . . . . (RM 52)

However, while this is suggestive of a possible distinction between freedom and basic well-being on the front of instrumental versus intrinsic valuation, I do not really comprehend what this distinction might be. So, rather than pursue what is likely to be a red herring, I shall assume that Gewirth holds that I must regard both my freedom and basic well-being to be "intrinsically" good, but only in sense 1; and I shall reply to Grunebaum on the basis of the general view that I stated in Chapter 2.

In Chapter 2 I distinguished three senses of "intrinsic" valuation.

1. X has intrinsic value for a PPA if it is of categorical instrumental value to PPA's agency—if it must be valued as a means to PPA's actions/purposes, whatever its purposes might be (must be valued *deontically as a means to its purposes*). (This can be called a case of "intrinsic" value in that a PPA, *with its continuing agency in mind*, that is to say, within the context of its being a PPA, or qua PPA, must

value its freedom and well-being *intrinsically.* The emphasis on this as being equivalent to categorical *instrumental* value is to insist that a PPA can act to terminate its agency, because it can view its being a PPA outside of its being a PPA—in its capacity as a thinking or valuing being. As such a being, it need not value its freedom and well-being as an end in itself.)

2. X has intrinsic value for a PPA if the PPA does not value X as a means to its actions/purposes, but as an end in itself.[10]

3. X has intrinsic value for a PPA if the PPA considers that it ought (morally, or in some other deontic sense) to value X, *as an end in itself,* or because X is a necessary means to what the PPA considers that it ought to value as an end in itself.

My view is that a PPA must value its freedom and well-being intrinsically in sense 1, but need not do so in sense 2 or 3. Grunebaum appears to be saying that a PPA need claim no right to its freedom and well-being, because it categorically needs its freedom and well-being, *unless* it must value some of its purposes intrinsically in sense 3, and that it *need* not value its freedom and well-being in this sense.

The real issue raised by Grunebaum's objection, which is partly obscured by Gewirth's reply, and perhaps missed altogether by Grunebaum (because he does not differentiate clearly, if at all, between contingent and categorical instrumental valuation), is whether the necessity for freedom and well-being requires me to value my freedom and well-being in a categorically instrumental manner or, if so, whether *categorical instrumental valuation* is sufficient to ground my rights-claim.

In other words, Grunebaum's contention has force only if the only sort of instrumental valuation possible is contingent upon my particular occurrent purposes (Stage I, therefore, being invalid) or if (4d) "PPAO ought not to interfere with my freedom and well-being as necessary means to my purposes" cannot be derived from (4c) "I ought to pursue my freedom and well-being as necessary means to my purposes."

In relation to the first option, Grunebaum seems to think that, because a PPA's valuation of its freedom and well-being derives from the fact that it values its purposes, it cannot be the case that a PPA must value its freedom and well-being independent of the sorts of values it attaches to its particular occurrent purposes. But, even if a PPA attaches no deontic value to its particular occurrent purposes, it must attach a deontic instrumental value to its freedom and well-being. That this value is deontic derives from the fact that it must value it for whatever its purposes, thus independent of the sort of values that it attaches to any of its purposes specifically.

On the second option Grunebaum says nothing, the premise for Stage II being treated as a contingent instrumental "ought," not as a strict one (deontic or categorical, albeit instrumental). Once it is seen to be a strict "ought," that it is an instrumental "ought" nonetheless merely means that a PPA is not prohibited from valuing termination of its agency in *sense 3*. Far from it being the case that deontic instrumental valuation is not correlative to rights-claims, it is precisely the instrumental character of my proactively required valuation of my freedom and well-being that explains why the rights I must claim are ones that I can waive (if I do not value my freedom and well-being in sense 3). To show this, of course, it must be shown that (4d) can be derived from (4c), and to do this it would be necessary to repeat Stage II of the argument as I have presented it. This is not necessary here, for Grunebaum does not attack the specific steps in this inference; he presents a general a priori objection to the stage, which does not properly comprehend what its starting premise is.

#33   **Ethical egoism does not prescribe that PPAO has a duty not to interfere with my freedom and well-being. Because the ethical egoist maxim "Every PPA ought to act in its own self-interest" has only "regional force," Gewirth's argument that ethical egoism is internally inconsistent fails.**

This criticism is made by Jesse Kalin (1984) in response to Gewirth's refutation of "universal ethical egoism" in *Reason and Morality*. The debate between Gewirth and Kalin is complex, and confusing, so it is necessary to begin with a statement of Gewirth's position.

Gewirth's Refutation of Universal Ethical Egoism

If it is dialectically necessary for me to hold that PPAO has a duty not to interfere with my freedom and well-being ([4d]), then it must be dialectically inconsistent for me to espouse any practical maxim that does not prescribe (4d). Ethical egoism "of the universalist sort," which holds "each person ought to act only for his own respective self-interest" (RM 82), does not prescribe (4d), and in fact denies it, by advocating that PPAO ought to interfere with my freedom and well-being (if to do so is in PPAO's self-interest). At the same time, ethical egoism upholds that my freedom and well-being are necessary goods ([4]; because my freedom and well-being consti-

tute, or are necessary means to, my self-interest). Thus, ethical egoism holds (4) and not-(4d) together.

Gewirth's arguments for (4) entailing (4d) (see RM 78–82, 89–97),
if valid, render ethical egoism *dialectically* inconsistent. Indeed, they
render any position that does not prescribe (4d) dialectically inconsistent.

However, as I understand Gewirth, he also claims that ethical
egoism is to be rejected because it is *internally* inconsistent (although
this charge is not always as clearly separated from the charge of
dialectical inconsistency as I would like).

Inasmuch as there is a separate argument that ethical egoism is
internally inconsistent, it is as follows: By accepting (4), I, as an
ethical egoist, must hold, employing *my criterion* of *my own* self-interest, that my freedom and well-being strictly ought to be protected
and not interfered with. At the same time, as an ethical egoist, I must
hold, employing *my criterion* of *PPAO's* self-interest, that it is not the
case that my freedom and well-being strictly ought not to be interfered with (because such interference might be in PPAO's self-interest). (See RM 83.)

> Universal ethical egoism requires that the egoist take impartially the posi-
> tion of each person acting for his own respective self-interest and that he
> have the criterion of his 'oughts' reflect their respective self-interests, even
> when this is opposed to his own self-interest as an agent, with its freedom
> and well-being. But as an agent, he must also regard his freedom and well-
> being as necessary goods, and hence he cannot impartially accept as crite-
> rion of his 'oughts' the self-interest of other persons when this conflicts with
> his freedom and well-being. Thus, a person cannot consistently be both an
> agent and a universal ethical egoist. (RM 84)[11]

According to Gewirth, attempted answers to this argument confront the ethical egoist with two interrelated dilemmas.

> If he is to avoid upholding incompatible and self-defeating directives
> ["PPAO ought not to interfere with my freedom and well-being" and "PPAO
> ought to interfere with my freedom and well-being"], he must at least incur
> equivocation, and his egoism cannot be universal. But if he avoids equivoca-
> tion and maintains universality, he must uphold incompatible and self-de-
> feating directives. (RM 86)

This dilemma arises because, in order to be a *universal* position,
the "ought" in "Each ought to act respectively for his own self-interest" must have the same sense no matter what PPA is addressed
by "each." As applied to my own actions, this "ought" is unquali-
fiedly prescriptive, involving my own endorsement (and, on its criterion of my own self-interest, entails my prescribing "PPAO ought
not to interfere with my freedom and well-being"—because such

noninterference is necessary for my self-interest). If it is unquali-
fiedly prescriptive, with the same illocutionary force when I apply it
to PPAO's actions, then the result is incompatible directives (for *I*
prescribe "PPAO ought to interfere with my freedom and well-
being," when this interference is in PPAO's self-interest). To avoid
this result, the "ought" I apply to PPAO's actions must not be un-
qualifiedly prescriptive (must not involve my unqualified endorsement). It must be either "hypothetical" ("*If* PPAO is to follow the
maxim of ethical egoism then it ought to act for its own self-interest"),[12] or "prima facie" ("PPAO ought to act in its own self-interest
provided that this does not interfere with my self-interest"). But then
"equivocation at least of illocutionary force" is involved, so that the
position is not universal. (See RM 85.)

Gewirth claims that this equivocation can be avoided by treating
the

'Formal' Basic Rule of the Universal Egoistic Life-Game: each and every
person ought to act only for his own respective self-interest . . . [as a] primary, definitive commitment to the universal life of struggle and conflict.
(RM 87)

By doing this, both the "ought" in "I ought to pursue my self-interest" and the "ought" in "PPAO ought to pursue its self-interest"
are given the same force. Both now carry the same *qualified* endorsement. Whatever my and PPAO's respective self-interested wants
might be, each of us ought to pursue these wants only if they involve conflict and competition. (See RM 86–87.)

However, this incurs a second dilemma:

If he maintains his universal egoism with its primary, definitive commitment
to the Formal Rules of the Universal Egoistic Life-Game, then he is not really
an egoist in the sense of a person whose primary, definitive commitment is
to the pursuit and maximization of his own self-interest, for he would endorse directives that violate his self-interest. If, on the other hand, he maintains this latter, egoistic commitment as his primary and definitive one, then
he cannot maintain his *universal* egoism with its primary, definitive commitment to the universal life of struggle and conflict. (RM 87)

Kalin's Response to Gewirth

As I have done, Kalin portrays Gewirth as having two arguments
against ethical egoism. The first is the argument that ethical egoism
prescribes contradictory directives, which can be avoided only by
incurring Gewirth's dilemmas (the charge of internal inconsistency). The second, which he calls the "direct" argument, is
Gewirth's argument that even an "amoralist" must accept a self-referring "ought" judgment, on the basis of which it must prescribe

that PPAO not interfere with its freedom and well-being (the charge of dialectical inconsistency, which, of course, I have presented as Gewirth's central argument for Stage II). Although Kalin says that these two arguments are related, the "first" drawing on the "direct" argument, he treats them separately and in fact implies that they are independent, because he says that

[w]hen the attempt to show egoism to be inconsistent fails, Gewirth will have to fall back on this more basic argument [i.e., the "direct" one]. (Kalin 1984, 130)

Kalin rejects both the inconsistency charge and the "direct" argument. I shall deal primarily with his treatment of the inconsistency charge here, and specifically with his rejection of the "direct" argument under #35.3.

Kalin maintains that ethical egoism does not involve contradictory beliefs, and can be both direction-giving and nonequivocal in its criteria and the meaning of its deontic terms. (See ibid., 132.)

He begins by restating what he says is the traditional way of formulating ethical egoism, namely, "A person ought, all things considered, to do an action if and only if that action is in his own overall interest," as

A person has conclusive reasons, all things considered, to do an action if and only if that action is in his own overall self-interest. (Ibid., 129)

He asks,

What must an egoist *believe* to be the case . . . if he believes (a) that only his own overall self-interest gives him (directly) reasons for acting, and (b) that only others' own overall self-interests give them (directly) reasons for acting? (Ibid., 131–132)

Gewirth, he says, answers (inter alia), with respect to himself (on the criterion of the egoist's own self-interest),

4. All other persons ought at least to refrain from interfering with my freedom and well-being[; and]
6. It is not the case that I ought at least to refrain from interfering with the freedom and well-being of others[;]

and with respect to others (on the criterion of others' self-interest)

iv. I ought at least to refrain from interfering with their freedom and well-being[; and]
vi. It is not the case that others ought at least to refrain from interfering with my freedom and well-being. (Ibid., 132)

Gewirth maintains that 4 contradicts vi, and 6 contradicts iv.

Kalin responds by saying that "what is in question is not action but belief . . . which is prior to action and governing of it" (ibid.). In line with this, 4 and 6 must be reformulated as (on the criterion of what is needful to me)

4*.   . . . I have conclusive reasons to have all other persons at least refrain from interfering with my freedom and well-being[; and]

6*.   . . . [I]t is not the case that I never have conclusive reasons to not refrain from interfering with the freedom and well-being of others.

Similarly, iv and vi must be reformulated (on the criterion of what is needful to others) as

iv*.   . . . [Others] have conclusive reasons to have me at least refrain from interfering with their freedom and well-being[; and]

vi*.   . . . [I]t is not the case that others never have conclusive reasons to not refrain from interfering with my freedom and well-being. (Ibid., 133)

According to Kalin, 4* is consistent with vi*, and 6* is consistent with iv*.

In attempting to identify what he sees as Gewirth's error, Kalin maintains that, according to ethical egoism, an agent's wants, needs, desires, and valuings have only "regional force." This means that only an agent's wants, needs, etc., give *that agent* (nonderivative) reasons for acting. My needs give me reasons to act; they do not (nonderivatively, i.e., independently of PPAO's self-interest) give PPAO any reason to do anything. PPAO's needs give PPAO reasons to act; they do not (nonderivatively) give me any reason to do anything. (See ibid., 134–135.) In holding that PPAO might have a good (indeed, a conclusive) reason (for PPAO) to harm PPA, PPA

is certainly not *giving* permission to others to harm him . . . . He is not *prescribing* that they harm him, though he does believe that this is what reason can tell them to do. (Ibid., 135)

Gewirth, says Kalin, supposes that by believing iv* and vi* "the egoist is *doing* something he cannot get away with. But he is *doing* nothing at all" (ibid.).

According to Kalin, Gewirth believes that the egoist must be prescribing that others harm it (when this is in their interests) because he supposes that "[w]hat a rational person necessarily judges when he makes practical judgments is what determinate ends are to be held as goods by everyone" (ibid., 136). If this were so, then what the egoist must mean, when it says that PPAO ought to pursue its own self-interest, is that it ought to be the case that harm to the egoist's freedom and well-being be brought about (when this is in PPAO's self-interest). If so, then there is a contradiction, and the egoist is caught in Gewirth's first dilemma. But, in fact, ethical egoism holds that

there is no one end that is to be held as unconditionally good by everyone. . . . [The egoist denies] that there is anything—any state of affairs—that ought to be the case. Rather, all there are are individual interests (and needs), and it is these that give their possessors reasons for acting one way rather than another. . . .

. . . [W]hile the egoist may think or say "A ought to do X" . . . , what he properly means is not that it ought to be the case that this state of affairs exist but only that "the most reasonable thing for A to do is X," which is consistent with the further judgment that there is nothing—no state of affairs at all— which is *the most* reasonable thing *to be done*. States of affairs are not reasonable (or good) in themselves, but only in relation to the interests (needs) of specific persons (and hence only good-to——, good-for——, or good-as——). (Ibid., 136–137)

Thus, the egoist can avoid Gewirth's first dilemma, for the "deontic validatives" in ethical egoism have the same sense in all their occurrences, viz., "the most reasonable thing for someone to do is what is in his own self-interest."

As far as the second dilemma goes, Kalin denies that the egoist is committed to unconditional endorsement of "a universal life of struggle and conflict." The only good that the egoist must endorse unconditionally is its own self-interest. Struggle is not to be set up as a good-in-itself, but may have to be accepted as a means to achieving the egoist's self-interest. (See ibid., 137–138.)

Kalin identifies the basic disagreement between Gewirth and the egoist as one about the nature and theoretical status of practical principles, and about what is involved in applying a principle universally or impartially. The egoist, in seeking to formulate ultimate principles, asks, "What am *I* to do?" In so doing, it begins with the belief that goods are only relative and that reasons for acting have only relative directive force. If this is so, then

universalization, outside some subsequent context of conventions and agreements [endorsement of which will be "essentially instrumental and thus contingent on promotion of one's overall self-interest"], is a matter of logical implication and formal consistency only. What it requires, and thus *commits* one to, are beliefs and their consequences consistent with [this] original body of belief. . . . [U]niversalization cannot add something new. Between persons, this sort of universalization requires only agreement in propositional holdings. (Ibid., 139)

As I understand this, Kalin is saying that from "It is rational for me to guide my actions by my self-interest" it follows that I must hold, by universalization, only that "It is rational for PPAO to guide its actions by its self-interest." It does not follow that I must endorse the consequences of PPAO's following its self-interest, in the sense of having a favorable attitude towards this.

On the other hand, according to Kalin, for Gewirth the fundamental question is, "What are *we* to do?" Gewirth has a "view of practical reasoning as a necessarily *interpersonal activity of sharing* principles" (ibid.). He is asking "What states of affairs are to be recommended as good to everyone?" on the assumption that there is a state of affairs that is good for everyone. On this basis, and only on this basis, is it natural to think of adopting ethical egoism as involving endorsement of the consequences of the principle applied to PPAO. To get this consequence, Gewirth must employ an augmented notion of "universalization," which rests, not on logic alone, but on this basis. (See ibid., 139–140.)

Here, I take Kalin to be saying that Gewirth can only get [Ethical egoism entails "I endorse the consequences of PPAO pursuing its own self-interest"] if I (an egoist) treat "I have a conclusive reason to pursue my self-interest" as entailing "PPAO has a conclusive reason to pursue my self-interest" (and conversely "PPAO has a conclusive reason to pursue its self-interest" as entailing "I have a conclusive reason to pursue PPAO's self-interest"). This, however, relies on more than just logical universalization; it relies on the assumption that goods are not relative, that practical judgments based on them do not have only relative prescriptive force, that what I have good reason to pursue (my own self-interest) PPAO has good reason to pursue (my self-interest). According to Kalin, an egoist does not hold this, so Gewirth's argument against the egoist fails.

At this point in his critique, Kalin turns to an examination of what he calls Gewirth's direct argument against ethical egoism. As I have said, I will deal with this in detail under #35.3. Here, it needs to be noted that he accepts that a PPA must advocate its own freedom and well-being in the sense that it must accept that it ought to pursue its own freedom and well-being ([4c] in my presentation). He claims, however, that (4c) does not entail (4d) "PPAO ought not to interfere with my freedom and well-being," where this is a genuinely "other-referring" ought, because "my prudential base" does not give PPAO a reason for acting. (See ibid., 143.)

Reply to Kalin

Gewirth (1984d, 215–219) claims that Kalin's attempt to rescue ethical egoism from self-contradiction employs two devices,

1.   changing ethical egoism from a practical to a theoretical doctrine, and
2.   the claim that, as prescriptions (or directives), the "oughts" in ethical egoism have only regional force.

The essential aspect of 1 is that, as *beliefs* about what it is rational for X to do on the criterion of its own self-interest, 4* and vi*, and iv* and 6*, are not contradictory propositions. This is correct, and Gewirth agrees! (See ibid., 216.)

Kalin claims that Gewirth holds that the ethical egoist, by holding its maxim, is doing something rather than believing something. However, because it is not acting on the basis of this maxim by propounding it, it is belief not action that is at issue. Gewirth responds that the ethical egoist, in propounding its maxim, might be doing something other than just believing that something is needful, or acting on its maxim. What it might be doing, and what Gewirth holds it to be doing, is *advocating* something, because "a practical purview" is crucial to any ethical doctrine (see ibid., 217); and, indeed, Kalin appears to recognize this when he says that the egoist's beliefs are both consistent and *action-guiding*, and when he holds that ethical egoism has prescriptive force, albeit only "regional."

Now, if ethical egoism is prescriptive, and tells the ethical egoist what it ought to do (in an advocative sense), and what PPAO ought to do (in the same advocative sense), then the ethical egoist incurs Gewirth's contradiction and dilemmas.

The role of 2 is to have us construe ethical egoism as prescriptive in telling the ethical egoist what it ought to do (what actions of its own must carry its advocacy), and in telling PPAO what PPAO ought to do (what actions of PPAO's must carry PPAO's advocacy), but not in telling the ethical egoist what PPAO ought to do (in a sense involving the ethical egoist's advocacy of this action), or in telling PPAO what the ethical egoist ought to do (in a sense involving PPAO's advocacy of this action). This would appear to rescue ethical egoism from the charge of incompatible directives, because when I (as an ethical egoist) say that I ought to pursue my self-interest, I am advocating my doing what I need to do in my self-interest; but when I say that PPAO ought to pursue its self-interest, I am not advocating that PPAO do what it needs to do in its self-interest. I am merely saying that this is what PPAO's self-interest requires PPAO to do.

However, whether or not this does rescue ethical egoism from the charge of incompatible directives,[13] it seems to me that any such rescue is still caught on the horns of a modified version of Gewirth's first dilemma.

Kalin claims that the deontic terms in 4*, 6*, iv*, and vi*

have one univocal sense, namely, "supported by conclusive reasons," and thus, exactly in *this* sense, "justified," "permissible," "right," and "not wrong." (Kalin 1984, 135)

This is true only if viewed externally, outside anyone's practical viewpoint. It is false if looked at from the practical viewpoint of PPAs. Stated by me, 4* and 6* give to "supported by conclusive reasons" the force of "must carry my advocacy." Stated by me, iv* and vi* intend "supported by conclusive reasons" to be neutral with respect to my advocacy (and the reverse applies when these propositions are stated by others). In the terms that Kelsen would have used, from my viewpoint 4* and 6* are "subjective 'oughts,'" they express what I intend, whereas iv* and vi* are "objective 'oughts,'" they express what I would be required to intend *if* I adopted the criterion that validates them. (See Kelsen 1967, 17–23.) In the terms that Gewirth uses in spelling out the first dilemma, from my viewpoint 4* and 6* carry my definitive endorsement, whereas iv* and vi* are "hypothetical." What I have conclusive reason to do on 4* and 6* is what I must do and must want to have done. What PPAO has conclusive reason to do on iv* and vi* is what PPAO must do and must want to have done, *and what* I must do/must want to have done *if* I advocate PPAO's pursuit of its interests (which as an ethical egoist, I [nonderivatively] do not advocate). In other words, when an ethical egoist addresses the ethical egoist maxim to itself, this is a practical doctrine (action-guiding, and intended to be so). When it addresses it to PPAO, it is a theoretical doctrine (and not intended to be action-guiding). Thus, under 2, ethical egoism is not a universal *ethical or practical* doctrine. If it is construed as such a universal doctrine, providing "supported by conclusive reasons" with an advocative sense, when said by me, regardless of who is being addressed, then it is inconsistent. On the other hand, if it provides a nonadvocative sense to "supported by conclusive reasons," whomever it addresses (which is what 1 presses), then it is not action-guiding at all.

About Kalin's response to the second dilemma, Gewirth is silent. It should be noted, however, that Kalin's response depends on the first dilemma failing to do its job. If the first dilemma fails (and I do not think that it does), then Gewirth has to show that the ethical egoist must conceive of life in terms of conflict and struggle. Kalin's argument is that this cannot be shown. Whether or not this is so I will not discuss, for Gewirth presents the second dilemma not as an independent argument, but as an elaboration of the first dilemma. Gewirth does not say that the ethical egoist *must* view life in these terms. He says that *if* the ethical egoist *is caught* by the first dilemma, then *the egoist could release itself* by viewing life in these conflictual terms. *But*, if it does so, then it is caught by the second dilemma.

Not surprisingly, Gewirth is unhappy about Kalin's discussion of "universalization." Kalin says that Gewirth makes the egoist's question "What are we to do?" in which "we" is given the collective meaning of "all of us together." Gewirth will only accept that this is the egoist's question if "we" is given the distributive meaning of "each of us separately." The "I" question cannot be primary, as this removes "the aspect of universality which makes a *universal* ethical egoist" (Gewirth 1984d, 218).

About Kalin's claim that Gewirth begs the question against ethical egoism by attributing to the ethical egoist the view that practical reason presupposes a "common good," which is related to this, Gewirth says nothing; but it is crucial.

The fact of the matter is that Gewirth and Kalin are talking at cross-purposes. What Gewirth is attacking as "universal ethical egoism," and what Kalin is defending as "ethical egoism," are simply not the same thing. Kalin defines "ethical egoism" as the view that a PPA's wants, needs, or interests, only provide *that* PPA with reasons for acting. This is equivalent to the position that there is no reason why a PPA should take favorable account of the interests of others in determining its own reasons for acting, and this is what Gewirth calls "amoralism." Now, what Gewirth calls "universal ethical egoism" is not a form of amoralism. It is, in fact, the view that what a PPA ought to do is to be determined completely by its own interests, yet to be determined completely by PPAO's interests. This is contradictory, and Kalin concedes that it is. Such a position does not exactly pose Kalin's aggregative "we" question, which presupposes that practical reason is guided by a "common good." But it does pose Gewirth's distributive "we" question.

Now, Gewirth's charge of inconsistency, leading to the dilemmas, is directed solely at "universal ethical egoism," as Gewirth defines this. It is not directed at "amoralism." Gewirth does not think that this argument shows that "amoralism" is *internally* inconsistent. Indeed, at no point does Gewirth argue that "amoralism" is internally inconsistent. He argues only that it is dialectically inconsistent. *This latter argument, however, is not the argument that a PPA must accept (4d)!* When (4d) is established, it is established that a PPA must consider that PPAO has a duty not to interfere with PPA's freedom and well-being. This, by itself, does not show that the PPA must treat the interests of PPAO as relevant to determining what it, PPA, ought to do. It also does not show that PPAO must treat the interests of PPA as relevant to determining what it, PPAO, ought to do. It only shows, that, *from PPA's viewpoint*, PPAO has a duty not to interfere with PPA's freedom and well-being. It is a tautology that, on the criterion of PPA's interests, PPAO ought not to interfere with PPA's interests. If PPA espouses this criterion, then PPA must consider that PPAO ought not to interfere with its freedom and well-being (because having its, PPA's, freedom and well-being is necessary for its, PPA's, interests to be fulfilled). The argument against amoralism requires, in addition, Stage III to be effected. It must be shown that, given the dialectical necessity of (4d), which poses neither Kalin's "I" question nor his "we" question (I am, at this point, not asking only, "What should I do for myself?" but also asking, "What should be done by you for me?" without asking "What should I do for you?" and, thus, without asking, "What should we do together?"), logical universalization alone compels a PPA to accept that it has a duty not to interfere with the freedom and well-being of PPAO. Only at this point does Gewirth purport to show that a PPA must take favorable account of PPAO's interests (specifically, its interests in freedom and well-being) in determining what it, PPA, ought to do.

Gewirth's reply to Kalin is not helpful. This is because he replies to Kalin as though Kalin were attempting to defend what Gewirth calls "universal ethical egoism," when Kalin is defending "amoralism" against the charge that it is internally inconsistent/incurs Gewirth's dilemmas (which Gewirth does not argue).

It is also tempting to argue that Kalin's discussion of Gewirth's "direct" argument is also directed at a red herring. As I have just pointed out, Gewirth's argument that (4d) is dialectically necessary is not intended to constitute a dialectical refutation of "amoralism." Kalin, however, clearly treats it as such. In this, he is mistaken. However, this leads to asking whether Kalin thinks that Gewirth's (4d) (which is prudential) can be established as dialectically necessary, and whether he thinks that such a demonstration can, when coupled with Gewirth's argument for the sufficiency of agency, yield a refutation of "amoralism" by purely logical universalization. Kalin's remarks on universalization, made during his discussion of the internal inconsistency charge, indicate that he thinks that universalization of (4d) cannot refute the amoralist. I shall discuss this when I examine Kalin's discussion of the "direct" argument (see #35.3).

**#34   The principle that "ought" implies "can" does not li-
cense the inference from "I ought to do Z" to "I ought
to be free to do Z," because an "egoist" can eschew this
inference.**

1 Davies

Colin Davies, in the course of a defense of "egoism" (which in my
terms is equivalent to "amoralism"), gives an argument for (4c) "I
ought to pursue my freedom and well-being" not entailing (4d)
"PPAO ought not to interfere with my freedom and well-being"
(this argument being directed at Gewirth's treatment in 1970a).

Gewirth says,

"I ought to do z [which is a means to the achievement of y]" entails "I ought
to be free to do z," where "to be free" means not to be interfered with by
other persons in doing z. For if it is right that other persons interfere with X's
doing z or prevent him from doing z, then it is false that he ought to do z.
(Gewirth 1970a in 1982b, 93)

For suppose X's doing z is impossible without other men's providing various kinds of essential conditions or services, which I shall call p. Hence,
when X says "I ought to do z," he must also accept the statement, "Other
men ought to do p." For since "ought" presupposes "can," if it is right that
other men not do p, without which X cannot do z, then it is false that X ought
to do z. To put it otherwise, if one endorses some end, then one must also
endorse the necessary means to that end, at least *prima facie* or in the absence
of superior counter-considerations. (Ibid., 94)

Davies seems prepared to concede that *if* this is valid, then it
follows by the use of the *logical* principle of universalizability that I
(an egoist) cannot deny, without contradiction, that I ought to refrain from preventing PPAO from doing z, or that I ought to provide
PPAO with p when my help is needed. *If* this argument is valid, then
I cannot be an egoist (amoralist). However, he claims,

This argument is invalid. The fact (if it is a fact)[14] that 'ought' presupposes
'can' does not show that 'I ought to do z' entails 'I ought to be free to do z.'
If X cannot properly say that he ought to do z unless he can do z, then all that
follows is that if he does properly say that he ought to do z, then he can do z.
If, however, X is someone (X') who believes that the rational consent of
others is relevant to the justification of his judgment about what he should
do, then 'I ought to do z' *does* entail 'I ought to be free to do z.' For X' cannot
both believe that others are right to prevent him from doing z and that he
ought to do z. But X' cannot appear in Gewirth's argument without begging
the question the argument is designed to answer, viz. how is morality to be
defended against the claims of egoism? X' is not a genuine egoist. The latter
is someone who denies that the rational consent of others is relevant to the
justification of his judgments about how he should treat them. For him, 'I

ought to do z,' does *not* entail 'I ought to be free to do z.' If he finds that others are preventing him from doing z, then, given that he accepts that 'ought' presupposes 'can,' he merely stops thinking that he ought to do z. Hence, unlike X', he can both believe that he ought to do z and that others are right to prevent him from doing z. His doing z is not in the interests of others and so they ought to stop him doing it if they can. (Davies 1975, 23)

As I understand this, Davies is claiming that "ought implies can" does not license the move from (A) "I ought to do z" to (B) "I ought to be free to do z" ("PPAO ought not [does wrong] to prevent me from doing z"). To get from (A) to (B) requires the assumption that I consider the interests of PPAO to be relevant to the justification of how I ought to act. To make this assumption, however, is to adopt a moral point of view, which begs the question against the "egoist," who holds that only the addressee's interests are relevant to how the addressee ought to act. On this maxim, "I ought to do z" and "PPAO ought to interfere with my doing z" are mutually consistent things for me to believe.

This requires careful analysis, but it will not stand up.

In the specific context of Gewirth's argument in *Reason and Morality*, z = pursuit/achievement of my freedom and well-being, and p = my freedom and well-being. However, the sequence that Davies questions is held to apply where z is anything that I strictly ought to do, and p represents the necessary conditions for my doing z.

Davies says that the following sequence is *logically* valid, and it is.

I do not have p → I cannot do z.

I ought to do z → I can do z → I have p. ∴

I cannot do z/I do not have p/PPAO prevents me having p → It is not the case that I ought to do z.

However, he claims that the following sequence is *logically* invalid.

I ought to do z.

If I do not have p/PPAO prevents me having p, then I cannot do z. ∴

(Because "I ought to do z" → "I can do z/I have p/PPAO does not prevent me having p") I ought to have p/PPAO ought not to prevent me having p.

Why? He says two things in support of his position.

1. This sequence requires the assumption that the criterion of "I ought to do z" includes the interests of PPAO. For me to adopt such

a criterion for what I ought to do, is for me to adopt a question-begging moral point of view. The "egoist" holds that my criterion of what I ought to do includes only *my* interests.

2. The "egoist," in saying "I ought to do z," is saying "It is in my interests to do z"; but, in saying "PPAO ought not to prevent me having p," it is saying "It is in PPAO's interests not to prevent me having p." However, there is no contradiction in saying "It is in my interests to do z" and saying "It is not the case that it is in PPAO's interests not to prevent me having p." Indeed, it claims that there is no contradiction in saying "It is in my interests to do z" and "It is in PPAO's interests to prevent me having p." So, for the "egoist," "I ought to do z" does not entail "PPAO ought not to prevent me having p."

However, for 1 to be correct, it must not only be sufficient for the sequence that my criterion include PPAO's interests. It must also be necessary. It is certainly sufficient. On such a criterion "I ought to do z" must mean "It is in PPAO's interests that I do z" But, if it is in PPAO's interests that I do z, then it cannot be in PPAO's interests to prevent me having p. This, however, does not show that it is necessary for the sequence that I adopt an other-regarding criterion for my "ought." Suppose that my criterion is solely my interests. "I ought to do z" means "It is in my interests to do z" If we keep this criterion constant, then "PPAO ought not to prevent me having p" must be read as "It is in my interests that PPAO not prevent me having p." For me to say "It is in my interests to do z, but it is not in my interests that PPAO not prevent me having p" is to contradict myself.

In other words, the sequence does not require me to adopt a moral point of view. It only requires that the criterion of "ought" be kept the same. Gewirth infers that "I ought to do z" → "I ought to be free to do z" → "PPAO ought not to prevent me having p," on the understanding that the criterion of all these "oughts" be the same, my interests. This is not to assume a moral point of view. The assumption is not that I take the "rational consent of others" to be relevant to my justification of how I ought to act. It is that I take my rational consent to be relevant to my justification of how others ought to act. Furthermore, Gewirth does not argue that from "I must consider (relative to my interests) that I ought to do z," it follows that "PPAO must consider (relative to its interests) that it ought not to prevent me having p." To hold that it does would be to infer that my prudential base justifies PPAO in having a moral base. Gewirth holds that I must consider there to be justification for PPAO having an other-regarding attitude to me, but that this justification is solely in my eyes, not in PPAO's. No assumption is made that PPAO will respect my reasons or that my justification provides any justification *for PPAO* why PPA ought to respect my reasons.

Of course, Davies might say that this is still question-begging. His egoist does not adopt such a criterion. His egoist specifies that what I ought to do is determined solely by my interests, and that what PPAO ought to do is determined solely by PPAO's interests. He does not specify that what PPAO ought to do is determined by my (the egoist's) interests.

This response, however, runs into problems. Davies is arguing that the egoist who finds that PPAO prevents it from doing z will conclude that it ought not to do z. But why should a PPA, who holds that what others do (in their interests) has no bearing on what it ought to do, conclude that it ought not to do z (when this is in its interest), because others are preventing it from doing z? If anything, to adopt such an attitude is precisely to take the moral viewpoint which Davies says the egoist disavows. It begins to look as though Davies' "egoist" is not an amoralist at all, but what Gewirth calls "a universal ethical egoist." This position is internally inconsistent. (See #33.) So, perhaps, this is just a slip on Davies' part. His egoist does not advocate that PPAO do what it is in PPAO's interests to do. When the egoist says that PPAO ought to interfere with its having p, it is merely stating the fact that this is what PPAO's interests require.

The problem with this, however, is that when I say "I ought to do z" (on the basis of my interests), I am prescribing, not just describing, what my interests require. No one would suggest that "I ought to do z" as a prescription entails "PPAO ought not to interfere with my having p" as a description of what is in PPAO's interests. That "ought implies can" will not license such an inference is not surprising. To appeal to this is to evade the pertinent issue, which is whether "I ought to do z" entails "PPAO ought not to interfere with my having z" *on the criterion of my interests,* for what Gewirth is claiming is that it does. He claims that I must consider that PPAO ought not to interfere with my freedom and well-being, because this restraint is required on the criterion of my interests, which is my criterion. I must conclude, therefore, that neither 1 nor 2 shows that "I ought to do z" does not *logically* entail "I ought to be free to do z."

However, Davies will still require an explanation of the validity of the second sequence as an application of "ought implies can." So, it is worth noting the difference between the two sequences. In the first, the question is whether I ought to do z. From "ought implies can" it follows that the answer is negative if I do not have p. But it also follows that, in a situation where I do not have p, I am not a PPA. It follows from this that the application of this sequence does not present an adequate picture of the context of Gewirth's argument. In the second sequence, on the other hand, the question is not whether I ought to do z—for it is assumed that I *am* a PPA to whom "I ought to do z" is properly addressed (it being assumed that I am able to do z if left to my own devices, and that this demand is justified)—but of what follows from "I ought to do z," given that "ought" implies "can," where the criterion of this "ought" is my interests. From the vantage point of my prospective purposive agency, I think about interference with my having p as a prospect for my agency, not as something I am suffering (which, by the first sequence, would excuse me from not obeying the directive), but as something I might suffer. So viewed, I do not look upon the "can" condition *merely* in terms of its implications for the "ought." I appreciate these implications—these being that I will be excused from my failure to carry out my obligation if I am deprived of p—but I also evaluate them in terms of the "ought" that at present binds me. I recognize that if I am required to carry out this demand, then I must have my freedom and well-being, that it would be an unreasonable demand to make that I should carry it out when I cannot. Any criterion that can reasonably demand that I do z would be unreasonable if it did not demand noninterference with my freedom and well-being.[15]

Thus, inasmuch as Davies thinks that the validity of the first sequence precludes the validity of the second, my response is that the two sequences are wholly compatible, because they apply in different contexts.[16]

2 White

Stephen K. White raises two objections. The first fits, more or less, under the present heading. The second raises points that relate more closely to objections raised by Jan Narveson (see #6 and #38) and N. Fotion (see #42.1) (and compare Lomasky #3.3). I consider both here, as they rest on the same basic analysis.

White's first objection is to Gewirth's inference from (4c) to (4d) elucidated in terms of the need to endorse the necessary conditions of an endorsed "ought," rather than in terms of "ought implies can" (which amounts to the same thing).

White accepts that even a "radical amoralist" must accept (1) "I ought to preserve my life" (I use his numbering), since life is a necessary good for any PPA. Correctly, he portrays Gewirth as holding that any PPA must infer (3) "All others ought to refrain from interfering with the preservation of my life," on the grounds of having to accept (2) "I ought to be free to preserve my life." That (2) entails (3) must be accepted because what (2) and (3) prescribe is necessary for (1) to be complied with. White does not dispute that (1) entails (3) via (2) *if* what (2) prescribes is necessary for (1). He claims that what (2) prescribes is not necessary for (1) *as the radical amoralist interprets (1)*.

[L]ife which is a generic good to an agent will always be a life of a certain kind—a life which the agent takes to be, in a basic sense, worth living. . . . [F]or a radical amoralist the outer limits of a life worth living are radically different from those of other agents. For him a worthwhile life is one lived in the context of potentially lethal threats and challenges from the human, as well as the natural, world. . . . Thus for the radical amoralist, (3) is not a necessary condition for maintaining the life *he* is referring to in (1). And insofar as (2) is other-directed, it also is not a necessary condition. (White 1982, 288)

Thus, for the radical amoralist (1) does not entail (3).

White's second objection is related to his first. White appreciates that Gewirth's concept of generic-dispositional well-being (WB_1) is defined purely in terms of generalized conditions and abilities, which are not dependent on the content of PPAs' particular occurrent purposes. He agrees that these conditions are necessary conditions for a PPA's agency. However, he claims that if a PPA is required to claim rights to its "necessary goods," a PPA will not be required to restrict its rights-claims to its WB_1. Relative to its particular "life plan" (its view of the sort of life worth living) a PPA will regard a set of purposes as core purposes. These core purposes will be the necessary conditions of the sort of life the PPA regards as worth living. In this sense, these core purposes (its WB_2) will be necessary goods for the PPA. However, whereas a PPA's WB_1 will not vary from PPA to PPA, a PPA's WB_2 will vary from PPA to PPA (according to varying "life plans"). A PPA's WB_1 will be a necessary, but not sufficient, condition of its WB_2. Reasoning from its WB_2, a PPA will be able to justify (at least to itself) a "rather expansive bag of rights." A PPA will have to universalize its rights-claims, and grant PPAO the same rights, but it will not have to respect the rights-claims of PPAO when these conflict with its own WB_2. Thus, an "egoist" who is not a radical amoralist will use moral principles only when it is in its self-interest to do so. It will not be committed to the PGC. (See ibid., 290–292.)

This is very confused.

1. The concept of a "generic/necessary good," which White employs in his first objection and which corresponds to a PPA's WB_2 in his second, is that of a necessary condition for all the purposes that

a PPA (according to its "life plan" [or SPR for its purposes]) would be willing to pursue. The concept of a "generic good," as Gewirth employs it, is that of a necessary condition for any and every purpose a PPA could possibly have. My WB_1 consists of generic conditions of my agency per se. My WB_2 comprises generic conditions of my agency as an egoist, radical amoralist, or whatever. In Gewirth's terms, my WB_2 contains elements that are not "necessary goods," for I, as a PPA, am not *categorically* required to value these purposes/conditions (insofar as they extend beyond my WB_1). If I do not value them, I do not deny that I am a PPA. I only deny that I am an egoist, radical amoralist, or whatever.

2. It follows that White's proposition (1), as interpreted by the radical amoralist qua radical amoralist, or by the egoist qua egoist, is not an "ought" that is categorically binding on a PPA. A PPA *might* take it as categorically binding, but there would be no irrationality in its not doing so. A PPA does not have to be a radical amoralist, or an egoist, and so does not *have* to pursue its WB_2 (beyond its WB_1). On the other hand, a PPA does have to value its WB_1 perfectly stringently. Its WB_1 comprises, and is conceded by White to comprise, necessary conditions for its purposes, whatever these might be, thus necessary conditions for its carrying out its life plan, whatever this might be. To be a radical amoralist, etc., I must be a PPA, and what I must value on the premise that "I am a PPA" must be valued by me if I am a radical amoralist. If there is any conflict here, then this shows that I rationally (logically) ought not to be a radical amoralist, etc.

3. From this it follows that a PPA, radical amoralist or not, has to interpret White's proposition (1) as Gewirth does, not as White would have it do; and this means that it would have to accept (3) via (2). Because (1), as characterized by Gewirth, is stringently justified, so is (3).

4. It further follows that a PPA would have no justification, on Gewirth's *logical criteria* of rationality, for claiming a right to its contingent WB_2 elements. But it would still have to claim a right to its WB_1.

5. The rights-claims that an egoist would be required to make *as an egoist* will not have as their sufficient condition the egoist's being a PPA. Consequently, an egoist would, *as egoist*, not necessarily have to grant the rights it claims to PPAs as such. On the other hand, the egoist, *as a PPA*, would have to grant rights to WB_1 to all PPAs. It would, *as a PPA*, have to accept the PGC, and reject its egoism.

Throughout his article White displays three errors.

1. A tendency to read the reductio ad absurdum strategy that Gewirth employs as operating on the contingent SPRs for their purposes that PPAs might happen to espouse, rather than from what is logically contained within the premise "I am a PPA."

2. A tendency to give "well-being" a particular occurrent interpretation. Gewirth, says White,

admits that well-being is a "continuum" between the general and the particular. [RM 60.] This insight, though, is quickly glossed with the assertion that well-being is still "primarily even if not exclusively" to be identified with general abilities and conditions. [RM 61.] But . . . Gewirth's "primarily" will still be too strong. He could justifiably say only that the general abilities and conditions are necessarily a part of well-being. (White 1982, 291)

Ironically, Gewirth, in fact, holds no more than that generic-dispositional well-being is *necessarily* a part of well-being. He does not ignore or degrade particular occurrent well-being in his characterization of well-being *in general*. What White fails to appreciate properly is that only in its generic-dispositional interpretation does well-being figure in the argument, because only such well-being is *necessarily* connected to being a PPA. It is precisely the fact that generic-dispositional well-being is *necessarily* a part of well-being, *whatever particular occurrent valuations this involves*, that is doing the work in the argument. In conceding that a PPA's WB$_1$ is a *necessary condition* of its WB$_2$, White has conceded the dialectical necessity of Gewirth's conception.

3. A tendency to read "the prudential standpoint" of a PPA (in Gewirth's usage) as making the criterion of rationality logical consistency with the particular occurrent purposes of PPAs, rather than as the normative standpoint logically implicated in the premise "I am a PPA." This is illustrated by claims like,

My . . . strategy will be to . . . show that at least some types of instrumentally rational individuals can be consistent in their judgments and yet reject Gewirth's supreme moral principle. (Ibid., 283)

The prudential calculus of an inductively and deductively disciplined egoist will not necessarily yield the moral perspective Gewirth wants. (Ibid., 286)

Gewirth's project only appears successful because his definition of well-being abstracts from the particular knowledge of the agent. This degree of abstraction, though, is unjustified . . . . The value of greater abstraction and generality is not in terms of greater prudential rationality, but rather greater impartiality or fairness. . . . While adopting his concept of well-being may be legitimate for helping to incorporate the value of fairness into moral choice, it is not . . . justifiable from a prudential rational standpoint. (Ibid., 292–293)

The problem with all of this is that the justification for Gewirth's "abstract" concept of well-being is not meant to be "prudence" or some wholly self-regarding *SPR* for my purposes. It is meant to be logical, and from a dialectically *necessary* standpoint it is justified. In the argument, "prudential" simply does not take the meaning of a wholly self-regarding SPR for my purposes, or of my particular occurrent purposes themselves. Any judgments or conceptions justified on such bases will be dialectically *contingent.* It refers to my proactive valuation of *my* purposes, which is immanent in my activity, howsoever this is indirectly and contingently rationalized. Furthermore, the "abstract" concept is not introduced in order to justify fairness: it is introduced as being all that is necessarily connected with agency per se. That this (ultimately) permits the PGC to be justified does not make the argument question-begging, for the features delineated by this concept *are necessarily* connected with agency, of which "egoistic agency," "radical amoralist agency," etc., are all species.

Finally, it is worth looking at a claim that White makes during his discussion. White claims that most PPAs

would not find, say, life worthwhile if it were one in which their brains were suspended in a chemical solution and commands were relayed through a computer to robots which carried out their purposes. (Ibid., 288)

Perhaps this is so (although we need to say something about how such an existence would be experienced to form any considered judgment on this). Anyway, I *might,* indeed, find such an existence intolerable, and would rather die than be subjected to it. But what is the significance of this? Does this mean, as I think White wishes to imply, that I need not accept the judgments that follow from the fact that I categorically need Gewirth's generic-dispositional well-being, and that I need only reason from my SPR for my purposes, and its specific necessary conditions?[17] The answer to this is negative. This is because I am only required to value my life in a categorically instrumental manner, not for its own sake; and, from this requirement, I am required to make rights-claims. These are, however, waivable rights. I must claim a right to noninterference with the necessary conditions of my agency per se which is *against my will.* What will determine whether or not I am willing to risk my life, or forfeit it, or have it interfered with will, indeed, be my SPR for my purposes (my "life plan"). But, in determining the conditions under which I would be willing to waive my generic rights, my SPR for my purposes would not determine whether or not I had to consider that I had these rights to waive. Dialectically necessary rights-claims, including the way in which they are to be qualified, can only derive from components necessarily connected with agency per se. They cannot be derived from features (particular occurrent purposes or SPRs for my purposes) that are dialectically contingent within the context of practical discourse per se. What is dialectically necessary *relative to dialectically contingent attachments* is still dialectically contingent, thus not a basis for *categorically binding* rights-claims, and thus not a basis for questioning inferences derived from attachments that *are* categorically binding.[18]

#35   From its being the case that *I* must consider that *I* prudentially ought to pursue my freedom and well-being, because I categorically need my freedom and well-being for my purposes, it does not follow that I must consider that *PPAO* prudentially ought not to interfere with my freedom and well-being (if this is equivalent to considering that I have a prudential right to my freedom and well-being), because PPAO does not categorically need *my* freedom and well-being for *its* purposes/PPAO is not necessarily given a reason not to interfere with my freedom and well-being/the notion of a prudential obligation/right is a contradiction in terms, incoherent, or only metaphorical.

1 Hare

According to R. M. Hare,

the step from the perhaps true premise that the agent wants something to the conclusion that *he* prudentially ought to seek it (and whatever is a necessary condition for it) may be all right; but this does not entitle us to conclude that he must think that other people prudentially ought to give it him; for it would not be true that they ought, and there would be no reason why he should think so, if to give it him would not be (and were known by him not to be) in *their* interests. (Hare 1984, 54)

As always, we should note that Gewirth does not argue that "I want X" entails "I *strictly* prudentially ought to seek X" (entails "I have a right to X"). He argues only that "I *rationally must* want X (proactively), for whatever my purposes" makes it dialectically necessary for *me* to hold "I (strictly) prudentially ought to seek X (etc.)," hence to hold "PPAO (strictly) prudentially ought not to interfere with my obtaining X," hence to hold "I have a (prudential) claim right to X."

If we assume that Hare understands this, then his objection is that, while he may be willing to concede that (4c) "I have a prudential instrumental duty to defend my freedom and well-being from interference" is dialectically necessary for me, it does not follow that (4d) "PPAO has a prudential instrumental duty not to interfere with my freedom and well-being (correlative to my having a claim right to my freedom and well-being)" is similarly necessary; and this is because it may not be in PPAO's interests not to interfere with my freedom and well-being.

However, when Gewirth claims that (4d) follows from (4c), he does not claim that *PPAO* must consider that PPAO has a prudential duty, that PPAO has a duty *on PPAO's prudential criterion*, that it is categorically in PPAO's interests, not to interfere with my freedom and well-being (or that I must think so). Thus, when (4d) states that I must consider that PPAO has a prudential duty not to interfere with my freedom and well-being, the prudential criterion is *mine, not PPAO's*. PPAO has, from my internal viewpoint, a duty not to interfere with my freedom and well-being *according to my prudential criterion*, in consistency with my criterion for my purposes, because I require my freedom and well-being for my purposes whatever they are. From my internal viewpoint, PPAO's duty is prudentially owed *to my interests, not to PPAO's*. (See RM 94; and Gewirth 1984d, 208.) Correlative to this duty, within my internal viewpoint, I have a prudential right to my freedom and well-being. Because this duty is other-referring (prescribed *to* PPAO), the correlative right is a claim right. It is prudential because its criterion is my prudential criterion. That its correlative duty is other-referring does not, however, make it a moral right, or the correlative duty a moral duty. The criterion of (4d) and (5) "I have a right to my freedom and well-being" is my prudential criterion, which is not necessarily moral as it does not necessarily take favorable account of the interests of PPAs other than, or in addition to, myself.[19] All that Gewirth needs to establish this claim is to show that (4c) entails (4d) *on my prudential criterion*. This depends on no more than the principle that "ought" implies "can," which can hardly be questioned.

We should note, however, that the reason why Hare presses this objection is that he considers that

> when I say that *other persons* prudentially ought to do something, I must mean that they ought to do it in *their* own interest; I cannot mean that they ought to do it in *my* interest. (Hare 1984, 54)

Hare does not explain directly why I cannot mean "they ought to do it in *my* interest." It is unlikely that he considers such a claim to be *unintelligible*, for he is prepared to concede that, on the basis of my valuing my purposes, I must prescribe that the necessary conditions (my freedom and well-being) for my purposes be supplied.

(See ibid., 56.) To concede this is to concede that I must consider that PPAO ought not to interfere with my freedom and well-being for the sake of my purposes (i.e., in *my interests*). In fact, what Hare appears to mean is that if (4d) is interpreted in this way, then it cannot be universalized by the *logical* principle of universalizability, and so Stage III cannot be effected. Gewirth must mean "they ought to do it in their interest" *if* Stage III is to be effected by the *logical* principle of universalizability. This objection must, therefore, be read in a more general context. In this context, Hare contends that any interpretation of (4d) that is dialectically necessary does not permit universalization to Stage III without begging the question (by presupposing the *moral* principle of universalizability). If, on the other hand, (4d) can be universalized by the *logical* principle of universalizability, then it must be interpreted as "PPAO ought not to interfere with my freedom and well-being in *PPAO's interest*." This, however, is not dialectically necessary, because PPAO does not categorically need my freedom and well-being. The relevance of Hare's present objection thus depends on the validity of his claim that "PPAO ought not to interfere with my freedom and well-being in *my* interest" cannot be universalized to Stage III by the *logical* principle of universalizability alone. I discuss this under #47.4.

2 Bond

According to E. J. Bond,

Gewirth's reasoning seems to be this. If my freedom and well-being are necessary goods, then others' not interfering with them is a necessary good. Therefore others are under an obligation to me not to interfere with them. But all he is entitled to say is that if I necessarily will, or regard as a necessary, self-regarding good, my own freedom and well-being, I must will or regard as a necessary, self-regarding good, that others do not interfere with it. I must believe, if you like, that, from my own point of view, *it ought to be the case that* others do not interfere in my freedom and well-being. But this is not the same as saying that others are *under an obligation* not to interfere in them. For this is to claim that there is for *them* an over-riding or commanding reason for respecting my freedom and well-being, and that does not follow at all. That can be the case only if non-interference in my freedom and well-being is my *moral* and not just my prudential due. . . . It is just nonsense to say that another person has a "prudential obligation"—prudential relative to my interests—not to interfere with my freedom and well-being. But that is what Gewirth is trying to tell us here. (Bond 1980a, 49–50)

Like Hare (#35.1), Bond concedes that *from my point of view* it ought to be the case that PPAO not interfere with my freedom and well-being. Bond, however, claims that it is *nonsense* to translate this as "On the criterion of my interests (which is the criterion of my dialectically necessary point of view in Stage II), PPAO *has an obliga-tion* not to interfere with my freedom and well-being." Why? Be-cause to say that X is under an obligation to do Y is to say that there is an "over-riding or commanding reason" *for* X to do Y.

This, however, is ambiguous. It is ambiguous as between "The speaker accepts an overriding or commanding reason why Y ought to be done by X" and "X accepts a reason for it to do Y as overriding or commanding." What Gewirth intends "PPAO ought not to inter-fere with my freedom and well-being" to mean is "I accept an over-riding or commanding reason why PPAO ought not to interfere with my freedom and well-being," and it would appear that Bond accepts that Gewirth can mean this. So Bond must be asserting that "X is under an obligation to do Y" means "X accepts a reason for it to do Y as overriding or commanding." When he goes on to say that "X has an obligation to do Y" does not follow from "From my point of view, it ought to be the case that X do Y" he intends to say that "From my point of view, it ought to be the case that X do Y" does not entail "From X's point of view, X ought to do Y."

Now, this is true, unless (as Bond states) the "ought" in question is a moral "ought" (the basis of which is X's interests as well as my own). Bond wishes to say that Gewirth illicitly reads this "ought" as a moral one in order to derive (4d). This, however, does not follow, unless Gewirth intends (4d) as "From PPAO's point of view, PPAO ought not to interfere with my freedom and well-being," and it is quite clear that he doesn't. Bond's charge, therefore, has to be that, whether or not Gewirth intends this, he *must* intend this if (4d) is to be correlative to a claim rights-claim/(4d) can be universalized to Stage III. Parallel to Hare, Bond's claim, that to say PPAO has an obligation relative to my interests is nonsense, must be read not as saying that it is nonsense *as such* to say this, but that it only makes sense to say this when this is interpreted as "From my point of view, it ought to be the case that PPAO not interfere with my freedom and well-being," and that, on this interpretation, Stage III will not work. Like Hare, Bond's present objection is dependent upon his objection to Stage III. I will consider this under #47.2.

Bond's objection must be placed in such a context, for to give a freestanding analysis of "X is under an obligation to do Y" (rather than of "X considers that it is under an obligation to do Y") in terms of "On criteria that X accepts, X ought to do Y," incurs severe diffi-culties.[20]

Suppose I am a Christian who accepts that God's commandments are to be obeyed, and that these are inscribed on the tablet of stone brought down by Moses from Mt. Sinai. As far as I am concerned, if this tablet says "Thou shalt not kill," then I must consider that there is an overriding or commanding reason why all persons ought not to kill. On my criterion of the tablet of stone, all PPAs are under an obligation not to kill. Of course, some PPAO, say X, might not accept this criterion. So, supposing that X does not accept some other criterion that prescribes "Thou shalt not kill," X will not *on its criterion* be required to consider that it is under an obligation not to kill. But it surely remains the case that *on the criterion* of the tablet of stone, X ought not to kill. Bond's analysis requires us not only to say that PPAO need not, *on its criterion*, accept that it is under an obligation not to kill, but that it makes no sense to say that *a criterion requires* PPAO not to kill unless PPAO accepts it. This would involve Bond in claiming that *the logical implications of a criterion* are relative to acceptance of the criterion. On such a view, "Napoleon was a Corsican" would not entail "Napoleon was a European" (given that Corsica is in Europe) for anyone who does not accept that Napoleon was a Corsican (or if Napoleon was not a Corsican). This is quite untenable. Furthermore, it makes no difference whether the criterion in question is moral, legal, prudential, or whatever. As Gewirth responds, such a freestanding analysis

would entail, for example, tha[t] an egoist cannot intelligibly address "ought"-judgments to other persons for his own self-interested reasons when these go counter to their own interests or other reasons. It would also entail, more generally, that no one can address even a moral judgment to other persons if they do not accept moral reasons. (Gewirth 1980b, 141)[21]

3 Kalin

In the second part of his article defending "ethical egoism" (for discussion of the first part, see #33), Jesse Kalin (1984, 142–144) turns to what he construes as Gewirth's "direct" argument against ethical egoism. This is Gewirth's argument that (4d) is dialectically necessary on the basis of (4c), that on the basis of being justified (from my point of view) in asserting "I ought to pursue my freedom and well-being," I am justified in prescribing to PPAO that PPAO not interfere with my freedom and well-being, correlative to which I am justified in holding that I have a right to my freedom and well-being. Gewirth claims that "universal ethical egoism" denies (4d). Such a demonstration must constitute a refutation of the rationality of a PPA espousing this position.

Kalin's response is as follows:

1. Gewirth *can* establish that I, on my "prudential base," must hold "All other persons ought at least to refrain from interfering with my freedom and well-being" (although Kalin only refers to my

basic well-being). This, he claims, can be rendered as "I have conclusive reasons [based on my prudential purposes] to have all other persons [at least] refrain from interfering with my basic well-being" (ibid., 143).

2. However, because my prudential base does not direct *others* with binding force, it does not give *them* a reason to refrain from interfering with my basic well-being. From "I have conclusive reasons (on my prudential base) to have PPAO not interfere with my basic well-being" it does not follow that "PPAO has conclusive reasons (on its prudential base) not to interfere with my basic well-being."

3. The most that can be inferred from 1 is "It is needful (prudent) (to me) for me to have a right to basic well-being" (ibid., 144). It cannot be inferred that I must consider that I have a right to my basic well-being.

4. Consequently, Gewirth has not refuted ethical egoism.

In the appendix to his article, Kalin considers the possibility that his reply to Gewirth might have focused on the wrong place. (See ibid.) There can be no doubt that this is so, although Kalin, even in his appendix, fails to see how. As I pointed out under #33, however, Gewirth's argument against "universal ethical egoism" is an argument against a particular *moral* position, whereas Kalin's defense of "ethical egoism" is a defense of amoralism. Gewirth does *not* consider that the demonstration that (4c) entails (4d) constitutes a demonstration that PPAs must take favorable account of the interests of others in determining what they themselves ought to do. Thus, the demonstration of (4d) is not held to refute Kalin's "ethical egoist," who holds that only a PPA's own interests give it reasons for acting. The demonstration that amoralism is dialectically inconsistent is given at a later stage in the argument. Kalin's primary error is to misconstrue the function of the demonstration that (4c) entails (4d).

In fact, when Kalin concedes 1, he concedes that (4c) does entail (4d). Kalin, however, by misconstruing Stage II as an argument against the amoralist, construes (4d) not as the proposition he concedes, but as the proposition that PPAO has conclusive reasons not to interfere with my freedom and well-being on *PPAO's* prudential base. Gewirth, however, makes no claim that this proposition can be inferred from (4c) by the principle that "ought" implies "can." He only claims that the proposition that I have conclusive reasons to have PPAO not interfere with my freedom and well-being on *my* prudential base can be inferred, and this Kalin concedes. What Kalin asserts in 2 is conceded by Gewirth.

3 is slightly more problematic. Gewirth claims that, correlative to

(4d), a PPA must claim "I have a right to my freedom and well-being." Just as "PPAO ought not to interfere with my freedom and well-being" is justified *for me* on my prudential base, so "I have a right to my freedom and well-being" is justified for me on my prudential base. According to Gewirth, even a Kalinesque ethical egoist (an amoralist) must consider that it has a right to its freedom and well-being, because, where the criterion for the having of rights is my prudential base, this criterion justifies (5) "I have a right to my freedom and well-being." Kalin, however, appears to deny this. The reason would appear to be that he construes this rights-claim as being correlative to acceptance by PPAO that PPAO ought not to interfere with my freedom and well-being (i.e., as being correlative to motivation on the part of PPAO to act in accordance with this rule, or to choice or commitment on the part of PPAO to follow this rule [or to motivation/choice/commitment to follow a criterion that validates this rule]). This is not so. Just as Gewirth does not think that establishing (4d) refutes the amoralist, he does not think that establishing (5) refutes the amoralist. In fact, it seems to me that (5) is equivalent to the proposition that Kalin grants that Gewirth can establish, viz., "It is needful (prudent) (to me) for me to have a right to freedom and well-being." If this does not say that I have a right to my freedom and well-being *on (according to)* the criterion of my interests, then I do not know what it says. If I adopt a criterion, then I must consider to be the case what that criterion validates.

I do not want to suggest that Kalin, once he realizes that his response is misdirected, will concede that (5) can be universalized to the PGC. This, if valid, *would constitute* a refutation of amoralism. I suspect that he would maintain, like Hare and Bond (#35.1 and #35.2), that Stage III will not go through on the *logical principle of universalizability* (LPU) unless (4d) is construed as an other-*directing* "ought." This would explain why he reads Stage II as attempting to derive an other-*directing* "ought," and hence as an attempted refutation of amoralism. For if (4d) *must* be an other-directing "ought" for logical universalization to yield a moral principle, then we must treat Gewirth as arguing that "ought implies can" (the logical operation of Stage II) licenses moving from an "ought" that is valid within my internal viewpoint to an "ought" that is valid within all internal viewpoints. Quite definitely, this is not what Gewirth is doing.[22] For Gewirth it is the LPU, applied first within my internal viewpoint to the other-referring "ought," which Kalin grants Gewirth can establish (but not the other-directing "ought," which Kalin attributes to Gewirth), and then externally, which licenses this conclusion. As with Hare (#35.1) and Bond (#35.2), the relevance of Kalin's objection, and the force of Gewirth's reply, depend upon whether or not an other-referring, but not other-directing, "ought" can be universalized to effect Stage III.

Well, can Gewirth get to the dialectical necessity of the PGC from the dialectical necessity of the proposition that Kalin is prepared to concede, without assuming that this latter proposition must be acceptable to others? I submit that he can.

If I must consider, on the basis that it is prudent for me (needful to me) to have freedom and well-being, that I have a "conclusive reason" to have PPAO refrain from interfering with my freedom and well-being (which Kalin concedes), then (by an argument formally analogous to the argument for the sufficiency of agency) "I categorically need my freedom and well-being" is, *for me,* a "conclusive reason" for having PPAO not interfere with my freedom and well-being. I would say that this is equivalent to "'I categorically need my freedom and well-being' is, *for me,* a sufficient reason for (justifies/validates) 'PPAO strictly ought not to interfere with my freedom and well-being.'"

What we have is that I must consider that my having a certain quality X (categorical need for my freedom and well-being) justifies having a certain state of affairs Y (noninterference with my freedom and well-being by PPAO) obtain. Well, then, by the LPU, if I (because I am a PPA) must consider that my having X is a "conclusive reason" for my having Y, then *I* must consider that PPAO's having X is a "conclusive reason" for PPAO's having Y. This means that PPAO's having a categorical need for its freedom and well-being is *for me* a conclusive reason to have all PPA's other than PPAO (and including myself) not interfere with PPAO's freedom and well-being. This is, in part at least, self-directing. So, even if it is not other-directing, we can say that I must consider that I ought not to interfere with PPAO's freedom and well-being. Since "I" stands for any PPA in this argument, we can get directly to the claim that every PPA must consider that it, at least, ought not to interfere with the freedom and well-being of any PPA other than itself. If this is so, then Kalin's objection must be mistaken.

This argument rests on the following contentions:

1.   It is a fact that it is in my generic interest that I have my freedom and well-being, and when my generic interest is used as the criterion of what ought to be, then it prescribes that I ought to have my freedom and well-being.

2.   This prescription is impersonal, in the sense that it addresses (prescribes *to*) *all* who are able to bring it about that I have my freedom and well-being. In justifying (4c) "I ought to pursue my freedom and well-being," the criterion of my interest jus-

tifies that the situation in which I pursue/achieve my freedom and well-being ought to be. This situation, with the criterion of my interest as the justifying criterion, is the situation
that ought to be brought about by those who can.

3.   Although only those who accept my interests as the criterion
        of "oughts," or logically must do so, are required to consider
        that I ought to have my freedom and well-being, those who
        accept this criterion are required to consider that, not only
        themselves, but all who can bring it about that I have my
        freedom and well-being ought to do so.

If these are correct, then my dialectically necessary viewpoint is
that my being a PPA (my categorical need for freedom and well-
being) is sufficient justification for the relationship between me (as
a PPA) and PPAO in which PPAO does not interfere with my freedom and well-being. It follows that the fact that PPAO is a PPA must
(from my point of view) be sufficient justification for the relationship between PPAO (as a PPA) and PPAs other than PPAO (who will
include myself) in which PPAs other than PPAO do not interfere
with the freedom and well-being of PPAO.

The view expressed in 1, 2, and 3 is that the value judgments of
Stage II are judgments of what has value relative *to the criterion of my
interests* (which defines my internal viewpoint as a PPA), but that
they are not judgments that are relative *on* this criterion. *On* the
criterion of my interests, my pursuit of my freedom and well-being,
my having freedom and well-being, and PPAO's not interfering
with my freedom and well-being are good, or what ought to be the
case, regardless of whether or not anyone accepts this criterion. As a
PPA, I necessarily must accept this criterion, so I must regard my
having freedom and well-being as good, or what ought to be the
case. But my (necessary) acceptance of this criterion does not determine that the criterion of my interests requires that I ought to have
my freedom and well-being. It only requires that I must consider
that I ought to have my freedom and well-being.

On this view, the scope of a criterion's action-guidingness depends on acceptance of the criterion, but the scope of its address
does not. It follows that I am required to consider that PPAO ought
not to interfere with my freedom and well-being for the same reason
that I am required to consider that I ought to pursue my freedom
and well-being: because these things are required by my interests,
and I (must) accept this criterion.

In other words, what is assumed is that it follows from

(1)   On my prudential criterion, PPAO ought not to interfere
        with my freedom and well-being; and

(2)   I must employ my prudential criterion as my criterion;
        that

(3)   *I must consider* that "PPAO ought not to interfere with
        my freedom and well-being" is what is justified, *whether
        or not* anyone else agrees.

Put even more briefly, the argument assumes that

(A)   "PPAO ought not to interfere with my freedom and
        well-being" prescribes what ought to be *according to me*

    (which Kalin seems to agree is the case) is equivalent to

(B)   *According to me,* "PPAO ought not to interfere with my
        freedom and well-being" prescribes what ought to be
        whether or not anyone else agrees (*simpliciter* or "in itself").

It seems to me that if Kalin maintains that the conclusion that he
says can be validly derived from (4c) does not universalize logically
to the PGC, then he must deny that (A) is equivalent to (B).

It might be thought that Kalin does deny that (A) is equivalent to
(B). After all, he holds that, for the egoist (amoralist), prescriptions
have only relative directive force (see #33). Explicating this, Kalin
says that the egoist holds that there is nothing that is good in itself,
no state of affairs that ought to be. States of affairs have value,
deontic or otherwise, only in relation to variable interests. There is
nothing that is good, or ought to be, according to everyone. Does
this not deny that I must use my generic interest as my criterion of
what ought to be "impersonally," or *simpliciter?*

It is not at all clear to me that it does. Kalin clearly wishes to assert
the following two propositions:

(C)   From (A) it does not follow that "PPAO ought not to
        interfere with my freedom and well-being" prescribes
        what ought to be *according to PPAO*; and

(D)   Amoralists (egoists) consider that the rational thing for
        X to do is what is in X's interests.

However, to assert (B) is not to deny (C). "According to me,
'PPAO ought not to interfere with my freedom and well-being' prescribes what ought to be *simpliciter*" does not entail "According to
PPAO, 'PPAO ought not to interfere with my freedom and well-
being' prescribes what ought to be."

(D) invites one of two interpretations.

(D1)   Egoists consider that, *according to X,* what ought to be
        (*simpliciter*) is what is in X's interests; and that, *according*

to Y, what ought to be (*simpliciter*) is what is in Y's interests.

(D2)   Egoists consider that what X ought to do (*simpliciter*) is
       what is in X's interests; and what Y ought to do (*simpli-
       citer*) is what is in Y's interests.

Kalin, clearly does not hold (D2), and this is the position that
Gewirth declares yields incompatible directives. (See #33.) (D1), on
the other hand, is wholly compatible with (B).

Now, Kalin holds that, on the criterion of my interests (which is
my criterion), I have conclusive reason to have PPAO not interfere
with my freedom and well-being. Is this not equivalent to "According to me, 'PPAO ought not to interfere with my freedom and well-
being' is conclusively justified"? If it is, then he accepts (B), for what
I wish to convey by (B) (with its talk of "what ought to be *simpliciter*") is that if my criterion justifies X being the case, then *I must think*
that *there is* conclusive justification for X being the case, whatever
might be justified on other criteria. If I must think that my categorical need for freedom and well-being is conclusive justification for
"PPAO ought not to interfere with my freedom and well-being,"
then I must concede that PPAO's categorical need for freedom and
well-being is conclusive justification for "I ought not to interfere
with PPAO's freedom and well-being."

It seems to me that if Kalin is to deny the validity of Stage III, on
the basis of a PPA's judgments of good and "ought" being "agent-
relative," then he must build into the idea of "agent-relativity"
rather more than is obviously involved in his claim that, for the
egoist, prescriptions have only relative directive force.

Perhaps Kalin's egoist holds that "I ought to do X" is *strictly* self-
referring. It does not even hold, which I have taken Kalin to accept,
that its interests are reasons *for it* why PPAO ought to do anything.
The allegation, now, is not that PPA's interests do not provide reasons *for PPAO* why PPAO ought not to interfere with PPA's doing X:
it is that PPA's interests need only, or can only, *refer* to PPA's actions,
not just that they only necessarily *direct* PPA's actions.

Remembering that the alleged inference is to "PPAO ought not to
interfere with my doing X *against my will*," I have two questions.

1. Is the "egoist" saying that (4d) follows logically from (4c), but
(as an egoist) it chooses not to lay a requirement on PPAO not to
interfere with the egoist's freedom and well-being? In this case, the
egoist is conceding that it must claim a right to its freedom and
well-being. What it is saying is that it chooses to waive this right. On
this, the egoist cannot deny that it ought not to interfere with

PPAO's freedom and well-being *against PPAO's will*. For, *as a PPA*, the egoist is required to universalize from the dialectically necessary proposition "PPAO ought not to interfere with my freedom and well-being *against my will*," not from the dialectically contingent proposition that expresses its willingness, *as an egoist*, to waive this requirement on PPAO. Thus, this way of construing the egoist's position does no damage to the argument.

2. Or, is the egoist saying that whether or not (4c) logically entails (4d) depends on whether or not it chooses to direct prescriptions based on its interests to PPAO? It seems to me that, if the egoist is not saying 1 (which does no damage to the argument), it must be saying 2. The only other alternative is to hold that it is dialectically *necessary* not to take "oughts" as other-referring. To do this, it must be contended (*a*) that egoism is dialectically necessary, and (*b*) that no PPA can rationally (in logical consistency with "I am a PPA") take "oughts" based on its interests as other-referring. I would like to see such a demonstration. (Here it is worth pointing out that "egoism" is an SPR for my purposes. The principle of egoism is not the same as a PPA's dialectically necessary criterion—which is neutral with respect to all SPRs for my purposes. [See RM 82.] A PPA cannot be taken to be an egoist without begging the question against moralists, for egoism has not been shown to be dialectically necessary. Kalin, however, is inclined to portray the starting point of Gewirth's argument as the position of egoism [see Kalin 1984, 128, 141], when this is not so.) But, if egoism is merely assumed to be dialectically contingent, then to press something that might damage the argument, the egoist must allege that the logic of "ought" is a matter of choice. The question of whether "ought" implies "can," or whether valuing X entails valuing the necessary means to X, must be made to depend on whether a PPA chooses to value the means to X. But, apart from anything else that might be said against this, the principle that *instrumental* "oughts" follow from statements of necessary means must, in consequence, be abandoned. Since the egoist relies on such inferences to ground *its* idea of prudence (an egoist, qua egoist, must do what is in its particular occurrent interests), such a position is fatal to the coherence of egoism. (See also #47.3.)

So, this line on "super agent-relativity" will not do.[23] However, if some "super agent-relativity" is not the basis of the objection, then it seems to me that Kalin must claim that the "ought" of (4d) is not other-referring or addressing, *because* not other-directing (see #35.2);[24] or that it is not other-referring in a practical sense, because it is only an "ought of evaluation" (see #35.10 and #47.6); or that the argument for the sufficiency of agency can only establish a basis for internal application of the LPU to effect the transition from the prudential to the moral on the basis of question-begging assumptions (see #50).

4 Raphael

D. D. Raphael perceives quite clearly that Gewirth holds that the "ought" I must direct at others is prudential rather than moral. He holds that the crucial step in the argument is the last sentence in the following passage, which he quotes (Raphael 1984, 87) from Gewirth:

[T]he agent is saying that because freedom and well-being are necessary goods for him, other persons strictly ought at least to refrain from interfering with his having them. And this is equivalent to saying that he has a right to them, because the agent holds that other persons owe him this strict duty of at least noninterference. (RM 79–80)

Raphael, note, is prepared to concede the claim made in the first sentence. However, he maintains that this "ought" judgment is not correlative to a claim rights judgment. This is because

[i]t is one thing for a person to advocate (as strongly as he can, because he regards it as a necessity for himself) that others should act or refrain from acting in certain ways. It is quite another thing for him to ascribe to those others a 'duty' (a moral, or quasi-moral, necessity for them, as contrasted with the necessity for himself) which they 'owe' to him. (Raphael 1984, 88)

Now, I don't know what this predication of "moral, or quasi-moral" necessities is about, for the rights-claim Gewirth attributes is prudential. Is Raphael saying that claim rights must be moral or "quasi-moral"? Or is he, like Bond, saying that I can only think that X owes me a duty if this claim is validated by criteria that X accepts? We need not agonize about this, however, for it does not matter. Whatever he has in mind, he must be wrong about it. We can leave "rights" talk out of the equation, and apply the LPU to the claim that Raphael accepts. This will get us to the PGC just as surely as the path that Gewirth selects. (See #35.3.)

5 Narveson

Jan Narveson concedes that the fact that I need my freedom and well-being in order to be able to act gives me a reason to do whatever I need to secure my freedom and well-being, but he objects, like so many others, that

in no such sense does my having a goal with that requirement, taken by itself, give anybody *else* a reason to do anything. (Narveson 1980, 661)

For this reason, any "ought" here cannot be regarded by me as a categorically binding commitment on others. Narveson claims that Gewirth's response to this objection in *Reason and Morality* (94–95), in which Gewirth insists upon the "ought" of (4d) being directed to others from my internal viewpoint for the sake of my purposivity,

evades the point, unfortunately. The question at issue is *whether* it actually *is* prudent, sensible, for A to issue, as it were, normatively expressed imperatives to or about others. . . . It is *not* true that I am committed, by my rational use of evaluative language, to the assertion of 'ought' judgments regarding others. Certainly I can express judgments of the desirability, from my point of view, of others doing this, that, or the other, but that's wishful thinking rather than the use of rationally-grounded normative language with any hope of having a "grab" on those others. And the latter is certainly all there is any point in being interested in at present. (Narveson 1980, 662–663)

First, we must separate this objection from Narveson's objections that were discussed in Chapter 5. Gewirth holds that if my prudential criterion (which governs my internal viewpoint as a PPA) entails "I strictly (instrumentally) ought to defend my freedom and well-being from interference," then my prudential criterion entails (by "ought implies can") "Others strictly ought not to interfere with my freedom and well-being against my will." For reasons discussed (and rejected) in Chapter 5, Narveson does not accept that the "ought" directed at myself is a strict one, so he doesn't accept that the "judgment of desirability" which I can (must?) make from my point of view (about others not interfering) is a strict "ought" judgment. However, I take it that Narveson is pressing an independent objection here.

On this assumption, I understand Narveson to be saying that *even if* I must make a self-referring strict "ought" judgment, *and even if* "ought implies can" requires me to make an other-referring "ought" judgment, this is beside the point. Why? Because the point is that a rational (prudent) PPA (A) is interested in directing claims at others (B) that will be practically effective in persuading, or simply getting, B not to interfere with A's interests. Even if A thinks (logically must think?) that B strictly ought not to interfere with its freedom and well-being, it is not necessarily going to be an effective ploy for securing A's interests for A to issue normative demands to B grounded in A's interests if these demands are not in B's interests, or if B does not care about A's interests. If A does not believe that B will take note of claims based on A's interests, then A will not issue these claims at B, for to do so is just wishful thinking. Because B might not accept claims issued on behalf of A's interests, A is not rationally committed to issuing such demands, even if A is logically committed to thinking that they are sound. Their "soundness" is "idealis-tic," not necessarily "realistic."

1. However, for the purposes of Gewirth's argument, which is to give a justification for the PGC that no PPA can deny without self-contradiction, a rational PPA is not a PPA who only does what is (or what it believes to be) in its interests. A rational PPA is one who only acts in ways that do not imply judgments that contradict "I am a PPA." This is because the enterprise in which Gewirth is engaged is moral epistemology, not practical politics. It is true that the baseline for the argument is "my prudential criteria." But Gewirth is inter-ested in what judgments I *logically* must accept on the basis of the valuations inherent in my having proactive purposive commit-ments. What Narveson appears to be interested in, which I am call-ing "practical politics," is the *prudent* (effective) way to achieve the purposes that I value.

2. When Gewirth says "I logically must claim that PPAO ought to do X," he means that I contradict "I am a PPA" if I do not consider this to be a valid claim. He does not mean that I logically must go up to PPAO and say to it "You ought to do X."[25] I might very well judge that it is wishful thinking on my part to do so, or even that it is imprudent (for PPAO might let me alone if I keep quiet, but attack me if I issue demands at it). It could well be the case that I logically ought to consider that PPAO ought not to interfere with my freedom and well-being, yet not say anything to PPAO about this, without contradicting myself.[26]

3. Neither 1 nor 2 denies that questions of practical politics are important questions for PPAs. 1 and 2 merely insist that they are different questions from questions of moral epistemology.

However, Narveson might wish to claim that questions of moral epistemology, so understood, are not important questions. To this I have two responses.

1. How, without engaging in moral epistemology, on a logical basis, are we going to decide what are important questions, and what are not, without begging the question?

2. If Narveson says this, then he needs to retract something he says earlier in his paper. He asks what a proof of the PGC consists of in Gewirth's terms, and says,

Gewirth's idea is to produce some features of the basic situation of all agents which require them to make, in effect, claims to the generic rights in ques-tion. If we can do that, then what we shall have shown is not exactly that everybody does have those rights, but rather that everybody is committed to recognize them. And since to recognize these rights is to commit oneself to the corresponding duties (as a matter of logic), this is to say that every rational agent must accept these duties. I imagine no one will quarrel with the suggestion that this Kantian gambit is enough to do, if one can bring it off: whatever it would mean to prove that there *are* these duties, independently of considerations of what we all must recognize, surely we have done the main thing if we can at any rate show that we really *must* accept the principles in question. (Ibid., 652)

Alternatively, Narveson might be tempted to claim that questions of moral epistemology and questions of practical politics are not distinct. To claim this, at the present juncture in the argument, is to claim that the answer to the question "Do I have, from my point of view, an exclusionary reason why others ought not to do Y?" depends on the answer to the question "Do I have a reasonable expectation that PPAO will respect (act in accordance with) my reason for having PPAO not do Y?"

Suppose, then, that I employ criteria Z that validate "PPAO ought not to interfere with my doing Y." Let us also suppose that PPAO does not accept criteria Z, and therefore does not accept that it ought not to interfere with my doing Y. If Narveson wishes to claim that questions of moral epistemology and those of practical politics are not distinct, then he would have us believe that it must be the case that I cannot be rationally (which means logically, as the "rational" criterion of the sort of moral epistemology we are considering is logical) required to employ criteria Z. But this means that I cannot be logically required to believe that PPAO ought not to interfere with my doing Y, unless PPAO considers that it ought not to interfere with my doing Y. This, surely, requires me to accept the criteria of PPAO as the criteria of what I am logically required to do. I submit that this is absurd, as it reduces the criteria of logic to the interests of others. (See #35.2.)

In a later article, Narveson expresses his present objection as the claim that Gewirth's major fallacy is that he does not appreciate that for rational agents, who act to maximize their utility, rights-claims are the objects of cost-benefit analysis. (See Narveson 1984, 102–104.)

To this Gewirth gives two replies, quite rightly seeing Narveson as suggesting an alternative moral epistemology—one that is not based on logical criteria of rationality, but on prudence—rather than a mere practical politics.

1. This puts

the *necessary* conditions of action on a par with all other "utilities" and "ben-

efits." But this is to overlook the rationally preferential status and the qualitative differentiation of the *necessary* goods of action as the essential preconditions of any agent's acting to obtain any *other* utilities and benefits.
(Gewirth 1984d, 230)

2. Any attempt to "emend" Gewirth's derivation by putting it in
terms of cost-benefit analysis and contractual bargaining will lead
to a diversity of rights-claims, as "the antecedently-held opinions,
values, and external resources of diverse protagonists," which form
the basis of this bargaining, will differ. But the whole point of moral
philosophy is

to critically evaluate and adjudicate [such claims, values, and opinions],
rather than taking them as definitive points of departure ([RM] 46–47). For
the claims are, as such, quite inconclusive, because they reflect or rest on
contingent, logically deniable, and sometimes seemingly arbitrary assumptions or principles. (Ibid., 230–231)

While Gewirth's scheme provides for calculations of comparative
costs in assessing rights-claims, this can only be done justifiably
after rights-claims have

been given a general validation. For this validation serves to establish what
are the justified criteria for estimating costs, as against the variable criteria,
relative to the contingent preferences of each person, that enter into cost-benefit analysis as usually conceived. (Ibid., 231)

Thus, it is Narveson's rejection of Gewirth's answer to the present
objection, rather than Gewirth's answer, that begs the question.

6 Regis

Gewirth says that a PPA wants its freedom and well-being to be
respected, not as a mere favor from others, but as a duty imposed on
others. (See RM 80.)

Edward Regis says about this that my wanting noninterference
entails nothing about the best way to secure it. This is an

empirical matter, and the agent cannot know in advance whether his freedom and well-being are better secured when granted as a favor from others
. . . or in some other way. (Regis 1981, 790)

This point is irrelevant. The argument is not about the prudent
way for me to behave. It is not about the best strategy for me to
adopt to secure my interests. It is about the judgments I must make
about my behavior and that of others, given that I want to pursue
some purposes and need my freedom and well-being in order to
pursue/achieve any purposes whatsoever by my agency. It is about
what judgments I must make if I am to make judgments consistent

with "I rationally *must* want my freedom and well-being not to be interfered with."

Regis, however, says that my wants do not set requirements that others are obligated to obey; they only set requirements in the sense of needs, of required means for the satisfying of my wants. (See ibid., 791.)

But although the fact that I need something to do what I want does not necessarily give PPAO a reason to provide me with what I need, it gives me a reason why PPAO should provide me with what I need. If I must want these needs met whatever I want, then I have a reason why PPAO should provide me with these needs, which I cannot eschew as a PPA.

However, Regis says that this reason gives me only a reason to prescribe that PPAO not interfere with my freedom and well-being. It does not follow that this prescription is justified, or that PPAO is obligated to obey it, although, if I am powerful enough, PPAO might be obliged to obey it. (See ibid.)

But why must justification be from the point of view of PPAO, or everyone's point of view? From my point of view, PPAO's not interfering with my freedom and well-being is a justified state of affairs. It is what my dialectically necessary criterion prescribes in requiring me to secure my freedom and well-being. That PPAO might not regard this state of affairs as justified is no reason for me to think that it is not—unless I am required to take favorable account of the viewpoint of PPAO, which I can hardly be required to do if I am not required to adopt the moral point of view. Gewirth does not suppose, at this stage, that I am required to adopt such a view—and Regis can hardly suppose that I am within the context of an objection that tries to show that I am not required to adopt such a view.

7 Golding

Martin P. Golding concedes, at least for the sake of argument, that Stages I and III are valid. He maintains that Stage II is defective. He claims that a "prudent amoralist" does not claim rights of any kind outside of the context of it being prudent to engage in "mutual cooperation and mutual undertakings." It is not logically committed to doing so, because its need for cooperation is contingent.

Gewirth argues that "My freedom and well-being are necessary goods" requires me (a prudent amoralist) to claim a right to my freedom and well-being, because

1.   my having my freedom and well-being carries my endorse-

ment; it is not a mere statement of a means-ends relationship;

2.   I conceive of my having freedom and well-being as my pru-
        dential due; and

3.   I make this claim on others because I need others not to inter-
        fere with my freedom and well-being.

Golding grants 1 but says that so does my pursuit of any of my purposes. Outside of the context of mutual cooperation and undertakings, that I want or necessarily want X does not prescribe anything to others. It might prescribe for me, but that is irrelevant. As far as 3 is concerned, he grants that demanding my freedom and well-being might be a rationally required demand; but outside the context of mutual cooperation and understandings, it is not made as a matter of moral right. (See Golding 1981, 170–171.)

Gewirth replies as follows:

Golding makes two false assumptions: that all prescriptive language must be "moral" and that it must always prescribe "*for* someone else" besides the speaker. In the first instance, the agent is advocating for himself. He is also prescribing *to* other persons. But there is this difference between prescribing *to* and prescribing *for* other persons: the latter, unlike the former, suggests that the other persons recognize or accept the prescription, or rules on which the prescription is based, or at least the authority of the prescriber. . . . But when the agent advocates his having freedom and well-being and hence prescribes *to* other persons that they at least not interfere with his having these necessary goods, he is not necessarily assuming that the other persons will accept his demand or the normative rules on which it is based . . . . (Gewirth 1982f, 71)

Furthermore, rights-claims, if intelligible at all, do not presuppose shared rules on which those prescribing and those addressed agree, as is shown by the situation in South Africa (ibid., 71–72). This is correct. We know perfectly well what Nelson Mandela meant when he said at his trial that the state had no right to prosecute and imprison him, and so did the South African government. He stated that he did not accept the criterion to which they appealed to justify their actions. This did not make their claim to have a right unintelligible to him; it merely made it unjustified as far as he was concerned.

As far as 2 is concerned, Golding claims not to understand what "due to" means on a prudential criterion.

The only sense that might be made of the agent's claim, on a prudential criterion, that a necessary good is due to him is that he has uttered the tautology that his necessary goods are necessary for him. If he means something more, I don't know what it is. (Golding 1981, 171)

Gewirth replies that the idea of a prudential "ought" is perfectly familiar.

It signifies the requirements a person must fulfill (or thinks he must fulfill) with a view to furthering his own self-interest or achieving his own purposes. Such an "ought" is prudential because its justificatory basis or criterion is prudential, consisting in the person's self-interest or in his achieving his own purposes. (Gewirth 1982f, 68–69)

Why should we not be able to say that PPAO owes me noninterference on my prudential criterion? It is perfectly clear what this means. It means that in order for me to do anything, PPAO ought not to interfere with my freedom and well-being, that on the criterion of my being able to do anything, PPAO ought not to interfere with my freedom and well-being. PPAO might not want me to do anything, so for PPAO this might merely be a means-ends statement. But I, as a PPA, want to do something so it is prescriptive for me.

Finally, we should note that Golding's terminology suggests that the argument is from "prudent amoralism." But, of course, it is from "I am a PPA." A PPA must accept (4d), not because this is validated by the principles of "prudent amoralism," but because the *"prudent amoralist"* denies that it is a PPA (and hence that it is the subject of any practical precepts, including the precepts of "prudent amoralism") if it rejects (4d).

8 Lomasky

Loren E. Lomasky considers that Stages I and III are both valid. As far as Stage II is concerned, he concedes that (4) "My freedom and well-being are necessary goods" entails that I, at least, possess some motivation to resist incursions upon my freedom and well-being. This is not quite equivalent to (4c) "I strictly ought to defend my freedom and well-being from interference," but we can let this pass, as Lomasky is prepared to accept that there is *a sense* in which I must claim "All others ought at least to refrain from interfering with my freedom and well-being." (See Lomasky 1981, 249.) In other words, he concedes that there is a sense in which (4) entails (4d). *However*, he claims that (4d) is ambiguous. The sense in which it is validly derived from (4) does not permit (5) "I have a right to my freedom and well-being" to be inferred. Conversely, in any sense correlative to (5), (4d) is not validly derived from (4).

The two interpretations of (4d) that Lomasky offers are

(A) "Would that all others at least refrain from interfering with my freedom and well-being" (i.e., "It ought to be the case that I am not interfered with");

[and] (B) "All others have reasons that justify at least their refraining from interfering with my freedom and well-being." (Ibid.)

According to Lomasky, "(A) is a judgement logically incumbent upon the agent" (ibid.). But the motivational force of (A) (through my [4c]),

applies only to the agent himself. Specifically, (A) makes no reference to any reasons potential interferers might have to refrain from doing so. Therefore, no *right* to non-interference can be adduced from (A). (Ibid., 250)

On the other hand, (B)

is strong enough to ground the existence of a right to non-interference. . . . Unfortunately, the inference can be shown to be invalid. . . . [I]f Gewirth were to invoke (B) as the preferred interpretation, he would be adopting a course that his own dialectically necessary method disallows. (Ibid.)

But why must it be the case that others must have (accept) a reason not to interfere with my freedom and well-being before I can (intelligibly) claim a right to my freedom and well-being? Lomasky asks us to imagine that there is a disease that threatens my basic well-being. I must accept that I ought to be free from this disease and that I ought to take steps to avoid this disease.

Clearly, though, it is illegitimate to jump from 'I ought to be free from [this] disease' to 'I have a right to be free from [this] disease.' For the latter claim makes sense only if there is some party against whom I have the right. By analogy, I cannot proceed from my desire to have freedom and well-being, or even my need to have them, to the claim that their possession is a matter of right. Unless others have reason to refrain from conduct inimical to my necessary goods, no right against them can obtain. (Ibid.)

However, whereas Lomasky is quite right to say that it does not follow from (4)/(4c) that I have a right (against the disease) to be free from the disease (that the disease has a duty not to infect me); it does not follow from this that (4)/(4c) cannot entail "I have a right to my freedom and well-being *against PPAO*" (which in the present context might be instantiated by "PPAO has a duty not to deliberately infect me with this disease"). The reason why we can readily assent to my not having a right (against the disease) to be free from the disease, is that we do not suppose that bacteria or viruses are PPAs. For me to have a right to Y against X is for X to have a duty not to interfere with my having/doing Y. This, however, can only be the case if it is in X's power to choose to refrain from interfering with my having/doing Y. We do not suppose that bacteria or viruses are PPAs, and in not so supposing, we do not suppose that they have this power. Lomasky's inference from this, that I cannot consider that I have a right to my freedom and well-being against PPAO unless PPAO has a reason to refrain from interfering with my freedom and well-being, is not established by analogy because bacteria and viruses cannot have reasons to refrain from interfering with my freedom and well-being. PPAO might not have a reason to refrain from interference with my freedom and well-being because I categorically need my freedom and well-being, but it does not follow that PPAO cannot accept this as a reason; and all that the necessary supposition for "rights" talk supposes (that PPAO can choose to refrain from interfering with what I have a right to) is that PPAO *could* accept my need for noninterference as a reason not to interfere, not that it *does* accept this need as such a reason.

(A) should, in fact, be rewritten as

(A')   I have a reason that justifies (for me) that all others at least refrain from interfering with my freedom and well-being.

Correspondingly, (B) is to be rewritten as

(B')   PPAO has a reason that justifies (for PPAO) that PPAO at least refrain from interfering with my freedom and well-being.

All that Lomasky's example shows is that a rights-claim must be *addressed* to a PPA. However, on the basis of (A'), I do address "My freedom and well-being ought not to be interfered with" to PPAO, for reasons that I consider justify the state of affairs that I prescribe. Lomasky claims that (A') is not correlative to a rights-claim, because a rights-claim presupposes that PPAO has a reason that justifies *for PPAO* that PPAO ought not to interfere with my freedom and well-being. This is false. If I say that I have a right to my freedom and well-being because I categorically need my freedom and well-being, I say that I consider that my need for freedom and well-being is a reason why PPAO ought not to interfere with my freedom and well-being. I do not say that PPAO accepts "I categorically need my freedom and well-being" as the reason why it ought not to interfere with my freedom and well-being. If a rights-claim is only intelligible when those to whom it is addressed accept the criteria on which it is based, then no rights-claim of any kind can be intelligible when addressed to those who do not accept the criteria on which it is based. But even if it is not intelligible to them, it is intelligible to me. And it really is going a bit far to say that the claim is unintelligible (either carte blanche or to them) simply on the grounds that they do not accept it. When South African racists claim that they have a right to rule as a minority (because they are white), I do not accept this claim, but it is perfectly intelligible to me. I am perfectly capable of assenting to the criterion, only I don't; and if I did, I would accept that they had the claimed right. Because I don't accept the criterion does not mean that they do not intelligibly claim a right. It just means that I don't accept that their criterion is a valid one for claiming it.

Lomasky claims that only by failing to recognize the ambiguity revealed by contrasting (A) and (B) can Gewirth profess to have demonstrated the necessity of a PPA's considering that it has a right to its freedom and well-being. (See ibid., 251.) Gewirth is fully conscious of this ambiguity. (See RM 94.) However, he does not think that (4d) has to be interpreted via (B) for his argument to work. He thinks that (A)/(A') is sufficient. Lomasky gives no reason why Gewirth cannot universalize (A') to the PGC.[27]

9 Singer

Gewirth maintains that in (4d) "PPAO ought not to interfere with my freedom and well-being" the "ought" is prudential and correlative to a rights-claim.

According to Marcus G. Singer,

1. Inasmuch as we can make sense of the notion of a "prudential right," it is not correlative to any "oughts" at all. Correlativity between rights and duties only holds where these are moral. (See Singer 1985, 297–298.)
2. Gewirth cites a number of examples of nonmoral (and nonlegal) contexts in which people talk of having rights. (See RM 69–71.) However, Gewirth's contention that rights are applicable in nonmoral and nonlegal contexts has only a linguistic basis. People might speak of, e.g., "intellectual rights,"[28] but talk of rights outside of legal and moral contexts is only metaphorical. (See Singer 1985, 299.)

On 1, his argument appears to be as follows.[29]

a. "A prudentially ought to do x" translates as "It would be imprudent for A not to do x." "A has a prudential right to x" translates as "A prudentially ought to have x" (which translates as "It would be imprudent for A not to have x" = "A would act imprudently not to have x"). According to Singer, the notion of it being imprudent for me not to have x is at least questionable.

And the air of strangeness in this last is due to the idea, which corresponds to a fact, that whereas one's doing x is ordinarily under one's control, one's having x is not—or not obviously—under one's control. (Ibid., 298)

However, even if we can use prudential "ought" in both "do" and "have" contexts, there is another problem.

b. "A has a prudential right to do x" can be read either as "It would be in A's interest for A to do x," or "It would not be contrary to A's interest for A to do x," or "It would not be imprudent for A to do x." From this it follows "that it is contrary to A's interest for B (or anyone else) to interfere with A's doing (having) x" (ibid., 299). However, this contains no prudential "ought." To establish that any-one other than A has any prudential obligation with respect to A's having/doing x, it must be established that if any other were to interfere with A's having/doing x, that this other would be doing something contrary to this *other's* interest. So, even if the idea of a prudential right is not disqualified by unintelligibility (by consideration *a*), it is not correlative to any other-directing "ought." (See ibid., 298–299.)

This is tremendously confusing. As Gewirth intends "A has a prudential right to x," this is to be translated as "It is in A's interest (where this specifically refers to A's categorical need for freedom and well-being) for A to have x" = "It is against A's interest for *B* to interfere with A's having x" = "B ought not *in A's interest* to interfere with A's doing x." When I say that PPAO prudentially ought not to interfere with my doing x, I say that PPAO ought not to interfere with my doing x on my prudential criterion, not on PPAO's. It is true that this is not necessarily directing for PPAO, meaning that, on the grounds that PPAO ought not to interfere with my doing x, because interference is not in my interest, it does not follow that interference is not in PPAO's interest. PPAO might accept that to interfere with my doing x is not in my interest, but not take this as a reason why it ought not to interfere with my doing x. But this does not mean that PPAO does not have an obligation *on the criterion of my interest* not to interfere with my doing/having x. PPAO can have an obligation on this criterion without having an obligation assertorically, or on some other criterion (say that of its own interest). What matters, because the argument is dialectical from my internal point of view, is what my prudential criterion validates. Other criteria are irrelevant.

In line with this, it is not true to say that "A prudentially ought to do x" translates as "It would be imprudent (on the criterion of A's interest) for A not to do x." Within the context of the argument, it translates as "A ought (on the criterion of *my* interest) to do x," regardless of who A is. "A has a prudential right to x" does not translate as "It would be imprudent for A not to have x," but as "It is against *my* interest for PPAO to interfere with my having x," correlative to "PPAO ought not to interfere with my having x in my interest." The "ought" here takes doing, not having, as its object, so there is no problem of the kind Singer raises under *a*. Furthermore, none of the initial translations of "A has a prudential right to do x," which Singer offers, will do. These are translations of "A prudentially does no wrong to do x," which can take a mere liberties sense as well as a claim rights sense, although he corrects this by (invalidly) inferring the correct claim rights reading "It is contrary to A's interest for B to interfere with A's having x" from them.

On 2, Singer claims that if, e.g., intellectual rights are really rights, then they must correlate with duties on the part of others. But he says that interference by others in such a context does not violate intellectual criteria unless it is of a form that also constitutes a moral offense (such as by threats, distortion, or hiding evidence). (See ibid., 299.)

This is irrelevant. That violations of criteria of "intellectual" propriety might also be violations of what Singer takes to be moral criteria shows nothing. What Singer has to show is that such violations are only violations of intellectual criteria *because* they are violations of moral criteria. Intellectual activity, of the kind Gewirth and Singer refer to, is guided by the goal of trying to discover what is true and what is false. Rights not to be threatened, etc., arise from the means required to pursue this enterprise rationally, and are internal to the enterprise itself. That the same rights might be secured on other criteria does not show that the rights are not secured independent of these criteria. Doubtless, if one has a moral point of view (which one takes to be overriding), and there is a conflict between what one's moral criteria validate and what other criteria validate, then one will not claim rights to what is validated by these other criteria. But it does not follow that one does not have rights *on* these other criteria. When Gewirth points to nonmoral rights and duties, he is pointing to the fact that rights and duties are held according to criteria for action or belief, and that these criteria are not all moral criteria.

Furthermore, it should be noted that Singer's willingness to accept that rights-talk is appropriate in legal contexts muddies the waters considerably. Although I would say that once Gewirth's entire argument is established then we have to view the legal enterprise as a moral one (see Beyleveld and Brownsword 1986), this has not yet been established. Without its being established there are plenty of nonmoral goals that we can give this enterprise. If so, to conceive of legal rights will be to conceive of nonmoral rights, and many would say that law serves the interests of the law giver. This would, in fact, make legal rights a species of prudential rights. So Singer's concession that rights-talk (correlative to other-directed duties) is appropriate in legal contexts might be construed as an unwitting concession of Gewirth's claims.

10 McMahon

Christopher McMahon alleges that Gewirth can establish that I must consider that PPAO ought to respect my freedom and well-being only if this "ought" is interpreted as an "'ought' of evaluation"

which reports the existence of sufficient reason, from some point of view, for regarding a particular event or state of affairs as desirable. In general, judgments employing the "ought" of evaluation are expressed only when action-guiding "ought"-judgments would be out of place—either because the object of the judgment cannot be realized by action . . . , or because no agent who can contribute to its realization has sufficient reason to do so . . . . But it appears that any judgment of the desirability of some state of affairs that can be made with the word "good" can be made with the "ought" of evaluation as well. (McMahon 1986, 269)

However, such an "ought" is not action-directing. To be action-directing, an "ought" judgment must be one that reports the existence of reasons for action sufficient to warrant the performance of some action by a PPA (either an "'ought' of rationality," in which the reasons are nonmoral [and typically prudential], or a "moral 'ought,'" in which the reasons are moral). Gewirth, however, cannot establish (4d) as an "ought" of rationality (as a prudential ought), because the fact that I need my freedom and well-being is not necessarily a reason for PPAO not to interfere with my freedom and well-being (unless we suppose that PPAO is altruistically motivated).[30]

Furthermore, McMahon claims that the notion of a "prudential right" is untenable. When Gewirth talks about prudential rights he is illicitly invoking moral rights. In relation to this, McMahon makes three claims.

1. Gewirth's claim that there are nonmoral and nonlegal contexts in which rights-claims can be made (e.g., epistemic ones) does not show that there are prudential rights. (See ibid., 272.) This is because prudential rights cannot be modelled on epistemic ones.

From the standpoint of theoretical reason [unlike that of practical reason], one is justified in exercising a right to be sure that some state of affairs obtains if and only if there is sufficient reason for believing it to obtain. And the considerations which establish this also establish that others ought to accept one's right-claim. (Ibid., 278)

On the other hand, all self-interested reasons are agent-relative.

From A has good reason to do X, one cannot infer that others have good reason to assist A.

2. On Gewirth's definition of a moral judgment, as one in which a PPA accepts moral (other-regarding) reasons for action in its own case,

few right-claims of any sort (that is, right-judgments made by the recipient) will count as moral judgments. (Ibid., 273)

3. Gewirth thinks that the type of right claimed is determined by "the occasion" of the claim (the reason for exercising the claim, for choosing to lay claim to a right), rather than by the "ground" of the claim (the reason for the claim to be respected). Conventionally, however, the type of right claimed is determined by its ground, not by its occasion.[31]

A moral right is not one which is exercised for moral reasons, it is one which is respected for moral reasons. Given this convention, a prudential right should be one which is respected for prudential reasons. (Ibid.)

Because Gewirth disavows this view, by insisting that the criterion of a prudential right is the PPA's own interests, it follows that Gewirth's analysis entails that,

while the reason an agent has for exercising his right to freedom and well-being is prudential, the consideration which he regards as establishing that others ought to respect his claim must be some *nonprudential* reason that he believes other agents have to promote his freedom and well[-]being (if he wants them to). (Ibid., 273–274)

This, however, means that any argument for my having to claim a prudential right to my freedom and well-being must include the premise that PPAO has a sufficient nonprudential reason to contribute to the maintenance of my freedom and well-being. But such a reason has the primary aspect of a moral reason: "it is a reason for an agent [the addressee] to promote the welfare of someone else" (ibid., 274). Thus, Gewirth's PPA, in Stage II, is one who operates on the maxim that others are morally motivated while it is prudentially motivated. Gewirth gives no reason why a PPA must accept this maxim, as he gives no reason that has force for PPAO why PPAO ought to respect my freedom and well-being. (See ibid.)[32]

In response to the allegation that (4d) is only validly derived as an "ought" of evaluation, Gewirth points out that, in being derived from (4) "My freedom and well-being are necessary goods," (4d) is not derived from an "ought" of evaluation. (4) is equivalent to (4c) "I ought to pursue my freedom and well-being," which is at least a self-referring action-guiding "ought." (See Gewirth 1988c, 250.) The

question, of course, remains whether (4d) "PPAO ought not to interfere with my freedom and well-being," as an action-directing
"ought," ≡ "There is sufficient reason for PPAO not to interfere with
my freedom and well-being," can be derived from (4c).

According to Gewirth, "There is sufficient reason for A (PPAO) to
do X (refrain from interfering with PPA's freedom and well-being)"
(= [10] in Gewirth's numbering) is ambiguous. This may mean

either (10a) "*A himself acknowledges and accepts that* there is sufficient
reason for him to do *X*," or (10b) "The speaker [e.g., PPA] of (10) holds, from
his own point of view, that there is sufficient reason for *A* to do *X*." (Ibid.,
251)

Thus, (4d) can be construed as an "ought" of rationality (an action-directing "ought"), but only if construed along the lines of (10b)
rather than (10a). Interpreted in line with (10b), (4d) is validly derived from (4c), and does

"report the existence of sufficient reason for others to act so as to maintain
my freedom and well-being" . . . ; but the reason in question is that of the
rational agent-speaker concerned for his necessary goods of action, not that
of the other persons about whom he makes the 'ought'-judgment. (Ibid., 252)

Interpreted in terms of (10b), (4d) expresses more than an "ought"
of evaluation; it is an action directive justified within my point of
view, even if not justified within PPAO's point of view.[33]

On the question of prudential rights, Gewirth responds to 1 by
stating that he did not intend to model prudential rights on epistemic rights as such.

I did not . . . use the example of epistemic rights to provide an exact parallel
to prudential or other rights, but only to show that rights and right-claims
may be based on various criteria (including intellectual ones) that are different from moral and legal criteria, so that a place is made for prudential rights
based on prudential criteria. (Ibid., 262 n. 9)

In response to 2 and 3, Gewirth has a number of things to say.

1. Gewirth holds that the classification of rights-claims depends
on the criteria that the upholder of the right employs to justify upholding it. Thus, from my point of view, a right is moral if my criteria that validate it are other-regarding. From the addressee's point
of view, the right is moral if the criteria the addressee employs that
validate it are other-regarding. The addressee might regard a claim
as moral that the claimant regards as prudential and vice versa. (See
ibid., 256, 258–260.)

I would add to this, first, that what McMahon calls the "ground" of the claim is ambiguous as between (*a*) the criterion by which the addressee justifies the rights-claim and (*b*) the criterion by which the claimant justifies the rights-claim. McMahon chooses to hold that no justification for a rights-claim exists unless the addressee's criterion justifies the claim. Simply by stating that the ground of the claim is the reason for it to be respected, McMahon suggests that the reason for holding the claim to be justified (which is surely what the ground of the claim is) is the reason for it to be respected *by others*. But why must justification always be justification in the eyes of others? Second, what he calls the "occasion" of the claim is ambiguous as between (*b*) the criterion that the claimant uses to justify the claim, and (*c*) the reason that the claimant has for wanting any right that is justified (under [*b*]) to be exercised (laid claim to). Only by saying that Gewirth confuses (*c*) with (*a*)/(*b*) can McMahon hold that Gewirth confuses "ground" with "occasion." In fact, Gewirth does nothing of the sort; he holds (contrary to McMahon) that the relevant "ground" for the dialectically necessary method *within a PPA's point of view* is (*b*) rather than (*a*), which is surely correct. If a PPA is not assumed (or yet shown) to take account of the interests of others, why should what it regards as justified depend on the views of others as determined by their interests? Third, we need to note that McMahon appeals to "conventional usage" (though it is not a usage I would consider normal). But, even if it is normal, that fact, by itself, has no bearing on the intelligibility of Gewirth's classification, or on its permissibility, and it does not render McMahon's usage immune from difficulties (as we shall see below).

2. McMahon's classification makes the idea of a prudential right impossible by definition. If the addressee does not recognize the claim then there is no rights-claim. If the addressee recognizes the claim, then it is moral. (See ibid., 256–257.)

This, it should be noted, follows from McMahon's taking (*a*) as the relevant ground. I should also add that since Gewirth's definition of a moral criterion is one that is other-regarding, *or* other-regarding *as well as* self-regarding, McMahon's claim that it will render few rights-claims moral strikes me as false.

3. McMahon's classification makes all rights-claims egalitarian universalist, as no rights-claim is made unless all PPAs accept criteria that require them to honor it. (See ibid., 257.)

Indeed, I think that, on McMahon's classification, it will certainly be false that there are any rights-claims made. Perhaps McMahon, and other advocates of a recognitional analysis of the intelligibility of rights-claims, would respond that only some addressees need to accept criteria that require them to honor it. However, I see no non-arbitrary reason for making such a specification.

4. The claim that Gewirth (or his PPA) attributes nonprudential reasons (and hence a moral point of view) to PPAO not to interfere with PPA's freedom and well-being, because Gewirth claims that it is not necessarily in PPAO's interests to honor PPA's rights-claim (that PPA's rights-claim is not necessarily validated by PPAO's prudential criterion), is unwarranted. Quite simply, this is because the argument focuses on PPA's reasons for claiming rights, not on PPAO's reasons for honoring such claims. Thus, no assumption is made about PPAO's having moral reasons to honor PPA's claim—because no assumption is made *at all* that PPAO *will* honor PPA's claim, *for any sort of reason*. (See ibid., 258–259.)

5.

The more general issue raised by McMahon about the concept of prudential rights and their distinction from moral rights is whether it makes sense to talk of rights and their correlative 'oughts' where it is not assumed that the respondents, the persons to whom the right-claims are addressed, have their own reasons for accepting or honoring the claims. (Ibid., 259)

Gewirth says that to talk about persons "having reasons to do X" can be looked at personally (addressees themselves accept certain reasons to do X) or impersonally (there are criteria that justify the addressees' actions of doing X whether or not they accept these criteria). For Gewirth, but not McMahon apparently, it makes sense to talk about rights-claims when the addressees do not have reasons to do X in the personal sense. The rights-claims that Gewirth's PPA addresses are, in effect, justified impersonally on the criterion of the PPA's interests, these claims having the personal aspect for PPA as well, because PPA accepts the criterion of its own interests (but not necessarily having the personal aspect for PPAO, because PPAO does not necessarily accept this criterion). Gewirth asks,

Can right-claims be addressed to persons where the claimants do not assume that there are certain *general* reasons, acceptable at least in principle to all rational persons, that justify the claims? (Ibid.)

Gewirth says that this must be answered affirmatively, unless we are to say that slaves cannot meaningfully direct rights-claims to their masters, or that there are no rights *on* the criteria of legal rules if these rules are not accepted by everyone. (See ibid., 259–260.)

And, indeed, it can be added that if we do not answer this question affirmatively, we would have to forfeit saying that there are *moral* rights according to X or Y or Z criteria if these criteria are not accepted by everyone.

#36 **"My freedom and well-being are necessary goods" cannot entail "I have a right to my freedom and well-being," because I can have a right to do X when X is not for my own good.**

According to Alasdair MacIntyre, "I have a right to have/do X" entails (*ceteris paribus*) "Others ought not to interfere with my attempts to have/do X, whether or not X is for my own good, and regardless of what kind of good is at issue." (See MacIntyre 1981, 64–65.)

MacIntyre appears to be saying that my judgment "X is a necessary good" cannot be a *sufficient* condition for my judgment "I have a right to X" because "X is a good (necessary or otherwise)" is not a *necessary* condition for "I have a right to X."

We must, of course, state this dialectically and within the context of the argument. So, MacIntyre is saying

(1) "I consider that I have a right to X" does not entail "I consider that X is good." ∴

(2) "I must consider that X is a necessary good (I must value X proactively for whatever my purposes)" does not entail "I must consider that I have a right to X."

Now, even if (1) is correct, I do not see how (2) follows from it. Furthermore, "My freedom and well-being are necessary goods" is, because of the *proactive* value that I attach to my purposes, equivalent to "I instrumentally prudentially (strictly) *ought* to pursue my freedom and well-being." It is all very well MacIntyre's saying that "good" is a completely different concept from "a right." But the sort of good we are talking about when we talk about "necessary goods" in Gewirth's argument is an "ought," and strict "oughts" belong to the same family of deontic concepts as "rights." To say that X is "good" in the argument is to say that I value it proactively. According to the argument, I rationally must value my freedom and well-being proactively, whether I, in fact, do so or not.[34]

In any case, whatever its bearing on (2) (which is all that is really at issue), is (1) true? There are doubtless senses in which it is. At the same time, however, the concept of "a right" is not wholly divorced from the concept of what is "good" or "a good."

Gewirth claims that

a necessary condition of any person's claiming a right to anything X is that X seems to him to be good. . . .

To lay claim to something X as one's right is contrasted with the situation where one makes no claim to have it as one's right. Such claiming or laying claim, when done explicitly, is a purposive action. . . . [I]n the case of all his actions the agent regards their purposes as good. Hence, unless the claimant regarded his claiming a right to X as having a purpose he considers good, he would not explicitly make the claim. To be sure, it might still be argued that this good purpose may consist in the claiming itself or in some goal beyond the X that is the direct object of the right-claim. But it is difficult to see how, in either of these cases, the purpose in question could be considered good without X itself being regarded as at least instrumentally good. This connection between rights and good also obtains when the person in question does not explicitly lay claim to X as his right but merely thinks he has a right to it. There would be no point in his thinking this unless he regarded X as directly or indirectly good [good in relation to the purposes he holds to be served by his having the right]. (RM 76)

MacIntyre, no doubt, disagrees, but he merely asserts (1) and provides no argument for it.

#37   "My freedom and well-being are necessary goods" cannot entail "I have a right to my freedom and well-being," because claims about rights are universalizable, whereas claims about necessary goods are not.

According to MacIntyre, the property of necessary universalizability, which belongs to claims about rights, does not belong to claims about

either the possession of or the need or desire for a good, even a universally necessary good. (MacIntyre 1981, 65)

I take it that MacIntyre is contending that from "I consider X to be good" (even from "I [because I am a PPA] rationally must value X proactively for my purposes, whatever they might be," coupled with my recognition that every PPA must make this same claim for itself—and this is the only legitimate interpretation of "X is a universally necessary good"), it does not follow that I rationally must consider that I ought not to interfere with PPAO's having/doing X. The objection is pertinent, because *if* "X is a necessary good (for me)" justifies "I have a right to X" (within my dialectically necessary viewpoint), and this latter universalizes to "PPAO has a right to X"—where the ground for "I have a right to X" is "I am a PPA" (which MacIntyre concedes is the case)—then "X is a necessary good (for me)" should universalize to "PPAO has a right to X" (or, at any rate, to a proposition from which this can be straightforwardly derived), where "I am a PPA" is the ground of "X is a necessary good (for me)." If Stage II is valid, then we ought to be able to apply universalization before connecting goods to rights, rather than only being able to universalize after connecting goods to rights. I take it that MacIntyre says that we cannot do this.[35]

I disagree! It seems to me that, from my internal point of view,

> ["I am a PPA" rationally requires me to claim "X is a necessary good" ($\equiv$ "I ought to pursue X for my purposes, whatever my purposes")] does rationally require me to claim "I ought not to interfere with PPAO having/doing X, whatever my purposes."

This is because "I am a PPA" *rationally requires*, within my internal viewpoint, my defense/pursuit of X. By the LPU (because, *within my viewpoint*, "I am a PPA" is a sufficient reason for "I ought to defend X from interference"), it follows that "PPAO is a PPA" rationally requires "PPAO ought to defend/pursue X," *not only within PPAO's internal viewpoint, but within mine as well. Within my dialectically necessary viewpoint*, "I am a PPA" justifies my actions to secure X. Since PPAO is a PPA, PPAO's defense of X must be held to be justified within my dialectically necessary viewpoint too. This means that it is not only PPAO who must advocate PPAO's defense of X. I must advocate it too. Since "A ought to do X" entails "A ought to be free to do X" (where the viewpoint and criterion of "ought" is the same), and A needs X (its necessary goods) in order to be free to do anything (thus to be free to do X), I must advocate that PPAO have X. This means that I must advocate that I not interfere with PPAO doing X.

Of course, this requires "I ought to pursue my freedom and well-being" to be validated by my prudential criterion as an impersonal good, as a state of affairs that ought to be brought about by those who can, on the grounds that I am a PPA. (I have defended this in my discussion of Kalin [#35.3].) If my being a PPA is what justifies the state of affairs of my being able to pursue my freedom and well-being, *within my viewpoint*, then X being a PPA must justify the state of affairs of X being able to pursue its freedom and well-being as well (within my viewpoint).

What MacIntyre fails to appreciate is that statements about necessary goods from my internal viewpoint as a PPA are statements of strict "ought," albeit only self-referring in the first instance, and these are universalizable both by the external and the internal applications of the LPU.

In giving this response, I do not wish to imply that MacIntyre is right to say that rights-claims (or, at any rate, deontic claims) are necessarily universalizable, whereas judgments of good are not. I see no reason why rights-claims that I make for myself must be granted to other PPAs *simply on the grounds that they are rights-claims;* and I also see no reason why "My having X is good, because I am a PPA," does not universalize to "PPAO's having X is good, because PPAO is a PPA."

In relation to the first point, what makes predication of a property P universalizable is that P is possessed (or claimed to be possessed) for a sufficient reason, the possession of a property R. If I possess (claim to possess) P because I have R, then (I must claim that) all who possess R must possess P. But, if R is a property that only I possess, then I do not have to grant P to anyone other than myself. The range of universalization depends on the range of predication of R, not on the sort of property that P is.

Regarding the second point, it follows from the first point that any claim of the form "X has P because X has R" universalizes logically to "All who have R have P." So, too, does any claim of the form "X's having Y has P because X has R" universalize to "Anyone's having Y has P if this anyone has R." If I judge that the state of affairs "my (X's) having freedom and well-being (Y)" is good (has P) because I am a PPA (have R), then I must hold that PPAO's having freedom and well-being is good because PPAO is a PPA. By having to judge that my freedom and well-being are necessary goods, I am required to judge that my freedom and well-being are good, on pain of contradicting that I am a PPA. By an argument analogous to the ASA, this requires me to judge that my having freedom and well-being is good, because I am a PPA. Internal application of the LPU then requires me to judge that PPAO's having freedom and well-being is good because PPAO is a PPA.

Of course, if the judgment of "goodness" here is merely a judgment of what is a desirable state of affairs, then this result, although justifying a moral position dialectically, would not, by itself, justify a *deontological* position; it would not necessarily require me to do anything to bring this state of affairs about. But, because the judgment of goodness in the argument is one of proactive value, a deontological result is secured.

This, however, should make it clear that the significance of judgments of necessary good being proactive (and hence deontic) is not specifically on the universalizability of these judgments, but on the deontological nature of Gewirth's theory. The universalizability of my judgments of necessary good depends on the goodness of my having freedom and well-being being impersonal *on* my prudential criterion. (See #13 and #35.3.) The specific significance of my having to attribute *necessary* goodness to my freedom and well-being is that I deny that I am a PPA if I do not judge my freedom and well-being to be good; and this, via an argument analogous to the ASA, has the result that I must cite being a PPA as the sufficient reason why my having freedom and well-being is good, which has the consequence that universalization of my judgment that my freedom and well-being are good requires me to judge that the freedom and well-being of *all PPAs* are good.

#38   I cannot, *on a prudential basis,* be required to consider that I have a right to my freedom and well-being, for, then (by universalization), I must concede that I have a duty not to interfere with the freedom and well-being of PPAO, and it is not necessarily in my interests to do so.

Jan Narveson contends that if I claim a right to my freedom and well-being, I must accept a duty not to interfere with the freedom and well-being of PPAO.[36] Because this is so, it cannot be the case that I am logically required to claim such a right on the basis of my having purposes that I want to achieve. If the achievement of my purposes is the criterion for my rights-claims, then it is also the criterion for the duties I acknowledge. However, for me to accept a duty not to interfere with the freedom and well-being of PPAO will not necessarily be conducive to my achievement of my purposes. Precisely because of the correlativity of rights and duties, and their universalizability, if it is not necessarily in my interests to concede a right to freedom and well-being to others, then it cannot necessarily be in my interest to claim a right to freedom and well-being for myself.

[I]f all we are given in the concept of a rational agent is that he has various purposes which he wants to achieve, and if all of his "necessary" evaluations are based on this fact alone, then what the agent must do is decide whether the duties he saddles himself with in claiming the rights in question are *worth it*. There can be no question of the agent's just mindlessly (as it were) insisting on these rights, whatever the price, and then (perhaps reluctantly) finding himself forced to acknowledge everyone else's rights as well. He must, as characterized by Gewirth, make a calculation on this point. And it is simply not a priori knowable whether the calculation in question must turn out favorable to rights. Doubtless it will for most of us, but that is a lot less than what Gewirth is trying to prove. (Narveson 1979, 429–30)

1. However, it is not true that *all* we are given in the concept of a

PPA is that it has various purposes it wants to achieve. We are also given that a PPA categorically needs its freedom and well-being. Given *both* of these things, *a rational PPA* (a rational PPA being, not one who acts for its particular occurrent purposes, but one who reasons logically from the [necessary and invariant] proactive evaluative relation to its purposes inherent in whatever its particular occurrent purposes) must (*a*) judge that it ought, *irrespective of its particular occurrent purposes*, to pursue its freedom and well-being for its purposes, and (*b*) accept all judgments that it is required to make in logical consistency with this judgment.

2. It follows that the criterion of a PPA's judgments is not the particular occurrent purposes that it has, but these in synthesis with the generic features of its agency—which, in synthesis, constitute the self-referring "ought" that begins Stage II. It is not open to the PPA to eschew this "ought" on any particular occurrent purposes, so it is not open to the PPA to eschew the logical implications of this judgment.

3. On the basis of this judgment, the PPA logically must claim a right to its freedom and well-being, which it must then universalize to all PPAs, because the ground of this claim is that it is a PPA. It might very well be the case that it has particular occurrent purposes that would not be served by granting rights to freedom and well-being to all PPAs. But the argument is not, as Narveson attempts to portray it, that it is in the interests of PPAs (interpreted as their particular occurrent purposes) to grant rights to freedom and well-being to all PPAs (to accept a duty for it not to interfere with the freedom and well-being of all PPAs). It is that I deny I am a PPA by not granting rights to PPAO that I must claim for myself on the ground that I categorically need my freedom and well-being.

4. Narveson seems to consider that I have a choice whether or not to claim a right to my freedom and well-being, depending on my particular occurrent purposes. But it is not my particular occurrent purposes as such that constitute my prudential criterion in Gewirth's argument, but my conative normality coupled with my perception that I need my freedom and well-being for whatever my purposes might be (that I would need to value my freedom and well-being proactively even if my purposes were different from what they happen to be) that constitutes this criterion. My particular occurrent purposes can affect whether I wish to lay claim to the rights I must consider I have, but not whether I must consider that I have these rights to lay claim to.[37]

#39   Stage II is invalid because it is not dialectically necessary to claim more than a right to try to obtain freedom and well-being.

According to Virginia Held,

someone who would be content for himself to be accorded only the right to try to act given his resources, since he was confident he could often enough win the contests that would result, might not go through the same reasoning that yields Gewirth's principle. He would rationally conclude that he would be better off winning these various contests among persons with rights to try to act in various ways, than he would be if everyone were accorded rights to have, and not just to try to have, what they actually need to act successfully. On the prudential grounds Gewirth goes through in developing his argument, the agent should assert this right. To have a chance to win such contests while others lose provides far larger rewards for the winners than would assuring to all the conditions for modest success.

Suppose the argument is presented to a successful or aspiring entrepreneur. He agrees: in eating this lavish meal, I act. I recognize that trying to act with the resources one has is a generic feature of all action. I assert that I have a right to try to do and [try to] obtain what I want through action,[38] and I acknowledge that others must have the same rights to try to do and [try to] obtain what they want through action. But I reject the view that everyone has a right to actually have what he or she needs to act successfully, and do not claim this for myself. Better, such an entrepreneur might suggest, that there be some rich and some poor than that all people have rights to have what they actually need, because in the latter case there would be none who could enjoy a meal like this . . . .

. . . The agent I have described would *want* others to compete, since he would expect them to lose, and winning such competitions would provide him more than would a non-competitive recognition of everyone's rights to have what they need to act successfully. The consistency that could be demanded of such an agent . . . is that he ask for no more assurance of his rights to actually have non-interference than he is willing to accord to others to actually have well-being. (Held 1979, 246–248)

What exactly is being claimed here is far from clear.

1. Of course, a PPA who demands a right to try to have its freedom and well-being, need not *on this demand* concede PPAO more than a right to try to have its freedom and well-being. But the question is whether it is dialectically consistent for a PPA to demand only a right to *try to have* its freedom and well-being, not to *have* its freedom and well-being.

Now, as far as its freedom and *basic* well-being are concerned, having these is a necessary precondition of trying to act at all, thus of trying to pursue its freedom and well-being. If, as a PPA, I must claim a right to try to have freedom and well-being (as Held seems to concede), then I must claim a right to *have* my freedom and basic well-being. As such, I must (as Held concedes by conceding universalization) grant a right to others to *have* their freedom and basic well-being.

Given this, the objection cannot threaten Stage II as such. At most it would require the argument to limit rights-claims to freedom and *basic* well-being. But even this is not the case. For, when I set out to achieve a purpose, I do so with the aim of succeeding. My attempt is pointless if I know that I am to be deprived of the general preconditions of successful action. For it to be rational for me to attempt to achieve purposes, I must have the general conditions of successful action. The criterion that requires me to try to pursue my freedom and well-being must, therefore, validate that I not be deprived of my nonsubtractive and additive well-being *generically interpreted* as well. Thus, Held's entrepreneur is being *dialectically* inconsistent.

2. Held's objection makes more sense if it is interpreted along the lines of Narveson's objection (see #38). For, with its particular occurrent purposes as its prudential base, the entrepreneur might well judge that it is in its particular occurrent interest to take the stance that Held describes.[39] But this misconstrues the nature of the argument. A PPA's "prudential base" consists of values and needs that pertain to its purposivity as such, not to what pertains to some, but not all, of its particular occurrent purposes.

3. It is possible that Held has in mind (at least partly) something akin to R. Randall Kelso's claim that Stage II assumes that PPAs are "risk-adverse" (*sic*). "Risk-preferrers" would not claim rights to their *basic goods* (rights to have them), because they might be willing to risk their basic goods being interfered with for the sake of being able to pursue additive gains (which, incidentally, he gives a particular occurrent interpretation. See Kelso 1982, 141–143). The argument, however, makes no assumption about PPA's being risk-averse rather than risk-preferring. Kelso's objection, like Narveson's (see #38) assumes that the argument is about what a PPA should do on the basis of a calculation of its utility interpreted in terms of its particular occurrent purposes and characteristics. (For discussion that picks up on this, see #54.) Somewhat ironically, Kelso has an argument of his own to the effect that "nonegocentric" behavior is demanded by the "logic of one's own consciousness." (See ibid., 156.) This argument is inadequate because it transparently assumes a moral point of view (what he calls "reciprocal thought"), but the irony is that Gewirth's argument is more akin to a "logic of consciousness," a logic of one's consciousness as a PPA (rather than as

a morally motivated being), than it is to a standard contractarian or utilitarian one.[40]

General Comments

In this chapter I have argued that

1. it is not open to a PPA to deny (4c) (that it ought to pursue its freedom and well-being), given its conative normality;

2. the assumption of conative normality does not violate the dialectically necessary method, as those who are not motivated to pursue their purposes are not PPAs;

3. the argument for Stage II does not presuppose that to deny (5) "I have a claim right to my freedom and well-being" is to grant PPAO a claim right to interfere with my freedom and well-being;

4. the inference from (4c) "I ought to pursue my freedom and well-being" to (4d) "PPAO ought to pursue my freedom and well-being" relies on no more than "ought implies can," where the criterion of both "oughts" is my interests, and both prescriptions are made from my point of view as a PPA. It is important to appreciate that the context of this operation is one in which I am a PPA to whom (4c) is properly prescribed, and the question is what prescriptions must be made to back the proper prescription of (4c), not one in which what is in question is whether I am a PPA to whom (4c) is properly prescribed;

5. "universal ethical egoism," as defined by Gewirth, is inconsistent. It is important not to confuse this position with amoralism. To confuse Gewirth's arguments against these two positions invites the mistaken reading that Gewirth attempts to refute amoralism in Stage II; and

6. various charges that Gewirth illicitly presupposes a moral point of view in order to derive (4d) "PPAO ought not to interfere with my freedom and well-being" either (a) do not attend to a number of key features of the argument, and/or (b) allege that the notion of "prudential duties/rights" is untenable, and/or (c) rest on the claim that, in order to effect Stage III, Stage II must conclude with (4d) interpreted as "From PPAO's point of view, PPAO ought not to interfere with my freedom and well-being."

On (a), the key features of the argument that must be attended to are

i.   that the "rights" and "duties" of Stage II are prudential rather than moral; and

ii.   that the argument is strictly from within a PPA's own viewpoint as a PPA.

Together these amount to the justification that a PPA claims for its having freedom and well-being, in Stage II, being justification for it, rather than justification for others or everyone. Related to this, it is necessary to distinguish between other-referring or -directed "oughts" (or prescribing *to* others) and other-directing "oughts" (or prescribing *for* others). Other-directed "oughts" that are not other-directing are not simply "'oughts' of evaluation," being possible other-directing "oughts" derived from a self-directing "ought."

On (*b*), I have argued that it is not unintelligible to talk of prudential rights and obligations, and have pointed to severe difficulties with making it a condition of the intelligibility of "PPAO has an obligation to do X" that PPAO agrees that it has an obligation to do X, or accepts the criterion according to which it has an obligation to do X. To deny the latter analysis is also not to commit oneself to the notion that diseases and natural objects have duties not to interfere with one's freedom and well-being.

To deal with (*c*) adequately, Stage III must be examined. I have, however, indicated in various places that I consider that arguments that universalization can only proceed from (4d), if this is interpreted as an other-directing "ought" (or if the PPA presupposes that it has moral justification for the claims of Stage II), rest on ignoring the fact that the LPU has an "internal" as well as an "external" application. This will be a major theme of the next chapter.

Finally, I argued that

7.   there is no difficulty in principle with deriving "rights" from "necessary goods," because the concept of a "necessary good" is a deontic concept. Furthermore, I have argued that "My freedom and well-being are necessary goods" is, in fact, universalizable to a proposition that requires me to take favorable account of the freedom and well-being of PPAO, by the internal application of the LPU, without supposing that it can ground even prudential rights-claims. In connection with this, and also in connection with direct universalization of (4d) to a moral claim, I have defended the position that criteria validate their requirements impersonally, which these universalizations require;

8.   it is vital not to confuse Gewirth's dialectically necessary method with a contractarian or utilitarian argument. A PPA's

dialectically necessary prudential base is not its particular occurrent purposes, but its proactive valuation of its freedom
and well-being which its *purposivity as such* requires it to
have. A PPA must accept the logical implications of this valuation, because to deny them is to deny its purposivity as such,
and thus that it is a PPA. It cannot eschew these implications
on the grounds that they do not suit its particular occurrent
purposes; and

9.   the fact that a PPA might be willing to have PPAO interfere
(or try to interfere) with its freedom and well-being does not
show that it need not consider that it has a right to its freedom
and well-being. The rights a PPA must consider it has are
inherently waivable. The rights-claim itself derives from dialectically necessary considerations. It is only the circumstances under which a PPA would be willing to waive these
rights that the dialectically necessary method permits to be
determined by dialectically contingent considerations.

8 Objections to Stage III

This chapter considers objections to Stage III, and specifically to the inference that, within my internal viewpoint as a PPA, "I have a prudential right to my freedom and well-being" entails "I (morally) ought not to interfere with the freedom and well-being of PPAO."

#40 Stage III cannot be valid because it relies on the principle of universalizability, which depends for its substantive implications on a PPA's contingent characteristics.

1 Ockleton

According to Mark Ockleton,

> Gewirth's conclusion, if it is sound, is sound because it depends on the principle of universalisation. A must hold that all others such as himself may make the same claims as he does, and are entitled to do so. But the PGC's dependence on the principle of universalisation has serious adverse consequences for its use in legal theory, because in any non-revolutionary society the law-maker . . . is unique. The principle of universalisation is limited to requiring him to admit that all other *law-makers* have the same rights: it does not compel him to act in the way in which he would hope his subjects would act towards one another, or towards him. The PGC does not . . . apply to the law-maker, and . . . cannot validate . . . a legal system. (Ockleton 1988, 236)

This is contradictory. Ockleton would have it that Stage III is both valid and invalid. He wishes to assert that the PGC, if valid, is valid as a moral principle because of the principle of universalizability, but that it does not apply to "law-makers." But, if the principle of universalizability licenses Stage III, then it licenses "All PPAs ought to respect the generic rights of their recipients as well as of themselves." A "law-maker," in issuing rules, is a PPA. As such, if Stage III is valid then the "law-maker," as a PPA, is logically compelled "to act in the way in which he would hope his subjects would act towards one another, or towards him"—and what he must hope is that they would not violate the PGC. If Ockleton's claim that the PGC does not apply to "law-makers" makes any sense, then we must take it that Ockleton is denying the validity of Stage III, on the grounds that the principle of universalizability does *not* require PPAs to accord the generic rights to other PPAs—that it only requires "law-makers" to grant the generic rights to other "law-makers." But Ockleton cannot do this if he concedes that Stage II is valid, for Stage II concludes that PPAs (and "law-makers" are PPAs) must claim the generic rights for themselves on the *sufficient* ground that they are PPAs. That they are "law-makers," or have any other contingent characteristics as individual PPAs, is irrelevant. They must, therefore, by the logical principle of universalizability (LPU), accord the generic rights to all other PPAs, and cannot, without contradicting that they are PPAs (and thus "law-makers"), issue rules that violate the PGC.

2 Geels

Donald E. Geels (referring to Gewirth 1967a) claims that Stage III is effected by the principle that whatever is right for one person must be right for any relevantly similar person in any relevantly similar circumstances.[1] However, he alleges that

[i]t is trivial to claim that whatever is right for one person must be right for any relevantly similar person in any relevantly similar circumstances (Geels 1971, 671),

because there is no determinate criterion of relevant similarity.

This is not true, for a PPA must claim that it has the generic rights (according to the argument for the sufficiency of agency [ASA]) for the sufficient reason that it is a PPA. Because a PPA logically must claim the generic rights, it is the property of being a PPA that is logically required to be the criterion of relevant similarities. A racist cannot make being a person of X race the relevant characteristic without contradicting that it is a PPA. By implication from holding that the PCC itself is not a tautology (ibid., 674), Geels, quite rightly, holds that "Only persons of X race have Y rights" is not a contradictory statement in itself. But this is irrelevant. What Gewirth holds to be a contradiction is the proposition that a PPA may rationally espouse such a principle, or act upon it.

#41   Stage III is valid if a PPA must claim the generic rights (in Stage II) on the grounds of "necessity." But although it is self-contradictory for a PPA whose criterion is prudential not to claim the generic rights, it would not be self-contradictory for a PPA to claim the generic rights on some other ground. Universalization, therefore, does not require a PPA to accord the generic rights to all other PPAs.

According to Richard B. Friedman, if a PPA must claim a right to its freedom and well-being on the grounds that its having freedom and well-being is "a necessity" (that it cannot do without its freedom and well-being as a PPA), then Stage III must be valid.

But it is not at all evident why a "rational agent," whose "criterion is prudential," *must* stake his claim to rights to freedom and well-being on the ground of their necessity. Strictly speaking, all that Gewirth's argument shows . . . is that it would be self-contradictory . . . for a rational agent, whose criterion is prudential, to refrain from claiming a right to the necessary conditions of action, but not that it would be self-contradictory . . . to claim these same rights *on some other ground.* (Friedman 1981, 152)

I deny "I am a PPA" if I deny "I have a right *to* the necessary conditions of agency," but not if I assert this right *on grounds*

other than necessity, on some title involving individual merit or desert. . . .
. . . For whereas the "fact" that certain things are necessary to action does entail that a rational agent, operating on a prudential criterion, must claim these things as rights, it does not entail that he must claim them on any particular ground. It entails only the rather sweeping consideration, that the ground on which he does choose to base his right-claim must be consistent with the prudential perspective he is postulated as adopting . . . . The logic of "diale[c]tical necessity" eventuates in a determinant right-claim, but not in a determinant title on which the claim is based. (Ibid., 153)

This is a highly relevant objection, for it is nothing less than a denial of Gewirth's ASA. According to this argument, if I contradict "I am a PPA" by not claiming the generic rights for myself (by not considering that I have the generic rights), then I must hold that my being a PPA (constituted by my having purposes that I wish to achieve, and my categorical need for freedom and well-being) is sufficient justification for my having the generic rights.

According to Friedman, I, as a PPA, have purposes that I wish to fulfill (IP), and I categorically need my freedom and well-being for my purposes (IC). It follows that I must claim a right to my freedom and well-being (MyR). In other words, the inference

(A)   "I am a PPA" ($\equiv$ "IP and IC") logically entails that I must
       claim "MyR"

is valid. Given IP ("my prudential criterion") and IC ("necessity"), I
must claim MyR.
    However, the inference

(B)   "I am a PPA" logically entails that I must claim "IC jus-
       tifies/entails/is sufficient reason for MyR"

is invalid. In other words, (A) does not logically entail (B). (A) logically entails

(C)   "I am a PPA" logically entails that I must claim "X
       (something I possess) justifies/entails/is sufficient rea-
       son for MyR";

but X in (C) need not be IC. If I claim that I have a right to my
freedom and well-being on grounds X, which are not my categorical
need for freedom and well-being (or my possession of any correlative properties that are necessary and sufficient to define me as
PPA), then I do not contradict "I am a PPA."
    This contention, *if valid*, would invalidate Stage III. For it is only
on the grounds that I must hold (within my internal viewpoint) [I
categorically need my freedom and well-being → *I have* a right to my
freedom and well-being] to be a valid inference, that I must hold, by
the LPU, that [PPAO categorically needs its freedom and well-being
→ PPAO *has* a right to its freedom and well-being] is a valid inference within my internal viewpoint; and thus be required to hold that
PPAO has a right to its freedom and well-being (because all PPAs *do*
categorically need their freedom and well-being).
    However, Friedman's contention is merely a denial of the ASA
(that [A] entails [B]), not an argument against it. Friedman says
nothing to show why (A) does not, as he alleges, entail (B). In particular, he says nothing about the *argument* for the sufficiency of
agency which Gewirth presents in order to demonstrate that (A)
entails (B).
    According to Gewirth, (C) is not consistent with (A), where X in
(C) is some property R that is more restrictive than being a PPA (or
having a categorical need for freedom and well-being for one's purposes).

The reason for this is that if the agent were to hold the position that he has
these [the generic] rights only for some more restrictive reason R (such as
merit, race, or profession), then he would contradict himself. For, according
to this position, if the agent were to lack R, he would have to accept for

himself, "I do not have the generic rights"; but it has previously been shown [and conceded by Friedman] that every agent *must* accept for himself, "I have the generic rights." Since this latter statement logically must be accepted for himself by every agent, he can avoid contradicting himself only by giving up the position that his rights are grounded on some criterion R that is more restrictive than his simply being a prospective purposive agent. (Gewirth 1982f, 76–77. See also RM 110 [passage quoted in Chapter 2]).

In fact, that (A) does entail (B) follows on one of the simplest logical transformations. If (p & q) → r, then it follows that p → (q → r). (A) can be rewritten as

(A')   Within my dialectically necessary viewpoint [(IP & IC) → MyR].

Where p = IP, q = IC, and r = MyR, it follows that

(B)   Within my dialectically necessary viewpoint [IP → (IC → MyR)].

Thus, IC is not merely the ground for my having to consider that I have MyR. It is also the "title" I must claim for MyR.

Is there any way in which this can be resisted? Friedman might wish to claim that, given IP and IC, it is dialectically necessary for me to claim MyR but that this does not mean that it is dialectically necessary for me to assent to [(IP & IC) → MyR]. In other words, he might wish to claim that my translation of (A) to (A') is fallacious. That I am required, on IP and IC, to consider that I have MyR, does not require me to hold that the reason I have MyR is (IP & IC).

However, this will not do. If I have a viewpoint that requires me to consider that X is the case, then the reasons why I am required to hold this viewpoint are reasons *within this viewpoint* why X is the case. This is established by Gewirth's formulation of the ASA (which, as I have said, Friedman does not attend to).

Alternatively, he might contend that he does not concede that I must consider that I have MyR, when he concedes that I must "claim" MyR. He concedes only that I must "lay claim" to MyR—i.e., that I must attempt to secure MyR. But if I must (ought to) try to secure MyR, then I ought (on the same criterion) to have my freedom and well-being, which implies that my freedom and well-being ought not to be interfered with, which in turn implies that I have MyR (in the *prescriptive* sense of "a right"): for I categorically need my freedom and well-being if I am to have any chance of securing my freedom and well-being, and it cannot be the case that I ought to try to secure my freedom and well-being if I lack the necessary means to secure my freedom and well-being.[2] Thus, if I am required to "lay claim" to MyR, I am required to consider that I have MyR.[3]

#42   Elitists need not accept the PGC, even if ordinary PPAs must, because they act, not as PPAs, but as superior PPAs.

1 Fotion

N. Fotion (1968) (responding to Gewirth 1967a) claims that a "fanatic" (read "elitist") can grant itself rights on the grounds that it is a superior PPA, yet refuse to grant these rights to other PPAs, who are not superior PPAs, without contradiction. Gewirth, he says, argues that the fanatic is being inconsistent because the fanatic is logically required to accept the PCC, which grants equal rights to all PPAs, while the fanatic's principle grants superior rights to itself.

Fotion objects that the fanatic does not accept the PCC. It operates on "Only superior PPAs have rights," and this principle does not logically entail the PCC.

To this Gewirth responds that his argument is not that the fanatic's *principle* logically entails the PCC.

Fotion's use of the fanatic's exclusivist claim suggests that he thinks of such argument as being of the *ad hominem* type which comprises two main elements: a material or substantive element or content consisting in the claims made by various protagonists (which reflect whatever interests or ideals they may be trying to promote), and a formal element involving a justificatory appeal to consistency. The trouble with this model is that since the content of the argument is a contingent one, in that it varies according to the particular desires of the respective claimants, the application of the justificatory formal element is unable to remove the arbitrariness which such variation involves. In the pattern of argument which I set forth, by contrast, the justificatory component is material as well as formal, in that the content must itself be necessary, not contingent. (Gewirth 1970b, 382)

It is as a PPA, not as a fanatic, that a PPA must embrace the PCC. The fanatic is a PPA, and as such must accept the PCC. By accepting the fanatical principle, it accepts what it cannot accept without contradicting that it is a PPA (and, hence, a fanatical *PPA*).

Fotion, however, anticipates this response. He appreciates that Gewirth might not be arguing

that the fanatic is logically committed to holding the non-fanatic's principle [the PCC] in trying to *assert* his own; but rather that in the very process of *acting* . . . he cannot help but act as an agent and, therefore, is forced . . . to adopt the non-fanatic's principle. (Fotion 1968, 263)

To this he objects that the fanatic is

not acting *as* an agent when he is acting as a superior agent even though agency is a part of or is included in the concept of 'acting as a superior agent.' When one is acting, it is by no means clear that he must be acting *as* an agent since, presumably, he may be acting as a superior agent . . . . (Ibid., 263–264)

Gewirth responds that

[e]ach of these statements is contradictory unless some special meaning is given to Fotion's italicized "*as.*" Isn't every superior agent an agent? Perhaps Fotion means that in claiming to be a *superior* agent the fanatic envisages himself as something more than a *mere* agent, where 'mere' signifies that one's agency is of the undistinguished, run-of-the-mill sort. But even if we assume that the latter interpretation makes sense as applied to agency, it is not the meaning I attributed to the *generic* sense of 'agent,' for it would signify rather a species of the genus agent. In the sense in which 'agent' signifies the genus of which 'superior agent' signifies a species, it is necessarily true both that all superior agents are agents and that all persons who act as (or while claiming to be) superior agents are agents. (Gewirth 1970b, 381 n. 1)

In effect, what Fotion fails to see is that agency, independent of the *content* of a PPA's particular occurrent purposes or its SPR for its purposes (represented here by the fanatic's principle), has a normative structure. Since this normative structure reflects judgments that a PPA must accept on pain of contradicting that it is a PPA independently of the *content* of its purposes (because these judgments are functions of the necessary conditions of its pursuit/achievement of any purposes), a PPA *might* reason from its SPR, but can only do so consistently with the assumption that it is a PPA *if* these reasonings are consistent with the judgments contained in the necessary normative structure of agency.

2 Simon

Robert Simon attempts to defend Fotion's position against Gewirth's response. He claims that Gewirth has *two* arguments against the fanatic: an *ad hominem* one (which we just have seen that Gewirth repudiates, such an argument being a misinterpretation of Gewirth's procedure by Fotion), and one that appeals to the necessity of claiming rights on the sufficient basis of agency. Simon, however, claims that the argument of the dialectically necessary method cannot succeed without falling back on an *ad hominem* argument (which, as Gewirth claims, is inadequate).

It may be granted that *if* the ASA depends on an *ad hominem* argument that cannot succeed, then all is up with the argument. But does the ASA not work in its own right?

Simon says that Gewirth's (dialectically necessary) argument rests on the view that

only what is universally and necessarily connected with its subject matter is

ultimately relevant to evaluation of that subject matter. Consider the application of this principle in some other area, say aesthetics. Suppose, for example, we had an acceptable account of what it is to be a work of art. According
to this account, features X and Y are the necessary and universal characteristics of such works. Now, since all works of art would possess X and Y, those
categorial features themselves would be inadequate for distinguishing between good and bad works of art. For that purpose, some other feature Z, or
at least the difference in degree to which art objects exemplify X and Y,
would be needed. If we were to restrict ourselves to X and Y alone, our
aesthetic evaluations would be depressingly uniform. (Simon 1975, 275)

Therefore, Gewirth cannot claim that it is by virtue of being a PPA
that the rights-claims are made without falling into vicious circularity.

He cannot claim that only the [generic] features of agency are categorically
connected with action for it is just the significance of that claim which the
aesthetics example calls into question. (Ibid., 276)

Thus, Gewirth must fall back on the claim that the fanatic's principle requires the fanatic to accept the PCC, which it doesn't.

What are we offered as an argument against the ASA? The sweeping claim that the dialectically necessary method will result in "depressingly uniform" judgments of what constitutes "good and bad"
PPAs.

However,

1.   on its own terms, Simon's argument cannot convict Gewirth's
      argument of a "vicious circularity": at most, *if his argument is
      relevant*, it can convict it of insignificance;

2.   the terms of Simon's argument, his use of the aesthetics anal-
      ogy, are wholly inappropriate.

First, Gewirth's argument is not concerned, directly, with what is
a good or bad PPA; it is concerned with the rights of PPAs.[4] In
addition, although the argument restricts dialectically necessary
rights-claims to the generic features, it permits any judgments of
value to be made and acted upon which are compatible with respect
for the generic rights. The uniformity of judgment required by the
argument is restricted to a particular level. Second, the application
of the dialectically necessary method is not contained in Simon's
description of what constitutes a work of art, or our evaluations of
this. Our judging works of art is external to our agency, not internal
to it. We are PPAs, and the significance of the generic features of
agency is for our ability to achieve the purposes we value. We are
not works of art, and the "generic features" of works of art are of no

necessary significance in relation to our purposivity. There is also no dialectical necessity about what constitutes the "necessary and universal features of such works" in Simon's account, unless we imagine the works of art judging the significance of their "generic features." All in all, I find it difficult to imagine what stance we would have to adopt to make the aesthetics model a test case for the adequacy of the dialectically necessary method. Simon certainly doesn't characterize it in the necessary way. This means that anything that follows from the aesthetics model, as he portrays it, is irrelevant for commenting on the dialectically necessary method.

#43   Gewirth's claim that superior PPAs do not have superior rights is an egalitarian assumption, which is question-begging.

According to Gewirth, although there are degrees of approach to being a PPA, there are no degrees of being a PPA. Those who do not possess the generic features in full must be accorded less than the full complement of the generic rights. They are to be accorded the generic rights in proportion to the degree to which they approach being PPAs. But, once they have the abilities sufficient to be PPAs, no superiority with respect to the abilities that make them PPAs is relevant to their possession of generic rights. They cannot, by virtue of possessing such superior abilities, claim superior rights. (See RM 121–125.)

    According to Susan Moller Okin,

Gewirth has to confront the argument that some people, being superior, should have more extensive rights than others. In order to do this, he argues that, whereas there are degrees of approach to being a prospective purposive agent, there are not degrees of *being* one. . . . [H]e denies that, above the minimum competency level of a "normal" adult, there are any degrees of prospective agency that are relevant to arguments about rights. . . . This assertion, however, is nothing but a camouflaged egalitarian premise. What Gewirth is really saying is that *although* in many respects human agents differ—*although* their purposes vary in number and intensity, and *although* they may have varying capacities to pursue these purposes—in one crucial respect, all human beings, *as purposive agents, are equal.* (Okin 1981, 232–233)

This assumption, however, is question-begging.

    What is question-begging? The assumption that PPAs are the subjects to which all practical precepts are addressed? Or the claim that being a PPA is the relevant criterion for the distribution of the generic rights? Neither of these contentions is question-begging. The first is necessary, given that "ought" implies "can."[5] The second is justified by Gewirth's argument for Stages I and II, and his ASA. Okin says nothing here that directly challenges the inferences or logical operations involved in making these claims. If PPAs are the relevant addressees of practical precepts, logically must claim rights to their freedom and well-being (because they are PPAs), and, hence, logically must claim that being a PPA is the sufficient ground for their having the generic rights, then being a PPA is the criterion of relevant similarity for universalization. To show that Gewirth's criterion of relevant similarity is question-begging, Okin has to show that the ASA is question-begging. She does not do so. Gewirth does not assume his criterion of relevant similarity in order to show that it is the criterion of relevant similarity. That the criterion *is* implicit in his premises, because his argument is logical, does not make the premises question-begging, *if* they are dialectically necessary; and there is no argument here to show that they are not.

#44   If superior PPAs could best provide for the purposes of all PPAs, then it is not necessary for PPAs to evaluate their own freedom as a necessary good, and thus not necessary for them to claim rights to their freedom on the sufficient ground that they are PPAs.

Gewirth presents the following specific argument against the view that PPAs with superior abilities may claim superior rights:

The basic argument [for superior rights] is that if an agent has rights to freedom and well-being, then a superior agent (which, ex hypothesi, the person of superior intelligence is) has superior rights to freedom and well-being. Now this argument commits a non sequitur. The antecedent of the argument, properly expanded, says that the reason why a person has rights to freedom and well-being is that he is a prospective agent who wants to fulfill his own purposes. The consequent says that if one prospective agent X has greater ability to achieve X's purposes than another prospective agent Y has to achieve Y's purposes, then X has superior rights to freedom and well-being. This consequent does not, however, follow from the antecedent, since the reason the consequent gives for having superior generic rights is quite distinct from the reason the antecedent gives for having the generic rights. Wanting to fulfill one's own purposes through action is not the same as having the ability to fulfill one's own purposes through action. While it is true that to act requires certain abilities, what is crucial in any agent's reason for acting is not his abilities but his purposes. (RM 124)

This, of course, follows from the ASA. Once being a PPA is the sufficient ground for having the generic rights (within a PPA's dialectically necessary viewpoint), and being a PPA does not vary in degree, then this must be so.

Gewirth, however, continues by saying that

[t]o justify the claim of superior rights, the argument from superior intelligence [for superior rights] would have to include one or both of two further assertions: (*a*) that those who have superior intelligence will necessarily use it to fulfill not only their own purposes but also the purposes of all or many other prospective agents; (*b*) that those who have superior intelligence also have more valuable purposes. Neither of these assertions, however, is plausible. (RM 125)

William O'Meara claims that (*a*) weakens Gewirth's argument fatally.

If we suppose that superior agents could in fact provide for the fulfillment of the purposes of all agents better than could the freedom of lower agents acting for their own benefits, then even lower agents would not have to evaluate their freedom as a necessary good for the achievement of other [*sic;* "their"?] purposes. (O'Meara 1982, 375)

As a result, the ASA would fail, because the whole argument would fail. Stage I would not be valid, and a PPA would not have to claim the generic rights (which it would have to claim if it had to claim "My freedom and well-being are necessary goods") on pain of contradicting "I am a PPA."

This objection is unsuccessful. The argument for superior rights does not merely require that we can, without contradiction, suppose that superior PPAs will cater for the abilities of inferior ones. It does not even require that an inferior PPA can, without contradiction, suppose that superior PPAs will cater for its needs. It requires that it be a necessary truth that superior PPAs will cater for the needs of inferior ones (better than they themselves will, in consequence of which inferior PPAs would not need to pursue their own freedom). But this is not a necessary truth, unless we make it true by an arbitrary stipulative definition of "PPA of superior intelligence." Given that it is not a necessary truth, even if an inferior PPA believes that superior PPAs will cater for its needs, the inferior PPA would have to maintain control of its freedom, just in case it were let down, and, in any event, would have to value its freedom to permit superior PPAs to cater for its needs.[6]

#45   Gewirth's theory must accord a higher degree of moral respect to PPAs with a higher degree of rationality.

1 Ben-Zeev

Aaron Ben-Zeev maintains that "rational" is an "attainment attribute" not a "status attribute." Status attributes cannot vary in de-

gree, and there are definite borderlines between having and not having them. Attainment attributes vary in degree, and there are no
definite borderlines for their possession. He claims that Gewirth's
theory rests on taking "rational" to be a status attribute. His evidence is that Gewirth holds that there are degrees of approach to
being a PPA, but not degrees of being a PPA, and that Gewirth holds
"rationality" to be a characteristic of being a PPA. (See Ben-Zeev
1982, 653.) Ben-Zeev's reasoning is that if "being a PPA" is a status
attribute, and "being rational" is a defining characteristic of PPAs,
then Gewirth must hold that "being rational" (and, hence, "being a
PPA") is a status attribute too.

However, he says that "rational," in the sense of having the ability to accept the reasons of deductive logic and the evidence of the
senses, is an attainment, not a status attribute. Being rational, in this
sense, can vary in degree, though he admits that it might be claimed
that

one may admit the existence of degrees of rationality, but still [*sic*; "maintain"?] that this attribute is given to all persons who overcome a certain
minimal threshold of rationality . . . . Overcoming this threshold will be
identical with the fulfilment of the sufficient and necessary conditions of a
status-attribute. (Ibid., 654)

However, he claims that it is difficult to locate this threshold in a
nonarbitrary way, and that this indicates "that such borderlines do
not exist" (ibid., 655). One of the difficulties this creates for Gewirth
is that,[7]

[s]ince 'rational' admits degrees of membership and indefinite borderlines,
there is no such identical unit as a rational agent; hence, this agent cannot
fulfil the function of a basic unit in the egalitarian rational theories [of which
Gewirth's is one]. That is not to say that rationality has nothing to do with a
moral theory, but the connection is not that of being a basic unit. A moral
theory which accepts my characterizations of 'rational,' but still claims the
dependence of moral attitudes on the degree of rationality, would also have
to claim that a higher degree of rationality renders a higher degree of moral
respect. (Ibid., 656)

Gewirth replies that the concept of a rational PPA enters into his
argument in two ways.

1. The argument is presented as conducted by a PPA who has
certain minimal rational capacities. Ben-Zeev recognizes that this
has the no-degree quality of a status attribute, but claims that it has
no clear borderline. This, however, is not so.

Just as there is no vagueness or fuzziness in the idea of rationality as involving elementary consistency and knowledge of the proximate circumstances of one's particular action,[8] so there is no vagueness or fuzziness in the idea of having the capacity for such rationality. The presence of the capacity can be tested for by appeal to the determinate minimal criteria of rationality itself. (Gewirth 1982d, 668–669)

Therefore, this capacity, which may be dispositional as well as occurrent, can be had equally by all PPAs; and, inasmuch as being rational characterizes being a PPA, being a PPA (like having this rational capacity) can be an all-or-nothing property.

2. The argument is dialectical in containing claims that are logically (rationally) implied by statements made by a PPA. The sufficient ground upon which each agent must claim the generic rights is

that he is a prospective agent who has purposes he wants to fulfil. Here it is the agent's purposiveness, rather than his rationality as such, that is shown to be crucial to the claiming and allocation of rights. Hence, so far as concerns the equal distribution of the rights, this is not affected by the prospective agent's degree of rationality. For his claiming of rights is based simply on his having purposes he wants to fulfil, not on his degree of rationality or of practical effectiveness in achieving his purposes. (Ibid., 669)

Gewirth's response to the specific objection that, although all PPAs must grant all PPAs rights, they do not have to grant them equal rights, because rationality is involved in being a PPA (in that agency requires certain practical abilities, and these can vary in degree), is that PPAs may vary in their degree of rationality, and the degree to which they have practical abilities. But they do not vary in what degree of these things they need in order to be PPAs (the *generic* abilities), and it is from the categorical need for the generic abilities that the generic rights are derived. The objection requires the practical abilities of PPAs to be viewed at the level of their particular exercise, whereas they are to be viewed at the generic level. (See ibid., 670–671.)

2 Wong

David B. Wong says that there

are ... degrees of wanting purposes fulfilled among prospective agents .... Part of the reason why children and mentally deficient persons approach but do not attain full-fledged prospective agency is that they have yet to form well-defined desires or are incapable of doing so. . . . Prospective agents differ in how well-defined their desires are. Some people know what they want better than others do. . . . It could be argued within the framework of Gewirth's theory that a person can only claim a right to something to the degree that he or she is capable of forming a well-defined desire for it. (Wong 1984, 201)

Therefore, it would not be self-contradictory for PPAs to accord superior rights to those with better-defined desires.

Initially, Wong appears to hold that an ability to form a "well-defined" desire qualifies one as a PPA. But he switches to talking about *PPAs* differing in their capacities to form "well-defined" desires. This is either contradictory, or else the predicate "well-defined" is being used in different senses when applied, on the one hand, as a condition of being a PPA, and on the other, as a property that full-fledged PPAs can possess in varying degrees. The theory grants beings who are PPAs the full generic rights. Once I have the capacities sufficient to be a PPA, then I have the generic rights in full. Varying properties that PPAs might possess, and still be PPAs, are irrelevant to the ascription of the generic rights.

There is no possible implication in Gewirth's theory that a PPA could be required to claim a right to X to the degree that it is capable of forming a "well-defined" desire for X. The theory does not grant rights to PPAs' "well-defined" desires. It grants rights, directly, only to possession of the generic features of agency. If I do X for E, I am not required to claim that I have a right to E, or to the necessary conditions of E that are specific to E. I am only required to claim rights to the necessary conditions of E that are the necessary conditions of my pursuit/achievement of any purpose whatsoever.

3 Puolimatka

According to Tapio Puolimatka,

Gewirth emphasizes rationality to the extent that moral rights are ascribed to the agent only in so far as he qualifies as a rational agent. This means that basic moral rights are made dependent on intellectual capabilities.

. . . Rational agency is defined by the ability to understand the essential features of action and their rational implications, of which Gewirth's theory purports to be an absolutely true account that is conclusively proved. This means that any rational agent will necessarily agree with it, at least after careful study. Anyone that is not convinced by Gewirth's argument is, by definition, mentally deficient. And as moral rights are ascribed to the agent to the degree that he approaches the status of rational agency . . . , and the agent qualifies as rational only to the extent that he rightly understands the logical implications of action . . . , it follows that an agent possesses basic moral rights only to the degree that he agrees with Gewirth's theory. (Puolimatka 1989, 73)

This is not so.

The generic rights are ascribed to PPAs who are rational *in the sense* that they act for purposes that are their reasons for acting. Such PPAs are *capable* of performing basic logical inferences.

However, it does not follow from this that the generic rights are only ascribed to PPAs who infallibly draw valid logical inferences, or only insofar as they actually reason validly. The subjects of the argument are PPAs *in referentia* (those who have the ability to follow logical inferences), not PPAs *in essentia* (those who necessarily reason validly and act in accordance with valid reasoning).[9] Thus, it does not follow from the validity of Gewirth's argument that one's rights depend on the degree to which one appreciates its validity.

Puolimatka's gibe about "mental deficiency" is gratuitous. Anyone who makes any sort of error of reasoning (or is even capable of such an error) displays, in a sense, "mental deficiency." This is a sense in which we are all mentally deficient, but this sort of "mental deficiency" does not disqualify one from being a PPA, and the distribution of the generic rights depends solely on possession of the qualities that define being a PPA.

#46   **Stage III rests on the premise "'Every X by virtue of property y claims Z' entails 'Every X by virtue of property y has Z.'" This is false.**

Gewirth says that

every agent must claim, at least implicitly, that he has rights to freedom and well-being for the sufficient reason that he is a prospective purposive agent. From the content of this claim it follows, by the principle of universalizability, that all prospective purposive agents have rights to freedom and well-being. If the agent denies this generalization, he contradicts himself. For he would then be in the position of both affirming and denying that being a prospective purposive agent is a sufficient condition of having rights to freedom and well-being. (RM 133)

Jeffrey Paul claims that this rests on the validity of the false proposition, "'Every X by virtue of property y claims Z' entails 'Every X by virtue of property y has Z.'" (See Paul 1979, 445.)

Paul, however, misreads this as an attempt to move from "I must claim that I have a right to my freedom and well-being, for the sufficient reason that I am a PPA" to the *assertoric* proposition "All PPAs have a right to their freedom and well-being." (See #23.1.1.) No such move is involved. Gewirth claims that Stage II establishes that I *must claim* π: [I am a PPA → I have a right to my freedom and well-being]. The general proposition this relies on (established by the ASA) is "'Every X by virtue of property y *must claim* Z' entails 'Every X *must claim* that it has Z by virtue of having y.'" π (as an instance of "I have Z by virtue of having y") is the content of my *dialectically necessary* claim. Applying the LPU to π we get τ: [PPAO is a PPA → PPAO has a right to its freedom and well-being]. Universalization, therefore, establishes that I *must claim* τ. It does not establish that τ is assertorically true, and is not intended to. The principle involved in this universalization is "If *an* X by virtue of property y *has* Z then *every* X by virtue of property y has Z," which is the LPU itself, applied internally to the content of my dialectically necessary claim π, to yield the *dialectically necessary claim* τ. Neither the ASA, nor the LPU, relies upon (or asserts) the false proposition Paul attributes.

#47   Stage II is valid if its conclusion is a prudential rights-claim (one validated by my interests). However, logical universalization of a rights-claim can yield a morally universal conclusion only if its premise is moral/based on the interests of all PPAs. Stage III thus rests on an equivocation between prudential and moral rights.

1 Schwartz

According to Adina Schwartz, Gewirth holds that

each agent has sound prudential reasons for claiming rights to freedom and well-being. Each must claim these rights for him/herself simply because he/she has purposes that he/she wants to fulfill.
 . . . Quite correctly, he claims that all rational agents must accept the "logical principle of universalizability: if some predicate P [*sic;* not italicized in RM] belongs to some subject S because S has the property Q . . . , then P must also belong to all other subjects S_1, S_2, . . . [,] S_n that have Q" ([RM] p. 105). On this basis, Gewirth infers that since each agent must claim that he/she has rights to freedom and well-being simply because he/she has purposes that he/she wants to attain, each is rationally bound to claim the same rights for all other purposive agents. The problem with this inference, however, is that Gewirth has only shown that each agent must claim these rights for him/herself on prudential grounds. Therefore, each agent is only logically bound to admit that all other agents have sound prudential reasons for claiming those same rights for themselves. Having so judged, an agent can coherently assert that he/she does not want others to achieve their goals. Therefore, he/she can argue, while it is prudent for each of them to demand rights to freedom and well-being, it is rational for him/her to refuse to grant such rights to any other purposive agent. (Schwartz 1979, 656)

Schwartz accepts that I must claim that I have the generic rights because I am a PPA. She claims, however, that it does not follow, by the LPU, that I must grant the generic rights to all PPAs, because I must only claim the generic rights on prudential grounds. Her reasoning appears to be that it follows from

(A)   I must consider that I have the generic rights, on my
        criterion of my interests,

that

(B)   PPAO must consider that it has the generic rights, on
        PPAO's criterion of its interests.

However, I am not rationally required (without begging the question) to take favorable account of the interests of PPAO. Therefore, it
does *not* follow from (B) (and, therefore, also not from [A]) that

(C)   I must consider that PPAO has the generic rights.

This is incorrect. (C) *does follow* from (A), on the LPU, *without* any
assumption that I must take favorable account of the interests of
PPAO!

My criterion of my interests is simply the essential conative aspect of "I am a PPA." (A) is thus equivalent to

(A')   [I am a PPA → I must consider that I have the generic
        rights].

   (B) is equivalent to

(B')   [PPAO is a PPA → PPAO must consider that PPAO has
        the generic rights].

   (B') follows from (A'), by the LPU, by making the following substitutions: S = myself; S_1, S_2, etc. = objects other than myself; P =
being required to consider that one has the generic rights; Q = being
a PPA.
   With these substitutions, the LPU

        [(S is Q) → (S has P)] → [(S_1, etc., are Q) → (S_1, etc., have
        P)] entails

{(A')   [I am a PPA → I must consider that I have the generic
        rights] entails

(B')   [Objects other than myself who are PPAs (PPAOs) must
        consider that they have the generic rights]}.

   However, from (A') it follows, by the ASA (see RM 110, quoted in
Chapter 2), that

(A")   I must consider that [I am a PPA → I have the generic
        rights] is a valid inference.

   Now, apply the LPU to the inference that is internal to my viewpoint, to [I am a PPA → I have the generic rights]. Here, the substi-

tutions into the LPU are different. S, S$_1$, etc., and Q retain the meanings they have in inferring (B') from (A'), but P (call it P') = the property of having the generic rights, rather than that of considering that one has the generic rights.

It follows that

(D)   [I am a PPA → I have the generic rights] entails

(E)   [PPAO is a PPA → PPAO has the generic rights].

Thus, it follows from

(A″)   I must consider that (D) is a valid inference

that

(F)   I must consider that (E) is a valid inference.

(F), however, entails

(C)   I must consider that PPAO has the generic rights.

In having to accept (C), I have to take favorable account of the interests of PPAO, but this demonstration does not *assume* that I must take favorable account of PPAO's interests. It is achieved by purely logical universalization of the dialectically necessary inference (D).

What Schwartz fails to appreciate is that the LPU has not only an "external" application, in which the property to be universalized is P (considering that I have the generic rights), but also an "internal" application to the inference (D), which I am required to accept in being required to consider that I have the generic rights—where the property to be universalized is P' (having the generic rights).[10]

2 Bond

According to E. J. Bond, in Stage III we start out with a prudential statement, and

by a simple process of universalization which is logically unavoidable, we derive a ge[n]uinely moral principle . . . . But if the initial statement is true only because it is an instantiation of the universal principle, how can the former be prudential while the latter is moral, i.e. how can a *prudential* statement be an instantiation of a *moral* principle?

Gewirth would say here that the principle is now moral since it now binds the agent to have concern for others, whereas the un-universalized statement was based entirely on his own interests. But something has gone wrong here. If the obligations you have to me because of my having the generic rights are only prudential obligations based on my interests, how do those very same obligations become moral when such claims are generalized? If we generalize a prudential statement, the result must be a prudential principle, viz. that everyone must concern themselves with the rights of others as these others' prudential due . . . . No magic can change this into a *moral* obligation. If, on the other hand, the universal principle is moral, then the singular instantiation of it is moral too. But I cannot, simply on the basis of my (necessarily) willing, desiring, or valuing certain things claim, as a deduction, that others are *morally* obliged to acknowledge my rights to these things. However, the particular rights claim, *to the extent that it is intelligible (vide supra)*[11] is already a moral claim, but not, of course, one that I can make simply on the basis of necessarily desiring, willing, or even regarding as good, the things in question. Nothing whatever directly follows for morality from the fact that I must necessarily will (or even value) certain things. In fact, the particular rights claim can only be made *on the basis of* the truth of the principle. And that must be arrived at by a different route. (Bond 1980a, 50–51)

First, as Gewirth responds,

Bond is mistaken when he asserts that the agent's singular rights-judgment "is true only because it is an instantiation of the universal principle" which says that all prospective agents have rights to freedom and well-being. Rather, the singular judgment is initially upheld by the agent *independently* of its relation to the generalization that follows from it when the sufficient reason is added to it. The singular judgment is upheld because it expresses the agent's recognition that, from the standpoint of his own agency-needs, other persons ought at least to refrain from interfering with his freedom and well-being. (Gewirth 1980a, 66; see also RM 145–147.)

The point here is that, although the singular prescription "I have a right to my freedom and well-being" can be derived from the general one, "All PPAs have rights to their freedom and well-being" (the PGC), this is not the route by which Gewirth derives the singular prescription in Stage II. Here, it is derived as a proposition validated by the prudential criterion of my own interests. This involves no assumption that I must take favorable account of the interests of PPAO.

Bond, however, makes another claim: if the singular prescription is a prudential one, then the general one must be a prudential one too. In Bond's words, Gewirth's argument makes "moral due . . . nothing but universal prudential due (prudential due from every point of view)" (Bond 1980b, 74). Bond, however, considers this to be unintelligible.

Bond concedes that "I have a prudential right (one on my own interests) to my freedom and well-being" can be universalized, purely logically, to a universal prescription, which he expresses as "Everyone must concern themselves with the rights of others as these others' prudential due." What this means is not at all clear. An instance of the latter is "I must concern myself with the rights of

PPAO as PPAO's prudential due." This must mean "(I must consider that) PPAO has a prudential right to its freedom and well-being." But, whose prudential criterion does "prudential" refer to here? Mine or PPAO's? We can get

(A)   I must consider that PPAO must consider (on the criterion of PPAO's interests) that PPAO has a right to its freedom and well-being (on the criterion of PPAO's interests)

(by external application of the LPU), *and*

(B)   I must consider that PPAO has a right to its freedom and well-being (in consistency with the judgment made on my interests that I have a right to freedom and well-being)

(by internal application of the LPU).

To concede that (B) is valid is to concede the validity of Stage III. So Bond must mean (A), though this seems to translate to "Everyone must concern themselves with *their own* rights as *their own* prudential due."

Granted, to establish (A) is not to establish that I must grant moral rights to PPAO. Although there are aspects of Bond's remarks that this does not explain, what I take Bond to be saying is that (B) cannot be established without supposing that the rights-claim of Stage II is a moral right (which cannot be established without begging the question). Only (A) can be established by purely logical universalization if this claim is prudential (validated on a nonmoral prudential criterion).

My response to this is that (B) can be established by internal application of the LPU, without assuming that the singular claim is moral, and that Bond fails to see how it can be established by the LPU by restricting the latter's use to its external application.[12]

3 Sterba

According to James P. Sterba,

Gewirth's argument can be summarized as follows:

(1)   All agents regard their purposes as good according to whatever criteria are involved in their actions to fulfill them.
(2)   Therefore, all agents must affirm a right to the freedom and well-being necessary to achieve their purposes.
(3)   All agents must affirm such a right on the basis of simply being prospective, purposive agents.

(4)   Hence, all agents must affirm that every prospective, purposive agent has a right to freedom and well-being.

Gewirth claims that the universalized right affirmed in the conclusion of his argument is a *moral* right and that every agent has to endorse that right under pain of self-contradiction.

Now there is an interpretation of Gewirth's conclusion that does follow from his premises; unfortunately, it is not the interpretation Gewirth intends. For from the generally acceptable premises of his argument, it does follow that all agents must affirm that every prospective purposive agent has a right to freedom and well-being, but the universalized right so deduced is still a prudential and not a moral right.

What a prudential right to freedom and well-being implies is an asymmetrically action-guiding "ought." This means that when an agent says that every prospective, purposive agent has a prudential right to freedom and well-being, the action-guiding implications are that the agent ought to take the steps necessary to secure or to retain the agent's own freedom and well-being, but not that the agent ought to take steps to secure or even steps not to interfere with the freedom and well-being of any other agent, except insofar as it is necessary for securing or retaining the agent's own freedom and well-being. And similarly for every other agent. (Sterba 1987, 55–56)

In claiming that universalization of "I have a prudential right to my freedom and well-being" only requires me to grant a "prudential right" to PPAO, Sterba claims that, while I must grant that PPAO ought to pursue its freedom and well-being, this does not entail that I must endorse this "ought" (i.e., want PPAO to pursue its freedom and well-being) or consider that I ought not to interfere with PPAO's freedom and well-being (except insofar as noninterference with PPAO's freedom and well-being is necessary to secure my own freedom and well-being). He contends that, because the right that I must grant to PPAO can be characterized in this way, Gewirth's argument "clearly fails." (See ibid., 57.) By implication, Gewirth is charged with equivocation between "prudential" and "moral" rights.

The first thing to note is that, in pressing this objection, Sterba characterizes the claim "I have a prudential right to my freedom and well-being" in a way that departs from Gewirth's intention. For Gewirth, "I have a prudential right to my freedom and well-being" means (is correlative to) (4d) "PPAO ought not to interfere with my freedom and well-being (on the criterion of my interests)." This is, of course, derived from (4c) "I ought to pursue my freedom and well-being (on the criterion of my interests)." In characterizing "I have a prudential right to my freedom and well-being" as "I ought to pursue my freedom and well-being," Sterba at best bypasses, or at least truncates, Gewirth's Stage II. This makes it rather difficult to identify which Gewirthian inference he is objecting to. Gewirth's derivation of the PGC does not proceed from "I ought to pursue my freedom and well-being (on the criterion of my interests)" by universalization alone.

Gewirth's sequence, of course, is as follows:

Sequence A

I must affirm, from the criterion of my internal viewpoint as a PPA, that I ought to pursue/secure my freedom and well-being (where this "ought" carries my endorsement).
On any criterion by which I ought to do X, I ought to be free to do X on the same criterion. ∴
From my own viewpoint, I ought to be free to pursue/secure my freedom and well-being. ∴
From my own viewpoint, PPAO ought not to interfere with my freedom and well-being (otherwise I will not be able to pursue/secure my freedom and well-being).
I must make this claim because I am a PPA. ∴
By the ASA, I must hold that [I am a PPA → PPAO ought not to interfere with my freedom and well-being] is a valid inference. ∴
By internal application of the LPU, I must hold [PPAO is a PPA → PPAs other than PPAO (and ∴ I) ought not to interfere with PPAO's freedom and well-being].
Every PPA must accept this process of reasoning. ∴
Every PPA must affirm that every PPA ought not to interfere with the freedom and well-being of any PPA.

Alternatively, we can alter the order of the derivation.

Sequence B

I must affirm "I ought to pursue/secure my freedom and well-being," on pain of contradicting that I am a PPA. ∴
By the ASA, I must hold that [I am a PPA → I ought to pursue/secure my freedom and well-being] is a valid inference, "I ought to pursue . . . " meaning "My pursuit . . . is the state of affairs that ought to be." (See #35.3.)
By the internal application of the LPU, I must hold [PPAO is a PPA → PPAO ought to pursue/secure its freedom and well-being] is a valid inference.
This proposition [PPAO is a PPA → PPAO ought to pursue/secure its freedom and well-being] is made from my internal viewpoint. It is not a statement of how PPAO must reason; it is a statement about how I must reason. The "ought" in "PPAO ought to pursue/secure its freedom and well-being" must, therefore, have the same

illocutionary force as that in "I ought to pursue/secure my freedom and well-being" ($\equiv$ "PPAO's pursuit/securing of its freedom and well-being is the state of affairs which ought to be"). I must, therefore, endorse this "ought." This means that I must endorse "PPAO ought to be free to pursue/secure its freedom and well-being," which entails "I ought not to interfere with PPAO's freedom and well-being."

Now, either of these sequences, if valid (and the validity of either entails the validity of the other), constitutes a refutation of Sterba's objection. In both, it is shown to be rationally necessary for me to accept "I ought not to interfere with the freedom and well-being of PPAO," without the derivation assuming that I adopt a moral point of view (take favorable account of PPAO's interests).

However, the proposition (4c) "I ought to pursue my freedom and well-being," which figures as the premise in these sequences, is not the same as Sterba's "I have a prudential right to my freedom and well-being." Sterba's premise is "I ought to pursue my freedom and well-being, *but* it is not the case that PPAO ought not to interfere with my freedom and well-being." Now, if Sterba means by this "I ought to pursue my freedom and well-being (from my point of view), *but* it is not the case that PPAO ought not to interfere with my freedom and well-being (from PPAO's point of view)," then this is compatible with Gewirth's sequences. For Gewirth's sequences do not *at any point* depend on assuming that PPAO ought not to interfere with my freedom and well-being from *PPAO's* point of view. For Sterba's premise to be different from Gewirth's, he must mean "I ought to pursue my freedom and well-being (from my point of view), *but* it is not the case that PPAO ought not to interfere with my freedom and well-being (from my point of view)." I shall call this latter premise "(4c)(weak)."

(4c)(weak) is still ambiguous. It can be (4c)(weak)(*a*) "I categorically instrumentally ought to pursue my freedom and well-being (on the criterion of my interests), *but* it is not the case that PPAO categorically instrumentally ought not to interfere with my freedom and well-being (on the criterion of my interests)." Alternatively, it can be (4c)(weak)(*b*) "I categorically instrumentally ought to pursue my freedom and well-being (on the criterion of my interests), *but* it is not the case that PPAO ought not to interfere with my freedom and well-being as ends in themselves (according to my SPR for my purposes)."

Now, (4c)(weak)(*b*) is consistent with Gewirth's position. As I have presented the argument in Chapter 2, to hold this is to hold that PPAO ought not to interfere with my freedom and well-being against my will, but to will PPAO's interference. It is to claim that I have a claim right to my freedom and well-being (on the criterion of my interests), but to waive this right. This rests on "I categorically instrumentally ought to pursue my freedom and well-being (on the criterion of my interests)" entailing (by "ought implies can") "PPAO categorically instrumentally ought not to interfere with my freedom and well-being (on the criterion of my interests)," and on this consequent being equivalent to "PPAO ought not to interfere with my freedom and well-being against my will" (this being correlative to "I have a [waivable] claim right to my freedom and well-being"). The argument of Stage II is that I *must* consider that I have a waivable claim right to my freedom and well-being on the basis of the dialectically necessary component of (4c)(weak)(*b*). Since the component that necessitates my considering that I have this right is itself dialectically necessary, the qualifying clause of (4c)(weak)(*b*), which is dialectically contingent, cannot constitute a denial that I have this right. It can only express that I might wish to waive this right for particular occurrent reasons. No damage is done to the argument by this, because the claim I have to universalize is that PPAO ought not to interfere with my freedom and well-being (because I am a PPA). This requires me to grant PPAO a waivable claim right to its freedom and well-being. I must accept that I ought not to interfere with PPAO's freedom and well-being against PPAO's will.

However, this rests on "I categorically instrumentally ought to pursue my freedom and well-being (on the criterion of my interests)" entailing "PPAO categorically instrumentally ought not to interfere with my freedom and well-being (on the criterion of my interests)" (thus, upon [4c][weak][*a*] being inconsistent).

It seems to me that if Sterba's objection does not simply rest on misconstruing Gewirth's argument, then it rests on contending that (4c)(weak)(*a*) is consistent.

It is not entirely clear to me whether Sterba merely holds that (4c)(weak) is dialectically consistent, or whether he holds that it is dialectically necessary. By defining a "prudential right" in terms of a "weak" "ought," and claiming that I contradict that I am a PPA by not claiming "I have a prudential right to my freedom and well-being," Sterba would appear to claim that (4c)(weak) is dialectically *necessary*. However, he also says that Gewirth's argument fails because (4c) *can* be characterized as a "weak" "ought," which implies that it is sufficient for (4c)(weak) to be dialectically consistent.

However, it does not matter which of these Sterba holds, for (4c)(weak)(*a*) is clearly inconsistent. The simplest way of demonstrating this is to say that "I ought to do X on criterion Y" entails "PPAO ought not to interfere with my doing X on criterion Y" by "ought implies can." However, it might be claimed that this holds only for certain kinds of "oughts." It does not hold for "oughts" of competitive games. In competitive games, it is quite normal to say things like "A ought to do X, but it is not the case that B ought not to prevent A from doing X." And we find Sterba saying that the PPA's "prudential" rights-claim is analogous to the "oughts" of competitive games. (See ibid., 56–57.)

However, in competitive games, the criterion of "A (may) ought to do (or try to do) X" and the criterion of "B may (ought) to (or try to) prevent A from doing X" is the rules of the game. For X, or prevention of X, to be validated by the rules of the game, they must be things that fall within these rules. A and B are directed to play the game according to the rules. The primary "ought" is "A and B ought to play the game according to the rules." "A ought to do X" and "B ought to prevent A doing X" should be stated as "A ought (according to the rules) to do X" and "B ought (according to the rules) to prevent A doing X." Although these are compatible, "A ought (according to the rules) to do X" is not compatible with "B ought to prevent A from doing X according to the rules" (i.e., B may not prevent A playing according to the rules of the game). Once we identify the primary "ought," the principle that "ought implies can" still applies to the "oughts" of competitive games. Given a redescription in terms of the primary "oughts," "A ought to do X" still entails that "B ought not to prevent A doing X."

However, Sterba claims that, although "prudential" "oughts" are in some ways analogous to the "oughts" of competitive games, they are different in that they are not "limited" by an allegiance to what I have called "primary" "oughts" of games. (See ibid., 57.) I do not know what he means unless he means that "A 'prudentially' ought to do X" (≡ "A ought to do X [on the criterion of A's interests]") is a statement of A's primary allegiance (i.e., not a function of a "higher allegiance").

Now, it is certainly true that "I ought to pursue my freedom and well-being" is presented as a dialectically necessary commitment, with it not being assumed that I consider any principles to override my self-interest. But, if this is so, then this means that I am not required to accept any rules that would permit PPAO to interfere with my pursuit of my freedom and well-being (along the lines of competitive games). "I ought to pursue my freedom and well-being (on the criterion of my interests)" being my "primary" "ought," will entail "PPAO ought not to interfere with my freedom and well-being (on the criterion of my interests)," just as "A ought to play according to the rules of the game" entails "B ought not to prevent A from playing according to the rules of the game." Far from it being the case (as Sterba alleges [see ibid.]) that the difference between "prudential" "oughts" and the "oughts" of competitive games shows that (4c) does not entail (4d), it is *this difference* which makes (4d) dialectically necessary on (4c).

Sterba does not see this because he thinks that Gewirth tries to move from the "prudential" to the "moral" by an argument by analogy between "prudential" "oughts" and the "oughts" of competitive games.

As one would expect, Gewirth does examine the asymmetrically action-guiding "oughts" of competitive games, but he concludes that any analogy here in fact supports his argument. For, as Gewirth points out, the asymmetrically action-guiding "oughts" of competitive games derive their force from the symmetrically action-guiding "ought" we express when we say that the game ought to be played according to its rules and related objectives. Accordingly, if the "oughts" of competitive games are to be taken as a model for interpreting Gewirth's conclusion [(4c) ≡ "I have a prudential right to my freedom and well-being"] then there too Gewirth thinks that we should find an "ought" which is symmetrically action-guiding. More specifically, Gewirth thinks that we should find a moral "ought." (Ibid., 56)

There are several problems with this. For example:

1. The discussion to which Sterba alludes (see RM 86–89) is one of "universal ethical egoism" (which is a moral position). What is being discussed specifically is whether a universal ethical egoist can avoid incompatible directives by modelling its "oughts" on the basis of a commitment to a life of struggle. Gewirth says that it cannot because such a commitment involves abandoning its primary commitment, as an egoist, to achieving its interests.

2. The more general issue addressed is not the move from the "prudential" to the "moral" (see #33 and #35.3), but the move from (4c) to (4d) (whether this is prudential or not), which, within the context of the derivation of the PGC, would be presumed to be prudential.

3. Sterba interprets "symmetrically action-guiding" to mean "action-guiding from both my and PPAO's points of view" (see Sterba 1987, 57), which implies that he thinks Gewirth is trying to derive "PPAO ought not to interfere with my freedom and well-being from PPAO's point of view (the criterion of its interests)" from (4c). However, in the context of Gewirth's discussion, "symmetrical" must mean "action-directed to both myself and PPAO from my point of view (on the criterion of my primary allegiance to the rules of the game [the game of conflict and struggle])."

4. In the context of the dialectically necessary derivation of (4d), Gewirth's point would be that (4c) and (4d) are not validated on my

presumption of "higher rules" that "limit" my action for my self-interest (since any allegiance to these has not been shown to be dialectically necessary). Nor would it be that PPAO's actions are limited (from PPAO's point of view) by the criterion of my interests. It is that PPAO's actions, as well as mine, are governed by the criterion of my interests (from my dialectically necessary viewpoint).

Ultimately, Sterba's refutation fails because he does not address the argument by which Gewirth attempts to make the move from the prudential to the moral. What Sterba has to refute are sequences A and B above, but his discussion totally fails to address these. In particular, he shows no appreciation of the distinction between other-referring and other-directing "oughts" and of the distinctive features of the internal application of the LPU.

4 Hare

I shall be concentrating on the two steps . . . : 'hence he must claim rights to freedom and well-being; hence he must accord the same rights to all agents . . . .' I shall argue that the first of these steps is only valid in a somewhat weak sense of "rights," if such a sense exists, in which a right-claim is not necessarily universalizable (i.e. in which we may claim a right without being thereby committed to extend it to others who have the same reasons for claiming it as we have). If there is no such sense, then the step is invalid. But even if there is such a sense, it is not that which is required in order to make the next step valid, viz. 'hence he must accord the same rights to all agents who have the same reasons for claiming them as he has.' In short, Gewirth is guilty of a fallacy of equivocation. (Hare 1984, 53)

According to R. M. Hare, the inference from (5) "I have a claim right to my freedom and well-being" to (9) "I must consider that PPAO has a claim right to its freedom and well-being"

relies on an insistence that, if what are claimed are *rights* (i.e. that others *ought* or *ought not* to do certain things), then it must be allowed that the same would apply if the roles were reversed. But this will only be so if the prescription to which the agent is committed is a universal one [i.e., a moral one]. And this has not been shown. It has been shown that he must prescribe that his purposes be achieved,[13] and that the necessary conditions for achieving them be supplied.[14] But it has not been shown that he must prescribe this universally—that is, prescribe that this be so whoever is in the roles in question.

It would thus be perfectly consistent for someone to admit that he was a purposive agent, and therefore bound to assent to *singular* prescriptions, and even to claim rights in the weak sense, if there is one, which is non-universalizable, but to refrain from prescribing universally, i.e. claiming rights in the strong, universalizable sense which compels him to accord them to others too. (Ibid., 56)

We need to be careful about terminology here. When Hare concedes that I might well be required to consider that I have a "weak right" to my freedom and well-being, he does not mean that I must consider that I have a mere liberty to my freedom and well-being. In Hare's use of "weak right," a weak right is a claim right (and claim rights are sometimes called "strong rights"), but a nonuniversalizable one. Hare appears to concede that I might well be required to consider that others have a duty not to interfere with my freedom and well-being (correlative to *my* having an other-directed right [of some sort] to my freedom and well-being), but in a way that does not require me to consider (by logical universalization) that I have a duty not to interfere with the freedom and well-being of PPAO, and thus to accord PPAO a similar right to its freedom and well-being. (See ibid.) In other words, Hare more or less defines a "strong right" as a "moral right," and a "weak right" as "a claim right that is owed to me on grounds that do not necessarily require me to accord this right to anyone else."

So, what Hare is claiming is not that Gewirth cannot establish that a PPA must consider that it has at least an *amoral right* (one grounded in its own interests) to its freedom and well-being (correlative to an other-referring duty of noninterference), which his "weak rights" terminology might suggest, but that Gewirth needs to construe the right in (5) as a moral one in order to effect *Stage III*. In Hare's view, if the right of (5) is an amoral claim right ("a weak right" in his terminology, "a prudential claim right"" in Gewirth's), then Stage III will not work; but if the right of (5) is moral, then (5) cannot be justified on the basis of the considerations that establish (4d).

Gewirth claims to effect the move to morality by *logical* universalization of (5).

According to Hare,

[t]here is indeed a sense in which prudential judgments are universalizable. . . . But this sense does not help Gewirth's argument. For if all he had shown was that an agent must claim that there is a prudential requirement on him to seek the necessary conditions for achieving *his* purposes, the universalization of this claim would only yield the claim that there is a prudential requirement on other similar agents in similar situations to seek the necessary conditions for achieving *their* purposes. Since they and their situations are similar, the necessary conditions will also be similar. But what Gewirth needs to substantiate is the universalized claim that there is a requirement on anyone, including the original agent, to seek the necessary conditions for achieving the purposes of anyone else who is similar and similarly placed. The agent would be committed to this claim if it were true in the *moral* sense of 'ought' that an agent is committed to claiming that all other persons ought

to supply the necessary conditions for achieving his purposes. But this has not been shown. (Ibid., 55)

Now, Gewirth does not apply the LPU to (4c), as Hare does here. He applies it to (4d)/(5) (which are derived from [4c]), and Hare, by conceding that a PPA must claim what he calls "weak rights," has conceded that (4d)/(5), *prudentially interpreted,* can be derived. But I take it that Hare would say that logically universalizing (4d)/(5) (prudentially interpreted) can only yield "(I must consider that) *PPAO must consider* that it has a right to its freedom and well-being (*PPAO must consider* that I have a duty not to interfere with its freedom and well-being)" and not "*I must consider* that PPAO has a right to its freedom and well-being (that I have a duty not to interfere with PPAO's freedom and well-being)."

However, Hare's application of the LPU is external, and he ignores internal application of the principle. Applying the principle internally, Gewirth reasons that if, *from my point of view,* [I am a PPA → I have a right to my freedom and well-being] is a valid (required) inference, then so too is [PPAO is a PPA → PPAO has a right to its freedom and well-being] *from my point of view.* There can be no doubt that this is valid.

Witness Bernard Williams.

[The step]—that if in my case rational agency alone is the ground of a right to noninterference, then it must be so in the case of other people—is certainly sound. It rests on the weakest and least contestable version of a "principle of universalizability," which is brought into play simply by *because* or *in virtue of.* If a particular consideration is really enough to establish a conclusion in my case, then it is enough to establish it in anyone's case. That must be so if enough is indeed enough. If the conclusion that brings in morality does not follow, it must be because of an earlier step. (Williams 1985, 60)[15]

Although *it is true* that, *simply* on the basis of holding that I have a claim right to my freedom and well-being (where this is not an egalitarian moral right), it is consistent for me to refuse to grant this right to PPAO (as Hare claims), this is the case only where I claim to have this right on the basis of properties that I possess, and that PPAO does not possess. However, where I consider—indeed, am required to consider—that I have a right *by virtue of being a PPA,* this "by virtue of" being a sufficient condition, I cannot consistently refuse to grant this same right to PPAO. I cannot then say that PPAO does not have this right because PPAO lacks certain of my properties, or even because PPAO lacks the property of being me. To do so is to deny that the property of being a PPA is the property that is the sufficient reason for my having the right. I cannot deny this at this point, because, by having to accept (5), I have to accept that my being a PPA is the sufficient justifying ground for my having a right to my freedom and well-being.[16]

Jan Narveson, who also agrees that Stage III is valid, puts this in the following way:

[Stage III] rests on the most straight-forward and widely accepted form of a universalizability principle. Why can't I consistently say, "I have these rights, but nobody else does"? The answer is that one could consistently say some things of that form, but not when *these* right-claims are made in the way Gewirth has in mind. . . . [A hypothetical agent A is,] in Gewirth's argument, . . . claiming these rights simply *in virtue of being an agent:* for he claims them, in Gewirth's view anyway, on the basis of wanting E, *no matter what E is.* If *that* is what gives A those rights,[17] then of course A must . . . allow that all other agents have them. (Narveson 1980, 655)[18]

Furthermore, Gewirth indicates that (4c) "I prudentially ought to pursue my freedom and well-being" can itself be universalized to a proposition that has moral import. According to Gewirth, Hare recognizes

that "prudential judgments are universalizable," but he applies this only to the move from (*a*) "there is a prudential requirement on [an agent] to seek the necessary conditions for achieving *his* purposes" to (*b*) "there is a prudential requirement on other similar agents {in similar situations} to seek the necessary conditions for achieving *their* purposes." Even within this limited framework, however, a transition from the prudential to the moral . . . can be made out. For if (*b*) is said by the original agent referred to in (*a*), then he is in the position of endorsing other agents' fulfillment of their own general agency-needs—and this endorsement is a moral one because the agent who says (*b*) thereby takes favorable account of the interests of persons other than or in addition to himself. (Gewirth 1984d, 211, quoting Hare 1984, 55; Gewirth's insertion in brackets; my insertion in curly brackets)

Unfortunately, this is not at all clear. Hare will say that if I say, "PPAO prudentially ought to seek its freedom and well-being" on the basis of "I prudentially ought to seek my freedom and well-being," then this does not commit me to endorsing that PPAO ought to seek its freedom and well-being, because the statement about PPAO refers to PPAO's prudential criterion, whereas the statement about me refers to my prudential criterion.

This, of course, is so if the move from (*a*) to (*b*) is effected by external application of the LPU, and (*a*) is a statement about what I must think from my point of view, and (*b*) is a statement about what PPAO must think from its point of view. This, however, ignores the fact that we can universalize from the prudential to the moral by internal application of the LPU; and it must be this that Gewirth has in mind.

Internal application of the LPU to (4c) yields "I must consider
(from my point of view) that PPAO strictly ought to pursue its freedom and well-being," where this "ought" is moral because advocated by me. (This is because my being a PPA is the sufficient ground
for "I ought to pursue my freedom and well-being," and the
illocutionary force of this "ought" is that my pursuit of my freedom
and well-being is the state of affairs which ought to be. This is explained under #35.3, #37 and #47.3.) Applying "ought implies can"
to this, we get "I must consider that I strictly ought not to interfere
with PPAO's freedom and well-being"; application of the principle
of correlativity then yields (9) "I must consider that PPAO has a
claim right to its freedom and well-being."

The point is that, although Gewirth's derivation in *Reason and
Morality* moves from (4c) to (4d) by "ought implies can," from this
to (5) (by the logical correlativity of other-referring strict "oughts"
and claim rights), and from this to (9) (by the internal application of
the LPU), we *can alter* the order of these logical transformations to
achieve the same result. This point is not just an interesting aside;
the validity of this contention is absolutely vital for the validity of
the argument as I understand it, for it is required as a matter of logic
(by the principle of transitivity in sequences of logical entailment).

Confronted with this, it is possible that Hare will claim that internal application of the LPU is not purely logical at all, that it is moral.
Why? Because in this application I claim a right to my freedom and
well-being for the sufficient reason that I am a PPA. Such a ground
is *universal*. If I claim my right on such grounds, then I must, of
course, grant this right to other PPAs. But, precisely because I am
claiming this right on grounds that require me to grant it to other
PPAs, the right I claim at the end of Stage II is already a moral right.

If Hare so wishes, he may define a "moral" right in this way. So
defined, the rights-claim of (5) is "moral," as are all the claims of
Stage II. But this terminology doesn't help Hare's cause one bit.

Hare claims that Gewirth cannot establish that the claims of Stage
II are moral without begging the question, but that he needs to do so
in order to effect Stage III. However, Hare concedes that Gewirth can
establish that I must accept the claims of Stage II on pain of contradicting that I am a PPA. The ASA shows that I must regard my
being a PPA as the sufficient ground for all these claims. If this
makes the claims "moral," which requires me to take favorable account of PPAO's freedom and well-being (by internal application of
the LPU), then it does not follow that the question has been begged.
The question has been begged only if the ASA is fallacious, or if its
application is question-begging. (See the discussion of #50.)

On such a definition of "moral," claims can be both prudential

and moral *within the same viewpoint*. The claims of Stage II are validated by my categorical proactive commitment to my freedom and
well-being. This, in Gewirth's terms, makes them prudential. At the
same time, these claims are required of me by virtue of my claim to
be a PPA, which (within my dialectically necessary viewpoint)
makes my being a PPA the sufficient ground for all the claims of
Stage II—which makes them "moral" in Hare's terms (but not in
Gewirth's).[19]

Gewirth defines the claims of Stage II as prudential, *rather than*
moral, because he is trying to establish that PPAs must adopt an SPR
that requires them to take favorable account of the interests of
PPAO, and the claims of Stage II, being validated by my interests, do
not, *as such*, require me to do so. What requires me to do so are the
additional considerations provided by the dialectical necessity of
these claims and the ASA. These considerations are, if the argument
is valid, already implicit in Stage II. Indeed, they are already implicit
in the premise. But this does not make the premise question-begging
unless the premise is not a necessary one.[20]

5 Harman

Gilbert Harman claims that, in general, all arguments that agents are
rationally committed to basic rights (and he specifically mentions
Kant and Gewirth)

> would have you consider a given situation from someone else's point of
> view, where this is supposed to show you that you have a reason to take the
> other person's interests into account in the present unreversed situation. To
> suppose that you do not have sufficient reason to take the other person's
> interests into account in this situation, is to suppose the other person would
> not have sufficient reason to take your intere[s]ts into account in the reversed
> situation. It is argued that, since you cannot accept the other person's not
> taking your interests into account in the reversed situation, you would be
> inconsistent not to take the other person's interests into account in the actual
> situation. (Harman 1983, 117)

This is not an accurate portrayal of Gewirth's strategy. Gewirth's
argument operates solely from within a PPA's own viewpoint, and
does not depend on how things look from PPAO's point of view. But
I shall let this pass for the moment.

Harman says that such arguments rest on an equivocation concerning what it is to "accept" a person's doing something. The sense
in which I cannot accept your ignoring my interests is

(A)   I do not want you to ignore my interests ≡ From my
       point of view it ought not to be the case that you ignore
       my interests.

From (A), however, it does not follow that

(B)   I cannot realize that, from your point of view, it ought to
        be the case that you ignore my interests (that you have
        sufficient reasons to ignore my interests).

Harman grants that there is a sense in which Gewirth can establish that I must suppose that PPAO must not (ought not to) interfere
with my freedom and well-being. This supposition is, however, ambiguous. It can mean either that

1.   (from my point of view, the point of view of my interests) it
        must not (ought not to) happen that PPAO interferes; or
2.   there is a "requirement on them [PPAOs] giving them reasons
        not to interfere" (ibid., 118).

Harman says (quite correctly) that from "My freedom and well-
being are necessary goods" the supposition in sense 1 ($\equiv$ to [A]) is
dialectically necessary, but that the supposition in sense 2 ($\equiv$ to [B])
does not follow logically.

But sense 2 of the supposition that they must not interfere is what is needed
to get to the supposition that you have a right to such noninterference and,
therefore, that others have a similar right. The supposition that you have
such a right does not follow simply from the thought that from your point of
view they must not interfere.

    Alternatively, the equivocation might be located at a later point in the
notion of a right. We might say that you have a "right" to noninterference in
the sense of a "justified claim" to noninterference because your self-interest
justifies you in making such a claim. Then others have a similar right; they
have a self-interested justification for a similar claim that they not be interfered with. However, it still does not follow that you have any reason to
accept their claim in the sense of being motivated not to interfere with them.
That follows only from a different notion of "right." (Ibid.)

Harman can hardly accuse Gewirth of not being aware of the
difference between senses 1 and 2, or (A) and (B). Gewirth takes a
great deal of trouble to distinguish these two things, and he agrees
that the "ought" of (4d) at the end of Stage II carries the meaning of
1, and absolutely insists that it not be given the meaning of 2. In
Stage II, the criterion of all "oughts" is my prudential criterion (my
interests), and all claims of Stage II are made from this perspective.
I must consider that PPAO ought not to interfere with my freedom
and well-being from my internal point of view as a PPA, on the
criterion of my interests (my categorical proactive evaluation of my
freedom and well-being). I prescribe this "ought" *to* PPAO, and this
means that I consider that I have a conclusive reason why PPAO

ought not to interfere with my freedom and well-being. But, in so
doing, I do not consider that PPAO will accept this reason, or that
PPAO will accept any reason not to interfere with my freedom and
well-being. The argument is conducted from my internal viewpoint.
What viewpoint PPAO might have doesn't come into it yet. When
Harman attempts to locate an equivocation "at a later point," and
says that Gewirth *can* claim that I must consider that I have a right
to my freedom and well-being, *if* "I have a right to my freedom and
well-being" means "I have a justified claim to noninterference with
my freedom and well-being," then he states Gewirth's position correctly. That is what Gewirth thinks he has established at the end of
Stage II.

Where Harman and Gewirth disagree is over what can be inferred
from my having to make this claim. Harman says that it follows (as
it does by external application of the LPU) that I must recognize that
PPAO must make the same claim, that PPAO must consider that it
has a justified claim to noninterference with its freedom and well-
being. But he contends that recognition of this fact does not give me
a reason not to interfere with PPAO's freedom and well-being. This
is because PPAO's justification is on the criterion of its interests.
This recognition only gives me a reason not to interfere with PPAO's
freedom and well-being if I adopt a moral point of view, by taking
favorable account of PPAO's interests. And such an assumption is
question-begging.

However, this is *not* how Gewirth argues. Gewirth argues that I
contradict "I am a PPA" if I do not consider that I have a justified
claim to noninterference with my freedom and well-being. True, this
claim is justified on the criterion of my interests. But the fact that it
is relative to my interests does not mean that I do not consider the
claim to be justified *simpliciter*.[21] True, I realize that it would not be
justified on the criterion of PPAO's interests. But the criterion of my
internal viewpoint is my interests, and *on that criterion*, which is
necessarily my criterion, I *have* a justified claim to noninterference
with my freedom and well-being. So, as far as I am concerned, it is
true that PPAO ought (*simpliciter*) not to interfere with my freedom
and well-being, whatever might be validated by some other criterion. By the ASA, Gewirth argues that [I am a PPA → I must consider
that PPAO ought (*simpliciter*) not to interfere with my freedom and
well-being] entails that I must consider that [I am a PPA → PPAO
ought (*simpliciter*) not to interfere with my freedom and well-being]
is a valid inference. In contrast with Harman's portrayal, Gewirth
does not now apply the LPU *externally* to this conclusion (though it
is perfectly valid to do so). He applies it *internally*, to the inference
A: [I am a PPA → PPAO ought (*simpliciter*) not to interfere with my

freedom and well-being]. In any system of reasoning in which A is a valid inference, B [PPAO is a PPA → All PPAs other than PPAO (including me) ought (*simpliciter*) not to interfere with PPAO's freedom and well-being] is a valid inference too. Since my internal viewpoint as a PPA is a system of reasoning in which A is valid, it is a system of reasoning in which B is valid too. But this means that I contradict "I am a PPA" if I do not consider that I ought not to interfere with PPAO's freedom and well-being.

But note: this conclusion is reached without assuming that I must take favorable account of PPAO's interests. It is also achieved without attending in any way to how the matter looks from the point of view of PPAO's interests. Only now does Gewirth apply the LPU externally, in order to generalize "I must consider that I ought not to interfere with PPAO's freedom and well-being" to "All PPAs must consider that they ought not to interfere with the freedom and well-being of any other PPA."

Harman is, therefore, mistaken when he claims that the conclusion that "I must consider that I ought not to interfere with PPAO's freedom and well-being" only follows from "I must consider that PPAO ought not to interfere with my freedom and well-being" in sense 2 of "PPAO ought not to interfere with my freedom and well-being." No equivocation between prudential and moral rights/ "oughts" is required to derive Stage III.[22]

6 McMahon

Stage II concludes that I must judge (4d) "PPAO ought not to interfere with my freedom and well-being." According to Christopher McMahon, if Stage III is to follow by the LPU, then this must be "an 'ought' of rationality *ascribing reasons for action to others*" (McMahon 1986, 271), but in this case (4d) is not validly derived. If, on the other hand, (4d) is an "ought" of evaluation, reporting

the existence of sufficient reason for me to regard . . . [action by others to maintain my freedom and well-being] as desirable from my point of view[, then it is validly derived.] . . .

. . . [But] then the requirement that relevantly similar cases be judged alike does not force acceptance of the PGC. (Ibid., 270–271)

As an "ought" of evaluation, Stage III does not follow by the *logical* principle of universalizability; all that follows is that I must accept that PPAO must, from its point of view, consider it desirable that I promote PPAO's freedom and well-being. This recognition does not, however, compel me to respect PPAO's prescription that I ought not to interfere with PPAO's freedom and well-being, because the ground of PPAO's prescription is its interests, and it has not yet been shown that I must take favorable account of PPAO's interests.

As McMahon defines an "ought" of evaluation, it is not only a judgment made by the speaker from its own point of view, it is also one that is

expressed only when action-guiding "ought"-judgments would be out of place—either because the object of the judgment cannot be realized by action . . . , or because no agent who can contribute to its realization has sufficient reason to do so . . . . (McMahon 1986, 269)

However, the "ought" of (4d) is neither an "ought" of evaluation, so defined, nor an "ought" of rationality. (4d) would be an "ought" of rationality, in McMahon's terms, if PPAO's interests required it not to interfere with my freedom and well-being, or if it had a viewpoint that required it to take favorable account of my interests—and thus to accept that it ought not to interfere with my freedom and well-being (and, more characteristically, the former). (4d) is based on my interests, not PPAO's, and it is not assumed that PPAO must take favorable account of my interests. But (4d) is not, therefore, merely an "ought" of evaluation. This is because it is assumed that PPAO *can* refrain from interfering with my freedom and well-being (if otherwise, PPAO would not be a PPA). (4d) is an action-guiding "ought" *from my point of view*. It says that PPAO has sufficient reason not to interfere with my freedom and well-being *on the criterion of my interests*. In other words, (4d) is validly derived as an "ought" giving reasons *to* others, *on my prudential criterion*, even if it is not validly derived as an "ought" giving reasons to others *on their criteria*. Correlative to this, I have a right to my freedom and well-being on the criterion of my interests, whereas a mere "ought" of evaluation would not be action-guiding (deontically prescriptive) on any criterion, and would not be correlative to a deontic rights-claim on any criterion.

Now, *if* (4d) were a mere "ought" of evaluation, then there is at least some plausibility in arguing that the most I could be required to claim is that I consider that it would be desirable from my point of view if I could have rights to my freedom and well-being. I would not be required to consider that, *on the criterion of my interests, I have* rights to freedom and well-being. Consequently, McMahon construes universalization as bearing on the *claiming* of rights, on the *making of judgments* about rights, where such claims and judgments are not to the *having* of rights from my point of view, but to the desirability, from my point of view, of my being able to have rights. If this is so, then I do not have rights on the criterion of my interests, and the only property I have that can be universalized is that of "claiming rights," where this means thinking it desirable for me to have rights if I could. All that would follow from universalization is that I must acknowledge that PPA must claim rights in the same sense—think it desirable, from its point of view, that it have rights to its freedom and well-being if it could.

However, since (4d) is not an "ought" of evaluation, Gewirth's response to McMahon is appropriate.

McMahon . . . construes the universalization as moving from *my making a judgment* that I have rights to *all other agents' making judgments* that they have rights. (Gewirth 1988c, 253)

Gewirth calls this "judgmental universalization," this being equivalent to what I have been calling external application of the LPU.

However, Gewirth's universalization moves from "From my point of view, I *have* rights to my freedom and well-being, because I am a PPA" to "From my point of view, all PPAs *have* rights to freedom and well-being, because they are PPAs."

Thus the universalization bears on the *having* of rights: it moves from *my having* the generic rights to *all prospective agents' having* them. I shall call this "possessive universalization." (Ibid.)

This, of course, is what I have been calling internal application of the LPU. If McMahon attended to this, he would see that Stage III is effected validly without any assumption that I must take favorable account of the interests of PPAO. If (4d)/(5) is "I must consider (on the criterion of my interests, which defines my viewpoint as a PPA) that I have rights to my freedom and well-being (for the sufficient reason that I am a PPA)," then we can use both judgmental and possessive universalization. The former yields "PPAO must consider (on the criterion of its interests, which defines its viewpoint as a PPA) that it has rights to its freedom and well-being (for the sufficient reason that it is a PPA)." The latter yields "I must consider (in consistency with the judgment validated by the criterion of my interests, which defines my viewpoint as a PPA) that PPAO has rights to freedom and well-being (because it is a PPA)."[23]

7 Puolimatka

According to Tapio Puolimatka, Stage III rests on an equivocation between prudential and moral rights. Gewirth

thinks that he is able to deduce all other kinds of rights, especially the most essential moral rights, from . . . prudential rights. (Puolimatka 1989, 66)

[But] the agent cannot proceed from (4) [Puolimatka's numbering] 'I have (prudential) rights to freedom and well-being,' to (5) 'All other persons ought to respect my freedom and well-being,' except in the sense (5') 'My own prudential point of view requires that all other persons ought to respect my freedom and well-being.' And from the agent's prudential standpoint (5') does not entail (6) 'All prospective purposive agents have rights to freedom and well-being,' except in the sense (6') 'All prospective purposive agents necessarily have to claim prudential rights to freedom and well-being.'

Thus, the statement (6) cannot be deduced from (4) and (5) without changing the meaning of the term 'a right' from prudential to moral. And this is, of course, illegitimate, as this is intended to be a strict deduction.

. . . Gewirth passes elusively from the agent's *believing* that he has rights to his admitting that other persons *have* rights, when in actual fact the agent needs only to admit that other people also (justifiably) believe that they have (prudential) rights. (Ibid., 67)

However, Gewirth does not claim to deduce *all* rights-claims (i.e., rights-prescriptions, e.g., logical ones) from the prudential rights-claim. Strictly speaking, he does not even claim to deduce moral rights-claims from prudential ones! He claims only to derive a PPA's (logically required) *commitment to a moral rights-claim* (the PGC) from its (logically required) *commitment to the prudential rights-claim* of Stage II. (See further below.)

Puolimatka's portrayal of Stage III is purely in terms of the external application of the LPU, ignoring the ASA and the internal application of the LPU. Gewirth does not move from a PPA's *believing* that it has the generic rights to PPAO's *having* them. The LPU is *not* used to move from a dialectically necessary claim to an assertoric one.[24] Gewirth moves from a PPA's having to believe that it has the generic rights, to the PPA's having to believe that PPAO has them. The ASA and internal application of the LPU enable him to do this without having to assume that a PPA adopts a moral point of view. I have spelled this out many times in connection with other objections under the present heading, and I will not repeat my analysis here.[25]

It is, however, interesting to examine why Puolimatka thinks that Gewirth is led into (nonexistent) equivocation between prudential and moral rights. According to Puolimatka, Gewirth's concept of "my prudential criterion" is "ambiguous." "Prudential," he says, covers any validation by my self-interest, even when I determine my self-interest in an altruistic way. "My prudential criterion" can stand for *any SPR for my purposes*. This allows Gewirth, conveniently, to forget that it is not necessary for me to espouse a moral SPR for my purposes. However, if my SPR for my purposes is amoral, it will not validate Stage III, while, if it is moral, it will not be necessary for me to go through the stages of the argument in order for me to be committed to taking account of PPAO's interests. That I do so will already be built into my SPR for my purposes. (See ibid., 71–72.)

However, this portrayal of "my prudential criterion" totally mis-construes the dialectically necessary method. Puolimatka thinks that Gewirth is trying to show that every possible SPR for my pur-poses entails the PGC, that the dialectically necessary method at-tempts to demonstrate that all SPRs for my purposes that are incom-patible with the PGC are *internally* inconsistent. Correlative to this, a PPA is portrayed as reasoning from its particular occurrent pur-poses, or from the SPR that it uses to rationalize these purposes.

In fact, "my prudential criterion," in the first instance, as em-ployed in the dialectically necessary method, stands neither for my particular occurrent purposes, nor for any SPR that I use to rational-ize them, but for my proactive evaluative relation to my purposes (IP). IP is invariant (because independent of the content of my pur-poses or SPR, and therefore neutral as between my espousal of moral or amoral SPRs) and is necessarily possessed by me as a PPA (unlike my particular occurrent purposes or SPR). IP is only *indi-rectly* (and contingently) moral or amoral, according to the content of my particular occurrent SPR, and the dialectically necessary method does not operate on contingent contents. Since "my pruden-tial criterion" does not represent the various indirect and contingent contents that might guide my purposes, Puolimatka's analysis is totally misguided.

Puolimatka's failure to appreciate this is shown graphically by his portrayal of the argument as one that requires a PPA to be mor-ally neutral at the beginning of Stage I, an amoralist from then on until the end of Stage II, and a moralist in Stage III (ibid.). The argument requires no such thing. For present purposes, we might characterize it as follows:

It is argued that, whether I am an amoralist or a moralist, I am a PPA, and *as a PPA* I proactively value my purposes (i.e., I possess IP). Stage I argues that, because I categorically need my freedom and well-being for whatever my purposes (IC), I must claim that my freedom and well-being are necessary goods. This claim is equiva-lent to "I ought to pursue my freedom and well-being" (SRO). The argument for Stage I is "IP & IC → SRO" within my internal view-point as a PPA. In having to hold SRO *because* of IC, I am required to prescribe, for the sake of my categorical needs, my freedom and well-being. Any judgments that *SRO* validates are, hence, "pruden-tial" in the specific sense that they are prescribed for the sake of my own categorical needs. SRO entails "PPAO ought not to interfere with my freedom and well-being" (ORO), which entails "I have a right to my freedom and well-being" (MyR). Thus, I must hold, at the end of Stage II, that "IP & IC → MyR." SRO, ORO, and MyR are all "generally prudential" in being dialectically validated by IP. They are also "specifically prudential," however, in that they are all prescribed for the sake of my own categorical needs, within my dialectically necessary viewpoint. Now, that I am required to claim MyR for the sake of my own categorical needs does not mean that I am required to be an amoralist in Stage II! For, the fact that I must prescribe for the sake of my own categorical needs does not mean that I am prohibited from prescribing (for myself) for the sake of PPAO's categorical needs as well. Stage II shows that I must, whether amoralist or moralist, claim MyR for the sake of my categorical needs, and only prohibits me from espousing SPRs for my purposes that do not grant that I have MyR. The universalization of Stage III (using the ASA and internal application of the LPU) then shows that I must grant PPAO a right to its freedom and well-being (PPAOR) because PPAO has OC (categorically needs its freedom and well-being). This result *shows* that I must take favorable account equally of both my own and PPAO's categorical needs. PPAOR is prescribed by me for the sake of OC. Thus, while the claims of Stage III are "generally prudential" in being validated dialectically on the basis of IP, they are moral (and not "specifically prudential," unlike MyR and the other prescriptions of Stage II) in being prescribed for the sake of PPAO's freedom and well-being as well as my own. PPAOR is necessitated, not by my *judgment* MyR, as validated by SRO (which is why PPAOR is not "specifically prudential"), but by the fact that I must claim that I have MyR for the sufficient reason that I have IC, as shown by the ASA (the universalization of the *inference* [IC → MyR] entailing that I must accept the inference [OC → PPAOR]).

In none of this is it supposed that IP, or any of the judgments or inferences dialectically necessitated by it, are rationalized by a moral SPR for my purposes. The argument works irrespective of my contingent rationalizations, not because it works on any and all that I might have, but because it is wholly independent of *the content of* any and all such *contingent* rationalizations.[26]

#48 "Ought implies can" does not permit Stage III to be derived.

Kai Nielsen (1984, 82–83, commenting on Gewirth 1970a) grants that an amoralist must accept [I want to have X, and I need to do Y to have X → I (prudentially) ought (have good reason) to do Y]. He insists that good reasons are not necessarily moral reasons (and they certainly are not from the amoralist's point of view). In this minimal sense he must accept "ought-talk." He also insists that [I have good reason to do Y does not → I have a right to Y].

He maintains that even if, in this minimal sense, [If I want to do X, I ought to do Y → All other persons who want to have X, ought to do Y], this does not entail "I ought not to interfere with others doing Y" or "Others have a right to do Y." I, if an amoralist, need only acknowledge that others have as good a reason to do Y as I have; and this does not entail that I endorse their doing Y, or consider myself not bound to interfere with their doing Y.

Gewirth tries to resist this by claiming, plausibly, that "'All persons who want to have Y ought to do Z [pursue the necessary conditions for securing Y]' entails 'All persons who want to have Y ought to be free to do Z.'" But again the amoralist is deliberately refusing to take the universalistic stance of the moral point of view. Given the aims of others, aims relevantly similar to his own, they (the others) indeed ought to do Y; and, since 'ought implies can,' they ought to be free to do Y. But the amoralist is not logically forced to consider things from the moral point of view or from others' points of view or to give others' points of view the same weight as his own or, indeed, any weight at all . . . . So for the amoralist, 'they ought to be free to do Z' does not entail that 'I ought to refrain from interfering with other persons doing Z if they want to have Y' . . . . (Ibid., 83)

The main thing that must be said about these comments is that they are not directed at a sequence of argument that Gewirth presents.

The prudential "ought" from which Gewirth derives that I must consider that I have a right to my freedom and well-being is a strict prudential "ought," not any prudential "ought." According to Gewirth, if I want X and need to do Y to have X, then this only entails that I must consider that I have a right to do Y, if Y is something that I need to do to get X, *whatever X might be.* Gewirth claims that only my freedom and well-being are things that I need to have (pursue), for whatever X might be. So, "I want X, and need to do Y to get X" only entails "I prudentially strictly (instrumentally) ought to have (pursue) Y" → "I have a claim right to (to pursue) Y," where Y is my freedom and well-being, the generic conditions of my agency. In Gewirth's argument we do not have [I have a good reason to do X → I have a right to do X]. We have [It is categorically irrational for me not to do X → I have a right to do X].

Gewirth does not confuse this "ought" with a moral "ought." The deontic concepts of Stage II do not

involve what Nielsen calls "taking the universalistic stance of the moral point of view." (Gewirth 1984d, 214)

The universalization to the moral point of view rests on the LPU, not on adoption of the moral point of view.

Gewirth does not just assume that "I prudentially strictly ought to have my freedom and well-being" entails "I prudentially have a claim right to my freedom and well-being." He argues that "I prudentially strictly ought to have my freedom and well-being" entails "I prudentially strictly ought to be free to have my freedom and well-being," which entails "Prudentially, PPAO strictly ought not to interfere with my freedom and well-being," which entails "Prudentially, I have a claim right to my freedom and well-being." The specific role that is accorded to the use of the principle that "ought" implies "can" is to effect the move from "According to criterion C (here my prudential criterion), I strictly ought to have Y" to "According to criterion C, I strictly ought to be free to do Z." It is not, as Nielsen suggests, to effect the move from "the prudential" to "the moral."

This sequence is conducted from within my internal point of view; what PPAO can (or must) think from its internal point of view simply doesn't come into it. Nielsen confuses matters here by talking about *whether I, as an amoralist, have to accept the claim of PPAO that I ought not to interfere with PPAO's freedom and well-being.* But, within this sequence, this is an irrelevant question. The relevant question is whether *I, amoralist or not, must (as a PPA) claim that PPAO ought not to interfere with my freedom and well-being.* Once this is recognized, there should be no difficulty in seeing that, *by Nielsen's own showing,* he should answer the relevant question affirmatively! For he concedes that [A ought to have or do Z → A ought to be free to have or do Z], by "ought implies can," and he appears to have no difficulty with the idea that *PPAO, from PPAO's point of view, must consider that PPAO ought to be free to do Z!* But, if this is so, then I, from my point of view, must consider that I ought to be free to do Z; and this, in turn, means that I, from my point of view, must consider that PPAO ought not to interfere with my doing Z, which, in turn, means (where this "ought" is strict) that I, from my point of view, must consider that I have a claim right to my freedom and well-being (and PPAO must consider, from PPAO's point of view, that PPAO has a claim right to its freedom and well-being). Nielsen says that this does not mean that I, if an amoralist, must endorse PPAO's self-directing "ought"; or that PPAO, if an amoralist, must endorse my self-directing "ought"; and thus that amoralists need not, on this basis, recognize that others have rights to their freedom and well-being. This is true, but it is irrelevant, for, at this point, Gewirth does not claim that I, if an amoralist, must endorse that PPAO ought to do Z, or consider myself bound not to interfere with PPAO doing Z. The move to "the moral" has not yet been effected.

This move is effected by applying the *LPU* in its internal application. Nielsen does not consider this step in its proper context; indeed, he does not consider it at all, because he does not differentiate between amoral and moral rights-claims, insisting (like Kalin (1984); see #35.3) on seeing Gewirth's argument in Stage II (in which Gewirth does not deploy universalization) as his refutation of amoralism.

#49   It is superfluous to characterize the rights-claim of Stage II as prudential. The PGC is validly derived from this claim by universalization, but the universalization is moral, not purely logical.

Marcus G. Singer claims that Gewirth's derivation of the PGC is valid, but falsely characterized. Singer specifically objects to the idea that (commitment to) a moral principle can be derived from purely prudential considerations. If the right I claim in Stage II is prudential, (commitment to) the PGC cannot be derived from it. According to Singer, however, (commitment to) the PGC can be derived from the rights-claim of Stage II by the LPU, but only because this claim is already a moral one, the LPU being put to a moral use, not a purely logical one. According to Singer, talk about prudential rights "only adds extraneous puzzlement" (Singer 1985, 297).

Singer's discussion is rather difficult to comment on. This is because at best he has an idiosyncratic way of characterizing Gewirth's argument, which is difficult to relate to what Gewirth actually does, and at worst he completely misportrays the argument.

Matters are complicated right at the beginning, by the following statement:

Gewirth's derivation of the principle of generic consistency goes this way. The agent reasons from within the perspective of agency:

	1. It is necessary for me to have these . . . for my freedom (F) and well-being (W-B);
ergo	2. I have a right to these (necessary goods);
ergo	3. Others have a duty not to interfere with my freedom and well-being.

But the right in 2 is a (so-called) prudential right. And the right necessary to derive 3 must be a moral right. Hence the derivation requires a transition from 2 to

2m. I have a moral right to have these necessary goods.

Though Gewirth talks of and presupposes the "correlativity of rights and strict 'oughts,'" the correlativity in question actually holds only between moral oughts and moral rights. A prudential right (R_p) has not been shown to be correlative to any moral oughts. It has not even been established that it is correlative to prudential oughts—or, indeed, any oughts at all. (Ibid., 297–298; ellipsis Singer's)

This is puzzling. If 1, 2, and 3 are meant (as I think they are) to represent the conclusions of Stages I, II, and III of Gewirth's argument, then what we should have is

(1')   My freedom and well-being are necessary goods; ergo

(2')   I have a (prudential) right to my freedom and well-being; ergo

(3')   PPAO has a (moral) right to its freedom and well-being ($\therefore$ All PPAs have a [moral] right to their freedom and well-being); (or) I have a (moral) duty not to interfere with the freedom and well-being of PPAO ($\therefore$ All PPAs have a [moral] duty not to interfere with the freedom and well-being of PPAs).

Granted, 3 might be regarded as an instance of (3') (in its general "ought" formulation), but Singer more than suggests that Gewirth attempts to derive 3 from 2 by the correlativity of rights and strict "oughts." Gewirth does no such thing if the "ought" of 3 is intended to be a moral "ought" in Gewirth's terms. The move from the prudential to the moral is effected by the internal application of the LPU, not by any presumption that prudential rights are correlative to moral oughts. When Gewirth appeals to the correlativity of rights and strict "oughts," both of these are prudential, and we remain in Stage II. Furthermore, Gewirth appeals to this correlativity, not to move from (5) "I have a prudential right to my freedom and well-being" to (4d) "Others have a prudential duty (prudential relative to my interests) not to interfere with my freedom and well-being," but to move from (4d) to (5).

There is, thus, more than a hint of confusing Stage III with elements of Stage II.

Singer does not provide an explicit statement of the defining features of a "moral" right, and his treatment of "prudential" right is not very helpful.

How is R_p: "A has an R_p [prudential right] to do x" to be understood? We can read it as either:

a   "It would be in A's interest for A to do x,"

or   *b*   "It would not be contrary to A's interest for A to do x,"
or   *c*   "It would not be imprudent for A to do x." (Ibid., 298;
                   Singer's brackets)

Now, remembering that Gewirth derives (5) from (4d) "PPAO
ought not to interfere with my freedom and well-being (on the criterion of my interests)," it is quite clear how Gewirth intends "A has a
prudential right to do x" to be understood—"It is categorically contrary to A's interest for B to interfere with A's doing x." None of *a*, *b*,
or *c* is equivalent, though (5) can be derived from *a* by "ought implies can" if doing x is categorically in A's interest.

"It is categorically contrary to A's interest for B to interfere with
A's doing/having x" quite clearly entails "On the criterion of A's
interest, B ought not to interfere with A's doing/having x." So, the
prudential rights-claim 2 *is* correlative to at least a prudential
"ought," and Singer is wrong to say that prudential rights have not
been established to be correlative to even prudential "oughts."
Granted, they are not correlative to moral "oughts," but Gewirth
does not claim that they are, and he claims that they are correlative
to prudential "oughts" only where the prudential criterion of the
right and duty is the same. "I have a prudential right to my freedom
and well-being" is correlative to "PPAO has a duty not to interfere
with my freedom and well-being (on the criterion of my interest),"
but it is not correlative to "PPAO has a duty not to interfere with my
freedom and well-being (on the criterion of PPAO's interest)."
Gewirth makes no attempt to move from the prudential (self-regarding) to the moral (other-regarding) or from other-referring "oughts"
to other-directing ones in Stage II (by the correlativity he claims).

At this point, Singer claims that, since the latter correlativity, and
correlativity with a moral "ought," do not hold, there is no way that
the move from the prudential to the moral can be effected. (See ibid,
299.) It begins to look as though Singer is pressing the objection that
the argument is invalid because it involves an equivocation between
a moral right (which cannot be established) and a prudential right
(which can).[27] But this cannot be right. For Singer now claims that
Gewirth tries to overcome these "difficulties" by appealing to the
LPU. We would expect Singer to say that he cannot succeed. But,
confounding our expectations, he claims that Gewirth can move validly from "I have a right to my freedom and well-being" to the PGC,
without begging the question! (See ibid., 300.)

How, according to Singer, is this done? Quite simply. If I must
claim a right to my freedom and well-being, on the grounds that I
categorically need my freedom and well-being (and, according to
Singer, I must), then I must grant this right to all others who satisfy

this ground (all other PPAs). (See ibid.) But isn't this exactly what Gewirth claims? Yes! But, according to Singer, in this derivation, the LPU is

> put to a moral and not merely a derivational use. And there is nothing in it that requires us to talk of . . . prudential rights as distinct from moral, legal, or political rights. (Ibid., 301)

> [T]alk about prudential rights is superfluous . . . . And what Gewirth is hereby talking about is what, in Kantian terms, can be described as what one must want if one is to want anything at all, must will if one is to will consistently, must find desirable if one is to have any desires at all. (Ibid., 300)

As I understand this, Singer is saying that I must claim a right to my freedom and well-being because having my freedom and well-being is something that I must will if I am to will anything at all, etc. This is sufficient justification for my considering that I have a right to my freedom and well-being. But this right is a moral right. I am justified in claiming a *moral* right to my freedom and well-being on the grounds that I must will having my freedom and well-being. As such, I must grant this right to all other PPAs who must also will having their freedom and well-being.

But, if this is valid, then Singer is just choosing to call what Gewirth calls a "prudential right" a "moral right." At this point we must distinguish between Gewirth's general and specific uses of "my prudential criterion." In the general use, my prudential criterion is "my proactive evaluative relation to my purposes" (IP); in the specific use it is "my categorical need for freedom and well-being" (IC, or, perhaps better, "my necessary proactive evaluation of my freedom and well-being" [SRO], derived from IP and IC). Anything validated by IP is "what I must will," thus "generally prudential." In this sense, all the dialectically necessary claims of the argument are prudential. Singer calls them "moral." In the specific use, on the other hand, the rights-claim of Stage II (MyR) is prudential in being prescribed for the sake of my having freedom and well-being (hence self-regarding), whereas the claim that PPAO has the generic rights (PPAOR) is not (because other-regarding). It is prescribed for PPAO's freedom and well-being, which is necessitated by universalization of (IC → MyR). Singer's specific reason for calling MyR "moral" is that it is claimed on grounds (a categorical need for freedom and well-being) that are universal and thus must be universalized. (See #47.4.) Since Singer agrees that MyR is validated on the criterion of my own interests and that universalization requires me to accept the PGC, and Gewirth agrees that I must will what MyR and the PGC prescribe, there is no substantive criticism of Gewirth here at all. There is only a statement of a terminological preference.

So, is talk of "prudential rights" superfluous? Well, in a way, it is. All terminology has alternatives. We could define "a moral right" differently from Gewirth, provided that we found some other way of drawing necessary distinctions. There are, of course, reasons for preferring one terminology to another. Singer claims that Gewirth's terminology is "unnecessary baggage distracting from the deduction" (ibid.). On the contrary, I think that it is much less confusing than Singer's preference. The second part of Singer's paper is not consistent with the first. If Stage II is valid, and all that is wrong with it is that calling its conclusion a "prudential right" is superfluous, then we can derive Stage III (Singer's part 2), but *according to part 1* we can't derive Stage III (which means that talk of "prudential rights" is not merely superfluous). This inconsistency almost certainly arises because Singer's terminology does not make various important distinctions (e.g., between self-regarding and other-regarding claims; between other-referring, other-directing, and other-regarding claims; and between criteria for prescribing "oughts" and criteria for specifying grounds for these "oughts" on the criteria for prescribing them). The difficulties that Singer has with characterizing Gewirth's argument correctly in its "prudential" formulation do not arise from any inherent difficulties with the notion of "prudential rights," or "prudential duties." At least, no difficulties arise if we attend to the precise way in which Gewirth defines these things. Singer's difficulties arise from not attending to Gewirth's definitions, from insisting on reading Gewirth's terminology through the looking glass of alien definitions.[28]

#50   Stage III is valid given Gewirth's universalization procedure as "possessive" rather than "judgmental" universalization; but this presupposes that a PPA values not only its own agency, but agency in general, and so the question is begged right at the start.

In response to the widespread claim that all that universalization yields, based on the fact that I must claim a right to my freedom and well-being (on my prudential criterion), is the recognition that PPAO must claim a right to its freedom and well-being (on its own prudential criterion), James Scheuermann says,

[P]erhaps universalization in Gewirth's theory yields this recognition by the original agent: 'If I claim prudential rights against all others for the sufficient reason that I am a prospective purposive agent, then I must claim prudential rights *on behalf of every other prospective purposive agent against myself* (among others).' In other words, 'for every other being which satisfies the sufficient reason for my (the original agent's) claim of prudential rights against them

(namely, being a prospective purposive agent), I am required to claim prudential rights *on behalf of that being against myself.'* Since every being which
satisfies this sufficient condition does so to the same degree as does the
original agent, the original agent is as committed to asserting their prudential rights against himself as he is to asserting his prudential rights against
them. He is thus rationally committed to taking "favourable account" of the
generic interests of others, and this, for Gewirth, is for the agent to be subject
to a moral requirement. (Scheuermann 1987, 304)

With one proviso, there is no "perhaps" about it. This reading of
the argument is the one that Gewirth intends—the internal application of the LPU, or "possessive" universalization. The external application of the LPU, or "judgmental" universalization, which critics
concede, is also valid, but not the route by which the move from the
prudential to the moral is effected.

The proviso that needs to be made is that, at the end of Stage II, a
PPA must claim a right to its freedom and well-being or deny that it
is a PPA. Saying that it must claim a *"prudential"* right does not
signify that it must claim this right *if* it contingently has a self-regarding SPR for its purposes, but need not claim this right if it does
not. Calling it "prudential" signifies "generally" that the claim to
having this right is dialectically necessary, but need not be claimed
for "moral" (other-regarding) reasons. "Specifically," it signifies that
it is dialectically necessary for a PPA to claim this right for self-regarding reasons at least (its categorical need for freedom and well-
being). (See Chapter 2, note 46.)

Now, Scheuermann says that it does not seem to him to be the
case that possessive universalization cannot get beyond "a Hobbesian conflict of rights claims" (every PPA having to claim rights for
itself that no other PPA has to recognize), or that it involves some
equivocation between moral and prudential rights.

But it is not so clear to me that the concept of a prospective purposive agent
is not so abstracted from the particular characteristics or identities of actual
agents that it does not imply a common noncompetitive good which all must
seek. Universalization may "work" on this reading only because the agent
universalizes not from *his* being a prospective purposive agent, but from the
fact that what is true of any arbitrarily chosen prospective purposive agent
(e.g. himself) is also true of any other. The agent can claim rights for all
others, then, because it is agency in general, not *his* agency in particular,
which he views as good from within the standpoint of his "prudential"
agency. If this is correct, then the fundamental problem in Gewirth's transition from the prudential to the moral is not the concept of prudential
rights,[29] but rather the concept of prudential agency which is its foundation.
(Ibid.)

This objection, which claims that the basis for employing possessive universalization to effect the transition from the prudential to the moral cannot be set up without characterizing the concept of being a PPA, or "prudential agency," in a question-begging way, appears to make four claims.

1.   For possessive universalization to effect the transition from the prudential to the moral, a PPA must be portrayed as universalizing from "the fact that what is true of any arbitrarily chosen prospective purposive agent . . . is also true of any other."

2.   To portray a PPA as universalizing from the basis portrayed in 1 is to suppose that a PPA values agency in general, not its own agency in particular, which is to suppose that PPAs consider there to be a "noncompetitive good which all must seek."

3.   However, these suppositions are question-begging.

4.   A PPA universalizes from *its* being a PPA, which involves valuing its agency in particular.

Scheuermann does not elaborate, and his remarks are open to interpretation. All I can do is try to read his mind, and hope that I get it right. Even if I misrepresent his intentions, however, my attribution presents an objection that needs answering.

Scheuermann does not question that a PPA must claim a right to its freedom and well-being, and I will assume that he does not question the formal principle (which is the basis of Gewirth's ASA) "If X (because it has y) logically must claim to have z, then X logically must claim that it has z because it has y."

According to possessive universalization, if X logically must claim that it has z because it has y, then X logically must claim that Q has z if Q has y. It follows from this that, if the property I must claim to be that by virtue of which I have a right to freedom and well-being is a property necessarily possessed by all PPAs, then I logically must claim that all PPAs have a right to freedom and well-being. Once it is granted that I (as a PPA) logically must claim that I have a right to freedom and well-being because I possess some determinate quality, the only way in which I can be rescued from logically having to consider that all PPAs have these rights is if PPAs other than myself do not necessarily possess this same quality.

Scheuermann contrasts a PPA who universalizes from *its* being a PPA with a PPA who universalizes from the fact that what is true of any arbitrarily chosen PPA is true of any other. He says that possessive universalization that "works" (that can effect the transition

from the prudential to the moral) operates on the latter basis, implying that possessive universalization that operates on the former will
not effect the transition from the prudential to the moral. He also
claims that a PPA universalizes from the former basis, which implies
that he grants that it is dialectically necessary for a PPA to adduce *its*
being a PPA as the property by virtue of which it has a right to
freedom and well-being. However, he does not consider that this
means that it is dialectically necessary for a PPA to adduce a property that is "true of" any PPA as the property by virtue of which it
has a right to freedom and well-being. This means that he holds that
I (as a PPA) must, indeed, consider "I have a right to freedom and
well-being *because* I am a PPA" to be dialectically necessary, but that
what is predicated of me by "*I am a PPA*," in this dialectically necessary statement, is not a property that is necessarily possessed by
("true of") all PPAs.

Thus, central to his objection is the claim that, *inasmuch* as "I have
a right to my freedom and well-being *because* I am a PPA" is dialectically necessary, the property predicated by "I am a PPA" is not
necessarily possessed by all PPAs. Conversely, he is required to
claim that *inasmuch* as predication by "I am a PPA" is predication of
a property that is necessarily possessed by all PPAs, "I have a right
to freedom and well-being *because* I am a PPA" is *not* dialectically
necessary.

What, then, is the property that Scheuermann alleges to be dialectically necessary for me to adduce as the property by virtue of which
I have a right to my freedom and well-being, but that is not necessarily possessed by all PPAs? What, by contrast, is the property that
is necessarily possessed by all PPAs, but that is not dialectically
necessary for me to adduce as the property by virtue of which I have
a right to freedom and well-being?

The key to both questions lies in Scheuermann's contention that a
PPA universalizes from *its* being a PPA. I take it that Scheuermann
intends this to signify that, in the dialectically necessary statement
"I have a right to freedom and well-being *because* I am a PPA," the
property predicated of me by "I am a PPA" is not one that is necessarily possessed by all PPAs, but is still one that I must possess as a
PPA.

Can we make any sense of this? Well, all PPAs (proactively) value
their own purposes. We might define a PPA as a member of the class
of beings who necessarily value their own purposes. I am a PPA
because I necessarily value my own purposes, and PPAO is a PPA
because PPAO necessarily values its own purposes. Now, as a PPA,
so defined, I necessarily value my purposes. But I do not necessarily

value PPAO's purposes. The property of necessarily valuing *my* purposes belongs to me as a PPA, but does not belong to PPAO. I shall call this property pvmp.

On the other hand, as a PPA (a member of the class of beings who necessarily value their own purposes), I possess a property that is necessarily possessed by all other PPAs. This property is the property of standing in a proactive valuational relationship to my own purposes. I value my purposes, and PPAO values PPAO's purposes. Although the relata "I" and "my purposes" in "I value my purposes" and the relata "PPAO" and "PPAO's purposes" in "PPAO values PPAO's purposes" are different, the relationship between "I" and "my purposes" and the relationship between "PPAO" and "PPAO's purposes" are *the same relationship*. This relationship, possession of the property that I shall call rpvp, is possessed by all PPAs. It is by virtue of possessing rpvp that I am a PPA (a member of the class of beings who value their own purposes). (See RM 118–119.) Being a PPA must be defined as possession of rpvp, and cannot be defined in terms of possession of pvmp. This is because, if we define being a PPA in the latter way, then, from my internal viewpoint, there can be only one PPA, myself. It will not then be coherent for me to talk about PPAO at all.

I take it that Scheuermann claims that it is my possession of pvmp by virtue of which I must claim the generic rights. If so, then the ASA establishes that I must hold

(A)   I have a right to freedom and well-being *because* I possess pvmp.

Application of possessive universalization to (A) requires me to grant the generic rights to all who possess pvmp. However, since only I possess pvmp (the property of *necessarily* valuing *my* purposes), possessive universalization does not require me to accord the generic rights to any PPAs (members of the class of beings who necessarily value their own purposes), other than myself.[30]

For possessive universalization to compel me to accord the generic rights to all PPAs (members of the class of beings who necessarily value their own purposes), it has to operate on

(B)   I have a right to freedom and well-being *because* I possess rpvp.

However, for (B) to be established as the dialectically necessary basis for possessive universalization (by the ASA), it has to be the case that the reason why I must claim that I have the generic rights is that I possess rpvp, rather than because I possess pvmp.

Scheuermann, in effect, claims that it is not dialectically necessary for me to claim the generic rights by virtue of my possessing rpvp, unless all PPAs (members of the class of beings who value their own purposes, or members of the class of beings who possess rpvp) necessarily value "agency in general." I take this to mean that a demonstration of the dialectical necessity of (B) has to employ the question-begging assumption that PPAs (possessors of rpvp) logically ought to value the purposes of PPAs (or, at least, their freedom and well-being) *whoever these PPAs might be* (or the false assumption that possessors of rpvp necessarily do value agency in general).

Now, I do not know why Scheuermann thinks this. Anyway, he cannot deny that all PPAs possess rpvp (see above), and he cannot claim that a being who possesses rpvp necessarily values agency in general, and cannot value its own agency *against* the agency of others. To possess rpvp is to necessarily value one's own purposes, and these need not be other-regarding. The issue of whether (B) is dialectically necessary is simply (the validity of the ASA accepted) one of whether or not I deny that I possess rpvp if I do not consider that I have a right to freedom and well-being. If, by failing to consider that I have a right to freedom and well-being, I do deny that I possess rpvp, then (B) must be dialectically necessary, and Scheuermann's objection must fail.

Since Scheuermann contends that it is dialectically necessary for me, by virtue of my possession of pvmp, to claim the generic rights, he contends that I deny that I possess pvmp if I do not consider that I have the generic rights. Correlatively, he must claim that PPAO denies that it possesses the property of necessarily valuing PPAO's purposes (pvPPAOp) if it does not consider that it has the generic rights. The key question may, therefore, be put as follows: "Do I deny that I possess rpvp if I deny that I possess pvmp?" If I do, then rpvp must be adduced as the sufficient condition for my claiming a right to freedom and well-being, and as the sufficient reason for which I have the generic rights under this claim.

Now, while X might be a possessor of rpvp and not possess pvmp, I cannot be a possessor of rpvp and not possess pvmp. *In my case*, possession of rpvp is sufficient for possession of pvmp. I cannot, therefore, deny that I possess pvmp without denying that I possess rpvp. Thus, by virtue of *my* possessing rpvp, I must claim a right to freedom and well-being (because I must claim a right to freedom and well-being if I possess pvmp, and I must possess pvmp if I possess rpvp). But, then (by the ASA) I must hold (B), and holding (B) commits me (by possessive universalization) to holding "PPAO (who also necessarily possesses rpvp) has a right to freedom and well-being." Thus, the basis (B), which is required for possessive universalization to effect the transition from the prudential to the moral, is dialectically necessary for me to hold *without* any assumption that I, as a PPA, must value agency in general.

This argument can be set up slightly differently. Scheuermann and Gewirth will agree that both of the following statements are true:

(C)   From my (DB's) internal viewpoint, I (DB) have a right to freedom and well-being *because* I (DB) value my (DB's) purposes.

(D)   From my (PPAO's) internal viewpoint, I (PPAO) have a right to freedom and well-being *because* I (PPAO) value my (PPAO's) purposes.

The central question is, "Is the reason I (DB) have for claiming a right to freedom and well-being (in [C]) the same reason as PPAO has for claiming a right to its freedom and well-being (in [D])?" This is equivalent to "Is the property I adduce as the sufficient ground for my right to freedom and well-being the same property PPAO adduces as the sufficient ground for its right to freedom and well-being?" Scheuermann's objection is that the reasons/properties adduced in (C) and (D) are different. In (C), the reason is "I am an X who values DB's purposes," the property "being an X who values DB's purposes." In (D), the reason is "I am an X who values PPAO's purposes," the property "being an X who values PPAO's purposes." According to Gewirth, the reasons/properties are the same. In both (C) and (D), the reason is "I am an X who values its own purposes," the property "being an X who values its own purposes."

I claim that Scheuermann must hold that, when I (DB) deny that I have the generic rights, I deny "I am an X who values DB's purposes," but do not deny "I am an X who values its own purposes." My response to this is that, although I (Y) can be an X who denies that I value DB's purposes and not deny that I am an X who values its own purposes, I (DB) cannot be an X who denies that I value DB's purposes yet not deny that I am an X who values its own purposes.

From this, I infer that "I (DB) value my (DB's) purposes" is merely an expression of the fact that I (DB) am a PPA (an X who values its own purposes), and that it is this fact that is the reason why I must claim a right to my freedom and well-being.

It might be objected that this does not show that the reason why I must claim I have a right is not that I have pvmp. It only shows that the reason why I must claim that I have a right because I have pvmp is that I have rpvp. "I have pvmp" represents the reason why I must claim a right to freedom and well-being, but "I have rpvp" represents the reason why I must claim this right for this reason; and it does not follow from the latter that "I have rpvp" is the reason why I must claim this right.

This, however, rests on holding that the relations "being a reason for," which are involved here, are not the same relation, or that (if they are the same relation) this relation is not transitive. This is false. "Being a reason for," here (in all its uses), means "logically entailing," and logical entailment is a transitive relation.

To elaborate: the objection accepts

(1)   I have rpvp → I have pvmp → I must hold [I have pvmp → I have a right to freedom and well-being].

It accepts that it follows from this that

(2)   I have rpvp → I must hold [I have pvmp → I have a right to freedom and well-being].

This may be portrayed as

(3)   Within my dialectically necessary viewpoint, I have rpvp → [I have pvmp → I have a right to freedom and well-being].

It follows, by the transitivity of logical entailment, that

(4)   Within my dialectically necessary viewpoint, [I have rpvp → I have a right to freedom and well-being].

This is equivalent to saying that I must hold "I have a right to freedom and well-being *because* I have rpvp."

To resist this, it might be claimed that (2) cannot be portrayed as (3). (2) must be portrayed as

(3')   I have rpvp → Within my dialectically necessary viewpoint [I have pvmp → I have a right to freedom and well-being].

This amounts to the claim that "I have rpvp" is not an operative within my dialectically necessary viewpoint. From my dialectically necessary viewpoint, "I have rpvp" operates as "I have pvmp." "I have rpvp" cannot be included within my dialectically necessary viewpoint without being portrayed as "I have pvmp."

However, although it is true that I reason from my proactive valuation of my purposes, it does not follow from this that "I have rpvp" cannot be an operative within my dialectically necessary viewpoint. This is because, if I *claim* "I have pvmp," then I *must claim* "I have rpvp," for I cannot have pvmp without having rpvp.

It follows from this that we can infer [I have rpvp → I have a right to freedom and well-being] (where this is a claim I must make) from [I have pvmp → I have a right to freedom and well-being] (where this is a claim I must make). This entails that (2) may be portrayed as (3).

In fact, although I reason from my proactive valuation of my purposes—and it might seem that, from such a basis, I am required to claim the generic rights for myself, and only for myself—my possessing pvmp cannot be separated from my possession of rpvp. Once this is appreciated, it becomes apparent that, in reasoning from my proactive valuation of my purposes, I am reasoning from *my* possession of the property rpvp (which necessarily belongs to all PPAs).

Scheuermann contrasts my reasoning from my proactive valuation of my purposes with my reasoning from what is true of all PPAs. However, for me to reason from what is true of all PPAs can be given at least two *different* meanings. It can mean that I reason from *my* membership of the class of PPAs, or that I reason from the assumption that any PPA can be substituted, from the start, for me in *my* dialectical reasoning. I can see that to portray me as reasoning on the latter basis would involve the assumption that I necessarily value the purposes of PPAO, that PPAs necessarily value "agency in general." But *my* reasoning from *my* membership of the class of PPAs involves no such assumption. All that this reasoning entails is that I reason from my proactive valuation of my purposes (whatever the content of these purposes), which (conversely) entails that I reason from my membership of the class of PPAs. It seems to me that Scheuermann has simply failed to see that the "objective" basis that Stage III requires is not an alternative to *my* reasoning from *my* purposes, but a presupposition of it.

Correlative to this, it seems to me that any force that Scheuermann's objection has derives from entertaining the idea that the property I have that requires me to claim the generic rights for myself (that of [necessarily] valuing my purposes) is a property that can exist independently of my possession of the relational property rpvp, a relational property that is possessed by all PPAs.

It is worth pointing out that if "I have pvmp" is viewed independently of "I have rpvp," then, as the basis for the argument, this has the consequence that, not only will possessive universalization not be able to effect the move from "I have a right to freedom and well-being *because* I am a PPA" to "PPAO has a right to its freedom and well-being *because* PPAO is a PPA," but "judgmental" universalization (*external* application of the LPU) will also not be able to effect the move from "I must consider, *because* I am a PPA, that I have a right to freedom and well-being" to "PPAO must consider, *because* it is a PPA, that it has a right to freedom and well-being." But no critic, to my knowledge, has questioned this latter inference.

To explain: to say that "having pvmp" is the quality I must adduce as that by virtue of which I have a right to my freedom and well-being, presupposes (correlative to the ASA) that "having pvmp" is the quality I possess that requires me to *claim* a right to freedom and well-being. Now, if we assume that "I have pvmp" is not to be viewed as a function of "I have rpvp," then we get not only (within my dialectically necessary viewpoint) that the sufficient condition for X having the generic rights is that X has pvmp, but also that the necessary and sufficient condition for X having to claim that it has the generic rights is that X has pvmp. I, and only I, have pvmp (the property of *necessarily* valuing my purposes); PPAO does not. But, from this, it follows that PPAO is not logically required to claim that it has a right to freedom and well-being on the grounds that I, as a PPA, am logically required to claim a right to freedom and well-being.

It is no use replying that PPAO must, *because* it has *pvPPAOp*, claim a right to freedom and well-being. To suppose that this is so is to suppose that it is because PPAO has rpvp that PPAO must claim a right to freedom and well-being. It is to suppose that I have pvmp, and PPAO has pvPPAOp, because we each have rpvp, and that having rpvp is the reason why I and PPAO must claim rights to our own freedom and well-being. Judgmental universalization can only be valid if Gewirth's possessive universalization is valid.

This suggests another point worth making. The logical relationship between "I have rpvp" and "I have pvmp" can, I think, be explained by the idea that purposes belong to a PPA by its act of valuing them. Possession of the property rpvp is to be viewed as the power or propensity of a PPA to exercise (freely chosen) preferences. "I have pvmp" then signifies that I possess this power or propensity, that I am a member of the class of PPAs. It is *my* exercise of this power or propensity that explains why *I* must claim the generic rights, not the fact that I have the nonuniversal property of possessing *my purposes*. To think that it is the fact that I have the nonuniversal property of possessing *my purposes*, is to portray purposes as belonging to a PPA independently of its act of valuation, or else to portray myself as the only being who possesses the power of valuation.

A further consideration must be borne in mind. In my discussion, I have assumed that Scheuermann accepts that I deny that I am a PPA if I do not claim a right to freedom and well-being (for he defends this thesis in the main body of his article), and that his disagreement with Gewirth is over what "I am a PPA" is to be taken as standing for. I remarked, at the beginning of my discussion, that, if these assumptions are correct, then "I am a PPA" is to be taken as the criterion according to which I must claim a right to freedom and well-being. In consequence, I am required to claim a right in terms of whatever contingent criteria (SPRs for my purposes) govern my pursuit of my purposes. These criteria might or might not be moral. They might be "moral" (other-regarding) or "prudential/amoral" (exclusively self-regarding). Gewirth expresses this in terms of my rights-claim being "directly prudential" (necessarily validated by my proactive valuation of my purposes), while capable (contingently) of being indirectly moral or "prudential." In the direct sense of "prudential," "I am a PPA" represents "my prudential criterion," and the right I must claim on the basis of it (in Stage II) is a "prudential" right. In the indirect sense of "prudential," the dialectically necessary right I claim will only be "prudential" if I contingently espouse a specifically nonmoral SPR for my purposes, one that is self-regarding *as against* other-regarding. To clarify matters, I shall refer to "my prudential criterion" ($\equiv$ "I am a PPA") as "my prudential (1) criterion," and "my prudential criterion" ($\equiv$ an exclusively self-regarding criterion for my purpose pursuit) as "a prudential (2) criterion." It is dialectically necessary for me to espouse my prudential (1) criterion, but not assumed to be dialectically necessary (or inconsistent) for me to espouse a prudential (2) criterion. I deny that I am a PPA if I do not claim a prudential (1) right to freedom and well-being. I do not deny that I am a PPA if I do not claim a prudential (2) right to freedom and well-being. I deny only that I guide my purposes by a prudential (2) criterion.

Now, if we were to suppose that the argument up to the end of Stage II showed only that I must claim a prudential (2) right, i.e., showed only that *if* I espoused a prudential (2) criterion, then I would have to claim a right to freedom and well-being, and not that I must claim a prudential (1) right, then I would not deny "I have rpvp" if I did not consider that I had a right to freedom and well-being. I would deny only that I reasoned from a prudential (2) criterion. When Scheuermann says that a PPA reasons from valuing *its* purposes, he could be interpreted as saying that Gewirth's PPA reasons from a prudential (2) criterion. Such a PPA values its agency as a competitive good (a PPA who reasons from a prudential [1] criterion might or might not value agency as a competitive good). Operating with a prudential (2) criterion, a PPA would have to claim a right to freedom and well-being. If we imagine this PPA saying "I must hold that I have a right to freedom and well-being *because* I value my purposes," then this reason would have to be given the meaning of "I value my purposes over the purposes of others." This could be interpreted to mean "I have a prudential (2) criterion," or it can mean "I am a X who values *my* purposes competitively." Universalizing from this basis would require me, in the first case, to grant the generic rights to all PPAs who reasoned from a prudential (2) criterion. In the second case it would require me not to grant the generic rights to any other PPAs at all. However, a PPA who reasoned on the second interpretation would be required to do so only because it was a PPA who reasoned from a prudential (2) criterion. So, despite initial appearances, it would have to grant the generic rights to all PPAs who reason from a prudential (2) criterion. Nevertheless, it would not have to grant the generic rights to all PPAs.

There are, however, numerous problems with this.

1. This is still a transition from the prudential to the moral, for, to be a morality, a morality does not have to be egalitarian universalist for all PPAs.

2. It is disingenuous to portray a PPA as inferring that it has a right to freedom and well-being *because* it has a prudential (2) criterion/has *its* purposes, on the ground that it must claim a right to freedom and well-being on its prudential (2) criterion. Such an inference operates only when the ASA can be applied (which presupposes the logical necessity of having to claim a right). But it is not dialectically necessary for a PPA to espouse a prudential (2) criterion (whereas it is necessary for it to espouse a prudential [1] criterion). So, *on* a prudential (2) criterion, a PPA is not required to apply possessive universalization.

3. However, to portray Gewirth's argument in this way is to portray it as an *ad hominem* one, and not as one employing the dialectically necessary method. Gewirth argues that a PPA must claim a right to freedom and well-being on its prudential (1) criterion. If it must, then *it* is required to universalize to the PGC even though a prudential (2) criterion does not. That is just what makes it untenable for a PPA to espouse a prudential (2) criterion, in the final analysis.

In short, if Scheuermann is basing his objection on this sort of thinking, then he is misconstruing Gewirth's argument.[31]

To conclude, my main discussion may be summed up in relation to the four claims that Scheuermann makes.

1. Scheuermann's first claim is true: for possessive universalization to do the job assigned to it, a PPA must be portrayed as univer-

salizing from its possession of a property that is possessed necessarily by all PPAs. This property is that which defines membership of the class of beings who are PPAs—viz., rpvp.

2. However, his second claim is false. "A PPA is a being who possesses rpvp" does not define a PPA as a being who values agency in general. It defines a PPA as a being who values its own purposes. As a being who possesses rpvp, I must value my own purposes. As a being who values my own purposes, I must claim a right to my freedom and well-being. If I deny that I have a right to my freedom and well-being, then I deny not only that I value my purposes, but that I possess rpvp. This requires me (by the ASA) to accept that I have a right to freedom and well-being because I have rpvp, even if I don't value agency in general. On this basis, possessive universalization requires me to grant all PPAs a right to freedom and well-being.

3. Scheuermann's third claim is true. To suppose that a PPA necessarily values agency in general (i.e., the agency of all PPAs) is question-begging or even false. But no such assumption need be made in demonstrating that a PPA must apply possessive universalization to "I have a right to freedom and well-being *because* I have rpvp."

4. His fourth claim is also true, *but only if* this means that a PPA reasons from its first-person perspective on "I have rpvp" ("I am a being who values its own purposes"), which requires *it* to say "I have pvmp" ("I am a being who values my own purposes"). It is false *if* this means that a PPA reasons on the basis of its purposes being valued as a property independent of its being a member of the class of PPAs (rather than from its act of valuing purposes by which it makes them its own).[32]

General Comments

There are two principal reasons why objections to Stage III fail to invalidate the argument:

1. failure to attend to Gewirth's ASA, which enables the LPU to be applied "internally" and the PGC to be given a determinate content, by making being a PPA the criterion of relevant similarity for the granting of the generic rights; and
2. failure to recognize that Gewirth's primary application of the LPU is internal or "possessive," not external or "judgmental."

It has also been necessary to point out

3.   that the argument is not contingently *ad hominem*. It does not operate on the implications of the contingent SPRs for their purposes that PPAs might happen to espouse. The argument is dialectically necessary, operating on features that PPAs must incorporate into their SPRs for their purposes if they are not to contradict that they are PPAs.

I have argued that

4.   the ASA does not fail in consequence of it being the case that

    a.   "superior" PPAs could possibly best provide for the purposes of all PPAs. It would only fail if it were a necessary truth that "superior" PPAs would so provide, and this is not the case;

    b.   "rationality" is, allegedly, an "attainment attribute." This is because a PPA claims the generic rights on the grounds of having purposes, not on its degree of rationality; and, inasmuch as rationality is necessary for a PPA to have purposes, it is a "status attribute";

5.   the internal application of the LPU does not fail because

    a.   the other-referring "ought" of Stage II is merely an "ought of evaluation," which permits only the external application of the LPU. This "ought" is action-guiding on the criterion of my interests, which is the criterion of my internal viewpoint as a PPA (and, even without the action-guiding aspect—which it, in fact, possesses—this "ought" is universalizable, albeit not to a deontological position); or

    b.   this application rests on an analysis of prudential agency, which requires a PPA to value agency in general, not merely its own agency. No such analysis is presupposed by this application.

We have seen

6.   that some critics misrepresent the role of various logical operations in the argument. It is not the case, as has been represented, that

    a.   Gewirth attempts to validate Stage III by the principle that "ought" implies "can." This principle is used to infer an other-referring prudential "ought" from a self-referring prudential one when used (as by Gewirth) prior to the internal application of the LPU (which, together with the ASA, effects the move to "the moral"); or

b. Gewirth attempts to validate Stage III by the principle of the logical correlativity between other-referring strict "oughts" and claim rights. In the sequence that Gewirth employs, the right that is inferred from an other-referring "ought," using this principle, is (like the "ought") a prudential one.

If judgments that a PPA must hold to be justified for the sufficient reason that it is a PPA, or that state what a PPA rationally must will to be the case, are called "moral judgments," then

7. it is true that all the judgments of Stage II, which Gewirth calls "prudential," are moral; and, as a matter of terminology, the concept of a "prudential right" becomes superfluous. However,

a. at a more significant conceptual level, the concept of a "prudential right" remains necessary. For we must still distinguish between other-regarding and self-regarding "moral" judgments, to represent Gewirth's distinction between moral and prudential judgments;

b. the fact that some critics wish to call "moral" what Gewirth calls "prudential" cannot be used to show that Gewirth equivocates or begs the question. Gewirth's task is to show how the reasons that require PPAs to make self-regarding judgments require them to make other-regarding judgments, and he does not assume that the judgments of Stage II are made for other-regarding reasons in effecting Stage III. Within the context of Gewirth's enterprise, refusal to accept his perfectly intelligible definitions only leads to confusion.

The most important thing to appreciate is that the internal application of the LPU effects the move from "the prudential" to "the moral" without assuming that PPAs must make other-regarding ("moral") "ought" judgments, and without assuming that PPAs have reason to believe that the addressees of their other-referring judgment (4d), will accept this judgment. From this it follows that

8. objections that (correctly) allege that (4d) "PPAO ought not to interfere with my freedom and well-being" cannot be shown

to be other-directing for PPAO (on PPAO's criteria) or moral by the considerations Gewirth provides in Stage II (see especially #35), fail thereby to invalidate Stage II as a sufficient platform for Stage III to be effected by purely logical universalization.

9   Miscellaneous Objections

There is no particular focus for the objections considered in this chapter. Most of them make general comments about the argument, not limited to any particular stage, that do not fit readily into the organization of the earlier chapters.

#51   The argument begs the question in its definition of morality.

According to Marcus G. Singer (1984), Gewirth's definition of "a moral position" takes sides in ruling out all possible forms of "egoism" and "self-interest positions."

It maintains that in a morality—or in morality—the interests of (some) others must be furthered, that this is what is required by morality, and that whatever system of rules does not require this is not a moral system or a morality . . . . (Singer 1984, 26)

He also complains that there are "moralities" that do not claim to set criteria that override all competing criteria, and that these are also excluded by Gewirth's definition. (See ibid., 25.)

According to Singer, this has the consequence that Gewirth is trying to establish the rational necessity for a PPA to adopt an SPR for its purposes in which the interests of others as well as its own are taken as overriding criteria *by definitional fiat*, rather than by argument or evidence.

This is incorrect. It is true that

1.   Gewirth does not call SPRs for a PPA's purposes that do not meet his defining conditions of a moral point of view "moralities";
2.   his definition is stipulative, rather than a statement of "ordinary" usage (although it does capture a common conception of what constitutes "a moral position"); and

3.   there are philosophers who define "a morality" differently.

But it does not follow from this that Gewirth is trying to establish that it is rationally necessary for a PPA to espouse "other-regarding" practical criteria, let alone the PGC, by definitional fiat.

The issue is not "What should we call 'a morality'?" It is "What practical criteria may a PPA rationally espouse?" Simply defining "a moral position" in a way that precludes a range of practical criteria from being called "moral" begs no questions.[1] Gewirth's definition is a statement of the sort of practical criteria that he attempts to show are rationally necessary. He does not argue *from the presumption that only such criteria are rationally necessary.* His reason for rejecting "egoism," "amoralism," and other "self-interest" positions is not that these are not "moral positions" according to his definition, or simply that they are self-interest positions. Gewirth allows PPAs, for the sake of argument, to adopt any practical criteria. The PPA who values X for purpose E may be motivated by any criteria. However, the dialectically necessary method reveals that there are certain things, necessarily connected to a PPA's conception of itself as a PPA, that require it to consider its freedom and well-being to be necessary goods. This judgment does not derive from the content of any specific practical criteria. A PPA must make this judgment, whatever practical criteria it might espouse, not by virtue of its practical criteria, but by virtue of its being a PPA. Any practical criteria it may rationally espouse must validate this judgment and any judgments that are validated by this judgment. Practical criteria that do not validate the judgments that a PPA rationally must make by virtue of conceiving of itself as a PPA are irrational for a PPA to espouse, in that such espousal involves a PPA in contradicting that it is a PPA. On this basis, Gewirth argues that a PPA may rationally espouse only the PGC.

Quite simply, as Gewirth says, he uses his definition to raise problems, not to settle them, for he does not *define* "a morality," let alone "PGC morality," *as rationally justified;* by his definition he only states the position that he sets out to prove is rationally justified. (See Gewirth 1984d, 200–201.)[2]

#52   The argument constitutes an exercise in coercive philosophy.

To read Gewirth is to experience the sense of being caught in an ever-tightening net from which all conceivable avenues of escape have been blocked in advance. This is "philosophy as a coercive activity," and Gewirth comes quite close to the extreme of propounding "arguments so powerful they set up reverberations in the brain: if the person refuses to accept the conclusion, he *dies*." (Regis 1984, 2, quoting Nozick 1981, 4)

This lurid imagery is fanciful; however, some might hold that the attempt to show that the PGC is dialectically necessary is

1.   "authoritarian," in that it attempts to impose ways of life on PPAs against their will, by not respecting their subjective viewpoints, and
2.   "coercive," in that it attempts to restrict their freedom of choice.

Against 1 it is to be pointed out that Gewirth's argument, by employing the dialectically necessary method *within PPAs' internal viewpoints*, does not impose the PGC against their will. On the contrary, it is held that the PGC must be espoused in consequence of the will of PPAs; espousal of the PGC is a self-imposition made by PPAs themselves. The argument does not, *by fiat*, exclude any SPRs for their purposes that PPAs might adhere to. By its dialectically necessary procedure, PGC-incompatible viewpoints are excluded for being incompatible with PPAs' own viewpoint of themselves as free agents.[3]

The answer to 2 follows from this. What the argument shows, if it is valid, is that PPAs who understand what it is for them to be PPAs—and this essentially involves, among other things, an understanding of what it means to be free—understand that to be a PPA is to be rationally bound to comply with the PGC. They understand that to violate the PGC is to deny that they are PPAs, and that this is to deny that they are beings who pursue purposes that they have freely chosen. Thus, the argument provides a dialectically necessary conception of "free action"—as action that is chosen by the agent to be in accordance with the PGC. For a PPA to conceive of "freedom of choice" differently is for a PPA to contradict that it is a PPA.[4]

#53   There are no human rights, and belief in them is on a par with belief in witches and unicorns, because every attempt to give good reasons for belief in these things has failed.

According to Alasdair MacIntyre,

the truth is plain: there are no . . . [human] rights, and belief in them is one with belief in witches and in unicorns.
   The best reason for asserting so bluntly that there are no such rights is indeed of precisely the same type as the best reason which we possess for

asserting that there are no witches and the best reason which we possess for
asserting that there are no unicorns: every attempt to give good reasons for
believing that there *are* such rights has failed. (MacIntyre 1981, 67)

MacIntyre asserts this *after* dismissing Gewirth's argument, and
not as an argument against it. Nevertheless, such a general statement really needs to be backed by adequate consideration of the
various attempts that have been made to establish that there are, or
that we must consider that there are, such rights. As Gewirth says,
MacIntyre does not provide the necessary coverage. He only considers Gewirth's attempt (and then only in part). (See Gewirth 1985a,
741–742.) MacIntyre, however, might be partially excused because
he does make it clear that he considers Gewirth's attempt to be the
best attempt to date. He treats Gewirth's arguments as

an ideal test case. If they do not succeed, that is strong evidence that the
project of which they are a part is not going to succeed. (MacIntyre 1981, 20)

The simple response to this is, of course, that neither MacIntyre's
arguments (see #26.1, #36, and #37) nor any others that I have examined refute Gewirth's argument. It is, thus, altogether premature to
talk about assimilating belief in human (or better, PPA)[5] rights to
belief in unicorns and witches.[6]

This response aside, MacIntyre's claim is objectionable in suggesting that, because X attempts to prove Y have failed, we can
conclude that Y cannot be proven (or is untrue). Even if MacIntyre
had shown that *all* attempts to prove that there are human rights
have failed, this would not make the truth plain that there are no
human rights. No one, to date, has proven Fermat's last theorem
(that there is no largest prime number). Does this make the truth
plain that there is a largest prime number?

What MacIntyre wishes to say (on the [false] presumption that
Gewirth's argument fails) is that we can now forget about human
rights. We need not take any future arguments seriously. To see how
untenable this is, we need only imagine this argument being applied
to the situation pre-Gewirth. We are told that every argument pre-
Gewirth to establish that there are (or that we must think there are)
human rights has failed. The truth is, therefore, plain—there are no
human rights. Ergo, we don't have to take Gewirth seriously. And,
indeed, I have had it thrust at me that it is a waste of time considering Gewirth's case, because other attempts to carry out his project
have failed.[7]

Kai Nielsen's attitude is more tenable.

Sometimes, rightly or wrongly, a philosophical account, even a closely reasoned and elaborately constructed philosophical account, will strike us as

being so utterly wrongheaded as not to be worth taking the very considerable trouble it would take to sort it out or to refute it. . . .

I must confess that that is something like the attitude I had toward Professor Alan Gewirth's central thesis about ethics . . . that there is a substantive
supreme principle of morality, the denial of which is self-contradictory . . . .
[To believe this thesis] is the equivalent in ethics of accepting the ontological
argument in the philosophy of religion. It just has to be wrong, and the task,
if one deals with it at all, is to locate the place or places where such an
argument went wrong. . . .[8]

However, it is not unnatural in turn to respond that that is being a little
dogmatic and that, if everyone were to react that way, cultural advance
would be impeded. . . . Such dogmatism . . . is intellectually stultifying. We,
given any careful challenge to a canonical doctrine, should rise to the occasion and follow the argument wherever it leads. . . . [T]here is enough force
in that response to motivate trying here to come to grips with such an ethical
rationalism. (Nielsen 1984, 59–60)

True, after considering Gewirth's argument, Nielsen also rejects it
(though, again, his arguments are invalid; see especially #13, #28,
#29, and #48). But, even if Nielsen were right in this, for the very
reasons that he himself gives, this should not inhibit our examining
any future scholarly attempt to demonstrate Gewirth's thesis.

#54   The argument presupposes the false premise that all
PPAs are in a situation of equal powerlessness.

1 Williams

Bernard Williams (1985, 62–63) maintains that if rational PPAs reflect on what laws they should (it would be reasonable for them to)
subject themselves to, on the assumption that they are rational PPAs
and no more, and, in particular, that there are no differences between rational PPAs with respect to power, then the answer they
would come up with might well be along the lines of Kant's categorical imperative (or Gewirth's PGC). But to ask what a rational PPA
should do as a rational PPA is not the same thing as to ask what it
would reasonably do if it were a rational PPA *and no more*. For "there
is no way of being a rational agent and no more" (ibid., 63). PPAs
differ in power, effectiveness, and position, and what a more powerful PPA might reasonably view as being in its interests is not the
same as what a less powerful PPA might view as being in its interests.

This is a reasonable objection, *provided that* we read Gewirth's
claim, that a rational PPA must bind itself by the PGC, as the claim
that, in order for a PPA to achieve its particular occurrent objectives
(whatever these might be), it is necessary for it to bind itself by the

PGC, or at least, that a PPA would best achieve its particular occurrent objectives if it bound itself by the PGC. For, if this is Gewirth's claim, then it is surely false. More powerful PPAs might well better achieve some of their objectives if they did not guide their conduct by the PGC.

But, of course, this is not what Gewirth is arguing. Gewirth's criterion of rationality is not prudence but logical consistency with "I am a PPA." He is not arguing that it is prudent to be moral, or to espouse the PGC. (See, e.g., #24, #35, and #38.) In "I ought to guide my conduct by the PGC," the "ought" referred to is not prudential, but logical; and the "ought" that is contained in the prescription that the PGC makes ("I ought to respect the freedom and well-being of all PPAs") is neither prudential nor logical, but moral.[9]

Furthermore, it is simply not true that Gewirth assumes that a PPA is rational and no more. Gewirth equips a PPA with any purposes, thus any set of justificatory frameworks for its purposes. He also allows a PPA to have any view of its position, and to be in any position. All he assumes is that for a PPA to be a PPA with specific contingent features, it must be a PPA, and that a PPA cannot rationally claim anything about itself that contradicts what it rationally must claim by virtue of being a PPA. To say that it may is on a par with saying that we may attribute properties to (Euclidean) triangles that are consistent with having two angles of the same magnitude, or one side 20 cm in length, or an angle of 90°, even if the properties in question would contradict that triangles, to be triangles, must have angles adding up to 180°. If Gewirth is mistaken in arguing that "I rationally must espouse the PGC" follows from "I am a PPA," then it is not because he supposes that PPAs are rational and no more, any more than to claim that triangles (must) have angles adding up to 180° is to suppose that triangles cannot vary in the lengths of their individual sides and the magnitudes of their individual angles.

Williams' objection is, in fact, somewhat akin to a statement made by Engels, which Gewirth considers in *Reason and Morality*. According to Engels,

[i]n order to establish the fundamental axiom that two people and their wills are absolutely equal to each other and that neither lords it over the other, we cannot use any couple of people at random. They must be two persons who are so thoroughly detached from all reality, from all national, economic, political, and religious relations which are found in the world, from all sex and personal differences, that nothing is left of either person beyond the mere idea: person—and then of course they are 'entirely equal.' They are therefore two complete phantoms conjured up. (Engels 1966, 108–109; quoted by Gewirth in RM 127–128)

In response, Gewirth comments that this statement is a pertinent comment on his argument, because his argument contends that

the actual differences among persons are irrelevant to the distribution of the generic rights. (RM 128)

To defeat this objection a

standpoint must . . . be found that abstracts from these . . . differences . . . , while at the same time it does not deny or ignore the differences, and it must also be able to subject the differences or their alleged moral implications to moral evaluation. (Ibid.)

According to Gewirth, the internal viewpoint of PPAs *as PPAs*, because of the generic and universal character of freedom and well-being as necessary conditions for agency, is such a standpoint. Because they are generic conditions, each PPA must claim rights to its freedom and well-being. Because they are universally generic conditions, these rights must be extended to other PPAs, thus producing a justified standpoint for moral evaluation. Because they are generic and universal, they must be valued in abstract from contingent features that pertain to, and differentiate, PPAs. But this does not mean that they are not of "real" concern to real people, because they are the necessary conditions for the

modes of conduct that characterize morality and practice in their full historical complexity. (RM 30)[10]

2 Held

John Rawls' theory of justice posits individuals who, before entering into civil society, are equal with respect to power and freedom, and ignorant of the particular characteristics that they will possess when they enter such a society. Rawls argues that it would be rational (in terms of utility) for such individuals to choose that society should be governed by certain egalitarian-universalist moral rules. Particular moral principles are rationally justified from "the original position" characterized by a "veil of ignorance." (See Rawls 1971.)

Gewirth considers that the assumptions that enable this theory to avoid inegalitarian conclusions are arbitrary.

Neither . . . has any independent rational justification: persons are not in fact equal in power and ability, nor are they so lacking in empirical reason as to be ignorant of all their particular qualities. (RM 20)

Thus, even if an egalitarian-universalist morality is justified *on* Rawls' assumptions, it has not been shown that a PPA cannot (rationally) refuse to reason on the basis of these assumptions. If PPAs are permitted to calculate their utility on the basis of knowing that they are more powerful than others, they might well conclude that their utility will be maximized under inegalitarian rules.

Virginia Held agrees. "The rich who vote for Reagan are not all fools" (Held 1985, 37).

From the class positions they now occupy, it would be contrary to their rational self-interest for the rich and privileged to take the point of view of those in an original position because, were they to do so, they would surely have to give up many actual advantages.

. . . Ideal theories such as Rawls's, . . . [sacrifice] the points of view of actual persons in actual situations. . . . And persons asking *why* they should choose to live their lives from the point of view of an ideal morality, rather than from the point of view of the actual life they are actually in, will receive no answer from these theories. (Ibid., 35–36)

According to Gewirth, his own theory avoids such problems of arbitrariness.

Held disagrees.

Gewirth thinks he can counter such arguments by requiring that it be only the *generic* features of action that are accorded attention, and to which all should be accorded rights. . . . But his suggestion that we limit our attention to these generic features of action seems arbitrary. It assumes that, in acting, we all claim rights to the same things: these generic features of action. But in acting, the rich may claim something quite different: the right to act with the resources already available to them, or the right to enter competitive contests.

If we require that in acting we are all so similar that we all claim the same thing, then Gewirth's theory is a theory of the ideal agent rather than of real agents, and it suffers from the same problems as . . . other ideal theories . . . . If, on the other hand, Gewirth's theory *is* a theory for actual agents in actual societies, then it is unpersuasive to assert that in acting all agents assert rights to the same things. (Ibid., 38)

Implicit in this objection is a mischaracterization of Gewirth's argument to the PGC. I will spell out this distortion and explain how Gewirth's theory is *both* nonarbitrary in reasoning from the generic features of action, and a theory binding on actual agents in actual societies.

Gewirth claims (Stages I and II) that PPAs, on pain of contradicting that they are PPAs, must claim rights to the generic features of action. Consequently (Stage III), they must accept that PPAO has rights to the generic features of action.

Held agrees that PPAs must universalize their rights-claims. But she does not see why a PPA must claim rights to the generic features of action rather than to the contingently necessary means for the particular actions the PPA pursues (as well, or exclusively). According to Held, in acting, different PPAs claim rights to different things. They claim rights to act for their particular occurrent purposes; hence, they must claim rights to the logically necessary means for these purposes; hence, they must grant rights to these things to PPAO.

The person who expects to win contests with others can say that in acting in such contests he claims the right to enter them. He can be quite willing to accord this right to others. An agent whose purpose in acting is winning out over others can reason that a logically necessary means to act successfully toward this purpose is to have occasions for such contests. He can agree that everyone ought to have such occasions, and if he is a fanatic supporter of a survival of the fittest approach to life, he can hold this view even if he does not expect to win himself.

. . . As R. M. Hare has shown, fanatics can universalize their judgments. Rationality alone has no satisfactory argument against them. (Ibid., 36–37)

There are three ways in which this departs from Gewirth's argument.

1. Held says that PPAs claim rights to their particular occurrent purposes, hence to the specific necessary conditions for *these* purposes. (Gewirth holds that PPAs *might* [but need not] claim rights to these things, but they *must* claim rights to the generic features of action [and must only to these features]. Gewirth does not say that PPAs all claim rights to the same things, and he does not claim that PPAs necessarily claim rights to all [or even any of] their particular occurrent purposes. He claims that they all *must* claim rights to the generic features of agency, whatever purposes they have, or rights they do claim.)

2. Consequently, Held has it that universalization operates on the rights PPAs do claim, or are willing to claim, as determined by their particular occurrent purposes (or by their SPRs for their purposes). (Gewirth has it that universalization only operates on the rights-claim to its generic features of agency, which a PPA must make, on pain of contradicting that it is a PPA.)

3. Because it is false to say that PPAs (necessarily) claim rights to their particular occurrent purposes, Held suggests that Gewirth's PPA espouses some form of deonticism, and isn't just *any* PPA. Thus, she portrays the argument as an argument from some deontic position, as one that alleges that the *judgments* licensed by all deontic positions entail the PGC by logical universalization (which, of course, is not the case). (Gewirth argues that PPAs, whatever their SPRs for their purposes, must accept the PGC on pain of self-contradiction, not because their denial of the PGC contradicts their SPRs for their purposes, or the requirements of achieving their specific

particular occurrent purposes, but because it contradicts that *they are PPAs.*)

Now, it is possible that Held will respond that she is perfectly well aware that Gewirth's argument is how I portray it. However, her objection does not rest on a mischaracterization of his argument; it spells out how various actual PPAs reason. To ask an actual PPA to reason from its necessary characteristics *as a PPA*, rather than from its particular occurrent features, is either arbitrary or assumes that PPAs are so similar that they will not find it in their rational interest to bind themselves by anything other than the PGC.

However, although a PPA is not necessarily a deontic egoist (say), a deontic egoist is necessarily a PPA. A PPA can eschew deontic egoism without contradicting that it is a PPA. A deontic egoist cannot deny being a PPA without denying that it is a deontic egoist. Thus, whatever a PPA must accept on pain of contradicting that it is a PPA, it must accept on pain of contradicting that it is a deontic egoist. Since the same logical relations hold between my being a PPA and *any* SPR for my purposes,

(S)   I contradict that I hold an SPR for my purposes if I hold anything that contradicts that I am a PPA.

Unless I possess the generic features of agency, I cannot pursue/achieve any purposes. I cannot be a PPA/successful PPA. Hence, I *must* value my possession of the generic features proactively, or deny that I am a PPA (hence, also, that I am a deontic egoist, or whatever). On the basis of this judgment, I must claim a right to my possession of the generic features. So, claiming a right to the generic features is *justified*, as being *logically required of me as a PPA*, whether I am a deontic egoist or not. It is, thus, not arbitrary for me to claim a right to my possession of the generic features. But, might it not be arbitrary to restrict my rights-claims (in Stage II) to my possession of the generic features?

As a deontic egoist (or as an upholder of some other SPR for my purposes), I might claim rights that go beyond (or even conflict with) the generic rights. If these claims conflict with the generic rights, then (by [S]), I contradict that I am a PPA (and hence that I hold any SPR for my purposes; hence that I hold *this* SPR for my purposes). I cannot coherently hold any SPR for my purposes that denies me the generic rights. If my SPR for my purposes does not deny me the generic rights, but merely grants me additional rights, then I do not deny that I am a PPA by espousing such an SPR for my purposes. However, what justification do I have for holding such an SPR for my purposes? I would not necessarily deny that I was a PPA if I held some other SPR for my purposes. As a PPA, I am not *logically* required to accept any inferences from SPRs for my purposes that merely prescribe consistently with my having the generic rights. Thus, at the end of Stage II, I am not *logically* required to universalize from the additional specifications of such SPRs for my purposes. I must, of course, universalize from them, *if* I hold them. But, since this "must" is conditional on my holding them, *and I am not logically required to hold them*, I am not *categorically* required to universalize from them. I could, faced with the consequences of universalization, simply abandon such SPRs for my purposes. However, *I am categorically* bound to universalize from the judgment that I have the generic rights; and this *categorically* requires me to accept the PGC and to reject all SPRs for my purposes that conflict with the PGC.

Thus, the answer to the charge of arbitrariness is that a PPA, regardless of its particular occurrent characteristics, is logically required to concentrate attention on the generic features as the basis of its rights-claims, and must restrict its *categorically binding* rights-claims to these features, because it is not logically required to attend to any other features. Only features that are *necessarily* connected with agency can yield requirements that are categorically binding on any (and, thus, all) PPAs. The generic conditions of agency are such features; the contingently necessary conditions of particular occurrent purposes (those necessary for some particular occurrent purposes, but not others) are not. (See, e.g., RM 149–150; Gewirth 1982b, 25–26; Gewirth 1985d, 20–21, which makes direct reference to Held 1985.) A PPA *may* make other rights-claims, *but only* if these do not contradict its categorically required rights-claims and their logical implications.

The answer to the charge that an argument that focuses attention on the generic features of agency does not address actual PPAs follows from the answer to the charge of arbitrariness. The only sense in which the generic features of agency are "abstract" is that they are universally and necessarily applicable to all PPAs *amid* their enormously varying particular occurrent purposes. In attending to the generic features, it is not assumed that PPAs are so similar that it will be in their particular occurrent interests for them all to make (wish to make) the same rights-claims. It is assumed only that PPAs, whatever their particular occurrent purposes, are PPAs (that they have purposes). It follows *logically* from *the fact that PPAs have purposes* that they must accept the PGC. It, therefore, follows logically, *for PPAs with varying particular occurrent purposes and characteristics*, that they must accept the PGC. For, whatever their particular occurrent characteristics, to deny the PGC is to deny that they have purposes, and this is to deny that they have *any* particular occurrent purposes (which, of course, includes the ones they have). Failure to assent to this can only derive from disagreeing that the argument is valid *on Gewirth's terms* (and Held, here at least, seems to concede that the argument is valid if Gewirth's terms are allowed), or from confusions that arise from misconstruing the criterion of "rationality," in Stages I and II, as I think Held does, as "prudence" (logical consistency with my particular occurrent purposes), rather than as logical consistency with "I am a PPA" (the claim that I have purposes).

My response can be presented differently.

The objection is that the argument requires a PPA to reason as "an ideal" PPA. It alleges that even if "ideal" PPAs logically must accept the PGC, "actual" PPAs need not.

An "actual" PPA is one who has various contingent purposes it wishes to pursue, which it rationalizes according to contingent SPRs. "Actual" PPAs vary in their contingent powers to achieve their purposes, and know that they do. (Call these contingent properties "CP.") An "actual" PPA does not reason just on the basis that it is a PPA; its starting premise is "I am a PPA with CP." I contend that, provided that Gewirth's argument is valid *if restricted* to the implicatures of the generic features of agency (and Held seems to concede that it is), then an "actual" PPA denies that it is an *"actual" PPA* if it does not accept the PGC. Why?

(A) "I am a PPA with CP" → (B) "I am a PPA" (characterized by my possession of the generic features) and (C) "I have CP." By virtue of (B), I logically must accept the PGC. By virtue of CP, I need not necessarily accept the PGC. Binding myself by the PGC will not necessarily best achieve my particular occurrent purposes. If I am an amoralist, and very powerful, it probably won't. However, if I do not accept the PGC, I deny (B), *and, by denying (B),* I deny (A). If I deny that I am a PPA, then I deny that I am *a PPA* with CP.

To this, I can imagine it being objected that, although I deny "I am a PPA with CP" if I reject the PGC, I do not deny that I have CP if I reject the PGC. If the price of denying the PGC is that I deny that I am a PPA, then I am quite happy to accept this. What matters to me is not claiming that I am a PPA, but achieving my particular occurrent goals.

However, this will not do at all. This is because (C') "I am a *being* with CP" → (B) "I am a PPA," insofar as having CP is relevant to the practical precepts I am willing to follow. I cannot claim that I act for some particular occurrent purposes X, without claiming that I have particular occurrent purposes for which I act (≡ "I am a PPA"). Thus, by denying the PGC, I deny "I have CP," insofar as CP is relevant to action.

Thus, Gewirth's argument to the PGC is not an argument from "abstract" or "ideal" PPAs (those who lack varying contingent features, or lack knowledge of which such features they possess). It is an argument from the *necessary* features that *"actual"* PPAs possess, regardless of their contingent differences, and the contingent purposes for which they act. Thus, the argument is directed at, and binding for, "actual" PPAs.

#55   The argument suggests that for rights to exist is for them to be demonstrated.

According to Arthur C. Danto, Gewirth's task

> is to demonstrate that there are human rights, and to demonstrate that such demonstration is necessary to the very existence of these rights. . . . As philosophers we should no doubt like to be able to prove the existence of human rights—prove that there are such rights in the event that the fool shall have said in his heart that there are none, even using his folly against him by showing his denial to entail *its* denial—but it is a bold claim that rights are things whose *esse est demonstrari.*
> Yet something like this seems to be claimed. (Danto 1984, 25)

Danto cites as evidence for this the following passages:

> That human rights exist . . . is a proposition whose truth depends on the possibility, in principle, of constructing a body of moral justificatory argument from which that proposition follows as a logical consequence. (Gewirth 1984b, 3)

> [F]or human rights to exist, or for all persons to have human rights, means that there are conclusive moral reasons that justify or ground the moral requirements that constitute the Nature of human rights . . . . (Ibid.)

> The existence of human rights depends on the existence of certain moral justificatory reasons . . . . (Ibid., 4)

Danto appears to be accusing Gewirth of what Roy Bhaskar has called "the epistemic fallacy," viz., "the conditions of knowledge of the existence of X are the conditions of the existence of X," or "X exists *iff* X is known (shown) to exist." (See Bhaskar 1978, 36.) However, such a charge takes no account of the fact that Gewirth holds that

> [t]he existence of human rights depends on the existence of certain moral justificatory reasons; but these reasons may exist even if they are not explicitly ascertained. Because of this, it is correct to say that all persons had human rights even in ancient Greece, whose leading philosophers did not develop the relevant reasons. (Gewirth 1984b, 4)

It is perfectly clear, as Gewirth points out in his reply to Danto (see Gewirth 1984c, 31), that Gewirth holds that rights, in the normative or prescriptive sense, can exist without being known or shown to exist. Furthermore, to say that rights can exist only if it is *in principle* possible to verify them is not to say that their existence depends upon their being verified.

It seems to me that Danto confuses two things: "justification" as it refers to *the existence* of sufficient reasons for the having of rights, and "justification" as it refers to *the recognition* of such reasons. To say that all PPAs have a right to X, in a sense that is binding on all PPAs, *is* to say that there is sufficient reason, on a criterion that there is sufficient reason to espouse, why PPAs ought not to interfere with PPAOs' doing or having X. A moral right to X *exists* only if there are sufficient reasons, on an other-regarding criterion, for not interfering with the doing/having of X by the rights-holder, and sufficient reason to espouse this criterion. But this is not to say that the existence of a moral right depends on its being demonstrated/recognized that the relevant sufficient reasons exist. The meaning of the right consists in its being a justified claim, but not in the demonstration of its being a justified claim. To hold that the meaning of a moral right consists in the latter is to commit the epistemic fallacy, but Gewirth does not hold this. He holds that the meaning of a moral right consists in the former, and does not thereby commit the epistemic fallacy.

#56   A supreme principle is neither possible nor necessary for the justification of moral judgments.

According to Renford Bambrough, it is impossible to derive a moral principle from premises that are neutral in relation to our ordinary moral thinking and practice. Moral epistemology can do no more than seek a summary articulation of this practice.

> The detailed character of the practice, examined with care, is the test for the accuracy of the articulation.
> . . . [A person's moral reasoning can be questioned; but only by appealing] against his practice to *the* practice which is also *his* practice. (Bambrough 1984, 50)

Bambrough is not saying that the PGC cannot be justified, but that it cannot be justified as "the supreme moral principle." For Bambrough, the notion that there might be a supreme moral principle goes hand in hand with a "foundations picture" of justification. In this model justification must take the form of a pyramid with a supreme principle as its apex. . . . [Justification takes] the form of an appeal to a hierarchy or pyramid of principles. (Ibid., 40–41)

His criticism of the *possibility* of a supreme moral principle involves two claims:

1.   "[t]he absurdity of requiring a single supreme principle as the foundation and justification of morality" (ibid., 41); and
2.   the impossibility "of inquiry or deliberation or discussion or disagreement without reference to what is, in advance of such inquiry or deliberation, known or understood" (ibid., 47).

I shall call 1 "the objection to ethical monism" and 2 "the objection to neutral foundations."

In support of 1 Bambrough holds that

a.   such a principle could not be used to teach children the difference between good and evil, right and wrong:

A child learns when to say 'It's not fair' or 'Thank you' or 'I couldn't help it' before meeting any conceivable candidate for the role of supreme principle (ibid., 41–42);

b.   no explanation of facts or concepts in any area could be given to persons who lack any observation or experience of the phenomena with which that area deals. (See ibid., 42.)

This leads on to what he has to say about 2. Bambrough holds that it is impossible to adopt a vantage point that is outside of our actual ongoing engagement in moral discourse. There is nowhere we can begin that is neutral with respect to our actual engagement in moral discourse. (See ibid., 42, 47–48, especially.)

His claim that it is *unnecessary* to seek a supreme moral principle follows on from this. According to Bambrough, the impossibility of neutral foundations does not mean that moral judgments cannot be justified. It merely means that justification must be conceived of in a different way from that which Gewirth envisages. When philosophers seek to justify mathematics they consider that anything

that purports to overturn or impugn our recognition that $7 \times 7 = 49$ or that the square on the hypotenuse of a right-angled triangle is equal to the sum of the squares on the adjacent sides would merely discredit itself by reductio ad absurdum.

. . . [W]hat is sought is a summary articulation of the structure of a practice. The detailed character of the practice, examined with care, is the test for the accuracy of the articulation. . . .

Gewirth suspects that we pragmatists and particularists are content to endorse familiar modes of argument simply because they are familiar. He is so attached to his conception of a justification that he does not recognize *as* a justification the only justification that can in the end be offered for a procedure or conclusion of physics or logic, mathematics or morals.

When we question somebody's reasoning we appeal against his practice to *the* practice which is also *his* practice. Socrates confutes Polus or Theaetetus by pointing out something that *he* recognizes to be so, and recognizes to be so only if what he said at first is *not* so. (Ibid., 50)

In response to 1*a*, Gewirth points out that

such a supreme principle as the Golden Rule plays an important part in moral education concerned with the *development* of children's moral conceptions. (Gewirth 1984d, 196)[11]

But, even if Bambrough were right about the process of learning being completely inductive and particularistic, the

order of *justification* need not be the same as the order of *teaching and learning*. (Ibid.)

In response to 1*b*, Gewirth maintains that "Euclid's definitions and axioms in geometry, Newton's law of gravitation [and] the laws of supply and demand in economics" have been presented as supreme principles, in the sense that

they have been held to *explain* all the other theorems or phenomena in the respective fields, without themselves being explained (in the same sense) by those theorems or phenomena. In a parallel way, the supreme principle of morality serves to *justify* all the right moral rules and judgments. (Ibid., 195–196)

In response to 2, Gewirth insists that how he arrives at his premises (the generic features of agency) does not matter, so long as they are generic, and every PPA must accept that they are (for it) necessary goods. Justification is a logical sequence. The PGC is justified dialectically on these ineluctable premises, and justifies other rules that are consistent with it. If these other rules can be arrived at inductively, this does not matter, for the PGC is not derived by assuming these rules. In other words, Gewirth claims that the sense in which our being immersed in an ongoing practice makes a neutral starting point impossible is irrelevant as an objection to his argument. (See ibid., 193–194, 196–197.)

In response to the claim that foundational justification is not necessary, Gewirth objects that Bambrough's conception of justification cannot deal with basic moral conflicts, including justified criteria for resolving them. Bambrough assumes that there is only one "practice" or "going concern" of morality. But how would this apply to the moralities of the Nazis and of Stalinist communism, as well as to that symbolized by Roosevelt and Gandhi? Bambrough's pattern of moral epistemology would enable us to resolve conflicts *within* any *one* of these moralities, but not *between discordant* moralities of the sorts I have mentioned. The latter conflicts provide a prime reason why a supreme moral principle must be categorical and determinate—features that Bambrough's conception cannot account for. (Ibid., 194)

Furthermore, in a sense, Gewirth's program does involve the sort of reductio procedures that Bambrough approves. The difference is that Gewirth holds that there are dialectically ineluctable anchor points for these procedures, whereas Bambrough restricts his anchor points to things that persons are contingently willing to accept. Bambrough's program, unlike Gewirth's, is strictly *ad hominem*.[12]

The question of Gewirth's ethical monism, and the question of neutral foundations for the PGC, are two separate issues. The first question concerns whether a single moral principle can be sufficient to cover all practical disputes. The second question is about whether any moral principle, whether or not it has total practical coverage, can be justified as dialectically necessary. In his reply, Gewirth treats Bambrough's attack almost exclusively as a treatment of the second question.[13] To some extent, this is justified, for Bambrough appears not to treat these as separate questions. He is inclined to portray Gewirth's program of justifying the PGC as one of justifying it from moral rules, which the PGC is then used to "justify"; so that either an attack on ethical monism or an attack on neutral foundations will serve to undermine this enterprise. If this is correct, then one may ask why Bambrough does not simply accuse Gewirth of circular argumentation. The answer is that this is precisely what Bambrough is doing in an indirect way. In this context, the following statement by Gewirth (directed at Bambrough's paper) is wholly appropriate:

My view is indeed "foundationist," but it is not *morally* foundationist. For I do not set forth some moral principle as self-evident, nor do I adduce such a principle as the starting point of my argument. (Gewirth 1984d, 192)[14]

Gewirth is quite right to complain that Bambrough takes no account of the way in which Gewirth argues for the dialectical necessity of the PGC, and says nothing bearing directly on the question of the validity of Gewirth's inferences. (See ibid., 193.)[15]

#57   We don't need an epistemology of rights.

Arthur C. Danto claims that

the project of constructing an *epistemology* of human rights reveals itself . . . [to be] a *pseudo problem*. (Danto 1984, 30)

He offers two reasons for this assertion.

1.   We are more certain that we have rights and what they are than we are of any argument for them.
2.   Establishing rights is not a matter of epistemological argument; it is a matter of declaring we have them, seeing if this is recognized—and, if it is not, then it becomes a matter of lobbying for them, or fighting for them. (See ibid.)

In response to 1, Gewirth points out that there is widespread disagreement between theorists and cultures about the existence of rights and what they are. Even in "our" own culture, there are currents antithetical to belief in human rights. So, it is incorrect to claim, in either context, that no argument or proof is needed. (See Gewirth 1984c, 33.)

To this it should be added that uncertainty about the validity of arguments for rights is beside the point. What matters is whether there are valid arguments available.

As far as 2 is concerned, this may be what the politics of rights amounts to when there is no agreement about the epistemological justification of rights-claims. But Gewirth's question is not about how we are to secure acceptance of our rights-claims, but of what rights-claims we may *justifiably* lobby and fight for. The fact that we want our rights-claims to be accepted, and might only be able to do so within a framework of declaration, recognition, and struggle (rather than one of rational justification), does not render an epistemology of rights unnecessary, or the problem of rational justification a "pseudo problem."

#58   It is unnecessary for Gewirth to construe moral judgments as true "by correspondence."

According to Gewirth,

the *PGC* and its entailed moral judgments are analytically true in that their predicates logically follow from the concept of being a rational agent. . . . This . . . may also be put in terms of correspondence. The *PGC* and the moral judgments that follow from it are true in that they correspond to the concept of a rational agent as this is involved in the normative structure of action. (RM 175)

R. M. Hare finds this notion of the PGC being true by virtue of correspondence problematic, and declares that Gewirth's theory

> does not need to be stated in this questionable way as a correspondence theory. He sets out to establish on conceptual grounds alone a theory which makes some moral judgments rational. He also . . . makes crucial use of the idea that by virtue of being agents we are committed to certain prescriptions (viz. that the necessary conditions be realized for achieving our purposes). All he needed to do was to show that these prescriptions, to which as agents we are committed, commit us in turn to certain *moral* prescriptions from which no agent who is consistent in his thinking can dissent. The notion of moral truth has no necessary part to play in this argument. So it was open to him to state his theory without reference to it, and entirely in terms of pre-scriptions. (Hare 1984, 57–58)

Hare runs together two distinct issues here: (*a*) Does Gewirth's theory need the notion of moral truth? (*b*) If the PGC can be said to be true, can it be said to be true by virtue of correspondence? To answer (*a*) negatively is to deny that the PGC is true on conceptual grounds alone; it is to deny that the fact that PPAs rationally must accept the PGC on pain of contradicting that they are PPAs is suffi-cient justification for saying that the PGC is true. To answer (*b*) neg-atively, on the other hand, is compatible with answering (*a*) affirm-atively. It is compatible with saying that the PGC is true on conceptual grounds, but not by virtue of any correspondence.

Now, Gewirth does not hold the PGC to be true in itself. When he speaks of the PGC's being analytically true, it is the complex judg-ment "PPAs rationally must accept the PGC on pain of contradicting that they are PPAs" which he holds to be true. (See Gewirth 1984d, 219. See also #18.1.) So, even on conceptual grounds, Gewirth does not advocate the assertoric truth of moral judgments. So, when Gewirth speaks of moral truth, he is really speaking of the necessity, or nonoptionality, of accepting a prescription with a determinate content. To say that this is not what "moral truth" means is a verbal quibble. I take it that Hare accepts that, if the argument is valid, then, in Gewirth's sense of "moral truth," the PGC is true on concep-tual grounds at least, and (*a*) is to be answered affirmatively.

In these terms, (*b*) asks whether it is true that "PPAs logically must accept the PGC" is true because this statement corresponds to what PPAs are logically required to accept (the normative structure of action). Now, in one sense of the "normative structure of action," it is tautologous, and hence unexceptionable, to say that the PGC corresponds to it. For it is a tautology to say that the dialectical necessity of the PGC corresponds to what is dialectically necessary. And it is clear that Gewirth means just this, for he says,

[T]he *PGC* is true by virtue of correspondence: it corresponds to what every agent logically must admit to be his duties, and hence it is true as stating the duties that necessarily pertain to every agent. (RM 177)

However, in putting forward the thesis that the PGC is true by virtue of correspondence, Gewirth has something deeper in mind.

The whole of my argument for the *PGC* . . . has undertaken to establish that the generic features of action provide objective, ineluctable contents for testing the truth or correctness [for which I think we should read "the dialectical necessity"] of moral judgments, parallel to the objectivity and ineluctability of the contents that observable facts provide for testing empirical and scientific propositions. The generic features of action serve this function not by directly being correspondence-correlates for moral judgments but rather by setting, through the normative structure of action [which here means that PPAs value their purposes], certain requirements for moral judgments, which must conform to these features on pain of contradiction. For the generic features of action supply necessary premises from which moral judgments logically follow. [Strictly speaking, this should read "from which agents are necessarily required to make moral judgments." Through the generic features of agency,] . . . action and agency provide the objective content or subject matter that deductively tests the truth or correctness of moral judgments. . . . [T]he *PGC* is true because it follows from the normative implications of the generic features of action. (RM 176)

As I see it, the main point of saying that the PGC is true by virtue of correspondence is to highlight the fact that the reason why the PGC, *with its specific content,* is dialectically necessary is that (given the proactive valuation by a PPA of its purposes) it categorically needs freedom and well-being. It is to say that this fact makes the PGC a necessary, determinate, and universally required prescription.

Again, given what Gewirth means by saying that the PGC is true by virtue of correspondence, the contention that it is true in this way is unexceptionable.

#59   The argument does not go far enough along the path of giving moral judgments correspondence correlates for truth.

According to E. M. Adams (1984), Gewirth holds that the PGC can be stated assertorically (that it represents "moral knowledge"). Adams, however, claims that Gewirth's theory does not allow for the PGC itself to be true, and so does not allow for "moral knowledge." The PPA derives the PGC as being logically necessary from premises that have no truth value, and thus the PGC itself has no truth value. We cannot collapse values into value attitudes and judgments and still have value knowledge.

Given Gewirth's account of the structure of agency, what role can moral knowledge, as conceived by him, play in action? Every agent, according to Gewirth's dialectical form of the *PGC*, is committed (and recognizes that other agents are likewise committed), on pain of inconsistency, to the judgment that he ought to respect the generic rights of others as well as his own. So what is added when an agent comes to recognize the assertoric *PGC* as a logical truth? In what way, if any, is the subjective normative structure of an agent altered by moral knowledge à la Gewirth? It would seem to have no added practical import whatever. . . . Thus Gewirth's logically true supreme moral principle seems to be a redundancy. If this is so, surely something has gone wrong. Any account of moral knowledge that renders it morally superfluous must be suspect. (Adams 1984, 11)

If all Adams is saying is that the PGC cannot be justified assertorically, only as dialectically necessary for every PPA to espouse, then the response is very simple: Gewirth does not, as Adams alleges, claim that the PGC can be justified assertorically, that the PGC is true *tout court* (see #18.1); it can be stated with assertoric force to all PPAs, because all PPAs must accept the PGC (the PGC being validated within the standpoint of any PPA). Adams is quite right that Gewirth's "assertoric transformation" adds nothing to the dialectical statement of the PGC, and in no way alters the subjective normative structure of agency as Gewirth analyzes it in the dialectically necessary method. The assertoric statement of the PGC is redundant in that it does not state anything more than that all PPAs must accept the PGC. This, however, does not mean that Gewirth cannot construe the PGC as "moral knowledge." It only means this if to construe the PGC as "moral knowledge" is to construe it as true *tout court*. But even if the PGC is not itself true, *it is true* that every PPA must act on it as if it were true. It remains true that PPAs who violate the PGC contradict themselves, and rationally ought to obey it. In this sense, the PGC represents moral knowledge. It is true that it is the supreme principle determining how PPAs ought to act if they are to be rational.

However, it seems to me that Adams is saying that, given Gewirth's analysis of the normative structure of agency, he cannot even derive the PGC as dialectically necessary, that he can only do so on a different analysis of this structure, but that *this* analysis *does* permit the PGC to be derived as an assertoric truth.

Adams says that Gewirth's analysis of "good" is "incomplete in that it leaves how 'good' is applied to objects a mystery" (ibid., 18). Gewirth's view is that to hold X to be good is to value or prize it, but this cannot be used to pick out what things to regard as good. A PPA

would have to say of at least some things that they were good even
if this attitude were not guided by principle. A PPA's judgment that
X is good is merely a description of the fact that it has a pro-attitude
to it. It is just an experience or feeling, and these cannot be contradictory. As such, reasoning is not permitted between a PPA's value
judgments. (See ibid., 13–14.)

On the other hand, according to Adams, PPAs distinguish what
seems good from their perspectives and what *is* good from their perspectives. They judge X is good when they judge that X has the
properties it ought to have. (See ibid., 15.) As a matter of fact,

agents do, from within their perspective as agents, assess their value experi-
ences and judgments epistemically. (Ibid., 18)

If Gewirth used this analysis,

he would have to conclude that the agent not only has the capacity and the
necessity to subscribe to certain value judgments, but that he has the capacity for value knowledge. (Ibid.)

There are several things wrong with this.

1. Gewirth does not analyze "I consider X to be good" as "I have
a pro-attitude to X for no reason." He analyzes it as "I judge that X
is good according to the criteria (I choose) that lead me to pursue X."
In this sense, Gewirth's PPA makes judgments that are epistemic.
But these judgments are relative to the PPA's criteria. That they are
judgments, properly speaking, permits logical reasoning between
them. (See Gewirth 1984d, 204.)

2. Although these judgments are relative to its criteria, a PPA's
judgment that its freedom and well-being are necessary goods is
relative only to its being a PPA. So, even if a PPA's particular occurrent goods are only seeming goods (when judged by its SPR for its
purposes, i.e., goods according to its motivations, not goods according to its rationalizations), its freedom and well-being must *be* good
from its perspective as a PPA. In other words, my judgment "My freedom and well-being are necessary goods" expresses "From my dialectically necessary viewpoint, my freedom and well-being *are* necessary goods." It does not express "From my dialectically necessary
viewpoint, my freedom and well-being are *seeming* (necessary)
goods." There is no SPR for my purposes that I can espouse, according to which my freedom and well-being are not judged to *be* good.
This, of course, does not mean that *others* are required to judge *my*
having freedom and well-being to *be* good, *according to their dialectically necessary viewpoints* (prior to Stage III). But it does mean that
others are required to judge *my* freedom and well-being to *be* good,

according to my dialectically necessary viewpoint. That others need not judge according to my dialectically necessary viewpoint does not negate the fact that my dialectically necessary criterion requires them to value my freedom and well-being. It is this that permits the PGC to be derived as dialectically necessary from *my viewpoint* as a PPA.[16] (See Gewirth 1984d, 219.)

3. Such an agent-relative analysis does not permit the PGC to be derived as more than dialectically necessary. Thus, if Adams intends his analysis, which in some ways is not different from Gewirth's (see my discussion under #23.2.1), to be able to secure an assertoric derivation, then the epistemic judgment that Adams attributes to PPAs cannot be agent-relative, but must be objective. But

Adams's nonrelativist interpretation of judgments of good incurs this problem: How, with regard to some object, are we to ascertain whether it "has the features or properties it ought to have"? . . . Even if we think of a good husband as one who does what "he ought to do," how do we ascertain what he ought to do? Doesn't the content of this "ought" vary with various cultures or societies? Hence, when husbands in different societies are called "good" because they do what they "ought to do," isn't the only common feature here the relativist one that the husbands in question are prized or valued for performing functions that are prized or valued in the respective societies? (Gewirth 1984d, 205)

In brief, Adams' analysis of judgments of value is either question-begging or does not go beyond Gewirth's in not permitting more than a dialectically necessary derivation of the PGC. Gewirth does not need an assertoric derivation to ground "moral knowledge." His position permits "moral knowledge" as relative to the purview of agency, which has an objective aspect in that this purview is common to all PPAs, who are the addressees of practical, and hence of moral, precepts.

#60 If the argument is valid, then the dialectically necessary method is redundant.

1. According to E. J. Bond,

[i]f the agent's reasoning is *in order*, we might well ask, where is the need for the dialectical method? Why not just look at the agent's arguments and see if they are sound? If they are, then the conclusion is established. But if they are not, the agent's reasoning, and his right claims, and his acceptance of the PGC, however psychologically necessary, is rationally unfounded. In the first case, the "dialectically necessary method" would seem to be unnecessary or redundant, and, in the second case, inadequate for the purpose at hand. (Bond 1980a, 51)

2. Bond portrays Gewirth's argument as follows:

"Freedom and well-being, as the necessary conditions of successful purposive actions, are necessary goods for all prospective purposive agents. This being so, all agents have rights to them. But if this is so, then, correlatively, all agents have obligations to respect the rights of all others to these necessary goods." This seems to be the genuine substance of the argument. Why all the fuss about the "dialectically necessary method"? . . . Gewirth tells us . . . that the PGC is detachable from its intentional ("dialectical") context, and can be affirmed objectively and categorically. Why, then, has Gewirth bothered with the "dialectically necessary method" at all? (Ibid.)

3. Bond says that the answer is to avoid problems of naturalism, and so as not to omit the conativeness that grounds a PPA's value judgments. But, says Bond (on naturalism), the dialectically necessary method is only necessary for moving from "I will X" to "I value X." This move is not necessary in order to get to "My freedom and well-being are necessary goods," for "that the agent must recognize as goods his own freedom and well-being . . . is objectively determinable" (ibid., 52), and it is this judgment that is important.

An agent who says that these must be good, since they are the enabling conditions of his successful action in general, is reasoning well. His argument is in order and can be taken, as it were, out of his head. (Ibid.)

4. On conativeness, Bond says that an objective approach does not omit conativeness. It recognizes that PPAs have purposes they wish to fulfill. Admittedly, it is only from a PPA's internal point of view that this means that a PPA must will its freedom and well-being. This is why Gewirth thinks the dialectically necessary method is necessary.

But we cannot move deductively from what an agent necessarily wills to any statement about what rights he has or even about what rights he thinks he has, since that . . . implies that a willing, which is not a proposition, has entailments . . . . (Ibid.)

Regarding 1: Gewirth responds that the very way Bond puts the question

shows that he accepts at least part of the very method whose needfulness he is disputing. For it is *"the agent's* reasoning" that is and must be used here. (Gewirth 1980a, 67)

Regarding 2: Gewirth points out that "Freedom and well-being are necessary goods *for* all agents" is ambiguous

as between meaning simply "beneficial to" and as meaning *"regarded as* beneficial by." The former meaning is assertoric, the latter dialectical. But if we interpret "goods for" as assertoric, as Bond seems to intend, then the next sentence as he here presents it does not follow: "This being so, all agents have rights to them." (Ibid., 68)

That I categorically need my freedom and well-being implies that *I* must *consider* that I have rights to them, not that I have rights to them and, without more, not that PPAO must consider that I have rights to them.

It is also to be pointed out that Gewirth does not hold that the PGC can be detached from its dialectical setting. It can be stated with assertoric force for all PPAs, because dialectically necessary for all PPAs, which is something different. (See #18.1.)

Regarding 3: It is objectively determinable that every PPA must regard its freedom and well-being as necessary goods. But it matters considerably what this means. If it means, as Gewirth intends, that every PPA must prescribe (will) that it have its freedom and well-being ($\equiv$ every PPA must consider [as required by its prudential criterion] that it ought to pursue its freedom and well-being), then this requires the dialectically necessary method. Only if it means no more than "Every PPA categorically needs its freedom and well-being" does it not. When Bond says that the PPA's prescription (reasoning) can be taken out of its head, he presumably means that every PPA can (must) recognize that a PPA must prescribe (or will) its freedom and well-being. But the inference from this that each PPA must consider that it has rights to freedom and well-being only follows from within each PPA's viewpoint. To take the argument further, the dialectically necessary method is (remains) necessary.

Regarding 4: Gewirth responds that

[a] "willing" is not indeed a proposition, but its thought-content can be expressed as a judgment, and this does have entailments. (Ibid., 69)

In reply to Gewirth's response, Bond says,

I really have just two points here. The first is that if this arbitrarily selected agent's reasoning is *sound*, then we can accept his argument *as such*, without adverting to his mental processes, in which case the "dialectically necessary method" would be redundant. . . . The second point is that, so far as the *force* of Professor Gewirth's argument is concerned, the method is not redundant at all. For it is not the agent's judgments, reasoning, or argumentation that is doing the work . . . —but rather his *will*. Professor Gewirth is really relying on what a rational human agent must necessarily will. (Bond 1980b, 74)

This, however, seems to amount to saying that the method is not redundant, only not sound (because relying solely[17] on what a PPA necessarily must will), and that in order to be sound it would have to be redundant (not rely on what a PPA necessarily must will).

However, there is no logical gap between "I must proactively will that I have X" and "I have a (prudential) right to X"; and, by the internal application of the logical principle of universalizability, we can move from this to the dialectical necessity of the PGC.[18] Thus, the dialectically necessary method is not unsound, and Bond's charge has to hold its own as a straightforward accusation of redundancy.

However, if the charge is that the dialectically necessary method, though sound, is redundant, then Gewirth's response to Bond's reply is appropriate.

Bond . . . overlooks the fact . . . that there are arguments which are sound only when given from a certain point of view or relative to a given perspective. In the present case the agent's arguments are agent-relative; they lose their soundness when taken out of relation to the agent's conative pursuits . . . . (Gewirth 1980b, 142)

In addition, it should be noted that the argument is run from a PPA's internal viewpoint. The question never arises as to whether "*we*" (as outside observers) should accept the PPA's reasonings. What matters is whether *the PPA* must accept the reasonings of the argument. "We" only enter into this insofar as we are asked to assess whether or not this is what *we (each of us) ourselves as PPAs* must accept *for (each of us) ourselves.*

#61   Even if the argument is valid on its own terms, it cannot be claimed that it has universal validity for PPAs, because there are alternative logics.

This is not an objection that I have actually encountered in written criticism of Gewirth.[19] There are, however, currents in modern philosophy that suggest such an objection. Gewirth's argument is that PPAs rationally must accept the PGC, and this means that canons of deductive and inductive logic, operating on "I am a PPA," from a PPA's internal viewpoint, require the PPA to accept the PGC. For Gewirth, "deductive logic" means, most centrally, the principle of noncontradiction, *modus ponens, modus tollens,* the principle of identity, and the predicative principle of sufficient reason (the logical principle of universalizability). Now, W. V. O. Quine (1963, 43) has said that the principle of noncontradiction is revisable, that it is not necessary for thought systems to operate with this principle; and views to the effect that there are no laws of thought are by no means uncommon—indeed, they are central to a number of schools of philosophical thought.[20]

Gewirth notes that "difficulties may be raised about the general justification of both deduction and induction," but says that in the present context it must suffice to note that, because they respectively achieve logical necessity and reflect what is empirically ineluctable, deduction and induction are the only sure ways of avoiding arbitrariness and attaining objectivity . . . . Because of these powers of reason, reliance on it is not a mere optional or parochial 'commitment' parallel to the commitments some persons may make to religious faith, aesthetic rapture, animal instinct, personal authenticity, national glory or tradition, or other variable objects of human allegiance. An important point of contrast is that concerning each of these other objects one may ask for its reason in the sense of the justification for upholding it; and any attempt at such justification must make use of reason in the sense of deduction or induction or both. Even if it is held that one or more of these objects is an intrinsic good needing no external justification, the question may always be raised of how it bears on or is related to other goods; and to answer such questions reason must be used.

It is indeed the case that there have also been historical demands that reason itself in turn pass various justificatory tests set by religious faith, aesthetic rapture, and so forth. But the very scrutiny to determine whether these tests are passed must itself make use of reason. For example, salient powers of reason must be used in order to check whether the products of logical and empirical rationality are consistent with propositions upheld on the basis of faith, or whether the use of reason is compatible with the experiencing of aesthetic feelings, and the like. Thus any attack on reason or any claim to supersede it by some other human power or criterion must rely on reason to justify its claims. (RM 22–23)

Some, at least, of Gewirth's critics are happy with this. Witness Kai Nielsen.

Brandt remarks correctly that Gewirth ([RM] 89) utilizes "a very astringent notion of 'rational': as accepting observed facts and the principles of deductive and inductive logic." On this astringent sense of 'rational,' . . . it is plain and uncontroversial that we ought to be rational. (Nielsen 1984, 65, quoting Brandt 1981, 39)

Plain it might be: uncontested it is not! No doubt it will be accepted that argumentation must employ reason, and that reasoning must be consistent. But the objection we have to consider is constituted by the claim that there are no necessary criteria of consistency, that the principle of noncontradiction is not *the* principle of consistency, merely a very widespread or established convention, rather than a universal law of inference or thought; so that avoidance of contradiction is only a reason for those who accept a particular convention.

This is not the place to deal fully with this question. I do, indeed, believe that there are some logical principles that are laws of thought, even if there are optional logics as well, and I have never been impressed by any arguments that claim that there are not.

I will simply state two considerations that figure in the arguments I would give to justify this claim.

1. The principle of noncontradiction, in stating that a statement and its denial cannot both be true *of the same set of circumstances*, is a principle presupposed in our assumed ability to delineate different classes of objects, and in our practice of denying that any statement is true. Anyone who says that the principle of noncontradiction is not a law of thought presupposes this principle by making such a statement. Anyone who asserts that there are alternative principles of consistency to this principle presupposes that there are different principles of consistency, and in so doing relies upon the principle of noncontradiction as a more fundamental principle of consistency.[21]

2. It is sometimes suggested (see, e.g., Quine 1963, 43–44) that the ultimate reason for entrenchment of the principle of noncontradiction in our thinking is that it is useful in ordering our experience, and that counterexperience could lead us to give it up. I disagree, and for two reasons: (*a*) being able to form the notion of a "counterexperience" presupposes use of the principle of noncontradiction, and (*b*) being able to infer that an experience is a counterexperience presupposes the principle of noncontradiction (as well as that of *modus ponens* [at the very least]).

Suppose, however, that I am wrong, and that there are no necessary logical principles. *If* there are no necessary principles of logic, then it must be conceded that the argument lacks the full-blown dialectical necessity that Gewirth claims for it, even if it is valid on its own logical principles. For it could then be said that a PPA who contradicts "I am a PPA" is not necessarily being "inconsistent."

Nevertheless, even on this extreme (and to my mind, untenable) hypothesis, we would still (if the argument is valid on its own terms) have the conclusion that a PPA who denies being bound by the PGC contradicts that it is a PPA. Any PPA who claims that this does not mean that it rationally must accept the PGC would then have to explain why it is not being inconsistent (irrational) by not accepting the PGC: and this, I submit, is a very tall order (indeed, I don't even know what it means). And, even if this can be done, PPAs who accept the principle of noncontradiction would have to accept the PGC. Even if this is not utterly conclusive, it would still be an enormously strong justification for accepting this claim; for anyone who did not accept it would, in consistency, have to give up everything that they believed on inferences that rest on the principle of noncontradiction. Necessary or not, this principle *is* so deeply entrenched in our thinking that the consequences of giving it up (if this is intelligible) are still mind-boggling.

If, in one sense, Gewirth can be asked to justify "reason" (as he defines it)—to justify rational commitment to the PGC in some "ultimate" sense—he nevertheless need not justify "reason" in this sense to justify that "reason" justifies the PGC. It is this latter claim that he is directly concerned to make; and whatever the "ultimate" status of "reason," if Gewirth is right, then he has still brought off a tremendous coup.[22]

General Comments

In this chapter we have seen that

1.   Gewirth's definition of morality, though not universally shared, begs no questions: it is used to raise his questions, not to answer them;
2.   the dialectically necessary method cannot be construed as coercive. The argument develops a conception of free agency as that which is chosen in conformity with the PGC from within any PPA's viewpoint as a PPA;
3.   the failure of previous attempts to prove a supreme moral principle doesn't provide evidence that Gewirth's argument is invalid;
4.   the argument, not being contractarian or utilitarian, does not presuppose that PPAs are in a situation of equal powerlessness; and a focus on the generic features of agency, rather than on contingently necessary conditions for pursuing particular occurrent purposes, is not an arbitrary basis for the making of rights-claims;
5.   the dialectically necessary method does not rest on "the epistemic fallacy";
6.   the argument is not *morally* foundationist; it does not reason from moral premises to the PGC;
7.   requirements for an effective politics of rights do not make an epistemology of rights redundant;
8.   the notion of "moral truth" is not redundant in Gewirth's argument, and can be given unexceptionable interpretations in terms of "truth by correspondence";
9.   the argument is not invalidated by its agency-relative perspective, and cannot be given a free standing assertoric formulation without begging the question; and
10.   the dialectically necessary method is not redundant.

10 Objections to Positive Rights

Gewirth holds that the PGC prescribes not only that PPAs ought to refrain from interfering with the freedom and well-being of other PPAs, but also that PPAs ought to assist other PPAs in securing or maintaining their freedom and well-being. (See, e.g., RM 217.) The generic rights, held to be dialectically necessary, are positive as well as negative.

A consequence of this claim is that the argument *from* the PGC supports, at the very least, a "welfare" or "supportive" state. (See RM 304–327.) And it also imposes duties on individual PPAs to make sacrifices for the well-being of others (Gewirth's doctrine of "the duty to rescue"). (See RM 217–230.)

A number of critics, at least one of whom (Roger Pilon; see below) supports Gewirth's claim that his argument renders *negative* generic rights dialectically necessary, claim that it does not establish *positive* generic rights and, especially, that it does not establish positive rights to *well-being*.

In this chapter, because the argument presented in Chapter 2 was presented in terms of "*at least negative* rights to freedom and well-being," I shall outline the argument for positive rights to both freedom *and* well-being. I shall then examine, and reject, objections to the thesis that the argument validates positive rights to both freedom and well-being.

It will not be possible to avoid, altogether, discussion of matters that properly belong to the argument *from* the PGC. This is because some objections treat the argument for positive rights as an application of the argument to the PGC, rather than as part of the argument to the PGC itself. In consequence, I will have to deal in detail with the "duty to rescue." As will be made clear during my discussion, this Gewirthian thesis belongs to the argument *from* the PGC, not to the argument *to* the PGC (with which this book is concerned).

The Argument for Positive Rights

Gewirth himself confesses that his argument for positive rights is not made as explicitly as it might have been in *Reason and Morality*. (See Gewirth 1984d, 229.) He states his argument more explicitly in Gewirth 1984d, 228–229. (See #66.1.)[1] However, rather than merely relying on this statement, I shall here state the argument in a form that is parallel to my presentation of the argument for "at least" negative rights in Chapter 2.

Within my internal viewpoint as a PPA,

(1)   I am a PPA

entails

(4)   My freedom and well-being are necessary goods ≡

(4c)   I ought to pursue my freedom and well-being.

(3)   I categorically need my freedom and well-being.

From the conjunction of (3) and (4c), the argument for negative rights infers

(4i)   My freedom and well-being ought not to be interfered with. ∴

(4d)   PPAO ought not to interfere with my freedom and well-being,

which is correlative to

(5′)   I have a negative right to my freedom and well-being.

By the *internal* application of the logical principle of universalizability, we get

(9′)   PPAO has a negative right to its freedom and well-being,

because, by the argument for the sufficiency of agency, I must adduce being a PPA as the property by virtue of which I have a negative right to my freedom and well-being.

By the external application of the logical principle of universalizability, we get

(12a′) Within every PPA's internal viewpoint as a PPA, "Every PPA has a negative right to its freedom and well-being" is dialectically necessary.

The argument for positive rights, instead of inferring (4i) from the conjunction of (3) and (4c), infers

(4k)   I ought to be provided with my freedom and well-being, when I am unable to secure my freedom and well-being by my own unaided efforts.

From this is follows that

(4l)   PPAO ought to assist me in securing my freedom and well-being, when I am unable to secure my freedom and well-being by my own unaided efforts. ∴

(5″)   I have a positive right to my freedom and well-being. ∴

(9″)   PPAO has a positive right to its freedom and well-being.

Hence,

(12a″) Within every PPA's internal viewpoint as a PPA, "Every PPA has a positive right to its freedom and well-being" is dialectically necessary.

The claim that PPAs must consider that all PPAs have both negative and positive rights to both their freedom and well-being rests, assuming that the argument for negative rights is valid, specifically on the validity of inferring (4k) as well as (4i) from the conjunction of (3) and (4c).

Now, from (3), it follows that

(4e)   I cannot secure my freedom and well-being if I do not have my freedom and well-being.

Given that I ought to do what is necessary to secure my freedom and well-being (≡ [4c]), it follows from (3)/(4e) together with (4c), by "ought implies can," that

(4m)   I ought to have my freedom and well-being.

As a *practical* directive, this is directed to PPAs, at those who can choose to do something to ensure that I have my freedom and well-being. Thus, it directs all PPAs to do what they can to ensure that I have my freedom and well-being. In the first instance, I am directed to do what I can to secure my freedom and well-being, and PPAO is directed not to interfere with my efforts. But, supposing that I am unable to do what is necessary to secure my freedom and well-being, PPAO is also directed to do what it can to secure my freedom and well-being, or at least what is necessary to enable me to secure my freedom and well-being. Since the directive from which this latter directive is derived prescribes that I ought to do what is necessary to secure my freedom and well-being, this latter directive is conditional upon my not being able to secure my freedom and well-being by my own unaided efforts. Thus, (4k) as well as (4i) follows from the conjunction of (3) and (4c), because both follow from (4m).

At this point in the argument, (4k) is a prudential "ought," being validated on the criterion of my own interests; and the correlative positive rights-claim is prudential in the same sense. The positive rights-claims of (9″) (and, hence, of the PGC) are, however, moral—being validated on the interests of PPAO—the internal application of the logical principle of universalizability requiring PPAs to take favorable account of the interests (the categorical need for freedom and well-being) of PPAs other than themselves, in addition to their own. This renders the duties that PPAO is subject to conditional upon further qualifications. For example, I am required to consider (correlative to my positive right to freedom and well-being) that PPAO has a duty to aid me in securing my freedom and well-being conditional not only upon this not being against my will,[2] and my being unable to secure my freedom and well-being by my own un-aided efforts, but also upon PPAO's positive intervention not in-volving a sacrifice of its own freedom and well-being comparable to or greater than my own.

The argument for positive rights to freedom and well-being may also be put in terms of the argument from attitudinal consistency. (See #13.) According to this argument, if I rationally must have a proactive negative attitude towards interference with my freedom and well-being, then I must consider that I have a negative right to my freedom and well-being. There is no logical gap between what I rationally must will to be the case (noninterference with my free-dom and well-being) and my having to consider that I have a (pru-dential) right to this being the case. If this is correct, and for the argument for negative rights to be valid it must be correct, then I am just as much required to have a negative attitude towards PPAO not aiding me in securing my freedom and well-being (when I am un-able to secure my freedom and well-being by my own unaided ef-forts, but PPAO is able to assist me). If so, I rationally must will that PPAO assist me (when such assistance is needed and possible), and so must consider that I have a positive (prudential) right to my freedom and well-being. It is just as much in my interests for PPAO to aid me in securing my freedom and well-being when I cannot do so, as it is for PPAO not to interfere with my freedom and well-being. If my prudential criterion validates "PPAO ought not to inter-fere with my freedom and well-being," then it must also validate "PPAO ought to assist me in securing my freedom and well-being, when I am unable to do so by my own unaided efforts."

Objections

#62   It is only rational to claim rights that PPAO would claim and accept. PPAO is more likely to grant me negative rights than to grant me positive rights; so I cannot be rationally required to claim positive rights.

Jan Narveson holds that Gewirth's PPA maximizes its utility. It makes claims based on weighing the costs and benefits of making these claims. Thus, if claiming rights entailed no costs to A, A would claim rights (positive as well as negative) to "absolutely everything he could ever want." But, if he claims rights, these (by universalization) entail duties on him. So he must

> weigh the cost, the duties to himself entailed by any proposed right, against the benefit, which is the advantage to himself from others' respecting his rights. . . . It is by no means obvious that it will be a good deal on my part to have you be disposed to give me an X if I should happen to need one, if the price is that I should in turn be disposed to give you an X if you should happen to need one. It is not even absolutely obvious that the benefit to me of your being disposed to refrain from depriving me of my X if I do have one outweighs the cost to me of my being disposed to refrain from depriving you of your X if I don't have one and need it. (Narveson 1984, 102–103)

In general, if I claim a right, then it is irrational (by which Narveson means "imprudent") to accept the duty entailed on myself, if others will not accept a duty on themselves. So, I should only claim rights that others would claim and accept because it is to their benefit (the benefit of their particular occurrent purposes) to do so. For Gewirth's derivation to work, there needs to be agreement between PPAs as to what rights it is in their individual benefit to claim. To establish invariability on this basis is a very tall order, but far greater in relation to positive rights than negative rights. Even if the theory can be made to work for negative rights, there seems to be little prospect of it being made to work for positive rights. (See Narveson 1984, 103–107.)

In response, it has to be said that there is almost nothing in this discussion that is properly directed at Gewirth's argument.

1.   Gewirth's PPA does not maximize its utility (weigh costs and benefits in relation to its *particular occurrent purposes*).
2.   Gewirth's criterion of rationality is not "prudence" (what is in a PPA's particular occurrent interests). It is logical, referring to what a PPA must assent to if it is not to deny that it is a PPA.

3.   Only proactive evaluation of a PPA's freedom and well-being (as necessary conditions of agency and successful agency) is necessarily related to its being a PPA, *in the sense* that it denies that it is a PPA if it does not pursue its freedom and well-being; so it is this to which a PPA's prudential criterion refers.

4.   On this basis, it does not matter what rights-claims PPAs might wish to make, or what conclusions they might be prepared to accept. What matters is what claims they logically must make, and what inferences they logically must accept.

5.   On this basis the invariability of rights-claims required for grounding both negative and positive rights is secured. I must claim that I ought to have my freedom and well-being/I logically must want to have my freedom and well-being (which entails prescribing/necessarily wanting both restraint from interference and necessary aid); and, because I must regard these prescriptions/desires as justified by my being a PPA, I must grant the correlative negative and positive rights to PPAO.[3] (See Gewirth 1984d, 229–232.)[4]

#63   **The doctrine of positive rights produces an incoherent theory—one that states that PPAs both have and do not have a right to freedom, for a PPA cannot retain its right to freedom while having a duty to assist PPAO.**

Douglas J. Den Uyl and Tibor R. Machan claim that

[t]he real problem is that one cannot retain one's right to exercise one's freedom at the same time one fulfills one's 'duty' to rescue. My freedom of movement is necessarily restricted if I am forced to part with some of my resources to take care of others. This problem does not arise if basic human rights are restricted to freedom rights; for no matter what my circumstances, I am free to do with my resources as I please, so long as I do not forcibly restrict others from doing likewise. In this latter case, each and every individual at any and all times (and irrespective of contingent technological and economic conditions) can exercise his right of freedom. This is true universality. What Gewirth offers is either a hypothetical and conditional universality (e.g., "If conditions are right, you may claim a right or exercise a duty"), or a system of rights which are 'possessed' but incapable of simultaneous application (transcendental rights). (Den Uyl and Machan 1984, 168)

This is similar to the view of Roger Pilon. According to Pilon, Gewirth's introduction of positive rights produces an inconsistent view.

If I have a general right to assistance then you have an obligation to assist me when I need it, even if you should not want to afford that assistance. But you also have a right to freedom. . . . Well either your action is going to be compelled, in which case you do not enjoy your right, or it is not, in which case I do not enjoy mine. There are no two ways about it, for the rights are in straightforward conflict. (Pilon 1979a, 1185–1186)

"Rights," according to Pilon, that can exist while being in conflict are not rights at all. A theory that generates both negative and positive rights is inconsistent; a theory with negative rights alone is consistent.

In a *qualified* form, this is echoed by Jan Narveson.

It will at once be evident that there is ample prospect of incompatibility between negative and positive rights. Indeed, if we assert full negative rights, then on the face of it we can assert no positive rights at all. For if someone has a positive right against B, then this means that B is required, whether he wants to or not, to perform certain actions that he might very well not wish to do: save someone from drowning when B prefers to lounge on the beach, or give $2,000 to the municipal government to spend on the local school system when B would prefer to spend it on a new piece of hi-fi equipment or on a nonpublic[5] school of B's choice, for instance. As Hobbes observed, obligation and liberty with respect to the same act are inconsistent. And, of course, positive rights may give rise to conflicting duties: my duty to help the poor can conflict with my duty to heal the sick; for that matter, my duty to help poor person C may conflict with my duty to help person D. Any theory of positive rights needs to supply us with procedures for sorting out such conflicts, if it is to be consistent. (Narveson 1984, 97)

A pure theory of negative rights does not obviously generate such conflicts.

A "pure theory of negative rights" is not, of course, a pure theory of unlimited liberty. All rights impose duties, and all duties are restrictions of liberty: if A has negative rights against B, there are acts which B may not perform. If we wish to assert as a generalization that people may do as they please . . . it will have to be hedged in some such way as with the clause "(within the limits of others' rights)." And of course a similar clause could be inserted after any general statement of positive rights as well; but there remains the important difference that with respect to an agent, A, the duties imposed by pure negative rights of others will not be inconsistent with each other, whereas the duties imposed by positive rights of others are quite likely to be so in practice, and thus to require sifting, balancing, and adjusting. (Ibid., 98)

To be fair to Gewirth, . . . Gewirth's duty to aid people is always a duty to do so when one can do so at "no comparable cost to oneself" . . . . But . . . this is obviously a fairly vague requirement . . . . (Ibid., 103)

Den Uyl and Machan, and to a lesser extent Pilon, risk confusing the issue with their terminology. Den Uyl and Machan talk about "freedom rights" versus "welfare rights" (see Den Uyl and Machan

1984, 167), and Pilon talks about "freedom rights" and "rights to assistance." Now, "welfare rights" could be taken to refer to what Gewirth calls "rights to well-being," and Den Uyl and Machan in fact take rights to "well-being" to be synonymous with "welfare" rights. Yet they also include the "right to life" under "freedom rights," placing rights to "housing, health care, and the like," under "rights to well-being/welfare rights." (See ibid.) Now, for Gewirth, the most fundamental right to basic well-being is the right to life, and rights to well-being are contrasted with rights to freedom. This contrast does not equate with the contrast between positive and negative rights, rights to assistance and rights to noninterference.[6] There can be both negative and positive rights to both freedom and well-being. On balance, though it is not always clear, I take it that Den Uyl and Machan (and Pilon) are not pressing for freedom rights against rights to well-being, but for negative rights to both freedom and well-being as against positive rights to either freedom or well-being.[7]

The objections made by Den Uyl and Machan, and Pilon, presuppose that rights cannot be had if they can be overridden: that rights must be absolute, and cannot be prima facie. But, as Narveson points out, this implies a theory of "unlimited liberty," which is untenable. To make a theory of universal negative rights consistent, it is necessary that these rights be qualified. Narveson is aware that a theory incorporating negative and positive rights can be made consistent by qualifying the rights, by specifying the criteria by which conflicts of rights are to be adjudicated. His objection really amounts to the contention that Gewirth provides no nonarbitrary criterion for doing so that is capable of providing determinate answers to questions in case of conflict. According to Gewirth, my positive right to aid overrides your negative right to noninterference, provided that your helping me does not incur a loss of your freedom/well-being comparable to the loss of freedom/well-being I will incur without your aid. Narveson complains, however, that this is vague.

This is not so. Costs are to be assessed by the "degree of necessity for agency." Although further discriminations can be made within these categories, rights to basic goods outweigh rights to non-subtractive goods, which outweigh rights to additive goods, and the right to life outweighs the right to basic freedom. (See, in particular, RM 338–354 for a discussion of principles for the ordering of rights in conflict.) If your saving my life involves you in some loss of additive well-being, then you clearly have a duty to forfeit this amount of your well-being; and the case is clearer still when it is only a particular occurrent good that you are required to sacrifice. The criterion of degrees of necessity is not arbitrary; it is part of the structure of the argument to the PGC itself.

Pilon, at least, writes as though PPAs have rights to any particular occurrent purposes that they wish to pursue, as though prevention of my pursuit of any particular occurrent purpose I might have constitutes a violation of my right to freedom. This not only leads to a "pure theory of liberty," it is also incompatible with the argument for negative rights which Pilon approves. Even the argument for negative rights only validates rights to freedom and well-being where these are interpreted as generic-dispositional capacities.[8]

#64   **A PPA may claim rights only to what is integral to its action. A PPA may claim negative rights to freedom and well-being because they are its property. It may not claim positive rights to its freedom and well-being because they are not its property.**

According to Roger Pilon,

even when . . . [the] generic features are characterized as the "necessary goods" of action—freedom and well-being[9]—and these in turn are claimed as rights, if they are *integral* to our action and thus are claimed *in* behaving conatively, we already *have* these goods, at least to a degree sufficient to be able to act and hence to be able to be claiming them in acting; thus we do not need to claim that others must afford them for us. (Pilon 1979a, 1180)

We have to limit rights to what is already inherent in action as such, if claims to them are to be necessarily implicit in action. (See ibid., 1181.) In claiming rights to its freedom and well-being, a PPA claims rights to its property, for freedom and well-being are its to claim. They belong to it. It has them. To claim positive rights is to claim what does not belong to it. Their possession is not contained in its action. (See ibid., 1181–1182.)

This comes very close to saying that "might" is "right," that what justifies my possession of freedom and well-being is my having freedom and well-being. But rights, as *justified demands*, are not implicit in *action*. Rather, if the argument is valid, then the *view that I have such rights* is implicit in *my internal viewpoint as a PPA*. The only sense in which rights are implicit in my action, in the way Pilon portrays this, is as *powers* to act. To define "rights" in this way is to employ a non-normative conception of "rights." It is to define a right to X in terms of having X. At best, such a definition is inappropriate in the context of an argument where the question of having a right to X is a question of *being justified* in having X. This conception makes a mockery of the dialectically necessary method.

In any event, within my internal viewpoint as a PPA, it is not my *having* freedom and well-being that justifies my right to freedom and well-being, but my categorical *need* for freedom and well-being for my *prospective* purposive agency. From the point of view of my *prospective* purposive agency, I need aid in securing my freedom and well-being, when I cannot do so by my own efforts, just as much as I need noninterference with my freedom and well-being. When I cannot secure my freedom and well-being by my own efforts, the *need* for assistance "belongs" to my *prospective* agency just as much as my *need* for noninterference.

Pilon claims that, if I am able to lay claim to my freedom and well-being, then I must already have my freedom and well-being, and therefore do not need to claim assistance in securing them. This ignores two things.

1.   There are levels of freedom and well-being. The freedom and well-being I must claim rights to is not limited to that re-quired to shout, "Help!" The level I must claim is the level I need to be able to pursue any of my freely chosen purposes (with general chances of success).

2.   This objection, if valid, would also make it redundant for me to lay claim to *negative* rights. If I am interfered with suffi-ciently, I will not be able to lay claim to negative rights either. On Pilon's way of conceiving the matter, if I can lay claim to noninterference, then I must already have these rights; it must be the case that they are not interfered with. Ergo, I do not need to claim them.

That I *have* my freedom and well-being might be as much a con-sequence of others aiding me as of their not interfering. I do not see how my having freedom and well-being can be conceived of as my property in a way that makes this possession *necessarily* indepen-dent of the behavior of others.[10]

#65   According to Gewirth, PPAO's positive duty to aid me in securing my freedom and well-being is conditional upon PPAO's not incurring comparable costs when it intervenes on my behalf. But cost-benefit considera-tions cannot enter into a deontological argument.

According to Roger Pilon, the qualification, that PPAO's duty to assist me is subject to such assistance's not involving comparable costs for PPAO, is incompatible with a deontological theory. Cost considerations cannot enter into a deontological argument, which

Gewirth's argument professes to be; and Gewirth does not, in any event, specify who is to assess these costs. (See Pilon 1979a, 1180.)

These statements are incorrect.

According to Gewirth (and I agree), an assessment of consequences (to be assessed by "costs/benefits") is compatible with a deontological theory. It is, however, important to distinguish between "utilitarian consequentialism" and "deontological consequentialism."

For the deontological consequentialist, a violent action against other persons is justified not if its consequences (or the consequences of a general rule upholding such actions) will serve to achieve more good than will any alternative action, but rather if the action, directed against the perpetrator of a severe injustice, will remove or remedy that injustice without leading to worse injustices, and only if it is quite clear that the severe injustice cannot otherwise be removed. . . .

To consider consequences by reference to this criterion is to recognize that the wrongness of actions may vary in degree, depending on the rights the actions violate, and that actions that are wrong when viewed without consideration of special excusing circumstances may nonetheless be required in order to prevent or remove worse wrongs. It is also true that rights are in part defined in terms of goods, and that rights and duties vary in degree of moral urgency according to the degree to which they affect well-being and hence the possibilities of purposive action. . . . Nevertheless, the criterion that the *PGC*'s consequentialism uses for ascertaining the rightness of an action refers not to the goods alone but to the entitlements to the goods of the parties affected, as ascertained by the consideration of equal rights to the conditions of agency. The question is how this equality of rights is to be maintained or restored. None of this is equivalent to utilitarian consequentialism that aims solely at maximizing goods regardless of the rights of the persons affected. The calculation that deontological consequentialism uses is not concerned simply with measuring amounts of goods and bads with a view to maximizing the former or minimizing the latter, without regard to their distribution; it is concerned rather with correcting or preventing unjust distributions of basic goods without incurring further or greater injustices. (RM 216)

The general point is that a deontological consequentialism assesses consequences in terms of *rights* and *duties*. In Gewirth's theory, rights are directly rights to the generic needs of agency. Some of these needs, however, are more radical than others, and this means that some of these needs must be sacrificed for others (which, in turn, entails that some rights take precedence over others, override them in case of conflict). You and I have equal rights. But I have a duty to grant you your rights only if doing so does not deprive me of rights that are equally or more important. When you are in dire need (e.g., your life is threatened), and I can aid you, Gewirth holds that I have a duty to aid you if my doing so does not (seriously) threaten my life. My doing so will incur "costs" for me. I may not want to be bothered, or it may even be the case that I can only do so at the risk of (nonfatal) injury. But, even if, as in the latter case, I forfeit rights that I have, your need (in relation to things that ground your rights) is greater than mine, so the rights I am required to forfeit are overridden. In this calculation it is not necessary to appeal to anything other than deontic considerations. To deny such a general view is to claim that there are no prima facie rights and duties at all in a "deontological" theory. There can be no doubt that Gewirth's theory is a theory of prima facie rights and duties, and if all that is at stake here is whether it should be called "deontological," then I am sure that Gewirth would not be at all bothered by his theory not being called deontological, provided that its inferences are sound.

The question is not *"Who is* to assess the costs?" but *"How are* the costs to be assessed in a dialectically necessary manner?" Like Narveson (see #63), Pilon ignores the criterion of "degrees of necessity" and Gewirth's general discussion of the conflict of rights.[11]

#66   Gewirth attempts to derive the dialectical necessity of
      claiming positive rights from the dialectical necessity
      of claiming negative rights, by arguing that to fail to
      aid a PPA in securing its freedom and well-being is to
      cause harm to the PPA's freedom and well-being. This
      is invalid because "not-doing" is not action.

1 Pilon, Narveson

According to Roger Pilon,[12] Gewirth's argument for positive rights is an argument from causality. Gewirth begins with an obligation on the part of PPAs not to cause harm to PPAO (not to interfere with PPAO's freedom and well-being), and then argues that to refrain from assisting PPAO in securing PPAO's freedom and well-being, in PPAO's time of need, is to cause harm to PPAO. Gewirth attempts to derive positive rights from negative rights.

Pilon's response is that "not-doings" are not "causally efficacious."

[F]or an agent to come under the prescription of the PGC at all, there must be a recipient of his action, a threshold condition the ordinary not-doing situation does not satisfy. Consider: at time t_1 A is standing on the shore "doing nothing"; at time t_2 B falls out of his boat; A could rescue B "without comparable cost," but instead he continues "doing nothing." If B is not a recipient of A's "act" at t_1, are we to suppose that he becomes a recipient of that same act at t_2, in virtue of *his* (*B*'s) act? (If so, then who is the causal agent here?) We could always change the description of *A*'s "same act," of course; but that would beg a very important question. I submit, in short, that *A*'s "agency" here simply does not make *B* a recipient; thus absent a plausible theory of not-doing causation, the PGC is powerless to impose positive obligations between generally related individuals. (Pilon 1979a, 1184)

[I]n a world of general relationships, (a) there are no obligations toward others *to* act, (b) there are no obligations *not* to act when doing so involves no recipient, and (c) when there *is* a recipient there is an obligation not to coerce or harm him, *i.e.,* to obtain his consent before involving him in transactions. (Ibid., 1184–1185)

According to Jan Narveson,

[m]any, including Gewirth, have argued for duties to rescue on the basis of the duty not to harm—the positive right on the basis of the negative one. Thus Mill, notoriously, argues that "a person may cause evil to others not only by his actions but also by his inaction, and in either case he is justly accountable to them for the injury." Likewise Gewirth: "An event . . . may be caused by a person's inaction . . . as well as by his positive action. A train wreck may be caused by a signalman's omitting to move a switch. . . . If the signalman's pulling the switch is expected and required in the normal operation of the railroad line . . . then his failure to pull it is the cause of the ensuing wreck" ([RM] 222).

But with all such arguments there is a fatal flaw. The signalman has an antecedent, professional (in this case) duty to pull switches at crucial times. His inaction is a cause because there is an antecedent basis for the positive duty, and thus for positive expectations for action on the part of affected persons. But whether there is such a duty is precisely what is at issue when the question is whether there is a general duty of aid. To argue that our negative duty to refrain from harming entails a positive duty to help when needed on the ground that not helping is in effect a kind of harming is to beg the question. (Narveson 1984, 98–99, quoting Mill 1910, 74, and RM 222)

To answer these objections it is necessary to look at the section of *Reason and Morality* entitled "The Duty to Rescue." Here, Gewirth presents us with the following example:

Suppose Carr, who is an excellent swimmer, is lolling in the sun on a deserted beach. On the edge of the beach near him is his motorboat, to which is attached a long, stout rope. Suddenly he becomes aware that another person, whom I shall call Davis, is struggling in the water some yards away. Carr knows that the water is about thirty feet deep at that point. Davis shouts for help; he is obviously in immediate danger of drowning. Carr sees that he could easily save Davis by swimming out to him, or at least by throwing him the rope from his boat. But Carr simply doesn't want to bother even though he is aware that Davis will probably drown unless he rescues him. Davis drowns. (RM 217–218)

Gewirth says that the PGC imposes a duty on Carr to rescue Davis.

Most directly, the *PGC* requires that an agent not only refrain from interfering with his recipients' freedom and well-being, but also that he assist them to have these necessary goods when they cannot have them by their own efforts and when he can give such assistance at no comparable cost to himself. By 'comparable cost' is meant that he is not required to risk his own life or other basic goods in order to save another person's life or other basic goods, and similarly with the other components of the necessary goods of action. To engage in such risk or to incur such cost would involve the possibility or actuality of losing his own life in order to save theirs, and this, rather than maintaining an equality of generic rights, would generate an inequality in his recipient's favor. In the situation as described, however, Carr can save Davis's life without risking his own. Hence, the *PGC* requires that he come to Davis's rescue. To put it somewhat more extensively: in failing to come to Davis's rescue, Carr drastically violates the equality of generic rights that the *PGC* prescribes for transactions between agents and their recipients. For Davis participates involuntarily and contrapurposively and indeed suffers basic harm in a transaction that is under Carr's control and in which Carr participates voluntarily and purposively. By his inaction, Carr lets Davis drown, thus imposing on him a maximally unfavorable inequality with regard to the rights of well-being. (RM 218–219)

Gewirth says that this account raises two interrelated questions.

a. In what way is Carr an agent in the situation as described? The PGC imposes duties on agents; but to be an agent, Carr must perform an action. Since he is inactive, how can he be held to perform an action?
b. In what way does Carr act on Davis? Since Carr remains passive and inert in the face of Davis's peril, how can it be held that there is a transaction between Carr and Davis, wherein Carr is the agent and Davis the recipient? (RM 219)

The answer to *a* is that nonaction and inaction are not the same thing.

Nonaction is the simple absence of any action . . . . [T]he person involved is not behaving voluntarily and purposively . . . . [O]n the other hand, . . . the inactive person unforcedly chooses to refrain in order to achieve some purpose of his own; he is aware of the proximate circumstances of his omission and intentionally engages in it. (Ibid.)

Because Carr's behavior is voluntary and purposive, it is a case of inaction, which is a category of action. His failure to rescue Davis is not a case of his doing nothing. He does something. He lolls on the beach. He chooses to do this rather than to rescue Davis. So, what he *does* is describable as "a failure to rescue Davis," as well as "lolling on the beach" (for, to loll on the beach *is* to fail to save Davis).

The answer to *b* is that Carr could have rescued Davis, and Davis would not have drowned if Carr had come to his rescue. Davis is Carr's recipient because his well-being is affected by what Carr voluntarily and purposively refrains from doing. (See RM 220–221.)

Gewirth asks a number of questions about this.

c.   How can Carr's inaction be a causal factor in Davis' drowning
      1. if Carr exerted no positive causal efficacy on Davis?
      2. if Davis would have drowned even if Carr had not been present at all?
d.   Why is Carr's inaction not a causal factor in every event that could have been prevented had Carr intervened? (See RM 221.)

Gewirth's answer to *c*1 is that Carr's inaction is attributable as the cause of Davis' death *because the PGC requires Carr to aid Davis* (to do the things necessary to save him that are in his power). (See RM 223.)

The answer to *c*2 is that, although the conditions of tide, Davis' health, swimming ability, etc., are sufficient to bring about Davis' death *when Carr is absent,* they are not sufficient when Carr is present. Carr's inaction must be added to these conditions, for Davis would not have drowned without this inaction. (See RM 223–225.)

The principal answer to *d* is that the PGC only holds PPAs responsible for events that they know about and are able to prevent (at no comparable cost to themselves), and, even then, only in relation to events that involve rights violations. (See RM 225–226.)

Gewirth concludes his discussion by considering objections to the thesis that the PGC grants positive rights. These include the objection that a scheme with positive and negative rights is inconsistent (examples of which I have replied to under #63). This discussion need not concern us here.

We can now return to Pilon's and Narveson's objections.

It is incorrect to say that Gewirth argues for positive rights on the basis of negative rights. To say this is to assume that the argument to the PGC only establishes negative rights, and that the discussion of the duty to rescue is a derivation of positive rights from these negative rights on the basis of a theory of negative causation. This, however, does not square with the fact that the attribution of causal efficacy to Davis' nonintervention relies on the PGC's establishing positive rights. Granted, this might merely fuel the charge of circularity. But to this it must be added that the discussion of the duty to rescue forms part of Gewirth's discussion of the direct *applications* of the PGC, not part of his argument *to* the PGC. This only makes sense if we suppose that Gewirth thinks that his argument *to* the PGC establishes the PGC as a principle of both negative and positive rights. Although Gewirth did not do much to underline this point in *Reason and Morality*, there is little excuse for thinking differently. Be that as may be, Gewirth has subsequently disavowed that he argues for positive rights on the basis of negative rights.

> My argument for positive rights is *parallel to*, and not *derived from*, my argument for negative rights . . . . Hence, Narveson's objection does not apply to my argument when he says that "the right not to have others interfering in one's pursuit of those purposes simply does not entail a right that others supply you with what you need in the way of fulfilling them." I do not hold that positive rights are entailed by negative rights. Rather, both sets of rights are entailed by the same considerations: that every agent logically must hold that he has both sets of rights because they are needed for his having the necessary conditions of action and of successful action in general. (Gewirth 1984d, 229, quoting Narveson 1984, 100)

I have presented the argument in the first section of this chapter. Gewirth states it as follows:

> Since well-being[13] is a necessary condition of action and successful action in general, every agent has a general need for its components. Hence, every agent has to accept (4a) [Gewirth's numbering] "I must have well-being." This 'must' is practical-prescriptive in that it signifies the agent's advocacy of his having what he needs in order to act either at all or with general chances of success. Now, by virtue of accepting (4a), the agent also has to accept (5a) "I have a positive right to well-being." For, if he denies (5a), then, because of the correlativity of positive rights and strict positive 'oughts,' he also has to deny (6a) "Other persons ought to assist me to have well-being when I cannot have it by my own efforts." By denying (6a), he has to accept (7a) "Other persons may not (i.e. It is permissible that other persons not) assist me to have well-being when I cannot have it by my own efforts." And by accepting (7a), he has to accept (8a) "I may not (i.e. It is permissible that I not) have well-being." But (8a) contradicts (4a). Since every agent must accept (4a), he must reject (8a). And, since (8a) follows from the denial of (5a), every agent must reject that denial, so that he must accept (5a) "I have a positive right to well-being."[14]

The further steps of this argument are also parallel to the argument for negative rights. Each agent logically must admit that the sufficient reason or ground on which he claims positive rights for himself is that he is a prospective purposive agent, so that he must accept the generalization that all prospective purposive agents have positive rights to well-being. Hence, he must also accept that he has positive duties to help other persons attain well-being when they cannot do so by their own efforts. Such help often requires a context of institutional rules, including the supportive state ([RM] 312ff.). (Gewirth 1984d, 228)

Admittedly, this raises questions about the precise role of the discussion of the duty to rescue. I will deal with this under #66.2. For the moment, it will suffice to say that I consider this discussion to be an explanation of features implicit in the argument to the PGC, which enable the PGC to be applied (as a principle of positive rights) to concrete situations, rather than an argument for positive rights on the basis of negative rights. The discussion of the duty to rescue, derivatively, contains replies to objections to the *general* idea that there can be positive rights. It shows how such objections (which do not address the argument to the PGC as such) can be answered once the PGC is in play.

In this context, it is to be observed that Gewirth's discussion of the duty to rescue contains replies to Pilon's and Narveson's specific objections, which they do not consider. To Pilon, the reply is constituted by the distinction Gewirth draws between nonaction and inaction, and by pointing out that, *given the PGC's prescription of positive rights,* it is correct (and nonarbitrary) to alter the description of A's act when B is drowning from the description of A's act when B is not. This does not beg the question, because the justification of the PGC as a principle of positive rights is prior to, and independent of, the application of the PGC in specifying positive duties in specific circumstances.[15] This point also serves as a reply to Narveson's objection. Narveson grants that causal responsibility via omissions can be identified in relation to rules. In the Carr/Davis situation, the rules are not institutional or professional, but those of the PGC (which bind all PPAs in a supremely authoritative manner). There is, again, no circularity in this, because the argument for positive rights is not an argument from negative rights.[16]

2 Mack

According to Eric Mack, Gewirth's explicit argument for positive duties is a direct application[17] of the PGC via his discussion of "the duty to rescue," and also an indirect application[18] of the PGC via the doctrine of consent.[19] However, in the absence of direct positive duties, individuals possessing negative rights will not be required to comply with institutionally based demands. (See Mack 1984, 147.)

So a failure of the argument for the duty to rescue will have broad repercussions for Gewirth's endorsement of positive (and enforceable) moral duties as direct and indirect implications of the *PGC*. (Ibid., 148)

Mack is aware that, at one level at least, Gewirth thinks that positive rights can be established without recourse to the discussion of "the duty to rescue," that the "duty to rescue" discussion does not provide the argument whereby it is established that the PGC requires PPAs to assist other PPAs in distress. This is stated at the beginning of Gewirth's treatment of the duty to rescue, his discussion being an application of the PGC, which already contains this positive requirement.

This might seem to imply that Mack is wrong to characterize the discussion of the duty to rescue as an attempt to derive positive rights by a direct application of the PGC. The natural characterization of such an attempt is as a derivation of positive rights from negative rights, it being held that the argument to the PGC is solely an argument for negative rights. This cannot be right if the argument to the PGC establishes positive as well as negative rights. However, Mack's characterization of the role of the discussion of the duty to rescue is much more complex than this.

Mack finds Gewirth's claim that the argument to the PGC is an argument for both negative and positive rights perplexing. Given Gewirth's positive as well as negative formulation of the PGC (see RM 218),

[s]eemingly, nothing could be easier than establishing Carr's obligation to rescue on the basis of Davis's "right to well-being." But suddenly the structure of Gewirth's argument becomes more complex. As part of a "more extensive statement" of it Gewirth repeats the claim that, "in failing to come to Davis's rescue, Carr drastically violates the equality of generic rights that the *PGC* prescribes for transactions between agents and their recipients." But as an explanation or justification of this strictly moral assertion, we are offered the mixed moral and causal claim that, "by his inaction, Carr lets Davis drown, thus *imposing* on him a maximally unfavorable inequality with regard to the rights of well-being" ([RM] 219; emphasis added). From this point on, within his discussion of the duty to rescue, Gewirth's primary concern is to defend the causal efficacy of inactions—specifically, the causal efficacy of conscious omissions of actions which would have prevented ills. (Mack 1984, 148–149)

What puzzles Mack is why an invocation of the PGC (as requiring assistance as well as noninterference) is not sufficient to condemn Carr. Why is it necessary to appeal to a negative causal responsibility thesis?

Apparently the reason . . . is that the *PGC* prescribes standards "for transactions between agents and recipients." That an upshot of Carr's refraining is Davis's loss of something to which he has a right, viz. his life, is not in itself enough to condemn Carr. What is necessary is that there be a rights-violating transaction in which Carr is the agent and Davis is the recipient. And what is essential to the existence of such a transaction is that Carr's action or inaction—in this case, his refraining from the rescue—be the cause of or a dominant cause of Davis's death. Only if this causal relation holds can Carr be judged blameworthy by the principles of a moral theory which prescribe not how the world shall be but, rather, which transactions among persons are morally obligatory and which are morally wrong. Gewirth's focus on interpersonal transactions is indicative of the deontological character he seeks for his moral theory. (Mack 1984, 149)

Labeling the values identified by one's theory of the good as 'rights' does not produce a deontic theory. Within Gewirth's theory, 'rights' do not function as moral side-constraints. Rather, each 'right' is part of the weighted and partially ordered system of goals to the value of which each agent is rationally committed. . . . Insofar as the *PGC* tells us what 'rights' persons have— i.e. what conditions of their existence we are rationally committed to value, and what the best balance of the possible realization of these values would be—and so establishes a ranking of sets of upshots, it has not yet told us about the rightness and wrongness of the actions of individuals. It has not yet functioned as a prescriber for transactions among agents and their recipients. The *PGC* cannot assume such a role until causal relations are established, until, for example, it is established that, by letting Davis drown, Carr *imposes* death upon him. Only when the disvalue constituted by Davis's death is so connected with Carr does it generate a judgment of wrongness. Only then does the *PGC* operate as a deontological principle. (Ibid., 151–152)

As I understand this, Mack concedes that the argument to the PGC *is* an argument for both positive and negative "rights," *but only in a sense of "rights" that is not deontic.* To establish the PGC, whether as a principle of *negative or positive rights,* as a *deontological* principle, we must be able to assign causal responsibility to others for a state of affairs in which what the PGC judges as the maximally favorable outcome is not attained. That is to say, we must be able to assign causal responsibility to others for violating our *nondeontic* "rights," as established by the argument to the PGC. To assign causal responsibility when positive actions are involved in these violations is straightforward—so, there is no problem with the argument to the PGC as an argument for negative deontic rights. But there are problems with assigning causal responsibility for omissions (negative actions). Such responsibility must be assigned if the PGC is to be a principle of *positive deontic* rights.

In other words, according to Mack, the role of the discussion of the duty to rescue is not to derive positive rights from negative rights, but to derive *positive deontic rights* from the *positive nondeontic "rights"* established by the argument to the PGC. In these terms, his acceptance that the argument to the PGC *is* an argument for both positive and negative "rights" is not inconsistent with his claim that Gewirth derives positive rights *from* the PGC.

According to Mack, Gewirth's claim that refraining from preventing evil is to cause evil comprises two assertions.

[O]missions of actions are causal factors in the harms that those actions would have respectively prevented.

[A]t least certain of these causally efficacious omissions of actions are the causes of, or at least dominant causes of, the evils that those actions would respectively have prevented. (Ibid., 152)

To be a causal factor in, or the cause of, an event has two types of conditions. Mack calls these

1.   the subjunctive condition: X is such a condition *iff* "X did not obtain" implies "Upshot Y would not have obtained." (If this condition were sufficient, then an omission is the cause of the harm if without the omission the harm would not have occurred);

2.   the immorality condition: X is such a condition *iff* X transgresses some moral norm entailed by the PGC. This condition is

one implication of what might be called the "abnormality criterion," viz., that some X can be singled out as the cause of some Y if X, among all events which satisfy the subjunctive condition, is the one which departs from the moral or statistical norm . . . . (Ibid., 152 n. 7)

In other words, if this condition is sufficient, then if the immorality condition is satisfied by an omission, then the omission is the cause of the harm that could have been prevented.

According to Mack, Gewirth's position could be that 1 is sufficient, or that 2 is sufficient, or that 1 and 2 are jointly sufficient. Alternatively, Gewirth might be saying either of the following:

a. The subjunctive condition is necessary and sufficient for an omission's being a causal factor in harm, while the immorality condition is necessary and sufficient to identify an omission as the cause, or the dominant cause, of the harm.

Carr's omission is a causal factor in Davis's drowning because, had the omission not obtained, the drowning would not have occurred. And this causal factor is the cause of the drowning because it is the factor which departs from the moral norm. (Ibid., 154)

b. The subjunctive and immorality conditions are each necessary and jointly sufficient conditions for an omission's being a causal factor in a harm; and the immorality condition is sufficient for singling out the omission as the cause, or dominant cause, of a harm that could have been prevented.

The immorality condition must be satisfied even for something to count as a causal factor. And if it is satisfied, that something will also count as the cause or dominant cause of some unhappy event. (Ibid., 155)

Mack says that he takes *b* to represent Gewirth's position, and that Gewirth holds that where an omission is legitimate it is not even a causal factor: if Carr omits to save Davis, knowing that, were he to save Davis, Davis would destroy humanity, then his omission is not a causal factor in Davis' drowning. (See ibid., 156.)

Mack objects to this account on the following grounds (see ibid., 157):

1. It obliterates the distinction between causal factors and dominant causes. Any X that satisfies the conditions for a causal factor will satisfy those for being a dominant cause.
2. It denies any sort of causal status to actions (viz., any *legitimate* omissions) that seem clearly to be such factors (if omissions have causal status).
3. If the subjunctive condition is necessary for causal factor status, then why not allow it also to be sufficient?

Mack also rejects the subjunctive condition as deployed in *a*, and the immorality condition as deployed in *b*, saying that Gewirth must be committed to one or another of these.

He rejects the view that Carr's omission to save Davis is a causal factor in Davis' drowning (according to the subjunctive condition in *a*) on the grounds that, without Carr's presence, factors such as the tide, water, Davis' inability to swim, etc., are already sufficient to lead to Davis' drowning. Carr's presence and omission to save Davis cannot thus be a necessary condition for Davis to drown, because this implies that the other factors were not (as they are) sufficient. (See ibid., 157–163.)

He rejects the immorality condition as in *b*, on the grounds that it implies that where Carr pushes Davis under the water in self-defense against Davis' unjustified attack, Carr is the cause of Davis' death, but not a causal factor in his death. (See ibid., 164.)

Furthermore, if the attribution of wrongdoing to an omission rests on the omission being a causal factor in the harm, then such an attribution cannot be used (as in the deployment of the immorality condition) to determine when the omission was a causal factor in the harm without begging the question.

On the other hand, if the theory can establish the wrongness of Carr's refraining without establishing a causal relationship between Carr's refraining and Davis' death, then the whole discussion aimed at establishing that causal relation is unnecessary and unmotivated; and Gewirth's moral theory can no longer be viewed as focusing primarily on persons' actions and their roles as agents and recipients. (Ibid., 165)

Mack sums up his critique in the form of a "destructive dilemma."

Either Carr's duty to rescue Davis requires the independent establishment of a causal relation between Carr's omission and Davis's death or it does not. If it does, then some appeal must be made to some combination of deployment of the subjunctive and immorality conditions. . . . But arguments have been advanced against . . . these . . . . Furthermore, any use of the immorality condition begs the question of whether Carr, through his omission, wrongs Davis. On the other hand, if Carr's duty to rescue Davis does not require the independent establishment of a causal relation between Carr's omission and Davis's death, then the argument in the section on the duty to rescue is, at best, superfluous, and Gewirth cannot lay claim to the causal strategy as a means of securing a deontological character for his moral theory. (Ibid., 165–166)

Gewirth provides an extensive response to Mack. (See Gewirth 1984d, 233–241.) He begins by clarifying his use of what Mack calls "the immorality condition" (which Gewirth prefers to call "the moral relevance condition").

Mack's interpretation of Gewirth's use of this condition is (*a*) too expansive, in that Gewirth applies it only to omissions or inactions, not to positive actions, and (*b*) too restrictive, in that Gewirth does not hold that the causal status of an omission depends on its violating the PGC.

According to this condition, in determining whether an omission is a causal factor in some harm, the relation of the omission to the *PGC*'s precepts (whether as violating or fulfilling them) is to be considered (see [RM] 225). (Ibid., 234)

Two versions of the moral relevance condition must be distinguished:

1.   an epistemological version: the PGC helps us to ascertain when causal responsibility for an event (usually a harm) is to be attributed to a PPA on account of its omission to do something; and
2.   an ontological version: the very fact that Carr's omission violates the PGC is what makes it a (or the) cause of Davis' drowning.

Gewirth intends the moral relevance condition to be understood only in the epistemological version (though he confesses that this was not made as clear as it might have been in *Reason and Morality*. See Gewirth 1984d, 234).

The moral relevance condition is needed for omissions rather than for positive actions, because omissions generate *a problem of negativity* (an omission is not necessarily describable as something done), and *a problem of diffuseness* (we need to pick out who, if anyone, to blame for Davis' drowning, because it is true of everyone that they did not rescue Davis).

The problem of diffuseness is solved in the following way. The PGC (in consequence of the argument to the PGC) upholds positive rights and requires positive actions on the part of PPAs to prevent certain harms. By the argument to the PGC, the PGC specifies the conditions under which assistance is to be provided. Assistance is to be provided

1.   only when a duty correlative to a generic right is violated;
2.   only when the PPA requiring assistance cannot assist itself; and
3.   only by those who
      a. are in a position to provide assistance,
      b. have the ability to provide assistance, and
      c. can provide assistance without comparable cost to themselves. (See ibid., 235.)[20]

However, if these conditions for assigning moral responsibility are to provide any basis for blame, then it must be possible to characterize those who fulfill 3a–c, given 2, as violating their duty by an omission. For this to be the case, the problem of negativity must be solved.

The problem of negativity is solved in the following way. To assign causal responsibility, an omission must be an inaction, not just a nonaction. It must involve choosing to refrain from doing something that one is required to do, when doing this is in one's power, etc. Because PPAs are morally required to provide assistance under specified conditions, when these conditions are fulfilled, their failure to provide assistance is to be characterized as inaction (which has the positive element of action). Doing anything other than what one is required to do constitutes a violation of one's duty for which one is culpable (causally responsible). In relation to his duty, Carr, who does not do *nothing* (he lolls on the beach), does something that he ought not to do in the circumstances; for his lolling on the beach, when Davis is drowning, is incompatible with what he ought to be doing. (See ibid., 236.)

Gewirth provides the following responses to Mack's objections to his use of the "subjunctive" and "immorality" conditions.

Mack asks, generally, why at least some cases in which Carr's refraining does not obtain, yet Davis drowns, should not count as relevant counterevidence to the claim that Carr's refraining satisfies the subjunctive condition and, in particular, why a previously sufficient set of positive conditions loses causal sufficiency simply because someone appears with the ability to prevent the outcome for which these conditions were sufficient.

Gewirth replies that, in the particular circumstances, Carr's inactivity is necessary for Davis to drown. In the situation where Carr is present, the conditions sufficient for Davis to drown when Carr was absent are no longer sufficient. The complete set of circumstances has changed. If Carr had aided Davis, Davis would not have drowned, and this is enough to show that the previous sufficient conditions are not here sufficient. (See ibid., 237–238.)

Gewirth's position is neither *a* nor *b*, in Mack's attribution.

The subjunctive condition does indeed indicate when an omission is a causal factor in some harm, but the indication holds only when that condition is given its particularizing interpretation[21] and only when it is interpreted according to the specifications provided by the moral relevance condition in its epistemological version. (Ibid., 238–239)

According to Mack, Gewirth's use of the immorality condition

1.   makes causal truths dependent on moral duties, and these in turn dependent on the conditions of these duties;
2.   makes an action of drowning someone in self-defense not a causal factor in the drowning; and
3.   is subject to a vicious circularity. The reason why Carr's omission wrongs Davis is that it causes Davis to suffer harm, and the reason why it causes Davis to suffer harm is that it wrongs him.

However, 1 applies only on the ontological version of the moral relevance condition. The epistemological version does not make causal truths dependent on moral duties, but provides clues for ascertaining truths about the causal responsibility of inactive persons for certain harms. 2 ignores that the moral relevance condition applies to actions that fulfill the PGC as well as to those that violate the PGC, and that the theory of causal responsibility is concerned with omissions (or inactions), not with positive actions. As far as 3 is concerned, the latter half of the circle is true only on the ontological interpretation of the moral relevance condition.

The first reason is a *ratio essendi:* it is the fact that Carr's omission causes Davis to suffer harm . . . that essentially grounds or constitutes the wrongness of the omission. The second reason, on the other hand, is a *ratio cognoscendi:* the wrongness of Carr's omission, as determined by the *PGC,* provides a clue to ascertaining his causal role, in accordance with the moral context of the raising of questions about the ascription of causal responsibility for harms occasioned by omissions. But the wrongness of Carr's omission does not itself constitute that omission's being a causal factor in Davis's suffering harm. (Ibid., 240–241)

Because 3 fails, Mack's destructive dilemma collapses.

Gewirth, rather surprisingly, does not comment on Mack's general comments on the nature of the argument to the PGC. However, I consider that Mack is mistaken in the two central claims that form the basis of his critique, viz.,

1.   the discussion of the duty to rescue attempts to provide an independent account of negative causality, which is needed to characterize the "rights" established by the argument to the PGC as deontic; and
2.   if the argument can be characterized as deontological without such a separate account, then the discussion of the duty to rescue is superfluous and unmotivated.

Mack is mistaken in 1 because the argument to the PGC, as given in "The Argument for Positive Rights" above, establishes that PPAs have positive rights to their freedom and well-being, in a full *deontic* sense.

Given this, 2 is negated. There are two basic (and nonredundant) functions performed by the discussion of the duty to rescue.

The discussion of the duty to rescue is not part of the argument to the PGC, it is a discussion of the implications of the PGC for specific situations, an example being the Carr/Davis case. It illustrates how the PGC specifies duties and causal responsibility in such a case.

Some philosophers are hostile to the idea of positive rights precisely because this requires an account of negative causality. The discussion of the duty to rescue provides an opportunity to explain how the PGC provides such an account. The discussion of the duty to rescue provides an opportunity to answer some standard objections to the idea of positive rights. As Narveson himself allows (see #66.1), omissions can be characterized as actions, *if* those who are guilty of them are subject to rules that direct that they ought to do things incompatible with these omissions. By the argument to the PGC, PPAs are bound to grant positive rights to other PPAs. Thus, Carr, in intentionally refraining from rescuing Davis, is doing things that he ought not to do. There is nothing question-begging or circular in this (as Mack, Narveson, and Pilon all allege), unless the argument to the PGC (as prescribing positive rights) is invalid.[22]

The root source of all Mack's errors lies in his interpretation of the discussion of the duty to rescue as adding something to the argument to the PGC by way of the justification of positive rights. This interpretation is guided, in turn, by his interpretation of the argument to the PGC as being, in the absence of an independent theory of negative causation, a "nonaggregative consequentialism of 'rights'" that does not offer "moral side-constraints" (Mack 1984d, 151.) In effect, Mack is saying something similar to Christopher McMahon (1986), who sees the argument as generating "oughts of evaluation" rather than prescriptions of duties. (See #47.6.) There cannot be a full identity of positions here, because, if McMahon is right, the argument would not be able to get beyond Stage II to any moral (other-regarding) action-guiding prescriptions at all, whether positive or negative. Nevertheless, Mack seems to be saying something along these lines, at least in relation to the argument for positive rights. Were this correct, then an independent theory of negative causal responsibility would be necessary to justify the establishment of positive *deontic* rights, and it is difficult to see how this could be achieved. But it is not correct, for the basis for Stage II is the self-referring strict "ought," "I ought to pursue my freedom and well-being." This is a full deontic prescription, and the "oughts" and "rights" derived from it, whether negative or positive requirements, are deontic as well. The discussion of the duty to rescue offers an explanation of how the theory is a deontological one, but it does not purport to turn a hitherto nondeontological theory into a deontological one. The theory is already established as deontological in the basic argument to the PGC (whether as establishing "at least negative rights," or positive rights as well).

General Comments

In this chapter we have seen, principally, that the argument to the PGC is an argument for both negative and positive rights to freedom and well-being. Objections to the PGC, as establishing positive rights *for* its applications, mistakenly treat the argument *to* the PGC *either* as establishing, at best, negative rights only, thus interpreting Gewirth's discussion of the duty to rescue (which is part of his argument *from* the PGC, already a principle of positive rights) as an attempt to derive positive from negative rights via a question-begging theory of negative causal responsibility, *or* as establishing nondeontic positive and negative "rights," which requires the discussion of the duty to rescue to provide a derivation of positive deontic rights from positive nondeontic "rights" via a similarly question-begging theory of negative causal responsibility. However, once it is seen that the argument *to* the PGC establishes positive deontic rights, and that the necessary theory of negative causal responsibility is logically implicit in it, a non–question-begging answer is available to objections to positive rights that raise questions about the coherence of negative causal responsibility.

In relation to the argument to the PGC, as a principle of positive rights, it has been necessary to point out that

1. the criterion of rationality employed by the argument is not one of "prudence";
2. the ground of a PPA's rights-claims is not that it *has* freedom and well-being, but its categorical *need* for freedom and well-being; and
3. the argument to the PGC establishes the PGC as a deontological principle, not merely as a principle of what are desirable states of affairs.

In formulating specific objections, critics have not always paid sufficient attention to

1. the distinction between inaction and nonaction;
2. the possibility of a "deontological consequentialism," and the difference between this and a "utilitarian consequentialism";
3. Gewirth's distinction between "the generalizing tendency" and "the particularizing tendency" in formulating causal conditions;
4. the need for any general theory of rights to be a theory of prima facie rights; and
5. Gewirth's discussion of the criteria for resolving conflicts between rights-claims.

Possible confusions between rights to freedom and rights to non-interference (negative rights), on the one hand, and rights to well-being and rights to aid (positive rights), on the other, have been noted. There can be (and are) negative and positive rights to both freedom and well-being.

11 Conclusion

In Chapters 4 to 10 I have examined a very large number of objections. In this chapter, I shall summarize this discussion. With all criticisms in view, it is possible to form a general picture of the critical reaction to the argument, and this picture reveals that, despite lack of widespread agreement about what, in the final analysis, is wrong with the argument, there is a core line of criticism. If the questions raised along this line can be answered satisfactorily, and they are relatively limited in number, then *many* of the critics should be willing to accept that the argument is valid. Indeed, rebuttal of *one* claim that critics make should suffice to convince these critics that the argument is sound. Having presented this core line, and the central critical claim within it, I shall indicate, very briefly,[1] why I consider that the questions raised should be answered in favor of the argument.

Summary of the Discussion of Objections
Chapter 4

Chapter 4 considered objections to Stage I of the argument. Stage I attempts to establish that a PPA contradicts "I am a PPA" if it does not consider its freedom and well-being to be necessary goods. There are basically two grounds upon which Stage I has been challenged. Other objections have been stated, but these can be regarded as a function of either

1. denying that a PPA must consider its purposes to be good; and/or
2. denying that freedom and well-being are generically necessary conditions of agency.

1 and 2 are the basic challenges, because if a PPA must value its purposes, and needs its freedom and well-being in order to pursue/achieve any purposes whatsoever by its agency, then it is per-

fectly clear that a PPA must value its freedom and well-being for the sake of its purposes, whatever its purposes might be. This, however, must not be misunderstood: it is not equivalent to the claim that PPAs cannot value/pursue their own self-destruction, or that it is irrational for them to do so (#4). They may rationally do so, but only as a particular occurrent purpose. *As generic-dispositional capacities for agency,* PPAs must pursue their freedom and well-being even with the end of self-destruction in mind. Without their freedom and well-being as generic-dispositional capacities, they cannot pursue/achieve even their own self-destruction. It is as generic means for agency that PPAs must value their freedom and well-being whatever their purposes, which might also be expressed by saying that the value that PPAs must attach to their freedom and well-being is categorical instrumental value.

1 picks up on Gewirth's claim that PPAs (in having purposes that they are motivated to pursue) display a positive attitude towards (desire for) their purposes, which is equivalent to *judging* their purposes to be good (attaching a positive *value* to their purposes). To this it is objected, not so much that PPAs need not attach *moral* value to their purposes—for Gewirth makes it perfectly clear that he does not assume all judgments of value to be judgments of moral value—but that the fact that PPAs *desire* their purposes does not entail that they *value* their purposes. Critics have variously claimed that

a. it is possible for a PPA to desire/pursue a purpose "capriciously" (for no reason), implying the absence of a valuation of this purpose (either positive or negative);

b. it is possible for a PPA to desire/pursue a purpose under a "compulsion" it would rather be rid of, thereby implying its negative valuation of this purpose.

The response to this objection (#3) is that PPAs, by definition, do not just pursue purposes that they desire. They pursue purposes that they choose to pursue. This is incompatible with the idea of a capricious or compulsive desire. Those who behave capriciously, or under compulsion, are simply not acting as PPAs. It is possible, of course, that a PPA will choose to pursue X, yet consider that it ought not to pursue X. However, such a situation does not disprove that the PPA values X (or prove that Gewirth has an incoherent conception of valuation according to which a PPA can both value and disvalue X). Valuation is always relative to a criterion. The PPA who chooses to do what it considers it ought not to do (X), desires X for a reason, and chooses to be motivated by this reason, by the value that this reason attaches to X. In judging that it ought not to be motivated by this reason, it judges that it ought to disvalue X, according to some (superior) criterion it *avows*, but which it does not choose to follow. It thus values and disvalues X. But there is no contradiction here, for the valuing and disvaluing involved are relative to different criteria. All that such a possibility shows is that the PPA does not necessarily attach a *definitive* value to X; and Gewirth's position is not that PPAs necessarily attach definitive value to their purposes, but that they attach positive value to their purposes according to whatever criterion they choose to be motivated by.

To this it has been objected that this conception of being a PPA is arbitrary (#1 and #3), or that it presupposes that determinism is false (#2).

The reply to the charge of arbitrariness is that the argument is concerned with what purposes it is rational for a PPA to choose to pursue, and thus with what practical precepts it is rational for a PPA to choose to be guided by, and that Gewirth's conception of a PPA is uniquely suited to such an aim. If the addressees of practical precepts are not capable of choosing to pursue their purposes, then practical precepts (because "ought" implies "can") are not rationally directed at them. Thus, Gewirth's definition of a PPA is not arbitrary.

As far as determinism is concerned, Gewirth's conception of a PPA presupposes that determinism is false only if determinism implies that it is not possible to be a PPA (to choose purposes freely). At one level, it is to be pointed out that determinism is not proven. At another, it is the case, even if determinism is true *and* incompatible with the rationality of practical precepts, that this does not affect the logical relationship between claiming to be a PPA and the judgments one is committed to by virtue of such a claim.

It is important to appreciate that the thesis that PPAs necessarily value their purposes is essential to Gewirth's argument. This is because, without this thesis, although it will still be true that PPAs must value their freedom and well-being whatever purposes *they value* (if freedom and well-being are generic conditions of agency), it will not be true that PPAs must value their freedom and well-being *whatever their purposes*. For me to deny "My freedom and well-being are necessary goods" will not be for me to deny "I am a PPA." It will merely be to deny "I am a PPA who values my purposes." Since all the deontic judgments of Stages II and III are claimed to follow from the fact that I must regard my freedom and well-being as necessary goods, the claim that these are dialectically necessary will fail if it is not the case that PPAs necessarily value their purposes. Furthermore, without the dialectical necessity of the claims of Stage II, the argument for the sufficiency of agency (ASA) will not be applicable,

which is necessary for the internal application of the logical principle of universalizability (LPU) to effect the move from self-*regarding*
(prudential) to other-*regarding* (moral) judgments.

It has been objected (#5) that Gewirth equivocates between two
senses of a generic feature of agency—a necessary condition of
agency, and a defining condition of agency—in purporting to establish that PPAs must value their freedom and well-being by an analysis of the concept of agency, and that the argument relies on equivocations between various senses of "freedom" and "well-being."

I argued that there is no equivocation between Gewirth's uses of
"generic feature" in establishing this conclusion, and that suspicion
of one arises only if it is not seen that a PPA necessarily values its
purposes. Other allegations of equivocation rest on failures to attend to Gewirth's definitions of terms and the role assigned to different senses of "freedom" and "well-being" in the argument.

The second main objection to the dialectical necessity of "My freedom and well-being are necessary goods" is 2, the claim that there
are no generic conditions of agency, no universal, uniform conditions for the pursuit/achievement of a PPA's purposes, whatever
these might be.

The response to this is that it rests on interpreting generic-dispositional conditions as uniform *particular occurrent conditions*, rather
than as *second-order, abstract, capacities* for the pursuit/achievement
of particular occurrent purposes (#6).

To the extent that Gewirth's specification of the generic needs and
their relative importance is debatable, these are nevertheless objective questions. Furthermore, the general validity of the argument
does not depend on exact specification of the generic needs, only on
its being clear that there are some generic needs (#7).

Chapter 5

Chapter 5 examined three sets of objections to the argument. The
first set of objections (#8–#14) focuses on the claim that a PPA can
want/value/need its freedom and well-being without having a
right to them, and without even considering that it has a right to
them. The second set (#15–#22) interprets the argument as asserting
that PPAs cannot violate the PGC (in the sense that it is *logically
impossible* for them to do so), or that the PGC is a logically necessary
truth. The third set (#23 and #24), which derives from the first or
second set, claims that the argument illicitly derives "ought" from
"is," or that the argument is incompatible with the autonomy of
morality. The first set constitutes objections to Stage II specifically,
whereas the second and third sets are general objections to the argu-

ment as a whole. The latter sets are appropriately dealt with together with the first because

1.   the relationship between needs and the duties and rights of Stage II (within a PPA's internal point of view) is where any connection between "is" and "ought" is initially made;
2.   the status in philosophical logic of the deontic claims of Stage II is identical to that of the PGC; and
3.   any claim that it is logically impossible for a PPA to violate the PGC must apply equally to the deontic claims of Stage II.

FROM NEEDS TO RIGHTS?

It is a misinterpretation of the argument to allege that it derives "A has a right to X" from "A wants/values/needs X" (#8, #10–#12). The argument is that *only categorical or generic* needs are connected to rights, and the argument is dialectical, not assertoric. The argument is that a PPA, whatever its purposes, rationally must want/value the generic needs of its agency proactively, and consequently must claim a right to the generic needs. It is incorrect to allege that, if the argument is valid, then a PPA should claim rights to all its purposes. Deontic requirements are conatively independent. A PPA must value having the generic features whatever its particular occurrent purposes. It contradicts that it is a PPA if it does not value its freedom and well-being proactively. It does not necessarily contradict that it is a PPA if it has one particular occurrent purpose rather than another (#9).

The objection that a PPA *can* be opposed to interference with its freedom and well-being without considering that it has a right to its freedom and well-being (#13) is misdirected. What is relevant is whether a PPA rationally may realize (*a*) that it *must* be opposed to interference with its freedom and well-being (whatever its purposes), yet (*b*) not consider that it has a right to its freedom and well-being.

I argued (in "The Argument from Attitudinal Consistency") that "I do not have a right to my freedom and well-being" is not dialectically consistent with "I *must* be opposed to interference with my freedom and well-being (whatever my purposes)."

It has been objected (#14) that the fact, if it were a fact, that PPAs could not help valuing their freedom and well-being would not entail that they have a right to their freedom and well-being.

This is also misdirected. When Gewirth claims that PPAs necessarily value their freedom and well-being, he claims that they must value their freedom and well-being *if they are to be rational* (i.e., if they are not to contradict that they are PPAs). This objection gives a nondialectical interpretation of the argument, and its interpretation of "necessity" is a misattribution of "psychological necessity" for "rational necessity," which is incompatible with the definition of a PPA as a being capable of choosing its purposes.

GROUNDING MORALITY IN LOGIC

Gewirth argues that a PPA contradicts that it is a PPA if it does not accept the PGC, or if it violates the PGC in practice. This he sometimes expresses as "The PGC is logically necessary." He argues that, because *every* PPA logically must accept the PGC, the PGC can be expressed assertorically *for every PPA*.

It has been objected that the argument reduces morality to logic (#15).

But, for this to be so, the "ought" in "PPAs ought not to interfere with the freedom and well-being of their recipients" (the PGC) must be a logical "ought," and the negation of the PGC must be a contradiction in terms. However, the "ought" of the PGC itself is moral. It is the "ought" of "PPAs ought to accept the PGC" which is logical. For a PPA to deny the PGC is for it to contradict that it is a PPA, not for it to assert a proposition that is a contradiction in terms. "The PGC is logically necessary" is to be read as "It is logically necessary for a PPA to accept the PGC," not as "The PGC itself is an instance of the principle of noncontradiction or the law of identity." It does not follow from the analyticity of "PPAs ought to accept the PGC" that the PGC itself is analytic, nor that "PPAs ought to accept the PGC" is a linguistic stipulation (#20).

It has been objected that Gewirth attempts to derive the assertoric PGC from the dialectical necessity of the PGC (a claim that is presupposed by #15 and #20), and that he needs to do so in order to achieve his objective of refuting moral relativism, but that he does not do so validly (#18).

However, at no stage does Gewirth claim that the validity or truth of the PGC can be separated from its dialectical linkage to what PPAs must claim. An argument that Gewirth presents to show that the force of "I must accept the PGC" is practical as well as theoretical, is misinterpreted as an argument for the derivation of the assertoric PGC from the dialectically necessary espousal of the PGC. The assertoric statement of the PGC, which Gewirth effects, is for practical purposes only. Given the universality of its dialectical grounds, the PGC can be stated with assertoric effect to PPAs. Gewirth does not need to justify the assertoric PGC *tout court* to achieve his aims. Even if he has not shown that moral relativism is assertorically false, he has still shown that it is dialectically inconsistent for a PPA to espouse moral relativism.

It has been alleged (#19) that the argument rests on a "conative theory of truth" which makes desire or need, rather than "assertoric or probative evidence," the criterion of truth.

This objection rests on the false premise that the PGC is asserted as an assertoric truth *tout court,* and it fails to appreciate that the assertoric truth that the argument does derive ("PPAs logically ought to espouse the PGC") is, *within the relative standpoint of agency,* established on the basis of assertoric evidence and standard requirements of logical consistency. The most that Gewirth can be said to claim is that PPAs must treat the PGC as true, that the PGC is "true *relative to the purview of agency,"* that it is "true *for PPAs," which means that PPAs must employ the PGC as the premise for their thought and practice.*

Because the argument is essentially dialectical rather than assertoric, it is untrue that Stage II can be established only by showing that it is necessarily true that I have a right to my freedom and well-being (#22).

The objection (#16) that immoral actions cannot be inconsistent is misdirected. Gewirth holds that PPAs who violate the PGC imply that it is rationally permissible for them to do so. In doing so, they imply the judgment "It is not the case that I ought to respect the freedom and well-being of my recipients as well as of myself." This judgment contradicts the PGC, which it is dialectically necessary for PPAs to espouse.

Objections that the argument makes intellectual error solely responsible for moral error (#17), and that it renders the PGC a logically inviolable rule (thus no rule at all) (#21), rest on the mistaken assumption that it is logically *impossible* for PPAs/rational PPAs to violate the PGC (PPAs logically *can't* violate the PGC). The argument, however, is that it is logically *impermissible* for PPAs to violate the PGC (PPAs logically *may not* violate the PGC). PPAs who are rational, *in the sense* that they inevitably do what they rationally ought to do, cannot violate the PGC. But those who are rational, *in the sense* that they can appreciate what they rationally ought to do, can violate the PGC, even when they appreciate that they ought not to do so. It is PPAs who are rational in this latter sense to whom practical precepts, and the argument, are directed. The argument claims that, in violating the PGC, PPAs are acting irrationally; but it does not follow from this that, if they were rational PPAs (in the relevant sense), then they could not violate the PGC, so that only intellectual inadequacy can be the explanation of moral error.

DERIVING "OUGHT" FROM "IS"

Gewirth does not attempt, *assertorically,* to derive that PPAs have rights to their freedom and well-being from the fact that they are PPAs (or that they categorically need their freedom and well-being). However, he does claim, in Stage II, that I must consider that I have a right to my freedom and well-being, on pain of contradicting that I am a PPA. Furthermore, he claims that this entails that I must consider that I have a right to my freedom and well-being for the sufficient reason that I am a PPA. Within my internal viewpoint as a PPA, [I am a PPA → I have a right to my freedom and well-being] is a valid (required) inference. In effect, because what constitutes my being a PPA is my having purposes that I wish to fulfill, and I categorically need my freedom and well-being, the claim is that, given my proactive valuation of my purposes, I am required to infer that I have a right to my freedom and well-being from the fact that I categorically need my freedom and well-being. Thus, *within my internal viewpoint as a PPA,* "ought" is derived from "is." Given the universalization *of this inference,* located within my internal viewpoint, in Stage III, the "is-ought" inference [PPAs categorically need their freedom and well-being → PPAs have a right to their freedom and well-being] is held to be dialectically necessary within every PPA's internal viewpoint as a PPA. Gewirth claims to have derived "ought" from "is." If his argument is valid, then it is clearly the case that he has done so *dialectically* (within every PPA's internal viewpoint as a PPA), though not assertorically (#23).

It has been objected that Gewirth has not derived "ought" from "is," even if the argument that the PGC is dialectically necessary is valid. The conclusion of the argument is that PPAs must accept the PGC (which is descriptive), not the PGC itself (which is categorically normative). To treat the argument as a derivation of "ought" from "is" involves an illicit transformation of a descriptive (dialectical) conclusion to a prescriptive (assertoric) one (#23.1).

Critics who press this objection have variously attributed the illicit switch from a "descriptive track" to a "prescriptive" one to

1. the use that Gewirth makes of the LPU;
2. Gewirth's treating [I do X for purpose E → I regard E as good] as equivalent to [I do X for purpose E → E is good]; or
3. Gewirth's attempting to derive the assertoric truth of the PGC from the dialectical necessity of the PGC by the principle that "I ought to do what I logically must consider that I ought to do."

These objections are in error because they suppose that Gewirth attempts to derive the assertoric truth of the PGC from its dialectical necessity. However, the procedures/premises attributed in 1, 2, and 3 are not used to infer the assertoric truth of the PGC, because Gewirth does not hold that the PGC may be treated as an assertoric truth (except for practical purposes). The LPU is employed solely to effect the move from dialectically necessary prudential claims to dialectically necessary moral ones. Gewirth does not hold 2 at all— he holds, instead, [I do X for purpose E → I regard E as good] to be equivalent to [*From my viewpoint as a PPA*, (I do X for purpose E → E is good)]; and 3 is used only to argue that the dialectical necessity of the PGC has practical as well as theoretical import for PPAs. Gewirth's derivation is dialectical, the inference from "is" to "ought" held to be dialectically necessary, within the standpoint of PPAs, not assertoric. These objections also ignore the fact that unless [I categorically need my freedom and well-being → I have a right to my freedom and well-being] is a valid inference *within my internal viewpoint as a PPA*, which implies that the "is-ought gap" is closed *dialectically*, the LPU will not be able to effect Stage III, the inference to the *dialectical necessity* of the PGC.[2]

It has been claimed that Gewirth's account of the "normative structure of agency" does not make it rich enough to permit the PGC to be derived (even dialectically) (#23.2). Gewirth requires explicit "ought" premises to be implicit in the notion of a rational PPA to derive a commitment to rights. These are present, but Gewirth does not allow for them by analyzing valuation in terms of desire.

In reply, I argued that this criticism is either misdirected or question-begging. It is misdirected because Gewirth does not construe "good" in terms of "desire" as such, but in terms of the free choice of purposes. The necessary valuation of my *freedom and well-being* that follows from this, given my categorical need for freedom and well-being, is an "ought" premise implicit in the standpoint of my agency, because of my proactive valuation of my purposes. If the claim is that these elements are not sufficient, then I argued that various suggested "emendments" were (in one case) question-begging or (in another) unnecessarily strong (or even incoherent, depending on how they were to be interpreted).

It has been objected (#23.3) that for a PPA necessarily to have to value its freedom and well-being is a firm grounding of "ought" in "is," but that such a grounding is tantamount to saying that a PPA must value what it is (for I cannot be a PPA without my freedom and well-being). This, it is said, is implausible, or else takes the point out of morality.

However, a PPA only has to value being a PPA if it must value its freedom and well-being as an end for its own sake rather than merely in a categorically instrumental manner (and only the latter is the case). This does not trivialize morality, principally because valuation of my freedom and well-being is not for what I have achieved, but for what I intend to achieve.

The autonomy of morality is removed if morality is reduced to logic or to prudence. However, the argument does not reduce morality to logic, nor does it contend that it is prudent to be moral (#24).

Chapter 6

Chapter 6 examined objections that derive from one or another interpretation of the idea that rights-claims presuppose a social context. The following claims have been made:

1.   PPAs cannot be required to claim they have rights to their freedom and well-being, because they do not always have these rights—this being shown by the fact that, throughout history, PPAs have been denied these rights/PPAs have violated these rights-claims (#25).
2.   The claiming of a right to X is not an intelligible performance unless there is a "socially established set of rules," but the existence of such rules is historically contingent (#26).
3.   It is unintelligible to claim a right when there is no one around who can violate the right. PPAs sometimes lead solitary existences, divorced from all social intercourse, and in such settings are not required to consider that they have rights to their freedom and well-being (#27).

However, 1 is open to various interpretations. Possible interpretations rest on one or more of the following errors:

a.   employing a recognitional sense of right, rather than the normative one that is appropriate to the argument;
b.   failure to appreciate that what is at issue is not what it is logically possible for a PPA to do, but what it is logically permissible for a PPA to do; and/or
c.   failure to distinguish different senses of being a rational PPA.

2 rests either on employing a recognitional rather than the appropriate normative conception of a right, or upon the claim that societies have existed that lacked the concept of a right. The latter claim is not, however, backed by suitable evidence (indeed, there is plenty of evidence that points in the contrary direction), and, even if it were

true, such a fact would be irrelevant—for what is at issue is not whether PPAs have had the concept of a right, but whether they are rationally required to do so.

3 rests either on thinking that what is at issue is the performance of laying claim to a right, rather than considering that one has a right, and/or on ignoring that the essential interactive or transactional aspect of having a right is constituted by the logically possible existence of other interacting PPAs, not by their actual presence. To say that I have a right is to specify how PPAs ought to act when interacting with me, and this does not suppose that they are interacting with me.

Chapter 7

Chapter 7 dealt with objections that, by and large, can be related directly to the structure of argumentation for Stage II that I presented in Chapter 2.

The first major inference in my sequence for Stage II is the inference from (4) "My freedom and well-being are necessary goods" to (4c) "I have an instrumental prudential duty to pursue my freedom and well-being."

It has been objected to this (#28) that an adeonticist can satisfy (4) by pursuing its freedom and well-being without considering that it ought to do so.

This, however, ignores that it is a condition of a PPA's rationality that it pursue its freedom and well-being. Given its proactive valuation of its purposes (its conative normality), a PPA must see pursuit of its freedom and well-being as a strict rational requirement, as an (instrumental) duty or strict "ought."

However, it has been objected (#29) that, even if a rational conatively normal PPA must accept such a self-referring "ought" prescription, the assumption of conative normality violates the dialectically necessary method, because it is alleged that PPAs need not be conatively normal. This is mistaken, because "conative normality" simply refers to a PPA's proactive commitment to its purposes, and possession of this property is a necessary condition of being a PPA.

It has been alleged (#30) that the inference from (4) "My freedom and well-being are necessary goods" to (5) "I have a right to my freedom and well-being" relies on the false presumption that to deny (5) is to grant PPAO a right to interfere with my freedom and well-being (which requires me to want/permit PPAO to interfere with my freedom and well-being, and which does contradict [4]). The denial of (5), however, might only commit me to "It is neither permissible nor impermissible for PPAO to interfere with my freedom and well-being," which does not require me to want/permit PPAO to interfere with my freedom and well-being.

However, this "weak" denial is still inconsistent with the dialectical necessity of (4), for, by this necessity, I am required to assent to "I *must* have a (proactive) negative attitude to (i.e., oppose) interference with my freedom and well-being," whereas the suggested interpretation of the denial of (5) is compatible with my not having a negative attitude towards such interference. Thus, the inference from (4) to (5) does not rely on an unjustifiably limited interpretation of the denial of (5).

It has been claimed that a PPA's need for freedom and well-being provides *motivation* for it to secure its freedom and well-being, and for it to demand noninterference with its freedom and well-being; but it does not provide *justification* for either of these activities, or for the demand made (#31).

This objection is premised either on

1.   the view that a PPA only *may* engage in these activities, not on the view that a PPA *must* engage in these activities; or on
2.   the view that the only kind of justification there can be is moral justification; or on
3.   the view that deontic claims, by their very nature, can only be "justified" if this justification is from *everyone's* point of view.

Regarding 1: These are activities that I cannot fail to engage in without contradicting "I am a PPA." I am, thus, justified on a criterion of rationality that takes precedence over all others. Regarding 2: All justifications are relative to criteria, acceptance of the justifications being dependent on acceptance of the criteria. Not all criteria are moral. The criterion here is my interests, in a sense that I cannot eschew as a PPA. Regarding 3: Deontic claims must, like any others, be justifiable from just one point of view, for the notion of justification from every point of view depends on the coherence of the notion of justification for each.

It has been objected (#32) that the instrumental nature of a PPA's valuation of its freedom and well-being means that a PPA must only claim rights if it claims rights to its particular occurrent purposes.

To be relevant, this objection must contend that even *categorical* instrumental valuation of my freedom and well-being is insufficient to ground a rights-claim to my freedom and well-being. However, as I argued in Chapter 2, this is so far from being the case that it is only because my dialectically necessary valuation of my freedom and well-being is (categorically) instrumental that the rights I must claim are waivable.

In *Reason and Morality*, Gewirth argues that "universal ethical egoism"—"Every PPA ought to act in its self-interest," which implies (4c) "I ought to pursue my freedom and well-being" (and [4c'] "PPAO ought to pursue its freedom and well-being"), but denies (4d) "PPAO ought not to interfere with my freedom and well-being" (because, in line with [4c'], PPAO might need to interfere with my freedom and well-being)—is either inconsistent or not a univocal *practical* doctrine. Thus, the existence of "universal ethical egoism" cannot be a refutation of the dialectical necessity of (4d) on the basis of the dialectical necessity of (4c). If (4c) and (4c') are stated with the same illocutionary force, then they are contradictory. For me to *prescribe* (4c') is to prescribe, in some circumstances, that PPAO ought to interfere with my freedom and well-being; and this entails that I ought not to interfere with PPAO interfering with my freedom and well-being, which entails the denial of (4c). (4c) and (4c') can be stated together only if one of these is a prescription endorsed by the speaker, whereas the other is not, or if neither is action-guiding from the speaker's point of view. This, however, is not "universal ethical egoism."

To this it has been objected (#33) that "ethical egoism" is consistent because it is not universally prescriptive in the way in which Gewirth portrays it. "Ethical egoism" states that the rational thing for me to do is to pursue my own self-interest, and the rational thing for PPAO to do is to pursue its self-interest. There is no equivocation of illocutionary force here either, because, in "ethical egoism," "A ought to do X" always means the same thing—"The most reasonable thing for A to do is what is in its own self-interest."

I argued that this restatement of "ethical egoism" does not rescue what Gewirth calls "universal ethical egoism" from inconsistency. It is true that a PPA can say "I ought (on the criterion of *my* self-interest) to pursue my own freedom and well-being, and PPAO ought (on the criterion of *its* self-interest) to interfere with my freedom and well-being" without contradiction. But this is not the position that Gewirth calls "universal ethical egoism," and Gewirth does not claim that it is self-contradictory. The critic who presses this objection, in fact, interprets Gewirth's claim that "universal ethical egoism" is inconsistent as the claim that what Gewirth calls "amoralism" is inconsistent. His defense of amoralism is that the amoralist does not endorse PPAO's self-interest (take favorable account of PPAO's self-interest in determining how it [the amoralist] ought to act). When an amoralist says that PPAs ought to pursue their own self-interest, it is saying that A's interests give A reasons to act, and B's interests give B reason to act; but this involves no endorsement by the amoralist of A's and B's actions in their own self-interest. A contradiction arises only if the amoralist advocates that what ought to be done is what is in its self-interest, *and* what is in the interests of others. But this begs the question against amoralism, for the amoralist does not hold that what is in the interests of others is relevant to what it (personally speaking) considers ought to be done. *All of this is correct.* But Gewirth does not claim that "amoralism" is *internally* inconsistent. He does, indeed, claim that it is *dialectically* inconsistent for a PPA to espouse amoralism, but his argument for this is not his argument against "universal ethical egoism." The objection to the claim that "universal ethical egoism" issues incompatible directives, in brief, errs in treating Stage II generally as Gewirth's argument against amoralism, when Gewirth does not claim to demonstrate that amoralism is dialectically inconsistent until Stage III. He claims, in Stage II, only that *even an amoralist* must hold, *on the criterion of its (the amoralist's) own interest,* that PPAO ought not to interfere with its (the amoralist's) freedom and well-being; and the critic who presses this objection, in fact, agrees that this is the case. His real disagreement with Gewirth has to be over whether this conclusion is a sufficient platform for Stage III to be effected by purely logical universalization, but this issue has no bearing on Gewirth's contention that "universal ethical egoism" is internally inconsistent.

It has been objected (#34.1) that the inference from (4c) to (4d) cannot be effected by the principle that "ought" implies "can," on the grounds that, on this principle, it does not follow from "I ought to do X" that "I ought to be free to do X," but only that "I can do X"; and it is alleged that (4d) can only be established (by "ought implies can") by supposing that PPAs take favorable account of the interests of others—which is question-begging.

I argued that this objection fails to appreciate that what is in question is not whether I ought to do X, but whether, given that I ought to do X (and therefore can, if not interfered with, do X), I ought not to be interfered with in doing X. In order to infer (4d) from (4c) it is not necessary to suppose that PPAs take favorable account of the interests of others. It is only necessary to keep the criterion of both "oughts" constant. The inference from (4c) to (4d) only requires a question-begging assumption if (4d) is interpreted as a moral "ought," or an other-directing "ought" from PPAO's viewpoint. To do this is to confuse the arguments for Stages II and III. (4d) is an other-directed "ought" from my viewpoint.

It has been objected (#34.2) that (4c) entails (4d) by "ought implies can" only where the conception of "life" involved in (4d) is dialectically necessary. It is claimed that the sort of "life" that it is dialectically necessary for PPAs to value varies according their contingent "life plans." "Radical amoralists" have a conception of "a worthwhile life" that does not permit (4d) to be derived from (4c) by the principle, correlative to "ought implies can," "I ought to do X → I ought to have the necessary means to X," because "radical amoralists" do not have to value a life of noninterference with their purposes by others.

In response, I argued that this objection, by trying to relativize the concept of "a generic good," misconstrues the dialectically necessary method as an argument from a PPA's SPR for its purposes, rather than as one from what is necessarily connected with its claim to be a PPA, and that considerations it adduces validly show no more than that a PPA can waive rights that it must think it has to waive (correlative to its having to regard [4d] as justified).

The most widely canvassed objection to Stage II consists in conceding that it might very well be the case that a PPA, on the basis of (4)/(4c), must consider that it ought to have its freedom and well-being, that its freedom and well-being ought not to be interfered with, *in some sense*. However, it is contended that this is not equivalent to a PPA's having to consider that PPAO has *an obligation* not to interfere with its (PPA's) freedom and well-being, and that it is not correlative to a PPA's having to consider that it has a right to its freedom and well-being. The general reason given for this is that, although the fact that I categorically need my freedom and well-being gives me a (categorical) reason to want my freedom and well-being (a [categorical] reason why I ought to have my freedom and well-being), it does not necessarily give PPAO a reason to want me to have my freedom and well-being, because PPAO does not categorically need my freedom and well-being for its purposes (#35).

Now, when Gewirth claims that I must consider that PPAO has an obligation not to interfere with my freedom and well-being, he claims that *I* must consider that PPAO strictly ought not to interfere with my freedom and well-being *on the criterion of my interests* (in consistency with my having to espouse [4c]). He does not claim that *PPAO must consider* on its criteria that it strictly ought not to interfere with my freedom and well-being. The objection would, thus, appear to be irrelevant.

However, the objection is usually accompanied by other claims that purport to make it relevant. One or more of the following claims are made:

1.   It is straightforwardly nonsense, or unintelligible, to assert that PPAO has an obligation not to interfere with my freedom and well-being on the criterion of my interests, or that I have a right on the criterion of my interests. To say that X has an

       obligation to do Y is to say that X has a categorical reason to do Y.

2.   "PPAO ought not, on the criterion of my interests, to interfere with my freedom and well-being" is not an action-guiding ought, but a mere "ought of evaluation," expressing what I must want to be the case, or consider to be desirable (from my point of view).

3.   The demand that PPAO not interfere with my freedom and well-being, unless expressed in a context in which PPAO has a reason not to interfere with my freedom and well-being, is idealistic, and not necessarily prudent.

4.   Even if it is intelligible to assert that PPAO has "an obligation" not to interfere with my freedom and well-being, or that I have "a right" to my freedom and well-being, relative to my interests, such a claim will not universalize, purely *logically*, to "PPAO has a right to its freedom and well-being" or to "I have an obligation not to interfere with PPAO's freedom and well-being," from my viewpoint. This universalization, by purely logical means, presupposes that PPAO necessarily has a reason (from its viewpoint) not to interfere with my freedom and well-being.

1 is incorrect. All prescriptions are relative to criteria. With my interests as the criterion, PPAO has an obligation not to interfere with my freedom and well-being. Granted, PPAO might not accept this criterion. But this does not mean that the criterion does not formally validate that PPAO ought not to interfere with my freedom and well-being. It does. And I must consider that PPAO ought not to interfere with my freedom and well-being because I must accept this criterion. Formally, the question of "oughts" and "rights" is not a question of what criteria I or PPA accept, but of what various criteria formally justify. To hold that it is a question of acceptance is to say that no one can direct any "ought" (even a moral one) *intelligibly* at anyone who does not accept the criterion of this "ought." But, even if PPAO does not accept that it ought not to interfere with my freedom and well-being, because this is in my interests, PPAO is perfectly capable of understanding that, on the criterion of my interests, it ought not to interfere with my interests, and that it would be required to think that it ought not to interfere with my freedom and well-being if it accepted this criterion. PPAO can also understand that my categorical need for freedom and well-being is a reason for me for PPAO not to interfere with my freedom and well-being, because PPAO's categorical need for freedom and well-being is a rea-

son for PPAO for me not to interfere with PPAO's freedom and well-being.

2 is also incorrect. (4d) is a statement of what I must think PPAO has reason to do on (relative to) the criterion of my interests, even if not a statement of what I must think PPAO has reason to do on the criterion of PPAO's interests. It is an action-guiding "ought" from my viewpoint, even if not an action-guiding "ought" from PPAO's viewpoint.

3 attempts to alter the terms of the argument. Rationality is to measured by "prudence," what is in my particular occurrent interests, not by what I must accept if I am not to contradict "I am a PPA." Alternatively, or in addition, it attempts to make questions of moral epistemology into questions of practical politics, or to switch the focus of the argument from moral epistemology to practical politics.

4 represents the bottom line on these claims, in that even if critics who press 1—3 accept the responses, they will still press 4. 4 implicates objections to Stage III in objections to Stage II, and the former are discussed in Chapter 8 (most specifically under #47).

It has been objected (#36) that rights judgments cannot be derived from judgments of good, because the latter are not even necessary for rights judgments.

However, even if the antecedent is correct (and Gewirth's contention that it is false is not discussed), no reasons are given for inferring the consequent. Furthermore, the objection rests on judgments of necessary goods being of a wholly different kind from judgments of rights. The concept of a necessary good is, however, a deontic concept, not merely a judgment of value, because of the proactive valuation of its purposes that characterizes being a PPA.

Related to this, it has been claimed (#37) that judgments of necessary goods, unlike judgments of rights, are not universalizable.

If this is correct, then the argument must be invalid. If the argument is valid, we must be able to switch the order of logical operations in moving from (4) to the PGC. We must be able to universalize (4c) to a moral claim, and only then invoke "ought implies can," and the logical correlativity of other-referring strict "oughts" and claim rights, to get to the PGC. I argued that this can, in fact, be done.

Related to the consideration expressed as #35.3 above, it has been claimed (#38) that it would be imprudent for me to claim a right to my freedom and well-being if this would entail (by universalization) that I must concede PPAO a right to its freedom and well-being against my interests. Thus, I cannot be required to consider that I have a right to my freedom and well-being on a *prudential* basis.

This objection, however, ignores the fact that the concept of "prudential," as it is used in Gewirth's argument, refers to what is necessarily related to being a PPA, not to particular occurrent purposes ("prudence").

It has been claimed (#39) that Stage II fails because it is not dialectically necessary to claim more than a right to try to obtain freedom and well-being. This is compatible with my advocacy of a competitive situation in which I do not claim a right to have my freedom and well-being.

This objection ignores the fact that, in being generic conditions of agency, my freedom and *basic* well-being are necessary preconditions of my even attempting to act (which includes trying to secure my freedom and well-being). Furthermore, my freedom and generic well-being generally are preconditions of successful agency, and there is no point in trying to secure my freedom and well-being if I am deprived of the preconditions of success. Thus, in claiming a right to try to secure my freedom and well-being, I must claim a right to have my freedom and well-being.

Chapter 8

This chapter dealt with objections to Stage III, and specifically with objections to the step by which Gewirth infers that a PPA, having to claim a right to its freedom and well-being on prudential grounds, must, by purely logical universalization, grant this right to PPAO.

It has been objected (#40) that the LPU cannot compel a PPA to grant the rights it claims for itself to other PPAs. For this to be the case, being a PPA must be the condition that a PPA needs to fulfill in order to have the rights (from its dialectically necessary viewpoint). However, the LPU does not establish any criterion of "relevant similarity."

This objection is correct *only insofar* as it is true that the LPU does not *itself* determine the criterion of relevant similarity for its application. However, the objection ignores the fact that Gewirth appeals to the ASA to move from the conclusion of Stage II, "Because I am a PPA, I must claim the generic rights for myself," to "I must claim 'I have the generic rights, because I am a PPA.'" By the ASA, "being a PPA" is established as the criterion of relevant similarity for the purposes of universalization.

The validity of the ASA has been denied implicitly (#41). It has been claimed that a PPA must, indeed, claim that it has the generic rights, on pain of self-contradiction, but that this does not entail that a PPA must make its being a PPA (or the fact that it categorically needs its freedom and well-being for its purposes) the justification for the rights it must claim. In other words, it is claimed that a PPA can satisfy the requirements of Stage II if it claims that it has the generic rights for any reason whatsoever.

This objection, however, fails to consider the ASA explicitly, and I argued that to reject the ASA requires the logical principle that $[(p \ \& \ q) \rightarrow r] \rightarrow [p \rightarrow (q \rightarrow r)]$ to be rejected.

It has been objected (#42) that elitists need not grant the generic rights to "inferior" PPAs, because there is nothing self-contradictory about the elitist's principle "All and only superior PPAs have the generic rights." This principle does not entail the PGC (PCC), which is a denial of it.

Gewirth, of course, does not argue that the elitist's principle is self-contradictory. He argues that the elitist denies that it is a PPA by espousing the elitist's principle.

To this it has been responded that

1.   the elitist acts not as a PPA, but as a superior PPA, so what follows from its acting as a PPA does not matter;

2.   the argument for the dialectical necessity of the PGC rests on the principle "Only what is universally and necessarily connected with its subject matter is ultimately relevant to evaluation of that subject matter"; but, as is seen from an "aesthetics analogy," this cannot, without vicious circularity, distinguish good from bad examples of a subject matter.

1 is, however, relevant only if Gewirth purports to deduce the PGC from a PPA's practical precepts, rather than a PPA's rationally required commitment to the PGC from its being a PPA. On the latter basis, "superior" PPAs are still PPAs. 2 misconstrues the argument as being about judgments of value rather than about deontic claims, and the "counterexample" that it deploys as a model for its contentions does not capture the features of an argument from a PPA's internal viewpoint.

It has been recognized (#43) that the argument rests on the premise that being a PPA is the criterion of relevant similarity for the granting of the generic rights, but it is objected that this is a question-begging assumption.

This, however, simply ignores the fact that such a proposition is not a starting premise, but one justified by the argument for Stage II together with the ASA.

It has been contended (#44) that, if "superior" PPAs could best provide for the purposes of all PPAs, then it would not be necessary for PPAs to consider their freedom and well-being to be necessary goods, thus undercutting the basis for the ASA and Gewirth's argument for the dialectical inconsistency of claiming superior rights on contingent characteristics.

This objection fails because the ASA and Gewirth's argument against superior rights only fail if it is a *necessary truth* that "superior" PPAs will best cater for the needs of all PPAs. This is true only if rendered trivial by a stipulation that "superior PPA" means "PPA who will best cater for the needs of all PPAs."

It has been objected (#45) that, because the theory attributes rights to PPAs on the grounds of their "rationality," it must grant superior rights to "more rational" PPAs. One critic (see #45.3) claims that the theory grants rights only to those who accept Gewirth's argument.

In general, these objections rest on misconstrual of the "rational properties" according to which the theory grants rights. Fundamentally, it is to a being who has reasons for action (who chooses its purposes) that the theory grants rights. Other senses in which "rationality" may be predicated of a PPA are irrelevant to the distribution of rights, except insofar as the designated properties bear on the capacity to do things for reasons at all.

It has been objected (#46) that Stage III rests on the premise "'Every X by virtue of property y claims Z' entails 'Every X by virtue of property y has Z,'" which is false.

Stage III, however, employs no such premise. The premises it does employ are

1.   "'Every X by virtue of property y *must claim* Z' entails 'Every X *must claim* that it has Z by virtue of having y,'" which is the form of the ASA; and
2.   "If *an* X by virtue of property y *has* Z, then *every* X by virtue of property y has Z," which is the LPU itself.

The objection's false attribution derives from a misguided interpretation of Stage III as attempting to derive the assertoric truth of the PGC from the dialectically necessary conclusion that every PPA must claim a right to its freedom and well-being.

The most frequent objection to Stage III (#47), which is also frequently linked to #35 (the most frequent objection to Stage II), is that, from the dialectical necessity of (4d) "PPAO ought not to interfere with my freedom and well-being"/(5) "I have a right to my freedom and well-being" (where these are claims validated on the criterion of my own interests), application of the LPU does not require me to grant the generic rights to PPAO. It requires only that all PPAs must consider that they have prudential rights (rights on the criteria of their own respective interests) to their own freedom and well-being. Only if Stage II establishes that PPAO has a categorical reason not to interfere with my freedom and well-being on the criterion of PPAO's interests (i.e., only if [4d] is established as other-directing [prescribing *for* PPAO] as well as other-directed [prescribing *to* PPAO]) can logical universalization require PPAs to grant the generic rights to PPAO. Since it is false that PPAO must consider, on the grounds of its own interests, that it ought not to interfere with my freedom and well-being, the moral conclusion follows only if it is assumed that PPAO must take favorable account of my interests (which ascribes a moral point of view to PPAO, and thus, implicitly, to all PPAs). Thus Stage III rests on an equivocation between moral and prudential rights. Insofar as Stage II is valid (establishing a prudential conclusion), Stage III does not follow logically. Insofar as Stage III is valid, Stage II is invalid (requiring a question-begging moral assumption to be made).

The primary response to this objection is that it applies the LPU only to a PPA's *act of claiming* that it has the generic rights ("judgmental universalization," or external application of the LPU). It ignores the fact that the LPU must also be applied to the *inference* that characterizes a PPA's dialectically necessary viewpoint, viz., "I am a PPA → I have a right to my freedom and well-being." This universalization ("possessive universalization," or internal application of the LPU) requires every PPA to accept the inference "X is a PPA → X has a right to its freedom and well-being." For possessive universalization to be applicable, it does not have to be supposed that PPAO has any reason to accept that it ought not to interfere with my freedom and well-being. It is sufficient that (4d)/(5) be other-directed (rather than other-directing).

Associated with this general objection it has been claimed that (4d), if validly derived, is not even other-directed. It is merely an "ought of evaluation," a judgment of desirability, from my point of view, which is in no sense action-guiding.

This is false. (4d) states what PPAO ought to do, according to the criterion of my interests. Anyone who accepts this criterion must accept that PPAO ought not to interfere with my freedom and well-being. This "ought" is action-guiding from the viewpoint of this criterion. This is my dialectically necessary criterion. Therefore, it is action-guiding from my viewpoint, even if not from PPAO's. Since the argument is conducted strictly within my viewpoint, what PPAO might think about it is irrelevant.

Another associated objection is that if the proposition arrived at by logical universalization is moral, then the proposition that is universalized must logically be an instance of a moral proposition.

However, although it is true that the proposition "I have a right to my freedom and well-being" *can* be derived from "Every PPA has a right to its freedom and well-being," it does not follow that the latter can be derived from the former only by assuming that the latter is true. The former is, in fact, derived without *assuming* that the latter is true. The fact that the latter is then derived from the former by universalization shows that the latter is *logically presupposed* by me in claiming to be a PPA. But the nature of the demonstration of this presupposition is such that it is independent of assuming what is shown to be presupposed.

It has been objected (#48) that "ought implies can" does not permit the move from "the prudential" to "the moral."

This objection misconstrues the role of this principle in the argument. It is used to derive my commitment to an other-directed "ought" from a self-directed "ought." It is not used to establish an other-directing "ought." The move from "the prudential" to "the moral" is effected by internal application of the LPU.

It has been objected (#49) that the move from "the prudential" to "the moral" cannot be effected by the correlativity of strict "oughts" and rights; and it has been claimed that it is superfluous to characterize the claims of Stage II as prudential. They are validly established as moral already.

However, the move from "the prudential" to "the moral" is effected by the LPU, not by the principle of correlativity. The contention that the deontic claims of Stage II are already (validly) moral rests on defining "the moral" in terms of what a PPA necessarily must will, not, as Gewirth does, in terms of what is validated by an other-regarding criterion. "The moral" can be defined in this way, but doing so simply requires us to redescribe the task for Stage III (the transition from "the prudential" to "the moral" [Gewirth]) as the transition from "the non–other-regarding moral" to "the other-regarding moral." It does not matter how we define "morality." What matters is whether the PGC is dialectically necessary. Given the features of the PGC, and the specific problems of justification that Gewirth addresses, Gewirth's terminology is more appropriate.

In general, I would say that failure to attend to "internal" application of the LPU is the main reason for objections to Stage III, and that this failure arises from inattention to the very existence of the ASA. However, it has been claimed (#50) that, although Stage III *is* validly derived by internal application of the LPU, this application requires the supposition that a PPA values agency in general, not only its own agency. This, however, is question-begging. This question-begging assumption is made by having universalization operate from the fact that I am a member of the class of beings who value their own purposes, not from valuation of my purposes specifically.

As I interpret this objection, it is an objection neither to the internal application of the LPU nor to the ASA *as such*. What it claims is that the ASA cannot establish "being a PPA" (being a member of the class of beings who value their own purposes proactively) as the criterion of relevant similarity for the purpose of universalization. This is because I must claim the generic rights for myself not because I am a member of the class of beings who value *their own* purposes proactively, but because I am a member of the class of beings who value *my* purposes proactively. Thus, the ASA establishes only that I must hold "I have the generic rights, because I am a member of the class of beings who value my purposes proactively." Internal application of the LPU to this does not require me to grant the generic rights to anyone other than myself. In order for the ASA to establish that I must hold "I have the generic rights, because I am a member of the class of beings who value their own purposes," it must be assumed that PPAs not only value their own agency, but the agency of all PPAs.

I argued that this is not so. If I must hold "I have the generic rights, because I am a member of the class of beings who value my own purposes," then *I* must hold "I have the generic rights, because I am a member of the class of beings who value *their own* purposes." This is, primarily, because I cannot be a member of the class of beings who value my purposes without being a member of the class of beings who value their own purposes. For me to deny that I have the generic rights is for me to deny not only that I am *that* (unique) PPA who necessarily values my purposes, but also that I am a PPA. Thus, if the ASA is valid, then "being a PPA" is established as the criterion of relevant similarity without supposing that I value any agency other than my own.

Chapter 9

Chapter 9 considered various objections that are not objections to specific steps or stages of the argument, and that were not dealt with in connection with such objections (or that have features that were not dealt with in this connection).

It has been objected (#51) that Gewirth's definition of morality, which requires moral reasons to be other-regarding and to override nonmoral reasons, begs the question against various practical viewpoints, and self-interest positions in particular.

This is not so. Gewirth's definition of morality is not used to settle the question of what practical position it is rational to adopt; it merely specifies what sort of position he argues to be dialectically necessary.

The argument might be viewed as coercive, in that it attempts to impose a viewpoint against the viewpoints that PPAs might wish to espouse, and thus attempts to restrict their freedom of choice (#52).

On the contrary, although the argument entails that PPAs rationally must adopt certain positions, that it is not open for them to espouse any position incompatible with the PGC and yet remain rational, it cannot force PPAs to act rationally. More importantly, if the argument is valid, then those who understand the implications of free choice will see that they can only be free by choosing to act in accordance with the PGC. It is the notion of being a *voluntary* purposive agent that yields rational commitment to the PGC.

It might be argued that the failure of previous attempts to prove a supreme moral principle counts against Gewirth's argument, and it has been claimed (#53) that the (purported) failure of Gewirth's argument is strong inductive evidence for the untenability of Gewirth's project (the provision of apodictic foundations for morality), implying that we need not take such a project seriously anymore.

However, Gewirth's argument is not invalid. Even if it were, it is dogmatic to claim that its failure is evidence that his project cannot succeed. As evidence for such a conclusion it presupposes that received wisdom should never be questioned. The only arguments for the untenability of Gewirth's project that are in order are those that attempt to prove its dialectical or assertoric incoherence. The only arguments against Gewirth's specific argument that merit any consideration are those that allege logical fallacies and errors, or arbitrariness in its premises.

The argument does not, as has been claimed (#54), presuppose that PPAs are all equally powerless, that PPAs are rational and no more—which they cannot be. This would only be the case if the argument attempts to derive commitment to the PGC from PPAs' contingent characteristics. It does not do so. Its foundation is in the generic features of PPAs, and all PPAs, whatever their contingent differences, share these generic features. The PGC is not solely directed at, and binding upon, PPAs whose contingent characteristics are so similar that it would be in their particular occurrent interest to bind themselves by the PGC. It is binding upon PPAs regardless of their contingent differences, for the PGC is derived from the necessary features of agency, which all PPAs possess. For PPAs to deny the PGC is for them to deny that they are PPAs, and hence that they are PPAs with whatever contingent characteristics they possess.

There are no proper grounds for alleging (#55) that the argument commits the "epistemic fallacy," that it implies that the existence of rights depends on their demonstration.

It has been claimed (#56) that neutral foundations for morality are impossible, and that justification can only take the form of *ad hominem* discursive critique.

However, the first claim is valid only on the assumption that Gewirth reasons from the contingent practical viewpoints of PPAs, and that no necessary starting point is available. This is untrue. PPAs must value their freedom and well-being because they are PPAs, and required consistency with this judgment is capable of ruling out various contingent positions as categorically irrational. This also has the implication that justification need not be only *ad hominem*.

The claim (#57) that an epistemology of rights is unnecessary, because establishing rights is a matter of practical politics rather than epistemological argument, misportrays Gewirth's project as practical politics and/or operates with a recognitional rather than a normative conception of rights.

It has been contended (#58) that Gewirth's claim that the PGC is true by correspondence with the generic features is problematic, and anyway unnecessary, as the PGC is shown to be dialectically necessary by conceptual analysis (if the argument is valid).

It is not entirely clear whether this is an objection to the notion of moral truth as such, or an objection to the notion of moral truth by correspondence specifically. However, Gewirth does not claim that the PGC *itself* is a truth—by correspondence or anything else. What is claimed to be true is that it is dialectically necessary for PPAs to espouse the PGC. This is established by conceptual analysis, but there is still point in saying that it is true by virtue of correspondence, because it is the fact that a PPA's freedom and well-being are generic conditions of its agency that constitutes the material reason why a PPA must espouse the PGC.

Conversely, it has been claimed (#59) that the demonstration of the dialectical necessity of the PGC requires an analysis of "good" that would also enable the PGC to be derived assertorically.

I argued, however, that Gewirth's concept of valuation is not agent-relative in a way that makes it invalid to derive the dialectical necessity of the PGC. It is agent-relative in a different way. This does not permit the PGC to be derived as an assertoric truth independent of the standpoint of agency. Any analysis that permits this is question-begging.

It has been claimed (#60) that the dialectically necessary method, if not redundant, is unsound, because it relies on deriving that a PPA must claim a right to its freedom and well-being from the fact that a PPA must will having its freedom and well-being. But if it is sound, then it must be redundant.

This "dilemma" vanishes once it is appreciated that there is, in fact, no logical gap between a PPA's necessarily valuing its freedom and well-being proactively and its considering that it has a right to its freedom and well-being (as established by the argument from attitudinal consistency [see #13]).

It might be objected (#61) that, even if the PGC is dialectically necessary on Gewirth's criterion of deductive and inductive rationality, this does not establish the PGC as dialectically apodictic, because there are alternative logics that are incompatible with the principles that characterize Gewirth's rationality criterion.

I expressed my view that, in relation to the specific principles to which Gewirth appeals, this is untenable: these principles are "laws of thought." However, even if this view is mistaken, the principles Gewirth relies on are so deeply entrenched in our thinking that it is well-nigh impossible to imagine what giving them up would involve. If Gewirth has established the dialectical necessity of the PGC in terms of these principles, then he has still provided morality with the strongest possible justification.

Chapter 10

Gewirth claims that his argument to the PGC establishes the PGC as a principle of positive as well as negative rights. I presented the argument for positive rights in a form parallel to my presentation (in Chapter 2) of the argument to "at least" negative rights. PPAs must claim positive rights to their freedom and well-being, because they need help to secure their freedom and well-being (when they cannot assist themselves) as much as they need noninterference with their freedom and well-being; and the prudential claim to positive rights is subject to the same universalization procedures as the prudential claim to negative rights. According to the PGC, PPAs have positive duties to assist PPAO in securing its freedom and well-being, when they have the ability to do so, when PPAO cannot assist itself, and when such assistance does not involve comparable costs (in terms of the forfeiture of rights) for PPA.

It has been objected (#62) that even if the argument for negative rights can be made to work, the argument for positive rights is on a much less sure footing. This is because it is less likely to be in my particular occurrent interests for me to grant you positive rights than negative rights.

This objection misconstrues the prudential aspect of the argu-

ment as indicating that the argument is an attempt to justify morality on the grounds of prudence (PPAs' particular occurrent interests). However, the prudential aspect refers to generic features, the
valuation of which is necessarily connected with being a PPA, so
that what is "prudentially required" is something that is logically
required by "I am a PPA." Positive rights must (logically) be claimed
for myself and granted to other PPAs (on the basis of my valuing my
freedom and well-being as necessary goods), whether or not claiming and conceding them is in my particular occurrent interests.

Some critics claim that a theory that grants positive as well as
negative rights to freedom and well-being is incoherent, because a
PPA cannot retain its right to freedom while conceding PPAO a right
to its well-being (#63).

However, it is a mistake to equate "rights to freedom" with "negative rights," "rights to well-being" with "positive rights." There
can be positive (aid) and negative (noninterference) rights to both
freedom and well-being. These critics, in fact, suppose that rights
cannot be prima facie, and, in effect, advocate a "pure theory of
unlimited liberty." The notion of universal rights to unlimited liberty is, however, incoherent, because I cannot grant PPAO even negative rights without imposing duties on myself, and thus (even according to these critics) restrictions on my negative right to freedom
(which, by their reasoning, disqualifies this as a right).

A critic who appreciates this claims that the difficulty with positive rights is that no prima facie qualifications can be stated non-
arbitrarily and unambiguously for positive as against negative
rights.

This objection, however, does not attend to Gewirth's criterion of
"degrees of necessity," and to other considerations for adjudicating
conflicting rights-claims that are necessarily built into the argument
to the PGC.

One critic, who considers that Gewirth's argument for negative
rights is valid (#64), claims that rights may only be claimed to what
is integral to a PPA's action. A PPA claims rights to its freedom and
well-being because they are its property. This means that it cannot
claim positive rights, because it does not own the freedom and well-
being of others; and, since in order to claim rights it must already
have its freedom and well-being, it does not need to claim that others must give it freedom and well-being.

This is a serious distortion of the argument. A PPA is not required
to consider that it has a right to its freedom and well-being because
it *has* its freedom and well-being *in its agency,* but because it categorically *needs* its freedom and well-being *for its prospective agency.* Furthermore, if having freedom and well-being means that I do not

need to claim a right to assistance when needed, then it means that I do not need to claim a right to noninterference either.

This same critic contends (#65) that the claim that positive duties to aid are subject to qualification (that aid does not incur comparable costs for the rescuer) is incompatible with a deontological theory. This objection ignores Gewirth's distinction between "deontological consequentialism" (in which rights are weighed against rights, according to the objective criterion of degrees of necessity for agency) and "utilitarian consequentialism" (in which "costs and benefits" are determined by the subjective preferences of PPAs, as determined by their particular occurrent purposes).

It has been alleged (#66) that Gewirth attempts to derive the dialectical necessity of positive rights from the dialectical necessity of negative rights by a theory of negative causality (according to which failure to aid a PPA in distress is to cause harm to the PPA). It is objected that omissions can only be construed as actions (inactions, rather than nonactions) by relating them to rules prescribing positive action in the circumstances in which omissions occur. Without positive rights being established, omissions cannot be construed as causes of harm, and Gewirth's derivation of positive rights from negative rights by a thesis of negative causality is viciously circular or question-begging.

However, Gewirth does not derive positive rights from negative rights. His argument for positive rights is parallel to his argument for negative rights. This objection treats Gewirth's discussion of the duty to rescue as part of the argument for the PGC's being a principle of positive rights (the argument to the PGC, thus far, only having established negative rights). Instead, the discussion of the duty to rescue is an application of the PGC, which is already established as a principle of both positive and negative rights. This discussion does not appeal to a theory of negative causality to establish the dialectical necessity of positive rights. It employs the PGC as a principle of positive rights to explain how omissions can be construed as causes of harms. The general purpose of this discussion is to exemplify one of the uses of the PGC in specifying rights and duties in concrete situations.

One critic perceives that, at one level at least, Gewirth's argument for positive rights is parallel to his argument for negative rights. He does not portray the discussion of the duty to rescue as an attempted derivation of positive rights from negative rights. However, he claims that the discussion of the duty to rescue is either superfluous, and Gewirth's theory is not deontological, or else its role is to establish Gewirth's theory as a deontological theory (the argument to the PGC having established only what outcomes PPAs must consider to be good, rather than what actions they must consider to be required or prohibited). A theory of causality (both negative and positive, which is seen to be the task of the discussion of the duty to rescue) is required to portray the theory as deontological (rather than as merely a "nonaggregative consequentialism of rights," which does not offer "moral side-constraints"). However, such a theory of causality, which requires the immorality of an action or inaction to be a condition of causal responsibility, is untenable and question-begging. It is question-begging, because it requires the theory to be established as deontological in order to assign causal responsibility; but it requires causal responsibility to be assigned in order to establish a deontological character for the theory.

This objection is also falsely premised. The argument to the PGC establishes the PGC as a deontological principle prior to the discussion of the duty to rescue (because the "oughts" in the argument are deontic, not merely "oughts of evaluation"). Thus, the discussion of causality in "The Duty to Rescue" is not designed to transform an otherwise nondeontological theory into a deontological one. This discussion is not superfluous. It functions to explain how the PGC, as a principle of positive rights, enables omissions to be characterized as causes of harms. It shows how the argument to the PGC enables a general objection to positive rights, that omissions are not actions, to be rejected. The objection is also mistaken in treating the theory of causal responsibility as applying to commissions as well as to omissions. Furthermore, it treats the theory as making immorality an ontological condition of causal responsibility, whereas the theory treats immorality only as an epistemological condition for the attribution of causal responsibility to omissions.

The Key Issues

If we ignore definite misinterpretations of the argument (e.g., failure to appreciate its dialectical character, or construing it as a dialectically contingent argument of some kind) and leave to one side objections to positive rights, then a general picture emerges.

Most critics are prepared to accept that a PPA must consider its freedom and well-being to be necessary goods. Stage I, in fact, only poses two issues.

(A)   Do PPAs have to value their purposes, not necessarily morally or definitively, but relative to the criteria that motivate them to pursue their purposes?

(B)   Are there any generic-dispositional conditions of agency?

If (A) and (B) are answered affirmatively, then Stage I must be valid.

It is uncontroversial that (4) "My freedom and well-being are necessary goods" commits me to

(4a)   I must want my freedom and well-being, whatever my purposes, as instrumental to my purposes.

It is also generally accepted that this requires me to accept

(4c)   I categorically ought to pursue my freedom and well-being as instrumental to my purposes (abbreviated SRO).

It is from this point that most critics begin to display serious disagreements with the argument. All who go along with the argument thus far, agree that a PPA must want its freedom and well-being (as generic capacities for action) not to be interfered with. Furthermore, almost all are prepared to accept that there is *a sense* in which a PPA must consider that it ought to have its freedom and well-being (that PPAO ought not to interfere with its freedom and well-being). Gewirth, however, claims that a PPA must consider that PPAO *has an obligation* not to interfere with its (PPA's) freedom and well-being ([4d]), correlative to which a PPA must consider that it has a *right* to its freedom and well-being ([5]).

Gewirth analyzes "A considers that B has an obligation to do X" as "On criteria that A accepts, B strictly ought to do X." (4d)/(5) are equivalent, or correlative, to "*From my viewpoint* (the point of view of my pursuit of my purposes), PPAO strictly ought not to interfere with my freedom and well-being."

So conceived, the derivation of (4d) from (4c) raises the following issue:

(C)   Does "I ought to do X, according to criterion Z" entail "I ought to be free to do X, according to criterion Z"? This may be expressed as "Does 'I ought to do X, according to criterion Z' entail 'I ought to have the necessary means to do X, according to criterion Z'?"

However, even if (C) is answered affirmatively, many critics are not willing to accept that (4d), so derived, is equivalent to "I must consider that PPAO has an obligation not to interfere with my freedom and well-being." They claim that "B has an obligation to do X" is to be analyzed as "There is a categorical reason for B to do X," and that "I must consider that PPAO has an obligation not to interfere with my freedom and well-being" is to be analyzed as

(4d*) I must consider that, *from PPAO's viewpoint*, PPAO strictly ought not to interfere with my freedom and well-being.

Their reasoning appears to be that deontic claims are action-guiding; they set requirements for others in transactions. (4d), they say, is not necessarily action-guiding, because it provides no reason, necessarily, for PPAO not to interfere with my freedom and well-being. Associated with this, it is sometimes said that (4d) is merely an "ought of evaluation," a statement of what is desirable from my point of view. The general issue raised by this is

(D)   Is it intelligible for me to hold that PPAO is bound to do X, even though PPAO does not accept any criteria according to which it is bound to do X?

An important subsidiary question is

(E)   Is (4d), as validly derived from (4c), merely an "ought of evaluation"?

Critics have, of course, not discussed my elaboration of what I term Gewirth's "argument from attitudinal consistency" (see #13). Supposing that they accept that there is at least a sense of "I must claim a right to my freedom and well-being" in which this argument is valid, I imagine that they might claim that there is, indeed, no gap between "I must want my freedom and well-being not to be interfered with" and "I must consider that I have a right to freedom and well-being" *in some nondeontic sense of "rights."*

Critics often write as though they believe that Gewirth thinks he can derive (4d*) from (4c). Though they deny that he can do so without begging the question (by attributing a moral viewpoint to PPAO, and thus to all PPAs), they generally seem to be prepared to accept that he can derive (4d), *in the sense* of an "ought" that expresses what "ought to be the case *from my viewpoint."*

Now, Gewirth claims to derive "I must consider that I ought not to interfere with PPAO's freedom and well-being" from (4d), thus interpreted, not from (4d*), by purely *logical* universalization. If he can do this, then, since "I ought not to interfere with the freedom and well-being of PPAO" will be shown to be valid according to criteria I must accept, it will be action-guiding from the addressee's point of view, and thus (according to the critics) a statement of obligation, even if (4d) is not, *provided that (4d) is not merely an "ought of evaluation."* Thus, the following issue is critical:

(F)   Does the dialectical necessity of "From my viewpoint,

PPAO ought not to interfere with my freedom and well-being" require me to assent, by logical universalization, to "From my viewpoint, I ought not to interfere with PPAO's freedom and well-being"?

Correlative to (F) is what I regard as the central objection to the argument. This is that

the dialectical necessity of (4d) does not require me to grant, by purely logical universalization, that I ought not to interfere with PPAO's freedom and well-being, *unless* it is assumed that PPAs necessarily take favorable account of the interests of others in determining what they ought to do. To assume that they do is to assume that PPAs are committed to the "moral point of view," which is question-begging.

Supposing that critics believe that Gewirth can show that (4c) "I ought to pursue my freedom and well-being" entails (4d) "From my viewpoint, PPAO ought not to interfere with my freedom and well-being" (≡ [5] "From my viewpoint, I have a right to my freedom and well-being"), they will not accept that this entails (by logical universalization)

(*)   From my viewpoint, I ought not to interfere with PPAO's freedom and well-being (≡ (9) From my viewpoint, PPAO has a right to its freedom and well-being).

They generally believe that logical universalization, operating on (5), can only establish

(5*)   From PPAO's viewpoint, PPAO has a right to its freedom and well-being,

and they point out that the right in (5) is validated on my interests, the right in (5*) on PPAO's interests. To get from (5*) to (*), they allege, and hence from (5) to (*), by logical universalization, requires the assumption that I take favorable account of PPAO's interests. To assume that this is so is to assume that I adopt a moral point of view, and this is question-begging.

Correlative to this claim, critics contend that if Stage II can establish (4d*) "From PPAO's viewpoint, PPAO ought not to interfere with my freedom and well-being" (≡ "From PPAO's viewpoint, I have a right to my freedom and well-being"), *on the grounds of (4c)* (on the grounds that I categorically need my freedom and well-being), *then* (*) could be established by logical universalization. For, *if* PPAO must consider that I have a right to freedom and well-being, because this is in my interests, *then* I must consider that PPAO has a right to its freedom and well-being, because this is in PPAO's interests. However, (4d*) cannot be inferred from (4c) without assuming that PPAO (and, therefore, all PPAs) espouse a moral point of view, which is, again, question-begging.

For these critics, the only question, therefore, is *where* the question is begged. Those who think that the question is begged in Stage II portray Gewirth as attempting to derive (4d*) from (4c) by "ought implies can" (see Kalin 1984, #33 and #35.3, and Nielsen 1984, #48), or as attempting to get from (4d) to "PPAO must consider that I have a right to my freedom and well-being" by use of the principle of the correlativity of strict "oughts" and claim rights (see Singer 1985, #49).

This objection rests critically on the claim that Gewirth cannot infer (*) from (5) by purely logical universalization. That is to say, it rests on a *negative* answer being given to the question raised by issue (F). If an affirmative answer can be given to this question, then the charge of equivocation collapses.

It is, therefore, of great significance that these critics ignore the actual procedures Gewirth employs in effecting Stage III. Gewirth reasons, by his ASA, that if I must *claim a "right"* to my freedom and well-being, *because* I am a PPA, I must claim "I *have a 'right'* to my freedom and well-being, *because* I am a PPA." Internal application of the LPU (possessive universalization—universalization of the inference internal to my viewpoint) then requires me to assent to "PPAO has a 'right' to its freedom and well-being, because it is a PPA."

This raises two issues, the validity of possessive universalization as such not being a serious issue. If the questions raised by these issues are answered affirmatively, then most critics should be prepared to accept the argument. These issues are

(G)   Is the ASA valid?

(H)   If the ASA is formally valid, then does it establish "being a PPA" as the criterion of relevant similarity for the purpose of universalization? The question here is whether I am required to claim a right to my freedom and well-being by virtue of being a PPA, rather than by virtue of being that PPA who necessarily values my purposes.

Although all these issues merit attention, it is important to note that there is a way of sidestepping, at least partially, the complications introduced by (D)–(F). If this argument is logically valid, then it must be valid to apply the ASA and possessive universalization to (4c) (SRO) in order to yield PPAORO: "I must consider that PPAO ought to pursue its freedom and well-being," where PPAORO is an "ought" that I *prescribe* to PPAO, a moral "ought" involving my endorsement of PPAO's interests. It can then be argued that I must prescribe that PPAO ought to be free to pursue its freedom and well-being. Since this involves PPAO's having its freedom and well-being, I must hold that I ought not to interfere with PPAO's freedom and well-being. To some extent, this also sidesteps issue (C). For there can be no question that I must consider that PPAO ought to have the means to do X if I prescribe that PPAO ought to do X.

In order for this to be valid, SRO must be validated, *relative to my dialectically necessary criterion,* as the state of affairs that *impersonally* strictly ought to be/is necessarily good. My dialectically necessary criterion must not validate SRO as *directed* only to me. In other words, although only those who accept my criterion must *prescribe* SRO, those who do accept my criterion must prescribe SRO. *According to my criterion,* SRO represents what "ought to be" *in-itself.* Those who accept my criterion must consider that what SRO requires is the state of affairs that ought to be in-itself.

In order for this not to be misunderstood, however, it is necessary to make some distinctions.

Given that I must claim (4c), if the ASA is valid then I must hold [I am a PPA → SRO]. [I am a PPA → SRO] could be represented as

1.   an assertoric inference. As such, it would be alleged that it simply is the case that the fact that I am a PPA entails SRO, that SRO is valid *in-itself simpliciter;*
2.   an inference that is valid impersonally *on a criterion.* This means that *on a criterion,* SRO (if validated) is validated as the state of affairs that ought to exist *in-itself;* from which it will follow that, *on this criterion,* all who can do something to secure the state of affairs prescribed by SRO ought to do so; or
3.   an inference that is subjectively valid on a criterion, one that is directed, with action-guiding implications, *on a criterion,* only to me.

The required universalization of SRO requires the dialectically necessary method to operate with 2. In particular (as 1 is obviously incompatible with the dialectically necessary method), 3 must be an untenable position. I, therefore, regard the following as perhaps the single most important issue in the argument:

(I)   Do criteria validate their prescriptions impersonally?

To deny that they do seems to involve one of two positions:

1.   holding that "I consider E to be good" to be equivalent to "From my viewpoint, I regard E as good," but not equivalent

to "From my viewpoint 'E is good'";

2.   holding that what a criterion requires depends on acceptance of the criterion.

I contend that all of the questions raised by the issues, here identified, are to be answered in favor of the argument.

(A) is to be answered *affirmatively* because PPAs *choose* their purposes. Negative answers to (A) ignore this feature of the argument. (See #3.)

(B) is to be answered *affirmatively.* Negative answers depend upon interpreting "generic conditions of agency" as "particular occurrent conditions of agency that are universal," rather than as "second-order capacities for purpose pursuit and achievement." (See #6.)

(C) is to be answered *affirmatively,* and is not often questioned. (But see #34.) My main reason for upholding this is that to give a negative answer to it is to hold that prescriptions are not validated impersonally *on* criteria. (See [I] below.)

(D) is to be answered *affirmatively.* To answer it negatively is to hold that it is unintelligible to address prescriptions to those who do not assent to their criteria. (See, e.g., #35.2 and #35.10.)

(E) is to be answered *negatively.* (4d) is an action-guiding "ought" from my point of view, even if not from PPAO's. It is true that to hold that A has an obligation to do X is to hold that there is a categorical reason why A ought to do X. But this reason need not be A's reason. It can be mine. (4d) is derived from (4c), *which is action-guiding* for me from my point of view. (4d) represents how, according to me, PPAO ought to act, in consistency with (4c). (See, especially, #47.6.) Because a PPA's "desires" are proactive, the argument from attitudinal consistency, if valid, establishes that I must claim a deontic right to my freedom and well-being.

(F) is to be answered *affirmatively.* Those who give a negative answer almost invariably fail to attend to the universalization procedure's being "possessive" rather than "judgmental." (See #47 generally.) To my mind, the clearest statements of the central objection associated with this issue are provided by R. M. Hare (1984), #35.1 and #47.4, and Gilbert Harman (1983), #47.5. The most detailed statement is provided by Christopher McMahon (1986), #35.10 and #47.6.

(G) is to be answered *affirmatively.* Although the validity of the ASA has been implicitly denied (see, especially, #41), it has only been addressed explicitly by one critic (see #44). It seems to me that the only way that the ASA can be denied is by denying $[(p \& q) \rightarrow r] \rightarrow [p \rightarrow (q \rightarrow r)]$.

(H) is to be answered *affirmatively*. Although I reason from my valuation of my purposes, I cannot make valuation of my purposes the property by virtue of which I possess a right to freedom and well-being, within my dialectically necessary viewpoint. I possess this property by virtue of being a PPA. I deny that I am a PPA if I do not consider that I have a right to freedom and well-being. By the ASA, I am required to make being a PPA the criterion of relevant similarity for the purpose of universalization, even if I reason from valuation of my purposes, and do not value the purposes of others. (See #50.)

(I) is to be answered *affirmatively*. Various critics hint that they might want to answer this negatively. (See, e.g., Allen 1982a, #23.1.2; Kalin 1984, #33 and #35.3; and Christopher McMahon 1986; see Chapter 8, note 31.)

Allen holds position 1 in response to (I). Since he thinks that the argument is valid, this is an inconsistent position for him to espouse. This position is to be rejected because it involves an infinite regress, which implies that to judge X is good, is to judge to judge X is good, etc.

Kalin and McMahon suggest that Gewirth does not hold an agent-relative view of "good." Baldly stated, this is false. Of the three interpretations of [I am a PPA → SRO], which I distinguished, Gewirth holds 2, which is an agent-relative view of judgments of good/"ought." They are mistaken if they attribute 1 to Gewirth, or the view that PPAs are committed to a common good. Furthermore, it is not entirely clear that they themselves hold 3 rather than 2. If agent-relativity of judgments is to damage the argument, then it must be held that 3 is a tenable position.[3] Inasmuch as Kalin or McMahon appear to hold 3, they appear to hold position 2 in response to (I). This is to be rejected, most basically, because it entails that the logical relationship between premises and a conclusion depends on the acceptance of the premises. On such a position it is impossible to know what a criterion requires without accepting it. This makes the whole idea of choosing criteria absurd. (It is for this reason that negative answers to [C] and [D] are also to be rejected.)

Given the importance of the validity of an SRO universalization, it is surprising that this has not been an explicit issue in the debate. Gewirth barely hints at such a universalization (see #47.4). Only Alasdair MacIntyre has raised an objection that draws attention explicitly to this issue. (See #37.) His objection is, however, unelaborated and couched in terms of universalizing judgments of necessary good, which he does not construe as self-referring deontic judgments.

All in all, my judgment is that, unless (G) and (I) are answered negatively, the argument must be valid. I do not see how they can be answered negatively, though, no doubt, critics will come up with suggestions. In consequence, I must conclude that the argument is valid.

Conclusion

Concluding his critique of Gewirth, Kai Nielsen says,

All bad fellows, it is sad to note, need not be irrational. (Nielsen 1984, 83)

However, having examined the objections that critics have brought against the argument, I find no good grounds for such dejection. On the contrary, Nielsen should be happy to note that, all things thus far considered, it has well and truly been demonstrated that it is irrational to act immorally: that PPAs contradict that they are PPAs if they do not guide their conduct by the PGC. It *is* logically necessary for PPAs to treat the PGC as the supreme principle of practical reasonableness. Gewirth has shown that Kant was right to proclaim a unity between theoretical and practical reason: the deductive and inductive principles of theoretical reason do have practical effect for PPAs. By his *dialectically* necessary procedure, Gewirth has shown how to derive "ought" (dialectically) from "is"; and the dialectically *necessary* nature of his argument has shown how the authoritative, substantive, and distributive questions of moral philosophy are to be answered in a way that is neither question-begging nor merely contingently *ad hominem.*

At the very least, I am confident that no critics have, thus far, managed to demonstrate any fatal flaw in Gewirth's reasoning. If there is such a flaw, then it has yet to be revealed. Much criticism of Gewirth derives from misinterpretation of his argument and from inattention to its details. I have tried to represent the logical structure of the argument in a way that, I hope, will make it much more difficult to misrepresent it, by making it clear what logical operations it employs, and what philosophical issues these raise. These issues, I contend, are to be resolved in favor of the argument. However, even if this is contested, focusing on these issues will, I hope, convince philosophers that, far from being merely a brave (but eccentric and fundamentally misguided) thesis, Gewirth's ethical rationalism is at least as tenable and well-founded a position as any on the foundations of ethics. It is, indeed, the best theory on this subject that has yet appeared.

Notes

Chapter 1: Introduction

1. I shall use the abbreviation RM for *Reason and Morality* (Gewirth 1978a) when referencing quotations and discussions.

2. Those who do (or intend to do) things voluntarily for a purpose they have freely chosen (purposive agents), and those who have the occurrent capacity to do so, which they have some disposition to exercise (prospective purposive agents).

3. A "strong" or "claim" right to do X is correlative to a duty on the part of other PPAs at least not to interfere with the doing of X by the right-holder against its uncoerced will.

4. This principle (which is also known as "the law of contradiction") states that a proposition and its denial cannot both be true of the same set of circumstances. Gewirth's project is to demonstrate the unity between theoretical and practical reason (the thesis that theoretical reason has practical effect) which Kant pressed in his *Critique of Practical Reason.*

5. For example, R. S. Peters 1966, A. Phillips-Griffiths 1967, and Thomas Nagel 1970. (See A. J. Watt 1975.)

6. I am persuaded that this assumption is warranted particularly by Martin Hollis (1977).

7. This, of course, is a defining feature of Weberian sociology as well as being central to H. L. A. Hart's insistence on the centrality of "the internal point of view." (See Hart 1961.) It finds its place in modern philosophical analyses of action as the thesis that the description of an action must be in terms of the reason for which it is performed.

8. In *Law as a Moral Judgment* (Beyleveld and Brownsword 1986), "natural law theory" was defined as any view that asserts that there is a necessary conceptual connection between law and morality (which I call legal idealism here). In more traditional usage, natural law theory additionally holds that there are moral principles that can be justified objectively by reason; and I follow this usage here.

Gewirth distinguishes his theory from "natural law theory" (see, e.g., Gewirth 1984a), whereas I view it as an example of such a theory. To some extent, there is no disagreement here, for different definitions of "natural law theory" are in play. Gewirth treats "natural law theory" as a stance that holds that moral principles can be derived assertorically from facts of human nature, whereas his position is that moral principles are to be derived dialectically from the concept of agency. Given my rather different definition of "natural law theory," however, Gewirth's theory falls within it. Other articles in which Gewirth discusses natural law theory are Gewirth 1984f and 1989. Gewirth 1967b is also of interest in this connection.

9. Which is the central contention of Beyleveld and Brownsword 1986.

10. *Reason and Morality* contains a sequence of argument that purports to establish the PGC as dialectically necessary within any PPA's internal point of view (argument *to* the PGC), and arguments applying the PGC to the resolution of familiar moral dilemmas (argument *from* the PGC). In this book I concern myself exclusively with the argument to the PGC. Subsequent to *Reason and Morality,* Gewirth has written a number of articles applying the PGC: 1979b, 1980d, 1983b, 1984e, 1985d, 1986b, 1986c, 1986d, 1986e, 1987a, 1987b, 1988b, 1990a, 1990b. For applications prior to *Reason and Morality,* see 1970c, 1970d, 1971c, 1974c, and 1975.

11. The revival of interest in objective morality is generally in utilitarian or contractarian terms, the most significant contributions being by Rawls (1971), Gauthier (1986), and Parfit (1984). Intuitionism is widely canvassed (see, e.g., Finnis 1980), and "moral point of view" theories are quite popular (see, e.g., Hare 1981, and Frankena 1980a). Habermas (1979 and in other writings) adopts an objectivist approach which, although not as severely rationalistic as Gewirth's approach, is closer to Gewirth's method than most others. (Gewirth and Habermas are compared by Phillips [1986] and White [1982].) By "moral objectivism" I mean any position that claims it is more rational to espouse some moral positions than others. The "objectivity" canvassed in these different approaches varies somewhat in both meaning and scope.

12. Gewirth's major replies to critics of *Reason and Morality* are contained in Gewirth 1980a and 1980b (to Bond 1980a and 1980b); 1981b (to Brandt 1981); 1982d (to Ben-Zeev 1982); 1982e (to Regis 1981); 1984d (to Adams 1984, Bambrough 1984, Singer 1984, Raphael 1984, Nielsen 1984, Hare 1984, Hudson 1984, Kalin 1984, Narveson 1984, Den Uyl and Machan 1984, Mack 1984, and Hill 1984); 1985a and 1985e (to MacIntyre 1981 and 1985, respectively); 1985b (to Singer 1985); 1985c (to Husak 1984); 1988a (to Williams 1985); and 1988c (to McMahon 1986). Brief comments on Held 1977, 1979 and 1985, and Haksar 1979 are to be found, respectively, in Gewirth 1982b, 37–38, 1985d, and 1982d. Subsequent to *Reason and Morality,* Gewirth has written a number of articles that summarize his argument to the PGC. The most important of these are Gewirth 1979a (which has been translated into Swedish), 1981b, and 1984b. (1990c has been translated into German.) Useful commentary on, and elaboration of, specific points are also contained in Gewirth 1978b, 1979c, 1980c, 1982c, 1982g, 1983a, 1984a, 1984f, and 1989. Of related interest are Gewirth 1986e and 1986f. Gewirth 1979a has been criticized by Morris (1981), Friedman (1981), and Golding (1981). Gewirth replies to these critics in 1982f. Gewirth 1984b has been criticized by Danto (1984), to whom Gewirth replies in 1984c. Gewirth 1988e is a general discussion of the "ethnocentric" objection (see Chapter 6), but does not address specific critics. Before *Reason and Morality* Gewirth wrote a number of articles developing the argument to the PGC: 1967a, 1969, 1970a, 1971a, 1971b, 1972, 1974a. And Gewirth 1974b is of related interest. Gewirth replies to criticisms of 1967a by

Fotion (1968) and Lycan (1969) in Gewirth 1970b. He replies to criticisms of 1974a by Grunebaum (1976), Veatch (1976), and Versenyi (1976) in Gewirth 1976.

13. Gewirth has not responded to the following articles: Geels 1971; Davies 1975; Den Uyl 1975; Simon 1975; Cohen 1979; Paul 1979; Pilon 1979a and 1979b; Narveson 1980; Lomasky 1981; Allen 1982a and 1982b; O'Meara 1982; White 1982; Seay 1983; Husak 1985; Heslep 1986; Loughran 1986; Allen 1987; Scheuermann 1987; Stohs 1988; and Paske 1989. He has not replied to the following reviews/review articles: Allen 1978; Collins 1979; Green 1979; Narveson 1979; Roberts 1979; Schumaker 1979; Schwartz 1979; Veatch 1979; Adams 1980; Mahowald 1980; Trigg 1980; Brooks 1981; Kelso 1982; Feldman 1983; and Lomasky 1986. He has not commented on critical remarks to be found in French 1979; Machan 1980; Okin 1981; Harman 1983; Bedau 1984; Fishkin 1984; Gamwell 1984; Golding 1984; Lomasky 1984; Wong 1984; Ewin 1987; Sterba 1987; Gould 1988; Pollock 1988; Arrington 1989; Barry 1989; Bittner 1989; Heslep 1989; Machan 1989; Puolimatka 1989; and Reiman 1990. He has not replied to four reviews of Gewirth 1982b that are relevant to the argument to the PGC: Overvold 1983; Waldron 1983; MacCormick 1984; and Pollis 1984. The criticisms to which Gewirth has not replied (in my opinion) differ widely in their importance, and Gewirth's replies to other critics will suffice (at least implicitly) as replies to some of these. I comment on all of these because much can be learned from examining the errors of critics, and I do not think that it is sound intellectual practice to exclude pieces from consideration on the unsupported judgment that they are "of poor quality" (especially when one is trying to establish an argument as a proof).

14. This statement must not be exaggerated. Although *most* commentators consider that there is *some* fatal flaw in the argument, this judgment is by no means universal. For example, apart from my own dissenting opinion (shared by Roger Brownsword in Beyleveld and Brownsword 1986), Derek L. Phillips states, "In my view, Gewirth has provided all that is required in the way of a rational justification for the rights to freedom and well-being" (Phillips 1986, 114); and James F. Hill declares, "I am in agreement with the major parts of Gewirth's moral theory, and believe that he has discovered the correct ground for making valid claims of moral right" (Hill 1984, 181). Lord Lloyd of Hampstead and M. D. A. Freeman consider that "[t]he force of Gewirth's logic cannot be gainsaid. . . . Critiques of it hitherto are not very convincing" (Lloyd and Freeman 1985, 440). Although they disagree with Gewirth's claim to have derived "ought" from "is," Paul Allen III (1982a), Gary Seay (1983), and Mark D. Stohs (1988) all contend that Gewirth has shown that it is dialectically necessary for PPAs to accept the PGC. Roger Pilon (1979a, 1979b) considers that the argument is a valid derivation of negative rights to freedom, and finds it unsuccessful only as an argument for positive rights.

Furthermore, the picture is complicated considerably by an appreciation that there is no *overwhelming* consensus among critics about what precisely is wrong with the argument. Indeed, my impression is that, with the exception of two steps in the argument, a majority opinion will be found *in favor* of each step in the argument. The two steps on which there appears to be a majority opinion *against* the argument are the step from the dialectical necessity of "I ought to pursue my freedom and well-being" to that of "Others ought not to interfere with my freedom and well-being" (the key inference in Stage II), and the step from the dialectical necessity of "I have a right to my freedom and well-being" to that of "Others have a right to their freedom and well-being" (the key inference of Stage III). Even here, however, detailed analysis reveals disagreements. There are many who are prepared to accept that there are senses of "ought" and "rights" in which both these steps are valid *individually*. Insofar as there is a majority core criticism, it is that there are no senses of these terms in which both of these steps are valid *simultaneously*. Although I shall endeavor to treat every criticism strictly on its own merits, I shall make special efforts to explain why this "core criticism" is mistaken.

15. We, for the most part, simply presented Gewirth's argument in some detail and, apart from dealing with some key criticisms, were content to refer to the existence of a wide range of criticisms and to the fact that Gewirth had replied to most of them (to our minds, satisfactorily).

16. Items by others that are significant in relation to Gewirth's argument from the PGC/PCC (either as criticisms or as applications) include Burrill 1971; Christie 1971; Davitt 1971; Corcoran 1973; Gillespie 1977; Pilon 1979a, 1979b, 1979c; Reamer 1979; Morris 1981; Okin 1981; Ben-Zeev 1982; Diller 1982; Heslep 1982; Reamer 1982; Von Magnus 1983; Kahn 1984; Den Uyl and Machan 1984; Mack 1984; Hill 1984; Narveson 1984; Raphael 1984; Singer 1984; Beyleveld and Brownsword 1986; Lomasky 1986; Phillips 1986; Pollock 1988; Bauhn 1989; and Machan 1989; as well as various reviews of Gewirth 1982b.

17. Articles criticizing Gewirth's principle of proportionality have some bearing in this regard. (See Morris 1981; Okin 1981; Ben-Zeev 1982; and Hill 1984.) In my opinion, aspects of the articles by Den Uyl and Machan (1984), Narveson (1984), Mack (1984), and Pilon (1979a, 1979b) confuse what belongs to the argument to the PGC and what belongs to the argument from the PGC. (See Chapter Ten.)

18. Levinson 1982. Gewirth replies in Gewirth 1982a.

19. Upton 1986. Gewirth replies in Gewirth 1988d.

20. I cannot, of course, guarantee that I have located all items. I have not commented on two articles in Dutch that I have located: De Roose 1987 and Keasberry 1986. If I have overlooked items, then these are most likely to be reviews, comments in books, comments in articles that are not specifically on Gewirth, or articles in foreign languages. After February 1990, I did not attempt to locate further items. I am reasonably confident that the bibliography is substantially complete for items published up until the middle of 1989.

21. See note 12 supra. The PGC, as against the PCC, does not appear until Gewirth 1974a.

Chapter 2: The Argument Presented

1. These general comments apply to "Preliminary Remarks" as well as to the actual sequence of the argument.

2. Objections to this concept of action being made central to morality are discussed under #1 and #2.

3. The numbers in this follow those of my presentation in "The Argument" in this chapter.

4. E. J. Bond (1980a, 40) objects to this on the grounds that actions cannot be consistent or contradictory, and D. E. Geels (1971) maintains that to act is not to presuppose normative propositions. These objections are discussed under #16.

5. This point is important in considering the sense in which the argument is an "is-ought" derivation, and in rebutting the objection that the argument reduces morality to logic. See #23 and #15. Gewirth does *not* contend that a being who violates the PGC cannot be a PPA—that it is logically *impossible* for a PPA to violate the PGC. He contends that it is logically *impermissible* for a PPA to violate the PGC. A "rational PPA," *in the sense* of one who acts rationally (i.e., as it needs to do if it is not to contradict that it is a PPA), cannot violate the PGC. A "rational PPA," *in the sense* of one with the capacity to perceive that it rationally ought to act in accordance with the PGC, can violate the PGC. PPAs who are rational in the latter sense are the addressees of practical precepts and the referents of the argument. This point is particularly important in relation to a number of objections discussed in Chapter 5 (see, especially, #21).

6. What this amounts to is discussed more fully in the first part of Chapter 3.

7. This definition explains why Gewirth considers that the move from the dialectical necessity of nonmoral judgments to the dialectical necessity of moral judgments is effected only in Stage III. This definition incurs objections that are discussed under #51.

8. This claim is discussed under #61.

9. Objections to Gewirth's foundationalism are discussed under #56 and #57.

Millard Schumaker contends that Gewirth's answer to the question "Why should I be moral?" is question-begging.

> Rationality is usually contrasted with stupidity on the one hand and emotional and mental imbalance on the other. But the alleged irrationality of immorality is clearly neither of these. The clever bank manager who successfully embezzles hundreds of thousands of dollars without being detected cannot be stupid and need not be emotionally disturbed. What, then, is irrational about his rather brilliant and level-headed criminal activity? On Gewirth's account his irrationality would seem to consist precisely in the fact that he is prepared to make exceptions in favor of himself; that is, he is irrational precisely because he is immoral. But if this is the reason to think him irrational, then reference to the irrationality of immorality is hardly an adequate answer to the question, Why should I be moral? (Schumaker 1979, 353–354)

Here, Schumaker ignores Gewirth's insistence that his operative criteria

of rationality are those of deductive and inductive logic. According to
Gewirth, to fail to act morally is to act irrationally, but this is not because
"irrationality" *means* "immorality." It is because to act immorally is to contradict that one is a PPA.

Schumaker is aware that Gewirth claims that a PPA must accept morality
on "pain of self-contradiction." But he thinks that the "contradiction" consists in not treating others like oneself, rather than in denying that one is a
PPA.

Schumaker makes another mistake. He considers that the "clever bank
manager" incurs "contradiction," but says,

> His contradiction can be painful only if he already accepts the
> authority of the moral law and so feels guilt and remorse. But to
> draw attention to this as a reason why one should be moral is
> once again to beg the question. (Ibid., 354)

The error lies in Schumaker's reading of "incurring the pain of self-contradiction." We are to understand that Gewirth argues that PPAs will be
motivated to be moral by the fact that to act immorally is to suffer some form
of emotional distress. But to say that X does Y on "pain of self-contradiction"
is to say only that if X does Y then X contradicts itself. It is not to say that if
X does Y then X contradicts itself *and that* this state of affairs causes X to
suffer anguish. Gewirth's argument is not that knowledge of the illogicality
of immorality (let alone its violation of the moral principle of universalizability) provides sufficient *motivating* reason to act morally (but see
Chapter 5, note 62—on Gewirth's view of the motivational force of his argument—for some qualification). Rather, it is that the illogicality of immorality
provides a categorical *justifying* reason for acting morally.

Finally, it must be noted that Schumaker interprets the question "Why
should I be moral?" as "Why should I follow the PGC?" whereas the question that Gewirth poses as the "authoritative question" is "Why should I
espouse some other-regarding criterion of practical reasonableness?"

10. Objections to the thesis that the PGC is a principle of positive as well
as negative rights to freedom and well-being are discussed in Chapter 10.

11. This is discussed further in the presentation of the argument and, e.g.,
under #35 and #47.

It is important to appreciate that Gewirth operates with a "normative" or
"prescriptive" sense of "rights," and not with a "recognitional" one. The
question of the existence of a right is one of justification rather than recognition. For A to consider that it has a right to X is for A to consider that it has
justification (according to criteria that A espouses) for the demand that B not
interfere with A's having or doing X. For A to be entitled to consider that it
has a right to X does not require that B refrain from interference with X or
that B espouse criteria that require B's noninterference. This raises issues
that are discussed especially in Chapter 6 (generally) and under #35 and #47.

12. Gewirth distinguishes "inclusive" from "exclusive" meanings of "additive goods." In the inclusive meaning,

> an additive good is any positive object of any purpose, whatever
> any agent aims to attain through action. (RM 56)

In the exclusive meaning,

> an additive good is only such a positive object of a purpose as is
> not comprised within basic and nonsubtractive goods. (Ibid.)

Gewirth uses the term "additive good" in its exclusive sense. (See ibid.)
13. According to Gewirth,

> [v]oluntariness involves a procedural aspect of actions in that it
> concerns the way actions are controlled as ongoing events. Pur-
> posiveness, on the other hand, in addition to having the distinct
> procedural aspect . . . also involves the substantive aspect of ac-
> tions, the specific contents of these events. Voluntariness refers
> to the means, purposiveness to the end; voluntariness comprises
> the agent's causation of his action, whereas purposiveness com-
> prises the object or goal of the action in the sense of the good he
> wants to achieve or have through this causation. Thus voluntar-
> iness is a matter of initiation or control while purposiveness is at
> least in part a matter of consummation. (RM 41)

> To interfere with someone's freedom is to interfere with his con-
> trol of his behavior, including his participation in transactions;
> such interference hence affects the procedural aspect of the be-
> havior. To interfere with someone's well-being, on the other
> hand, is to interfere with the objects or goods at which his behav-
> ior is aimed; it hence affects the substantive or purposive aspect
> of his behavior. . . . [A]lthough killing, libeling, and insulting are
> interferences both with well-being and with freedom, they have
> the former aspect as removing or diminishing certain goods re-
> quired for action, but they have the latter aspect insofar as they
> are inflicted through violence, coercion, deception, or other pro-
> cedures whereby the recipient participates in the transactions.
> Such actions interfere with their recipient's freedom and rational
> autonomy in that he does not give his unforced, informed con-
> sent. (RM 251–252)

Marcus G. Singer claims that Gewirth has a "preposterously narrow"
view of well-being, which does not include "autonomy" (Singer 1984, 32).
But, as Gewirth responds, a PPA's valuing and need for autonomy are included under its valuing and need for freedom, which itself might be included under the category of well-being, but which is taken account of as a
separate category because of Gewirth's distinction between the procedural
and substantive aspects of action. (See Gewirth 1984d, 203.) In this regard, it
might also be noted that Gewirth maintains that there is a

> close connection between freedom and well-being. Since the
> agent controls his behavior with a view to various purposes,
> interference with this control will seem more or less important to
> him according as the purposes to which his actions or behaviors
> were directed are more or less important. . . .
>   . . . The agent's freedom or control . . . largely consists in his
> having the unhindered powers or abilities required for achieving

the purposes to which he directs his behavior. As such, this freedom, even as procedural, is a component both of additive and of
basic well-being . . . . (RM 254–255)

Nevertheless, the procedural aspect of action (freedom) and the substantive component (well-being), for which the procedural aspect is a means, are
conceptually distinct. (See RM 256.)

14. Central to this discussion is Gewirth's distinction between "conative"
and "achievemental" modes of purposive action. In the conative mode a PPA
values what it needs to attempt to achieve its goals. However, "[t]he point of
trying is to succeed, so that the concept of action takes on a further normative connotation, that of successful action" (RM 58). In the achievemental
mode, a PPA also values what it needs to succeed in its purposive activity.

15. E. J. Bond (1980a, 47–48 n. 3) accuses Gewirth of equivocating between
two senses of "a generic feature of agency." This is discussed under #5.1.

16. D. D. Raphael says that he is puzzled how

the two concepts of freedom and well-being can cover everything that should be covered: how, for example, does the right to
life fit in[?] . . . [Gewirth] does not appear to discuss the right to
life as such, [though] one can imagine that he might subsume it
under either or both of the rights to freedom and well-being.
(Raphael 1984, 85)

Such a query reveals a very casual reading of *Reason and Morality*. It is
perfectly clear where the right to life fits in. As Gewirth responds,

I include life among the "basic goods, which are the general
necessary preconditions of action" ([RM] 54). I point out that
"among these basic goods there is also a hierarchy, headed by
life" ([RM] 63), and I include the right to life among the "basic
rights" which are rights to the basic goods ([RM] 211–212).
(Gewirth 1984d, 202–203)

Objections to Gewirth's specification of the contents of the generic features of agency are considered under #6 and #7.

17. I will generally forgo these parenthetical qualifications.

18. This is discussed under #3.

19. "Agents may not always have purposes clearly in view; in particular,
'purposive' must not be identified with 'purposeful,' where the latter con-
notes a deliberate, resolute design and its determined pursuit" (RM 38). That
purposiveness is present even in habitual action would be shown by a PPA's
resistance to interference with such action.

20. The term "subjective viewpoint on practical reasonableness," with its
abbreviation SPR, is mine, not Gewirth's.

21. In addition to this distinction between reflective appraising and non-
reflective valuing, Gewirth points out that the value that I attach to E must
be at least instrumental according to whatever criteria lead me to try to
achieve E; but it may, in a certain sense, also be intrinsic, as E

need not consist in some further end to which the action is regarded as a means; the agent may want and hence value the action for itself. (RM 50)

That is to say, the means X and the purpose E may coincide.

Ways in which "intrinsic" may be contrasted with "instrumental" are discussed further in this section, under the elucidation of (4a).

Gewirth, additionally, points out that a PPA

may also value the action only as having been arbitrarily chosen by him from among various alternatives, where he had to make some choice but was indifferent as to the alternatives. (RM 50)

22. See the discussion of this in "Preliminary Remarks."

Peter A. French totally misconstrues the argument when he claims that

we appear to have . . . a *logical* necessity for being moral that is based on the contingent fact that to be an active agent . . . one must be free and enjoy a certain level of "well-being." (French 1979, 109)

Were the need for freedom and well-being to be only *contingently* connected with being a PPA, there would be no logical necessity for a PPA to judge its freedom and well-being to be necessary goods, and the argument would break down completely. It is a contingent matter whether or not X is a PPA. But it is analytic to the concept of a PPA that X needs (must have) freedom and well-being to be a PPA. It is only what well-being consists of that is in any manner contingent.

23. Although a PPA necessarily values every purpose it has, *necessarily* regards all its purposes as *goods,* a PPA does not *necessarily* regard every purpose it has as a *necessary good.* To regard something as a necessary good is to regard it as necessarily good. I must regard my freedom and well-being as necessary goods because I must regard them as good *irrespective* of my purposes. On the other hand, I need only regard a particular occurrent purpose as good *if I have that purpose.* Gewirth distinguishes "what I am interested in" from "what is in my interests." (See RM 61.) I am interested in all my purposes, but all my purposes are not necessarily in my interests. My freedom and well-being are in my interest, even if I am not interested in my freedom and well-being. In Chapter 5 I shall show that a failure to appreciate this distinction and its implications is a major source of resistance to Stage II.

Rüdiger Bittner (1989) claims that if I consider X to be good, it does not follow that I consider whatever is necessary to achieve X to be good. If this is to be relevant, he must be claiming that if I wish to pursue X then it does not follow that I must (relative to my desire for X) consider that I ought to pursue whatever is necessary to achieve X, and, hence, that it does not follow from the fact that my freedom and well-being are my categorical agency needs that I must consider that I ought to pursue my freedom and well-being for whatever my goals (consider that my freedom and well-being are necessary goods). His reasoning is that

often the necessary conditions for achieving a goal are not such that actions will in turn be aimed at them. Often these conditions are simply given. And whether or not in some other situation in

> which they are not given we will make an effort to bring them
> about is not yet decided by our using them to reach some goal in
> the present situation in which they are given. (Bittner 1989, 29)

That one might already have the means to pursue/achieve one's purposes is irrelevant. The requirement to pursue the means is a requirement to
ensure that one has them if they are not given, and to protect them when they
are given but threatened. I find his second point too unclear to comment on
with any confidence. It is to be noted, however, that the question is not what
I will do, but what I ought to do if I wish to do X and M is necessary for me
to do X.

That the dialectically necessary method proceeds only on judgments of
value that a PPA cannot deny without contradicting that it is a PPA cannot
be stressed too strongly. Judgments that a PPA cannot deny without contradicting that it is a PPA are justified in the sense that it is logically necessary for a PPA to espouse them. Any judgments that follow logically from the
judgment "My freedom and well-being are necessary goods" are similarly
logically necessary for me to espouse. Judgments, or qualifications to the
dialectically necessary judgments, that are functions of the value I attach to
specific particular occurrent purposes are not logically necessary in this
sense. If I did not have these purposes, I would not contradict that I was a
PPA. So, if I did not make judgments corresponding to my specific particular
occurrent purposes alone, I would not contradict that I was a PPA. Relative
to the criterion of logical necessity, such purposes, and the judgments that
derive from them, are unjustified (arbitrary). They are only not impermissible if they are consistent with judgments that are dialectically necessary. The
dialectically necessary judgments derive from my voluntary purposivity as
such, from my relation to my purposes which makes those purposes the
purposes I choose to act for, not from the *content* of the purposes specifically.
This relation is constant, regardless of the varying content of my purposes,
and is possessed universally by all PPAs, regardless of variations in the
content of their purposes. (See further #50.) The generic features of agency
relate to me as necessary conditions for this relation, not as necessary conditions for my specific particular occurrent purposes, *although* they are necessary conditions for all my particular occurrent purposes, in that I cannot
have specific particular occurrent purposes without having this relation. In
this sense, the focus on the generic conditions of agency per se, and the
judgments through which the dialectically necessary method operates, are
abstracted from my particular occurrent purposes. This, however, must not
be misunderstood. The operative inferences of the dialectically necessary
method must still be made by "real embodied" PPAs with specific contingent characteristics, for they are "immanent" within action for specific particular occurrent purposes. The dialectically necessary method does not operate on the assumption that PPAs are "rational and no more." It operates on
what PPAs must accept regardless of the differences that they contingently
have, and which characterize them as different PPAs. (See #54.) *Within the
dialectically necessary method,* no question can arise of having to choose be-

tween treating the generic features as the necessary conditions of agency and treating the contingently necessary conditions of specific particular occurrent purposes as the necessary conditions of agency. The latter conditions include the former, but not vice versa. The latter are not conditions of agency per se, but conditions of specific actions; and what are conditions of agency per se are also conditions of specific actions. "Real embodied" PPAs must adopt the position of "an abstract rational agent" (insofar as the argument can be said to operate on such a position), because what defines "an abstract rational agent" defines a "real embodied" PPA *as a PPA* at all. Ignoring the conditions of actions that are not *generic conditions* of action per se is not arbitrary. It is justified by the dialectically necessary method, which operates on the principle that a PPA cannot rationally espouse judgments that contradict judgments that are logically necessary for it to espouse. (See the first part of Chapter 3.) The focus on necessary, or generic, contents that the argument employs cannot be questioned without questioning the primacy of logical criteria over other criteria of "reason." Any suggestion that the focus on necessary contents is arbitrary can only be taken seriously as a suggestion that the dialectically necessary method is itself arbitrary. This, however, can be sustained only by claiming that logical criteria are not primary within the field of reason-in-general, or that they are not ineluctable. (For the bottom line on this see #61.) In my opinion, this is not sustainable for the simple reason that to request a *justification* for the use of the dialectically necessary method is, implicitly, to commit oneself to criteria of formal logic.

Failure to appreciate such considerations is very likely responsible, at least partly, for misconstruing the argument as an *ad hominem* one, which requires the PGC to be derived from the *specific contents* of particular occurrent value judgments. The argument, however, proceeds from the judgments implicit in a PPA's voluntary purposivity as such, which are independent of the specific contents of PPAs' particular occurrent judgments, but implicit in any PPA's voluntary purposive relation to whatever its purposes (this relation being implicit in a PPA's *making* whatever specific value judgments it makes). (See the first part of Chapter 3.) The judgments that follow from the specific particular occurrent judgments that a PPA might make cannot count as counterexamples to a PPA's dialectically necessary judgments. (This must be borne in mind when considering objections based on the particular occurrent espousal of various SPRs.)

All these matters must be borne in mind throughout. However, they are especially important in relation to the objections raised by Puolimatka (1989), Narveson (1979), (1980), (1984), White (1982), Collins (1979), Held (1977), (1979), (1985), Fotion (1968), Simon (1975), Okin (1981), Williams (1985), Allen (1987), Kalin (1984), and Scheuermann (1987).

24. The argument against the ethical egoist is considered in most detail under #33, the argument concerning historical contingency in Chapter 6. The argument against the adeonticist is considered below, and further under #28, #29, and #30. There is no literature responding to Gewirth from the perspective of the radical social critic. Although critics make occasional mention of "fanatics" being able to evade the argument, there is nothing very concerted

about this (the most direct remarks being by Gamwell [1984, see #23.2] and by Held [1985, see #54.2]). One article which might seem to falsify this statement (Fotion 1968, see #42.1) portrays "the fanatic" as what Gewirth would call "an elitist."

25. *On the contrary,* I shall argue for the adequacy of the argument from attitudinal consistency under #13; and the sequence for Stage II that I personally favor is, in any case, best read as an elaboration of the direct argument.

26. Gewirth, in *Reason and Morality,* refers to his target here as "the amoralist." But, in Gewirth 1984d, 207, he makes it terminologically explicit that his target is the "adeonticist," which, despite his terminology in *Reason and Morality,* should be clear from his insistence that the move to "the moral" occurs only in Stage III. This terminological switch is not a change in Gewirth's position, because in this section of *Reason and Morality* Gewirth is trying not to refute amoralism, but to show that even an amoralist must accept deontic prescriptions. Only the adeonticist is refuted by such a demonstration.

27. As will be seen below, the prima facie qualification is a function of the fact that I might hold an SPR for my purposes that requires me to will interference with my freedom and well-being as an end in itself in certain circumstances.

It is also to be noted that, in his reply to Bond 1980a, Gewirth says that he never uses the term "prudential obligation" which Bond attributes to him. (See Bond 1980a, 50, and Gewirth 1980a, 66.) This is true and extends to "prudential duty." However, I see no harm in this usage, as Gewirth does say that he uses "strict ought" synonymously with "duty" and "obligation," and does not attribute to the latter two terms the more restrictive meanings that are sometimes assigned to them. (See RM 67.)

28. The qualification "at least," attached to "refrain," arises because Gewirth maintains that I must also hold, under certain conditions, that PPAO has a duty to aid me in securing my freedom and well-being. (See RM 67.) Gewirth discusses these conditions most fully under "The Duty to Rescue" (RM 217–230). I agree that an aid requirement also follows, but I shall expound the argument in the more restricted form here (as Gewirth tends to do in the main presentation of his argument), and present and defend the argument for a positive duty in Chapter 10, where I also discuss the relation between the argument to the PGC and Gewirth's discussion of the duty to rescue.

29. In the more restricted version of the argument, this is (at least) a negative claim right.

30. I say "in my view" because Gewirth, in various places, has a number of things to say about a PPA's "instrumental" and "intrinsic" valuation of its freedom and well-being which I do not find entirely clear; and it is just possible that the view I have expressed here differs from Gewirth's position. This is discussed in Chapter 7 (#32) in connection with an objection raised by James O. Grunebaum (1976) and Arval A. Morris (1981).

31. I shall use either of these interchangeably.

32. Kai Nielsen (1984) considers that this assumption of conative normality violates the dialectically necessary method. This is discussed under #29.

Vinit Haksar misses the assumption of conative normality. Referring to Gewirth's view that egalitarianism is to be defended by appealing to the fact that "human beings have purposes," Haksar says,

> [T]here seems something missing in the view that the having of purposes is the only relevant thing from the point of view of worth . . . . In short, we must not only have ideals we must also pursue them with zest. (Haksar 1979, 67)

To this Gewirth (correctly) responds,

> Haksar fails to note that my full statement refers to agents as having 'purposes they want to fulfil,' and that this wanting supplies the conative element whose need he posits. (Gewirth 1982d, 669 n. 2)

The point that (4c) is action-directing, not merely attitude-directing, is important in replying to objections considered under #37 and #35.10/#47.6.

33. The 'oughts' . . . of other persons . . . are quite strict. The actions and, more usually, the omissions of which they are predicated are regarded by the agent not merely as preferable or fitting, as generous, supererogatory, or matters of grace, but rather as required or mandatory, so that he holds that he is entitled to redress and his respondents are subject to severe censure and other appropriate countermeasures, at least by himself, if the required conduct is not forthcoming. This mandatoriness is a logical consequence of the fact that the objects of the generic rights are necessary goods and are so regarded and claimed by the agent. (RM 67)

This is not entirely clear. It might look as though a strict "ought" is simply a prescription that I am required to do X. However, such "oughts" may be hypothetical, dependent upon what I contingently want to do. A strict "ought" is not hypothetical in this way. It specifies a mandatory requirement. This mandatoriness is here linked to the objects of the rights-claims being necessary goods, and what is special about necessary goods is that I am required to want them (proactively) for whatever I want. If this conative independence is what accounts for the mandatory character of the "oughts" of Stage II, then a strict "ought" must be one in which the requirement to do something is conatively independent, and not dependent upon the addressee's particular occurrent goals. This is made explicit in my definition.

34. This is to be contrasted with "ought" in the sense of recommendation.

35. "I shall here use 'obligation' and 'duty' interchangeably with these strict 'oughts,' although the former terms are sometimes used in more restricted and specific senses to signify the requirements that stem, respectively, from prior agreements and from one's job, office, or station" (RM 67).

36. This, of course, simply correlates with what was said in the discussion of (4a) about the valuation of my freedom and well-being being at least instrumental, rather than necessarily intrinsic.

37. Which means, such interference as is viewed by me in its aspect of thwarting my achievement of the purposes I will.

38. Gewirth considers that serious difficulties with the notion of "duties to oneself" severely restrict the scope of such duties. (See RM 333–338.) Of particular importance in the present context is the objection that

> if a person has duties to himself, then, because of the correlativ-ity of duties and rights, he also has rights against himself. But any right-holder can always give up his right and thereby release the respondent of the right from his duty. On the other hand, no person can release himself from a duty. Hence, the notion of duties to oneself is contradictory, since it implies that a person both can and cannot release himself from his duties to himself. (RM 334)

Although Gewirth's discussion is in the context of duties deriving from the PGC, this objection also has to be met here.

39. For Gewirth's general view on the epistemological primacy of rights, see Gewirth 1986a and 1988d. For a criticism, see Upton 1986. This issue, although of interest, is of no direct relevance to the validity of the argument to the PGC.

As far as I am aware, Gewirth has not made this linkage between the instrumental nature of the self-referring ought of (4c) and the waivable na-ture of the generic rights.

In what follows, in the interests of brevity, I will sometimes simply refer to "my duty to defend my freedom and well-being from interference." All the qualifications introduced here are to be taken as read.

40. There are some passages in *Reason and Morality* that might be thought to cast doubt on the claim that Gewirth holds the deontic judgments of Stage II to be only "at least prima facie." For example:

> [A] rights-judgment need not be set forth independently; it may, instead, figure as a subordinate clause wherein the attribution of rights to the subject is only conditional. [But] . . . the agent who is the subject of the generic rights is assumed to set forth or uphold the rights-judgment himself, . . . not merely condition-ally or tentatively but in an unqualified way. (RM 65)

Does this mean that I must consider that I have an unconditional, unqual-ified, conclusive, or absolute right to my freedom and well-being? No, it doesn't! We must be careful to distinguish predication of "unconditional versus conditional," "unqualified versus qualified," "conclusive versus ten-tative," or "prima facie versus absolute" *to the right I claim*, from predication to *the grounds upon which I claim this right*.

What I take Gewirth to hold is that I have conclusive, rather than prima facie, grounds for claiming a right to my freedom and well-being (conclu-sive, because I logically must claim this right—avoidance of self-contradic-tion taking precedence over all other criteria of justification [because it is a necessary condition for all justifications (see RM 194, 73)]), but that the *right* I have conclusive grounds for claiming is, *on these grounds*, not necessarily more than prima facie.

In the present context, this amounts to the claim that I have a conclusive reason to hold that I have at least a prima facie (conditional) duty to pursue my freedom and well-being; but it is not the case that I must hold only tentatively (prima facie) that I have a duty to pursue my freedom and well-being.

If there are occasions when Gewirth might seem to be saying that I logically must hold that I have an absolute right to my freedom and well-being, then, apart from when he is talking about an adeonticist's attitude towards its *basic* well-being, these must be taken to be functions of Gewirth's not taking sufficient account of the possible ambiguity that I have drawn attention to. My attribution of this view is, to some extent, derived from the logically required judgments that I consider that a PPA must make; but Gewirth does, in fact, state quite explicitly that the deontic judgments of Stage II are being asserted to be not necessarily more than prima facie. (See Gewirth 1984d, 207. However, even here some interpretive construction is required. For, although Gewirth is here replying to Nielsen [1984, 71], who claims that [4d] requires a *ceteris paribus* qualification, the places in *Reason and Morality* where Gewirth says that he in fact insists on such a qualification [see RM 206, 258] insist on a prima facie qualification to the rights-claims of *the PGC*, not directly to the deontic judgments of Stage II. But this is, implicitly, good enough. For there would be a contradiction in claiming that the rights I must claim on the basis of my logically necessary acceptance of the PGC are prima facie, whereas I logically must claim definitively absolute rights to these same things in Stage II.)

41. For objections to the argument for being based on motivational grounds, see #31.

42. Only one SPR for my purposes may be excluded at the outset. This one prescribes that it is impermissible for me to pursue any purposes whatsoever by my agency. I provide an argument for this in the first section of Chapter 3. It should be noted that this consideration does not figure explicitly in Gewirth's discussions.

43. Remember that "my freedom and well-being" stands for a structure that has hierarchically arranged components.

44. I could be a particularist deontic egoist, holding that I have claim rights against other PPAs, but that they have no claim rights against me.

45. That the PGC is an absolute principle does not entail that the rights it secures are absolute. Gewirth does, however, consider that there is at least one absolute right. (See Gewirth 1981a.) The claim he discusses is that of a mother not to be tortured to death by her son. But this is only a specific example of the general right for an innocent person not to be killed by PPAs against its uncoerced will. This is criticized by Levinson (1982). (See Gewirth 1982a for a rejoinder.) The absolute nature of this right is ultimately a function of life being at the apex of a PPA's basic well-being.

46. The distinction between directly and indirectly "prudential" criteria is suggested by Gewirth's comment that "the criterion of the 'oughts' in (7) [≡ (4c)] and (8) [≡ (4d)] is directly neither moral nor legal but rather prudential" (RM 93), which implies that the criterion could be moral or legal indirectly.

In my discussion of objections I shall not always attend to these conceptual distinctions *explicitly.* I shall generally speak of "my prudential criterion" (the criterion of my interests) as "my proactive evaluative relation to my purposes," or even as "I am a PPA," though, on occasion, I shall refer to it "specifically" (i.e., in terms of "[4]/[4c]" or "my categorical need for freedom and well-being"). When the issue at hand is the move from the "prudential" to the "moral," the specific characterization is, strictly speaking, more appropriate. When the issue concerns contrasts between a dialectically necessary method and dialectically contingent ones, it matters only that the criterion be a dialectically necessary one. My varying, and sometimes loose, terminology on this point is a function of the fact that attending to all these precise nuances, in every case, would produce an unnecessarily technical exegesis at every turn. However, my varying terminology will incur no fallacies, as what matters *in the final analysis* is not how (as "prudential," "moral," or whatever) we designate the PGC and the claims leading to it, but simply whether or not they are dialectically necessary. All the "criteria" I shall variously refer to as "my prudential criterion" are dialectically necessary features or claims.

I shall frequently refer to "my prudential criterion" as "the criterion of my interest/s." Corresponding to the general characterization of this criterion, my interest is in my pursuit/achievement of my purposes. Corresponding to the specific characterization, my interest is in my having freedom and well-being. It is important to appreciate that, in the dialectically necessary method, "the criterion of my interests" never stands for a dialectically contingent content. Thus, it *never* stands for my particular occurrent purposes, or for some self-regarding SPR for my purposes, or for the specific needs of my purposes. It stands for the invariant proactive evaluative relation or "interest" I have in my purposes, or for my generic needs, not for my purposes themselves (unless these are established as dialectically necessary).

47. Gewirth runs this argument with reference to my basic well-being. However, he states that the argument may be run for the other generic features as well (see RM 95), and I present it here in composite form. It can be run in this form because the point of trying to achieve X is to succeed in achieving X. (See RM 58.)

48. The point about "can" implying "ought" is taken from Scheuermann 1987. Of course, from "I can do Y" it does not follow that "I ought to do Y." But from "Y ought to be done" it follows, *ceteris paribus,* from "I can do Y" that "I ought to do Y." This is not simply an application of "ought implies can." For, although it follows from this that an "ought" is *only* directed at those who can fulfill it, it does not follow that it is directed at all who can fulfill it. However, "can implies ought"

> is plausible when interpreted as stating the idea that when there
> is a general and standing requirement to bring about or to pre-
> vent some state of affairs, such a requirement is practically bind-
> ing on those who by virtue of their (special) circumstances are
> (alone or best) able to satisfy it. (Scheuermann 1987, 300)

It is to be noted, however, that in relation to an "ought" prescribing noninterference, as against "aid," all PPAs are equally in the required "special" position, so that in this case "I ought to do X" implies "I ought to do X *iff* I can."

Colin Davies (1975, 23) contends that the principle that "ought" implies "can" does not enable (4d) to be inferred from (4c). This is discussed in #34.1.

49. (See, e.g., RM 94.) Scheuermann (1987, 296–303) provides a valuable discussion of these points. In Scheuermann's terms, (4d) is "subjunctively" other-directing rather than unconditionally other-directing. These matters are discussed further in my consideration of objections to (4d) in Chapter 7.

The claim that (4d) does not follow from (4), in any sense that can ground the rest of the argument, is the most frequently voiced objection to Gewirth's argument.

Fred Feldman fails to appreciate that the argument proceeds on only dialectically necessary judgments. He objects to the inference from (4)/(4c) to (4d) (which he calls "(12)") on the grounds that

> my freedom and well-being may not be the only necessary goods. Perhaps the freedom and well-being of some other person are also necessary goods, and can be maintained only at the expense of some interference with my freedom and well-being. I see no reason why an agent, even at this early stage of the argument, could not be sensitive to this possibility, and hence reject (12). (Feldman 1983, 480)

However, while a PPA *might* regard PPAO's freedom and well-being as necessary goods (and the dialectical necessity of [4c] does not *prohibit* a PPA from espousing such a moral viewpoint), such a viewpoint has not yet been shown to be dialectically necessary. In *having* to accept (4c), a PPA *must* accept (4d). In not *having* to adopt a moral viewpoint, a PPA does not *have to deny* (4d). The assumption of such a viewpoint is question-begging. In any case, it could hardly constitute an invalidation of the argument to the PGC, as it looks like a statement of the PGC itself. The impact of such an as yet dialectically contingent assumption cannot be a denial of (4d); it can only be a dialectically contingent qualification of it. If this qualification leads me to allow my freedom and well-being to be interfered with, this cannot be regarded as a denial of (4d). It must be regarded as a case of my releasing PPAO from its duty, (or, given that [4d] is correlative to [5] [see below], as a case of my waiving the right correlative to this duty).

50. (See Hohfeld 1964, 36ff.; RM 66.) Martin P. Golding points out that there may be a concept of "other-referring duties" that is not correlative to rights because the duty cannot be waived by the recipient of the duty. (See Golding 1984, 129.) This may be correct, and Gewirth himself refers to "rights" that cannot be waived by the rights-holder. (See RM 335.) However, as I pointed out above, the rights-claim here is correlative to an other-referring duty derived from a self-referring instrumental duty, and this guarantees that the rights-claim here is one that can be waived by the rights-holder.

However, to avoid any confusion on this point, it should be said that my right to have my freedom and well-being not interfered with *against my will is* inalienable. What I can waive is any right to freedom and well-being which I may wish to claim *under* this inalienable right!

51. Gewirth discusses the intelligibility of the notion of a "prudential right" in RM 68–71. This discussion, and objections to this concept, are considered under #35.

52. Richard B. Friedman (1981, 153) claims that Stage II does not establish that a PPA must specifically claim rights to its categorical needs, on the grounds of such needs. This is considered under #41.

53. The dialectical necessity of this claim makes the property of being a PPA the criterion of relevant similarity for the logical principle of universalizability (see [7] below). The use of this criterion in conjunction with the logical principle of universalizability enables the argument to overcome the complete variability of content permitted by the formal moral principle of universalizability "[W]hatever is right for one person must be right for any similar person in similar circumstances" (RM 105) (this principle being the logical principle of universalizability in its moral application). (See RM 104–128 generally.) Ignoring the ASA is responsible for a number of objections to Stage III. (See Chapter 8.) The ASA is analyzed further in Chapter 3 "The Formal Structure of the Argument." Although Gewirth refers to the ASA as the argument *from* the sufficiency of agency, I shall generally refer to it as the argument *for* the sufficiency of agency. The ASA is an argument from the sufficiency of agency for having to claim the generic rights, to the requirement to claim agency as the sufficient reason for having the generic rights. Calling it an argument *from* the sufficiency of agency concentrates attention on its premise. Calling it an argument *for* the sufficiency of agency concentrates attention on its conclusion.

54. The logical principle of universalizability must not be confused with the moral principle of universalizability, or with other moral consistency principles like the "Golden Rule." Although it is used to generate the conclusion that a PPA must accept a substantive moral principle, it is not such a principle, nor does its use presuppose that a PPA accepts a moral point of view. (See RM 105.)

55. Gewirth formulates this as follows:

> [I]f some predicate P belongs to some subject S because S has the property Q (where the 'because' is that of sufficient reason or condition), then P must also belong to all other subjects S_1, S_2, . . . , S_n that have Q. (RM 105)

There are a number of ways in which this can be stated. I shall use yet another formulation in my formal summary in Chapter 3.

56. The inferences from (6) to (9) and from (6) to (11) both employ the same logical principle of universalizability. The application of this principle is, however, different in each case. In the inference from (6) to (11), what is universalized is the property of *considering that one has a right* to one's freedom and well-being, or the property of having an SPR according to which one has this right, on the grounds of being a PPA. In the inference from (6) to (9), what is universalized is the property of *having a right* to one's freedom and well-being on the grounds of being a PPA, which is the judgment internal to one's dialectically required SPR. Gewirth calls the universalization from (6) to (11) "judgmental universalization," because it bears "on the *claim-*

ing of rights, on the *making of judgments* about rights"; he refers to the universalization from (6) to (9) as "possessive universalization," because it "bears on the *having* of rights" (Gewirth 1988c, 253). In my formal summary in Chapter 3, I shall characterize "judgmental universalization" as "external application of the logical principle of universalizability," and "possessive universalization" as "internal application of the logical principle of universalizability." This distinction is crucial in replying to one of the main objections to Stage III. Objections to Stage III are discussed in Chapter 8 (see, especially, #47).

57. This is now definitively prima facie. A PPA must conceive of its rights to freedom and well-being as conditional upon its not interfering with the freedom and well-being of other PPAs against their will.

58. In general terms, according to the PGC, a PPA has a right to its freedom and well-being provided that it does not interfere with the freedom and well-being of PPAO. Gewirth gives a general analysis of principles for the resolution of conflicts of duties in RM 338–354. Important among these is the principle of degrees of necessity for action derived from the hierarchical structure of the necessary goods, which are the objects of the generic rights.

59. Gewirth formulates this in a number of different ways, one statement being "Act in accord with the generic rights [rights to freedom and well-being] of your recipients as well as of yourself" (RM 135). My formulation is equivalent. Obviously there can be formulations in terms of duties because of the logical correlativity of other-referring duties and claim rights.

60. See generally RM 158–161, the whole matter being discussed extensively on 150–161. This "assertoric conversion" is discussed further in Chapter 5, "Grounding Morality in Logic" (especially #15–#18).

61. The PGC differs from other "consistency principles," like the "Golden Rule," in that the former has "a necessary content as well as a necessary form" (RM 164); it does not merely state that like cases must be treated alike (for it has a determinate content, see RM 165–166); and it has a dialectically necessary justification (see RM 166–169, and generally RM 162–171). The "Golden Rule" states that I ought to treat others as I wish them to treat me. The PGC is, in fact, a "rationalized" version of this rule, as it can be expressed as "I ought to treat others as I *rationally must wish* them to treat me," because, according to the argument, I rationally must wish others not to interfere with my freedom and well-being (and to aid me in securing my freedom and well-being, when this involves no comparable cost to themselves). (See Gewirth 1978b, where this is discussed extensively.) Superficially, the PGC is similar to John Stuart Mill's view that harm to others is the only justification for restricting a person's freedom. But this principle, within Mill's epistemology, cannot be given a nonarbitrary and justified specification of "harm." (See RM 232.)

Chapter 3: Two Summary Formulations

1. "Practical rationality" is sometimes thought of as involving efficient means-ends calculation, with "practical reasonableness" involving attention to moral requirements. So defined, Gewirth's position is that practical rationality and practical reasonableness both commit a PPA to rationality in the

sense of not acting against reason (in the sense of what is required by deductive and inductive reason). He argues that practical reasonableness is justified by reason in this sense, and that where practical reasonableness and practical rationality conflict, reasonableness is superior in terms of reason. (See Gewirth 1983a.) In contrast with this usage, I here use "practical reasonableness" and "practical rationality" as synonyms and attach a sense to them rather different from those above. A viewpoint on practical reasonableness/rationality is a viewpoint on what it is permissible/impermissible/not impermissible for someone to choose to do, whether such a viewpoint is a moral position or not.

2. Martin P. Golding expresses his skepticism about Gewirth's enterprise in the following way:

> Professor Gewirth employs a strategy of argument that might be called the ideal philosophical procedure. This strategy involves the derivation of powerful or rich conclusions from weak or minimal premises . . . . Contrary to popular belief, philosophers sometimes do reach the same conclusions on some issue, but they usually do so by means of arguments that employ substantive premises over which disagreement is sharp. More often, perhaps, there is little or no unanimity on premises and conclusions. In either case, the soundness of the arguments is thrown into question and the conclusions cannot be said to be firmly established. So it is tempting to seek premises that are very weak in terms of philosophical commitment, which in consequence are likely to be acceptable to a wider range of thinkers and are likely to result in more generally accepted conclusions. The risk in employing this strategy is obvious: the weaker premises often will be inadequate to sustain the particular conclusions that one wants to reach. (Golding 1981, 165)

Kai Nielsen makes some stronger statements. He believes that in Gewirth's "astringent sense of 'rational' . . . it is plain and uncontroversial that we ought to be rational" (Nielsen 1984, 65). However,

> Gewirth, like Kant, is trying to get categorically binding moral principles (principles binding on every rational agent)—including categorical right-claims—from the sheer concept of agency. . . . [T]rying to get so much out of a bare concept of agency is like trying to squeeze blood out of a turnip . . . . (Ibid., 79)

Although, as both Golding and Nielsen admit, ingrained incredulity is no argument, and the proof of the pudding is in the eating, there is no doubt that there is a widespread conviction that an argument of Gewirth's type cannot succeed.

3. That the argument has a strictly practical purview must not be forgotten. This is important (for example) in relation to an objection made by E. J. Bond (1980a) (see #3.1), and also in relation to one made by Jesse Kalin (1984) (see #33).

4. Gewirth does not say anything like this, but I take this to be implicit in his strategy.

5. For Gewirth's statement of the ASA see RM 109–110. I have quoted this passage in Chapter 2. For more on the ASA see the next section of this chapter. See note 11 infra, especially.

6. Here, it must not be forgotten that the prima facie qualification pertains to possible overriding considerations to the right I have conclusive reason to think that I have (because its condition is that I am a PPA, which I necessarily am in the context of the argument), rather than to the justification for my having the right. (See Chapter 2, note 40.)

7. The sense in which Gewirth maintains that a PPA has an absolute right to life (see Gewirth 1981a) is consistent with this. My absolute right is a right not to be killed against my will when I do not act to endanger the life of PPAO against PPAO's will.

8. The way in which, within my dialectically necessary internal viewpoint, the generic requirements ground my claim to freedom and well-being is analyzed in the next section of this chapter.

9. An interpretation of the argument as an argument from prudence is most explicit in Jan Narveson's account. (See Narveson 1979, 1980, and 1984. This is discussed under #6, #35.5, and #38.) It is also, to cite just one example, implicit in Bernard Williams' critique. (See Williams 1985, #54.1.)

10. The dialectical necessity of the PGC as against its assertoric truth is discussed in Chapter 5, "Morality, Logic, and 'Is-Ought.'" For misportrayal of the argument in this way in the present context, see, e.g., #42 and #47.7.

11. Gewirth's argument for the sufficiency of agency (see RM 109–110) may, in the present context, be presented as follows: {IP} & IC → {MyR}. IP and IC pertain to me necessarily as a PPA. If I claim MyR, I must adduce some ground, some feature I possess by virtue of which I consider that I have MyR. Suppose that I adduce D, which is something that does not pertain to me *necessarily as a PPA* (which means something other than IP or IC—though, in the present context, this means something other than IC, with IP being given). By virtue of this claim I would be required to consider that I do not have MyR if I do not have D, even though I have IC (which I necessarily have as a PPA). But, as a PPA, I *must* consider that I have MyR, even if I do not have D. Therefore, I must adduce IC as the feature by virtue of which I have MyR. I must hold that (IC → MyR).

This may be expressed rather differently. Although IC necessarily pertains to me *assertorically* (see note 12 infra), it is dialectically necessary for me to hold that IC. {IP} & IC may, thus, be written as {IP & IC}, and the inference that {IP} & IC → {MyR}, may be written as {IP & IC → MyR}. From p & q → r, it follows that p → (q → r). So it follows that {IP → (IC → MyR)}.

Of course, it also follows that {IC → (IP → MyR)}. In fact, it hardly matters which of IP and IC we state as the sufficient condition for MyR; both, within the dialectically necessary method, stand for necessary aspects of being a PPA. The main reason for preferring IC to stand as the sufficient condition, in this context, is that it is customary in arguments with evaluative conclusions to have an evaluative premise as the major premise, and factual conditions as minor premises. The argument here is that, on my proactive (i.e., "conatively normal") evaluative commitment to my purposes (IP), given the fact that I categorically need my freedom and well-being in order to achieve any purposes by my agency (IC), I must hold that I have a claim right to my freedom and well-being (MyR).

12. "[I]t is important to distinguish two questions: (c) What characteristics or abilities must one have in order to be an agent? (d) What aspect of being an agent is the justifying ground for claiming to have the generic rights? . . . [The answer to the first question does not constitute the answer to the second question.] The criterion for answering (c) refers to the generic abilities of action, whereas the criterion for answering (d) refers to the desire to fulfill one's purposes among persons who have these abilities. Thus it is not the case that two completely different criteria are used to answer (c) and (d). Rather, the answer to (d) takes as decisive one component or aspect of the answer to (c). What justifies this specification of criteria is that the determination of the characteristics required for being an agent is not itself subject to the views, claims, or desires of agents, as is the determination of what aspect of agency serves to justify for each agent his claim to have the generic rights. . . . Thus the answer to (c) falls outside the dialectically necessary method, unlike the answer to (d). Once it is determined what constitutes being an agent, the dialectically necessary method takes over, with its focus on what must be claimed or upheld by every agent from within his own standpoint in purposive agency" (RM 123).

13. See #50 for discussion of an objection to this, which maintains that IC must be written as "I am an X who categorically needs freedom and well-being for *my* purposes," and that IC can only be written as "I am an X who categorically needs freedom and well-being for *its* purposes" if it is assumed that I reason from (my) proactive valuation of purposivity in general (i.e., [my] proactive valuation of the purposivity of all PPAs), and not just of my own purposivity, thereby assuming that I take favorable account of PPAO's interests (which is question-begging).

14. This states, "If I must hold 'I am an X who has C' is a sufficient reason for (validates, or justifies) 'I am an X who has R,' then I must hold that there is an X for which 'X has C' validates 'X has R.'"

15. This states, "If there is an X, such that X has C is a sufficient reason for inferring that X has R, then for all X, X having C is a sufficient reason for inferring that X has R." (H) is a substitution instance of the logical principle of universalizability, $(\exists x)[(x \text{ has } \sigma) \to (x \text{ has } \rho)] \to (x)[(x \text{ has } \sigma) \to (x \text{ has } \rho)]$. Where "$\to$" is interpreted as "material implication," this is a proposition of the predicate calculus; but it holds for any calculus that employs the notion of sufficient reason.

16. It is to be recalled that Gewirth calls the internal application "possessive universalization" and the external application "judgmental universalization." (See Chapter 2, note 56.)

17. This universalization, being internal, commits my dialectically necessary viewpoint to advocacy of PPAOs' pursuit of their F&WB. The parallel external universalization, whereby PPAO must advocate its pursuit of its

F&WB, is also logically necessary, but does not negate the validity of the internal universalization. As I read Gewirth, and this does require a degree of interpretation, he points to the possibility of internal universalization being applied to {IC → SRO} in his reply to R. M. Hare 1984. (See Gewirth 1984d, 211–212.) (See #47.4 for some comments on this aspect of Gewirth's reply to Hare.)

18. On this analysis, it is the internal application of the LPU, operating with Gewirth's criterion of relevant similarities (as being a PPA or a correlate), that effects the move from the prudential to the moral. From what has been said above, it can be seen that this move can be made before it is shown that I must claim MyR. Gewirth only makes the move from the prudential to the moral after showing that I must consider that I have MyR, because it is at this point that he chooses to deploy the LPU and the ASA.

My formalization of the argument also enables us to clarify Gewirth's concept of "my prudential criterion." Most basically, IP is "my prudential criterion." Indirectly (and contingently) IP might express a nonmoral criterion or a moral one (depending upon whether I pursue *my* purposes for self-regarding or other-regarding reasons). But IP directly, as dialectically necessary, is morally neutral (and "prudential" in expressing my proactive evaluative relation to *my* purposes). IP (dialectically) validates all the value judgments in the argument. Relative to IP, *all* these judgments, *including the PGC,* are "prudential." The PGC is, nevertheless, a *moral* principle, whereas MyR (and the other dialectically necessary judgments of Stage II) is not. This is because the dialectically necessary *ground* of the PGC is OC as well as IC—the dialectically necessary ground of the dialectically necessary judgments of Stage II being IC alone. The PGC is "prudential" ("generally prudential") in being upheld in consistency with IP, "moral" in being grounded (partly) in OC (the PGC being derived as the union between PPAOR—which is grounded in OC—and MyR). MyR is "generally prudential" in being upheld in consistency with IP, "specifically prudential" in being grounded in IC alone. The explanation of this is as follows: It is dialectically necessary for me to hold (IC → SRO), and (SRO → ORO → MyR). But PPAOR, unlike MyR, is not derived from *my judgment* SRO (which I ground in IC) or from MyR. It is derived from *my inference* (IC → MyR). Universalization of this inference does not yield (IC → PPAOR), but (OC → PPAOR). Nevertheless, both MyR and PPAOR are dialectically necessary in terms of IP.

19. The objection from the adeonticist, stated most forcefully by Kai Nielsen (1984) and Bernard Williams (1985), is the objection most relevant to this inference. (See #28–#30.) If I am right in my interpretation of James P. Sterba 1987, then he also objects to this inference. However, Sterba has (at best) an idiosyncratic way of portraying the argument's structure, which leads him to question this step in the context of an objection to Stage III. (See #47.3.)

20. Richard B. Friedman (1981) considers that Gewirth has shown that a PPA must claim MyR, but not on the "grounds of necessity." I take this to be a denial of the validity of the ASA as I have here portrayed it. (See #41.) The validity of the ASA is questioned explicitly by William O'Meara (1982). (See #44.)

21. Gewirth's claim to have derived "ought" from "is" *dialectically,*

though not *assertorically*, is discussed in Chapter 5, "Deriving 'Ought' from 'Is.'" (See, especially, the general analysis of #23.)

22. Objections to Stage III generally characterize the universalization process in terms of the external application of the LPU exclusively. William O'Meara (1982) and James Scheuermann (1987), at least, seem to be aware of Gewirth's appeal to the internal application of the LPU. O'Meara, however, questions the ASA, which is necessary to ground this application. (See #44.) Scheuermann does not seem to question the ASA as such, but suggests that its application cannot form a basis for internal application of the LPU (which is capable of effecting the move from the prudential to the moral) without employing a question-begging conception of "prudential agency." (See note 13 supra.)

23. Colin Davies (1975) claims that "ought implies can" cannot effect this move in the case of an "egoist." (See #34.1.) Kai Nielsen (1984) would have us believe (falsely) that Gewirth infers the move from the prudential to the moral by use of this principle. (See #48.)

24. See, for example, #35 and #47. Marcus G. Singer (1985) claims (falsely) that Gewirth uses this principle to effect the transition from the prudential to the moral. (See #49.)

Chapter 4: Objections to Stage I

1. Moral judgments are also made about the quality of a PPA's character. But to say that X is a morally good or bad person is to say that X acts, tends to act, or generally intends to act in morally good or bad ways, so that judgments of "agent morality" are analytically derivative of judgments of "act morality." The sole point of this remark is that to derive a moral principle from the concept of action does not beg the question against "virtue ethics." The virtues are dispositions to act well; their relevance is for action (which was appreciated by Aristotle—a proponent of "virtue ethics." See *Nicomachean Ethics*, especially Bk. 2 passim).

2. Which is also why the concept of reason employed in the justification must be the most generally applicable and inescapable one, viz., deductive and inductive logic.

3. There are some problems about whether Gewirth regards all human beings as PPAs. See Chapter 7, note 1.

4. The articles that Den Uyl deals with refer to "the principle of categorial consistency" (PCC), rather than to the PGC. As I have indicated in the Introduction, I shall treat all criticisms of Gewirth's earlier work as criticisms of his argument to the PGC in *Reason and Morality*

5. Peter Allen (1987) presses an objection that may be classified under #1. Allen contends that Gewirth's view, that moral precepts are directed at hearers who can control their behavior through their unforced choice, is arbitrary. "We could just as easily focus on other aspects of moral precepts such as their context-ridden nature," this being that "moral precepts address persons not as unencumbered individuals who can make their own decisions de novo but rather as bearers of social roles defined by institutional rules" (Allen 1987, 44).

These simply are not alternatives. To direct a practical precept at X is senseless if X cannot choose to obey it, and, thus, equally senseless if X cannot choose to disobey it. Institutional rules, as practical precepts, must be assumed to be directed at voluntary agents. That these agents may choose on the basis of contextual situations, rather than *in vacuo*, doesn't matter. What matters is that they are capable of reflecting on these factors and deciding for themselves what considerations they will and will not follow.

Connected with his assertion, Allen claims that Gewirth employs two conceptions of agency: one is a logical abstraction (focusing on the generic features), which grounds "the viewpoint of the agent," and the other is "phenomenological" in that agents are assumed to have varying ends. (See ibid., 45–46.) He alleges that Gewirth switches from "a purportedly logical or formal standpoint to a seemingly phenomenological one as it best suits his assumptions" (ibid., 41). Of course, there are not two conceptions of agency here at all. Agents are assumed to act for purposes that can vary. But they are assumed to do so *as PPAs* whose abilities *to act* are dependent upon their possession of the generic features. The whole argument is that, because freedom and well-being are categorically necessary conditions of guiding one's behavior by practical precepts, PPAs rationally ought to measure these precepts by the PGC regardless of the purposes that they might otherwise choose to follow, or be commanded to follow. As phenomenological agents, they rationally ought to follow the PGC, if this is open to them. Not to do so is to deny that they are agents (whatever contingent features might characterize their agency. See also #54).

6. Peter Allen's view (see Allen 1987, 47) that Gewirth's agents are not real "persons," because real persons very often lack the rational capacities and capacities for unforced choice that Gewirth's agents have, is irrelevant. What Gewirth is interested in is the justification of practical precepts. This question only arises in connection with beings with the capacities Gewirth attributes. If we direct practical precepts at ourselves or others, then we presuppose that these addressees are PPAs. That is all Gewirth's argument assumes. The validity of the argument is not affected by some (or even all) "persons" not being Gewirthian agents. All that this affects is the extent to which we may direct practical precepts at persons with propriety.

7. R. Randall Kelso objects to Gewirth's definition of "action" as "voluntary purposive behavior." This, he says, is taken by Gewirth to refer only to rational conscious decision making, ignoring the role of the emotions and "action" that is under the control of unconscious drives. (See Kelso 1982, 138–140.)

However, as I have just pointed out, Gewirth does not restrict actions to behaviors involving conscious deliberation. Furthermore, this objection misses the point that a conative aspect is involved in any *motivating* reason or purpose. Most importantly, Kelso fails to comprehend why Gewirth defines action in the way he does. The voluntariness condition arises because Gewirth is interested in practical precepts, the issuing of which presupposes that their addressees have the ability to guide their actions in conformity with the precepts. The rationality condition arises in one sense (that of a purposivity condition) because practical precepts prescribe purposes; and it arises in another sense (that of the ability to understand and follow "good" reasons or justifications—which is applied to PPAs rather than to their actions) because Gewirth is interested in the rational justification of practical precepts.

R. E. Ewin (1987, 53) says that, to say that a PPA must value a purpose is to say no more than that a PPA has it, for PPAs may act for purposes forced on them by circumstances; and that it is not clear that, in habitual action, PPAs act for any purposes at all.

However, PPAs only act when they choose their purposes. Furthermore, to act, a PPA need not be aware of its purpose at the time. Habitual actions were once done for conscious purposes, and retain them dispositionally. If the behavior in question does not have this character, then it is not action.

8. It must be noted that Gewirth holds that there is a sense in which a PPA *can* have "a capricious purpose," but this sense is different from Heslep's, because the PPA still values it. According to Gewirth, a PPA

> may also value the action only as having been arbitrarily chosen by him from among various alternatives, where he had to make some choice but was indifferent as to the alternatives. . . . Even in the case of arbitrarily chosen actions he at least wants to perform some action rather than none. So long as this wanting is not a case of forced choice . . . , it constitutes a valuing on the part of the agent so that, to this extent, he regards the purpose or object of his action as good . . . . (RM 50–51)

> [T]here are no indifferent actions, 'indifferent' meaning that the agent does not care at all whether he performs the action or not. For even if he regards his action as morally indifferent or as not making any difference on some other specific criterion, by the very fact that he aims to do the action he has a pro-attitude toward doing it and hence a positive or favorable interest in doing it. (RM 40)

Suppose that I am presented with two purposes, A and B, between which I am indifferent. Suppose I choose to pursue A. In so doing, my reason is not directly that I have a pro-attitude to A over B. But I have chosen to pursue A. My valuing A does not derive from a preference for A over B. It derives indirectly, from the fact that I have chosen to pursue A rather than B, which implies a pro-attitude to the pursuit of some purpose (rather than none). By my choice, this "indeterminate" preference is transmuted into a determinate preference for A.

It should also be noted that, although I might be indifferent as between A and B prior to my choice, it does not follow that I will be indifferent as between (A or B) and C, in which case I might have a direct preference for A over C, if not over B. The fact that my preferences or valuation of my purposes might be relative in this way does not damage Gewirth's argument.

9. D. D. Raphael claims that voluntariness does not necessarily form part of the ordinary conception of action, and that persons generally do not conceive of their well-being in the restricted manner in which Gewirth does—as capabilities for action. (See Raphael 1984, 86–87.) Gewirth (1984d, 202) ac-

cepts that this might well be the case. But, since his object is not to analyze "ordinary" usage of terms, but to justify practical precepts, the giving of which presupposes that the ability to comply or not is under the agent's control, the former fact, if it is a fact, is irrelevant.

> The term 'agent' as I have used it here is to some extent a techni-
> cal term or a term of art; it is not as current in ordinary language
> as is, for example, 'bachelor.' The term is defined through con-
> sideration of the characteristics understood to pertain to the pos-
> sible addresses of practical precepts that are held to be based on
> reason. (RM 171)

And, as far as the latter consideration is concerned, "the concept of well-being need not be dependent for its relevant meaning on what the majority of people understand by it"; it only matters that what Gewirth identifies as "well-being" is "intelligibly related to the conative pursuits that are charac-teristic of all persons as actual or prospective agents" (Gewirth 1984d, 202).

10. Many of Heslep's criticisms are repeated in Heslep 1989.

Bernard Williams also contends that a PPA can act for some purpose without regarding it as good. (See Williams 1985, 58–59.) To this Gewirth responds that Williams fails to distinguish between

> definitive judgments of goodness and judgments that ascribe
> only some minimal, even tentative, good or value to one's pur-
> poses. In my argument I held that the agent need not accept more
> than the latter . . . . (Gewirth 1988a, 145)

However, although this distinction must be made, Williams' objection is rather different. He explains in a footnote that

> [t]he point is not that a desire is not enough to give one a reason
> for acting. I have already said that it is enough (Chapter 1). The
> truth is that not every reason for action is grounded in an evalu-
> ation. (Williams 1985, 210 n. 9)

However, it follows from my commentary on Heslep's critique that this is false if a PPA's reasons for acting are purposes that the PPA has chosen.

11. See Lomasky 1981 for these other reasons. These are discussed under #35.8.

12. In his reply to Bond, Gewirth quotes from page 53 of *Reason and Mo-rality* (apparently in support of the view that a PPA must value its freedom *for its own sake*), that cases of surrendering one's freedom

> may correctly be regarded as pathological, because, so far as the
> historical record indicates, they mainly occur when basic well-
> being—persons' ability to obtain the minimal necessities re-
> quired for agency—is so severely threatened that only surrender
> of their freedom seems to offer any relief. (Gewirth 1980a, 64)

I am puzzled by this point, whether it be directed at showing that a PPA must value its freedom intrinsically or only categorically instrumentally, as it appeals to contingent considerations, which are alien to the dialectically necessary method.

It is to be noted that this reply also applies to W. D. Hudson's claim that Gewirth's argument presupposes that PPAs must consider it to be good that they are what they are. (See Hudson 1984, 125.) The context of Hudson's objection is, however, the question of the argument as a derivation of "ought" from "is," and it is discussed under #23.3.

13. Gewirth, of course, would not assent to such an assertoric formulation.

14. Mark Ockleton objects to the claim that a PPA must consider its freedom and well-being to be necessary goods, on the grounds that

> there are historical examples of people who, although apparently being purposive agents, have not wanted to make this claim. (Ockleton 1988, 236)

However, (a) the argument is not that persons who do not value their freedom and well-being (defined as capacities for agency) cannot be PPAs. It is that they deny that they are PPAs. The latter claim cannot be refuted by pointing to the historical record in this way. (b) Ockleton cites no examples, so it is unclear what he considers to be a case of not considering my freedom and well-being to be good. If he means things like people committing suicide, then this is not a counterexample, for even the suicide values its freedom and well-being as capacities for carrying out its suicidal purpose, and it is only freedom and well-being as generic capacities that are the subject matter of this claim.

15. This is in spite of his quibbles about this discussed under #4.

16. Williams' objection (see note 10 supra) has a similar aspect. He objects to "I must consider my purposes to be good," but not to "I must value my freedom." (See Williams 1985, 59.)

17. *Strictly speaking*, the basic goods are also "apparent" goods in the argument, features that *seem* good to the agent, or that *are* good *from the agent's point of view*. Although the basic needs are the same for all PPAs, so are the nonsubtractive and additive needs, and it is as generic needs that Gewirth views the nonsubtractive and additive goods as things that a PPA must regard as necessary goods.

18. Gerald H. Paske raises an objection that can be classified under the present heading, although, as will be seen, it might also be considered as an objection to Stage II.

According to Paske, a PPA need not accept "My freedom is a necessary good." The dialectical necessity of this proposition depends on freedom being a generic condition of my agency. But, in arguing this, Gewirth equivocates on the meaning of "freedom."

> Voluntariness is a generic feature of action. Freedom is not. "Freedom," in the sense of being free from the interference of other creatures, is helpful, but . . . it is not a generic feature of action. (Paske 1989, 55)

A PPA does not categorically need noninterference; it only needs to be able to overcome it.

This is rather mysterious as an objection to Stage I. Action is voluntary purposive behavior. In order to act a PPA must have "freedom," which Gewirth defines as the capacity to control one's behavior by one's unforced choice. This follows from the definition of action. If I do not have "freedom" in this sense, I will not be able to act voluntarily. "Freedom" is not defined as "noninterference." For one thing, noninterference with what?

Perhaps Paske has it in mind that, in Stage II, Gewirth holds that I must claim that PPAO ought not to interfere with my freedom (and well-being) on the basis of "My freedom (and well-being) are necessary goods." The argument for Stage II relies on the premise that I categorically need "noninterference" *with my freedom* (and well-being). On the basis of (4) "My freedom and well-being are necessary goods," I must hold (4c) "I ought to pursue my freedom and well-being." If PPAO "interferes" with my freedom and well-being, I will not be able to carry out this directive. So, by "ought implies can," I must hold (4d) "PPAO ought not to interfere with my freedom and well-being."

If this is what he has in mind, then Paske might be claiming that this sequence is invalid because I do not *categorically* need noninterference with my freedom (and well-being). If I do not categorically need noninterference with my freedom (and well-being), (4c) will not entail (4d).

However, whether or not I categorically need noninterference with my freedom and well-being depends on what we mean by "noninterference." There is an ambiguity in the phrase "to interfere with my freedom and well-being." This can mean "to *prevent* my having freedom and well-being," or it can mean "to *attempt to prevent* my having freedom and well-being" (or "to place obstacles in my path to having freedom and well-being"). In the former sense, it is nonsense to say that I do not need noninterference, but only need to overcome it. If there is interference, then (by definition) I will have failed to overcome it. In needing freedom, I need noninterference with it. So, in this sense, I do categorically need noninterference with my freedom (and well-being). In the latter sense, on the other hand, I do not categorically need noninterference, for I *might* be able to overcome it.

Stage II, however, only relies on my needing freedom and well-being in the former sense. From this we *can* derive that PPAO ought not to do what will prevent my having freedom and well-being. From this, we can also derive "PPAO ought not to attempt to prevent my having freedom and well-being (against my will, of course)" not because I *necessarily* could not defend myself successfully against such an attempt, but because I could not be certain that I would do so.

Of course, a PPA *may* choose to permit PPAO to interfere with its freedom and well-being (in either sense of "interfere"), for in "PPAO ought not to interfere with my freedom and well-being" it is understood that this is what PPAO ought not to do *against my will* (which is correlative to this "ought" being categorically instrumental). The rational permissibility of choosing a scenario that endangers my freedom cannot be construed as a denial that PPAO ought not to interfere with my freedom and well-being. It only signifies that such a choice is a choice to waive the justified requirement I have (from my point of view) that PPAO ought not so to act.

Thus, Paske's objection is mistaken, as it relies on a misinterpretation of the relevant conception of "interference," and hence of "freedom." (For a similar objection to Stage II, see #34.2.)

19. Strictly speaking, Gewirth begins from the desires *that they choose to follow*.

20. Narveson's particular occurrent interpretation of the "generic features" is brought out clearly in a later article. In this article Narveson says that additive and nonsubtractive goods

> will in fact vary among people, for they seem clearly to be attached to the particular sets of purposes people are pursuing. . . . [As far as the basic goods are concerned,] we may accept that such things as "life and physical integrity (including such of their means as food, clothing, and shelter)" and possibly also "mental equilibrium and a feeling of confidence as to the general possibility of attaining one's goals" ([RM] 54) are standing goods. Even here, though, we should be careful to appreciate that there is ample room for variation about specifics—one man's meat, as they say, being another man's poison. (Narveson 1984, 101)

Here, Narveson quite clearly fails to appreciate that my additive and nonsubtractive goods are to be given a generic-dispositional interpretation as well (as capacities for maintaining and extending my purposivity, which are independent of my particular occurrent purposes). When Narveson agrees that the basic needs are standing goods, but says that they are subject to relative judgments, he seems to be trying to have it both ways.

Glen O. Allen (1978, 128), similarly, claims that the generic rights are virtually devoid of determinate content, and that they might readily be "called into the service of indiscriminate human whim."

21. James O. Grunebaum (1976) and Arval A. Morris (1981) make a similar claim, but they focus on different alleged implications. (See #32.)

Reminiscent of Narveson (see note 22 infra), Tapio Puolimatka claims that "derived goodness cannot consistently be said to be more necessary than the goodness from which it is derived" (so a judgment of necessary good cannot be derived from one of good). Like Grunebaum, he says, "The prerequisites for these actions can be good only as instrumental to the given purposes" (Puolimatka 1989, 60).

He errs in thinking that in "good" and "necessary good," "good" has different meanings. The meaning is the same—proactive valuation. The predicate "necessary" signifies that its subject *must be* made a purpose by the PPA, which is not the case with "contingent" goods. Consequently, he errs in not distinguishing instrumental valuation from categorical instrumental valuation.

It is to be noted that Narveson's objection resembles a feature of one made by Stephen K. White (1982), who insists that a PPA can reason from the prerequisites of the range of purposes it would be willing to pursue, and need not reason from the prerequisites of its agency per se (the range of purposes it could possibly have). (See #34.2.)

22. In an earlier piece, Narveson says that Gewirth slips from thinking that I must value my freedom and well-being to thinking that I must value my freedom and well-being necessarily (from "It is necessary for me to think my freedom and well-being are good" to "It is necessary for me to think that my freedom and well-being are necessary goods").

> What about the rights which Gewirth thinks are supported by this argument? They are, of course, rights to "freedom and well-being," more specifically to "generic freedom and well-being," which presumably would be some kind of minimum of same. [No! See above.] (Gewirth slips quickly into and then stays permanently with the term "necessary goods," as if it were not only necessary that the agent think these things good, but also that he think they are "necessary goods" as well; after this, the notion of necessity, I believe, slides over in the direction of what is minimally necessary . . . .) (Narveson 1979, 430)

As I show in what follows, however, there is no "slippage." The inference from "I necessarily value my purposes" to "I necessarily attach necessary value to my freedom and well-being" is justified.

23. When Bond (1980a, 45) says that a PPA's valuation of its freedom and well-being does not go beyond its valuation of its particular occurrent purposes (see my discussion of #5), he makes the same claim as Narveson. This is mistaken for the same reason—failure to appreciate that because my freedom and well-being are categorical agency requirements (and not particular occurrent purposes), I must value them irrespective of my particular occurrent purposes, simply because I am a PPA with (by definition) some purposes. Narveson's allegation of a "slippage" from the necessity of valuing my purposes to the necessity of valuing my freedom and well-being necessarily, hints at Bond's allegation of an equivocation between senses of "a generic feature of agency," though I do not think that quite the same objection is being made.

24. Gewirth cites Maslow 1954, 80ff., and Towle 1957. (See RM 370 n. 6.)

Chapter 5: Objections to Stage II

1. Alasdair MacIntyre (1981) presents two objections that might have been considered here. They are considered under #36 and #37.

2. Williams' query might be prompted by the same error I have attributed to Narveson (1980) and Bond (1980a). See #5 and #6.

3. According to Glen O. Allen,

> [l]et it be granted that every agent values his own freedom and well-being as necessary conditions to action; it is nevertheless not obvious that so valuing them entails claiming them as rights. (Allen 1978, 128)

However, the rights-claim is required by the fact that a PPA *rationally must* value its freedom and well-being as categorically necessary conditions, not by the fact that it *just does* (or even that all PPAs do) so value them (which is not necessarily true).

Arthur C. Danto concedes that freedom and well-being being necessary goods, and my having rights to them, may well be valid inferences from my first-person perspective; but he does not see that "I need X to do Y (to rape)" entails that I have a right to do X, even in the first person. (See Danto 1984, 28–29.)

As Gewirth responds, a PPA's dialectically necessary rights-claims only derive from, and have as their object, *categorical needs*. (See Gewirth 1984c, 32.) If X is my freedom and well-being (generic-dispositionally interpreted), then I need X to rape. But I also need X to do anything. My rights-claim does not derive from the fact that I need X to rape (or for any other specific particular occurrent purpose), but because I need X to do anything at all.

4. This is, in effect, what I have called Gewirth's argument from attitudinal consistency.

5. For example, E. M. Adams claims that a PPA must regard its freedom and well-being as necessary, i.e., "unconditional, indispensable" goods. But this does not

> warrant the conclusion that . . . he must, on pain of inconsistency, regard them as rights, which entail obligations on the part of others. All the connection between "good" and desire would seem to warrant at this point would be that the agent, with his judgment that his freedom and well-being are indispensable goods, would, on pain of inconsistency, desire, and even regard as an indispensable good, that others not interfere with his freedom and well-being and that they assist him under certain circumstances in the maintenance and enhancement of them. (Adams 1980, 585)

R. M. Hare says,

> Let us admit for the sake of argument that the agent must *want* his purpose to be achieved (at any rate want it *ceteris paribus*), and that if one wants the purpose to be achieved, one must *want* whatever is a necessary condition for its achievement. . . . Can I not want something without thinking that I ought to have it? (Hare 1984, 54)

We are, of course, invited to answer "Yes!" (though note that Hare has slipped from "must want" to "want").

According to E. J. Bond, on the basis of "My freedom and well-being are necessary goods," Gewirth is entitled to say that

> I must will or regard as a necessary, self-regarding good, that others do not interfere with it. (Bond 1980a, 49–50)

But this is not the same as considering that I have a right to my freedom and well-being.

Bernard Williams appreciates that I necessarily want my "basic freedom," and hence "I must be opposed to courses of action that would remove it" (Williams 1985, 59). He asks rhetorically, "But does this, in itself, generate any prescription that leads to obligations or rights?" (ibid., 61).

I could offer more citations, but this is hardly necessary. Anyone who accepts Stage I (without misinterpreting it), but rejects Stage II, must make this claim.

6. Gewirth holds that

> a necessary condition of any person's claiming a right to any-thing X is that X seems to him to be . . . directly or indirectly good according to whatever criteria he accepts in the given situation. By 'indirectly good' I refer mainly to two kinds of cases. One is where the claimant does not regard as good the specific object of his right-claim but holds that this object, insofar as he claims a right to it, is a specification of some more general good. . . . A second kind of indirect good is found where a person has and claims a certain right by virtue of certain rules he upholds and regards as good, even though he may not regard as good every application of the rules. (RM 76)

7. Gewirth expresses this by saying, "But even if it is a necessary condi-tion of someone's claiming a right to X that X seem to him to be good, it is hardly a sufficient condition" (RM 77).

8. In some formal modal calculi any proposition strictly implies a neces-sary truth. This is because such calculi are merely designed to ensure that false conclusions are not inferred from true premises. We could not, how-ever, know that (β) was true on the basis of "Napoleon was an emperor," and the sense of "entailment" I am employing here would require this to be the case.

9. Which covers cases (–C2) and (–C3) above.

10. This aspect of voluntary agency was emphasized in Chapter 4. For a discussion of some complications that might be thought to arise from this assertion, see my discussion of #21.

Jeffrey Reiman commits a similar error to Veatch's when he says that, for Gewirth, a PPA's dialectically necessary deontic judgments are matters of "sheer inescapable fact," "a kind of compulsion that grabs hold of the rea-soning faculties of a prospective agent," and, as such, are "blind" and carry "no warrant" (Reiman 1990, 62).

11. Gewirth argues that my acceptance of this self-referring "ought" en-tails that I must hold that I have a right to my freedom and well-being. However, Veatch does not consider this sequence. This sequence is, of course, that presented by Gewirth in arguing that even an amoralist must consider that it has a right to its freedom and well-being (see RM 89–95), which I have presented as the central argument for Stage II. For general discussion of the argument as an "is-ought" derivation see #23. Narveson (1980) does consider at least part of this sequence (see #11), but he fails to treat its "ought" premise as a *strict* self-referring one.

12. The general use of this criterion is discussed under #61.

13. Glen O. Allen (1978, 128) also claims that Gewirth holds that an act is wrong because it is illogical.

14. Bond then adds (in a footnote) that he considers the statement "Every agent ought to act in accord with the generic rights of his recipients as well

as of himself" to be analytically true. This is because it is analytically true that rights are to be respected.

> But this is empty analyticity, quite lacking in content. . . . It is the statement "Every agent ought to respect the freedom and well-being of his recipients as well as of himself" that Gewirth must show to be, with its content, analytic or logically necessary. (Bond 1980a, 43 n. 1)

However, although "Every agent ought to act in accordance with the rights of his recipients as well as of himself" is analytic, Gewirth does not try to argue that "Every agent ought to grant himself and his recipients rights to freedom and well-being" is analytic itself on that account. Inasmuch as Gewirth does state the PGC as "Every agent ought to respect the generic rights of his recipients as well as of himself," it is clear that he is expecting the reader to realize that "generic rights" refers to "rights to freedom and well-being." With this reference, the principle is not an "empty analyticity." Indeed, as he points out in his reply to Bond (see Gewirth 1980a, 54–55), he considered this objection about "empty analyticity" on pages 151–152 of *Reason and Morality*. And, of course, it is not the PGC that is contended to be analytic, but the statement that every PPA ought to accept the PGC.

E. M. Adams makes a comment that is well-nigh identical to Bond's when he says,

> I have no quarrel with Gewirth's APGC [assertoric PGC] as such. It is, I think, analytically true. This is so by virtue of the conceptual connection between "ought" and "rights," if not because of what is entailed by "agent." (Adams 1980, 591)

15. "No deontic statement with content can be logically necessary" can mean either (a) "No deontic statement with content is itself a necessary truth (the negation of which *is* a contradictory proposition, because the proposition states, once the meanings of its terms are understood, that A = A)" or (b) "No deontic statement with content is such that it is logically necessary for a PPA to hold it (the denying of which by a PPA involves the PPA contradicting that it is a PPA)." Gewirth holds that (a) is true, but (b) is false. These two should not be confused. This is discussed below.

16. Another way of explaining Bond's confusion is to point out that "Denial of X is contradictory" is ambiguous. It can mean either that the act of denying X lands the denier in contradiction, or that the proposition that –X is a contradiction. These are not equivalent, and when Gewirth says that denial of the PGC is contradictory, he means the former, not the latter. Bond's objection can be seen to arise from reading Gewirth to be saying "A proposition that is the negation of the PGC is a contradiction" or by taking this statement to be equivalent to Gewirth's position.

17. For Gewirth's reply to Bond, see Gewirth 1980a, 55–62, and Gewirth 1980b, 138–139. Although my reply is to much the same effect as Gewirth's, I have not followed the form or ramifications of his response. All these matters, and more besides, are discussed extensively in RM 150–161 and 171–190. Bond barely alludes to this discussion.

According to Jeffrey Reiman, if Stages II and III are valid, then Gewirth has shown that a PPA contradicts itself by not accepting the PGC. However, he claims that Gewirth would still not have shown that a PPA is *morally* required not to interfere with the freedom and well-being of PPAO, for "the simple reason that logical requirements are not moral requirements" (Reiman 1990, 109).

In connection with this, Reiman makes four claims.

a.   If I deny that PPAO has the generic rights, then I deny that I have the generic rights. However, it does not follow that I must concede PPAO the generic rights, for I might have been wrong to claim these rights for myself. (See ibid., 110.)

b.   That I contradict myself by not affirming the PGC as the supreme moral principle does not show that I do wrong by violating it. (See ibid., 111.)

c.   Gewirth does not show murder to be any worse than calling a bachelor "married." (See ibid., 127.)

d.   Gewirth's theory is about moral discourse, not about morality. (See ibid., 181.)

Regarding *a:* I *cannot* rationally consider that I am wrong to claim the generic rights for myself. If Stage II is valid, this claim is dialectically necessary. Inasmuch as Reiman appreciates this, he claims that it might be the case that I *have* no rights even if I must think that I do. However, this is beside the point, as the dialectically necessary method seeks to establish only that I must consider that I (and ultimately PPAO too) have the generic rights. It does not seek to establish assertorically that I have them. It is not necessary to have an *assertoric* conclusion to Stage II in order to obtain the *dialectical necessity* of the PGC by universalization.

Regarding *b:* The PGC *itself* states, "I *morally ought* to refrain from interfering with PPAO's freedom and well-being." If I (logically) must *accept* the PGC, I (logically) must *accept* that I do *moral* wrong by violating the PGC, which is all Gewirth alleges.

Regarding *c:* The argument makes morality a requirement of logic only in the sense that it provides logically necessary reasons for PPAs to adopt a moral principle. The "ought" prescribed by the PGC is not logical because the reasons to adopt the PGC are logical. Within the argument, murder is wrong because it interferes with PPAO's categorical needs. It is only the wrongness of not accepting this reason for the wrongness of murder that is logical. Calling a bachelor "married" is not necessarily wrong according to the criterion of PPAO's categorical needs.

Regarding *d:* This is true, insofar as the argument is about what PPAs must consider to be right and wrong, not about what is *assertorically* right or wrong. But what a PPA *must* think has assertoric force for it for all practical purposes. Moral discourse is itself about morality.

These errors are generally produced by attempting to construe the argument as an assertoric derivation of the PGC.

18. Peter A. French says, "The logical necessity generated by the law of contradiction is concerned with propositions, not with acting" (French 1979,

111). This ignores the fact, which is all that is relevant (given the argument's dialectical context), that some propositions prescribe for actions.

19. For further discussion around this point see #21.

Tapio Puolimatka accuses Gewirth of reducing morality to logic (see Puolimatka 1989, 162), and specifically raises Cohen's objection. (See ibid., 185 n. 31.)

Peter A. French claims that

> the attempt to create a logical necessity for being moral, if it did convert moral judgments into assertions of requirements that one can only fail to meet on pain of irrationality, would in the end make a sham of choice and hence of the very freedom morality is meant to protect. If I must do *x* or I am irrational and I do not do *x*, then I certainly cannot be held blameworthy for not doing *x*, for I am irrational. But I must be held blameworthy for those of my irrational acts that violate the generic rights of others, or Gewirth's formulation of morality has no point. (French 1979, 109)

The first sentence is ambiguous. It states either (*a*) If I (logically) ought to obey the PGC, then I am not free (able) to make my own choices (and to disobey the PGC); or (*b*) If I (logically) ought to obey the PGC, then I am not free (rationally permitted) to make choices that disobey the PGC.

a is false. Although *b* is true, it does not deny the freedom the PGC is meant to protect. (For some related discussion see #52.)

In the rest of the passage, French seems to say that irrational PPAs cannot be blamed for doing wrong. However, this is true only if an "irrational PPA" is one without the capacity to reason correctly. But excusing the mentally deficient, in this sense, from moral responsibility, hardly removes the point from morality. If an "irrational PPA" is one with this capacity who errs in reasoning, or who refuses to follow its correct reasoning, then I do not see why it cannot be held culpable for violating the PGC. It is capable of correct reasoning and does not *have* to violate the PGC.

20. Fred Feldman (1983, 477) also alleges that Gewirth uses this principle to derive the assertoric truth of the PGC from its dialectical necessity. (See also #18.2, #23.1.1, and #23.1.2.)

21. Arthur C. Danto claims that something

> as fragile and threatened as human rights are needs some better protection than an argument with itinerant operators, dependent upon the eccentricities of first-person implicatures and the internal presuppositions of points of view. (Danto 1984, 30)

Gewirth replies that there is nothing eccentric about these implications, as they are based on the generic features of agency and, therefore, rationally necessary and binding on all PPAs. The conclusion that all PPAs must accept the PGC is quite sufficient to give human rights a firm rational basis. (See Gewirth 1984c, 33.)

The point is that, as far as PPAs are concerned (and they are all who matter practically), a universal dialectically necessary justification is as good as an assertoric one. It won't, of course, be sufficient to guarantee that human rights are respected. But neither would an assertoric demonstration of the PGC. Getting PPAs to act rationally is a matter of practical politics, not one of moral epistemology alone.

22. I confess to having something of an allergy to talk of "relative truth." This is, however, acceptable enough if what it means is only that certain conclusions are *valid* on some premises and not on others.

23. It is to be noted that a number of other commentators (e.g., Paul Allen III [1982a], Jeffrey Paul [1979], and Gary Seay [1983]) portray Gewirth as claiming to have established the PGC in itself as a necessary truth. These are considered under #23.1, as the main interest of their comments lies elsewhere.

24. It is understandable that Gewirth might wish to distance himself from any doctrine that bears the label "synthetic a priori," for this doctrine is associated with Kantian transcendentalism specifically, and with traditional epistemological rationalism more generally, and there is strong resistance (albeit misconceived) to both of these nowadays.

25. After all, determinism *might* be true. See the discussion of #2.

26. For a discussion of Kant's position, see Beyleveld 1980.

Tapio Puolimatka completely misconstrues Gewirth's view of the nature of the statements validated by the dialectically necessary method. No doubt picking up on Gewirth's claim that the PGC is "true by correspondence," as well as being validated by conceptual analysis (see #58 for a discussion of this), he launches into a very confused discussion. This discussion interprets the PGC as a necessary truth about the world, which is established by conceptual analysis from a definition of agency that is derived from statements that are supposed to be analytically true, though derived from experience. This has the effect of interpreting the PGC as an alleged analytic truth derived from experience, with the claim that the PGC is true by correspondence being interpreted as the claim that conceptual analysis can establish its "empirical truth." To this Puolimatka objects that elements in the statements defining the concept of action "that are derived from empirical experience cannot be analytically true" (Puolimatka 1989, 42), and that conceptual analysis alone is not sufficient to establish something as necessarily true about the world (meaning "empirically true"). (See ibid., 42–47.)

a. However, Gewirth's definition of action is not derived empirically. It is derived from the features that behavior must be supposed to have if it is to be the object of practical precepts, themselves defined according to necessary requirements set by the question that guides the argument. (See #1.3.)

b. The PGC is derived dialectically from this concept of action. That the PGC must be espoused by PPAs (defined according to the procedures in *a*) is analytically true. This analyticity is, however, material—in the sense that it is not a stipulation, but a specification by conceptual analysis of features that PPAs, if they were to exist, must (accept they) possess. For them not to accept these features would be for them to deny that they were PPAs as defined.

c. The relevance and force of the argument, in the real world, is, however, an empirical matter. It depends on the extension of the term "PPA" as defined, or on the degree to which persons employ, or presuppose, this concept in their discourse and practice.

In this, empirical considerations relate solely to the scope of the argument, conceptual analysis solely to the validation of its inferences. Puolimatka's objection conflates these two issues.

d. Puolimatka's discussion requires the PGC to be interpreted as an assertoric truth derived from assertoric truths, which again totally misconstrues the enterprise.

27. This distinction has relevance for the objection made by Cohen (1979, #17), and also for those of Veatch (1979, #14), Versenyi (1976, note 28 infra), Nielsen (1984, #22), and Hudson (1984, #23.3). Reading the focus of the argument in terms of its practical prescriptive capacity as directed to PPAs *in essentia,* rather than at PPAs *in referentia,* may also contribute to all readings of the argument as attempting to establish the PGC as an analytic truth *tout court.*

28. Laszlo Versenyi (focusing on Gewirth 1974a) claims that Gewirth argues that the PGC is logically derived from the concept of action. If so, then it is logically impossible for a PPA not to conform to the PGC. However, if it is not possible not to conform to the PGC, then the PGC is a pointless command, empty of content, and as a command (which has as its point purposes that it is logically possible not to achieve) contradicts the notion of a purposive agent. Conversely, if an imperative has content, then it cannot be derived logically from the concept of action. (See Versenyi 1976, 265–273.)

What has been said in reply to Lycan can also be said in reply to Versenyi. In particular it is to be noted that the argument has the consequences that Versenyi alleges only if it is directed at PPAs *in essentia:* it has none of these consequences if directed at PPAs *in referentia.* Versenyi's criticism of Gewirth also has other features that do not merit consideration, as they rest on a severe distortion of the argument. I refer, in particular, to his construal of the PGC as commanding a PPA to be purposive (which means, for Versenyi, to be voluntary as well as to pursue purposes). Gewirth's reply to Versenyi concentrates on this aspect. (See Gewirth 1976, 288–289.)

29. Furthermore, Nielsen claims, it cannot be necessarily true, without at least a *ceteris paribus* qualification, that PPAO ought to refrain from interfering with my freedom and well-being. However, it is quite clear that Gewirth holds that this "ought" need only be prima facie (as he points out in response to Nielsen). (See Gewirth 1984d, 207.) I have commented on some possible complications to this reply in Chapter 2, note 40.

Fred Feldman (1983, 479) errs straightforwardly in interpreting the rights-claims of Stage II as absolute.

30. Nielsen's misreading of Gewirth's position could possibly be attributed to a failure to appreciate that the PPAs to whom the argument is directed are PPAs *in referentia,* not PPAs *in essentia.* See the discussion of #21.

31. The doctrine of the "is-ought gap" I take to be the view that no categorical prescription can be derived from premises that do not contain categorical prescriptions.

32. See note 34 infra.

33. Roger Trigg says that, by making well-being a precondition of action, Gewirth runs the risk of making the argument either not morally neutral or else totally vacuous. As Gewirth specifies the preconditions of agency, the argument yields specific rights (which makes the conclusion not morally neutral). Yet Gewirth asserts that the generic features of action are prescribed in all moralities, and this makes the argument vacuous (as it cannot now choose between moralities. See Trigg 1980, 151).

Trigg's dilemma is spurious.

a. His idea of moral neutrality is odd. He appears to allege that the argument is not morally neutral if it has a determinate conclusion that precludes or rejects certain positions. This dovetails with his claim that, because certain of Gewirth's conclusions are controversial (there are positions that reject them), the argument cannot be morally neutral. (See ibid., 150.) Well, in *this sense,* Gewirth's argument is not morally neutral. But so what? If it were, it would be vacuous. What matters is that Gewirth has not arbitrarily introduced assumptions generating a morally determinate conclusion. Avoidance of such a question-begging strategy is the only critical sense in which the argument must be morally neutral. On this front, Trigg suggests that Gewirth has *made* well-being a precondition of action. Gewirth has done nothing of the sort. Well-being *is* a precondition of action (where this is the sort of behavior that is the address of practical precepts). It is not open to him to specify anything else.

b. The second horn of Trigg's dilemma involves a misreading of what Gewirth says. Gewirth (see RM 356, the source of Trigg's attribution) does not say that all moralities prescribe the generic features (i.e., prescribe that PPAs have rights to freedom and well-being). He says that "the generic features are found in the actions prescribed by all moralities and other practical precepts." This means that the generic features are preconditions of all actions prescribed by moralities and other practical precepts. So, if their precepts (those of any SPR) are to be followed, those at whom they are directed must have the generic features. From this it follows that all moralities, *on pain of reductio ad absurdum*, must (not "do") prescribe that their addressees have the generic features. This does not make the argument vacuous. On the contrary, it is because this is so that the argument can have a determinate conclusion that is arrived at in a non–question-begging way.

34. W. D. Hudson says that, due to its conative normality, a PPA

> not only sees that he needs the capabilities of action if he is to go on being an agent, but he wants to do so and is therefore prepared to insist upon having these capabilities. (Hudson 1984, 126)

However, Hudson does not see how a PPA can be required to claim rights to these capabilities on this account. But, as we have seen in "From Needs to Rights?" it is not on this account that a PPA must claim the generic rights. Due to its conative normality, a PPA *is required* to want the capabilities of action, whether it actually wants them or not, and *is required* to insist upon having them, whether it wants to or not. Just wanting its generic features or just being prepared to insist on having them does not come into it. It is on the basis of this stringent requirement that a PPA is required to go on and claim rights to its generic features.

35. Gewirth says that, at the point where it is shown that a PPA must claim that its freedom and well-being are necessary goods,

> from the standpoint of the agent the 'fact-value' gap, even if not the 'is-ought' gap, is already bridged in action. (RM 57)

However, I think that the "is-ought gap" is also bridged at this point, because the *proactive* valuation of its purposes renders the PPA's judgment of necessary goods as a self-referring strict "ought."

36. To be somewhat pedantic, this depends upon what is meant by "agent." The statement is true for "PPAs *in essentia*," but not for "PPAs *in referentia*." (See #21.) I would also say that this is logically prescriptive rather than descriptive in the case of PPAs *in referentia*.

37. If so, then it is likely that he accepts that "I logically must consider that I have rights to my freedom and well-being" entails "All PPAs logically must consider that all PPAs have rights to their freedom and well-being" (and thereby that all PPAs must take favorable account of the interests of PPAO), but does not consider that "I must *claim rights* to my freedom and well-being" entails "I must *consider that I have rights* to my freedom and well-being."

38. The general question raised concerns the way in which a PPA's dialectically necessary judgments are "agent-relative." I comment on this in connection with criticisms made by Paul Allen III (#23.1.2), E. M. Adams (#23.2.1 and #59), Jesse Kalin (#35.3 in particular), James Scheuermann (#50), and Christopher McMahon (Chapter 8, note 31). Some general comments are also made on this in Chapter 11.

39. It is to be noted that Paul seems to think that there is a gap between "I must claim a right to X" and "I must consider that I have a right to X." As Gewirth uses "claim" here, there is no gap. Gewirth means the latter when he says the former. Of course, "claim" may also be used in the sense of an act of demand. If Paul is saying that I must demand a right to my freedom and well-being but not consider that I have a right to my freedom and well-being, then he is not objecting to Stage III but to Stage II.

40. Loren Lomasky (1981, 249) interprets Paul as offering such a critique.

41. I consider this aspect of Paul's criticisms further under #46. Since I find it impossible to detach this aspect from his central objection, which relates to the argument not being a successful derivation of an assertoric "ought" conclusion from "is" premises, my two discussions of this aspect involve considerable repetition.

42. Allen runs the argument in terms of freedom only, and says nothing about well-being.

43. Gewirth does not claim this, if "I have a duty" is meant to be an assertoric statement *tout court*. (See #18.)

44. It is to be noted that E. M. Adams is inclined to interpret "E is good" in [I do X for purpose E → *Within my standpoint as a PPA, E is good*] as *meaning* "E is judged to be good." This is not plausible, says Adams, because

then we get an infinite regress. "E is judged to be good" means "E is judged is judged to be good" and so on ad infinitum. (See Adams 1984, 20.) Indeed, we do. But Gewirth does not mean by "E is good" that "E is judged to be good." What Gewirth means when he says that E seems good to the agent is that E *is* good from the *agent's point of view.*

Furthermore the universalization from Stage II to Stage III needs to operate on a judgment that I *have* a right to my freedom and well-being, albeit *from my point of view.* (See the internal application of the LPU in Chapter 3, "The Formal Structure of the Argument.") If Allen is right in his criticism, then the argument to Stage III will not work *even dialectically,* as Allen thinks it does. Allen says (see the above quote from page 223) that Gewirth validly infers the PGC from "E is good" within a PPA's standpoint. This is right, but incompatible with Allen's general criticism, for this can't be right *unless* Gewirth is able to infer "Within my standpoint [I pursue E → E is good] is a valid inference" (i.e., that "E is good" is true *relative to my standpoint,* as Gewirth might prefer to put it).

45. See "Grounding Morality in Logic," especially #18.

46. See Alasdair MacIntyre's objections discussed under #36 and #37.

47. Allen 1982b covers much the same ground vis-à-vis Gewirth as Allen 1982a.

48. W. D. Hudson asks whether Gewirth hasn't adulterated the "is," and thus begged the question. He claims that, in the derivation, "I do X for purpose E" is not treated as a pure indicative, but as a speech act with "both constative and prescriptive illocutionary force." (See Hudson 1984, 119–122.) Gewirth replies that he does not take it to be prescriptive. He takes it to be descriptive. There is a difference between implicit inclusion of a premise and explicit inclusion. There is an implicit inclusion here, meaning that it exists in the PPA's relation to the facts of agency, and this is revealed by analysis. It is not added *by Gewirth* to the analysis, and its presence, therefore, begs no questions. It is also in response to this charge that Gewirth claims that he really couldn't care whether the "is" is a pure fact or not, as long as it is dialectically necessary and the PGC follows from it with dialectical necessity. (See Gewirth 1984d, 222–223.) Gewirth also points out that "if the purely factual is that which is the case independently of anyone's *variable* commitments or *contingent* evaluations, then the 'do' aspect of ['I do X for purpose E'] reflects the purely factual nature of things" because the "do" is not something that I can dispense with as a PPA; so, if it includes value, then this is also indispensable. (See ibid., 223.) This, indeed, makes the factuality of "I do X for purpose E" unassimilable to institutional facts, which is what Gewirth is primarily at pains to point out here (because I can decide not to engage in promising, etc.). However, I do not think that this really bears on the question of factuality as such (though it bears on the question of the type of fact): it bears rather on the dialectical necessity of the implicit evaluative component.

49. In connection with #23.1 generally, the following criticisms are to be noted:

a. Richard Brooks claims that Gewirth begins with what seems good to the agent, but later moves (unsuccessfully) to conclusions about what is good. (See Brooks 1981, 293.) Gewirth makes no such move, so he cannot make it unsuccessfully.

b. Hugo Adam Bedau claims that Gewirth's argument is not strong enough, because it doesn't prove that PPAs *have* the generic rights.

> The reason is that the assertoric propositions, 'I have rights to freedom and wellbeing' and 'Every agent has rights to freedom and wellbeing,' have not been derived or established at all. For all we know from Gewirth's argument, these two propositions may be false. Yet some such assertoric propositions must be true if we have human rights. To put this another way, Gewirth's argument at best shows that any moral agent [any agent!] in effect must say, 'If I am to act, then I and every other agent have [must consider that I/we have] the human moral right to freedom and wellbeing.' But it is difficult to see how this hypothetical proposition constitutes an explanation of why we have the rights we do, if we have any rights. (Bedau 1984, 66)

There is some confusion here about what's hypothetical and what's dialectical, but we can let this pass. The answer to this is that it doesn't matter whether we have rights or not. What matters is that we are justified in holding that we do. If we must claim that we have rights, then we must hold that we do, and are justified in so doing. We don't have to have rights in order to be logically required to claim (consider, hold) that we do.

c. Arthur C. Danto says that Gewirth's argument does not cross the fact/value gap, because there are differences between what is valid from first-person and third-person perspectives. From my point of view, it may be crossed in the first person, but not in the third person, because to say that PPAO must judge that E is good is not to make a value judgment. (See Danto 1984, 27–28.)

Quite! As Gewirth replies,

> I was making a point about the crossing of the fact/value gap only from within the agent's *first-person* perspective, not from any *third*-person perspective. (Gewirth 1984c, 32)

It cannot be overemphasized that the entire argument is from within my internal viewpoint as a PPA, until the concluding stages of Stage III, when claims I must make are shown to be valid within any PPA's internal viewpoint (about any PPA), and that the argument never transcends this dialectical purview—except for practical purposes.

d. The article by Mark D. Stohs (1988), considered under #18, might be included under this heading.

50. This "ought" is thus equivalent to (ω) in my presentation of the argument as a reductio in Chapter 3.

51. It is vacuous, in this context, to analyze proactive "good" in terms of "ought" if this "ought" is not strict. On the other hand, if this "ought" is strict, then it will not be accepted by the adeonticist.

52. It is doubtful, however, that this is what Adams has in mind. See #59.

53. This transition was explained in Chapter 2. It is also discussed under #31.

54. Gewirth claims that the argument cannot be made to rest on a premise such as "Every agent ought to act according to what follows from the concept of an agent" or "What logically must be accepted by every agent is right" *where* the criterion of "ought" or "right" is *moral*. If such premises are assumed,

> then the whole argument for the *PGC* will rest not on factual and logical antecedents alone but on a normative or evaluative premise; moreover, the question will then arise of the truth or warrant of this premise. (RM 155)

55. Though he seems to forget that he has granted this when he presents the objection referred to in note 34 supra.

56. See the discussion of categorical instrumental "ought" in Chapter 2. See also #4 and #32.

57. There is another possible interpretation of Hudson's objection. This has Hudson attributing to Gewirth the view that a PPA is a being who necessarily follows the PGC (as against one who necessarily ought to follow the PGC). But to say that I ought to follow the PGC when I can't do otherwise (while remaining a PPA) is nonsensical. If this is what Hudson has in mind, then his objection is akin to Lycan's or Versenyi's (see #21), and is to be dealt with by drawing the distinction between PPAs *in essentia* and PPAs *in referentia*, and by pointing out that the subject of the argument is a PPA *in referentia* who can violate the PGC.

58. It is worth pointing out again (see #23.1.1) that the logical necessity of a PPA's "claiming" a right to freedom and well-being does not essentially refer to a PPA's act of presenting a claim to a right, but to its considering that it has a right. Considering that X is the case may, of course, be classed as an act; so this point has no real bearing on Hudson's discussion. However, the point is important in its own right, and should not be obscured by the way in which Hudson states the case.

59. This objection is not stated in this form by any critics of *Reason and Morality*. But the general question needs to be considered.

60. Gewirth's notion of the generic features of agency as "categorical interests" may be viewed as giving content to the notion of "real interests."

61. In Gewirth's terminology (see the quote below from RM 361–362), prudential and moral criteria are "external" to each other.

62. The transition from the prudential to the moral and social is . . . , in the first instance, not motivational but logical. The reason why the agent must endorse the generic rights of his recipients is not the Hobbesian prudential or contingent one that if he violates or fails to endorse these rights for others he may probably expect them to violate his own rights, but rather the logically necessary one that if there is a sufficient condition that justifies the agent's having the generic rights [within the agent's standpoint of course], then it must justify that these rights are had by all other persons who satisfy that sufficient condition. . . . [I]f the

basis of the *PGC* as a moral principle were only prudential, its
validity or requiredness would be contingent on the degree to
which an agent could not in fact pursue his purposes without
endorsing other persons' having the generic rights. . . . Since,
however, the basis of these obligations is logical, their validity is
necessary independent of such considerations. (RM 146)

When the agent says 'I have rights to freedom and well-being,'
he makes or accepts the statement for his own self-interested
reasons, or at least for reasons bearing on his pursuit of his own
purposes . . . . The case is different, however, with the subsequent step where the agent's right-claim entails the generalization, 'All prospective purposive agents have rights to freedom
and well-being.' For this generalized judgment is not set forth by
the agent for his pursuit of his own purposes or for his own
self-interested reasons; on the contrary, it imposes restrictions on
his acting for these purposes or reasons. (RM 190)

The argument is, therefore, not prudentially reductive. But does this not
create another problem, one about the motivational or prescriptive force of
the PGC? The judgments of Stages I and II have motivational force for a PPA
because they are advocated for the sake of its own purposes. But a mere
logical relation does not carry motivational force. So might it not be the case
that the PGC is not a practical-prescriptive principle, despite its being impossible for a PPA to deny it without self-contradiction?
Gewirth's answer to this is that

the *PGC* must have prescriptive force for the agent because it
follows logically from his individual right-claim, which admittedly has prescriptive force for him [provided that this is properly interpreted]. (RM 191)

To interpret this properly, it must be understood (*a*) that the PPA's judgments in Stages I and II are judgments made "within the context of the
agent's overall acceptance of rationality" (RM 192). This means that if a PPA
refuses to accept the judgment that it ought not to interfere with PPAO's
freedom and well-being, then it cannot consistently uphold its individual
rights-claim. This does not show that logical consistency merely provides a
reason for making judgments, but not a reason for acting in accordance with
them, for a reason for me to judge that I ought to do X is a reason for me to
do X. (See RM 194.) Furthermore, (*b*) for a rational PPA, the question of
motivation is not the question of whether it is in fact motivated to accept the
judgment, but the question of whether it rationally ought to accept the judgment, and (*c*) "by virtue of the *PGC*'s being rationally justified the rational
agent is in fact motivated to accept it, since, being rational, he accepts what
is rationally justified" (RM 195). Still further, (*d*) "every agent ought to be
motivated to accept the *PGC*, where the criterion of this 'ought' is initially
not moral but rational or logical" (ibid.).
I am not totally sure of considerations (*c*) and (*d*). As formulated, these
(and [*c*] in particular) *might* run foul of the distinction between PPAs *in*

essentia and PPAs *in referentia,* which is necessary to answer certain objections. (See #21.) Anyway, whether or not this is so, (*a*) is adequate by itself, and it is this to which Gewirth appeals in summing up his discussion of motivation.

> [T]he *PGC,* because of its derivation, is . . . not open to the strictures of Hume and other critics of ethical rationalism. . . . [A]n intrinsic part of the principle's justification rests on its having a necessary content referring to the freedom and well-being that every agent must regard as his rights. This content is a direct source of human motivations . . . . Thus, the agent can reject the *PGC* only by surrendering the logical right to uphold . . . evaluative and prescriptive judgments . . . that express the purposive strivings necessarily characteristic of all agents. . . . [T]he *PGC's* derivation shows how reason can be practical; but 'reason' now includes not only logical form but also the conative content, itself ascertained by conceptual analysis, that in the argument is necessarily combined with this form. (RM 196)

Chapter 6: Objections to Stage II
1. The general philosophical considerations with which this chapter deals are relevant to the two "main" objections to Gewirth's argument (#35 and #47). Many examples of these objections rest on the contention that X can only consider that Y has an obligation not to interfere with X's doing/having Z (that X has a right to Z against Y) if Y accepts this, or accepts the criterion that X employs to validate it. This contention is at least implicit in many of the objections dealt with in this chapter. My reasons for rejecting this contention are given mainly under #35. (See, e.g., #35.2.)

2. Related to the distinction between prescriptive and recognitional senses of "a right," it is to be noted that Arthur C. Danto thinks that, at the end of Stage II, Gewirth's PPA is required to think that it has rights when all that has been shown is that it has a need for them. However, says Danto, the only way in which a PPA can acquire rights is for others to recognize that it has them; and this means that arguments for my having to think that I have them from the internal point of view are beside the point. (See Danto 1984, 30.)

I find this far from clear. Obviously, if my thinking that I have a right to X is my thinking that others will think that they ought not to interfere with my doing X, or that they will not interfere with my doing X (grant me a right in the recognitional sense), then my thinking that I have a right will be mistaken if others do not recognize my right in the prescriptive sense, or if they interfere with my doing X. But Gewirth argues that I must think that I have a right to my freedom and well-being in the prescriptive sense, which, from my internal point of view, requires neither that others will refrain from interfering with my freedom and well-being, nor that others recognize that I have a right to my freedom and well-being in the prescriptive sense. Is Danto saying (*a*) that I cannot be required to think that I have a right to my freedom and well-being *in the prescriptive sense* unless others recognize that I have such a right/do not interfere with my freedom and well-being? Or, is he saying (*b*) that I must think that I have a right in *the prescriptive sense*, but that showing this is irrelevant to showing that others must recognize my right in the prescriptive sense/will not interfere with my freedom and well-being?

If (*a*), then Gewirth's response is that

> [t]o make rights dependent entirely on declaration and recognition would mean that slaves and other oppressed groups would have no rights even in the sense of moral justification. (Gewirth 1984c, 34)

If (*b*), then the response is that, by the universalization of Stage III, it can be shown that *I (as a PPA)* must recognize the right of others to *their* freedom and well-being, and hence that others (as PPAs) must recognize my right to freedom and well-being, so establishing that the result that I must think that I have a right to my freedom and well-being is not irrelevant to showing that others must recognize this claim. Of course, this does not show that others will refrain from interference with my freedom and well-being, or even that they will grant that I have a right in the prescriptive sense. However, this is irrelevant, because the argument is about what PPAs are justified in doing, not about what they can do. It is an epistemology of rights, not an ontology of action. It is Danto's objection that is beside the point.

Jesse Kalin, in an appendix to his critique of Gewirth (Kalin 1984; this critique is discussed under #33 and #35.3), considers the possibility that Gewirth might be arguing that the fact of agency itself entails a right to freedom and well-being. Kalin asks how the fact of agency can generate rights to freedom and well-being, rather than merely a need for them. He offers two suggestions.

a.   The generic necessity of freedom means that the "intention and effort to act must include an intention and effort to appropriate (lay claim to) such a right" (ibid., 144). (Surely "appropriation" must mean the securing of noninterference, which is somewhat stronger than merely "laying claim to" a right to noninterference, but I shall let this pass).

b.   Gewirth might hold that "in acting an agent necessarily assumes permission to act and hence implicitly claims the rights supposed by such permission" (ibid., 145).

To *a*, Kalin responds that nothing follows about *having* rights from this. All that follows is that it

> might be useful or perhaps particularly beneficial . . . [to have them. Agency] without power or the assurance of noninterference is not worth much. But this fact in itself does not establish or presuppose any right to such power and noninterference. (Ibid., 144, 145)

To *b*, Kalin responds that all that is actually happening, if such an entitlement does not exist and is only being assumed, is that the agent hopes to have such an entitlement, which will depend on whether others are willing not to interfere.

However, apart from the fact that suggestion *a* attributes a nondialectical mode of argumentation, and requires Gewirth to establish that PPAs *have* rights (and not just that they must consider that they have them), both of these objections operate with an effective or recognitional sense of "having a right," rather than the normative or prescriptive sense that Gewirth employs. Kalin is insisting that I cannot consider that I have a right to X unless those who owe me duties of noninterference under such a right are willing not to interfere/do not interfere/consider that they ought not to interfere. Whether or not *I* can consider that I have a right (and, indeed, whether I have a right) is made to depend on the behavior/criteria for behavior *of others*.

Unless Kalin is going to argue that the prescriptive sense of having a right is unintelligible, his objections are irrelevant. (But see note 5 infra.)

3. Trigg is by no means alone on this matter. See, e.g., #21.

4. Of course, according to the argument, a PPA must only consider that there are these duties.

5. Gewirth's position is, of course, just the reverse of MacIntyre's. Whereas MacIntyre claims that rights-claims presuppose the existence of socially established rules, Gewirth holds that a

> legitimate community presupposes the claiming and respecting of rights (*RM* 74–75) (Gewirth 1985a, 747),

and that social rules (ought to) exist for the sake of rights rather than the other way around.

Jesse Kalin (in connection with objections considered under note 2 supra) states that he is aware of the fact that Gewirth adopts this position (which is a function of Gewirth's concentration on the prescriptive sense of having a right). However, he claims that Gewirth's arguments on this issue

> are unsatisfactory and fall far short of refuting the institutional analysis of rights (as contrasted with justifying reasons) which makes them contingent social achievements. In this regard, Alasdair MacIntyre's otherwise heavy-handed criticism of *Reason and Morality* [see #36 and #37] fastens on a central error. (Kalin 1984, 146)

This is a bit difficult to assess, as Kalin does not tell us why Gewirth's arguments are defective. Furthermore, Gewirth does not have to show that an institutional analysis of rights is untenable, *if* all that such an analysis does is present a recognitional sense of having a right. He only has to refute such an analysis if it denies the intelligibility of an analysis of "having rights" in terms of justifying reasons. Once this is appreciated, the ball is firmly in Kalin's and MacIntyre's court. They have to show that the idea that others strictly ought not to interfere with my freedom and well-being on *my criteria* is an unintelligible one. (On such a claim, see especially #35.2, #35.3, and #35.10. For an interesting discussion of difficulties with various versions of the thesis that rights are to be analyzed in terms of social rules [and not the other way around], which I largely endorse, see Ronald Dworkin 1978, Chapter 3, especially 48–58.)

6. Bear in mind (whatever we are to make of MacIntyre's qualification about "custom" and "positive law" rights) that he is claiming that the concept of a prescriptive right is nonuniversal, and not merely that the concept of a human right is socially variable and contingent.

7. This quotation also has direct relevance for the reply to Narveson in #25.3.

Richard Brooks claims that if persons do not believe in individual rights, Gewirth's theory will lack moral appeal and "the appearance of objectivity," and that in societies without such a belief, which is contingent, Gewirth's claims would lack appeal, meaning, and the appearance of objectivity. (See Brooks 1981, 292.)

However, the argument is not dependent on the contingent beliefs of PPAs. True, if they don't like the conclusion, they might be hostile to the argument. But the argument is not about what they will accept, or will think objective. It is about what they rationally must accept, and it *is* objective on its criteria. Furthermore, the claim about meaning is simply false. It just does not follow from "I believe that there are no generic rights" that "I consider that the statement that there are generic rights is meaningless." Peter Allen's contention that discourses about rights make no sense, are unintelligible, in contexts where individual autonomy is not considered to be of some value (see Allen 1987, 48), is similarly untenable.

Derek L. Phillips defends Gewirth against MacIntyre's criticism.

> Gewirth could . . . avoid MacIntyre's criticism by totally ignoring the term *rights*. He could simply restate his questionable step in terms of such notions as duty or wrongness. (Phillips 1986, 108)

Up to a point this is correct (for qualification see Gewirth 1986a and 1988d), and also means that we can universalize on the basis of (4d), rather than (5), to yield "All PPAs are logically required to conclude that they ought not to interfere with PPAO's freedom and well-being." (See Chapter 3, "The Formal Structure of the Argument.") As Phillips says, "With such a reformulation, [talk of] rights disappear[s]. But the basic moral injunction remains the same: we ought not to interfere with other people's freedom and well-being" (ibid., 109).

Gewirth provides a general discussion of the "social" and "ethnocentric" (see #26.2) objections, which is not focused on any particular critics of his argument, in Gewirth 1988e.

8. "Emotions" (as "proactive attitudes") are incorporated in the specification that PPAs are conatively normal. The argument is essentially about what motivating attitudes PPAs may rationally pursue. This is shown most clearly by stating it in terms of the argument from attitudinal consistency (see #13). It is true that *particular occurrent* emotions (or attitudes) are not employed *as criteria* for what is permissible. To do so would, however, beg the question against those with different attitudes.

9. Golding, incidentally, agrees with Gewirth (contrary to MacIntyre #26.1) that the concept of rights was implicit in much earlier discourse before it became defined in the Middle Ages. (See Golding 1984, 125.)

10. *Any* agent, according to Gewirth, or *even* prudential self-interested ones, but not *only* prudential self-interested ones.

11. The "perhaps" should be emphasized. Golding (1981) claims that there are other reasons why a PPA is not required to claim rights to its freedom and well-being, and in the 1984 paper he tells us that he stands by the 1981 criticism. For this see Chapter 7, note 6 and #35.7. Golding also criticizes Stage III. See Chapter 8, note 10.

12. Tibor R. Machan claims that

> [t]he element of choice in human life depends for its culpable suppression upon others. This gives the right to freedom from suppression a social moral standing. But capability or capacity [for action?] is something one would have to worry about even (especially) if one were all alone. The right to it would have to pertain apart from human community life (i.e., others who should respect it), which is a curious result. (Machan 1980, 113)

There are two points to make about this. First, Machan appears to suggest that Gewirth's argument would have me claiming rights against rocks and trees. This is not so. It does not do so because for me to claim a right is for me to claim that others ought not to interfere with what I claim a right to. "Ought" implies "can," so this claim can only be directed at those who are capable of refraining *voluntarily* from interference with my freedom and well-being. Only other PPAs meet this requirement. So, despite the fact that I would still have to worry about my freedom and well-being without the presence of others, I would not claim rights (in any sense that involved other-referring duties) against the non-PPA forces that were capable of harming me. (See, also, Chapter 7, note 21, and #35.8.) Second, the same point can be made against Machan as I make against Golding. Living alone, I would still have a right to my freedom and well-being against "others who should respect it" (i.e., other PPAs who might come along). Living alone would not have the consequence that, having to consider that I have rights to freedom and well-being, even while alone, I would have to consider that these rights were held against non-PPA forces with which I was in contact. It would, indeed, be curious if Gewirth's argument had the consequence that rights-claims (rights-prescriptions) are not other-referring; but to be other-referring it is not necessary for contingent circumstances to pertain in which the others referred to are actually present. There is nothing curious about the idea that rights can pertain when actual social interaction is absent.

Chapter 7: Objections to Stage II

1. To say that PPAs are conatively normal *by definition* does not introduce an arbitrary element into the argument. That PPAs are *proactively* motivated to pursue their purposes is not an *arbitrary* stipulation. Beings who are not so motivated do not move from passivity to activity for their purposes (on account of what they value). Whatever they might value or desire has no *practical* significance for them. Practical precepts, however, prescribe *for behavior*. Where the guiding question of the enterprise concerns what purposes may be *pursued*, a PPA *cannot* be defined in any other way. Practical precepts

have *no relevance* for those who *do* nothing on the basis of the things they value or desire.

Gewirth says, variously, that all human beings are at least potential PPAs, that most adult human beings are PPAs (e.g., RM 171) and that human beings are not necessarily PPAs. From time to time (see especially Gewirth 1979a), he says that his argument establishes that all PPAs must grant human beings the generic rights, that the claim that the generic rights are basic *human* rights is dialectically necessary for all PPAs. His argument for this involves what he calls the "principle of proportionality." According to the argument, what justifies for every PPA that it has the generic rights is that it is a PPA. Gewirth says that there are no degrees of *being* a PPA; one is either a PPA or one is not. If one is a PPA, then one has (it is dialectically necessary to hold that one has) the generic rights in full. One has no grounds for claiming a superior degree of the generic rights to other PPAs, for being a PPA is the *sufficient* reason for having the generic rights. There are, however, *degrees of approach* to being a PPA. Children, mentally deficient persons, and animals have varying degrees of approach to being PPAs, and (according to the principle of proportionality) they do not have the generic rights *in full*, but do have them in proportion to the degree to which they approach being PPAs (the extent to which they have the generic abilities). In being at least potential PPAs, all human beings have the generic rights at least in part. (See RM 119–125.)

Gewirth's claim that his theory is a theory of human rights, and that it grants "marginal agents" rights, has occasioned difficulty. For example:

a. James F. Hill (1984) agrees with the major parts of Gewirth's theory, and says that he believes that Gewirth has discovered the correct ground for the making of valid claims of moral rights; but he argues that Gewirth is wrong to think that marginal agents fall within its scope by application of the principle of proportionality. According to Hill, marginal agents do not have the generic rights, either in part or in varying degrees. Any duties we have towards them do not derive from their having the generic rights to some degree.

b. Aaron Ben-Zeev (1982) argues that the principle of proportionality may justify children's having the generic rights in part as potential (developing PPAs), but it cannot be used to grant the generic rights, even in part, to senile persons. Gewirth's theory would deprive some human beings of the generic rights.

c. Douglas N. Husak (1984) argues that Gewirth has not shown that PPAs must grant rights to all human beings (biologically defined) equally, even if his argument to the PGC is valid. PPAs only have to grant rights to PPAs. The principle of proportionality does not show that PPAs have rights to the degree to which they have the generic abilities.

d. Richard Brooks (1981, 294) claims that, by resting the argument on the agent's purposiveness and voluntariness, Gewirth gives up the notion of the rights of nonhumans.

e. Arval A. Morris (1981) accuses Gewirth of having an "elitist conception of human rights," because the theory assigns rights to PPAs, and not to human beings as such.

It seems to me that Gewirth's theory is essentially a theory of the rights of PPAs, and not a theory of human rights as such (which is conceded by Gewirth [1982f, 77]). From this it follows that there are some human beings (those who are not even marginal agents) who do not have the generic rights, and that nonhuman beings might have the generic rights (contrary to Brooks' assertion). The question of the rights of "marginal agents" is, however, a more complex one. I do not discuss this, because I view its importance as being for the argument *from* the PGC, rather than the argument *to* the PGC, with which this book is solely concerned; so I shall not discuss any of the above claims in detail. This said, there are a number of general points that must be noted.

a. As any true rationalist should, I hold that "counterintuitive" conclusions carry no disconfirmatory weight whatsoever against *clearly valid* applications of the PGC (assuming the argument to the PGC to be valid). As a *matter of logic, if* the PGC is dialectically necessary, and *if* it denies certain human beings the generic rights because they are not PPAs, then we must accept that these human beings do not have the generic rights. The fact that this may offend our sensibilities is neither here nor there as a reason to reject valid inferences from dialectically necessary premises. We cannot weigh what *is* dialectically necessary against judgments derived from dialectically contingent assumptions, thereby placing logically necessary judgments in a "reflective equilibrium" with judgments validated by other criteria. To derive these other judgments from their criteria requires the use of logic, and so they cannot countermand judgments that are logically necessary. If they conflict with dialectically necessary judgments, then they must be dialectically inconsistent; and if they are dialectically inconsistent, we contradict that we are PPAs if we espouse them. To attempt to say that, in some "metalogical" way, we may nevertheless espouse such judgments is incoherent. Since a PPA who espouses such judgments denies that it is a PPA, the "metalogical" property "may espouse these judgments" cannot be predicated *of a PPA.*

However, *in practice,* since applications of the PGC are not always simple and clear, I agree with Gewirth that

> [i]n tracing these applications, there is an important place for the inductive confrontation of the supreme principle with widely held beliefs and judgments about lower-level moral rules. . . . [T]hese beliefs . . . provide valuable further tests for the principle insofar as they stem . . . from a historical and ongoing arena of discussion and debate that fosters reflective thought. (RM 199)

However, these tests cannot be regarded as conclusive until supported by a dialectically necessary validation.

b. As an essential qualification to this I, like Gewirth, do not concede that the argument grants no rights to marginal agents. Gewirth replies to Hill in Gewirth 1984d, 225–227, to Ben-Zeev in Gewirth 1982d, to Husak in Gewirth 1985c, and to Morris in Gewirth 1982f.

c. Correlative to the question of whether marginal agents have rights is the question of whether superior agents have superior rights. This is pertinent to the validity of the argument, as it bears on the quality of being a PPA being the sufficient ground for the generic rights within my dialectically necessary viewpoint, on the argument for the sufficiency of agency, which is crucial for Stage III. This is discussed in Chapter 8, especially #42–#45.

d. Susan Moller Okin (1981) claims that basing the argument on "I am a PPA" is arbitrary. If so, then the stance I have adopted in a is untenable. This claim is considered and rejected under #43.

e. A question might be raised about the extent to which the practical import of the PGC is narrowed by conative normality's being a definitional requirement of being a PPA. The answer is, Not very much! Conative normality is, after all, something that is characteristic of most adult human beings. In practice, we are required to treat human beings as conatively normal (as PPAs) unless we have compelling evidence that they are not PPAs. It follows that, even if some human being P is not conatively normal, PPAs are still required to treat P as though he or she were a PPA unless they have knowledge of P's conative abnormality (whereupon the principle of proportionality comes into play).

2. I feel sure that Nielsen does not take him to mean this either. I am puzzled by this objection and the emphasis that Nielsen puts on it, for he makes it abundantly clear that he regards it as conclusive. (See Nielsen 1984, 79.)

However, Tapio Puolimatka explicitly, and mistakenly, suggests that Gewirth might be using his definition of conative normality "to imply a criterion for discriminating between desires," hence as a covert normative standard (Puolimatka 1989, 175 n. 8). To repeat: the predication of "conative normality" is merely the predication of proactivity.

Alasdair MacIntyre thinks that the predication of "conative normality" is the predication of individualistic as against communitarian motivation. Gewirth, he says, operates with

> a conception of social life as an arena in which self-interested individuals contend for advantage and aggrandisement . . . .
> And Gewirth's conception of conative normality is in fact not a conception of normal human behavior, but of the behavior taken to be normal in the individualist social order of modernity. (MacIntyre 1985, 237)

This is mistaken. "Being conatively normal" (as Gewirth intends it, "being proactively motivated to pursue one's *own purposes*") does not imply that one's purposes are "individualistic," "egoistic," or whatever, as against "communitarian," or "altruistic," etc. (See Gewirth 1985e, 250; and RM 71.)

That MacIntyre misses the import of "conative normality" is shown by another objection he raises in the same article. Gewirth often expresses the implications, within my viewpoint as a PPA, of my categorical need for freedom and well-being, as "I *must have* freedom and well-being." (See, e.g., RM 81.) MacIntyre (1985, 235–236) says that he finds the meaning of this "must have" mysterious—if it is not merely a statement of need. What it, in fact, expresses is a strict instrumental "ought to have" (*based on*, though *not equivalent to*, the statement of my categorical need for freedom and well-being), which is prescriptive on account of my intention to act. Given this intention (my "conative normality"), Gewirth contends that my categorical need for freedom and well-being is a strict reason *for me* why I ought to (must) have my freedom and well-being.

3. The analogy employed here is somewhat inappropriate, unless Williams wishes to hold that tigers are PPAs. On the supposition that tigers are not PPAs, Gewirth would not hold that I have a right to my freedom and well-being in any sense that would imply that tigers have a duty not to interfere with my freedom and well-being. At the same time, if tigers are not PPAs, then not even the later stages of the argument require me to grant them rights of any kind that require me to forfeit any level of my generic rights in cases of conflict.

4. Which is how Williams seems to interpret it on pages 60–61 of his book.

5. For more on this, see my discussion of Narveson's objection under #35.5.

6. Kai Nielsen's general position is that an "amoralist"

> might reject the whole category of permissible/impermissible as incoherent or mystificatory while (1) still believing that his freedom and well-being are necessary goods for him and (2) being quite categorically resolved to protect them: to not permit, if he can help it, others interfering with him. He might consistently and firmly hold (1) and (2) and still not make any claim about what it is impermissible for others to do even vis-à-vis him. He sees the above situation as an arena for the conflict of interests— a situation where people with at least potentially conflicting interests may be set against each other—and he is resolved to protect his interests come what may, but he need not, even implicitly, conceptualize things in terms of rights or entitlements or in terms of what is permissible and what is not. (If a person refuses to permit something, it does not follow that he thinks it is impermissible . . .). Moreover, if I deny that I have rights to freedom and well-being (perhaps because I regard rights-talk as incoherent or otherwise unsuitable), it does not follow that I must regard interfering with my freedom and well-being as permissible. (Nielsen 1984, 81)

This is essentially the same position as Williams is defending. To back it up, Nielsen makes a number of claims.

a.   A PPA can be opposed to interference with its freedom and well-being without claiming any rights to them (ibid., 72). Not to claim a right to my freedom and well-being is not necessarily to display indifference to interference with my freedom and well-being (ibid., 77).

b.   In order to establish Stage II, Gewirth has to show that it is necessarily true that PPAO ought not to interfere with PPA's freedom and well-being. But this is contingently false (ibid., 71).

c.   To recognize that my freedom and well-being are necessary goods is to be resolved to pursue my freedom and well-being, and from this it does not follow that I must consider that non-pursuit of my freedom and well-being, or interference with my freedom and well-being, is impermissible (ibid., 75–77; and see the quote from 81 supra). (Related to this, Nielsen claims that trying to ground any deontic claims in "My freedom and well-being are necessary goods" involves reducing "ought" talk to "expressions of intentions" [ibid., 79–80].)

d.   Even if Gewirth can show that (4c) entails (4d), establishing (4c) involves an assumption of conative normality, which violates the dialectically necessary method (ibid., 78–79).

e.   (4c) does not logically entail (4d) because this inference requires adoption of the "universalistic stance of the moral point of view" (ibid., 83).

I have replied to *a* under #13; to *b* under #22; to *c*, in effect, under #28 (the point being that it is not a question of my being resolved to defend my freedom and well-being, but of my being rationally required to do so—a point that Nielsen recognizes but tends to forget or to obscure in his discussion. I comment on the related claim about reduction to intentions under #31.3). *d* has been dealt with under #29; and *e* will be discussed under #48.

According to Martin P. Golding, a denial of "I have a right to X" can be "strong" or "weak." The strong denial implies "Others have a right to interfere with my having X" (in a sense that implies that I ought not to resist such interference). The weak denial does not imply this. When the "prudent amoralist" denies that it has a right to its freedom and well-being, it is not making a strong denial. However, Gewirth's argument requires the prudent amoralist to be making a strong denial. (See Golding 1981, 172–173.)

I take this to be the same claim as Williams is making. Rather revealingly, Golding says that to make a weak denial of "I have a right to X" does not imply that any alternative rights-claim or *normative* utterance is true. By (weakly) denying "I have a right to X" I do not imply that anyone ought to do anything. But this is just the problem. By having to hold that my freedom and well-being are necessary goods, I have to hold that *I* ought to resist interference with my freedom and well-being. If denying "I have a right to my freedom and well-being" does not entail that I ought to resist interference with my freedom and well-being, then by holding that I may hold such a weak denial of "I have a right to my freedom and well-being," the "prudent amoralist" denies that it *ought* to (rationally must) resist interference with its freedom and well-being. It therefore contradicts that it is dialectically necessary for it to hold "My freedom and well-being are necessary goods." Thus, both the weak and strong denials of "I have a right to my freedom and well-being" are dialectically inconsistent with "I am a PPA." Golding's "prudent amoralist" does, indeed, make only the weak denial. So much the worse for its position. This position is dialectically inconsistent, and Gewirth does not have to assume (falsely) that it involves the strong denial in order to show this.

7. There is another possibility, which is that Veatch considers that all justification must be moral, meaning that what Gewirth calls "prudential justification" is unintelligible. (For him simply to define all justification as

moral is, of course, to trivialize the objection.) Objections of this kind are considered under #35.

Rüdiger Bittner (1989, 28–29) raises an objection against Stage II that I do not find clear. As I understand him, he claims that "(I must consider that) my freedom and well-being are necessary goods" does not entail "(I must consider that) I am entitled to my freedom and well-being," because the fact that my categorical need for freedom and well-being gives me good (indeed, the best possible) grounds for "demanding" noninterference with my freedom and well-being (should I wish to do so) does not entail that I must consider that such a demand is justified (i.e., a demand that I am entitled to). If this is a correct interpretation, then Bittner's objection is akin to those considered under the present heading and, in particular, to that brought by Regis (1981). Bittner himself (see 1989, 163 n. 62) attributes his objection to Adams (1980), MacIntyre (1981), and White (1982). This seems to me to be correct only insofar as all these commentators object to Stage II. Bittner's objection seems to me to have a different thrust from these others (which also differ from each other in detail).

8. Arval A. Morris borrows this objection from Grunebaum. According to Morris, the argument

> requires an agent to value his freedom and well-being only in-strumentally—as necessary conditions for his actions. Moreover, his actions are instrumental to his purposes. Thus, the conclu-sion of [Stage I] . . . should reflect two instrumentalities . . . (1) "My freedom and basic well-being are instrumental goods serv-ing as necessary conditions of my action[s] . . . ," and (2) "My actions are the necessary conditions for my achieving my pur-pose[s] . . . ." (Morris 1981, 163)

According to Morris, this means that a PPA will be required to claim a right to its freedom and well-being only if it claims rights to its particular occurrent purposes, and will be required to claim a moral right to its free-dom and well-being only if it claims moral rights to its particular occurrent purposes. In other words, Morris claims that the instrumentality of its free-dom and well-being entails that a PPA is required to attach to its freedom and well-being only whatever value it attaches to its particular occurrent purposes. Morris, however, now gives this objection a different twist from Grunebaum. He claims that it further follows that, because Gewirth argues that the rights-claim that concludes Stage II is not morally justified, Stage III cannot be valid. I consider this latter objection under #47 (see Chapter 8, note 26 for specific comment on Morris' objection). My reply to Grunebaum will do service as my reply to the rest of Morris' objection.

Fred Feldman also presses Grunebaum's objection. (See Feldman 1983, 478.) His discussion raises no additional issues.

9. The requirement for moral valuation to ground rights-claims is more clearly attributable to Morris (1981) than to Grunebaum.

10. This is, perhaps, the sense of "intrinsic" value that Gewirth appeals to in his reply to Grunebaum when he says that a PPA must value some of its pur-poses for their own sakes. I do not, however, see that it follows from this that a

PPA must value its freedom and well-being in this sense. From the fact that it must value at least some of its particular occurrent purposes in this sense, it follows only that a PPA must value its freedom and well-being in sense 1, not that it must value its freedom and well-being in sense 2 or sense 3.

11. This actually switches from talking about ethical egoism being inconsistent in itself to ethical egoism being dialectically inconsistent (for it to be inconsistent for me, as a PPA, to hold ethical egoism). The latter is Gewirth's general intention, the former his specific intention here. He can apply the specific intention because ethical egoism itself espouses (4).

12. A prescriptive "ought" is more or less equivalent to a Kelsenian "subjective ought," a hypothetical one to a Kelsenian "objective ought." (See Kelsen 1967, 17–23.)

13. It is to be noted that Gewirth does not appear to think that it does. (See Gewirth 1984d, 217–218.) However, I do not fully understand Gewirth's reasoning, so I will not comment on it.

14. What is the doubt about "ought presupposes can"? Perhaps Davies has in mind the existence of "strict liability" rules in law, whereby persons are held responsible for outcomes that they did not bring about directly, and that they could not have prevented. For example, if A stores dangerous material on A's property, and this material leaks onto B's property causing damage, A is liable in English law for this damage, even if A was not negligent in storing the material and took all the steps A was able to prevent leakage (certain statutory defenses excepted). At first sight this looks like a case of "A ought to prevent leakage of dangerous material A owns onto B's property, even if A cannot prevent this leakage." There are, however, at least two possible responses to this. The first is to say that, if so, because "ought" *does* presuppose "can," the law is an ass. The second is to say that the law does not issue any such directive to A. The directive it issues is that innocent parties should be compensated for any damage to their property caused by the leakage of dangerous material. A is to be held liable for the damage, because A stands to gain by the storage of the material, and this is not something that A has to do. A could choose not to store the material on A's property, or not to engage in activities that require A to store the material on A's property. If A chooses to store the material on A's property, then the possibility that A will be liable to pay damages to B is a risk that A chooses to accept. So construed, the injunction "A ought not to cause damage to B's property" is one that presupposes that A can prevent damage caused (by choosing not to store the dangerous material on A's property), and does not constitute even a prima facie exception to "ought implies can."

That Gewirth would give the second reading is apparent from what he says about "strict liability" in *Reason and Morality*.

> The behaviors dealt with in provisions for strict liability and collective responsibility are actions in the relevant sense only insofar as the persons addressed can at least prospectively control their behavior so as to conform to these provisions. Where this ability to control is absent, the idea of reason-giving that is essential to moral and many other [Gewirth surely needs to say

"all"] practical precepts is also absent, unless the control in question is exercisable by the persons addressed at some stage prior to the behavior in question. That there is such prior ability to control one's behavior is, indeed, an assumption of these legal precepts. (RM 35)

15. It is worth noting that, in *Reason and Morality*, Gewirth does not express the entailment between (4c) and (4d) as being effected by "ought implies can." He elaborates, instead, upon his alternative formulation, which expresses it as a matter of having to endorse the necessary means to an endorsed end.

If a person accepts that he ought to do X, on some criterion of 'ought,' then he must also accept that he ought, according to that same criterion, to be free to do X in that his doing X ought not to be prevented or interfered with by other persons. . . . For insofar as such nonprevention or noninterference is a necessary condition of one's doing X, one's acceptance for oneself of the requirement that one do X entails at least an implicit acceptance of the requirement that there be no interference with one's doing X. To reject the latter requirement, so far as one is aware of it, would be to reject also the former requirement, for one cannot rationally both accept that something ought to be done and reject a necessary condition of its being done. . . . [T]he inference from doing X to being free to do X is quite direct. And if one believes that the necessary condition of one's performing some action is repugnant or otherwise unacceptable, then, where it is indeed necessary to the performance of that action, one will not accept the requirement that the action itself be performed. (RM 91–92)

Davies makes no comment on this alternative formulation. This formulation makes it quite clear what the context of the second sequence is. This is an application of "ought implies can," but a slightly different one from that of the first sequence. The first sequence just states that "can" is a condition for "ought." The second sequence states "I ought to do X," and "I ought to do X" implies "I can do X, so I ought to be able to do X (ought to have the necessary conditions for doing X)." This *affirms* that I ought to do X, notes that this could not be the case if I could not do X, and concludes that, because "I ought to do X" is directed at my prospective agency, I ought to be able to do X so as to be able to meet my demand to do X.

16. There is another way in which the inference from (4c) to (4d) might be explained, which owes much to James Scheuermann (1987).

What is involved in my thinking that I ought to do z, or more generally in my prescribing that X ought to do z? To be rationally justified (on my criteria) in prescribing "X ought to do z," where this means "X does wrong by not doing z," three conditions must be satisfied.

a. I need a justification for holding z, or what it would achieve, as a state of affairs that ought to be. I must hold that a state of affairs in which z, or its end, does not exist is wrong. Without this, I have no grounds for requiring X to do z. This has a subcondition, which is that z is a possible state of affairs to be brought about (though not necessarily by X). Since this "ought" is abstracted from any addressees, we may, following Scheuermann (see 1987, 298), call it a "metaphysical" "ought."

b. It must be the case that X can do z. If X cannot do z, then demanding that X do z will not have any effect in bringing about the state of affairs z, or its end, which ought to be. There will be no point in *requiring* X to do z.

c. I need a justification for requiring *X* to do z. It does not follow from the fact that X can do z, and that z metaphysically ought to be, that X is the right subject upon whom to place responsibility for securing z. X is the appropriate addressee if X fulfills *b*, and if X is as well or better placed to do z than any other (available) PPA. (This might include the proviso that X not be placed under a greater burden by the requirement than any other addressee who fulfills *b*, but it only clearly does so on a moral criterion.)

These conditions are at least partially independent.

If *a* is satisfied, then I have a justification for z to be brought about by those who fulfill *b* and *c*. But, because those who might not be able to bring about z (because their doing z is interfered with) would be able to bring about z if their doing z is not interfered with, if *a* is satisfied then I have justification (on the same criterion that justifies *a*) for the state of affairs being brought about in which those who could do z (unless they are prevented from doing z, and who fulfill *c*) do not have their doing z interfered with. But this means that *a* provides justification for "Those who can refrain from interfering with X doing z, ought to refrain from interfering with X doing z." Those who fulfill *b* and *c*, in relation to this prescription, are other PPAs. Thus "X ought to do z" entails "Other PPAs ought not to interfere with X doing z."

To put it otherwise, justification of "z is the state of affairs that ought to be (if possible)" is directly justification (on the same criterion) for the metaphysical "ought" "Interference with z being brought about ought not to be." Those who are capable of fulfilling *b* and *c*, in relation to this metaphysical "ought," are other PPAs. Therefore, other PPAs ought not to interfere with X's doing z, where this is a strict practical "ought," and not merely a metaphysical one.

17. It must not be thought that Gewirth's generic "life" is equivalent to such a life. Such a life is a particular occurrent specification of conditions that would satisfy Gewirth's generic "life." I must claim a right (which I may waive) to such a life, but such a life does not exhaust what I must/may claim a right to.

18. According to James Collins,

> in the concrete, the individual values his ability to be an agent
> not for general abstract purposiveness but because of his specific
> desires, that is, *his* goods. (Collins 1979, 71)

From this he infers that a PPA's justification for its claims is not its being a PPA, but its "concrete" (contingent) self-interest. (See ibid., 72.)

But, even if PPAs *do* value their freedom and well-being only for purposes they would be willing to pursue, it still follows from the fact that freedom and well-being are categorically necessary conditions for agency that they *logically must* value their freedom and well-being (as generic conditions of "abstract purposiveness"), or deny that they are PPAs, but do not (in the same sense) *have* to value the contingently necessary conditions of their particular occurrent purposes (for they do not *have* to have these specific purposes).

19. Christopher McMahon (1986) questions this way of classifying rights/duties. See #35.10.

20. Whether or not Bond will accept my broader contextual interpretation of his objection, his reply to Gewirth makes it clear that he is offering it as a freestanding analysis.

> What Professor Gewirth is saying is that others are under an obligation, related to what is prudential for *me*, not to violate my generic rights. I am denying that this makes any sense. A person can only intelligibly be said to have a duty, or to be under an obligation, . . . if *he* has sufficient reason for doing whatever he is said to be obliged to do. (Bond 1980b, 73)

21. Neil MacCormick (reviewing Gewirth 1982b) objects to the inference from (4c), which he expresses as "I must have freedom and well-being" (which he calls [2]), to (4d) "Others must at least refrain from interfering with my freedom and well-being" (which he calls [3]), on the grounds that (3) is not correlative to "I have a right to my freedom and well-being" *unless* (3) is other-*directing*. He holds that (2) does not entail (3) if (3)

> is equivalent to (3A) "All other persons have reason to aim for my freedom and well[-]being as necessities for my pursuing my purposes." All that it authorises is (3B) "I have reason to ensure if possible that all other persons refrain from removing or interfering with my freedom and well-being as necessities for my pursuing my purposes." That *my* interest in my own potential for agency will be served by *your* refraining from removing or interfering with my freedom and well[-]being does not entail that *you* have any prudential reason of *yours* for so refraining. (MacCormick 1984, 347)

He concedes that (3B) is equivalent to "By reference to my interests, PPAO ought not to interfere with my freedom and well-being" (see ibid., 350), but he continues,

> [F]or it to be the case on some normative ground NG that I have a right that you so refrain, it has to be the case that NG also specify or constitute some reason for your so refraining. So long as NG is for any and each agent nothing more than the interest he or she has in securing the necessary generic conditions for his or her being an agent, it cannot be the case that on that ground any one agent can posit any mandatory reason for action by any other agent directed solely at favouring, protecting or respecting the generic interest of the first party. (Ibid., 347)

This, with the focus on rights rather than other-*directed* obligations, is

essentially the same view as Bond's. Since Gewirth infers only (3B) (not [3A])
from (2), the two central questions are

a.   Must rights-claims be other-*directing*, and not merely other-*di-
      rected?* I think not, for the same reasons as I think that claims that
      others are under an obligation to do something need not be ac-
      cepted by these others to be intelligible.
b.   Can Gewirth universalize to the PGC from (3B) (other-*directed*)?
      MacCormick thinks not, claiming that universalization requires
      (3A) (other-*directing*) to be established (see ibid., 350), which is
      not dialectically necessary. However, as I argue in #35.3 (and in
      #47), this is mistaken. It follows that if I am right about *b,* then it
      does not matter if I am wrong about *a.*

MacCormick also claims that it is irrational to suppose (as taking [3B] to
be other-*directed* does) that PPAO *could* take my reasons for wishing PPAO to
act in certain ways as good reasons *for PPAO* to act in these ways.

> One might as well say that if Canute has reason to wish the tide
> not to rise, Canute must suppose that the tide has reason not to
> rise. (Ibid., 350)

This analogy is inappropriate in two ways. First, for the two cases to be
comparable, MacCormick must say ". . . Canute must suppose that the tide
could have reason not to rise." Second, the cases are not comparable: the tide
isn't a PPA and (under this assumption) *could not* take my reasons for it not
to rise as its reasons not to rise. But PPAO *could* accept my reasons as binding
on it, even if it doesn't. (See also my discussion of Lomasky under #35.8.)

As a Hartian legal positivist, MacCormick's position on the conditions of
intelligibility of a rights-claim is a very peculiar one. According to H. L. A.
Hart, it is a necessary condition for the existence of a legal system that the
officials adopt the system's secondary rule of recognition as a standard for
their conduct. It is not necessary that other persons regard the secondary
rule of recognition as providing *them* with good reasons for acting. (See Hart
1961, 113.) This means that legal rights and duties are determined by criteria
the officials espouse. But, from MacCormick's analysis, it follows that we
cannot view rules validated by the secondary rule of recognition as even
legal rights (with correlative duties), if the *addressees* of these rules do not
accept the secondary rule of recognition as a standard for their conduct. This
contradicts Hart's "definition" of a legal system, *unless* MacCormick says
that legal rights and obligations are addressed *solely* to the officials. But this
is a thoroughly un-Hartian view. (See ibid., 35–38.)

There are wider implications here. It is a necessary, though not sufficient,
condition for the coherence of Hartian theory that it be intelligible to hold
that persons are under obligations when they do not accept the criteria that
validate these obligations. Yet, if this is so, then we cannot object (on
MacCormick's account) to (3B) being dialectically necessary and correlative
to a rights-claim. Since MacCormick holds that there is no difficulty with
universalizing such a claim to the PGC (see MacCormick 1984, 347), then the
necessary condition for the coherence of Hartian legal positivism becomes a

sufficient condition for the dialectical necessity of the PGC. But the dialectical necessity of the PGC entails that all practical reasoning *rationally* must be viewed from the moral viewpoint of the PGC; and this is fatal to Hartian legal positivism (see Beyleveld and Brownsword 1986). In short, on MacCormick's reading, the necessary condition of the coherence of Hartian legal positivism becomes a sufficient condition for its untenability.

22. Kai Nielsen (1984) also construes Gewirth as trying to effect the move from the prudential to the moral via "ought implies can." See #48.

23. For some possibilities, see (*a*) my discussion of Paul Allen III's claim that Gewirth cannot infer "From my viewpoint, E is good" from "I regard E as good" (under #23.1.2), and (*b*) my discussion of Christopher McMahon's claim that Gewirth's argument does not work if a PPA's judgments are viewed as "agent-relative" (in Chapter 8, note 31).

For Kalin's views on the agent-relativity of evaluation, in a context not involving criticism of Gewirth, see Kalin 1968, 1970, and 1975. The possible interpretations of "agent-relativity" that I discuss above are not derived directly from Kalin's discussion in these latter articles. In these articles, Kalin discusses two views of evaluation (more or less those premised on his "I" and "we" questions [see #33]); but it seems to me that Gewirth's argument does not rest exactly on either of these, so that Kalin's general discussion of these questions is not all that helpful.

24. Gewirth suspects that Kalin has some such view in mind, for he retorts,

> What Kalin fails to see here is that to direct a practical 'ought' to other persons does not require that *they* have reasons for complying with it; it is sufficient if the person who does the directing has reasons for upholding the 'ought' which he addresses to others. When slaves say to their masters, "You ought to free us," this 'ought' is perfectly intelligible as reflecting the slaves' own reasons for saying it; it need not also reflect reasons for acting had or upheld by the masters. (Gewirth 1984d, 218–219)

Kalin does say that (4d) is not *properly* other-referring ("directed") because not other-directing. (See Kalin 1984, 142.)

25. Narveson says he is unsure about what Gewirth means on this point. (See Narveson 1980, 654.)

26. David B. Wong says,

> Perhaps it is not the justifiability of the claim [to a right to freedom and well-being] that is rooted in prudential considerations, but the *action* of A's making the claim against others that is so rooted. . . . As a prudent, purposive agent, A surely has nothing to lose and everything to gain from making the claim. But A might have something to lose. There are places in the world where claiming one's rights would not only be silly and beside the point but dangerous to one's health. The prudent thing to do may be to keep silent and make plans for escape or for overthrowing the authorities. (Wong 1984, 82–83)

But it *is* the justifiability of the claim Gewirth is talking about, and the argument is about what PPAs logically must accept, not about what actions are prudent.

27. See Kalin #35.3, and #47 (where this is discussed in relation to other critics). It should be noted that Lomasky's specific objection bears some resemblance to comments made by Tibor R. Machan (1980). (See Chapter 6, note 12.) See also my discussion of Neil MacCormick's objection (note 21 supra). MacCormick's objection is *very* similar to Lomasky's, and might have been dealt with here instead.

28. Most of Gewirth's examples are of this kind, rights to do X on intellectual criteria.

29. I find Singer's article far from clear, so this interpretation is somewhat conjectural.

30. If McMahon is right about this, then universalization of (4d) to a moral claim, even if this is valid, will not yield a deontological morality directing "interpersonal transactions." Somewhat ironically, James Collins claims that if the argument is valid it is to be rejected *because* it *only* deals with "inter-personal transactions." Gewirth's theory (*a*) is a morality independent of "attitudes" and (*b*) has no place for "heroism." (See Collins 1979, 73–74.)

However, (*a*) is false, which can be seen by the fact that Stage II can be stated in terms of the argument from attitudinal consistency. (See 13#.) (*b*) ignores Gewirth's extensive comments on supererogation (see, e.g., RM 188–190, 228, 229, 330) and on virtues (see, especially, RM 243–244, 332–333).

Collins also claims that Stage II is invalid because an other-directing "ought" cannot be derived from (4c). (See Chapter 8, note 22.)

31. David B. Wong claims that (without the question-begging assumption that PPAO thinks morally) (4c) does not entail (4d), when the latter is interpreted to be correlative to a rights-claim, *as rights-claims are "usually" interpreted* (i.e., as other-*directing*), and that, although (4d) and (5) can be validated as not other-directing, this will not yield the conclusion Gewirth requires (although he does not say why). (See Wong 1984, 81–82.)

However, I doubt that Wong's "usual" conception is the usual one, and, even if it is, there are severe difficulties with it, as I discuss below. Wong's objection, like so many (perhaps all) others under the present objection heading, really reduces to the claim that only an other-directing "ought" claim can be universalized purely logically to the PGC. This is rejected under #35.3 and #47.

32. Robert C. Roberts, and Robert L. Arrington (like David B. Wong—see note 31 supra) make similar claims to McMahon here, as part of objections that fit under the present heading.

Roberts says that, according to Gewirth,

> the reason I give for claiming that the other person has this obligation is my own absolute need as an agent for . . . [my freedom and well-being]. But now the question is this: What kind of person could accept *that* as a reason for acknowledging that he is under obligation to respect my freedom and well-being? And the answer is: Only a moral person. . . . Thus on . . . [Gewirth's inter-

pretation] of "prudential right-claim," the person who makes the claim does not limit himself to prudential considerations; he assumes the moral point of view. . . . [I]n making the prudential right-claim he assumes that other people adopt the moral point of view toward himself. (Roberts 1979, 81)

Arrington objects that

[w]e cannot charge people with obligations whose grounds they do not recognize *and cannot reasonably be expected to recognize!* Do I have any justification for thinking that another agent, *not conceived of as a moral agent but only as a prudential one,* has a reason to recognize my prudential right to my own freedom? . . . This is highly doubtful. . . . But if I cannot attribute to the other person a reason for granting me my freedom, a reason he can be expected as a rational, prudential agent to accept, I cannot attribute to him a duty, not even a prudential one, to respect my freedom/well-being. And if I cannot attribute a prudential duty to him, I can hardly claim a prudential right against him, for . . . rights and duties are logically correlative. (Arrington 1989, 108)

Both of these are covered by my response to McMahon. Given that rights-claims, and obligation-claims on others, do not have to be other-*directing*, and Gewirth does not assume (nor need he assume for Stage III to be effected [see #35.3 and #47]) that PPAO recognizes *any* reason to respect my claims (see below), these objections simply collapse.

33. Here, again, as with some other critics considered under the present heading, and R. M. Hare and E. J. Bond in particular, it should be noted that McMahon's objection is bound up with the contention that (4d) can only be universalized if interpreted in terms of (10a). McMahon's presentation of this is discussed under #47.6.

34. Fred Feldman says,

[I]t seems to me that there is a large gap between claims about what is good (even necessarily good) and claims about what people ought to do. (Feldman 1983, 480)

Millard Schumaker says,

As I see it, the right and the good just are not that closely related. (Schumaker 1979, 353)

James S. Fishkin claims that there is a

gap between an agent's claim that freedom and well-being are good or desirable (that they are goods necessary for his prospective purposive action) and that he has a "right" to them. (Fishkin 1984, 92)

These commentators all ignore that Gewirth's concept of a "necessary good" is the concept of a rationally required proactive commitment to my freedom and well-being, which makes it a deontic concept. Since they do not construe (4) as (4c), it is not surprising that they do not see how (4) validates (4d)/(5). Fishkin claims that the fact that my freedom and well-being are *universal goods* does not help the inference. (See ibid., 93.) However, it is not the universality of the goods that does the work, but their *necessity* for my purposes, within my viewpoint.

35. According to Jeremy Waldron, reviewing Gewirth 1982b, Gewirth has difficulty in showing that an amoralist is committed

> to anything more than a *firm resolve* to have the necessary goods of agency. Such a resolve is no doubt strongly prescriptive but it is not palpably evaluative or universalizable. But even if an agent *is* committed to some evaluative claim, we still have to be convinced that this must be understood and dealt with as a claim of *right*, rather than as a weak consideration of value which can be fed into a utilitarian calculus. I suppose any moral consideration with prescriptive import can be represented *notationally* in terms of rights. But the rights Gewirth relies on in his political philosophy have a distinctive force or weight against other moral considerations, and they are brought into relation with one another in a distinctive sort of way (equalizing rather than maximizing, for example). I can find no argument which shows that agents are necessarily committed by their actions to moral claims with these distinctive (and highly controversial) features. (Waldron 1983, 16)

This, initially, raises MacIntyre's present objection. It then moves to considerations that suggest Christopher McMahon's claim that Stage II validates only an "ought of evaluation" (see #35.10 and #47.6), or Eric Mack's assertion that Gewirth has produced only a nondeontological nonaggregative consequentialism of rights. (See #66.2.) His remarks are too cryptic for me to interpret them further.

Rüdiger Bittner (1989, 25–28) objects to Gewirth's argument for the PCC in Gewirth 1970a. I do not consider his discussion in any detail, but it is worth noting two claims that he makes. Translated and interpreted into the context of the argument in *Reason and Morality*, these are (*a*) that "I must, on the grounds that I am a PPA, believe that I ought to do X" does not entail that "I ought to do X" is assertorically true; and (*b*) that, unless this belief is assertorically true, the LPU cannot require me to assent to "I must believe, on the grounds that PPAO is a PPA, that PPAO ought to do X" (where this "ought" involves my endorsement, being something that I prescribe). (See Bittner 1989, 27–28.)

While the first claim is correct, it is irrelevant, for the second claim is shown to be false by my reply to MacIntyre's present objection.

36. I am, in fact, not required to do so carte blanche. By the *logical* principle of universalizability, I am only required to concede the rights I claim for myself to those others who satisfy the grounds or characteristics on which I claim (consider that I have) the rights. In Gewirth's argument, I am rationally required to claim the generic rights on the sufficient grounds that I am a PPA, and it is for this reason, not my mere claiming of the generic rights, that I must grant them to all PPAs.

37. For more discussion on how Narveson attempts to construe Gewirth's argument, see #35.5.

Neil MacCormick (reviewing Gewirth 1982b) claims that, not only *can* a PPA deny Stage II without self-contradiction, an amoralist PPA *must* deny Stage II in order to avoid self-contradiction. Since MacCormick holds that Stage III is valid, his reasoning appears to be that acceptance of Stage II will mean that the amoralist will have to concede rights to PPAO even though to do so would be against its particular occurrent interests (thus contradicting its espousal of amoralism. See MacCormick 1984, 348–349). This is essentially the same objection as Narveson's.

Granted! The amoralism of a PPA is contradicted by the PGC. But the argument is not an argument from the amoralist PPA's amoralism, or from its particular occurrent purposes, but from the amoralist PPA's being a PPA! The argument is not invalidated by showing that amoralism does not entail the PGC. Such a claim misconstrues the dialectically necessary method. It is irrational to espouse amoralism if being a PPA requires the PGC to be espoused. (In any event, on the premise of amoralism Stage III isn't valid, because any rights-claim validated by amoralism does not necessarily present being a PPA as the justification for the rights-claim.)

38. Gewirth does *not*, as this suggests, contend that a PPA must claim rights to all its particular occurrent purposes.

39. In an earlier piece, Held argues that this is so.

> Gewirth's argument [in Gewirth 1967a, 1970a, 1971a, 1972, and 1976] may indicate that, if I argue for myself that when it is in my interest to do so I ought to take advantage of my neighbor, or give priority to reasons of self-interest, then I must be willing on grounds of consistency to recognize that my neighbor ought to act in the same way. However, if I think that the facts are such that it will often and in important ways be in my interest to act this way, and only seldom and in trivial ways in his interest for him to act this way, then Gewirth's argument does not show that it would be incoherent or irrational [meaning logically inconsistent with considerations of prudence!] for me to do so. (Held 1977, 712)

40. Kelso's talk of risk preference being a basis for denying Stage II suggests that he thinks that, because a PPA might be willing to have its freedom and well-being put at risk, it need not claim a right to freedom and well-being. However, since risk preference or aversion is a contingent property of PPAs, and voluntariness and purposivity are not, the PPA's rights-claim being derived from the latter properties, risk preference can bear only on the circumstances in which the PPA would be willing to waive the rights it must think it has, not on whether it must think that it has these rights to waive.

Mark Carl Overvold (reviewing Gewirth 1982b) concedes that a PPA must regard its freedom and well-being as necessary goods; but, like Held, he states,

> I see no reason for thinking that he must go on to claim a right to

these things as opposed to concluding simply that he ought to try to secure them. (Overvold 1983, 242)

Overvold does not elaborate.

Chapter 8: Objections to Stage III

1. This is not an accurate portrayal of Gewirth's universalization principle, which is purely logical, as against formally moral.

2. See my discussions of the objections by Virginia Held (#39) and Colin Davies (#34.1).

3. Friedman claims that in order to show that I must hold (IC → MyR), additional assumptions are required. These, he says, could be (a) moral: "necessity of a thing to a distinctively human life constitutes an independent moral title to that thing" (Friedman 1981, 154); or (b) prudential: to claim MyR on any grounds other than IC would be imprudent. (See ibid., 154–155.) He appreciates that Gewirth would regard (a) as transparently question-begging, so he attributes an implicit acceptance of (b). This, however, requires the PPA to be abstracted from ordinary circumstances, and to be assumed to occupy a Rawlsian "original position." However, to put the PPA in this position presupposes an outlook

> according to which variations in individual abilities are seen as morally arbitrary and thus not allowed to enter into the determination of the principles governing the allocation of the basic goods. (Ibid., 156)

So (b) does not enable Gewirth to derive (IC → MyR) without making a question-begging moral assumption.

Now, both (a) and (b) are question-begging. But we have just seen that Gewirth requires neither to secure (IC → MyR). Within my dialectically necessary viewpoint, where [(IP & IC) → MyR], [IP → (IC → MyR)] follows purely logically, without any additional assumptions.

Friedman, however, claims that even [(IP & IC) → MyR], which he has apparently conceded to be dialectically necessary, is necessary only on the assumption that PPAs are roughly equal in power, so that it will not be prudent for a powerful PPA to decide to live by its wits and not enter into any discourse of claiming rights. The argument is, thus, implicitly contractarian. (See ibid., 156–157.)

This, however, misconstrues the argument as making my prudential criterion my particular occurrent purposes, whereas it is what pertains to my particular occurrent purposes whatever they might be (my judgment that my freedom and well-being are necessary goods). (See my discussion of Narveson's objections under #35.5 and #38.) Even a powerful PPA contradicts that it is a PPA if it does not claim MyR, because this is required in consistency with (4c) "I ought to pursue my freedom and well-being," which a PPA cannot deny without denying that it is a PPA. (On the specific question of an assumption of "equal power," see #54.)

It is of the utmost importance to appreciate that "my prudential criterion" stands for my proactive evaluative relation to my purposes, whatever they might be. Thus, it does not stand for any particular occurrent viewpoint like that of prudence, for I need not be an egoist. As Gewirth uses the concept of "prudential," my prudential criterion is necessarily my criterion as a PPA. To deny what follows on my prudential criterion is to deny that I am a PPA. Friedman sometimes writes as though what a PPA contradicts if it denies MyR is that it is a rational "prudent amoralist" (who additionally assumes equal or inferior power). This is not the case. A PPA, whatever its SPR for its purposes, denies that it is a PPA (that it is proactively motivated to pursue its purposes) if it denies MyR.

According to Fred Feldman,

> [i]t might be that I would claim a right to a free lunch if and only if I were hungry. Yet, if I were to make that claim, I might attempt to justify it by appeal to the fact that I am a citizen. (Feldman 1983, 481)

I think that this is intended to be a counterexample to the ASA inference, which employs the principle "'I *must claim* [I have X], *if* I have Y' → 'I must claim [I have X *because* I have Y].'" If so, for it to be relevant, it must be expressed as "Suppose I *must* claim a right to a free lunch *if* I am hungry. Yet, if I were to make that claim, I might (without inconsistency) attempt to justify it by appeal to the fact that I am a citizen."

But such a justificatory appeal *is* inconsistent (unless being a citizen at least entails that I am hungry—in which case the stance does not refute the ASA). I cannot consistently hold both that *if* I am hungry I *must* claim a right to a free lunch, and that I have this right because I am a citizen. Holding that I have this right because I am a citizen requires me to hold that *if* I were not a citizen, then I would not have this right, *even if* I were hungry. This directly contradicts "*If* I am hungry, then I must hold that I have this right."

4. In part, a "good" PPA is, on Gewirth's theory, one who has or works to inculcate the "moral virtues," characteristics that dispose it to act in accordance with the PGC. (See RM 243–244.) However, the theory also permits supererogatory judgments. (See RM 189–190.)

5. "Ought implies can" enters centrally into the argument in Stage II, in inferring (4d) from (4c). This principle is also, however, central to the reasoning that only PPAs (those who can choose their purposes, and actions, freely) are the addressees of practical precepts.

6. O'Meara also claims that it is not self-contradictory for me (a superior PPA) to assert that my purposes are more valuable than those of inferior PPAs. (See O'Meara 1982, 374.) If this means that "I have superior rights" is not internally inconsistent, then this claim is question-begging, as what is at issue is whether it is dialectically inconsistent. If it means that a PPA just thinks that it has better purposes, then this is not self-contradictory. But the validity of the argument for superior rights does not depend on this being not self-contradictory; it rests on its being a necessary truth that *all* my purposes are more valuable.

7. The other difficulty concerns the rights of marginal agents and the principle of proportionality. (See Chapter 7, note 1.)

In connection with the principle of proportionality, it is to be noted that Robert D. Heslep (1989, 33) thinks that Gewirth uses this principle to argue for "superior" agents having superior rights. However, the inegalitarian argument attributed to Gewirth (see RM 120) is an objection to Gewirth's egalitarianism, not a position that he holds. Gewirth *rejects* it on pages 122–123 of *Reason and Morality.*

8. At this point, Gewirth quotes Aristotle.

> The agent, insofar as he acts voluntarily, knows 'who he is, what he is doing, what or whom he is acting on . . . ' (Aristotle, *Nicomachean Ethics* III.1. 1111a2ff.). (Gewirth 1982d, 668 n. 1; ellipsis Gewirth's)

9. For more on this distinction, see #21. For some discussion related to Puolimatka's claim, see #17 and #25.3.

10. It is possible that Schwartz, even though she might accept the general principle upon which the ASA rests ("If I must *claim that I have X,* because I am y, then I must claim that *I have X because I am y*"), will claim that I have missed the import of the fact that I claim my right to freedom and well-being on "prudential" grounds. The problem is not with internal application of the LPU as such. Rather, it is that the fact that I claim my right on "prudential" grounds means that the property I must adduce as the sufficient ground for my having this right is not that of being a PPA (my being a member of the class of beings who proactively value their own purposes), which is required for the internal application of the LPU to yield the PGC, but my being a member of the class of beings who proactively value *my* purposes—which does not yield the PGC by internal application of the LPU.

I discuss this objection in detail under #50. However, the short answer to such an objection is that it rests on the untenable claim that I do not deny "I am a member of the class of beings who proactively value their own purposes" if I deny "I am a member of the class of beings who proactively value my purposes" (which I do if I do not claim that I have a right to my freedom and well-being on prudential grounds). Alternatively, the objection supposes that I can avoid contradicting "I am a PPA" by denying that I have a right to my freedom and well-being, provided that I assert that I have a right to my freedom and well-being *according to the criterion* of my own interests, which supposes that, as a PPA, I do not have to value my own purposes proactively.

R. B. Brandt presses the following objection:

> Gewirth correctly affirms that agents want their motivating goals and also want freedom to act and their own purpose-fulfillment generally; he wants the latter two as necessary to any goal-achievement. Gewirth then argues that a person who understands this must claim a *right* to freedom and well-being, on the ground these are necessary for all purpose-fulfillment. The right-claim is a demand made on others, based on a reason. Other persons, of course, can [must!] make similar demands on him, based on symmetrical reasoning, and in consistency he must concede that these demands are as valid against him as his against others. What I do not see is why these reciprocal prudentially-based demands are demands which the persons addressed

are in any way bound to honor. So I fail to see how Gewirth's theory gets off the ground. (Brandt 1981, 39–40)

Gewirth points out that his

argument did not directly refer to *others* making "similar demands" or to "symmetrical reasoning." It referred rather to the *agent's* logically having to recognize that all other prospective agents have the same rights he claims for himself. (Gewirth 1984d, 211)

This is true, but altogether too brief. What Brandt means by "symmetrical reasoning" is external application of the LPU. He grants that all PPAs must, on the criterion of their own interests, claim rights to their own freedom and well-being. Each PPA must hold that every other PPA's claim against it is as valid as its own against PPAO. However, it does not follow from this that PPA need recognize PPAO's claim, because PPAO's claim is validated on PPAO's interests and it cannot be assumed that PPA must take favorable account of PPAO's interests. I must accept that PPAO's claim is as justified *on its terms* as mine is *on my terms*, but it cannot be assumed that we must respect each other's terms.

What Brandt fails to appreciate, however, is that on the criterion of PPA's interests (which is *its* criterion as a PPA for what *is* valid), "I (PPA) am a PPA → I have a right to my freedom and well-being" is a valid inference. By *internal* application of the LPU to this *inference,* it follows that I must consider that PPAO has a right to its freedom and well-being (because PPAO is a PPA). To deny this is to deny that my being a PPA is a sufficient ground for my having a right to my freedom and well-being within my viewpoint.

Following on from his claim that rights and rights-related duties only arise in a social context (see #27), Martin P. Golding claims that the question is not whether Robinson can or must claim a right to freedom and well-being against Friday, but whether Friday should concede these rights to Robinson. He says that Friday will not be required to do so if he does not claim any rights for himself. (See Golding 1984, 131–134.)

But if Robinson must claim the generic rights for himself because he (Robinson) is a PPA, then Friday also must claim the generic rights for himself because he (Friday) is a PPA. Furthermore, Golding fails to see that the argument for Stage III, conducted from Robinson's viewpoint, is independent of what Friday thinks or must think from Friday's viewpoint. Robinson must claim the generic rights for the sufficient reason that he is a PPA, and so must grant these rights to Friday, because Friday is a PPA. From Friday's point of view we get similar reasoning. But neither Robinson nor Friday reasons from the fact that the other must claim rights for himself.

11. This refers to preceding comments in Bond's objection. (See #35.2.)

12. I am not at all sure that this is the right interpretation, for it does not take account of Bond's contentions about various claims being unintelligible. I have commented under #35.2 on his claim that "PPAO has a duty not to interfere with my freedom and well-being *in my interests*" is unintelligible per se. I have not commented on the claim that "Moral due is universal prudential due" is unintelligible. This is basically because I am not sure what

he is attributing, and do not see that any interpretation of such a statement that can be *correctly attributed* to Gewirth is unintelligible. The only relevant question here is whether it is true that I have to grant rights to the freedom and well-being of PPAO because I must consider that, *on the criterion of my interests* (having to regard my freedom and well-being as necessary goods), I have a right to my freedom and well-being. If this is true, and it is, then it does not matter what we call these rights. It will be true that I contradict that I am a PPA if I do not grant these rights, or if I interfere with PPAO's freedom and well-being, and that is all that matters.

13. Yes! But not in a strict "ought" sense.

14. Again, not in any strict "ought" sense.

15. Williams thinks that it is not dialectically necessary for me to claim a right to my freedom and well-being.

16. By Gewirth's ASA. (See RM 110.)

17. Narveson should add "in A's dialectically necessary viewpoint."

It should be noted that there is an ambiguity here. This does not signify that I must claim my right on the *content* of E, whatever that content. It signifies that I must claim it by virtue of my proactive evaluative relation to my purposes entailed by my choosing purposes.

18. The basis of Narveson's critique is his denial of Stage I, of the dialectical necessity of "My freedom and well-being are necessary goods" in a generic-dispositional interpretation. (See #10–#12, #35.5, and #38.)

19. E. M. Adams claims that

> Gewirth maintains that the agent's rights-claim [in Stage II] is a prudential judgment, not an ethical one. But this contention is a consequence of his conception of morality as concerned with furthering the important interests of persons other than or in addition to the agent. And he thinks that the reason for the agent's rights-claim is the fact that his freedom and well-being are necessary conditions of his acting and acting successfully in the pursuit of any of his goals. Hence the rights-claim is said to be a prudential judgment. Nevertheless the agent's rights-claim entails a judgment about what others ought to do for a reason that is not to them prudential. Therefore, from within his own standpoint, the agent claims that his freedom and well-being are reasons why others ought to do or to refrain from doing certain things. It is on the basis of this, Gewirth argues, that an agent must, on pain of inconsistency, acknowledge that he ought to respect the freedom and well-being of others as their rights. So it would seem that even on Gewirth's conception of morality, which I think is too restricted, the agent's rights-claim would have to be counted a moral judgment. (Adams 1980, 585–586].

Why? Because Gewirth says,

> "every agent must claim these rights for the *sufficient reason* that he is a prospective agent who has purposes he wants to fulfill" (emphasis added), and that, therefore, every agent "must accept the generalization that all prospective purposive agents have

rights to freedom and well-being." [RM 48?] This sounds like straight ethical-reasons talk that transcends purely logical inference. I cannot escape the conclusion that either Gewirth has operated from suppressed premises that transcend his account of the conceptual situation or he has mixed ethical intuitions with logical insights in his proof of the DPGC. (Adams 1980, 586)

Adams mixes formal and material considerations here. The move from [I am a PPA is a sufficient reason for "I have a right to my freedom and well-being"] to [PPAO has a right to its freedom and well-being] is purely logical, even if the premise is moral. What Adams must mean is that in [I am a PPA is sufficient reason for "I have a right to my freedom and well-being"], the sufficient reason is not purely logical (but moral). Indeed, it is not purely logical—it is prudential. Within my viewpoint as a PPA, in which I logically must accept [I am a PPA → (is sufficient reason for) I have a right to my freedom and well-being], the criterion of sufficient reason, the criterion for "I have a right to my freedom and well-being" is my interests. Logical necessity applies here in that I deny that I am a PPA if I do not accept this criterion and what it validates. It is not true that, on Gewirth's own account, "I have a right to my freedom and well-being" is moral. If Adams wants to say that the right is moral because the ground of the sufficient reason here makes the right universalizable to all PPAs, then he may do so, if he likes. But then, like Hare, he will not be able to extract any equivocational capital out of it. He will simply be using "moral" in a different way from Gewirth.

On the other hand, Adams might be making the false claim (also suggested by McMahon [#35.10]) that Gewirth assumes that PPA considers that PPAO accepts a nonprudential reason not to interfere with PPA's freedom and well-being. PPA does not assume that PPAO accepts *any* reason not to interfere with PPA's freedom and well-being.

I don't know what Adams means when he says that Gewirth's definition of "moral" is too narrow. Gewirth's definition of "moral" is not meant to cover "ordinary usage," though it accords with much of it. It is designed to highlight and specify what Gewirth wishes to prove. It does not matter whether or not we call the PGC "a moral" principle. It only matters that we are obliged to accept and obey the PGC on pain of contradicting that we are PPAs. The same goes for all the inferences in the argument. It does not matter how we label them, it only matters that they are dialectically necessary.

20. Further matters relating to this are discussed in note 31 infra.

21. To contend that I consider X to be justified *simpliciter* is not to say that it is justified assertorically, or from every PPA's viewpoint. Matters relating to this are discussed under #35.3.

22. R. E. Ewin (1987, 59–60) claims that Stage II is defective because Gewirth cannot establish that I must consider that I have a right to my freedom and well-being. All that can be established is that, *from my point of view*, PPAO ought to give me my freedom and well-being. However, this "ought" is not correlative to a rights-claim—as PPAO is given no reason to act by the criterion of this "ought." Even if we can say it is correlative to a rights-claim, this does not help, for all that universalization can establish is

that I ought, *from the point of view of PPAO*, not to interfere with the freedom and well-being of PPAO.

This is well-nigh identical to Harman's objection, except that Ewin does not use it, explicitly, to allege equivocation between moral and prudential rights, but to support his own contention that "rights can be explained only if we start with consideration of community and the relations between people" (ibid., 60).

James Collins presses what is essentially the same objection as Ewin's. (See Collins 1979, 72–73.)

23. I discuss a further aspect of McMahon's critique in note 31 infra.

In considering McMahon's critique, I have posited the plausibility of holding that an "ought" of evaluation will not universalize, merely to show how this would contribute to holding that only external application of the LPU is applicable. I do not, in fact, think that it is correct to say that (4d), as an "ought" of evaluation, will not universalize to an other-regarding position. If I am required to consider my having freedom and well-being to be desirable (impersonally good *relative to* my prudential criterion) because I am a PPA, then I am required to consider that it is desirable that PPAO have its freedom and well-being. (See #13 and #37, also #35.3 and note 31 infra, on the concept of "impersonal good.") The implication of (4d) being only an "ought" of evaluation, which *would* damage the argument, is that the derived other-regarding judgment would not be deontic. It would accord desirability to states of affairs, but it would not prescribe duties. (See #37.) An independent theory of causal responsibility for outcomes would be required to render it deontological. While there might be no difficulty about this regarding negative rights, there are problems regarding positive rights. (See #66.2.) Complications like this can be ignored, however, because (4d) is an action directive from my viewpoint, the concept of desirability employed in the argument being proactive. (See #37.)

24. Compare Jeffrey Paul's claim, discussed under #46, that Gewirth uses universalization to move from the dialectical to the assertoric.

25. Puolimatka claims that Gewirth tacitly admits to using the principle of universalizability in its moral application, because the principle, logical in itself, only yields the desired result when applied to a moral rights-claim. (See Puolimatka 1989, 68–69.) Since the latter claim is false, Gewirth admits to no such thing. He admits only to using the same *logical* principle as is employed in the universalization of moral judgments. (See RM 105.)

26. Arval A. Morris (1981), Ronald M. Green (1979), and Brian Barry (1989) all press objections that can be classified under #47 generally.

According to Morris, if a PPA does not claim a moral right to its freedom and well-being, Stage III will not work. Prudentially based rights-claims will not universalize to moral ones. (See Morris 1981, 164.)

This is false, if the prudential criterion is one that is necessarily connected with "I am a PPA," as it is shown to be in Gewirth's argument. For, then, to deny that I have the prudentially based rights is to deny that I am a PPA, and hence, to deny that I have these rights because I am a PPA is to deny "I am a PPA." Once this claim is secured, internal application of the LPU requires me to grant these rights to all PPAs on the grounds that they are PPAs; and, on

Gewirth's definition of "moral," these rights are moral.

According to Green,

> [i]t may well be the case that an individual who values the ge-
> neric goods must believe that he "ought" to be free to enjoy them,
> and (somewhat less certainly) that he then makes the correlative
> claim that he has a "right" to these goods. But if so, the "ought"
> here indicates only a logically necessary condition of free action
> which either will not, in fact, be met (prompting the conclusion
> that the agent cannot act as freely as he wishes), or which can be
> satisfied in any of a number of ways (including the agent's own
> forcible defense of his liberty and well-being). What this "ought"
> and any correlative "right" claim do not necessarily imply, how-
> ever, is that others should restrain their behavior on the agent's
> behalf or show him any kind of moral respect. But it is just this
> idea which seems to be required if a universalization of one's
> own prudential "ought" and rights claim is to have any moral
> significance, as Gewirth seems to believe it has. (Green 1979, 188)

However, the "ought" here does not just indicate a logically necessary
condition of free action. *On my prudential criterion* it indicates that PPAO
ought to restrain its behavior on my behalf. (See #34.1.) This does not mean
that PPAO must show me moral respect. The criterion of this "ought" is not
moral. It also does not mean that PPAO ought, *on PPAO's prudential criterion*,
to refrain from interference with my freedom and well-being. And it is not
true that this "ought" must be moral in order for universalization to have
any moral significance. Internal application of the LPU to the inference I am
dialectically required to accept, [I am a PPA → I have a right to my freedom
and well-being], entails that I must grant these rights to PPAO (that I must
hold that I ought not to interfere with PPAO's freedom and well-being), even
when the criterion of the right I must claim is my interests. What matters for
this universalization is not the criterion of the right but the ground upon
which the criterion grants the right.

According to Brian Barry (who, as late as 1989, considers only Gewirth
1970a!), "I ought to do x because it is necessary for the achievement of y,
which I want" can be universalized purely logically to "PPAO ought to have
x because it is necessary for the achievement of y, which PPAO wants." Stage
III, however, cannot be established in this way because the first "ought" is
(for me as an amoralist) only action-guiding for me, the second only action-
guiding for PPAO. Moral motives must be attributed to PPAO for Stage III to
be effected. (See Barry 1989, 288–289.)

However, use of the ASA combined with internal application of the LPU,
requires even the amoralist to *endorse* "PPAO ought to have x." This is explained in *Reason and Morality*, but Barry does not consider this. (Nor do
most other commentators, but it requires a very cavalier reading of *Reason
and Morality* to say, as Barry does, that the argument in *Reason and Morality*
adds nothing substantial to that in Gewirth 1970a.)

27. Matters are complicated further still by Singer's claim that talk of
prudential rights is only metaphorical. In my discussion under #35.9 I have

taken Singer to be charging equivocation. However, this does not square with the second half of his paper. See below.

28. James Scheuermann considers that

> Singer is right when he says that all that Gewirth is talking about when using the concept of prudential rights is "what one must ... will if one is to will consistently, must find desirable if one is to have any desires at all." And if that is true, then it is hard to avoid Singer's conclusion that "talk about prudential rights is superfluous ... " That is, if Gewirth's derivation of the Principle of Generic Consistency by way of the concept of prudential rights is successful, it can also be shown to be successful without the use of this concept; the derivation could be conducted simply in terms of the necessary volitions of rational agents. But if this is taken to be a criticism, it is not one which I think is very significant. There may still be good reasons to employ the concept of prudential rights, e.g. the desire to provide a basis for our concept of moral rights, clarity of exposition, and so on. (Scheuermann 1987, 303; ellipses Scheuermann's)

I agree with this entirely, and it is worth noting that my formulation of Stage II in terms of the argument from attitudinal consistency (see #13) is, effectively, an argument "conducted simply in terms of the necessary volitions of rational agents."

Gewirth replies to Singer in Gewirth 1985b. Gewirth does not attempt to analyze what lies behind Singer's comments, and restricts himself (in the main) to correcting Singer's presentation of his argument. I do not think that Gewirth is entirely correct to say that Singer holds that the derivation of the PGC can proceed in terms of moral rather than prudential rights throughout. Gewirth is correct to say that this would be question-begging *given Gewirth's definitions of terms*. But it seems to me that Singer is not operating with Gewirth's terms (which is the source of his difficulties). Singer really wants to talk about "non–other-regarding moral" rights—rather than about "prudential" rights—and "other-regarding moral" rights (at least in part 2 of his paper), though he does not make this explicit. (On the other hand, in part 1, Singer does not recognize non–other-regarding moral rights, and this is the source of the inconsistency in his critique.)

Robert L. Arrington claims that the dialectically necessary claims of Stage II could be called "moral" claims, and that this might help Stage III. This leads him to a very confused and unnecessarily lengthy discussion in which he attempts to refute this suggestion. (See Arrington 1989, 109–112.)

This suggestion is, indeed, to be rejected. Such a linguistic stipulation achieves nothing. All it does is change the way we talk about Stage III. The argument's task is now to be described as that of effecting the move from the self-regarding "moral" rights of Stage II to the other-regarding ones of Stage III. What is at issue is whether PPAs must accept other-regarding rights-claims, not whether we should call them "moral." But Arrington makes a mountain out of a molehill by attempting a *material* refutation of a nonmaterial suggestion.

29. Scheuermann's article consists mainly of a (generally convincing) defense of the intelligibility of Gewirth's concept of a prudential right. This takes the form of presenting the argument for Stage II along the lines I have adapted in Chapter 7, note 16.

30. It should be apparent that I am interpreting Scheuermann's objection as a version of what Gewirth calls "the individualizability objection."

> The individualizability objection holds that when the agent gives a sufficient justificatory reason for his having the generic rights, this reason may be so individualized that it pertains only to the agent himself. The point is that since the agent claims the generic rights for himself, his reason for this claim must consist in his own having of his own purposes that he wants to fulfill for himself. Hence, as formulated by the agent, his reason for his right-claim must include 'egocentric particulars'—expressions whose denotation is relative to the speaker himself, such as 'I' and 'my.' The agent would be in the position of saying, 'I have the generic rights because *I* want to fulfill *my own* purposes.' Since other persons may not have or want to fulfill the agent's purposes, the agent's reason for his right-claim comprises characteristics of himself that are not had by other persons, and his reason is not the same as the reasons other persons give for their right-claims. Thus the universalization of the agent's right-claim would be not, 'All prospective agents who have purposes they want to fulfill have the generic rights,' but rather, 'All prospective agents who have *my* purposes that *I* want to fulfill have the generic rights.'
> . . . Thus . . . the universalization of the agent's right-claim would be logically restricted so as to entail only that the agent himself has the generic rights, not that all prospective agents have them. (RM 115–116)

Gewirth considers two versions of this: first a version based on indexical expressions. The PPA is portrayed as arguing

> 'I have the generic rights because I am a prospective agent named X who wants to fulfill X's purposes.' The universalization would now be: 'All prospective agents named "X" who want to fulfill X's purposes have the generic rights.' (RM 116)

Gewirth replies to this in terms of the ASA.

> [O]ne would ask the agent, 'Wouldn't you claim the rights to freedom and well-being even if your name weren't "X"?' If he replies, 'No; only one's having the noble name "X" justifies one's having these rights,' then he can be refuted by the consideration . . . that the rights to freedom and well-being must be claimed, at

least implicitly, by every agent who acts for purposes he regards as good. Hence, X would claim to have these rights for a justificatory reason even if his name were not 'X.' It follows that . . . his justificatory reason can be sufficient without including or having in the background his being named 'X.' (Ibid.)

Second, Gewirth considers a version that turns on a PPA being the unique PPA that it is.

In response to this, he argues that my and PPAO's reasons for acting may be considered the same reason, even though the relata in "I want to benefit myself" and "PPAO wants to benefit itself" are different. The reason is constituted by the same qualitative *relation*. (See RM 117–119.)

I treat Scheuermann's objection as a version of the latter type. My response draws, in part, on Gewirth's: it is more detailed, however, adduces considerations Gewirth does not mention, and attends to the specific features of Scheuermann's remarks to which Gewirth (of course) was not responding. Scheuermann makes no mention of Gewirth's discussion. The reason for this might be that this is not the objection he has in mind (improbably, I think); or it might be that Scheuermann's remarks are more in the nature of suggestive comments, coming as they do at the end of an article with a different focus.

31. It is to be noted that Scheuermann is not the only critic who contends that Gewirth presupposes that PPAs are committed to the idea that having freedom and well-being ("agency in general") is, in some sense, a "noncompetitive" good. Jesse Kalin (1984) does so, as does Christopher McMahon (1986), to cite just two examples.

According to Christopher McMahon

Gewirth . . . may think that . . . , from his own point of view, an agent must judge the maintenance of the generic conditions of his agency to have impersonal value—that is, to be good not just for him but in itself. If Gewirth's argument is interpreted in this way, then the whole of my previous account of it is mistaken. [The bulk of McMahon's critique is considered under #35.10 and #47.6.] For my account has proceeded on the assumption that an agent's judgment of the necessary goodness of his freedom and well-being is a judgment of their supreme agent-relative value. . . .

But . . . this interpretation . . . merely pushes back the point at which the question is begged. For if analysis of the concept of agency establishes that each agent must be regarded as judging the maintenance of the generic conditions of his or her agency to have impersonal value, then analysis of this concept establishes that agency has, initially and prior to deductive elaboration, not just a normative but a moral (or at any rate, proto-moral) structure. And . . . the success of . . . [the] argument . . . requires that it proceed from a concept of agency which is not explicitly moral. (McMahon 1986, 279–280)

(Of course, if it is only analysis that reveals such a structure—and if the argument is valid, then such a structure must be revealed—then the concept of agency is not being assumed to be *explicitly* moral. It is only explicitly moral if the argument does not work without assuming explicitly that the structure of agency is moral. I shall assume that McMahon appreciates this, and is claiming that the argument does not work unless we suppose, explicitly, that the concept of agency is moral.)

First, what exactly is McMahon saying? We saw under #35.3, that Gewirth *does use* an agent-relative analysis of good and "ought." When a PPA says "I (PPA) ought to have my freedom and well-being," this is a judgment validated by the PPA's dialectically necessary criterion. The PPA is required to make this judgment because this judgment is validated by its dialectically necessary criterion. No assumption is made that this is assertorically a true judgment, or that PPAO will accept this judgment (that it is validated by PPAO's dialectically necessary criteria), or that PPA's dialectically necessary criterion is other-regarding (moral). Now, McMahon suggests that Gewirth considers that a PPA regards its generic features as good, not just for itself, but in themselves. This is ambiguous. If McMahon means that a PPA assumes that every PPA's generic features are necessary goods, or that PPAO regards its (PPA's) generic features as necessary goods, then Gewirth attributes no such view to a PPA. If, on the other hand, he is saying that a PPA regards its judgments, which are valid relative to its dialectically necessary criterion, as prescribing what is valid (justified *simpliciter*, in the sense that these are the judgments that are to definitively guide the PPA's thinking and acting), then Gewirth does attribute this view. In the latter sense, but not in the former, Gewirth holds that a PPA's judgments are judgments of "impersonal value" or "good-in-itself." But, these judgments are judgments of what is good-in-itself *from the PPA's viewpoint* (i.e., relative to the PPA's dialectically necessary criteria). According to Gewirth, criteria specify what *on the criteria* ought to be, or are, good, independent of anyone's espousal of the criteria. *Criteria* do not prescribe only *to* those who accept them, though they only prescribe *for* those who accept them. They prescribe *what* they prescribe *impersonally*. Who considers that what they prescribe is binding depends on the personal dimension of acceptance.

Now, Gewirth's argument certainly rests on the latter view. It does not rest on the former. To espouse the latter does not entail espousing the former. If McMahon thinks that Gewirth espouses the former, or that the latter entails the former, then he is mistaken. But, perhaps, he appreciates that Gewirth holds the latter and thinks that this is mistaken or, at least, not dialectically necessary.

What, then, could it mean to say that a PPA's judgments are not about what, from its point of view, are good-in-themselves?

a. McMahon might wish to assert that a PPA may (or must) recognize that PPAO might have a different point of view, and thus think that different things are good. This, however, is compatible with Gewirth's view.

b. McMahon might mean that a PPA need not take its view to be privileged over other viewpoints. If this means that a PPA has no grounds for thinking that its viewpoint has assertoric privilege, then I agree. But the argument does not need to deny this. On the other hand, if this means that a PPA is not bound to reason in terms of its viewpoint, then this is untenable.

Alternatively, if this means that I must temper my judgments because PPAO might not agree, then this seems to involve just the moral viewpoint that Gewirth wishes to avoid; and Gewirth certainly doesn't hold this, or need to.

c. So, perhaps, McMahon wishes to assert that it is not necessarily true that *according to* my prudential criterion my having freedom and well-being ought to be. My criterion, perhaps, prescribes only that my having freedom and well-being ought to be *according to me*, or according to anyone who accepts this criterion. However, if "according to me" signifies that only those who accept the criterion consider themselves bound by it, then this is compatible with Gewirth's view. This denies Gewirth's view only if it signifies that the content of what is *formally* validated by the criterion depends on acceptance of the criterion. This, however, is barely intelligible. If the content of a criterion's prescriptions is not impersonal (fixed independent of acceptance), then there is no way of knowing what a criterion requires prior to acceptance, and thus no choice between criteria to accept can ever be presented. Criteria are differentiated precisely by the fact that they validate different things.

We must also consider how Scheuermann's objection relates to this suggestion. Scheuermann (see Chapter 7, note 16) holds that if a PPA judges that it ought to pursue its freedom and well-being, where this "ought" has the sense of what ought to be the case "impersonally," then Stage II must be valid. The idea is that the criterion provided by my agency (my "prudential (1) criterion," [see above]) validates "I ought to pursue my freedom and well-being." I need my freedom and well-being to bring this state of affairs about, so this criterion must prescribe that I have my freedom and well-being. As such, this "ought" must be other-referring. It will be directing, however, only for those who espouse this criterion (and only I necessarily do so). This means that, on this criterion, I have a right to my freedom and well-being, though only those who must espouse this criterion must consider that I have this right. Scheuermann agrees with Gewirth that this is so. As such, he cannot be pressing the view I have just suggested McMahon might hold. However, according to Gewirth, possessive universalization now requires me to grant the generic rights to PPAO. Scheuermann disagrees. For it to do so, he says, I must be supposed to value freedom and well-being as a "noncompetitive good," and this is not dialectically necessary. But, when he says this, he does not question that it is dialectically necessary for me to hold that my prudential criterion validates its prescriptions "impersonally" in the way I have just outlined; and it seems to me it is this that McMahon might (here) be denying. McMahon's "impersonal good" does not seem to me to be the same as Scheuermann's "noncompetitive good," and so Scheuermann's objection seems to be different from that which I am attributing to McMahon here.

32. A criticism that *at least superficially* suggests the objection I have attributed to Scheuermann is stated by Carol C. Gould. However, I think her objection is different, and based on a more obvious error.

> The transition from the merely prudential to the moral status of
> the individual's rights-claim comes, according to Gewirth, from

the fact that the agent claims the rights to freedom and well-being as generic rights, as rights which hold for all prospective agents as necessary conditions for their action. But this is already to include in the notion of agency something more than Gewirth himself allows in his account of the individual agent acting prudentially in pursuit of his or her own purposes. For if the right claimed by the agent is a generic right, then it is already surreptitiously moral at the outset, and its universalizability is assured even as the agent acts presumably only prudentially. (Gould 1988, 69–70)

Gould misinterprets the sense in which a PPA claims "generic" rights in Stage II. "Generic," as Gewirth (here) employs it, refers to the generic *conditions* of *my agency*, to my freedom and well-being. According to (5), I must claim that I have the generic rights, meaning that I must claim that I have a right *to* my freedom and well-being. "Generic rights" is not used in the sense of "rights belonging to all PPAs." (5) does not state that I must claim rights that belong to all PPAs, merely that I must claim rights to the categorically necessary conditions of my agency. That I must also recognize that freedom and well-being are categorically necessary conditions of PPAO's agency requires me (by the ASA and the internal application of the LPU) to grant PPAO these rights. As a result, I must accept that freedom and well-being are "generic rights" in Gould's sense of this term. But the universalization that produces this result does not assume that this is so.

Chapter 9: Miscellaneous Objections
1. As W. D. Hudson declares,

Whether or not this conception of the moral 'ought' accords with the ordinary use of the word is a debatable matter. (Hudson 1984, 109)

But Hudson also appreciates that Gewirth is well aware of this, and that the pertinent question is whether he can derive rationally necessary commitment to "the moral," as he defines this, from "I am a PPA." (See ibid., 109–110.)

2. Singer would appear to have changed his mind about this objection by the time of his 1985 article. (See #49.)

3. Richard Brooks says that Gewirth's "ethical principles are not 'objective' in the sense of not being debatable" (Brooks 1981, 295). I am not sure what Brooks means by this. He surely cannot mean that Gewirth holds his position dogmatically, without argument, or that he does not hold his argument to be open to question. I take it that he means that, if the argument is sound, then the PGC cannot be rejected without error, and PPAs are rationally prohibited from adopting other principles. I cannot see that this constitutes any sort of objection. (On the other hand, if Brooks means the opposite of what I have taken him to be saying, then all that needs to be said is that a position does not have to be beyond dispute in order to be either correct or firmly grounded.)

4. Gewirth alludes to this in RM 138.

5. Douglas N. Husak (1984, 1985) also holds that it is clear that there are no human rights. However, his argument is that Gewirth's argument, even if valid, does not establish that beings have the generic rights by virtue of being biologically human; it establishes that they have the generic rights by virtue of being PPAs. MacIntyre's denial is as much a denial of PPA rights as of human rights.

6. Gewirth, I think somewhat unfairly, treats MacIntyre's assimilation of belief in human rights to belief in unicorns and witches as a freestanding argument against human rights, and objects to this mainly on the ground that there are empirical correlates for rights, but not for witches and unicorns (in that empirical facts could not establish that there are witches and unicorns, whereas we can point to phenomena that are undeniably violations of human rights). (See Gewirth 1985a, 740.) This is not a very good response. I am not at all sure that nothing could be good empirical evidence for witches and unicorns; and the claim that certain actions are undeniably violations of human rights, while true (if Gewirth's argument is valid), is question-begging by itself. It needs to be backed by an explicit appeal to Gewirth's argument.

7. Derek Parfit points out that the attempt to provide an objective (nonreligious) basis for moral judgments is a relatively recent enterprise as a concerted endeavor within moral philosophy. (See Parfit 1984, 453.) On this evidence, the inductive basis for MacIntyre's claim is slim, even if inductive evidence were relevant.

8. Gewirth notes that Nielsen seems to overlook that Kant, whom many take to have refuted the ontological argument, held Gewirth's general epistemological thesis, indicating that the two arguments might not be as analogous as Nielsen suggests they are. (See Gewirth 1984d, 199.)

9. In "I *ought* to guide my conduct by 'I ought to pursue my freedom and well-being,'" the "*ought*" is logical rather than prudential, although the "ought" in "I ought to pursue my freedom and well-being" is prudential; and the same applies to the "*ought*" in "I *ought* to hold that PPAO ought not to interfere with my freedom and well-being." The reason why the "ought" in the PGC is moral rather than prudential is that the universalization that takes us into the moral is logical rather than prudential: I am logically, rather than prudentially, required to take favorable account of the interests of PPAO, on the grounds of logically having to impose a prudential duty on PPAO not to interfere with my freedom and well-being for the sufficient reason that I am a PPA.

10. This paragraph is my interpretation of RM 128, taken together with RM 29–30.

Something like Williams' objection (or Virginia Held's, #54.2) is also pressed by

a.   Richard B. Friedman (1981, 155–157). (See Chapter 8, note 3);

b.   Peter Allen, who claims that Gewirth's argument only works on the assumption that PPAs are persons abstracted from real social, historical, and political relationships. (See Allen 1987, 44–48); and *c.*   Richard Brooks, who says that Gewirth's starting point assumes away contingent historical situations that give expression to ethical and legal claims: "To illustrate, a dialogue with the Iranian students holding American hostages would not yield as a starting point their recognition of the need to start with their status as purposive and voluntary agents. Rather they would begin with their claims as radical Moslems at a certain point in Iran's history" (Brooks 1981, 292).

The response given to Williams/Engels (and Held [below]) applies equally to all of these. Additionally, it is to be pointed out that Brooks' example has bearing on the politics of debate, but not on its epistemology. Moslems at a certain point in Iran's history or not, the Iranian students are (were) still (presumably) PPAs, and thus rationally committed to the PGC (if the inferences from "I am a PPA" are valid), whether they assent to this or not.

11. Lansing Pollock asks how a theory as "complex" as Gewirth's could be taught to children, or even to adults without many years of philosophical training, and objects that it would have to be left to moral experts to tell us how to act on it.

Ultimately,

> [i]f we want moral theories to be serviceable as action-guides, a satisfactory theory must be simpler than Gewirth's. (Pollock 1988, 237)

However, although a theory must give clear prescriptions to function as an action guide, its *justification* does not have to be simple for it to function in this way. Most people use and learn arithmetic without being able to prove any of its basic principles. Provided that the argument to the PGC is valid, there is no problem leaving its proof to experts. The PGC itself is not more difficult to understand than other general principles, like the "Golden Rule" (and is, in fact, clearer, because of its determinate content). As far as applications go, the more clear-cut applications can be taught as rules of thumb. These rules cover the standard prohibitions against violence, theft, dishonesty, killing, etc., which are common to most societies in any case. Difficult cases can be left to individual decision, in the first instance, and adjudicated by "moral courts" interpreting the "PGC constitution," in the last instance. (See Beyleveld and Brownsword 1986, Chapters Seven to Nine, for some discussion of this.) In any event, whatever practical difficulties are faced here cannot be used to question the validity of the argument *to* the PGC.

12. Gewirth replies, in a vein similar to this and the preceding quoted paragraph, to W. D. Hudson (who talks about "the distinctively moral way of thinking" as the ultimate justification for moral judgments [Hudson 1984, 113]), and to Hare (who presses for a "rationalist prescriptivism," which resorts to a form of reflexive, but contingent, *ad hominem* critique for its justificatory arguments [see Hare 1984, 57–58]). (See Gewirth 1984d, 220–221.)

William K. Frankena (1980a) holds a view epistemologically similar to that of Hare; the basis of moral justification is the moral point of view (MPV).

This was criticized by Gewirth (1980c), on the grounds that it cannot answer two questions: (*a*) Why should one adopt the MPV? (*b*) How does the MPV serve as the basis of morality? To this Frankena responds,

> A MPV theory like mine cannot actually give decisive answers to Gewirth's questions, because it cannot demonstrate clearly and certainly that one should be moral or that one must adopt a certain moral principle rather than another. Now, Gewirth believes that he can demonstrate both of these things . . . . Like many of the critics of his earlier articles and recent book, however, I have doubts that he has actually succeeded in doing so. I admit argument and proof are wanted, but I am not convinced that proof is possible. To one who believes that he has such arguments and proofs, my kind of view, even with its best foot forward, must seem quite inadequate; for him we have something much better. To me, however, being doubtful about this, and also about intuitionism, my kind of theory seems to be the best we can do and hence to be, in a second[-]best sense, worth putting forward. If I were more content with my presentation of my kind of theory, I might even suggest that, when better is not available, second-best is first-best after all. (Frankena 1980b, 126–127)

This is admirable on its own terms, but since Gewirth has provided a proof, first-best is all that will do, and second-best is no good at all.

(In this general connection, it is worth noting that the idea that apodictic epistemological foundations for physics, mathematics, and the like cannot be given, and that philosophers must rest content with justifying propositions in these disciplines by appealing to principles embedded in received practice (which Bambrough asserts), although characteristic of certain schools of philosophy, is by no means uncontentious. Philosophers have, at various times, sought apodictic foundations for empirical science and mathematics; and Bambrough's characterization of justification in/of these disciplines should not be accepted without argument.)

13. Marcus G. Singer has criticized Gewirth explicitly on his treatment of the first question (see Singer 1984), and Gewirth replies to this in Gewirth 1984d, 197–199. However, I have not considered this, as it applies more importantly to the use that Gewirth makes of the PGC than to his argument to the PGC (with which I am solely concerned).

Robert L. Arrington claims that the PGC is open to two radically different interpretations—as a principle of negative rights, or as one of both positive and negative rights. He infers from this that Gewirth has not demonstrated that there is only one fundamental moral principle. (See Arrington 1989, 113.)

This is incorrect. The PGC is demonstrated as a principle of both positive and negative rights. (See Chapter 10.) Even if it were not, this would not show, as Arrington thinks it does, that there are two fundamental principles. It would show only that it is uncertain what the fundamental principle is.

14. Richard Brooks says that Gewirth's theory (which he calls "ethical humanism") lacks "moral appeal" because it is not based on "sympathetic" ethical principles. (See Brooks 1981, 302–304.)

However, the question of its appeal is epistemologically irrelevant. What matters is its rational necessity. More to the present point, however, the justification of the PGC is not based on any ethical principles at all.

Brooks also says that Gewirth's system does not offer a complete and satisfactory ethical basis for legal rules and institutions, because these are not universally based on ethical humanism. (See ibid., 304.)

However, the test of Gewirth's theory, which is not an ethical anthropology, is most definitely *not* its conformity with existing institutions and practices, which might not be rationally justified. The situation is quite the opposite: as a moral epistemology, it is the theory that is to provide the test for the justifiability of historical institutions and practices.

Tapio Puolimatka thinks that some moral notions are universally experienced as indubitable, and that a conclusive justificatory argument is unnecessary. (See Puolimatka 1989, 166.) He claims, further, that Gewirth tacitly accepts this when he says that the search for proof is not just a search for certainty but also an attempt to make our deepest convictions coherent. (See RM ix.) He claims that this is an admission that Gewirth's argument begins from moral premises based in intuition. (See Puolimatka 1989, 167.) To support his claim that logical proof is unnecessary, Puolimatka claims that the acceptance of logic is basically intuitive.

> If reason in its intuitive function must operate as the basis for the deductive function, we can suppose that moral intuitions can, in a similar way, ground our moral thinking and behaviour without making them somehow irrational. (Ibid., 169)

However, Gewirth does not reason from moral premises. His argument does not begin from "our moral convictions." Puolimatka's inference is a total non sequitur. There is no universal consensus on moral notions. It is just this that makes the need for a justificatory argument so pressing. It is true that the most basic logical principles cannot be proved independently. If this is what Puolimatka means by the "intuitive function," then this is correct. But the intuition attaching to this is fundamentally different from the "intuition" attaching to moral notions. Negation of the principle of noncontradiction presupposes the validity of the principle of noncontradiction. Negation of a moral notion does not presuppose the validity of this notion.

15. It may also be noted that Gewirth considers the question of a supreme moral principle under three headings: "Is it needless to justify a supreme moral principle?" "Is it impossible to justify a supreme moral principle?" "Can a supreme moral principle be justified inductively?" (See RM 7–21.) Much of this discussion has a direct bearing on Bambrough's critique, but Bambrough does not deal with it.

The impotence of contingent *ad hominem* critique is illustrated by James N. Loughran's comments on *Reason and Morality*.

According to Loughran,

> it is surely not enough to take the human agent merely as free and purposive—not if the goal is to present morality as categorically binding and other-directed. The conclusion will be too

> much at odds with the first premise. Something else must be
> included as essential to the initial description of human agency.
> (Loughran 1986, 149–150)

Why is it not enough to begin with voluntariness and purposivity? Because the argument requires even an egoist (amoralist?) to accept a moral principle, and this

> is paradox of the highest order. Even the most logical, the most
> "rational" among us must feel that something is wrong with the
> argument. I for one, or at least the egoist in me, feel tricked. But
> I think I know where to locate the fundamental weakness of the
> argument: not at its derivations, conclusion, or applications: but
> at its starting point. (Ibid., 149)

Loughran appears to be saying that it just can't be right to say that the egoist logically must accept a moral principle when egoism disavows morality: there just must be a flaw in the argument.

If Loughran understands the dialectically necessary method, if he understands that Gewirth argues from what the egoist must hold *as a PPA*, then this is absurd. The egoist is a PPA, a voluntary purposive agent. So, even for the egoist, Gewirth's starting point is dialectically necessary. If there is nothing wrong with the derivations, then the egoist (as a PPA) must accept the PGC, and the starting point must be adequate; it cannot be at odds with the conclusion. What Loughran says only makes sense if he maintains that the egoist can refuse to accept what it must accept as a PPA, that it may reason from its egoism even when this conflicts with its reasoning from its agency. Only if this is so will a moral conception of agency, which the egoist disavows, be necessary. However, such a conception will be treated by the egoist as question-begging. According to Gewirth, either the egoist, *as a PPA*, must accept the PGC, or else any argument for morality will beg the question against the egoist. (Alternatively, Loughran, like Tapio Puolimatka [see Puolimatka 1989, 56], thinks that the argument to the PGC is "inherently paradoxical" because it requires the prescriptions of egoism to entail their denial. But this simply misinterprets the dialectically necessary method as an assertoric one.)

Loughran's critique is confused at the very beginning, and it is thoroughly unclear what his criticism of Gewirth is. I shall, therefore, pass it over without further comment, and look briefly at Loughran's own position.

Loughran, in fact, denies that it is necessary to begin with a neutral starting point. He says that there are three basic features relevant to human agency: "purposiveness" (the having of interests and goals which give direction to one's life and a measure of the success of one's choices and achievements), "personalness" (awareness of oneself as a self against others), and "aesthetic nature of life" (the propensity to seek satisfaction and equilibrium as opposed to their opposites). This, which Loughran derives from Lawrence Becker (1973), *on the surface* does not appear to be incompatible with Gewirth's starting point. However, as Loughran explicates "personalness," it takes priority over the other two categories, and involves capacities and dispositions for rationality, freedom, creativity, communication, love, self-respect, *etc.* (Loughran 1986, 153)

The inclusion of the disposition to love definitely makes this a moral category. So, Loughran wishes to begin with a moral conception of agency. How, then, does he propose to justify this against the egoist? We are told that all "normal" human beings, by which Loughran means the statistical norm (see ibid., 150), possess personalness. This fact, we are told, generates a *presumption* that what it is rational to value is what these "normal" persons, thinking logically in terms of these capacities, will value. The onus is, therefore, on the skeptic (egoist) to *prove that this is not so.* Loughran does not think that the skeptic can do this. Egoism is disarmed by requiring the egoist, rather than the moralist, to prove its position.

Now, if demonstrating "the rationality of morality" means demonstrating that it is *"not irrational* to adopt a moral point of view," then we may, indeed, presume that adoption of a moral viewpoint is not irrational ("rational"), pending proof that it is irrational. But, equally, pending proof that egoism is irrational, it is "rational," in this sense, to be an egoist. But Loughran clearly thinks that the fact that the statistical norm of humanity are moralists creates a presumption that egoism is irrational, that moralism is *rationally required.* This is, obviously, not so—unless we make the criteria of rationality the criteria of the statistical norm; and this is question-begging. To demonstrate that morality is *categorically* binding, nothing other than a dialectically necessary starting point will do.

Like Loughran, Neil MacCormick tries to place the onus of proof solely on amoralists.

> The boot is on the other foot. It is amoralism into which human beings have to argue themselves, having learned the arts of rationality in a social existence in which it is taken for granted that each of us can have as his/her own end some disinterested interest in others' well being, and ought to have. The question is not then whether one can construct morality out of amoralism, but whether one should abandon morality in favour of amoralism. (MacCormick 1984, 351)

This is ethnocentric, and question-begging against the amoralist. From an epistemological point of view, the onus of proof rests equally on the shoulders of the moralist and the amoralist. Note also, that Gewirth *does not,* as this suggests, try to construct morality out of amoralism. The argument is that PPAs, *as PPAs,* must accept the PGC. It is not an argument from *any* SPR for my purposes.

Robert L. Arrington claims that the PGC is not "the kind of first principle that actually operates in our moral thinking" (Arrington 1989, 115). We take our moral principles to be absolutely obvious. The PGC is not absolutely obvious, as it requires an intricate proof.

However, the issue is not whether we (who?) take something to be indubitable, but whether we are justified in doing so. The rules Arrington cites are not obvious to all. Independent of proof, we have no proper grounds for treating them as indubitable. To reject the argument to the PGC on grounds like this is to abandon reason for dogma. Furthermore, it seems to have escaped Arrington's notice that the PGC validates the very rules he cites as obvious.

16. See also, e.g., #35.3, #35.10, #47.5, #47.6, and especially Chapter 8, note 31.

17. Bond holds that a supreme moral principle can be derived from what a PPA necessarily must will, but only by adding a metaphysical, not logically necessary premise that

> *qua* rational, sentient, conative agents, we are all on the same and hence an equal footing. (Bond 1980b, 74. See also Bond 1980a, 52–53.)

18. On the first claim, see the argument from attitudinal consistency in #13. Compare also #49 (Singer 1985) and Chapter 8, note 28 (Scheuermann 1987). On the second claim, see, especially, #47 and #50.

19. This statement is no longer true. After this was written and, unfortunately, too late for me to comment on it, an article by Michael Davis (1991) came to my attention in which he presses this very objection. A reply by Gewirth is, however, forthcoming in the same journal.

20. Bruce Aune (1970) attributes this view to "pragmatism," which he treats as an epistemological stance opposed to "empiricism" and "rationalism." It is also to be found in the writings of Nietzsche and various wings of "postmodernism," and is also stated by Engels (1954, 214–216); and this list is by no means exhaustive. Note, too, Bambrough's claim (see #56) and Puolimatka's claim (note 14 supra) that logic can be given only a discursive justification.

21. Note that the principle of noncontradiction is not a "two-valued" principle. It does not assert that if a statement is not true, then its denial must be true, but such an interpretation figures strongly in some attempts to dispute the necessity of this principle. (See, e.g., Aune 1970, 104–122.) It simply says that a statement and its denial cannot both be true (of *the same* set of circumstances), which permits both a statement and its denial (in the form of a *contrary*, if not as its strict *contradictory*) to be false.

22. In the present context, it is appropriate to cite Quine's remark to the effect that people and societies who ignore the principles of deductive and inductive logic possess the noble property of becoming extinct. (See Phillips 1986, 109, for this citation.)

Although this is only tenuously related to the present objection, it is worth noting that Peter Allen says that the notion that truth and reasons are things to be discovered, rather than invented, is hard enough to sustain in the physical sciences, let alone in moral philosophy. (See Allen 1987, 48–49.)

It is received wisdom in *some* quarters that physical science is conventional, and that morality is more certainly so. But, confronted with Gewirth's argument, this is no argument, just rhetoric and hearsay. Indeed, the logical validity of Gewirth's argument effects a reversal of such "wisdom."

> [I]n the final analysis, . . . the *PGC* and its derivative moral rules can attain, in a substantial, nonvacuous way, a degree of necessity or stringency superior to that found in the laws of the natu-

ral sciences. For there is a unity of subject and object in morality that is not found in any of the natural sciences, including psychology insofar as it is an empirical discipline. Morality sets rational requirements for rational agents; hence, the whole enterprise is under the control of reason . . . . (RM 364)

It is no exaggeration, I think, to say that if Gewirth's argument is valid, then the system of morality governed by the PGC has a comparable status to arithmetic vis-à-vis justification.

Chapter 10: Objections to Positive Rights

1. Robert L. Arrington's claim that

[n]owhere in the proof does Gewirth show that an agent *must* demand her positive rights and not just her negative ones (Arrington 1989, 114)

is false.

Tibor R. Machan makes the truly extraordinary statement that

[i]n Gewirth's doctrine of human rights there is a failure to ground the political principles in a more fundamental ethical theory. (Machan 1989, 123)

Whether he is referring to the lack of an argument for negative or positive rights, this is unwarranted. Gewirth's political principles are grounded in the PGC and the argument to it.

2. This being a condition of all the deontic claims in the argument, in consequence of the categorical *instrumental* valuation of its freedom and well-being to which a PPA is committed. (See Chapter 2.)

3. If I do not have to claim these rights on the grounds of being a PPA, then I do not have to grant these rights to all other PPAs. Narveson does not appear to take account of this here, although he does appreciate the point. (See Narveson 1980, 655, and #47.4.)

4. On 1–4, see also #35.5 and #38, and discussions in #47.7 and #54.2. On 5, see "The Argument for Positive Rights" above.

5. In England, a "nonpublic school" would be a "public school" or an "independent school."

6. This is appreciated and, indeed, emphasized by Narveson. (See Narveson 1984, 100.)

7. If "welfare rights" are equated with "rights to well-being," then Den Uyl and Machan's stated view, that "freedom does not diminish another's welfare" (Den Uyl and Machan 1984, 170), is open to the following response:

If a person should be "free to do with his resources as he pleases," then he should be free to drive 100 miles per hour down city streets, dump his garbage from his windows, and pollute the air with carcinogenic chemicals. In none of these activities would he "forcibly restrict others from doing likewise." Such examples show the falsity of the authors' assertion that "it is not necessarily the case that maximizing a person's freedom diminishes another's welfare—indeed, freedom does not diminish

[another's] welfare." On the contrary, unrestricted freedom conflicts with welfare, with basic well-being, just as the duty to provide welfare operates to restrict certain freedoms. I have tried to
indicate the criteria for dealing with such conflicts; but the
authors' exclusive espousal of the right to freedom still leaves
them with conflicts that need resolution. Their libertarian qualification—"so long as I do not forcibly restrict others from doing
likewise"—would not prevent persons from doing the kinds of
life-threatening actions mentioned above. (Gewirth 1984d, 246,
quoting Den Uyl and Machan 1984, 170)

8. Machan (1989) persists in referring to the issue of negative and positive
rights as the issue of rights to freedom and rights to well-being, as though
rights to freedom are always negative, and rights to well-being always positive. He continues to insist that rights cannot be traded. "[T]o speak of
trading off rights is a category mistake" (ibid., 113). He holds that the right
to freedom (which he prefers to call the right to "liberty") is absolute (see
ibid., 116), and he objects to a system of prima facie rights, on the grounds
that there is no criterion for determining priority between rights (see ibid.,
119–120).

9. Pilon professes to be a convinced disciple of Gewirth—as far as the
argument for negative rights is concerned. He prefers Gewirth's earlier formulations of the argument, those in which the supreme principle is the PCC
rather than the PGC (in which Gewirth talks about "categorial rules" rather
than "necessary goods"). (See Pilon 1979a, 1173 n. 8.)

10. According to Tibor R. Machan,

[w]e have a *right* to freedom because autonomy or sovereignty is
something that one would always possess were it not for others'
taking it away. Freedom cannot be given, only taken and then
regained. . . . Wellbeing is a different kind of value. We may lack
wellbeing *quite apart from what others do or don't do to or for us.*
(Machan 1989, 198)

Similarly, Loren E. Lomasky holds that well-being (for which he gives a
list that includes particular occurrent purposes) can be supplied by PPAs
through their own efforts or by others, but that "liberty" (which he construes
as "noninterference") must be supplied by (all) others. Lomasky appears to
argue that I can claim a positive right to freedom, but only negative rights to
well-being (as Gewirth uses "freedom" and "well-being"); otherwise he is
asserting the tautology that I can only claim negative rights to negative
rights, and positive rights to positive rights. (See Lomasky 1986, 17.)

For Gewirth, a right to noninterference is a negative right, a right to aid is
a positive right. As far as *rights*-claims are concerned, freedom is the ability
to act according to my choices, and well-being constitutes the other generic
capacities for action or successful action. The confusions of terminology introduced by Machan and Lomasky make their comments difficult to assess.
Without going into this, it seems to me that whatever *relevance* (for Gewirth's
argument to positive rights) the distinctions have that Machan and Lomasky
are trying to draw, these distinctions are taken account of by the way

Gewirth distinguishes between positive and negative rights. Positive rights are conditional upon my not being able to secure my generic needs by my own unaided efforts, whereas negative rights are not.

11. Tibor R. Machan says that Gewirth's theory is a form of utilitarianism, and that it is not deontological. (See Machan 1989, 120–121.) However, he fails to comment on Gewirth's explanation of the difference between his theory and utilitarianism.

12. It is to be noted that Pilon repeats the objections given in Pilon 1979a (covered in this chapter) in Pilon 1979b, and indicates a similar general view in Pilon 1979c.

13. Gewirth states the argument here in terms of well-being only, but it may be stated in terms of freedom and well-being without alteration. This argument is reproduced in all essentials in many of Gewirth's articles applying the PGC. For example, in Gewirth 1985d, 24, 1986c, 182–184, 1987a, 67–68, and 1987b, 248–249.

14. Just as my presentation, in "The Argument for Positive Rights" above, is parallel to my presentation in Chapter 2, so Gewirth's presentation is parallel to his formulation in Gewirth 1984d, 205–206 (quoted under #30).

15. It is to be noted that B (or Davis) is not, as Pilon implies, *acting* by falling out of his boat—unless he is committing suicide. But to suppose that he is departs from the Carr/Davis scenario, and introduces complications that need not be considered here. (Gewirth discusses the application of the PGC in relation to duties to prevent suicides in RM 264–267.)

16. The question of circularity, or question-beggingness, is dealt with more fully, in a slightly different context, in the discussion of Mack 1984 that follows.

17. "Direct application of the PGC" refers to rules that can be deductively derived from the PGC.

18. "Indirect application of the PGC" refers to rules promulgated by the exercise of "discretion" by persons or institutions whose authority is granted by direct application of the PGC.

19. In effect, the doctrine (held to be a direct application of the PGC) that institutions having authority must be freely elected by those over whom authority is held. (See RM 304–311.)

20. Gewirth emphasizes that this discussion is restricted to the context of direct personal interactions, and that, in larger-scale social situations, duties fall on governments and institutions according to other aspects of his argument from the PGC.

21. "The generalizing tendency thinks about the event as a member of a whole class of similar events, and about its conditions in terms of the whole general realm of physical possibility. The particularizing tendency thinks about the particular event as it actually occurred amid all its particular circumstances of time and place, and about its conditions in terms of the limited range of possibilities actually present and operative on that particular occasion" (RM 223–224).

22. One of the main reasons for Gewirth's lengthy preoccupation with the duty to rescue is undoubtedly his sensitivity to the political implications of the doctrine of positive rights. As Den Uyl and Machan state, this doctrine

places Gewirth's position "well left of center . . . politically" (Den Uyl and Machan 1984, 169); and Machan complains that

> Gewirth and other defenders of the welfare state and opponents of capitalism substitute the principle of welfare rights for the virtue of generosity. (Machan 1989, 122)

Being based at the University of Chicago, with its strong tradition of right-wing libertarianism, especially in the field of economics, would, I imagine, serve to make Gewirth more sensitive to this. As Henry B. Veatch says,

> Gewirth finds himself having to tread very warily here, considering that some of his own most loyal students are libertarians, and, while wholeheartedly accepting the PGC, they tend to be no less insistent that it scarcely commits one to thus helping others, as opposed to merely not interfering with them or injuring them. (Veatch 1979, 408)

Whether these students, notably Roger Pilon, should be called "loyal" is another matter. For, as I have emphasized, the question of positive rights is not a question of the application of the PGC, but one of the argument to the PGC itself. I see no way to resist the claim that the PGC is a principle of positive rights without rejecting the argument to the PGC altogether. Indeed, what Pilon wishes to do in the name of the argument to the PGC (to defend the right of corporations—business interests—"to exist and to operate free from outside interference, independent of whether it does or does not serve some larger public interest" (Pilon 1979b, 1248) and, in essence, to make "private property" the basic moral epistemological category) strikes me as an attempted "hijack" of his "master's" theory comparable (in the scope of its "heresy") to that which Fichte effected with Kant's transcendental philosophy, thereby laying the foundations for later German idealism and Hegelianism.

Given this, it is ironic that R. Randall Kelso (1982) attempts to tar and feather not only the rigorous style, but also the substance, of Gewirth's moral philosophy with the brush of the right-wing libertarian views of the Chicago school of economics generally. Such a costume fits Pilon, but it is a travesty of Gewirth's position.

Chapter 11: Conclusion

1. More detailed analysis is to be found in the discussion of objections relating to these questions in the earlier chapters.

2. This point is of particular importance in relation to the analysis of Paul Allen III (1982a), who claims that [I do X for purpose E → I regard E as good] is not equivalent to [From my internal viewpoint as a PPA (I do X for purpose E → E is good)], yet holds the argument to be valid.

3. It seems to me that E. M. Adams (1980, and 1984) (see #23.2 and #59), who claims that Gewirth's analysis of valuation is subject to a regression, treats the interpretations under 1 and 3 (as involving position 1 in response to [I]) as exhaustive alternatives, ignoring the interpretation under 2, which is, in fact, Gewirth's.

References

Adams, E. M. 1980. "Gewirth on Reason and Morality." *Review of Metaphysics* 33:579–592.

———. 1984. "The Subjective Normative Structure of Agency." In Edward Regis, Jr., ed., *Gewirth's Ethical Rationalism: Critical Essays with a Reply by Alan Gewirth*, 8–22. Chicago: University of Chicago Press.

Allen, Glen O. 1978. Review of *Reason and Morality*, by Alan Gewirth. *Philosophical Books* 19/3:126–129.

Allen III, Paul. 1982a. "A Critique of Gewirth's 'Is-Ought' Derivation." *Ethics* 92:211–226.

———. 1982b. "'Ought' from 'Is'? What Hare and Gewirth Should Have Said." *American Journal of Theology and Philosophy* 3:90–97.

Allen, Peter. 1987. "Agency and Objectivity: Alan Gewirth's Theory of Human Rights." *Bracton Law Journal* 19:37–52.

Arrington, Robert L. 1989. *Rationalism, Realism, and Relativism: Perspectives in Contemporary Moral Epistemology*. Ithaca, New York: Cornell University Press.

Aune, Bruce. 1970. *Rationalism, Empiricism, and Pragmatism*. New York: Random House.

Bambrough, Renford. 1984. "The Roots of Moral Reason." In Edward Regis, Jr., ed., *Gewirth's Ethical Rationalism: Critical Essays with a Reply by Alan Gewirth*, 39–51. Chicago: University of Chicago Press.

Barry, Brian. 1989. *Theories of Justice*. Berkeley: University of California Press.

Bauhn, Per. 1989. *Ethical Aspects of Political Terrorism: The Sacrificing of the Innocent*. Lund, Sweden: Lund University Press.

Becker, Lawrence C. 1973. *On Justifying Moral Judgments*. New York: Humanities Press.

Bedau, Hugo Adam. 1984. "Why Do We Have the Rights We Do?" *Social Philosophy and Policy* 1/2:56–72.

Ben-Zeev, Aaron. 1982. "Who Is a Rational Agent?" *Canadian Journal of Philosophy* 12:647–661.

Beyleveld, Deryck. 1980. "Transcendentalism and Realism." Paper presented to the Theory Group of the British Sociological Association, University of Sussex, September.

Beyleveld, Deryck, and Brownsword, Roger. 1986. *Law as a Moral Judgment*. London: Sweet and Maxwell.

Bhaskar, Roy. 1978. *A Realist Theory of Science*. 2d edition. Hassocks: Harvester Press and Atlantic Highlands, New Jersey: Humanities Press.

Bittner, Rüdiger. 1989. *What Reason Demands*. Translated from German by Theodore Talbot. Cambridge: Cambridge University Press.

Bond, E. J. 1980a. "Gewirth on Reason and Morality." *Metaphilosophy* 11:36–53.

———. 1980b. "Reply to Gewirth." *Metaphilosophy* 11:70–75.

Brandt, R. B. 1981. "The Future of Ethics." *Nous* 15:31–40.

Brooks, Richard. 1981. "The Future of Ethical Humanism, the Re-introduction of Ethics into the Legal World: Alan Gewirth's *Reason and Morality*." *Journal of Legal Education* 31:287–305.

Burrill, Donald R. 1971. "Professor Gewirth's Principle of Moral Rightness." In Erwin H. Pollack, ed., *Human Rights (Amintaphil I)*, 281–285. Buffalo: Jay Stewart Publications.

Christie, George C. 1971. "Some Thoughts on the Nature of Institutional Obligations." In Erwin H. Pollack, ed., *Human Rights (Amintaphil I)*, 275–280. Buffalo: Jay Stewart Publications.

Cohen, Stephen. 1979. "Gewirth's Rationalism: Who Is a Moral Agent?" *Ethics* 89:179–190.

Collins, James. 1979. Review of *Reason and Morality*, by Alan Gewirth. *Modern Schoolman* 57 (Nov.): 69–74.

Corcoran, James. 1973. "Gewirth's Deontologism." *Ethics* 83:313–321.

Danto, Arthur C. 1984. "Comment on Gewirth: Constructing an Epistemology of Human Rights: A Pseudo Problem?" *Social Philosophy and Policy* 1/2:25–30.

Davies, Colin. 1975. "Egoism and Consistency." *Australasian Journal of Philosophy* 53/1:19–27.

Davis, Michael. 1991. "Gewirth and the Pain of Contradiction." *Philosophical Forum* 22/3:211–227.

Davitt, Thomas E. 1971. "Response to 'Obligation: Political, Legal, Moral' by Alan Gewirth." In Erwin H. Pollack, ed., *Human Rights (Amintaphil I)*, 286–290. Buffalo: Jay Stewart Publications.

Den Uyl, Douglas J. 1975. "Ethical Egoism and Gewirth's PCC." *Personalist* 56:432–447.

Den Uyl, Douglas J., and Machan, Tibor R. 1984. "Gewirth and the Supportive State." In Edward Regis, Jr., ed., *Gewirth's Ethical Rationalism: Critical Essays with a Reply by Alan Gewirth*, 167–179. Chicago: University of Chicago Press.

De Roose, Frank. 1987. "Alan Gewirth en de Come-back van de Categorische Imperatief." *Tijdschrift voor Filosofie* 9/3:479–491.

Diller, Ann. 1982. "Gewirth's Principle of Generic Consistency and Heslep's Applications to Teaching." *Philosophy of Education: Proceedings* 38:261–264.

Dworkin, Ronald. 1978. *Taking Rights Seriously*. New impression (corrected) with appendix. London: Duckworth.

Engels, Frederick. 1954. *Dialectics of Nature*. 2d revised edition. Moscow: Progress Publishers.

———. 1966. *Anti-Dühring: Herr Eugen Dühring's Revolution in Science*. New York: International Publishers.

Ewin, R. E. 1987. *Liberty, Community, and Justice.* Totowa, New Jersey: Rowman and Littlefield.

Feldman, Fred. 1983. Review of *Reason and Morality*, by Alan Gewirth. *Nous* 17/3:475–482.

Finnis, John. 1980. *Natural Law and Natural Rights.* Oxford: Clarendon Press.

Fishkin, James S. 1984. *Beyond Subjective Morality: Ethical Reasoning and Political Philosophy.* New Haven: Yale University Press.

Fotion, N. 1968. "Gewirth and Categorial Consistency." *Philosophical Quarterly* 18:262–264.

Frankena, William K. 1980a. "The Carus Lectures." *Monist* 63/1:3–68.

———. 1980b. "Reply to My Three Critics." *Monist* 63/1:110–128.

French, Peter A. 1979. *The Scope of Morality.* Minneapolis: University of Minnesota Press.

Friedman, Richard B. 1981. "The Basis of Human Rights: A Criticism of Gewirth's Theory." In J. R. Pennock and J. W. Chapman, eds., *Nomos XXIII: Human Rights*, 148–157. New York: New York University Press.

Gamwell, Franklin I. 1984. *Beyond Preference: Liberal Theories of Independent Associations.* Chicago: University of Chicago Press.

Gauthier, David. 1986. *Morals by Agreement.* Oxford: Clarendon Press.

Geels, Donald E. 1971. "How to Be a Consistent Racist." *Personalist* 52:662–679.

Gewirth, Alan. 1953. "The Distinction between Analytic and Synthetic Truths." *Journal of Philosophy* 50:397–425.

———. 1967a. "Categorial Consistency in Ethics." *Philosophical Quarterly* 17:289–299.

———. 1967b. "Some Misconceptions of the Relation between Law and Morality." In *Proceedings of the Seventh Inter-American Congress of Philosophy*, 1:208–222. Quebec: Les Presses de l'Université Laval.

———. 1969. "The Non-trivializability of Universalizability." *Australasian Journal of Philosophy* 47/2:123–131.

———. 1970a. "Must One Play the Moral Language Game?" *American Philosophical Quarterly* 7:107–118. Reprinted in Alan Gewirth, *Human Rights: Essays on Justification and Applications*, 79–99. Chicago: University of Chicago Press, 1982.

———. 1970b. "Some Comments on Categorial Consistency." *Philosophical Quarterly* 20:380–384.

———. 1970c. "Civil Disobedience, Law, and Morality." *Monist* 54:536–555. Reprinted in Alan Gewirth, *Human Rights: Essays on Justification and Applications*, 290–309. Chicago: University of Chicago Press, 1982. Reprinted in Paul Harris, ed., *Civil Disobedience*, 107–124. Lanham, Maryland: University Press of America, 1989.

———. 1970d. "Obligation: Political, Legal, Moral." In J. R. Pennock and J. W. Chapman, eds., *Nomos XII: Political and Legal Obligation*, 55–88. New York: Atherton Press. Reprinted in M. G. Singer, ed., *Morals and Values: Readings in Theoretical and Practical Ethics*, 348–363. New York: Alfred A. Knopf, 1973. Reprinted in Alan Gewirth, *Human Rights: Essays on Justifica-*

tion and Applications, 256–289. Chicago: University of Chicago Press, 1982.

———. 1971a. "The Justification of Egalitarian Justice." *American Philosophical Quarterly* 8/4:331–341. Reprinted in R. E. Flathman, ed., *Concepts in Social and Political Philosophy,* 352–366. New York: Macmillan, 1973.

———. 1971b. "The Normative Structure of Action." *Review of Metaphysics* 25/2:238–261.

———. 1971c. "Some Notes on Moral and Legal Obligation." In Erwin H. Pollack, ed., *Human Rights (Amintaphil I),* 291–296. Buffalo: Jay Stewart Publications.

———. 1972. "Moral Rationality." The Lindley Lecture, University of Kansas. Reprinted in J. Bricke, ed., *Freedom and Morality,* 113–150. Lawrence: University of Kansas Press, 1976.

———. 1974a. "The 'Is-Ought' Problem Resolved." *Proceedings and Addresses of the American Philosophical Association* 47:34–61. Reprinted in Alan Gewirth, *Human Rights: Essays on Justification and Applications,* 100–127. Chicago: University of Chicago Press, 1982. Reprinted in George Sher, ed., *Moral Philosophy: Selected Readings,* 316–351. New York: Harcourt Brace Jovanovich, 1987.

———. 1974b. "Ethics." In *Encyclopaedia Britannica,* 15th edition, 6:976–998.

———. 1974c. "Reasons and Conscience: The Claims of the Selective Conscientious Objector." In Virginia Held, Sidney Morgenbesser, and Thomas Nagel, eds., *Philosophy, Morality, and International Affairs,* 89–117. New York: Oxford University Press. Reprinted in Alan Gewirth, *Human Rights: Essays on Justification and Applications,* 329–357. Chicago: University of Chicago Press, 1982.

———. 1975. "Civil Liberties as Effective Powers." In R. B. Ashmore and L. C. Rice, eds., *Moral Values in Contemporary Public Life,* 3–10. Milwaukee: Department of Philosophy, Marquette University. Reprinted in Alan Gewirth, *Human Rights: Essays on Justification and Applications,* 310–328. Chicago: University of Chicago Press, 1982.

———. 1976. "Action and Rights: A Reply." *Ethics* 86:288–293.

———. 1978a. *Reason and Morality.* Chicago: University of Chicago Press.

———. 1978b. "The Golden Rule Rationalized." *Midwest Studies in Philosophy* 3:133–147. Reprinted in Alan Gewirth, *Human Rights: Essays on Justification and Applications,* 128–142. Chicago: University of Chicago Press, 1982.

———. 1979a. "The Basis and Content of Human Rights." *Georgia Law Review* 13:1143–1170. Reprinted in J. R. Pennock and J. W. Chapman, eds., *Nomos XXIII: Human Rights,* 119–147. New York: New York University Press, 1981. Reprinted in Alan Gewirth, *Human Rights: Essays on Justification and Applications,* 41–67. Chicago: University of Chicago Press, 1982. Reprinted in Morton E. Winston, ed., *The Philosophy of Human Rights,* 181–201. Belmont, California: Wadsworth Publishing Co., 1989. Translated into Swedish as "Mänskliga Rättigheters Grund och Innehäll." In Per Bauhn, ed., *Teòrier om Rättig Heter,* 40–80. Stockholm: Bokförlaget Thales, 1990.

———. 1979b. "Starvation and Human Rights." In K. E. Goodpaster and K. M. Sayre, eds., *Ethics and Problems of the 21st Century,* 139–159. Notre Dame, Indiana: University of Notre Dame Press. Reprinted in Alan

Gewirth, *Human Rights: Essays on Justification and Applications*, 197–217. Chicago: University of Chicago Press, 1982. Reprinted in C. C. Rostankowski and M. G. Velasquez, eds., *Ethics: Theory and Practice— Readings in Moral Philosophy*, 238–259. Englewood Cliffs, New Jersey: Prentice Hall, 1984.

———. 1979c. "On Deriving a Morally Significant 'Ought.'" *Philosophy* 54:231–232.

———. 1980a. "Comments on Bond's Article." *Metaphilosophy* 11:54–69.

———. 1980b. "Reason and Morality: Rejoinder to E. J. Bond." *Metaphilosophy* 11:138–142.

———. 1980c. "Limitations of the Moral Point of View." *Monist* 63/1:69–84.

———. 1980d. "Human Rights and the Prevention of Cancer." *American Philosophical Quarterly* 17:117–125. Reprinted in Alan Gewirth, *Human Rights: Essays on Justification and Applications*, 181–196. Chicago: University of Chicago Press, 1982. Reprinted in T. Attig and D. Scherer, eds., *Ethics and the Environment*, 170–177. Englewood Cliffs, New Jersey: Prentice Hall, 1983. Reprinted in Michael D. Bayles and Kenneth Henley, eds., *Right Conduct*, 2d edition, 283–295. New York: Random House, 1989.

———. 1981a. "Are There Any Absolute Rights?" *Philosophical Quarterly* 31:1–16. Reprinted in Alan Gewirth, *Human Rights: Essays on Justification and Applications*, 218–233. Chicago: University of Chicago Press, 1982. Reprinted in Jeremy Waldron, ed., *Theories of Rights*, 91–109. Oxford Readings in Philosophy. Oxford: Oxford University Press, 1984.

———. 1981b. "The Future of Ethics: The Moral Powers of Reason." *Nous* 15:15–30. Reprinted in Alan Gewirth, *Human Rights: Essays on Justification and Applications*, 163–178. Chicago: University of Chicago Press, 1982.

———. 1982a. "There Are Absolute Rights." *Philosophical Quarterly* 32:348–353.

———. 1982b. *Human Rights: Essays on Justification and Applications.* Chicago: University of Chicago Press. Translated into French by Bruno Baron-Renault as *Droits de l'Homme: Défense et Illustrations.* Paris: Les Editions du Cerf, 1987.

———. 1982c. Introduction to Alan Gewirth, *Human Rights: Essays on Justification and Applications*, 1–38. Chicago: University of Chicago Press, 1982.

———. 1982d. "On Rational Agency as the Basis of Moral Equality: Reply to Ben-Zeev." *Canadian Journal of Philosophy* 12:667–671.

———. 1982e. "Why Agents Must Claim Rights: A Reply." *Journal of Philosophy* 79:403–410.

———. 1982f. "Replies to Some Criticisms." Addendum to "The Basis and Content of Human Rights," *Georgia Law Review* 13 (1979): 1143–1170, as reprinted in Alan Gewirth, *Human Rights: Essays on Justification and Applications*, 67–78. Chicago: University of Chicago Press, 1982.

———. 1982g. "Can Utilitarianism Justify Any Moral Rights?" In J. R. Pennock and J. W. Chapman, eds., *Nomos XXIV: Ethics, Economics, and the Law*, 158–193. New York: New York University Press. Reprinted in Alan Gewirth, *Human Rights: Essays on Justification and Applications*, 143–162. Chicago: Chicago University Press, 1982.

——. 1983a. "The Rationality of Reasonableness." *Synthèse* 57:225–247.

——. 1983b. "Individual Rights and Political-Military Obligations." In Robert K. Fullinwider, ed., *Conscripts and Volunteers: Military Requirements, Social Justice, and the All-Volunteer Force*, 89–105. Maryland Studies in Public Philosophy. Totowa, New Jersey: Rowman and Allanheld. Reprinted in Alan Gewirth, *Human Rights: Essays on Justification and Applications*, 234–255. Chicago: University of Chicago Press, 1982.

——. 1984a. "The Ontological Basis of Natural Law: A Critique and an Alternative." *American Journal of Jurisprudence* 29:95–121.

——. 1984b. "The Epistemology of Human Rights." *Social Philosophy and Policy* 1/2:1–24. Extracted in Lord Lloyd of Hampstead and M. D. A. Freeman, *Lloyd's Introduction to Jurisprudence*, 5th edition, 229–245. London: Stevens and Sons.

——. 1984c. "Reply to Danto." *Social Philosophy and Policy* 1/2:31–34.

——. 1984d. "Replies to My Critics." In Edward Regis, Jr., ed., *Gewirth's Ethical Rationalism: Critical Essays with a Reply by Alan Gewirth*, 192–255. Chicago: University of Chicago Press.

——. 1984e. "Practical Philosophy, Civil Liberties, and Poverty." *Monist* 67/4:549–568.

——. 1984f. "Natural Law, Human Action, and Morality." In R. Porreco, ed., *The Georgetown Symposium on Ethics: Essays in Honor of Henry B. Veatch*, 67–90. Washington, D.C.: University Press of America.

——. 1985a. "Rights and Virtues." *Review of Metaphysics* 38:739–762. Co-published with *Analyse und Kritik* 6 (1984): 28–48.

——. 1985b. "From the Prudential to the Moral: Reply to Singer." *Ethics* 95:302–304.

——. 1985c. "Why There Are Human Rights." *Social Theory and Practice* 11/2:235–248. Reprinted in Morton E. Winston, ed., *The Philosophy of Human Rights*, 247–256. Belmont, California: Wadsworth Publishing Co., 1989.

——. 1985d. "Economic Justice: Concepts and Criteria." In K. Kipnis and D. T. Meyers, eds., *Economic Justice: Private Rights and Public Responsibilities*, 7–32. Totowa, New Jersey: Rowman and Allanheld.

——. 1985e. "A Brief Rejoinder." *Analyse und Kritik* 7:249–250.

——. 1986a. "Why Rights Are Indispensable." *Mind* 95:329–344.

——. 1986b. "Professional Ethics: The Separatist Thesis." *Ethics* 96:282–300.

——. 1986c. "Economic Rights." *Philosophical Topics* 14/2:169–193.

——. 1986d. "Human Rights and the Workplace." *American Journal of Industrial Medicine* 9:31–40.

——. 1986e. "Reason and Nuclear Deterrence." *Canadian Journal of Philosophy*, supplementary volume 12:129–159.

——. 1986f. "The Problem of Specificity in Evolutionary Ethics." *Biology and Philosophy* 1:297–305.

——. 1987a. "Private Philanthropy and Positive Rights." *Social Philosophy and Policy* 4/2:55–78.

——. 1987b. "Moral Foundations of Civil Rights Law." *Modern Schoolman*

64:235–255. Also in *Journal of Law and Religion* 5/1 (1987): 125–147.

———. 1988a. Review of *Ethics and the Limits of Philosophy*, by Bernard Williams. *Nous* 22/1:143–146.

———. 1988b. "Ethical Universalism and Particularism." *Journal of Philosophy* 85:283–302.

———. 1988c. "The Justification of Morality." *Philosophical Studies* 53:245–262.

———. 1988d. "Rights and Duties." *Mind* 97:441–445.

———. 1988e. "Human Rights and Conceptions of the Self." *Philosophia* (Israel) 18:129–149.

———. 1989. "Are There Any Natural Rights?" In David Weissbord, ed., *Mind, Value, and Culture: Essays in Honor of E. M. Adams*, 249–268. Atascadero, California: Ridgeview Publishing Co.

———. 1990a. "Human Rights and Academic Freedom." In Steven M. Cahn, ed., *Morality, Responsibility, and the University: Studies in Academic Ethics*, 8–31. Philadelphia: Temple University Press.

———. 1990b. "Two Types of Cost-Benefit Analysis." In Donald Scherer, ed., *Upstream/Downstream: Issues in Environmental Ethics*, 205–232. Philadelphia: Temple University Press.

———. 1990c. "The Rational Foundations of Ethics." Translated into German by K. Steigleder as "Die Rationalen Grundlagen der Ethik." In K. Steigleder and D. Mieth, eds., *Ethik in den Wissenschaften: Ariadnefaden im Technischen Labyrinth?* 3–34. Tübingen: Attemptoverlag.

Gillespie, Norman C. 1977. "Abortion and Human Rights." *Ethics* 87:237–243.

Golding, Martin P. 1981. "From Prudence to Rights: A Critique." In J. R. Pennock and J. W. Chapman, eds., *Nomos XXIII: Human Rights*, 165–174. New York: New York University Press.

———. 1984. "The Primacy of Welfare Rights." *Social Philosophy and Policy* 1/2:119–136.

Gould, Carol C. 1988. *Rethinking Democracy: Freedom and Social Cooperation in Politics, Economy, and Society.* Cambridge: Cambridge University Press.

Green, Ronald M. 1979. Review of *Reason and Morality*, by Alan Gewirth. *Religious Studies Review* 5/3:187–190.

Grunebaum, James O. 1976. "Gewirth and a Reluctant Protagonist." *Ethics* 86:274–277.

Habermas, Jürgen. 1979. *Communication and the Evolution of Society.* Boston: Beacon Press.

Haksar, Vinit. 1979. *Equality, Liberty, and Perfectionism.* Oxford: Clarendon Press

Hare, R. M. 1981. *Moral Thinking.* Oxford: Clarendon Press.

———. 1984. "Do Agents Have to Be Moralists?" In Edward Regis, Jr., ed., *Gewirth's Ethical Rationalism: Critical Essays with a Reply by Alan Gewirth*, 52–58. Chicago: University of Chicago Press.

Harman, Gilbert. 1983. "Justice and Moral Bargaining." *Social Philosophy and Policy* 1/1:114–131.

Hart, H. L. A. 1961. *The Concept of Law.* Oxford: Clarendon Press.

Held, Virginia. 1977. "Rationality and Reasonable Cooperation." *Social Research* 44:708–744.

———. 1979. Review of *Reason and Morality*, by Alan Gewirth. *Social Theory and Practice* 5:243–250.

———. 1985. "Reason and Economic Justice." In K. Kipnis and D. T. Meyers, eds., *Economic Justice: Private Rights and Public Responsibilities*, 33–41. Totowa, New Jersey: Rowman and Allanheld.

Heslep, Robert D. 1982. "Teaching and Gewirth's Principle of Generic Consistency." *Philosophy of Education: Proceedings* 38:253–260.

———. 1986. "Gewirth and the Voluntary Agent's Esteem of Purpose." *Philosophy Research Archives* 11:379–391.

———. 1989. *Education in Democracy: Education's Moral Role in the Democratic State*. Ames: Iowa State University Press.

Hill, James F. 1984. "Are Marginal Agents 'Our Recipients'?" In Edward Regis, Jr., ed., *Gewirth's Ethical Rationalism: Critical Essays with a Reply by Alan Gewirth*, 180–191. Chicago: University of Chicago Press.

Hohfeld, Wesley N. 1964. *Fundamental Legal Conceptions as Applied in Judicial Reasoning*. New Haven: Yale University Press.

Hollis, Martin. 1977. *Models of Man: Philosophical Thoughts on Social Action*. Cambridge: Cambridge University Press.

Hudson, W. D. 1984. "The 'Is-Ought' Problem Resolved?" In Edward Regis, Jr., ed., *Gewirth's Ethical Rationalism: Critical Essays with a Reply by Alan Gewirth*, 108–127. Chicago: University of Chicago Press.

Husak, Douglas N. 1984. "Why There Are No Human Rights." *Social Theory and Practice* 10/2:125–141.

———. 1985. "The Motivation for Human Rights." *Social Theory and Practice* 11/2:249–255.

Kahn, Shari Lynne. 1984. "The Right to Adequate Treatment versus the Right to Refuse Antipsychotic Drug Treatment: A Solution to the Dilemma of the Involuntarily Committed Psychiatric Patient." *Emory Law Journal* 33:441–485.

Kalin, Jesse. 1968. "On Ethical Egoism." *American Philosophical Quarterly Monograph* no.1:26–41.

———. 1970. "In Defense of Egoism." In David Gauthier, ed., *Morality and Rational Self-Interest*, 64–87. Englewood Cliffs, New Jersey: Prentice Hall.

———. 1975. "Two Kinds of Moral Reasoning: Ethical Egoism as a Moral Theory." *Canadian Journal of Philosophy* 5:323–356.

———. 1984. "Public Pursuit and Private Escape: The Persistence of Egoism." In Edward Regis, Jr., ed., *Gewirth's Ethical Rationalism: Critical Essays with a Reply by Alan Gewirth*, 128–146. Chicago: University of Chicago Press.

Keasberry, Helen. 1986. "Alan Gewirth en het Onbehagen in de Ethiek." *Algemeen Nederlands Tijdschrift voor Wijsbegeerte* 78/3:189–198.

Kelsen, Hans. 1967. *Pure Theory of Law*. Translated by Max Knight from 2d revised, enlarged edition (1960). Berkeley and Los Angeles: University of California Press.

Kelso, R. Randall. 1982. "Reason, Morality, Wealth: Gewirth, Posner and the

University of Chicago Approach." *Oklahoma City University Law Review* 7/1:131–175.

Levinson, Jerrold. 1982. "Gewirth on Absolute Rights." *Philosophical Quarterly* 32:73–75.

Lloyd of Hampstead, Lord, and Freeman, M. D. A. 1985. *Lloyd's Introduction to Jurisprudence.* 5th edition. London: Stevens and Sons.

Lomasky, Loren E. 1981. "Gewirth's Generation of Rights." *Philosophical Quarterly* 31:248–253.

———. 1984. "Personal Projects as the Foundation for Basic Rights." *Social Philosophy and Policy* 1/2: 35–55.

———. 1986. Review of *Reason and Morality*, by Alan Gewirth. *Vera Lex* 6/1:16–17.

Loughran, James N. 1986. "The Moral Ideal of the Person." *International Philosophical Quarterly* 26:147–159.

Lycan, W. Gregory. 1969. "Hare, Singer, and Gewirth on Universalizability." *Philosophical Quarterly* 19:135–144.

MacCormick, Neil. 1984. "Gewirth's Fallacy." *Queen's Law Journal* 9/2:345–351.

Machan, Tibor R. 1980. "Some Recent Work in Human Rights Theory." *American Philosophical Quarterly* 17:103–115.

———. 1989. *Individuals and Their Rights.* La Salle, Illinois: Open Court Publishing Co.

MacIntyre, Alasdair. 1981. *After Virtue: A Study in Moral Theory.* Notre Dame, Indiana: University of Notre Dame Press.

———. 1985. "Rights, Practices, and Marxism: Replies to Six Critics." *Analyse und Kritik* 7:234–248.

Mack, Eric. 1984. "Deontologism, Negative Causation, and the Duty to Rescue." In Edward Regis, Jr., ed., *Gewirth's Ethical Rationalism: Critical Essays with a Reply by Alan Gewirth,* 147–166. Chicago: University of Chicago Press.

McMahon, Christopher. 1986. "Gewirth's Justification of Morality." *Philosophical Studies* 50:261–281.

Mahowald, Mary B. 1980. Review of *Reason and Morality,* by Alan Gewirth. *Philosophy and Phenomenological Research* 40:446–447.

Maslow, A. H. 1954. *Motivation and Personality.* New York: Harper and Brothers.

Mill, John Stuart. 1910. "On Liberty." In John Stuart Mill, *Utilitarianism; Liberty; Representative Government,* 65–170. Everyman's Library. London: J. M. Dent and Sons.

Morris, Arval A. 1981. "A Differential Theory of Human Rights." In J. R. Pennock and J. W. Chapman, eds., *Nomos XXIII: Human Rights,* 158–164. New York: New York University Press.

Nagel, Thomas. 1970. *The Possibility of Altruism.* Oxford: Clarendon Press.

Narveson, Jan. 1979. Review of *Reason and Morality,* by Alan Gewirth. *Political Theory* 7:428–431.

———. 1980. "Gewirth's Reason and Morality—A Study of the Hazards of Universalizability in Ethics." *Dialogue* 19:651–674.

———. 1984. "Negative and Positive Rights in Gewirth's *Reason and Morality*." In Edward Regis, Jr., ed., *Gewirth's Ethical Rationalism: Critical Essays with a Reply by Alan Gewirth*, 96–107. Chicago: University of Chicago Press.

Nielsen, Kai. 1984. "Against Ethical Rationalism." In Edward Regis, Jr., ed., *Gewirth's Ethical Rationalism: Critical Essays with a Reply by Alan Gewirth*, 59–83. Chicago: University of Chicago Press.

Nozick, Robert. 1981. *Philosophical Explanations*. Cambridge, Massachusetts: Harvard University Press.

Ockleton, Mark. 1988. Review of *Law as a Moral Judgment*, by Deryck Beyleveld and Roger Brownsword. *Legal Studies* 8/2:234–238.

Okin, Susan Moller. 1981. "Liberty and Welfare: Some Issues in Human Rights Theory." In J. R. Pennock and J. W. Chapman, eds., *Nomos XXIII: Human Rights*, 230–256. New York: New York University Press.

O'Meara, William M. 1982. "Gewirth and Adams on the Foundation of Morality." *Philosophy Research Archives* 8:367–381.

Overvold, Mark Carl. 1983. Review of *Human Rights*, by Alan Gewirth. *Philosophical Books* 24/4:241–243.

Pap, Arthur. 1958. *Semantics and Necessary Truth*. New Haven: Yale University Press.

Parfit, Derek. 1984. *Reasons and Persons*. Oxford: Clarendon Press.

Paske, Gerald H. 1989. "Magic and Morality: Remarks on Gewirth and Hare." *Journal of Value Inquiry* 23:51–58.

Paul, Jeffrey. 1979. "Gewirth's Solution to the 'Is-Ought' Problem." *Personalist* 60:442–447.

Peters, R. S. 1966. *Ethics and Education*. London: George Allen and Unwin.

Phillips, Derek L. 1986. *Toward a Just Social Order*. Princeton, New Jersey: Princeton University Press.

Phillips-Griffiths, A. 1967. "Ultimate Moral Principles: Their Justification." In P. Edwards, ed., *Encyclopaedia of Philosophy*, 8:177–182. London: Collier-Macmillan.

Pilon, Roger. 1979a. "Ordering Rights Consistently: Or What We Do and Do Not Have Rights To." *Georgia Law Review* 13:1171–1196.

———. 1979b. "Corporations and Rights: On Treating Corporate People Justly." *Georgia Law Review* 13:1245–1370.

———. 1979c. "On Moral and Legal Justification." *Southwestern University Law Review* 11:1327–1344.

Pollis, Adamantia. 1984. Review of *Human Rights*, by Alan Gewirth. *Graduate Faculty Philosophy Journal* (New School for Social Research) 10/1:183–186.

Pollock, Lansing. 1988. "Evaluating Moral Theories." *American Philosophical Quarterly* 25 (July): 229–240.

Puolimatka, Tapio. 1989. *Moral Realism and Justification*. Helsinki, Finland: Suomalainen Tiedeakatemia.

Quine, Willard Van Orman. 1963. "Two Dogmas of Empiricism." In Willard Van Orman Quine, *From a Logical Point of View*, 2d revised edition, 20–46. New York: Harper and Row.

Raphael, D. D. 1984. "Rights and Conflicts." In Edward Regis, Jr., ed.,

Gewirth's Ethical Rationalism: Critical Essays with a Reply by Alan Gewirth, 84–95. Chicago: University of Chicago Press.

Rawls, John. 1971. *A Theory of Justice.* Cambridge, Massachusetts: Harvard University Press.

Reamer, Frederic G. 1979. "Fundamental Issues in Social Work: An Essay Review." *Social Services Review* (June): 229–243.

———. 1982. *Ethical Dilemmas in Social Service.* New York: Columbia University Press.

Regis, Jr., Edward. 1981. "Gewirth on Rights." *Journal of Philosophy* 78:786–794.

———. 1984. Introduction to Edward Regis, Jr., ed., *Gewirth's Ethical Rationalism: Critical Essays with a Reply by Alan Gewirth*, 1–7. Chicago: University of Chicago Press.

Reiman, Jeffrey. 1990. *Justice and Modern Moral Philosophy.* New Haven: Yale University Press.

Roberts, Robert C. 1979. Review of *Reason and Morality*, by Alan Gewirth. *Philosophical Investigations* (Millikin University) 2/2:78–82.

Scheuermann, James. 1987. "Gewirth's Concept of Prudential Rights." *Philosophical Quarterly* 37:291–304.

Schumaker, Millard. 1979. "The Pain of Self-Contradiction." *Journal of Religion* 59/3:352–356.

Schwartz, Adina. 1979. Review of *Reason and Morality*, by Alan Gewirth. *Philosophical Review* 88:654–656.

Seay, Gary. 1983. "Fact and Value Revisited: Why Gewirth Is Not a Cognitivist." *Journal of Value Inquiry* 17:133–141.

Simon, Robert. 1975. "The Trouble with Categorial Consistency." *Philosophical Studies* 27:271–277.

Singer, Marcus G. 1984. "Gewirth's Ethical Monism." In Edward Regis, Jr., ed., *Gewirth's Ethical Rationalism: Critical Essays with a Reply by Alan Gewirth*, 23–38. Chicago: University of Chicago Press.

———. 1985. "On Gewirth's Derivation of the Principle of Generic Consistency." *Ethics* 95:297–301.

Sterba, James P. 1987. "Justifying Morality: The Right and the Wrong Ways." *Synthèse* 72:45–69.

Stirner, Max. 1982. *Der Einziger und Sein Eigenthum.* Translated by S. T. Byington as *The Ego and His Own,* edited by James J. Martin. Sun City, California: West World Press.

Stohs, Mark D. 1988. "Gewirth's Dialectically Necessary Method." *Journal of Value Inquiry* 22:53–65.

Towle, Charlotte. 1957. *Common Human Needs.* Revised edition. New York: National Association of Social Workers.

Trigg, Roger. 1980. Review of *Reason and Morality*, by Alan Gewirth. *Mind* 89:149–151.

Upton, Hugh. 1986. "Rights and Duties—A Reply to Gewirth." *Mind* 95:381–385.

Veatch, Henry B. 1976. "Paying Heed to Gewirth's Principle of Categorial Consistency." *Ethics* 86:278–287.

———. 1979. Review of *Reason and Morality*, by Alan Gewirth. *Ethics* 89:401–414.

Versenyi, Laszlo. 1976. "On Deriving Categorical Imperatives from the Concept of Action." *Ethics* 86:265–273.

Von Magnus, Eric. 1983. "Rights and Risks." *Journal of Business Ethics* 2:23–26.

Waldron, Jeremy. 1983. "By Rights." Review of *Human Rights*, by Alan Gewirth. *The Times Higher Education Supplement*, May 27, 16.

Watt, A. J. 1975. "Transcendental Arguments and Moral Principles." *Philosophical Quarterly* 25:40–57.

White, Stephen K. 1982. "On the Normative Structure of Action: Gewirth and Habermas." *Review of Politics* 44:282–301.

Williams, Bernard. 1985. *Ethics and the Limits of Philosophy*. Cambridge, Massachusetts: Harvard University Press.

Wollaston, William. 1964. "The Religion of Nature Delineated." In L. A. Selby-Bigge, ed., *British Moralists*, II, 361–384. Indianapolis and New York: Bobbs-Merrill Co. Inc.

Wong, David B. 1984. *Moral Relativity*. Berkeley: University of California Press.

Author Index

This index lists persons mentioned in the text or notes who have works cited in References. For other persons named or alluded to, see Subject Index.

Subject Index

Abstraction. *See* Generic features of agency: as abstract conditions; PPA: abstract/ideal and real

Acceptance of criteria. *See* Criteria, acceptance of

Action: categorial rules of, 119, 484; conative versus achievemental modes of, 404; evaluation inherent in (*see* Evaluation); habitual, 404, 422; indifferent? 71–74, 405, 422; ontology of, 442; phenomenological versus logical concept of? 421; procedural aspect of, 403–404; procedural context of, 29; prospective and present, 142, 151, 196, 342, 369, 386; purposive versus purposeful, 404; rationalizing phenomenology of versus theoretical speculation about, 49; rights integral to? 341–342, 386, 442; rights/rights-claims needed for? 150–152; self-contradictory? (*see* Contradiction); subject matter of moral/practical precepts, 40–41, 66–69, 139, 158, 250–251, 335, 362, 366, 401, 420–421, 423, 433, 435, 445, 452–453, 463; substantive aspect of, 403–404; successful action versus, 20, 82, 88, 89–90, 151, 238, 404; unconscious drives and, 421. *See also* Definition of action; Foundational base for rights; Freedom of action; Impossibility; Omissions; Ordinary usage; Preconditions of action; Reasons for action

Ad hominem arguments, 2, 139, 247–250, 299, 301, 320, 384, 396, 407, 477, 479–481

Adeonticism, 2, 22, 26, 34, 35, 47, 50–51, 55, 137, 164–166, 177, 370, 407, 408, 411, 419, 438; refutation of, 2, 35, 50–51, 164–165, 408

Aesthetics analogy? 249–250, 378

Agency. *See* Action

Agent. *See* PPA

Agent-relativity of evaluation, 15, 115, 130–132, 134, 173, 175–176, 194–195, 207–213, 218, 220, 226, 228, 240, 325–326, 329, 332, 366, 367–368, 384, 393–394, 395, 436–437, 457, 472–474; super-, 211–213. *See also* Assertoric transformation of PGC: relative to PPAs; Dialectically necessary method: internal viewpoint of PPA employed by; Egoism: regional force of directives in? Evaluation: relative on criteria? Evaluation: relative to criteria

Aid. *See* Positive rights

Altruism, 35, 36–38, 226, 279, 448

Amoralism, 1–2, 22, 26, 34, 35, 47, 51, 54, 55, 56, 93, 164–166, 173, 177, 183, 190–191, 192, 195, 196–201, 206–207, 210, 218–220, 239, 279–281, 281–284, 305, 315, 372–374, 408, 429, 449–450, 460, 461, 463, 469, 480, 481; burden of proof on? 481; deontic, 34, 47, 51, 55; not internally inconsistent, 190, 280, 372–373; prudent, 218–220, 450, 463; radical, 196–201, 373–374; refutation of, 1, 51–54, 190–191, 206–207, 239, 284, 373, 408, 450 (unnecessary? 481); universal ethical egoism versus, 190–191, 239, 372–373

Analytic/synthetic distinction, 117

Analyticity, 116–117. *See also* PGC: analyticity of

Anthropology, 155, 157, 479

Apodictic status of: foundations of empirical science and mathematics, 478, 482–483; foundations of morality, 2, 66, 317–320, 383, 478–482; PGC, 1, 385; principle of noncontradiction, 1